ROSEMARY BROWN'S

Big
KITCHEN
INSTRUCTION
BOOK

ROSEMARY BROWN'S

Big

KITCHEN

INSTRUCTION

BOOK

ROSEMARY CARLETON BROWN

Illustrations by Deborah Zemke

GRAMERCY BOOKS
New York

This 2000 edition is published by Gramercy Books™,
an imprint of Random House Value Publishing, Inc.,
280 Park Avenue, New York, New York 10017,
by arrangement with Andrews McMeel Publishing.

Gramercy Books™ and design are trademarks of
Random House Value Publishing, Inc.

Random House
New York • Toronto • London • Sydney • Auckland
http://www.randomhouse.com/

Printed and bound in the United States of America

Library of Congress Cataloging-in-Publication Data
Brown, Rosemary, 1945–
[Big kitchen instruction book]
Rosemary Brown's big kitchen instruction book / Rosemary Carleton Brown ;
illustrations by Deborah Zemke.
p. cm.
Reprint. Originally published: Kansas City : Andrews McMeel Pub., c1998.
ISBN 0-517-16221-0
1. Cookery. I. Title: Big kitchen instruction book. II. Title.

TX651.B75 2000
641.5—dc21
00-039411

8 7 6 5 4 3 2 1

■ ■ ■

To Jack and Adam,
with love

Contents

■ ■ ■ ■ ■

▪ 125 ▪
CHICKEN AND POULTRY
▪ *Cooking chicken every way to Sunday, including roasting, stir-frying, grilling, and casseroles* ▪ *Selection and safe handling of poultry* ▪ *Preparing the traditional Thanksgiving turkey* ▪ *Tips and checklists for a hassle-free holiday dinner* ▪

▪ 143 ▪
FISH AND SEAFOOD
▪ *If it lives in water, here's how to cook it* ▪ *Popular varieties of fish* ▪ *How to recognize the different market forms* ▪

▪ 151 ▪
EGGS, QUICHES, AND SOUFFLES
▪ *The versatile egg, and all you need to know about it* ▪ *The short-order cook's guide to breakfast eggs and omelets* ▪ *Assembling delicious quiches* ▪ *Preparing a stunning soufflé from a basic recipe* ▪

▪ 161 ▪
PASTA AND PASTA SAUCES
▪ *Italian and American favorites, including lasagne, manicotti, meat sauce, and pesto* ▪ *Names and descriptions of dozens of shapes of pasta* ▪ *Matching up pasta with the most appropriate sauce* ▪ *Charts and tips for cooking pasta* ▪

▪ 175 ▪
RICE, GRAINS, AND STARCHES
▪ *American and ethnic recipes for rice, pilafs, and other popular grains, including couscous, kasha, and quinoa* ▪ *Scrumptious side dishes, including delicious dressing for holiday turkey and Yorkshire pudding to serve with roast beef* ▪

▪ 185 ▪
VEGETABLES

▪ Mouth-watering recipes to make you wish that summer lasted all year long ▪ More than twenty kinds of vegetables, with instructions for cleaning them, cutting them up, and cooking them ▪ Techniques for preparing vegetables, including steaming, baking, boiling, and sautéing ▪ An herb-taster's guide to over a dozen fresh herbs ▪

▪ 237 ▪
SALADS AND SIDE DISHES

▪ Delicious recipes for rounding out the menu ▪
How to identify and prepare more than a dozen varieties of salad greens ▪

▪ 249 ▪
SAUCES AND SALAD DRESSINGS

▪ The perfect complement, including sauces, salad dressings, and gravy ▪ Master recipes for Béchamel (white sauce), Hollandaise sauce, and Vinaigrette, with variations for each ▪

▪ 257 ▪
BREADS

▪ Foolproof yeast rolls and a dozen ways to shape them ▪ Detailed directions for turning out prize-winning biscuits ▪ Delectable breads and muffins ▪ Bread-making terms ▪ Breakfast favorites, including French toast, pancakes, and waffles ▪

▪ 271 ▪
CAKES AND FROSTINGS

▪ How to bake a cake from scratch or make a mix taste more like homemade ▪ Tips for better cakes and frostings ▪ Charts for every cake-maker, including how to determine the amount of batter or frosting needed for all shapes and sizes of cakes ▪ Heavenly cakes, from angel food to chocolate, and luscious frostings and glazes for them all ▪

Acknowledgments

■ ■ ■ ■ ■

"Have you talked to Rosemary lately?"
"Not in the last few days. Do you suppose she's had the baby yet?"
"I hate to call over there again. I know she's getting tired of people asking."
"It seems like she's been on the nest forever. Isn't it about time?"
"You can't rush these things. The baby will come when it's good and ready."
"I know. But it's been almost twenty years!"

At long last the baby has arrived, and it's a whopper! In fact, the original manuscript weighed in at twelve pounds. And if I do say so myself, I haven't seen a baby this beautiful since our son, Adam, was born. However, I can't take all the credit myself, since there were some very talented people who helped me through the labor.

My husband, Jack, has been my number one taste-tester for thirty years. Not only does he love my cooking, but he has a wonderful sense of humor, which I especially appreciated when I was just learning the ropes in the kitchen. He's also an incurable romantic. (I'm hoping no one finds a cure.) He's great fun to be with, he's the light of my life, he's full of great surprises, and he's the twinkle in my eye. But beyond all these outstanding qualities, he's also extraordinarily gifted. Throughout this book project, I've relied heavily on his superb advice, his professional expertise, his impeccable judgment, and his artistic eye. His generous praise for my accomplishments in the kitchen has fueled my confidence and intensified my motivation. Every woman should be this blessed. *Sweetheart, I love it when you dive into one of my concoctions, close your eyes, nod your head, and sigh, "Best I ever had." You spur me on to new heights. Thanks for being so supportive for all these years. You'll never know how precious your encouragement has been to me.*

Adam, our son, joined my taste-testing team as soon as he graduated from Gerber. However I wouldn't be completely truthful if I said that the only reviews he's given my cooking have been raves. I think the problem was that his taste buds needed to mature before he could fully appreciate my culinary talents. He often verbalized something other than praise for the vegetables that he discovered on his plate. But over the years, he learned to keep his mouth shut—especially when he knew what was for dessert. *Honey, I'm so glad that you finally acquired a taste for my cooking, even if those vegetables were somewhat of a challenge at first. I look forward to the time when your own children are gathered around your dinner table, gagging at the sight of their green beans, and trying to hide their broccoli in their milk. Just remember to keep plenty of peanut butter in the pantry,* and they'll grow up to be big and strong, just like their daddy.

Although I can't put a date on the conception of this book, I'm certain that the project was well underway by the early spring of 1980, when the Junior League of Nashville asked me to present a home-management workshop. That was just a few months before my mother passed away, and I remember how delighted she was when I told her about my upcoming project. *Mama, thanks for your patience, and for taking the time to show me the right way to do things. I think of you so often—and especially whenever I have the opportunity to pass along something you taught me.*

After that first workshop, one thing led to another. Pretty soon my business, *Neat Ideas*, involved space planning and kitchen designing projects, as well as home-management seminars. When I was invited to present my very first out-of-town workshop, I took the loose-leaf manuscript for the manual I'd written to the typesetter, and from there to the printer. The result was a spiral-bound volume entitled *Getting Your Home in Order*. In the beginning, my daddy kept my self-published book business afloat by buying up cases of those books to give his friends. He was so proud of his little girl. *Daddy, I'll be forever grateful for the wonderful start you gave me, and for all those cherished father-daughter times we shared. Oh, how I wish you were here now to share my joy.*

From the earliest days of my home-management seminars, my dear friend Lynn Samuels has stuck closer than a sister. I remember enjoying coffee with her so many mornings on the screened-in porch overlooking her lovely garden. Our brainstorming helped pave the way for what this book has finally evolved into. *Lynn, you're a world-class cheerleader. I count your loyal friendship and your steadfast encouragement among my dearest treasures.*

I'm greatly indebted to so many people who, through the years, have contributed to my knowledge of food, cooking, and kitchen management. It's difficult to say when my culinary quest began, since I've surrounded myself with cookbooks ever since I was old enough to read them. I received my first junior cookbook as a gift for my tenth birthday. In addition to the burgeoning shelves of cookbooks that I've accumulated since then, I've devoured innumerable cooking magazines, beginning with my first subscription to *Gourmet* during my college days. Since the advent of the Internet, I've taken more than a few surfing safaris. And I've attended some superb cooking classes as well. I clearly remember participating in my very first cooking school; it was taught by Mary Walton Caldwell in the summer of 1971, when I was pregnant with Adam. Since I was eating for two then, I managed to consume more than my fair share of our class projects. In recent years, Hilda Pope's unique zest for cooking has fanned the flame that was ignit-

ed years ago. I've always believed that the most effective way to learn to cook is to be exposed to those who have a passion for it. I count my good friend Daisy King among those enthusiastic cooks, and I'm thankful that she has always been eager to share her kitchen wisdom with me. *To those who have passed along their knowledge, skill, and inspiration, thank you for keeping the fire kindled all these years.*

I have been blessed with a wealth of friends. Along the way, many people have offered their own special brand of encouragement. Many times, they had no idea that their words were so well-timed. Although there's not room here to list them all by name, I'll never forget the phone calls, cards, and e-mails that kept me going when I was tired or discouraged. Add to those the countless prayers that sustained me and helped me bring this endeavor to fulfillment. *To all the generous people who took time to offer a few kind words, to call, to write, and to pray for me, thank you. I know that I couldn't have made it without your support.*

Many thanks to my illustrator, Deborah Zemke, for creating artwork that captured the very essence of all that I'd imagined and hoped for. Her unique talent and personality are projected so clearly in her whimsical drawings.

My proofreaders, Estelle Laurence and Claire Caterer, deserve the Sherlock Holmes Award for going over my manuscript and page proofs with a magnifying glass, uncovering errors and inconsistencies that others (myself especially) had overlooked. Their precise and meticulous attention to detail was a work of art in itself.

There are so many creative, competent, and dedicated folks at Andrews McMeel Publishing, and I've benefited

greatly from the skills, talents, and special gifts of a number of them. My editor, Jean Zevnik, has worked tirelessly and conscientiously to help bring this book to press. Polly Blair has done a splendid job of overseeing the production, and her excellent staff has painstakingly followed through on the tiniest details. It's been such a pleasure to hear JuJu Johnson's cheerful voice when I call the Andrews McMeel editorial department in Kansas City. But I think the grand prize at Andrews McMeel goes to Chris Schillig, who caught my vision for this project the very first time I unveiled the prototype. Had it not been for her perseverance and expertise, this book might still be a dream in a loose-leaf binder. Chris, thank you a thousand times over for going to bat for me, and for helping to turn my vision into a reality.

Finally, I'd like to express my gratitude to the One who has watched over not only this project, but my entire life as well. He has seen to it that so many different people were in the right place at the right time, just when I needed them. He has provided the inspiration, the talent, the skill, the resources, the technology, and the wisdom necessary to accomplish such a great undertaking. He has ultimately made it possible for me to arrive where I am today. When He looked down on that little hospital in Blackwell, Oklahoma, on Easter Sunday, 1945, He knew the wonderful plans that He had in store for that tiny newborn baby girl who lay abandoned there: plans to prosper me and not to harm me, plans to give me hope and a future. I lift up my eyes to the hills—where does my help come from? My help comes from the Lord, the Maker of Heaven and Earth. *Thank You, Lord, for Your amazing grace.*

Introduction

■ ■ ■ ■ ■

Now close your books and take out a sheet of paper. We're going to have a test.

Even if you haven't seen the inside of a classroom in decades, those two sentences are probably still powerful enough to tie your stomach in knots. To this day, I have a recurring dream that a psychiatrist would probably have a field day with. I'm lounging on the bed in my dorm room, daydreaming about life after graduation. Suddenly, I remember that I'm registered for a class that I've forgotten to attend. I haven't even bought the textbook. Naturally, I don't have the first page of notes, nor do I have the slightest idea who I can borrow them from. I'm not even sure if I know where the class meets. And there's a big test in the morning. For a fleeting moment, I consider the possibility of simply dropping out of the class, but then I realize that I might not have enough hours to graduate. And it's spring semester of my senior year. Frantically, I try to figure out how I can get myself out of this mess. I wake up in a cold sweat.

Most of us hate taking tests, and yet we face them in one form or another almost daily. A *test* can be defined as *one or more questions, exercises, or situations that help to determine a person's knowledge, ability, or aptitude.* Some tests reveal skill or understanding gained through study, experience, or a combination of the two, while other tests reflect innate talent, character, or just plain common sense. The kitchen is a prime testing ground, since managing it requires not only technical skill, but also creativity, ingenuity, and endurance. We're tested day in, day out, evenings, weekends, and holidays. And in most cases, there's little time off—even for good behavior.

Besides revealing our strengths, reliable tests also expose our weaknesses. Consider one test with which most of us are painfully familiar: It's six o'clock and dinner is nowhere in sight—physically, mentally, or otherwise. The pizza delivery man came to the rescue last night, so that option is out. The night before that, it was take-out Chinese. There are no "get out of jail free" cards left, and the clock is ticking. Furthermore, there are very few raw materials to work with. The cupboard is bare, with the exception of a bumper crop of canned green beans, a twelve-pack of paper towels, and a vast assortment of jelly received as gifts over the last decade. The freezer is chock-full of large UFOs (unidentified frozen objects), each of which would probably take at least two days to thaw and identify. So it looks like it's going to be scrambled eggs again tonight. Why does this keep happening?

We frequently operate in crisis mode because we're just too tired to think after a busy day. In the kitchen, we're faced with too much to do, not enough time to do it in, and probably too few square feet in which to operate. Indeed, kitchens can get out of control more easily, and overwhelm us more quickly, than any other room in the house. Granted, they should be busy places—but not war zones. The bottom line is this: We need clever ideas, fresh inspiration, and probably a crash course in home economics. Clearly, many of us are organizationally challenged. We need to set aside time to arrange our space, stock our pantry, and develop a strategy. The problem is, many of us simply don't know how.

One good daydream could solve most of our problems: We arrive home after a nerve-racking day. At the door, we're met by a grandmotherly figure who takes our hand and leads us to an overstuffed chair, next to a plate of warm oatmeal cookies. She hands us a new spiral notebook and a sharp #2 pencil with a clean eraser. Then, in a reassuring voice, she wisely reveals the solutions to all our chronic kitchen problems. She tells us we can take our time with this little exercise, since we don't have to cook dinner tonight. She's already fixed it, and it's staying warm on the back of the stove. We smell the homemade yeast rolls. She waxes eloquent, dictating enough simple dinner menus to last us for the rest of our lives. Naturally, she speaks only as fast as we can write, and she stands by our side patiently, never losing her temper, until we have all the answers neatly transcribed into the notebook. Then we hop up from the chair and dive into the homemade yeast rolls.

It's a shame it's only a daydream, because a lot of the information she imparts to us has slipped through the cracks into the generation gap between what our mothers and grandmothers knew, and what we need to find out. Most of us haven't been to class, we haven't taken any notes, and we haven't bought the textbook. Until now. This *Big Kitchen Instruction Book* bridges that generation gap, and contains everything you need to know to set up your kitchen and keep it running smoothly. In fact, it's almost as good as the daydream, except that you'll have to supply the oatmeal cookies and yeast rolls.

I've spent countless hours in the kitchen, and I've learned a lot over the years—much of it by trial and error—from how to arrange things conveniently in my cupboards to the secrets of making fantastic soup. I've also learned that unless I want to redecorate the ceiling, I shouldn't try to stir the homemade blender mayonnaise with a rubber spatula until after I've turned the blender off. But by far the most important lessons I've learned are about working smarter, not harder.

Most of my accumulation of kitchen knowledge is gathered together right here for you, so you won't have to figure things out the hard way. The *Big Kitchen Instruction Book* is a storehouse of valuable information, organized and indexed to put all the facts you need right at your fingertips. In one volume you'll find recipes, reference material, and a simple plan for fitting together all your kitchen chores into a workable system. And although this book is filled with some of the best recipes you've ever tasted, I hope that's not all you discover here. If it is, you'll be missing out on some very important features.

The first part of the book could very well revolutionize the way you work in the kitchen. First of all, you'll learn how to streamline your space and clear away the obstacles and bottlenecks that slow you down. Then you'll discover how to stock up on everything you need, from pots and pans to pantry staples, and how to arrange it all to make the most of whatever space you have to work in, no matter how limited. You'll find convenient solutions for all kinds of kitchen problems, and you'll appreciate the tips on planning meals, shopping for groceries, saving at the supermarket, and getting dinner on the table, including dozens of delicious but doable dinner menus. The *Big Kitchen Instruction Book* will take apart all the pieces of the kitchen puzzle and put them back together for you into a plan that you can understand and work with.

At the heart of this book is a marvelous collection of recipes, including most of the basics you'd expect to find in a cookbook several times this large. As you thumb through it, you'll notice the memo pads in the sidebars—perfect places for you to add more recipes, discoveries, personal experiences, or even sticky notes, so the book can grow with you and become part of your own personal legacy. The more you add, the more valuable this book will become to you, or whomever you pass it along to.

The reference section is unique. I don't believe you'll find anything as comprehensive in another cookbook of any size. It's a collection of facts and charts that will guide you in making all kinds of food-related decisions, from pointers on selecting a fresh pineapple, to advice on how long to keep a can of baking powder, to knowing how many crackers to crush when you need a cup of crumbs.

I hope this book will become like a trusted friend that you turn to often for inspiration and advice, and that in years to come you'll say that it's still your very favorite cookbook. The *Big Kitchen Instruction Book* is ideal for beginners. Like a set of training wheels on a bicycle, it will gently guide you through uncertainty and keep you from falling. It's a simplified kitchen encyclopedia that will teach you how to achieve terrific results in a reasonable amount of time. But although it's perfect for someone who's just getting started, this book is certainly not for beginners only. It's for cooks of all ages and abilities: students, brides, working professionals, busy young mothers, empty nesters, and even grandmothers who have been cooking for decades.

Too few people today seem to enjoy the time they spend in the kitchen. My goal in writing this book has been to add to my readers' enjoyment of cooking, and to transform the time they spend in the kitchen into a pleasant and creative experience. I look forward to sharing many things that I've learned in over a quarter of a century of managing a home. So whether you're just moving into your first apartment, or you've been keeping house for years, from my heart to yours, God bless, and bon appétit!

Rosemary Brown

S.O.S for the Kitchen

Chapter 1

The Game Plan

■ ■ ■ ■ ■

■ ■ ■

Lucy and the Chocolate Factory

In the fall of the year that I started the fourth grade, my family got a television set. Although we weren't the first family on our block to have one, we were by no means the last. We never could have imagined how the Monday night TV lineup would evolve through the years. Who could have known that one day, viewers from coast to coast would watch eighteen testosterone-charged men crashing into each other on a playing field on a weekly basis? In those kinder, gentler times, instead of being glued to the tube watching the Redskins, we were riveted to the antics of a zany redhead and her Cuban bandleader husband.

In one of the classic episodes of *I Love Lucy,* the audience is treated to a slapstick comedy involving role reversal. Ricky Ricardo and Fred Mertz reach the conclusion that running a home is no big deal, and they decide that they're more than capable of holding down the fort. Fred, clad in a ruffled apron, sashays around behind the vacuum cleaner, armed with a feather duster. Ricky assumes full

responsibility for the kitchen, armed with his mother's recipe for *arroz con pollo.* A little knowledge is a dangerous thing. Meanwhile, Lucy and Ethel, liberated women of the fifties, set out for the local chocolate factory to join the work force as bonbon wrappersons.

As Ricky confidently begins preparing the chicken and rice recipe, he discovers that the kitchen is a hard-hat area, a little rice goes a long way, and it's easier just to have dinner delivered. (These are truths that women have grasped since the dawn of time.) While Ricky and Fred keep house, Lucy and Ethel get acquainted with the twin wonders of the assembly line and the conveyor belt. Their supervisor, who looks as if she eats barbed wire for breakfast, orders them not to allow a single bonbon to pass their station without a wrapper. As the candy moves down the conveyor belt in a slow and orderly fashion, Lucy and Ethel glow with smug assurance, certain that the task of bringing home the bacon will be a piece of cake. Actually, it will be a box of candy, but no one knows that at this point in the show.

Gradually, someone off-camera begins to turn up the speed on the conveyor belt, and Lucy and Ethel have to pick up the pace just a wee bit. As the speed increases, stress mounts in the workplace, and the bonbon surplus disappears first into their mouths and then into their pockets. Faster and faster the candy zips past, and Lucy and Ethel are challenged to find more innovative places to stash the extras: under their caps and down the fronts of their blouses.

When all is said and done, Lucy, Ethel, Ricky, and Fred all reach the same conclusion: Dealing with food in any form, whether it's *arroz con pollo* or chocolate bonbons, can produce stress.

■ ■ ■

Who's in Control Here?

When you're dealing with food, you've really got to know what you're doing. It helps to know these things before you get started, but even if you're currently up to your eyeballs in poorly-stocked cupboards and kitchen chaos, it's not too late for you to learn how to master the one room in your home that gets out of hand faster than any other. And that's what this book is all about: learning how

to take control of your kitchen, so that instead of dreading the thought of spending time there, you can actually start enjoying it.

Unfortunately, because food plays such an important role in our lives, the kitchen is one place where "Just Say No" just won't work. There's no way around it. Some people have a love-hate relationship with their kitchens similar to the unfortunate arrangement that Henry VIII had with his wives: they can't live with them, and they can't live without them. I know one woman who painted her kitchen black, kept all the lights turned off, and put a folding screen in front of the doorway. Her decorating scheme left little doubt about her sentiments. But unless you plan to eat all your meals out, sooner

or later you're going to have to come to terms with your kitchen.

■ ■ ■

Crying Won't Put Dinner on the Table

Babies have a unique approach to dealing with hunger. They cry. So simple, yet so effective. An ear-piercing squall is sufficient to cause their dinner to materialize magically out of nowhere. Unfortunately, we adults have to go through a few more steps to get from here to dinner.

First, it's bumper cars in the supermarket parking lot. Then comes the showdown at the O.K. Corral, as we disengage several buggies in our search for one that doesn't need a wheel alignment. Dodging displays of cans, bot-

COMMON KITCHEN COMPLAINTS

Complaint: *I grew up in a disorganized home, and no one ever taught me how to manage a kitchen. Besides, I never got around to taking home economics when I was in school.*
Response: You're fresh out of excuses! The S.O.S. Plan described in this chapter will provide you with tools for managing your kitchen, which you can also apply to other disorganized areas of your life.

Complaint: *My kitchen is too small to hold all my stuff.*
Response: You're probably harboring more than your share of kitchen clutter. Chapter 2, "The Streamlined Kitchen," (pages 9–16) will show you how to free up space where you thought there wasn't any hope.

Complaint: *Naturally, I'd like a larger kitchen (who wouldn't!), but my main problem is that nothing is arranged conveniently. I wear myself out retracing my steps.*
Response: This problem is fairly easy to remedy. Read Chapter 3, "The Organized Kitchen," (pages 17–40) to find out the most accessible places to put everything.

Complaint: *I never seem to have the right ingredients on hand. So instead of heading back to the store for the fourth time that week, we frequently order in or eat out.*
Response: You simply need to replenish things as you use them up. Read Chapter 3, "The Organized Kitchen," (pages 17–40) for advice on keeping your shelves stocked.

(continued)

tles, and cleaning products, that resemble the Great Pyramid at Giza, we maneuver around abandoned carts in the middle of aisles, veer out of the way of preschoolers with tiny shopping buggies (provided by store managers who undoubtedly want to detain us as long as possible), and watch grocery stockers zealously rearranging our favorite foods so that it's impossible for us to find what we're looking for. We try to be polite as we edge past people who appear to be long-lost friends, joyfully reunited in the middle of the frozen foods section after years of painful separation. We patiently move at a snail's pace in the no-passing zones, behind middle-of-the-aisle shoppers who seem to be wading through pits of molasses. After the "paper or plastic" interrogation, we fight traffic all the way home. We hope we didn't forget to pick up aspirin.

Our final reward is hauling, unpacking, washing, trimming, slicing, dicing, and blowing the whistle to round up family members for dinner (some of whom mysteriously disappear three minutes before we're ready to put the food on the table). After a quick meal that takes a frac-tion of the time to eat that it took to prepare, there's a big mess to clean up. It's wearisome just thinking about it. But I have good news: It's so much easier if you have a plan.

One of the main benefits of creating an efficient kitchen is the extra time you'll find to devote to other pursuits. If your kitchen is disorganized, you'll wear yourself out running around in circles, with far less time to enjoy yourself. The choice is up to you.

Creating a well-run kitchen will require a commitment of time, energy, and money. But your investment will pay enormous dividends. You'll need to develop a strategy first, and then follow through with it. And you'll have to exercise some self-discipline to stay on top of things. One of my friends calls it "Planning Your Work and Working Your Plan." This book will show you how to do both.

■ ■ ■

Back to School

In college, I had a social psychology professor whose first lecture made a lasting impact on his students. Dr. Weinstein assigned us a simple quote to memorize: "Human behavior is organized around the anticipated responses of others." He warned us that we'd better know it backwards and forwards if we wanted to pass his course. From time to time he would interrupt his lectures to give a selected student in the class an opportunity to recite the carefully-memorized motto. Word for word. Pass or fail. No in-between. Did we listen up, or what? It's been more than thirty years, and I can still rattle it off. Like the lyrics to songs that we crooned as teenagers, it's amazing how some things in our brains just won't turn loose.

■ ■ ■

From Distress to Success with S.O.S.

If this were the first day of class in a college course in Kitchen Management, and if I were your professor, I'd probably say, "Welcome to Kitchenology 101. Let me review my credentials for you.

"I've been involved in this field for over a quarter of a century, and I've had plenty of hands-on experience. Not only have I prepared thousands of meals and cleaned up after same, but I've packed my share of lunches, served my share of snacks, and hosted my share of dinner parties. I've cruised supermarket aisles morning, noon, and night, as well as

the day before Thanksgiving, and all those afternoons the weatherman erroneously predicted six inches of snow.

"Furthermore, I've put in considerable time doing research. I've read books, newspapers, and magazines, I've surfed the Internet, and I've conducted countless interviews.

"As a professional organizer, I've been hired to go into people's homes as a consultant, to offer suggestions to help them organize their space and use their time more efficiently. I've given seminars, conducted workshops, and rolled up my sleeves to get down to the real nitty gritty. In short, I've paid my dues. I know what it's like to try to work around homework papers on the kitchen table at dinnertime, and I've cultivated the art of holding a telephone on one shoulder while using both hands to wash dishes.

"During the countless official and unofficial hours I've spent examining the factors that make a kitchen run smoothly, I've isolated

three key ingredients that spell the difference between distress and success in the kitchen. These three elements will make up the core of your kitchenology curriculum, and from here on, we'll refer to them collectively as the S.O.S. Plan. This plan is easy to remember, simple to implement, and has far-reaching applications. Not only can you apply this wonder-working formula to your kitchen, but you can use it to untangle other areas of your life that might be in disarray, from a messy desk, to a fund-raising project for the YWCA. Although it's not a cure for the common cold, this plan will be a veritable gold mine for you, if you'll

simply put it to work. Now Hear This: If you want to pass this course, memorize the Plan!"

∎ ∎ ∎
Drum Roll and Fanfare!

S ▪ STREAMLINE

O ▪ ORGANIZE

S ▪ SYSTEMIZE

Hopefully, the Plan will stick with you like glue! Since a picture is worth a thousand words, here's a visual image for you. Just close your eyes and conjure up that familiar little yellow and red box of soap-filled

---

> **COMMON KITCHEN COMPLAINTS (CONTINUED)**
>
> **Complaint:** *I'm overworked, and I just don't have time to figure out a plan for managing my kitchen.*
> **Response:** You have it backwards: You don't have time *not* to work out a plan! Chapter 4, "The Systemized Kitchen," (pages 41–63) is full of ideas for creating a strategy.
>
> **Complaint:** *I'm tired of coming up with new ideas for what to fix for dinner.*
> **Response:** Once you learn how to recycle your menus in Chapter 4, "The Systemized Kitchen," (pages 41–63) you won't worry about this anymore!
>
> **Complaint:** *My freezer is full of stuff that I can't identify, and I usually can't find what I'm looking for.*
> **Response:** Contrary to popular misconceptions, the freezer is not an electric trash can. Get rid of the "UFO's" (Unidentified Frozen Objects) and read Chapter 4, "The Systemized Kitchen," (pages 41–63) to find out how to keep up with what's in there.
>
> **Complaint:** *I'm never quite sure how much to buy to end up with the right amount of a particular ingredient for a recipe.*
> **Response:** Look through the "Food Math" section (pages 377–392) to see exactly how much equals what.
>
> **Complaint:** *I don't have much cooking experience, so I avoid recipes that look too complicated, or whenever I don't understand the terminology.*
> **Response:** All the recipes in this book are simple and straightforward. But to answer any questions you might have on terminology, refer to the "Food Terms" section (pages 359–376) for help.

scouring pads. Now focus on those three big letters jumping off the side of the box. You can't miss them. Don't forget them! Set a box of them on your kitchen windowsill to remind you of their intrinsic value. Before we get into details, here are some definitions and an S.O.S. Catechism to go along with those letters:

"S" STANDS FOR STREAMLINE:
To unclutter by removing dead wood.

Q: Why is streamlining your kitchen important?

A: Streamlining is the key to getting rid of anything that isn't productive, attractive, or enjoyable, to enable you to make room for things that are.

To streamline your kitchen, just move out the stuff that gets in your way. Clearing the decks is like a shot in the arm. You'll have more energy, and you'll feel more in control.

"O" STANDS FOR ORGANIZE:
To arrange in a meaningful pattern.

Q: Why is organizing your kitchen important?

A: Organizing is a stress-reducer. It saves you time and energy when you need to find things quickly. Organizing has two goals: (1) to bring a sense of harmony to your surroundings, and (2) to simplify whatever jobs you need to accomplish.

To organize your kitchen, just put things where they belong. It's that simple. And since you're in charge of your kitchen, you're the one who gets to decide where things should go. Once you've arranged things the way you like them, put them away when you're finished using them.

"S" STANDS FOR SYSTEMIZE:
To create a logical process for dealing with recurring chores.

Q: Why should you systemize your kitchen?

A: Systemizing prevents important jobs from (1) piling up, (2) being overlooked, or (3) getting squeezed out of your schedule. Systemizing really isn't complicated at all. First, decide the best and most effective way to do a job. Then do it the same way every time, without spending any more mental energy reinventing the wheel. Because you'll develop a rhythm, you'll be able to work faster. Then, as you learn simpler or better ways of doing something, you can fine-tune your system.

Systemizing your kitchen boils down to developing routines for handling repetitive chores, such as planning menus, shopping for groceries, and doing the dishes. Dressmakers use patterns and financial analysts use spreadsheet templates. With a plan, you won't have to face kitchen chores each day wondering, "Now what should I do next?" Instead, you'll be sailing through work that used to bog you down. Most important, you'll feel like you're in control. And that feeling is invigorating!

■ ■ ■

Watch That First Step!

Each component of the S.O.S. Plan—streamlining, organizing, and systemizing—is interdependent. You mustn't skip any steps—especially the first one. If you do, I guarantee that you'll work harder, not smarter. Streamlining your kitchen will make organizing it and systemizing it so much simpler. Don't organize clutter. Get rid of it! It's an albatross around your neck. Now turn to the next chapter for some serious motivation to clear your decks.

Chapter 2

The Streamlined Kitchen

■ ■ ■ ■ ■

STREAMLINE:
To unclutter by removing dead wood.

■ ■ ■

In Your Dreams

Temptation lurks in the racks next to the supermarket checkout lanes. In plain sight, right there next to the candy, chewing gum, and tabloids. It's those home remodeling magazines, with enticing headlines plastered all over the covers: "CREATE THE KITCHEN OF YOUR DREAMS." Right. Just as soon as I get my hands on the winning Powerball ticket, or Ed McMahon shows up at the door with my check. Impossible, you say? Maybe not.

Close your eyes for a moment and fantasize about what it would be like to move into your dream home. You know, a house like the one you saw last month in *Architectural Digest.* It's all yours now. The movers have finished dragging the last carton of books up the steps and their van is pulling out of the driveway. Now you have it all to yourself, as you sit in the middle of your new kitchen on a packing crate full of dishes, sipping the iced tea you

bought at the drive-through several miles back. Maybe the ice in your drink has melted, but your dreams certainly haven't. You've finally arrived in the home you've been dreaming about all your life. You have yet to put the first box of Hamburger Helper in the pantry. The cabinets are as bare as Old Mother Hubbard's cupboard. Nary a twist-tie, expired pizza coupon, or broken ballpoint pen litters the drawers. The countertops are as clean as the driven snow. This kitchen is so streamlined that it squeaks.

Now let your imagination carry you one step further: If you were starting from scratch, what would you add to the kitchen picture? Or maybe the more important question is, what would you leave out?

■ ■ ■

The Narrow Road to Kitchen Fitness

Homes are like people: They have an annoying tendency to put on weight over the years—especially if no one is keeping an eye on things. And the kitchen seems to fall prey to this malady more than any other room in the home. Why? Because we spend so much time in there, engaged in plenty of other activities besides cooking, eating, and cleaning up. There's no guarantee that whatever goes into the kitchen will go out.

Truly, the kitchen is the last frontier for clutter-busting. Activities that we don't always tolerate in other rooms, like art projects, seem to be excused, condoned, or even encouraged in the kitchen. And since kitchens are often the first place we stop when we come inside, we often drop things off there "just for the time being." Things like coats, purses, papers, and shopping bags. Kitchens are inviting places for family members to socialize, as well—either tethered to the telephone, or visiting with anyone who happens to be working in there. The problem is, the longer someone stays in the kitchen, the greater the likelihood that they'll leave something behind when they leave. Kitchens are such busy places, too. We're often in high gear there—hurriedly dashing in, throwing the mail on the counter, slinging groceries into cabinets, rummaging to find our fa-

vorite knife, moving books and papers off the kitchen table to make room for dinner, cleaning up after everyone, and often just giving the mess a "lick and a promise" until we have a little more time. Who are we kidding? There's never a little more time. The bottom line is that it takes lots less energy to prevent clutter in the first place, than it does to get rid of it once it's put down roots.

In addition to clutter that's generated by so many different activities, it also results from another phenomenon. Our lifestyles change. To illustrate this point, just look around and count the things that are taking up space in your kitchen that haven't served a useful purpose in years.

When was the last time you fired up your automatic weenie-cooker? How about that electric crêpe pan? Or even the waffle iron? Every Saturday morning? I doubt it. Have your preschoolers become teenagers? Then how long has it been since you whipped up a batch of GI-Joe popsicles? The point is that from time to time, all of us need to reevaluate the way we use our kitchen space, and then clear out the relics from the past.

If you're just setting up a kitchen for the first time, here's a golden opportunity to start out on the right foot.

Let these words serve as a warning beacon to motivate you to form good habits from the outset. Then you'll be less likely to get bogged down in kitchen clutter in the months to come. But unless your kitchen is brand new, you'll probably need to roll up your sleeves and get down to some serious clutter-busting.

• • •
Once Upon a Time...

...there was a woman named Clara who was convinced that the reason she avoided cooking at all costs was because her kitchen was a disaster area. She knew she'd be magically transformed into a gourmet cook if only she had a new kitchen. She rattled on incessantly about how much she hated hers. Clara claimed she never needed to learn new jokes. All she had to do was take one look at her kitchen and report the facts. One day, after concluding that the only solution to her culinary frustration was a complete kitchen makeover, Clara decided to take matters into her own hands. She clipped coupons and entered contests until she'd saved enough money to go for the whole enchilada: new cabinets, appliances, countertops, wallpaper, and flooring. It was a long, uphill battle, but Clara was a woman with a mission. Finally, she'd saved enough money to begin her project.

Once she'd located the perfect contractor, she was sure she had it made. Unfortunately, the contractor dropped a bombshell on her fantasy world the morning he announced that all the stuff in her kitchen would have to be moved out before he could move in and get started. Everything had to go. No exceptions. This was not good news, because Clara was chronicled in the *Guinness Book of Records* as the owner of the world's largest collection of salt and pepper shakers.

Fortunately, Clara did have a screened-in back porch just off her kitchen, so she packed her things in boxes and piled them up on the porch. After she finished racking and stacking, Clara and her family settled in to what seemed like an eternity of home-delivered pizzas, carry-out Chinese food, drive-through burgers, and pickup barbecue. She was on a first-name basis with everyone who delivered any variety of Meals on Wheels. Finally, when the last workman left, it was time for Clara to clean up and put away everything in the boxes. (Did I say everything? Actually, not quite. Read on.)

• • •
The Moment of Truth

As the days of construction turned into weeks, and the weeks turned into months, Clara stayed busy working on her cross-stitch motto, "Remodeling always costs twice as much and takes twice as long as you'd planned." When she wasn't embroidering or phoning in her dinner orders, she sat and gazed at all those boxes stacked up on her back porch. As she reflected on her life in general and her kitchen in particular, Clara grappled with the age-old question that has mystified philosophers and politicians for centuries: "How did I get myself into this mess?" She knew that the single motivating factor that had led her to embark upon this remodeling project was the simple fact that she'd lost control of her kitchen. She had become the victim of her own procrastination, carelessness, and lack of discipline, as she had gradually allowed her kitchen to become a repository for paraphernalia and gadgets that she didn't need, never used, or probably shouldn't have kept in the kitchen in the first

place. The shocking truth was that her original kitchen hadn't needed a face-lift in the first place. What it had needed instead was bypass surgery.

As Clara gazed out at her porch and reminisced, her daydream carried her back to a vision of her kitchen, B.C. (Before the Contractor). Clearly, she saw her kitchen table: a miniature landfill, groaning under the weight of unclaimed papers, catalogs, and junk mail. She viewed her kitchen counters, which resembled a tiny freeway at rush hour, with small appliances in gridlock. Her cabinets, like a string of volcanoes on the Pacific Rim, threatened to erupt in a tidal wave of empty margarine tubs and cottage cheese cartons. Rusty knives and fondue forks lurked in her drawers like man-eating sharks, waiting to draw blood whenever she rummaged for her measuring spoons. A treacherous tower of warped foil pans (remnants of a life misspent over TV dinners) loomed from the top shelf of the pantry when she reached for a roll of paper towels. Her stunning collection

UNCLUTTERING YOUR REFRIGERATOR

▪ Clean out one shelf or bin of your refrigerator every day or so. Dividing this job into smaller parts makes it less objectionable, and helps you stay on top of it.

▪ Check expiration dates often on perishable products like cottage cheese and lunch meat. Many times we think we have a well-stocked refrigerator, but when we reach for something, we're disappointed to discover that it's gone bad.

▪ Transfer leftovers into smaller containers as you use part of them up. This frees up space in your refrigerator, and helps refresh your memory as to what food needs to be eaten quickly.

▪ Keep small bottles and jars of condiments in a plastic box or tote tray, so they won't migrate all over the refrigerator shelves.

UNCLUTTERING YOUR FREEZER

▪ Unidentified frozen objects belong in the garbage. If you don't know what's in there, what makes you think you'll eat it? Prevent UFO's in the future by labeling things carefully, and keeping a list of what you've frozen.

▪ Put partially-used bags of frozen veggies inside a large plastic zip bag, so they won't fall off the back of the shelf into Never Never Land.

▪ About once a month, empty your ice maker or ice trays into a heavy-duty plastic zip bag and start fresh.

▪ Those bags of ice left over from the Fourth of July block party two summers ago probably taste like silver fur by now. One bag is usually enough to keep on hand for emergencies.

of grocery sacks under the kitchen sink had been eerily transformed into a luxury condo by a burgeoning colony of cockroaches. And like a three-dimensional Salvador Dalí creation, her leggy houseplants alternated with pairs of prizewinning salt and pepper shakers on the windowsills.

The ringing telephone suddenly jolted Clara back to reality, with the realization that it would have cost her much less money just to rent a dumpster and have a garage sale. Like Ebenezer Scrooge, she was convinced

by her ominous visions that it was time to turn over a new leaf.

So when the contractor finally finished up the job, and Clara faced the stacks of boxes on her back porch, she made some resolutions. From here on out, she would fill her brand new cabinets and counters only with things that were useful, essential, attractive, and/or in good working order. She took a solemn oath to stop accumulating freebies, doodads, and dust catchers. She marched right down to the home improvement center and invested in an industrial-size trash can.

Then she sold the rest of her junk at a garage sale, laughing all the way to the bank about the people who had actually paid her for the opportunity to clutter up their own kitchens! The moral of this story is simple:

■■■
Non Carborundum
Clutterati Kitchenorum

Freely translated that reads, "Don't let kitchen clutter get you down." The cases may not agree, but the experts do: Kitchen clutter is a menace. Consider some of the facts:

■ It's **dangerous.** It can fall on your head, trip you up, slice your fingers, ruin your manicure, and cause gruesome accidents too horrifying to mention in a publication of this nature.

■ It's **unhealthy.** It attracts dust, grime, pests, rodents, and creepy-crawly things, not to mention more of its own kind.

■ It's **unsightly.** When you're forced to gaze at it for hours on end, it's distracting, disgusting, and discouraging, not to mention depressing, disheartening, and demoralizing.

■ It's **wasteful.** It eats up your time because you can't find what you need.

■ It's **expensive.** It drains your wallet because you have to replace things you already have, but can't find because they're buried somewhere under the clutter. And it consumes valuable real estate. After all, it's what keeps the people who manufacture storage sheds in business.

■ It's **time-consuming.** It takes a lot of maintenance: moving, dusting, cleaning, polishing, sorting, repairing, and rearranging.

■ It's **exhausting.** You either have to work around it, or you have to move it to get to whatever else you happen to need at the time.

An ounce of prevention is worth a pound of cure. Because it's easier to keep up than it is to catch up, it's simpler to hold clutter at bay than it is to dislodge it after it's become entrenched. It has strong roots, and usually puts up quite a fight when challenged. And unfortunately, it sneaks up on most of us. So here are some pointers to help you unclutter your kitchen. Mastering this one skill will improve your performance in the kitchen dramatically.

■■■
Get a Grip

Clutter must be related to rabbits, since it always appears to be engaged in repopulation efforts. Clutter's theme song is "Ain't No Mountain High Enough." That's why eliminating it can seem overwhelming. You need to take advantage of every opportunity to put it in its place (which is frequently the trash can). Here are some ideas to get you started:

■ Stop (and train your family to stop) using the kitchen as a dumping ground for things that don't belong there—overcoats, baseball gloves, library books, junk mail, etc. Contrary to what some people believe, the kitchen is not a landfill. Experts tell us that there are over a quarter of a

million items in the average home, and if only six of them are out of place in one room, things start looking pretty messy.

■ Utilize the storage space in your kitchen strictly for things that you need in the kitchen. Yes, you might need a hammer or a screwdriver occasionally. Maybe even a pair of pliers. But you definitely won't be needing the hedge trimmer.

■ Find somewhere else to store the things that you only use occasionally—especially the ones that take up big chunks of space, like the ice cream freezer, turkey roaster, and any special holiday dishes, decorations, or centerpieces.

■ Eliminate multiple generations of kitchen equipment and small appliances. If something's broken, get it fixed. If it can't be repaired and you buy a new one to replace the old one, for heaven's sake, get rid of the old one! No one needs three broken mixers. Don't be seduced into thinking

that you need to keep the old ones for the spare parts. Trust me. Every time they design a new model, they create all new parts that are guaranteed to be 100 percent incompatible with the old ones.

■ Don't allow yourself more than one junk drawer. That's asking for trouble. If one junk drawer isn't enough, face it. You have too much junk.

■ Just because you have a complete set of something doesn't mean you have to keep the entire, unexpurgated set in the kitchen. If your dishware service includes cups and saucers that you never use because you prefer mugs, pack up those cups and saucers.

■ Set a numerical statute of limitations on freebies—fast-food glasses, margarine tubs, frozen food trays, and grocery sacks.

■ Get rid of all your paraphernalia from Fantasy Land: all those gourmet gadgets that you can't identify, can't remember why you bought, and honestly can't ever imagine yourself using.

■ Try to break yourself of the habit of setting things down in the kitchen "just for the time being," when they really don't belong there. Things end up blending into their surroundings, and pretty soon they look as if they have a right to be there. Although every square foot of empty counter-

top seems to be crying out for someone to put something down there, train yourself to resist that temptation! When it comes to things on kitchen counters, less is more.

···
Getting Down to Business

After hearing such an inspiring pep talk, you should be really fired up by now. Why not strike while the iron is hot? Just run to the kitchen, roll up your sleeves, and start busting some clutter! Once you build up a head of steam, you'll be amazed at how satisfying this exercise can be! (Maybe it can even be categorized as aerobic. Who knows?) As you sort through your belongings, be brutally honest with yourself as you ask, "Does this object truly enhance my life?" If the answer is "Yes," the next question is, "Do I use it exclusively in the kitchen?" If the answer is still "Yes," ask yourself, "Do I have room for it in there?" If the answer is "No," then you need to move it somewhere else, maybe to the basement, attic,

garage, or storage closet. Remember that you should allocate the most easily accessible storage space to the things you use most often. (More about this later.) If an item scores a "Yes" on all three counts, it's earned its place.

···
Is This a Waltz or a Rumba?

You're the one in charge of deciding whether to take a slow, methodical approach involving one shelf or one drawer at a time, or to go all out and engage in a frenzied marathon of clutter-busting. My advice, however, is not to pull everything out of all the cabinets at once. You may not realize quite what you're getting into when you begin. Personally, I prefer the one-shelf-at-a-time approach. That way, I don't bite off more than I can chew and create a big, unmanageable mess. If something else comes up that I need to deal with, it's simple to stop at a moment's notice. I can keep going as long as my enthusiasm holds up, call it quits whenever I run out of steam, and pick up wherever I left off later on.

Some storage areas, like the silverware drawer, are so small that you can tackle them while you're talking on the phone or waiting for something to finish cooking. Others, like the pantry, need a little more intensive concentration.

···
Sorting It All Out

Regardless of the tempo you choose, remember that you can stop whenever you get overwhelmed. The clutter predicament didn't happen overnight, and it won't disappear that quickly either. Just focus on one shelf, drawer, or part of the counter at a time. Move everything out, wipe off the area or vacuum it, and go through the process described below. You'll need about four containers to sort through your belongings. You can use laundry baskets, cardboard cartons, paper sacks, or plastic bags.

1. The first container (and my personal favorite) is the trash can. Like Clara, I vote for the industrial size. It's for things that you probably should have thrown away some time ago: broken ballpoint pens, expired coupons, and packages of food much older than they should be. Many times, there's more than one package of the same thing opened, such

as cereal or crackers. Consolidate the two packages into one container (assuming they're both fresh) and toss away the empty one. Some of your trash can be recycled, so you might want to set out a separate container for that.

2. The second container is for anything in good enough condition to give away or sell at a garage sale, if you can deal with the thought of a garage sale. (For many people, that speculation evokes about as much anxiety as the thought of having gum surgery. For these folks, the best thing to do is just give all the usable stuff to charity.)

3. The third container is for things that you want to keep, but that belong in another room or storage area. This is where those boots, library books, and hedge trimmers go. A laundry basket is handy for this.

4. And now for the fourth container: the Ambivalence Box. It's for people who have difficulty deciding whether to fish or cut bait when it comes to dealing with some of their belongings. Let me explain.

To understand how all kinds of different people relate to clutter, it's necessary to determine an individual's rating, based on the Standardized TTTT (Trash Tolerance Threshold Test). Individuals with a high score (also insensitively referred to as pack rats) can deal with an incredible amount of junk without blowing a fuse. They can stack and pile things until there is only a narrow path through their home or office. At the opposite end of the clutter-clutching spectrum are the people who go ballistic at the sight of a single out-of-date catalog. (Thanks to Freud, there's an unkind term for these folks as well.) They're the ones who have a trash can stationed between their mailbox and their front door, so that they can toss out the junk mail before they wipe their feet on the doormat.

Each type of individual has one of two possible reactions when forced to get rid of junk: terror or ecstasy. For those of you who have had a meaningful bonding experience with each and every one of your belongings, no matter how worthless those things may be, let me help you over the hump by telling you about a little crutch that's helped lots of people deal with postpartum clutter depression. I call it the Ambivalence Box. You put into this receptacle everything that you think you might need someday, but you're not really sure whether, where, or when.

As you fill up each container of items for which you feel some de-

gree of ambivalence, tape it shut and write the date on the box with a magic marker. Make absolutely no notation whatsoever regarding the contents of the box. Then stash it out of the way. Sooner or later, you'll probably trip over it trying to find something else. If the expiration date on the box is over one year old, the stuff is ripe. Don't open it. Just put it in the car and take it to the nearest charity pickup location. You'll never remember what's in it, which means you'll never miss it, and someone else will benefit by your generosity. Trust me.

I've given you plenty of good reasons to unclutter your kitchen, as well as ways to tackle the job. Perhaps you'll read through this section and think this can't possibly apply to you. If that's the case, either you scored very low on the TTTT, or you're in denial about your junk-ridden lifestyle. When you can look in the mirror and see yourself as others see you, follow these steps to a life of freedom from clutter. Then move along to the next chapter to find out how to get organized.

Chapter 3

The Organized Kitchen

■ ■ ■ ■ ■

■ ■ ■

First Things First

If you still haven't jumped on the streamlining bandwagon, now's the time. You have to be lean and mean to delve into the deeper mysteries of kitchen management, and you can't do it with a bunch of excess baggage! If you still have too much junk in your kitchen, don't try to organize it! Flip back to Chapter 2 (pages 9–16) for a refresher course in clutter-busting.

■ ■ ■

Time for Some Decisions

To have an organized kitchen, you don't need to be a June Cleaver clone. Being organized isn't synonymous with being rigid, inflexible, or compulsive. Your life won't be drained of all spontaneity, nor will you have to stay up late at night alphabetizing all your coupons. To the contrary, you'll actually have more time for the things you enjoy. Being able to work in an organized kitchen is a huge relief, and all it involves is deciding what goes where, and putting

it there. Since you're the one in charge, you get to make the decisions, so it will be easier for you to follow through. Your objective is to be able to find what you want when you need it, and to be able to get to it easily.

In this chapter, we'll explore the most convenient ways to arrange all your kitchen gear. Then we'll discuss exactly which tools, equipment, utensils, and supplies you'll need, so that when you're working in the kitchen, you won't be frustrated. We'll even make recommendations for loading your pantry, refrigerator, and freezer shelves with the kinds of foods that will enable you to put together a wide variety of simple meals: the ingredients that will save you from making extra trips to the supermarket.

The lists that follow will provide you with some guidelines as you try to decide whether something's essential, or if it's just taking up valuable space. Personally, I prefer to use a larger percent of my kitchen cabinet space for pantry items, rather than to store every size and shape of cookware known to man. If you decide later that you want to become a gourmet chef, you can always add some fancier equipment than what's suggested below. For now, though, it's best to keep things simple.

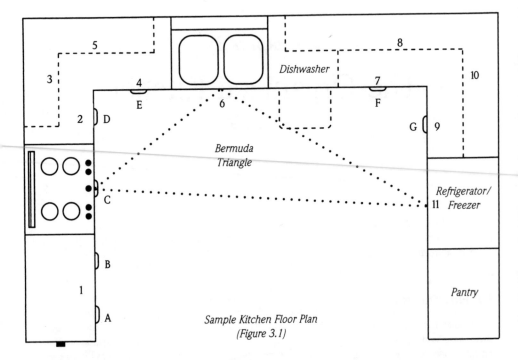

Sample Kitchen Floor Plan
(Figure 3.1)

If you're just setting up house-keeping, you'll probably need to buy several things. Remember that most kitchen equipment, especially knives and saucepans, will have to stand up to heavy use over the long haul. So instead of going for the el-cheapo stuff, get the best you can afford. If you invest in high-quality tools, they'll last longer and give you so much more satisfaction whenever you use them.

There are lots of places to find kitchen tools and gadgets, from discount stores to the Internet. I've included the names, toll-free numbers, and Web sites of several established companies that offer catalogs specializing in kitchen gear. You might want to contact them for a free catalog.

• • •

Designing Your Work Centers

In a tiny apartment kitchen, storage space is obviously at a premium. But even if you have a larger kitchen, it's important to plan your space carefully. Professional kitchen designers subdivide the kitchen into several areas called *work centers*. The primary ones are arranged around the stove, the sink, and the refrigerator, plus an area that's sometimes called the mixing or food preparation area. In larger kitchens, substations can be set up for hobbies like making bread or arranging flowers. Planning these areas simply involves some common sense. The best way to decide where something should go is to ask yourself what other things might be used along with it. Then group all the related items together.

First, we'll examine a standard kitchen floor plan (see Figure 3.1). We'll make some general storage recommendations, and then we'll talk about some of the specific tools and equipment you'll need for running your kitchen.

In this floor plan, notice that the drawers are labeled with letters, and the cabinets are labeled with numbers. The dishwasher and the upper cabinets are indicated by dashed lines. Dotted lines mark the path connecting the stove, the sink, and the refrigerator, an area that's often called the *work triangle*. (At some times of the month this zone is called the Bermuda Triangle.) Since people spend a lot of time traipsing over those dotted lines, kitchen planners recommend that the total distance around the triangle not exceed 21'–24'.

The arrangement of the stove, sink, and refrigerator will dictate the storage plan for everything from pots and pans to paper towels. Although this floor plan may not look like your kitchen, the rationale for what goes where remains the same, no matter how your appliances are arranged.

Moving clockwise around the floor plan from the lower left corner, we'll take each drawer, cabinet, and countertop in turn, and make suggestions for the best use of each storage space or work area. The cabinets above the counter are referred to as *wall cabinets*, and the cabinets below the counter are called *base cabinets*. Pretend that there is a dining area just out of the picture to the left, which you face as you stand at the stove. There is a window above the sink,

and a cordless phone or one with a long cord mounted on the end of the cabinet between the kitchen and the eating area to the left. There's an oven below the cooktop.

A: The drawer close to the telephone should probably be designated as the catch-all or junk drawer, where you store pens, notepads, markers, labels, tape, rubber bands, the telephone directory, and a few tools, like a hammer, screwdriver, and a pair of pliers. Put a small box or jar in the drawer to collect any tiny parts you find that probably belong to something important, but you're not sure what. And make room for a small first-aid kit here. Since this drawer is outside the Bermuda Triangle, it would help keep innocent bystanders out of your way, should they decide to wander into the kitchen and rummage around for something while you're working.

B: Since this drawer to the left of the stove is also close to the dining area, it would be a good place to store placemats, napkins, and kitchen linens, plus anything that goes straight to the table and back. Put the birthday candles and matches here, too.

You'll probably want to keep the countertop to the left of the stove as bare as possible, to leave room for serving meals, clearing the table, and setting down bags of groceries as you bring them in.

1: The base cabinet to the left of the stove would be the most logical

place to store serving containers and accessories: platters, vegetable dishes, carving board, and bread basket. You can keep candles for the table down here as well.

C: The drawer underneath the stove is wide enough for the broiler pan, roasting pan, and wire cooling racks.

The stovetop is the traditional place for a set of salt and pepper shakers, and you'll probably want to keep a teakettle on one of the back burners.

D: The drawer to the right of the stove should be for tools and gadgets: tongs, pancake turner, potato masher, long-handled spoons, meat and candy thermometers, and a timer, unless there's one built into the stove.

On the countertop above this drawer, you could keep a crock with mixing spoons and wire whisks—so handy to be able to pull out whatever you need while you're at the stove.

2: The base cabinet to the right of the stove is where the pots and pans should go. Saucepans can be nested inside one another, and you can hang your favorite skillet from a screw inside the cabinet door. Keep tall bottles of oil and vinegar there too, and a container to collect drippings. Be sure to make room for a fire extinguisher. If you have more pots and pans than you can fit into this cabinet, an attractive solution would be to install a pot rack over the stove.

3: The wall cabinet to the right of the stove is the place for any herbs, spices, seasonings, and condiments that you add to foods while you're preparing them at the stove, plus croutons and other ingredients for salads and salad dressings.

E: Unless you have a knife block or a magnetic rack mounted on the wall, the drawer to the left of the sink would be a convenient place for cutlery, plus other tools like the vegetable peeler, scissors, can opener, bottle opener, and corkscrew.

The countertop to the left of the sink seems to be the most logical place for the coffeemaker, since it's close to the water faucet. If you don't have a built-in microwave oven, a

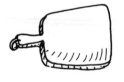

good location for a table-top model would be in the back corner of this countertop.

4: The base cabinet to the left of the sink is ideal for cutting boards and anything that involves working with water or liquids: a salad-spinning basket, steamer basket, pitchers, strainers, and funnels. It's also a good place for a salad bowl. Hang your colander on a hook inside the cabinet door.

5: The cabinet above the counter to the left of the sink is a good spot for microwave dishes, containers you use for leftovers, and the coffee filters, sweetener, creamer, and a few mugs.

6: The wastebasket can go on one side of the cabinet beneath the sink, and the plastic liners and cleaning supplies can go on the other side. Installing a slide-out tray will make these things much more accessible. A paper towel dispenser can be installed on the inside of one of the cabinet doors, if you're short on wall space close to the sink.

On the counter either to the left or the right of the sink, you can keep a pump dispenser with soap, a bottle of hand lotion, and a small jar for brushes and the rubber spatula that you use to scrape plates.

F: The drawer to the right of the dishwasher would be a good place to store measuring spoons and cups, as well as any other utensils used for mixing and baking, such as spatulas and the rolling pin. You can keep a box of plastic sandwich bags here as well.

On the countertop to the right of the sink is just the spot for a set of canisters containing your baking staples: flour, sugar, rice, oatmeal, etc. Here's also the most logical place for your food processor.

7: This base cabinet to the right of the dishwasher would be convenient for cake pans, casseroles, baking dishes, and other bakeware. You can keep a kitchen scale, sifter, grater, and other food preparation equipment there too. Mount a rack inside the cabinet door to hold boxes of waxed paper, plastic wrap, and foil.

8: Since this wall cabinet is right next to the dishwasher, it's a good place for glasses, plates, and other everyday dishes. You can stand in one place and unload the dishwasher without taking a single step.

G: Also close to the dishwasher, this drawer to the left of the refrigerator is a convenient place to put everyday flatware: knives, forks, spoons, and various serving utensils.

The countertop next to the refrigerator would be the perfect place for the bread box and toaster oven, since it's close to the butter, spreads, and sandwich fixings in the refrigerator. You can keep your favorite cookbooks there, too.

9: Small kitchen appliances that you don't keep on the counter can be stored in this base cabinet to the left of the refrigerator: an electric mixer and mixing bowls, blender, etc.

10: The wall cabinet to the left of the refrigerator can be designated as the breakfast and sandwich center, with your favorite cereals, unrefrigerated sandwich fixings like peanut butter, and your baking supplies.

11: A turntable in one of the shelves inside this deep cabinet over the refrigerator will make it easier to reach things at the back of the cabinet. Store bulky things there, like a covered cake plate and an ice bucket.

The Pantry: Expand your space by installing shallow racks on the insides of the pantry doors, just deep enough to hold canned goods. Use turntables on some of the pantry shelves for small jars and bottles, and store boxes on the other shelves. Below the bottom shelf, you might use a vinyl-coated wire drawer system for bulky bagged items like chips. Hang your apron on a hook inside the door. If there's room, put a broom and a dustpan in there as well, or better yet, an electric broom.

Now that we've covered the general layout, here are the lists of specific items you need in the kitchen. Items followed by an asterisk (*) are nonessentials, but nice to have. They can be added later on. The potential list of gadgets could fill many pages, so if cooking is your hobby, you'll probably want a number of things that aren't included in these lists.

Sink Center

Cleanup Equipment and Supplies

Keep all your dish brushes clean by running them through the dishwasher every so often. Launder dishcloths and towels with bleach to keep them smelling fresh.

- **Bleach:** For disinfecting cutting boards. (You could use disinfectant spray cleaner instead.) I keep a small, clearly-labeled squeeze bottle filled with bleach here, and use it to remove stains on the counter.

- **Dish Brush**

- **Dishcloths:** (These are the size of washcloths.) You'll need about a dozen. I prefer them to sponges for wiping off sticky jars and counters.

- **Dish Drainer and Mat*:** This is optional if you have a dishwasher.

- **Dishpan:** You can use this for soaking things or washing them by hand, even if you do have a dishwasher.

- **Dish Towels:** You'll need at least a dozen; two dozen is better. I keep

my multicolored assortment folded up in a wicker basket on the counter, so they're always handy. You'll use these for drying dishes, vegetables, and salad greens, and also for wiping your hands.

■ **Dishwasher Powder*:** Not necessary unless you have a dishwasher.

■ **Dishwashing Liquid:** Everybody needs this. It's also a substitute for hand soap, in case you run out.

■ **Disinfectant Spray Cleaner:** For sinks, counters, and cutting boards, unless you put them in the dishwasher. Be sure to use this or bleach to disinfect any surface where you've placed raw meat, poultry, seafood, or produce, so as to reduce the risk of cross-contamination. And use it to wipe off sticky drawer pulls and handles on your cabinets and appliances.

■ **Glass and Countertop Cleaner:** For light cleaning of countertops, cabinets, and kitchen surfaces.

■ **Hand Lotion**

■ **Hand Soap:** I like the antibacterial kind in a pump dispenser better than bar soap, since there's no glop to clean out of a soap dish.

■ **Nonabrasive Cleanser:** I prefer the kind with bleach, since it's more effective for cleaning stains off sinks and countertops.

■ **Nylon Scrubbing Pad*:** If you have any Teflon-coated skillets or pans, you'll need one of these for scrubbing them.

■ **Oven Cleaner:** Even if you have a self-cleaning or continuous-cleaning oven, you might still need this to clean the racks.

■ **Paper Towels:** Since I use cloth dish towels for so many things, I don't use too many paper towels. But they're unbeatable for draining bacon, wiping off poultry after rinsing it, and cleaning up messy spills.

■ **Polishes:** You'll need some for brass, copper, silver, or any other metals you have that require polishing.

■ **Rubber Gloves:** Dermatologists recommend cotton-lined neoprene gloves, because of the absorbent lining. (It took an office visit for me to glean this little bit of information.)

■ **Rubber Plate Scraper:** This is great for scraping dishes at the sink, as well as for stuffing things down the disposal—when the motor is turned off, of course.

■ **Scouring Pads or Steel Wool*:** If you have a scrub brush and a nylon pad, you may not need any of these. But nothing removes gunk from oven racks quite as well.

■ **Scrub Brush:** I use one with a long handle for cleaning out the sink.

- **Sponges:** Except for special scrubber-sponges, I prefer dishcloths, since sponges tend to harbor bacteria. But if you do use sponges, be sure to disinfect them in the dishwasher, or put them through the washing machine in a mesh bag. Otherwise, they get smelly. Keep a separate one in a distinct color just for wiping up spills on the floor.

- **Vegetable Brush**

- **Wastebasket:** Buy the largest one you can find that will fit under your sink. Be sure to line it.

- **Wastebasket Liners:** You can use grocery sacks or plastic bags specially designed for this purpose. I prefer the drawstring variety, since you can cram more trash into them. If you use a size larger than you think you'll need, it can extend over the sides of the wastebasket, allowing for any overflow that occurs before someone decides to take out the trash.

Cutting and Spreading Tools

Knives should be stored in a knife block or on a magnetic bar—either fastened to the inside of a drawer, or mounted on the wall. Have knives professionally sharpened about once a year. I take mine to a neighborhood meat market, and use a sharpening steel between times. Sizes indicated below refer to the length of the blade.

- **Apple Corer or Corer/Sectioner*:** This gadget removes cores and slices apples and pears into 8–12 sections.

- **Bottle Opener/Church Key**

- **Can Opener:** I much prefer a heavy-duty manual can opener to the electric variety. Be sure to wash off the tops of cans before you open them, and run your can and bottle openers through the dishwasher regularly, to prevent an accumulation of gunk.

- **Carving Knife and Fork—8"–10":** For carving cooked meats.

- **Chef's (Cook's) Knife—8"–10":** For chopping foods. Test it before you buy it to be sure that it's comfortable, and that it fits your hand well.

- **Corkscrew**

- **Cutting Boards:** I keep several sizes for cutting up raw and cooked foods. Mine all go into the dishwasher.

- **Egg Slicer*:** This gadget can also be used to chop eggs: Slice the egg once. Then turn it 90° and slice it a second time, holding it over the bowl where you want the egg to fall.

- **Paring Knife:** 3"–4".

- **Poultry Shears*:** These are only necessary if you intend to cut up and disjoint whole chickens, rather than buying them already cut up at the supermarket. You can use plain scissors for cutting up cooked poultry.

- **Scissors:** I keep two pairs: red for opening packages, and blue for snipping herbs and cutting up other foods like cooked chicken. The blue pair goes into the dishwasher.

- **Serrated Knife:** My small one has a 3"–4" blade and a red plastic handle, and I reach for it almost every day to slice things like tomatoes and citrus fruits. I have a larger one with an 8"–12" blade, which is a must for slicing bread, since it keeps the loaf from getting squashed. You can also use it to slice cold ham and turkey.

- **Sharpening (Honing) Steel:** If you don't know how to use one, ask your butcher to demonstrate.

- **Spatulas—Narrow Metal Blade:** A long one is handy for frosting cakes, and a shorter one is nice to have for spreading sandwiches.

- **Utility Knife:** You'll find that you use this often for trimming and slicing fruits and vegetables. It should have a blade 6"–8" long.

- **Vegetable Peeler—Swivel Blade:** You'll need to replace this from time to time, since there's no simple way to sharpen the blade.

- **Zester*:** For stripping citrus peel from lemons, limes, and oranges.

Miscellaneous

- **Aspirin or Substitute**

- **Bandages:** You probably don't need a whole box of them in the kitchen. Just put several in an old tin bandage box, and keep a tube of first-aid cream in there too.

- **Coffee Filters:** I usually keep a stack of filters in the drawer next to the coffeemaker, and a full box in the pantry. You can use a paper towel for an emergency substitute.

- **Coffeemaker:** Clean it out about once a month with a commercial cleaner, or mix a few tablespoons of vinegar in a quart of water. Be sure

A-TO-Z CHECKLIST OF STORAGE ORGANIZERS AND SPACE SAVERS

If you like to shop from home, look through cookware and organizing catalogs, or surf the Internet. Away from home, you can shop at stores specializing in housewares and kitchen products. You may be surprised at the variety of kitchen organizers you'll discover in places like hardware stores, variety stores, discount stores, linen stores, and office supply stores. Many times a particular organizer designed to store something totally unrelated to the kitchen can be improvised for a perfect solution to a difficult storage problem. For example, vertical file racks do a great job of keeping cookie sheets and muffin tins neatly arranged and easy to remove. You can snap as many together as you need.

- **Add-a-Shelf:** These freestanding shelves are made of vinyl-coated steel wire or particle board, and are shaped like an upside-down "U." They help you take advantage of wasted space between or above shelves. Sometimes these are called "helper shelves." You'll find full-depth shelves, as well as shelves that are half as deep as a wall cabinet, for arranging shorter items double-decker style towards the back of the cabinet, with taller items towards the front. Some slide out to expand, and others are fixed in width. They are available in various sizes, widths, depths, and heights. Use them to increase storage space for spices, canned goods, and other nonperishable foods, as well as for all sorts of kitchen equipment. They'll double your shelf space for juice glasses and other squatty glasses or mugs.

- **Baby-Wipes Dispensers:** These come in two shapes: cylindrical and rectangular. Cut the lid off the rectangular ones and use them as drawer organizers. Use either style to hold odds and ends that would otherwise get jumbled up, such as cookie cutters or cake decorating supplies.

- **Bakers' Racks:** These are attractive as well as functional. Use them for platters, large serving pieces, or cookbooks. If you put one in a sunny spot, you could even put a small herb garden on it.

(continued)

---

to run plain water through the coffeemaker a couple of times after cleaning it.

- **Colander:** Get one that's not wobbly. I have two: one with large slits for draining pasta and berries, and another one with tiny holes that I use to press the water out of chopped spinach and steamed squash.

- **First-Aid Cream**

- **Funnels:** One with a narrow mouth helps you pour liquids or ground spices into bottles. One with

a wide mouth is good for filling jars with pickles, or freezer containers with soups and sauces.

- **Garlic Press*:** Unless I'm using whole garlic cloves, I prefer to buy minced garlic in a jar. One of my high school friends used to say that her mother kept her in line by making her wash the garlic press before she went out on dates.

- **Juice Reamer:** For squeezing lemons, etc. The old-fashioned glass kind works well.

- **Pitchers:** A plastic one with a lid, for mixing frozen juice, plus another one for serving water at the table.

- **Salad Spinning Basket:** I think this is the easiest and most efficient way to dry salad greens and herbs.

- **Steamer Basket**

- **Strainers:** A small one (3"), with fine mesh, and a larger one (5"), with medium mesh, are both handy.

Cooking Center: Cooktop, Oven, and Microwave

Pots and Pans

- **Broiler Pan and Rack:** New ovens usually come with a set of these. But since I usually grill food instead of broiling it in the oven, I don't use mine very often.

- **Double Boiler*:** The 2–3-quart size is standard. If you don't have one, you can improvise by setting a small pan or metal bowl inside a larger pan. Unless directions state otherwise, always cook food over (not in) hot (not boiling) water.

- **Dutch Oven:** These come in two styles: one looks like an extra-deep saucepot with double handles; the other style resembles one saucepot turned upside down on top of another one. They're often used for cooking soups, stews, or pot roasts on top of the stove.

- **Electric Skillet*:** Although this isn't technically a necessity, my T-Fal Gourmet Skillet is one of my favorite

appliances, and I use it several times each week. You can plug it in anywhere there's an outlet, so you can isolate foods that might splatter. In addition to the standard 3-quart sauté pan that comes with it, you can order other sizes as well. One is a larger pot that can be used as a slow cooker or a soup kettle. A griddle and a ridged skillet, called a health grill, are also available. Since the base has a temperature dial, it's good for slow simmering, or any in situation where you need precise temperature control.

- **Microwave Dishes:** If you're not sure if a container is suitable for microwave use, do this: Pour a cup of water into a glass measuring cup and set it in the microwave next to or on top of the container in question. Heat it for 1 minute on "High." If the water heats, it's fine to use. If the container heats, it's not microwave-safe.

- **Rack for Roasting Pan:** Usually these are V-shaped and adjustable. They elevate the roast so that it doesn't stew in its own juices.

- **Roasting Pan:** Mine is heavy, and measures 16" x 12" x 3½". It holds a whole beef tenderloin, a large turkey, or two turkey breasts.

- **Saucepans:** I have an extra-small (1-pint) size for melting butter, which is nice, but not essential. Three sizes you'll need are: small (1–1½-quart), medium (2–2½-quart), and large (3–4-quart). They all should have tight-fitting lids.

- **Saucepots:** These are shaped like wide saucepans, but they have a small handle on each side, in place of one long handle. Because they're wider than saucepans, and allow for better evaporation, they're good for reducing sauces. If they're ovenproof, they can double as casserole dishes.

- **Sauté Pan and Cover:** This 3–5-quart pan looks like a large skillet with straight sides, and can double as a chicken fryer. It's great for making spaghetti sauce or soup, since you can sauté ground beef, onions, or mushrooms, and then add any liquid ingredients to the same pan.

- **Skillet:** A 10" size with a nonstick finish is essential. Be sure you have some sort of cover that fits your skillet. A smaller 8" size is optional, but it's handy for omelets.

- **Stock Pot or Large Soup Kettle:** A 6–8-quart size is good for cooking pasta and large quantities of soup or stock. I use mine frequently, since I cook a lot of both.

- **Teakettle:** A 2–3-quart size is fine.

- **Wire Cooling Racks:** You'll need at least two of these, preferably the large rectangular size. I recently found a boxed set of three with folding legs that allow you to stack them. This would be a great idea for anyone with limited counter space.

Cooking Utensils, Tools, and Gadgets

- **Basting Brush:** Some cooks prefer a bulb baster, which looks like a giant eye dropper. Personally, I've always had trouble controlling them. The juices gush out at the most inopportune times.

- **Fork:** A 2-tined, long-handled variety is good for piercing raw meats to help them absorb marinade, but I prefer tongs for turning things once the cooking has begun.

- **Ladle:** I have a large one for soups, and a smaller one for sauces.

- **Pancake Turner:** I have a small one for getting brownies out of the pan, plus a larger one for flipping pancakes. Sometimes I use both of them at the same time for tricky things like turning quesadillas.

- **Potato Masher:** I like the kind with a round head and holes better than the variety with a wavy wire base. It's just personal preference.

A-TO-Z CHECKLIST (CONTINUED)

- **Baskets and Bins:** These can be made of many different materials, from vinyl-coated steel wire, to plastic (similar to miniature laundry baskets), to wicker. Some even have prongs for attaching to peg board. The smaller ones can be used in drawers for small gadgets. Larger ones work well inside cabinets, where it might be easier to pull out a basket or bin and select what you need, than to wrestle around trying to retrieve something on the back of a shelf that's difficult to reach. Attractive baskets, such as those made of wicker, can be used on countertops to hold things like colorful dish towels or napkins (cloth or paper).

- **Book Racks:** The one-shelf freestanding variety can be used on the counter to hold cookbooks. Some types can be attached to the wall. If you have an extensive collection of cookbooks, you might want to use a small, furniture-sized bookcase backed up to the end of a counter.

- **Canisters:** There are all kinds, from imported Italian designer crockery to utilitarian plastic and glass. They're wonderful for storing dry staples, such as flour, rice, and pasta. You can keep them either in wall cabinets, at eye level, or base cabinets, below the counter. The more attractive ones can be stored out on the countertop. For the others, you can make colorful labels with markers and "ball-style" printing. To keep the labels from smearing, use indelible ink or cover the labels with a wide piece of clear tape.

- **Carry-All Caddies and Totes:** Although these are most often used to hold cleaning supplies, they can also be used for many other things. Try one in the refrigerator to hold mustard, relish, and other sandwich condiments. When you're fixing sandwiches, all the condiments can be easily removed from the refrigerator, and then replaced in one quick motion. These caddies come in several different sizes, each of which is particularly well suited for a different purpose.

(continued)

- **Spoons:** I have two large metal ones: a long-handled basting spoon that I use to stir spaghetti sauce or chili, and to scoop fat out of the pan when I'm browning ground beef. I also have a slotted one for removing vegetables from the steamer, or crumbled bacon from a skillet. In addition, I have a pasta serving spoon with funny teeth, that also makes it easier to lift a few strands from the pot to see if it's cooked al dente. Then I have a couple of wooden spoons for stirring sauces. Finally, I have several spoons made of nylon, melamine, and various indeterminate materials, in assorted sizes and colors. You'll find that you add to your spoon collection through the years, and the old favorites are difficult to part with.

- **Thermometers:** A meat thermometer is an absolute must! It measures internal temperatures up to about 200°. There is simply no other way to get an accurate reading to find out how well done something is. You can also use one to verify that leftovers are reheated to a safe internal temperature: 140°. I have one of the instant-read styles. I have another thermometer designed for candy, which registers temperatures up to 400°. It has a clip on the side so you can snap it onto a saucepan and watch the action.

- **Timer:** It should make a loud noise.

- **Tongs:** These are just the thing for turning things as they cook, or for holding foods as you dip them into breading mixtures.

- **Wire whisk:** You might want to have more than one.

Miscellaneous

- **Apron:** Unless you get a little messy in the kitchen, you're not getting involved enough with your cooking! I like the cobbler-style apron that slips over the head and ties on both sides.

- **Barbecue Tools*:** If you do much grilling, you might want a long-handled turner and tongs. A pair of fireproof mitts is also nice to have. However, the chef's hat is optional.

- **Burn Ointment:** Ask your doctor to prescribe a jar of Silvadene cream. It's expensive, but there's nothing like it for a painful burn. Otherwise, buy a tube of the over-the-counter variety.

- **Drippings Container:** You can use an empty can, or you can order a Fat Trapper from Range Kleen, (888) 364-5566. It's a white plastic box, about the size of a large bag of coffee beans, which comes with disposable foil-lined bags for drippings.

- **Fire Extinguisher:** This is a must, and everyone in the family should know where it is and how to use it. You need a smoke detector, too.

- **Oven Thermometer:** This is the only way to be sure that the thermostat on your oven is accurate.

- **Pot Holders:** You'll need at least two, and preferably four. I use them under hot pots or baking dishes when I set them on the counter, as well as for removing things from the oven.

- **Salt and Pepper Shakers:** You might want several sets, as well as a pepper grinder.

Food Service Center

Tableware and Serving Utensils

- **Dishware:** You'll need something to serve food on: plates, cereal and salad bowls, mugs, etc. If you rarely use cups and saucers, there's no need to keep them in the kitchen.

- **Flatware:** Unless you're exclusively into finger foods, you'll need some knives, forks, spoons, soup or dessert spoons, and maybe steak knives. Iced tea spoons are good for fishing things out of tall, skinny jars.

- **Glassware:** I like the French bistro-style. They're inexpensive, and come in assorted sizes for everything from juice to iced tea.

- **Pie Server:** Until you've tried to get the first slice of pie out of the pan with a pancake turner, you don't know how handy these are.

- **Salad Fork and Spoon**

- **Serving Forks and Spoons:** A plain and a slotted tablespoon, a meat fork, a sugar spoon, and a gravy ladle will do nicely. (These are called *completer sets*.) Add extra serving spoons and other special pieces as you need them.

- **Stemware:** This type of glassware is a little more elegant than tumblers for serving drinks. A balloon shape is a good all-purpose style.

- **Sugar Bowl and Cream Pitcher:** These don't have to match your dishes. A container for artificial sweetener is also nice to have, as well as a small dish for empty packets or used tea bags.

Table Linens and Accessories

- **Beverage Napkins**

- **Birthday Candles:** Don't wait until the big day to get these.

- **Candles for the Table***

- **Dinner Napkins**

- **Matches:** Use the long-handled kind for lighting a grill or the pilot light on a gas oven. My favorite type is a pistol-style butane lighter.

- **Paper Doilies*:** These are nice for dressing up a plate of brownies or a dessert. The rectangular ones can be used as placemats on lap trays. Look for assorted sizes in variety stores, kitchen specialty shops, or stationery and party goods stores.

- **Paper Napkins:** I keep a stack in an oblong basket on the counter, next to my dish towels. That way, they're handy to grab when you're having a quick sandwich or bowl of cereal.

- **Paper Plates:** Good for picnics, and handy for microwaving.
- **Pepper Mill**★
- **Placemats:** I like the ones that you can toss in the washing machine.
- **Tablecloths**★

Serving Accessories

- **Bread Basket:** An inexpensive wicker basket is fine. If you only have one, be sure it's long enough to hold French bread. A smaller one for biscuits or rolls also comes in handy.
- **Carving Board:** One made of wood is nice, preferably with a groove to catch the juices. If you use it for cutting up raw meat, be sure to disinfect it afterwards. It's really better to have separate cutting boards for raw foods.
- **Cheese Board**★
- **Hot Pads/Trivets:** Besides the utilitarian ones you use in the kitchen, you'll need a couple that are nice enough to bring to the table.
- **Lap Trays:** They're great for eating in front of the TV, and when you serve dinner buffet-style.
- **Platters:** Several assorted sizes.
- **Salad Bowl:** This can be wooden, Lucite, glass, or pottery.
- **Serving Dishes and Bowls**
- **Serving Trays**
- **Small Dishes for Condiments:** Ramekins work just fine.
- **Snack Dishes and Baskets:** For popcorn and chips.

A-TO-Z CHECKLIST (CONTINUED)

- **Cereal and Cracker Canisters:** These plastic containers with tight-fitting lids are ideal for keeping opened boxes of cereal or crackers fresh. They also make it easy for you to see how much you have left. Some have flip-top lids, which make it simple to dispense cereal. (This kind is also useful for storing dry pet food or detergent.) Other box-types have airtight lids, some of which are hinged, which make them good for crackers and cookies.

- **Cup Hooks:** These can be used for lots more besides hanging up cups and mugs. They can be mounted underneath cabinets or shelves, or they can be attached to vertical surfaces. If you have ceramic tile or another type of hard-surface backsplash behind your countertops, and want to hang up something there, such as a copper mold, try this solution: Screw a small cup hook to the underside of the wall cabinet that hangs above the backsplash, as close as possible to the back edge, where the cabinet joins the backsplash. Then thread about 18″ of nylon fishing line through a ring in the copper mold. Tie a knot in it, and hang the line from the hook. Adjust the length as desired. It's practically invisible, and whatever you have on display can be easily removed for cleaning or polishing.

- **Cup Stackers:** These hold 3 or 4 teacups without toppling over.

- **Cutlery Trays:** These are designed to hold knives, forks, spoons, etc. Some are 2-tiered, with a sliding upper tray. They're also useful for organizing "junk" drawers.

- **Dishpans:** These can be used for lots more things than washing dishes. Set them on pantry shelves to store bulky containers of pasta or bags of snack chips. Or put one under the sink to organize your cleaning products.

- **Dishware Racks:** Because these are designed just for this purpose, they do a good job of maximizing your space. Some are plastic and some are vinyl-coated steel wire.

(continued)

Mixing, Baking, and Food Preparation Center

Bakeware and Ovenware

- **Baking Dishes:** The 2- and 3-quart ovenproof glass rectangular pans are a must. I also like the 4-quart size for extra-large things, like big batches of brownies.

- **Biscuit Pan:** This is a small rectangular baking pan for biscuits, rolls, etc. I prefer to use an 8″ or 9″ round cake pan for biscuits, but I use my biscuit pan for heating rolls.

- **Cake Pans—Flat:** You'll need 2–3 round ones (8″–9″) for layer cakes. You'll need a 9″ x 13″ rectangular pan for sheet cakes. One with a snap-on lid is good for transporting, refrigerating, or just keeping cakes fresh. For cornbread or gingerbread, you'll need an 8″ or 9″ square pan.

- **Cake Pans—Tube:** A 10″ size is good for angel or pound cakes. A Bundt pan (12-cup) can be used for fancy cakes and for congealed salads.

- **Casseroles and Covers:** Two sizes, 1½- or 2-quart and 3-quart, will do.

- **Cookie Sheets:** You'll need at least two, and they can have a ½″ lip or not, whichever style you prefer. I like the ones with a lip, since you can use them for preparing oven-fried chicken, and the juices won't run over the sides.

- **Custard Cups:** These usually come in sets of six, which is the minimum number you need.

- **Jelly Roll Pan—10″ x 15″*:** This can double as an extra cookie sheet.

- **Loaf Pan:** You'll need two (9″ x 5″ x 3″) pans for things like banana bread and meatloaf. You may want some of the smaller sizes for holiday baking.

- **Muffin Tin—Standard Size*:** If you make muffins and cupcakes, you'll need at least one.

- **Pie Pan—8″–9″:** I prefer ovenproof glass pans, but metal or ceramic is fine. You might want several, since they're handy to use for holding ingredients for breading chicken and the like.

- **Quiche Pan*:** You can always use a deep-dish pie pan instead.

- **Ring Mold*:** If you buy one, the 6–8-cup size is most useful.

- **Springform Pan*:** For making cheesecake, you'll need a 9″ size.

- **Tart Pans*:** These have removable bottoms. I have several sizes, but the 8″ or 9″ round one is standard. I used to think these were just for a gourmet cook. Now I know how nice they are to have. However, beware of using a tart pan for quiche, since the liquid ingredients can leak out.

Cooking Utensils, Tools, and Gadgets

- **Biscuit Cutter:** You'll need one about 2½″ in diameter for cutting out rolls, biscuits, cookies, etc.

- **Flour Sifter*:** As long as you're buying one, get a fairly large size.

- **Grater:** The 4-sided box style is good, but if you have a food processor, you may not use a grater too often.

- **Ice Cream Scoop or Spade:** This beats trying to dip out frozen goodies with a flimsy-handled spoon!

- **Measuring Cups for Dry Ingredients:** It's nice to have 2 sets of the standard ¼-cup, ⅓-cup, ½-cup, and 1-cup size. I also enjoy my set with ⅛-cup, ⅔-cup, and ¾-cup sizes, which I ordered from a catalog.

- **Measuring Cups for Liquids:** Although I have a 1-cup, 2-cup, and 4-cup glass nesting set, the one I use most often is a 2-cup plastic beaker style. I also have a 2-quart glass pitcher that I use for making tapioca pudding and peanut brittle in the microwave.

- **Measuring Spoons:** I have several sets. Besides the standard ¼-, ½-, and 1-teaspoon, plus 1-tablespoon sizes, my sets have ⅛-teaspoon and ½-tablespoon measures as well. I also have 2 individual plastic measuring spoons

with sliding measures: one that measures up to 1 teaspoon, and the other that goes up to 1 tablespoon. These are handy if you need to measure an odd amount, like ¾ teaspoon.

- **Pastry Blender*:** If you don't have a food processor, you'll need this for making pie crusts from scratch, or for cutting butter or shortening into flour.

- **Pastry Brush:** It's nice to have a separate one for brushing melted butter or olive oil on bread, or egg whites on unbaked rolls, plus another one for basting meat as it cooks.

- **Pizza Cutting Wheel*:** In some families, this is standard equipment. In others, it's optional.

- **Rolling Pin:** Get a full-size version. I think the marble ones are too heavy.

- **Rotary Egg Beater:** Since I bought a small cordless electric mixer, I don't use this too often.

- **Rubber Spatulas:** You'll need at least two of these, preferably both wide and narrow sizes. You might also like one shaped like a spoon.

Containers

- **Mixing Bowls:** Start out with a set of 3–4 nested bowls, preferably in stainless steel, since they can be chilled for whipping cream. Add others made of glass, melamine, or crockery, as desired. A giant one (6- to 8-quart or larger) isn't absolutely essential, but it's nice to have for mixing up extra-large batches of cole slaw or potato salad.

- **Ramekins***: These little white containers that look like miniature soufflé dishes are quite versatile. They make attractive cups for baked custard, and they can double as small snack or condiment dishes. You can also prepare individual soufflés or other desserts in them.

- **Soufflé Dish:** The 2½–3-quart size is most useful, and it can also do double duty as a serving dish. I have a nested set of several different sizes, and use them for heating and serving foods directly from the microwave.

Consumables

- **Foil:** I like to have both the regular and heavy-duty weights on hand. I also use the super-heavy-duty weight for cooking fish on the grill. I fold up the edges to resemble a cookie sheet, add the fish, and then pour the melted butter or basting sauce on top. About halfway through the cooking time, I punch holes in the foil with a sharp fork, and let the juices run out onto the coals. It makes the grill smoke up, and gives the fish a delicious flavor, while keeping it from falling apart on the grill.

- **Kitchen Twine:** You'll need this for tying chicken or rolled roasts, and for other purposes as well. It's especially made to use with food, so don't try to substitute package-wrapping string.

- **Muffin Cup Liners—Paper***: Heavy foil liners can be used on a cookie sheet without a muffin pan.

A-TO-Z CHECKLIST (CONTINUED)

- **Door Racks:** These come in two varieties: vinyl-coated steel wire with fixed shelves, or aluminum slats with adjustable shelves. They are available in sizes as small as two-shelf units, or as large as ten-shelf units. Widths vary, and depths are generally about 5", or just the size that fits on a hinged closet-type door, allowing the door to be closed without bumping into the shelves in front of it. Smaller sizes are available that can be mounted inside cabinet doors, but care must be taken to hang them so that when the door is closed, they don't hit the items stored on the shelves.

- **Drawer Dividers:** These come in all varieties. Most are plastic, although some are vinyl-coated wire or wire mesh. Some are designed for kitchen cutlery (knives, forks, and spoons). Others are plastic snap-together rectangular modules, ranging in size from about 2" square to over a foot in length. Some have a smaller tray that slides over the contents stored in the tray below. You can even buy self-adhesive plastic strips to create custom dividers. Be sure to check office supply stores for things that can be adapted to kitchen use.

- **Extra Shelves:** These can be made from wood shelving or particle board. They're available at the lumberyard, and are attached with brackets. Often there is wasted space above the upper shelf in a pantry or closet. Although this storage area may require a step stool to reach, it's still useful for stashing seldom-needed items.

- **Glassware Tracks:** These are usually made of vinyl-coated steel wire, and are mounted under shelves to allow stemware to be suspended from the shelf upside down. They free up some shelf space underneath the glassware.

- **Hooks:** Brass hooks that are often used for robes can be attached to the outside ends of cabinets to hang potholders and dish towels. Just be sure they don't jut out too far. They're useful for hanging aprons inside the pantry door, as well.

(continued)

- **Parchment Paper***: Use this for lining baking pans. It keeps cookies from spreading as much as they would if you used just non-stick spray.

- **Plastic Bags and Wrap:** You'll need an assortment of bags in different sizes and weights: both the zip kind and the plain ones.

- **Toothpicks:** Good for testing cakes, wrapping bacon around meats, and for anchoring frosted cake layers so that they don't slide around.

- **Waxed Paper:** For rolling out pie crusts or biscuits, or for shaping hamburger patties.

Miscellaneous

- **Blender:** Even if you have a food processor, blenders are great for mixing smoothies and other drinks.

- **Canisters:** Whether they're the decorative or the utilitarian variety that you keep tucked away in a cabinet, you'll need some to keep dry staples fresh after you open them. I began collecting see-through canisters years ago, and I use them for storing all my dry staples: sugar, flour, Bisquick, rice, macaroni, noodles, and tapioca, to name a few. I can tell at a glance when I'm getting low on anything.

- **Covered Cake Plate***: I have several sizes, from small to jumbo.

- **Electric Mixer—Portable**: I have a small cordless one with a single whisk or beater attachment. It's not quite powerful enough to whip cream, but it's handy for sauces and eggs, and you can use it anywhere.

- **Electric Mixer—Standard***: The portable variety works almost as well for some things, but the standard size is nice for making cakes, and it's essential for beating mixtures for any extended length of time.

- **Food Processor***: Although I have friends who don't use one, I don't know what I'd do without mine!

- **Immersion Blender***: If you make pureed soups very often, you'll appreciate the convenience of not having to transfer it to a blender or food processor.

- **Kitchen Scale**: I use mine for weighing pasta and meat, especially when I'm freezing several portions of cooked chicken, ham, or roast. That way I know exactly how much is in each package.

- **Toaster Oven or Toaster**: I vote for the toaster oven. Besides, the top of it is a great place to warm plates and bowls for soup or pasta.

Refrigerator and Freezer Center

- **Freezer Bags**: Buy the kind you can write on, in several different sizes.

- **Freezer Containers**: Handy for freezing soups and other liquids.

- **Freezer Labels**: I use a sheet of peel-off office labels for this purpose.

- **Indelible Marking Pen**: If you use a regular pen to mark food for the freezer, you may not be able to read the label if it gets wet.

- **Refrigerator Dishes—Covered**: I've collected an assortment over the years. All of mine are married. The rule is that if they're missing their mates, they get evicted!

- **Ice Bucket and Tongs***: If you have company and someone offers to fill the water glasses for you, this is nice to have.

- **Ice Pick**: Better than dropping a big block of ice into the sink to break it into pieces!

- - -

Stocking the Shelves

Now hear this! A well-stocked pantry is one of the best keys I know to being able to prepare good meals in a hurry. Avoiding those extra trips to the store helps you sidestep one of the biggest annoyances of getting dinner on the table. Having plenty of ingredients tucked away in your refrigerator, freezer, and pantry will add hours to your week, and will open up many creative possibilities. When you roll up your sleeves to cook, it's so satisfying to discover that all the ingredients you need are right there waiting for you. Some of these items are available in low-fat or low-sodium varieties. Choose the kinds you prefer.

Refrigerated Foods

- **Bacon**: I prefer the center-cut variety. It costs more per pound, but seems to go further, and is less fatty.

- **Breadstick or Biscuit Dough**: If you keep these on hand, check the expiration date fairly frequently, since they don't last forever.

- **Butter—Salted and Sweet**: I use the sweet (unsalted) kind fairly often, both for cooking, and for serving at the table. I much prefer butter to margarine.

- **Carrots**: I like the baby size, since they don't have to be peeled. They're quite versatile. I use them in salads and soups a lot.

- **Celery**: Good for salads, as well as for stuffing with spreads.

- **Cheese—Cheddar or Colby**: I keep packets of shredded cheese in the refrigerator to save time. It's easy to make your own with a food processor. It freezes well for several months.

- **Cheese—Cottage**: This is good with fruit or tomatoes for a quick lunch, and a versatile ingredient for casseroles. You can also process it in a blender and add herbs for a spread.

- **Cheese—Cream**: I keep both the soft kind in the tub, for spreading, and the block kind, for cooking.

- **Cheese—Parmesan:** There are few pasta dishes that this doesn't improve. My husband, Jack, loves the kind that comes in the can. (I think it goes back to his childhood.) We call it "box cheese." Personally, I'm not too fond of it. I prefer the freshly grated variety.

- **Cheese—Processed:** This is the only way to make perfect chile con queso. Besides, our dog loves it when I stuff some inside a hollow shank bone. It keeps her busy for hours.

- **Cheese—Sliced:** Buy it in small quantities, since it seems to get moldy pretty quickly.

- **Coffee and Decaf:** I only keep a small amount in the refrigerator. The rest goes into the freezer.

- **Cookie Dough:** Make your own, or let the Pillsbury Dough Boy help you out. The chocolate chip slice-and-bake cookies are delicious, and the sugar cookies can be rolled and cut out with cookie cutters.

- **Cream—Half and Half:** Just a little bit in cream soups makes them so much more delicious. Add a touch to pasta with butter and Parmesan cheese for a real treat!

- **Cream—Whipping:** This usually keeps for a while unopened. Once you whip it, you can freeze leftover dollops on waxed paper. Transfer them to a plastic bag and keep them in the freezer for up to a month.

- **Cucumbers:** In the summer, they're essential for gazpacho or for

A-TO-Z CHECKLIST (CONTINUED)

- **Ice Cube Bins:** Not to be confused with ice cube trays, these are about the size of a large shoe box, and hold several trays' worth of ice cubes. Great for storing bottles of herbs and spices on shelves. Also good for storing condiments or other smaller items in the refrigerator. Their built-in handles make it easy to slide them off shelves.

- **Knife Blocks:** If your drawer space is limited, here's a safe way to store sharp knives on the counter.

- **Lid Racks:** This is a simple way to keep saucepan lids neat.

- **Magnetic Clips:** These can be used for a variety of purposes. Try one on the door of the refrigerator to hold your grocery list.

- **Magnetic Holders:** There's a variety of these available for things such as storing a notepad and pen or a calendar on the refrigerator door. There are also magnetic picture frames.

- **Magnetic Strips:** These can be mounted on the wall or inside drawers. They hold knives and other cutlery, or anything that's magnetic. Because they keep sharp utensils from sliding around, they offer an added safety bonus.

- **Nails, Screws, and Pegs:** These simple pieces of hardware can help you make the most of your storage space. Besides using them on walls, you can attach them inside cabinet doors, for things like hanging up a skillet or a colander.

- **Nesting Bowls:** You'll save a lot of storage space if your bowls and other containers fit together in a nest.

- **Paper Towel Holders:** These can be mounted on the wall, hung from the underside of a wall cabinet, or attached to the inside of a cabinet door.

(continued)

marinating with Vidalia onion slices. Any time, they're great in salads.

- **Eggs:** These keep for several weeks, and besides the obvious breakfast and baking uses, scrambled eggs make a real "comfort food" supper.

- **Garlic—Minced or Chopped:** For my money, this beats the daylights out of cutting up the stuff by hand.

- **Ginger:** Fresh minced ginger now comes in little jars. What a time-saver!

- **Green Onions:** These make a nice addition to salads, beans, or South-western dishes.

- **Horseradish:** A dose of this turns plain chili sauce into a great seafood dip, and horseradish is also good with roast beef. Not only that, it'll clear out your sinuses pretty quickly!

- **Juice—Cranberry:** This is my morning juice of choice, and is good for mixing with other juices and soda.

- **Juice—Lemon:** I like the Minute Maid brand that comes frozen in a tall squeeze bottle. I keep one in the refrigerator, and a spare one in the freezer.

- **Lemons and Limes:** I probably use limes more than lemons, although I keep both on hand. A squeeze of fresh lemon is often just the thing for zinging up a bland soup.

- **Lettuce:** It's nice to have a variety: iceberg to shred for tacos, Boston or Bibb for sandwiches and serving under cold vegetables, and romaine and other leafy varieties for salads. I also like mesclun (sometimes called *gourmet mix*), which is available in many supermarkets.

- **Margarine:** The only kind I use is the squeeze variety, for spreading on toast without tearing it. Otherwise, I'm a real butter fan.

- **Mayonnaise:** Whether you prefer the high-test or the lower-fat variety, this is great as a spread, and for binding salad ingredients together.

- **Milk:** Even if you don't enjoy it as a beverage, you'll need a little for cereal and cooking.

- **Mustard—Dijon and Yellow:** Good for sandwiches, and for spreading on meat before grilling. I also like the grainy kind to serve with ham.

- **Parsley:** Use the curly-leaf variety for garnishes, and the flat-leaf kind for everything else.

- **Pesto:** Mix with a little butter or olive oil and toss with pasta, blend a dab with some soft cream cheese and use it as a spread, or use it to add a little zip to tomato basil soup.

- **Pie Crusts:** If you don't make your own, the Pillsbury brand is the next best thing. I keep some in the refrigerator, and a backup box in the freezer.

- **Salad Dressing—Assorted:** If you don't have time to make it fresh, keep several bottled varieties on hand.

- **Sausage—Italian—Sweet or Hot:** Slice and brown in a skillet, and then add a jar of pasta sauce and a can of diced tomatoes, for a quick and simple pasta sauce.

- **Sausage—Kielbasa:** Good for a quick supper, either heated in a skillet or cooked on the grill. Or add bite-sized chunks to black beans and serve over rice.

- **Sour Cream:** High-fat, low-fat, or no-fat, this is a very versatile ingredient for cooking and baking.

- **Tortillas:** I keep both corn (6″) and flour (8½″) varieties on hand.

- **Yeast:** This is necessary only if you bake rolls or yeast breads.

- **Yogurt—Plain and Flavored:** The plain variety is a good low-fat substitute for sour cream.

Frozen Foods

- **Angel Food Cake:** The perfect emergency dessert! Slice it frozen, let it thaw for a few minutes, and spoon some ice cream over it. Top with fresh fruit, Raspberry Sauce (page 312), or Hot Fudge Sauce (page 310).

- **Beef—Ground:** Freeze ground beef in ½-pound packages, and use it as needed, for spaghetti sauce, tacos, or vegetable beef soup.

- **Chicken Breasts:** You can do a zillion things with individually frozen boneless, skinless chicken breasts:

soups, salads, stir-fry, and beyond. You can also buy just the chicken tenders or nuggets.

- **Corn:** White corn (sometimes called "shoepeg") is my favorite, since it's sweeter and more tender. I use it often as an ingredient in soups, salads, and casseroles.

- **Dinner Rolls:** Frozen yeast rolls are nice to keep on hand. Buy them at the bakery, or use commercial brands.

- **English Muffins:** These are good for breakfast, and they make a nice base for mini-pizzas or creamed chicken.

- **French Bread:** Keep a loaf in the freezer for unexpected dinner guests.

- **Ham Bones:** Pick some up when you buy spiral-sliced ham. They're delicious for making soups, and you don't even have to thaw them first.

- **Ham Slices:** I keep several packages of spiral-sliced ham in the freezer for sandwiches and casseroles.

- **Ice Cream and Frozen Yogurt**

- **Juice—Lemon:** I always keep one on reserve in the freezer.

- **Juice—Orange:** Although we enjoy fresh-squeezed orange or grapefruit juice, I keep a can of orange juice concentrate in the freezer just in case.

- **Muffins:** Don't let leftover muffins get stale. Wrap them in a plastic bag and stash them in the freezer.

- **Nuts:** These turn rancid if they stay at room temperature for too long, so I keep them in the freezer. Buy whatever kinds you use most often. I like slivered almonds, pecan halves and chips, pine nuts, and walnut pieces.

- **Onions—Chopped:** My neighborhood supermarket now carries my favorite Bland Farms frozen Vidalias! Great for soups and casseroles, and to stir into beans.

- **Party Rye Bread:** These make a perfect crust for bite-size pizzas.

- **Pasta (Cheese-stuffed shells, ravioli, tortellini):** The stuffed shells are one of my favorite busy-day standbys. With a jar of pasta sauce and a little grated Parmesan cheese, dinner is just a microwave away.

- **Peas—Baby Green:** I sprinkle these in salads sometimes, and also use them in my favorite Red, White, and Green Bean Salad (page 213).

- **Peppers:** These also come in a tricolor mix that's great for soups, stir-frys, and casseroles.

- **Pie Crusts:** Thaw these in the refrigerator or at room temperature, but not in the microwave.

- **Pork Tenderloin:** I like to package these individually and keep several on hand in the freezer. They thaw quickly, and are simple to grill or roast whole. They can also be cubed and used for stir-fry.

A-TO-Z CHECKLIST (CONTINUED)

- **Peg-Board:** There are lots of options here, with a wide variety of attachments available. Look for these components in hardware or home building supply stores.

- **Pot Racks:** These can be quite attractive hung on a wall or suspended from the ceiling over a cooktop or island. Use hooks to hang cookware, baskets, and other items. Some have a shelf incorporated into the design.

- **Pull-Out Drawers:** Some are made of plastic, and some are vinyl-coated steel wire. Some are designed to be mounted on tracks in base cabinets, and others are free-standing units intended for use in the pantry, below the lowest shelf.

- **Quilted Cases for China and Glassware:** This is a convenient, safe way to store holiday dishes, glassware, and other fragile things that you don't use very often.

- **Racks:** These are made of vinyl-coated steel wire or heavy plastic. Some are free-standing, and some can be mounted inside cabinet doors to hold small items such as spices. Others are specially made for boxes of waxed paper, foil, and plastic wraps, as well as for cleaning supplies and other items. Some, such as spice racks, are made of wood or decorative metals, and are attractive enough to be displayed.

- **Rolling Baskets and Carts:** These can be made of heavy plastic, vinyl-coated steel wire, wood, or metal. All kinds of configurations are possible. Some have butcher-block tops for chopping. Some have slats on the sides to accommodate a variety of depths of drawers. Others accept only one depth of drawer. Some have casters, enabling you to roll them easily from place to place. Often the casters are removable.

- **Rubbermaid, Tupperware, and Other Plastic Containers:** What did we ever do without them? They make excellent canisters, and since they're airtight, they keep foods fresh. When you're not using these containers to store food, you can use them to store equipment and gadgets.

(continued)

- **Pound Cake:** A great emergency dessert with fresh fruit or ice cream.

- **Puff Pastry:** You can make lots of easy hors d'oeuvres with this. Look for recipes right on the package.

- **Raspberries:** Use these to make a quick dessert sauce (page 312).

- **Sandwich Bread:** I always keep an extra loaf in the freezer. The secret is not to leave it in there too long. When I buy a fresh loaf, I take the frozen one out of the freezer, so my stock stays rotated.

- **Shrimp—Frozen Cooked:** The kind with tails attached is good for shrimp cocktails. The peeled kind is delicious with pasta and salads.

- **Spinach—Chopped:** I use this often for my favorite dips and soups.

- **Turkey Breast:** My favorite brand is Norbest.

- **Veggies—Mixed:** These are convenient for vegetable soup and stir-frys.

- **Whipped Topping:** I prefer real whipped cream, but this will do in a pinch.

Herbs, Spices, and Flavorings

Buy small sizes, since the larger sizes tend to get stale. Keep them in a cool, dark place, and mark the date on the container when you buy it.

- Allspice
- Basil
- Bay Leaves
- Caraway Seeds
- Cayenne
- Celery—Salt and Seeds
- Chili Powder
- Cinnamon—Ground and Sticks
- Cloves—Ground and Whole
- Cream of Tartar
- Cumin—Ground
- Curry Powder
- Dill—Seeds and Weed
- Extracts—Vanilla, Almond, and Lemon
- Garlic—Powder and Salt
- Ginger—Ground and Crystallized
- Lemon Peel
- Lemon Pepper
- Liquid Smoke
- Meat Tenderizer
- Mint Leaves—Dried
- MSG
- Mustard—Dry and Seeds
- Nutmeg—Ground and Whole
- Onion Juice
- Onions—Dehydrated
- Onion Salt
- Oregano
- Paprika
- Parsley Flakes
- Pepper—Cracked and Ground
- Peppercorns
- Pepper Flakes—Red
- Pickling Spice
- Poppy Seeds
- Rosemary
- Salt—Table and Kosher
- Sesame Seeds
- Thyme
- Turmeric

Pantry Shelf

- **A-1 Sauce:** We like the "Bold and Spicy" flavor. Pour it over cream cheese and serve it with crackers.

- **Anchovies:** My husband, Jack, likes them on pizza. His half only.

- **Apple Juice:** It's especially good in the winter, heated up with a cinnamon stick and a few cloves.

- **Applesauce:** You can also use this as a low-fat substitute for part of the oil in baking cakes.

- **Apple Slices:** Sprinkle with some cinnamon, and microwave them for a good side dish with pork.

- Apricots—Dried and canned

- **Artichoke Hearts:** Great in salads and dips.

- **Asparagus:** Although it tastes nothing like fresh, it still is an easy side dish when chilled and served with Lemon Mayonnaise (page 253).

- **Bacon Bits or Pieces:** Use as a salad topping or in a quiche. I prefer the real bacon bits.

- **Baking Powder:** Check the expiration date on the can before you ruin a batch of biscuits. This usually only stays at its optimum freshness for about 6 months.

- **Baking Soda:** Use it for cooking, cleaning, and deodorizing.

- **Barbecue Sauce:** Heat it up with an equal part of orange marmalade for a great dip for chicken fingers.

- **Beans—Baked, Black, and Kidney:** Black beans and rice are one of my favorite pantry-shelf suppers. Season them with the same ingredients you'd use if you were making them from scratch. Kidney beans are great to add to chili.

- **Beans—Dried:** Good if you have the time. I also like the multi-bean soup mixes. Be sure to add the juice of a lemon whenever you cook beans.

- **Beef Broth:** I always keep 3–4 cans on the shelf, and add some to my spaghetti sauce, tomato aspic, and vegetable soup.

- **Beets—Julienned, Whole, and Pickled:** For an easy side dish, toss with a little vinegar, mayonnaise, and a pinch of sugar. Chill and serve on a lettuce leaf.

- **Bisquick:** This also makes a great substitute for flour, when you're breading chicken or pork chops.

- **Black-eyed Peas:** Mix with some salsa for a tasty dip.

- **Bouillon—Cubes, Crystals, or Stock Base:** I prefer the stock base (liquid or paste), since it's not as salty.

- **Bread Crumbs:** Progresso is a good brand.

- **Bulgur Wheat:** The backbone of Tabbouleh (page 183).

- **Cake, Muffin, and Bread Mixes:** Keep an assortment of your favorites.

- **Cereal:** Whatever kinds you enjoy.

- **Chicken—Canned White:** You can use this to make instant chicken salad or a chicken casserole.

- **Chicken Broth:** I always keep 3–4 cans on the shelf. Now it comes in a resealable carton as well. Chicken broth makes a great soup starter, and adds flavor depth to rice and grains. It's also a low-fat seasoning for mashed potatoes.

- **Chili Sauce or Cocktail Sauce**

- **Chili Seasoning Mix:** My favorite is Wick Fowler's 2-Alarm (see Special Ingredients, page 68).

- **Chocolate Morsels—Semisweet**

- **Chocolate Squares—Unsweetened**

A-TO-Z CHECKLIST (CONTINUED)

- **Shelf Dividers:** These are useful for making narrow, upright boundaries for things like cookie sheets, trays, and muffin tins. Vertical letter trays, available at office supply stores, can be used for this purpose as well.

- **Shoe and Sweater Boxes:** Generally made of plastic, these aren't just for using in bedroom closets. Some are stackable, and others are the pull-out variety, like small chests of drawers. Look for these in the closet section of large variety stores. The smaller sizes can be used to store things like salad dressing mixes, seasoning packets, or small boxes of pudding or gelatin. The larger sizes can be used to store noodles and other dried pasta or baking supplies. The smaller ones can be used in wall cabinets, while the larger ones are useful in base cabinets or pantries. If you label the drawers, you can easily tell what's inside.

- **Specialized Organizers:** Different kinds are available for dishes, teacups, saucepan lids, paper and plastic wraps, paper plates, paper towels, paper napkins, paper and plastic grocery bags, coffee filters, etc. Some of them mount on the inside of cabinet doors.

- **Step Shelves:** These are often plastic, and resemble tiny stair steps. Some are adjustable in width. They can be used to store small bottles, spice jars, or small canned goods. By elevating the products stored at the back of the "stairs," they enable you to see clearly what's at the back of the shelf.

- **Step Stool:** Although this isn't technically a storage device, it is an absolute necessity for gaining access to your otherwise hard-to-reach areas. Buy a heavy-duty one, and be sure it's sturdy. They also make a style that rolls around.

- **Tins:** Most often used for holiday cookies and treats, these can also be used to store sets of small items, such as pastry tips or cookie cutters. Several can be stacked on a shelf, but label them to show what's inside.

(continued)

- **Chocolate Syrup**
- **Clam Juice**
- **Clams**
- **Cocoa—Baking:** I use this more often than the unsweetened squares.
- **Coconut—Shredded**
- **Coffee & Decaf—Instant:** I use the instant variety only for cooking.
- **Cornbread Mix:** Use this for corn sticks, cornbread, or corn cakes.
- **Cornmeal—Regular and Self-Rising**
- **Cornstarch**
- **Corn Syrup**
- **Couscous:** Although considered a grain, this is actually tiny pasta. For richer flavor, prepare it using chicken broth as part or all of the liquid.
- **Crabmeat**
- **Crackers and Cookies:** Keep an assortment on hand, and be sure to rewrap them tightly after opening, since they get stale easily.
- **Cranberry Sauce:** A quick and colorful side dish for chicken or pork.

- Dried Fruits—Apricots, Currants, Raisins, and Cranberries: Use these for snacking, baking, and adding to salads.

- Flour: All-purpose is usually all you need. Check the Food Substitutions section (pages 393-398) if your recipe calls for another kind.

- Fruit Cocktail

- Garlic: Unless I need whole garlic cloves, I usually prefer the minced or chopped variety that comes in a jar.

- Gelatin—Fruit-Flavored and Un-flavored

- Grapefruit Sections: Toss with some Kraft Catalina dressing, and serve on a lettuce leaf, for a quick side dish.

- Green Beans: I use the canned variety chilled or in salads most often.

- Green Chiles—Chopped

- Honey

- Jalapeño Peppers

- Jelly, Jam, Preserves, and Marmalade

- Ketchup

- Lemon Curd: A great topping for gingerbread.

- Lentils

- Macaroni

- Maple Syrup: Once you try the "real thing," you'll be hooked.

- Marshmallows: If they're not fresh, don't use them for Rice Krispies squares.

- Mayonnaise: Keep an extra jar on hand.

- Milk—Evaporated and Sweetened Condensed: Be sure not to confuse them. They're definitely not interchangeable!

- Mushrooms—Canned and Dried

- Non-stick Baking Spray: There's also one that contains flour, for preparing cake pans.

- Noodles—Egg and Ramen

- Nuts—Dry-Roasted

- Oatmeal

- Olive Oil

- Olives—Green, Stuffed

- Olives—Ripe (Whole and Sliced)

- Oranges—Mandarin

- Pancake Mix: You can substitute Bisquick. See the recipe on page 266.

- Pasta—Assorted

- Pasta Sauce: My favorite brand is Classico with Sun-Dried Tomatoes (see Special Ingredients, page 68). I always keep a couple of large jars on the shelf. I use it on pasta, to make soups, and to spread on pizza.

- Peach Halves and Spiced Peaches

- Peanut Butter

- Pears

- Pesto: Besides the refrigerated kind, there's a concentrate made by Amore that comes in a tube (see Special Ingredients, page 68).

- Pickapeppa Sauce: Pour over cream cheese for a quick snack spread.

- Pickle Relish

- Pickles—Slices and Gherkins

- Pimientos and Roasted Red Peppers

- Pineapple—Crushed

- Pineapple Juice

- Pineapple—Sliced

- Pudding and Pie Filling Mix

- Rice—Assorted Varieties: My favorite is popcorn rice (see Special Ingredients, page 68).

- Salad Dressing Mixes: I prepare the Italian flavor for salad dressing, and also to use as a marinade.

- Salmon: Easy croquettes.

- Salsa: I've started adding this to soups, and discovered a new treat.

- Sesame Oil

- Sherry

- Shortening: I prefer Crisco sticks. It's so much easier to measure shortening by cutting off part of a stick than scooping it out of a can.

- Soft Drinks and Mixers

- Soup Mixes—Dried: In addition to using these for soups, I also make dips with them.

- Soups: Find several varieties that your family likes, and keep them on hand. We like the Progresso ready-to-serve brand.

- Soy Sauce

- Stuffing Mix: Pepperidge Farm herb-seasoned stuffing mix can be crushed in the blender or food processor, and used in place of dried bread crumbs. Add it to meatloaf as it comes from the package.

- Sugar—Brown, Granulated, and Powdered

- Sugar Substitute

- Sun-Dried Tomato Paste: The Amore brand comes in a tube (see

A-TO-Z CHECKLIST (CONTINUED)

- **Turntables:** These can be used in the refrigerator, as well as on cabinet or pantry shelves. They come in different sizes, and some have multiple tiers. They make items accessible that might otherwise be difficult to reach.

- **Under-Cabinet Shelves:** This is a specialized type of shelf, made of vinyl-coated steel wire, that clamps onto the shelf above it. It's useful for storing platters and other large, flat pieces.

- **Under-Cabinet Storage Units and Appliances:** These compact storage units, such as cookbook holders, are designed to utilize the otherwise-wasted space underneath wall cabinets. Look for these products in catalogs and home building supply stores. Also shop for small appliances (such as coffeemakers and toaster ovens) that mount under the cabinet, thereby freeing up valuable counter space.

- **Vegetable Bins:** These are useful for storing lots of things besides potatoes and onions. Try them for bulky packages of snack foods, or use them to organize large bags of flour, sugar, rice, pasta, etc.

- **Zipper Plastic Bags:** These are great for keeping up with loose packets of seasonings, salad dressing mixes, soft drink mixes, etc.

Special Ingredients, page 68). Mix a squirt with cream cheese for a great spread on Crostini Crisps (page 78).

- Tabasco Sauce

- Taco Sauce

- Taco Seasoning Mix

- Taco Shells: Call the toll-free number of the brand you like best, and ask them how to decipher their date code. Once you do that, you'll never have a problem with stale taco shells again.

- Tapioca: Good for pudding, and the best way to thicken fruit pies.

- Tea—Bags, Loose, and Mixes

- Teriyaki Sauce

- Tomatoes—Diced: When they started doing the dicing at the factory, I stopped buying whole canned tomatoes. These are such a time-saver to add to soups and pasta sauce!

- Tomatoes—Sun-Dried: These snap up the flavor of soups, salads, and spreads.

- Tomatoes and Chiles—Ro-Tel (see Special Ingredients, page 68): Look for the kind with diced tomatoes.

- Tomato Juice: Good as a beverage, and to make tomato aspic.

- Tomato Paste: It's actually cheaper to use a few tablespoons from a 6-ounce can and throw the rest away than it is to buy the 4½-ounce tube.

- Tomato Puree: This is somewhere between tomato paste and tomato sauce in thickness. It's the consistency that's used in pizza sauce.

- Tomato Sauce
- Tuna: I prefer albacore tuna packed in water.
- V-8 Juice
- Vegetable Oil
- Vinegar—Balsamic, Cider, Distilled, White, Wine, and Raspberry
- Water Chestnuts
- Worcestershire Sauce

Fresh Produce

- Apples
- Avocados
- Bananas
- Onions—Sweet and Yellow
- Potatoes—Russet
- Tomatoes—Roma

■ ■ ■

Stashing the Crown Jewels

Once you've made the substantial investment required to stock your refrigerator, freezer, and pantry, you need to give some careful thought to how you arrange everything on the shelves. Your kitchen is first and foremost a workroom, and it needs to be set up with that in mind. Here are some basic storage guidelines that I call:

Ten Commandments for Storage

1. First come, first served: Store items as close as possible to the first place you plan to use them. Keep the coffeemaker and any other equipment that uses water next to the kitchen sink. Keep the placemats close to the table. Keep the bread close to the toaster. Keep spoons by the stove.

2. Divide and conquer: Use dividers to partition drawers, so that things don't get tangled up and jumbled together. This will make it easier to find what you need, and will simplify putting things away. You can use inexpensive plastic dividers, or you can recycle small boxes and other types of containers.

3. Birds of a feather flock together: Store similar items together. Keep canned goods together, snack foods together, herbs and spices together, dairy products in the refrigerator together, paper and plastic wraps together, etc.

4. Partners in crime: Store things together that are used for the same types of jobs. For example, keep supplies for packing lunches in one area: sandwich bags, lunch boxes, thermos jars, individual packages of snacks, etc. Ideally, this would be close to where you keep the bread and spreads.

5. Keep it in bounds: Use containers to corral things that might otherwise spread out all over the neighboring territory. Store mixing spoons and wire whisks in a big crock on the counter. Keep packets of seasoning mixes in a small box or basket on the shelf.

6. Lay down the law: Decide exactly what is and what is not to be stored in each area, and then enforce the law! Kitchen counters should not become repositories for junk mail. This principle may involve a little effort until new habits are formed, but the results will be well worthwhile.

7. One fell swoop: Plan your storage so that you have easy, single-motion access to whatever you use most often. Keep those things front and center, and not behind or underneath other things that you only use occasionally. Avoid arrangements that force you to move something you use once a month to get to something else you use every day. For example, don't store your favorite skillet on a shelf underneath the heavy chicken fryer, which you use maybe three or four times a year. Better yet, hang that skillet on the inside of a cabinet door.

8. The Princess and the Pea: Stack only identical items. Don't make more work for yourself by creating layers of things that have to be moved to get to something at the bottom of the pile. This is especially important for things you use on a daily basis. Stacking a dozen dinner plates on top of each other is fine, but don't make stacks of stacks. It's not a good

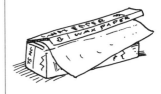

idea to put the salad plates on top of the dinner plates, where they have to be shifted each time you need to get out a dinner plate.

9. **Location, Location, Location:** Reserve your most accessible storage space for whatever you use most often. Zone 1, between eye-level and hip-level, should be for things you use almost every day. Zone 2 storage might involve a little reaching or bending, and is for things you use maybe once a week or so. Zone 3, where you have to pull out the kitchen stool or get down on your hands and knees, should be set aside for things you only need to use occasionally.

10. **Plain brown wrapper:** If you stash something in a container that you can't see through, label it. This will save you hours of futile searching.

■ ■ ■

Recipe Collections

It's a fact of life: Navy collects lint, and cooks collect recipes. Some cooks are quite discriminating, while others are pack rats, clipping everything they can find from newspapers, magazines, package labels, and anything else that isn't nailed down. Although chronic clippers have good intentions, often their recipes get shoved to the back of a drawer, never to see the light of day. What's the solution? I have two. Now that I have a computer scanner (a Visioneer PaperPort), I just scan in all the recipes that I tear out of newspapers and magazines, filing them into categories on my hard drive. It's so fast, and it eliminates all those little scraps of paper littering my desk. When I'm ready to try a recipe, I print out a copy to work from. As I'm preparing it, I make notes of any changes that I think improve or enhance the recipe, and if I like it well enough, I copy it into one of the sidebars of my *Big Kitchen Instruction Book.* (Fortunately, mine is a looseleaf version!) Before I bought a computer scanner, I used to keep a large accordion file with individual slots for different recipe categories. As soon as I'd clip a recipe, I'd stuff it into the folder. Then, whenever I was watching an old movie on TV or enjoying some other mindless activity, I'd go through the file and get more realistic. If the recipe was something that I knew in my heart of hearts I'd never fix, I'd toss it. If it was something that honestly sounded good enough to try, I'd put it in a looseleaf scrapbook with clear plastic peel-back pages. After I prepared the recipe, if I thought it warranted a place in my permanent collection, I fine-tuned it to my liking and copied the revised version into my looseleaf cookbook. Naturally, I'd discard any recipe that I didn't think measured up. Either the computer version of my recipe system or the accordion file version works pretty well, and they both seem to be more convenient than keeping an index card file. Whenever I discover a good recipe in another cookbook, I make a cross-reference notation in my *Big Kitchen Instruction Book,* so I can find it easily the next time I want to use it.

■ ■ ■

Holding Down the Fort

Streamlining and organizing your kitchen takes time. After you've made such a valiant effort, you'll appreciate the advantages of having a well-stocked and well-organized kitchen, and you'll want to keep things under control. It's all a matter of holding your ground, and not allowing yourself to get sloppy or to slip back into any bad habits. Protecting your investment of time and energy is much easier if you just discipline yourself to take the small steps necessary to stay on top of things each day. The next time you're tempted to set something down where it doesn't belong "just for the time being," remember that a few minutes spent putting something back where it belongs is truly time well spent.

"Cooking with love means never having to feel chained to your stove, never feeling that getting dinner on the table is a teeth-gritting experience rather than a charming interlude."

—Francis Anthony

Chapter 4

The Systemized Kitchen

■ ■ ■ ■ ■

SYSTEMIZE:
To create a logical process for dealing with recurring chores.

■ ■ ■

The 2,000-Piece Kitchen Puzzle

Managing a kitchen is like working a giant jigsaw puzzle. There are so many pieces involved that you need some kind of system to fit them all together. But once you locate the corners and straight edges, you begin to get some sense of direction.

Like painting the Golden Gate Bridge, the job of getting meals on the table every day never seems to end. Just when we finish cleaning up from one, it's time to start working on the next one. And there's never any letup—even on weekends or holidays. As a matter of fact, the pace only intensifies. The solution is to figure out how to get the job done as quickly and painlessly as possible, using the

least amount of energy. Figure 4.1 shows some of the big kitchen puzzle pieces we'll be fitting together.

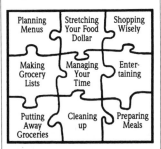

Planning Menus	Stretching Your Food Dollar	Shopping Wisely
Making Grocery Lists	Managing Your Time	Entertaining
Putting Away Groceries	Cleaning up	Preparing Meals

The Kitchen Puzzle (Figure 4.1)

■ ■ ■

Eeny Meeny Miney Menu

It's 5:00 P.M. Do you know where your dinner is? Meal planning can tax the creativity of the most resourceful individual. The math is a little unsettling: 365 days a year, times three meals a day, equals a total

of 1,095 meals per annum. Each meal must be planned, shopped for, prepared, and cleaned up after. No wonder most women will tell you that their favorite thing to make for dinner is reservations! Besides the meals, there are lunches to pack, soup to take to a sick friend, a plate of cookies or a loaf of banana bread for the new neighbors down the street, and perhaps a pan of brownies to indulge in over the weekend. But here's the good news: You don't have to start from scratch each and every time you plan a meal. You can repeat favorite dishes and entire menus on a fairly regular basis. Although the definition of "fairly regular" is open to a wide variety of interpretation, nevertheless I've discovered that three weeks is about the average memory retention when it comes to food. After that magical 21-day period has passed, you're not as likely to get comments like, "But we just had that!" If you give some thought to the types of food your family enjoys, and spend a little time planning, you can recycle the menus that you've created until the cows come home. Here's an analogy to help you get the picture. An experienced seamstress might alter a favorite blouse pattern until it fits perfectly, and then stitch it up several times in assorted fabrics with different types of sleeves, collars, buttons, and trims. None of the creations looks like the same blouse, and yet all the blouses are based on the same pattern. Likewise, once you work out your own master framework of menu plans, you can modify the basic plan countless times. Whenever you're feeling creative or energetic, you can make substitutions. If you're tired, you can stick to the same old tried and true stand-bys.

■ ■ ■

A Basic Repertoire of Menus

Here are some figures you should aim for as a beginning goal for planning menus. Once you have these down pat, you can start expanding and fine-tuning your repertoire. Don't let this exercise become as difficult as making New Year's resolutions. These menus don't have to be the essence of perfection! You can polish them up a little later. Of course you'd like every one of them to be low-cost, high nutrition, and easy enough to prepare in twenty minutes. But that's not

all going to come together right at the outset. If you hold yourself to severely high standards at the beginning, you'll get the cook's equivalent of writer's block. Just aim for menus that are doable, and you can fine tune them later on.

■ A week's worth of different breakfast menus: With 7 menus, you won't have to get too creative before you've had your morning coffee. As long as you know what day it is, you'll know what's coming even before you roll out of bed. (If this is Tuesday, it must be oatmeal.) And because you know

what's ahead, you can get a jump on things the night before. For some ideas to get you started, check the inset box above.

■ A week's worth of different lunch menus: Having 7 menus will make packing lunches a breeze (see the tips in the box above), plus you'll have an opportunity to fix a few things ahead for the weekends. The ingredients will be written on your grocery list, and you'll be prepared.

■ Three weeks' worth of different dinner menus: As I mentioned earlier, folks tend to forget what they've eaten. By the time you rotate through 21 different dinners, no one is likely to remember just how recently they had the same meal.

■ Two or three foolproof, simple company menus: These should be uncomplicated meals that you can prepare partially in advance, saving your energy so you can enjoy the evening with your guests.

■ ■ ■

The Dinner Challenge

Breakfast and lunch menus are truly no-brainers. By combining different kinds of cereal, fruit, yogurt, bread, and perhaps eggs and bacon occasionally, coming up with breakfast menus is no problem. Likewise, lunch. Sandwiches, soups, salads, and fruits can be put together in infinite combinations. But dinner presents somewhat more of a challenge. Since this is the meal where families traditionally gather, planning it might warrant a little more thought. This process may be easier than you think, though. Here's one approach: Get out a legal pad and start making a list of all the different dishes your family enjoys. Don't bother creating entire menus yet—just write down some favorite dishes. Let this be a free association list of anything you or your family would like to see on the dinner table. At my house, the list would have to include tacos, twice-baked potatoes, spaghetti, and salmon croquettes, not

to mention quesadillas and some of my world-class soups. (Tortilla Soup, page 93, happens to be the current favorite.) In the summer, the list would also include Silver Queen corn on the cob, Bradley tomatoes, little yellow crookneck squash, gazpacho, and my award-winning Red, White, and Green Bean Salad (page 213). Thinking of one favorite dish frequently brings another one to mind. Take a survey among family members, and don't limit your thinking to main dishes. Include vegetables and side dishes, salads, and soups. Put a star next to things that are extra simple to fix, as well as any that can be prepared in advance, or made up in large quantities and frozen. Especially valuable are recipes that can be put together with ingredients you normally keep on hand in the pantry, refrigerator, and freezer. (These score bonus points!) Once your page begins to fill up, start making notes alongside the main dishes, writing down whatever side

dishes would be natural accompaniments. Certain foods seem to be traditional go-togethers. By keeping these natural flavor partners in mind, you'll make your menu-planning project even simpler. Several that come to mind might be ham and pineapple, pork and apples, barbecue and baked beans, chicken and rice, roast beef and potatoes, etc. Don't worry right now about being too specific, or about completing each menu—that will come a little later. For now, just make notes of foods that seem to go well with each other.

■ ■ ■

It's as Easy as Flipping Pages

Have you ever seen a child's book with pictures of different animal heads, bodies, and legs on each page, and the pages are split so that you can create all kinds of ridiculous-looking

combinations, like a horse head, a gorilla body, and ostrich legs? What I'm about to describe is an idea based on the same principle, but something that you can use for creating menus. I call it a *Flipper Book*. Take a small spiral memo book (about 4″ x 6″). Sometimes you can find these memo books made up of index cards, which might be even better, since the pages are heavier. Now cut the pages into four equal strips, so that each strip is still attached to the spiral binding and turns independently of the others. Begin writing the names of your favorite recipes in your Flipper Book in this order: On the top group of strips, write all the main dish recipes, including soups. On the second group of strips, write the names of all the starchy recipes, including sandwiches, potatoes, rice, corn, noodles, etc. On the third group of strips, write the names of green vegetable and salad recipes. And on the bottom strips, write the names of other vegetables and side dishes, such as carrots, beets, fruits, and relishes.

■ ■ ■

Menu-Planning Guidelines

Before you start creating complete menus from the ideas you've written in your Flipper Book, let's discuss some guidelines for planning menus. Eating is much more than an exercise in survival. It involves not only our sense of taste but our sense

USDA FOOD GUIDE PYRAMID

■ **Bread, Cereal, Rice, and Pasta:** 6–11 servings a day: a slice of bread, half an English muffin or hamburger bun, a small roll, ½ cup cooked cereal, rice, or pasta, 1 ounce ready-to-eat cereal, or 4–6 crackers.

■ **Vegetables:** 3–5 servings a day: 1 cup raw leafy vegetables (spinach or lettuce), ½ cup chopped raw or cooked vegetables (cabbage or carrots), or ¾ cup vegetable juice.

■ **Fruits:** 2–4 servings a day: ¾ cup fruit juice, ½ grapefruit, ½ cup chopped, cooked, or canned fruit, 1 cup melon chunks, ½ cup berries, ¼ cup raisins or dried fruits, or a medium apple, banana, orange, peach, or pear.

■ **Meat, Poultry, Fish, Dried Beans, Eggs, and Nuts:** 2–3 servings a day (a total of 5–7 ounces of cooked lean meat, poultry, or fish): The following counts as 1 ounce cooked meat: ½ cup cooked beans or peas, an egg, an ounce of nuts, or 2 tablespoons of peanut butter.

■ **Milk, Yogurt, and Cheese:** 2–3 servings a day: a cup of milk or yogurt, ½ cup of cottage cheese, 2 ounces of processed cheese, or 1½ ounces of natural cheese.

■ **Fats, Oils, Sweets, and Alcoholic Beverages:** Use these sparingly.

USDA Food Guide Pyramid (Figure 4.2)

of smell, touch, and sight. (In the case of potato chips, it involves our sense of hearing as well.) For that reason, a good menu should appeal to more than just our taste buds. One key in planning is variety. Avoid using a particular main ingredient for more than one dish in any given menu. For example, if you're having macaroni and cheese, don't serve broccoli with cheese sauce at the same meal. This is especially important when planning company meals, since you might not know about your guests' food preferences or diet restrictions. Besides, an ingredient you love might

not be one of their favorites. Some other types of variety you should consider include:

1. Variety in nutritional composition: Many people use the USDA Food Guide Pyramid (Figure 4.2) as a pattern for planning balanced meals. This is a good starting place. However a number of experts now claim that the dietary standards illustrated by this pyramid place too heavy an emphasis on carbohydrates. The reasoning is that too many carbohydrates, especially simple carbohydrates (such as those found in sugar and flour), can cause the body to produce too much insulin, which can in turn lead to obesity. For that reason, many nutritionists are now recommending that the Food Guide Pyramid be re-shaped to resemble the Washington Monument, with protein and carbohydrate intake more equally balanced.

2. Variety in color: You can make the meal look as good as it tastes by choosing contrasting colors. Simple garnishes like a sprig of parsley or dill, a few carrot sticks, or some strips of sweet peppers can do a lot to enhance the presentation. Look through food magazines for inventive ways to use color. If you're serving white fish, don't serve mashed potatoes and cauliflower alongside. Instead, try foods like wild rice and spinach.

3. Variety in taste: In the same menu, mix spicy with bland, or sweet with tart. Think how good the combination of flavors in mango salsa tastes. Contrast is very pleasing to the palate, and enhances the flavors of each dish on the menu.

4. Variety in texture: Pair crisp or firm foods with soft ones, and serve crunchy foods with smooth ones. For example, serve broccoli cooked al dente along with mashed potatoes, or crisp raw veggies with a creamy dip.

5. Variety in temperature: Every hot dish improves when it's served with one that offers a chilling contrast, and vice versa. No matter what the season, composed salads with chilled vegetables are a welcome contrast for an otherwise hot meal. Conversely, even when the temperature soars in August, a hot, spicy dish tastes good.

■ ■ ■

Here Comes the Bride

Another factor to take into consideration is the ease of preparation of the entire menu. If it takes substantial time or effort to prepare a particular dish for one meal, try to team that dish up with other foods that are much simpler to fix. Even better, try to avoid preparing a whole meal from scratch. As you plan your menus, try to incorporate a combination of leftovers, make-ahead dishes, quick-and-easy-to-throw-together recipes, and convenience foods, alongside things that are prepared from scratch. To illustrate this principle, I've taken the traditional prescription for dressing a bride, "Something old, something new, something borrowed, something blue, and a silver sixpence in her shoe." I've loosely adapted it to form a menu-planning yardstick that's easy to remember. It goes something like this:

1. Something Old: For each menu, take advantage of your refrigerator and freezer by including something that you might have prepared a while back. This could be spaghetti sauce, chili, or twice-baked potatoes from the freezer, that can be heated up in the microwave. Or it might be bean salad encore, since it keeps well for several days in the refrigerator.

2. Something New: This is anything you prepare initially for that particular meal. It might be pasta that you cook to go with the spaghetti sauce you took out of the freezer. It could be fresh steamed broccoli or asparagus that becomes the something old several days from now when it reappears in a salad. Perhaps it's a marinated flank steak that will provide leftovers for weekend sandwiches. As you prepare the "new" foods, you'll save yourself even more time in the future with a concept that I call *coattail cooking*. This means that dishes that will appear later in future meals "ride on the coattails" of tonight's dinner. Here are some examples: Cook more pasta than you'll eat at one meal, toss the extra pasta with a little olive oil, and then stash it in the refrigerator. It becomes the foundation for pasta salad several days later. Steam more broccoli than you need for dinner and drizzle some Italian dressing

over what's left over. Tomorrow night it becomes marinated broccoli salad with a few pine nuts sprinkled on top. If you're grilling flank steak, toss two on the grill instead of one. Slice the extra one, put it in a plastic zipper bag, and toss it in the freezer for quick sandwiches. Or whenever you're in the mood for stir-fry, your meat is all ready, a sack of mixed vegetables is on stand-by in the freezer, and the rice is waiting on your pantry shelf. When you cook pork tenderloin, prepare black bean and yellow rice salad to serve with it that night. Use the leftover salad to make quesadillas tomorrow, and then use the leftover pork tenderloin for stir-fry on the next night. Cooking with this piggyback technique is an important habit to cultivate, and will save you hours of time and lots of energy. It's a skill that will improve the more you use it. Pretty soon it will become second nature for you to double up. Instead of cooking the same thing twice, cook twice as much. It makes more sense to clean up a mess one time than to clean up the same mess two different times.

3. Something Borrowed: This might be described as disguised leftovers, such as last night's garlic bread, sprinkled with a little Parmesan cheese and browned in the toaster oven. It might be the cooked rice that was left from Sunday's stir-fry that you add to Wednesday's cream of mushroom soup. It could be the dabs of this and that tossed into a chef's salad.

Menu Planning Card (Figure 4.3)

● ● ●

Playing with Building Blocks

Now it's time to create some menus from the building blocks that you've written in your Flipper Book. To do this, you'll need some index cards. (See the Menu Planning Card, Figure 4.3, for a sample format.) You could use a notebook instead of the cards, but the cards are easier to rearrange. The goal of this exercise is to help you create a menu-planning system—a permanent collection of menu ideas, that will keep you from having to dream up new ones every week for the rest of your life! I've included dozens of menu ideas from my own collection on pages 64–66. All the recipes described in my menus are included in this book. If you like, turn there now to get some ideas. After you've looked through them, set them aside and put on your thinking cap. Keep your materials handy, so you can work on them at

4. Something Blue: I had to use poetic license here, so I decided that fresh ingredients in the refrigerator would be blue from the cold. This represents the salad greens for the tossed salad, or a can of pickled beets or asparagus spears chilling until dinnertime.

5. A Silver Sixpence: This represents all those ingredients that are worth their weight in gold: the things that comprise a good cook's bag of tricks. I'm referring to those convenience foods that come to the rescue in many forms. It might be canned bread sticks from the refrigerator case at the supermarket. It could be prepared pie crusts, or maybe a delicious soup mix that you discovered at a kitchen specialty shop. It could be frozen chopped onions, canned diced tomatoes, minced garlic, or pesto in a jar. It's whatever makes your life in the kitchen easier, less complicated, and more enjoyable.

your leisure. This is a good project to play around with while you're watching TV.

Start by experimenting with different combinations of recipes in your Flipper Book. Begin with the main dish and then choose starches, vegetables, salads, and side dishes that provide the types of variety described earlier. If the main dish requires a lot of time or effort, select side dishes you're likely to have in the freezer, or things like rice and steamed vegetables, which are simple to prepare. Match up side dishes that require a little more effort with main dishes that are easier to fix. When you discover a particular combination you like, write it down on a card. Keep in mind the principles of using leftovers and preparing extras to enjoy later on.

If you use a layout like the Menu Planning Card, you'll have places to fill in every piece of the menu puzzle (except for bread and dessert, which you can add or not, as you like). There's also a place for notes. You might use that note space to indicate minor variations of the menu, side dish substitutions, and so forth. You can also jot down creative ways to use leftovers from that particular menu. You might want to indicate special situations for which this menu is particularly appropriate, such as "busy-day meal," "good for casual company," or "can be fixed with ingredients I normally have on hand." (I call these "Look, Ma—No Grocery Cart" menus.) If you're using index cards to record your menus, use the back of the card if you need extra space. You might want to clip together several different cards with the same main dish. The column to the right side is for jotting down any additional ingredients you'll need to buy to prepare that menu, above and beyond the staples that you normally keep on hand in the freezer, refrigerator, or pantry. This ingredients list will vary in length, depending on how well stocked your pantry is. One of the nice features of having these menus written down is that whenever you decide to prepare a particular menu, you can tell at a glance what items you need to add to your ongoing grocery list, without getting out the cookbook and checking the list of ingredients. (We'll talk more about that grocery list later.) You might not have an entry on each line for every menu. That's fine. Just keep things simple and flexible. You can always decide later on to fill in some of the blanks, or to add extra dishes or make substitutions. The important thing is to create a stack of menus to begin with. Fine-tuning comes later on.

■ ■ ■
Pulling Rabbits
out of Hats

Each week, or however often you plan menus, just pull out some ideas from your collection and recycle them. You'll never again have to sit down in front of a blank sheet of paper, waiting for inspiration to strike. Once you create your skeleton crew of 21 dinner menus, you can add variety, just as you'd do if you were building a wardrobe: Start with several basic pieces, and change accessories to create different outfits. Translating that technique into menu planning, you'd simply repeat the same 21 main dishes, substituting different side dishes, perhaps switching vegetables, depending on what was in season. Before you know it, you'll have twice as many menu possibilities. Keep up the process, and pretty soon you'll have a substantial collection of menus to rely on for years to come. Writing down your brainstorms will make planning menus as easy as thumbing through your cards and making selections.

Grouping the menus by categories (chicken, ground beef, fish, pasta, etc.) will make it easier for you to find an appropriate menu when you want to use a particular main ingredient. Divide your card file into sections that correspond to the main-dish recipe sections in this book. You can also add sections with menus for cookouts,

meals that travel well (picnics, tailgate suppers, and covered-dish or potluck dinners), meatless menus, light suppers, busy-day dinners, freezer-to-microwave meals, etc. Break down the categories into hot-weather and cold-weather favorites, if you like. Indicate which dishes you can make in large quantities and freeze. That way you can cook and clean up once, but enjoy the dish several times. You could use colored index cards, or color-code your menus with magic markers or stick-on dots to indicate entire menus that can be pulled from the freezer or pantry shelf, for days when you haven't had time to go to the store. These emergency meal ideas will prove to be a gold mine in days to come!

TRIMMING SOME FAT FROM YOUR DIET

- Remove the skin from chicken and other poultry. If you do this before cooking, you'll reduce the fat even more.
- Instead of butter or margarine, use non-stick cookware and sprays.
- Don't be a Frequent Fryer. Roast, grill, or broil meats, poultry, and fish, and bake or steam vegetables as often as possible.
- When baking, replace 1 whole egg in a recipe with 2 egg whites.
- When baking cakes, replace some of the oil with applesauce.
- Choose canned foods like tuna packed in water or broth instead of oil.
- Select plain frozen vegetables, instead of those prepared with butter or rich sauces.
- Use fat-free marinades.
- Substitute ground turkey or chicken for ground beef.
- To enrich sauces and soups, try evaporated skim milk or nonfat dry milk instead of cream.
- When preparing soups that have residual fats, chill them and skim off the congealed fat. Then reheat and serve.
- Substitute plain yogurt or sour half-and-half for sour cream.
- Use low-fat or fat-free spreads, mayonnaise, and salad dressings.
- Trim visible fats from meats before cooking.
- To make dips, use yogurt cheese or process low-fat cottage cheese in the blender.
- Substitute low-fat cheeses for higher-fat varieties.

One Week at a Time

Once you've created a collection of dinner menus, you can begin grouping them together. You may want to write down the week's menus on a sheet of paper and post them on the refrigerator door as a reminder. If you save these sheets each week, you'll develop a permanent record. That may not sound too exciting right now, but believe me, it will be worth more to you later on than you can imagine! I've often commented that I wish I'd written down all the meals I served the first year I was married. Even though I've learned so much since then, it would have been fun to go back and reminisce.

Sticky Menus

If you like, you can go further than planning just one week's worth of menus at a time. Here's a way to arrange menus for an entire month: Take a pad of sticky notes (1½″ x 2″) and write one menu on each one. Then take a sheet of 8½″ x 11″ paper and rule it off in 7 columns and 4 rows, as shown in Figure 4.4. Now arrange the menus so that you can take advantage of leftovers and extras prepared for the freezer. Duplicate menus that you like particularly well and post them once every week or two. (We do this with tacos!) Keep rearranging the menus until you're pleased.

Getting Inspired

Fresh sources of inspiration are always welcome, so browse through magazines, newspapers, and cookbooks, and swap ideas with friends. As you collect recipes, gather pictures as well. There are lots of cooking magazines on the newsstand, and many of them feature different themes in each issue, depicting mouth-watering photographs of food that's been prepared and styled by experts. Sometimes they even offer menu plans for the entire month. Often the themes are geared to holidays or foods that are plentiful or popular during that particular season. Usually the table settings are as attractive as the foods themselves, so you'll get some ideas from those as well. Even when the featured menus might be a little too complicated or time-consuming to prepare, the pictures can still provide you with creative inspiration for attractive food arrangements. You'd be amazed at how easy it is to turn simple foods into something special just by taking some extra care with the presentation.

Frequently, cookbooks include recipes with suggestions for side dishes, accompaniments, garnishes, and other serving hints. Save these ideas. You might transpose them to an entirely different menu. Also pay close attention to the way food is served in restaurants: how it's arranged on the plate, and which side dishes and accompaniments are offered alongside. I've come up with some great meal ideas just by reading restaurant menus. You can learn so much by observing what's going on around you. You'll be surprised how indispensable your personal reference collection will become, as you accumulate new ideas through the years. You might want to compile a set of clippings and other ideas for entertaining. In addition to menus, collect ideas for flowers and decorations as well. Be sure to document your own parties, including guest lists and even photographs. And always be an astute observer when you're a guest in someone's home. If a particular menu worked well for someone else, chances are you could adapt it to work just as well for you.

Sun #1	Mon #1	Tues #1	Wed #1	Thurs #1	Fri #1	Sat #1
Sun #2	Mon #2	Tues #2	Wed #2	Thurs #2	Fri #2	Sat #2
Sun #3	Mon #3	Tues #3	Wed #3	Thurs #3	Fri #3	Sat #3
Sun #4	Mon #4	Tues #4	Wed #4	Thurs #4	Fri #4	Sat #4

Sticky Menus Worksheet (Figure 4.4)

■ ■ ■

Comparing Strategies

There are a wide variety of menu-planning strategies. Of course there are some folks who have no strategy at all—the ones who think that "Rush-Hour-Traffic" is synonymous with "Dinner-Hour-Dysfunction." Actually, they do have a strategy of sorts: to locate the drive-through with the shortest line. But aside from that approach, there are several more fruitful ways of dealing with menu planning, each of which is best suited to a different lifestyle. Choose one of these plans, or combine several, and modify the plans to suit your needs.

Plan #1: Write out specific menus for a week at a time or longer. If your family's schedule is fairly predictable, this method will probably work quite well for you. If your plans change or you eat out one night, simply bump that night's dinner menu to the following night.

Plan #2: Choose a category for each day of the week, and plug different menus into the basic framework. This type of plan works well for families with a recurring weekly event on a certain night each week, such as sports, church, or classes. Here are a few examples:

■ **Monday:** Pasta

■ **Tuesday:** Meat: Beef, Pork, etc.

■ **Wednesday:** Soup and Sandwich

■ **Thursday:** Chicken or Poultry

■ **Friday:** Fish, Eggs, or Meatless

■ **Saturday:** Family Favorite (Tacos, Hamburgers, Pizza, etc.)

■ **Sunday Night Supper:** One-Dish Meals or Skillet Suppers

■ **One Day a Week:** Prepare a food that generates plenty of leftovers, such as a turkey breast or a roast.

Plan #3: Perhaps the most flexible method is to keep the ingredients for about 10–15 different dinner menus on hand at all times on the shelves of your freezer, refrigerator, and pantry. This is much simpler than it may sound, especially if you use the "Stocking the Shelves" list (pages 31–39). It's not difficult to load up the freezer with an assortment of chicken breasts, fish, pork tenderloin, ground meat, and vegetables from the supermarket, along with homemade spaghetti sauce, chili, and casseroles. If you keep the supply replenished as things are used up, you can decide what to serve the night before, and defrost whatever is necessary. With a weekly stop at the grocery store to replenish your supplies, and to stock up on fresh produce, milk, and bread, you can be ready to put a meal on the table without too much advance preparation. Naturally, a microwave oven is an important tool that makes this plan work effectively. This is my preferred method of menu planning. In addition to replenishing my supplies, I often buy many of the same fresh ingredients at the store each week, and decide what to do with them when I get home.

■ ■ ■

Makin' a List and Checkin' It Twice

Brain space is far too valuable to waste it trying to memorize your grocery list. Designate a place of honor in your kitchen for a written list. Set it next to the kitchen phone, hang it on a clipboard inside the pantry or a kitchen cabinet, or anchor it to the re-

---

ABOUT YOUR APPLIANCES...

You've invested a considerable amount of money purchasing the best appliances you can afford, so try to get as much mileage from them as possible.

■ Save the booklets that come with each appliance, and keep them handy. Not only do you need the booklets to explain safety precautions and cleaning procedures, but you can get lots of good ideas from them as well. Read them to learn about special features that can save you time or effort. Many times we think we know everything a particular appliance is supposed to do, and we overlook special features.

■ Sometimes buying a new appliance (a microwave oven or a food processor, for instance) entitles us to a complimentary class that gives helpful tips about using the appliance. The class might help us feel more familiar with some of the special features, and it also might be a source for quick and easy recipes. Take advantage of these free bonuses.

■ If you're online, check out the manufacturers' Web sites. There might be new attachments for the appliance that weren't available when you bought it.

■ Get the most out of your appliances, searching out all their possible uses.

■ Use your food processor as a chef's assistant, to shred large quantities of cheese, chop batches of onions for the freezer, grate carrots, and perform other tedious chores.

■ Use your toaster oven as a plate warmer. Set plates or soup bowls on top while things are cooking. (Don't forget to turn it off!)

---

frigerator door with a magnet. Be sure to keep a pen or pencil handy. Now keep a watchful eye on what gets used up. Train yourself and your family to write things on the list as soon as you notice the supply beginning to dwindle. You know you shouldn't wait until your gas gauge is pointing to "Empty" before you fill up your car. It takes a lot longer to walk to the nearest gas station if you run out of gas, than it does to fill up before you're down to the last quarter of a tank. Likewise, don't look the other way or procrastinate until you've polished off the last piece, drop, bite, spoonful, or squirt of your favorite food. By then it's too late. Every time you remember something you need to buy—including anything from toilet paper to toothpaste—write it on the list. Keep pads of sticky notes all around the house for jotting things down on, and then attach them to the master list. And although I'm not suggesting that you go through your trash, nevertheless, if you happen to look in the kitchen wastebasket and notice that someone's tossed out an empty milk jug, cereal box, or peanut butter jar, be sure it's written down on the list. When you plan your menus, add the key ingredients to your grocery list. Whenever you find out that you need something for a special event (company dinner, bake sale at your child's school, etc.), make a note of it. Pretty soon, you and your grocery list will have developed quite a warm relationship. And when it's time to go to the store, don't leave home without it!

∎ ∎ ∎

Preparing for the Big Trip

It helps if you can plan your weekly grocery shopping expedition right after you've cleaned out the refrigerator. Not only will it remind you of things you're about to run out of, but it also simplifies putting away the groceries when you get home. It's exasperating to arrive with a trunk filled with bulging sacks—especially things that have to be refrigerated—when all the shelves are packed and there's no room to squeeze anything else in sideways. Before you go to the store, eyeball your pantry shelves as well, just to be sure you or someone else didn't use the last bit of something and then forget to write it on the list.

∎ ∎ ∎

Divide and Conquer

Navigating the crowded aisles at the supermarket is tiring enough in itself. But even worse is realizing, after you're in the home stretch and you've finally waded through the dairy section, that you've forgotten to pick up chicken broth or breakfast cereal. So you have to backtrack, like a salmon swimming upstream, propelling the grocery cart up the down staircase as you retrace your steps.

Give yourself a break. It's so much simpler in the long run if you just take a few minutes to plan your shopping strategy. Instead of scrawling your list in no particular order on the back of an old envelope, divide it into categories on a legal pad. Better yet, arrange the categories in the same general order as the aisles of your favorite supermarket, often with produce at one end, dairy at the other, meats along the back wall, and frozen foods somewhere inside the Arctic Circle. You can use one like the sample shown on page 53, or design your own and run off copies. Keep a stack of extras handy so that you can begin with a fresh one each week. If you use colored paper, your list will be easier to find if it migrates into another stack of papers, and you'll be able to locate it more quickly in your purse.

∎ ∎ ∎

Unexplained Memory Lapses

It goes without saying that you should write everything you need on the list. Just as surely as you think you'll remember something, you'll forget it. Even if you just need a few things, chances are better than even that if you trust your memory instead of using a list, you'll arrive home only to discover that you've forgotten something crucial. When you go grocery shopping, take your week's menu plans as well, just in case you

did forget to write something important on your list. Oftentimes, it's just too easy to forget the obvious, once we get focused on our mission. Use a clipboard to snap together your grocery list, menus, and any coupons you may have. I set my clipboard next to my purse in the child's seat of the grocery cart. A child who's old enough can check things off for you as you go. Attach a ballpoint pen or mechanical pencil, or use a stick-on pen with a bungee cord. People have stopped me in the supermarket to look more closely at this wondrous arrangement, and I've actually been asked for my used list by people standing in the checkout line next to me. You too can be a supermarket celebrity once you start using one.

If you can't find a particular item on your list, mention it to the customer service representative. If possible, make a substitution on the spot. Otherwise, circle the item while you're waiting in the checkout line. If you can't do without it that week, unfortunately you'll have to go elsewhere to finish up your shopping.

Hopefully, you can wait for your next shopping trip. This is one reason why having a backup supply at home is so important. It helps get you through another week without a special trip to the store. In my neighborhood, I can choose among several different supermarkets, and I often alternate from week to week, since some stores carry items that others don't stock. Once you get home, be sure to transfer the things that you circled on your old list to a new list before you throw the old one away.

· · ·

The Kitchen Pantry Master List

How many times have you had the nagging feeling that there's something important that you need from the store, but you just can't remember what it is: perhaps you were about to put it on your list, but the phone rang? Your child mentioned something he needed for school, but you were in the car, and didn't write it down. A blank piece of paper staring you in the face is no help as a reminder. What you need is something like a Sears catalog for the kitchen: everything you ever wanted to pick up at the store, but forgot to write down.

Think how helpful it would be to have a list of every item around your home that has to be replenished—from light bulbs to blank VCR tapes. You could use the list to jog your memory. With a tool like

that, you'd be much less likely to forget something critical. This list could be simple or very detailed—whatever appeals to you, and whatever helps you remember those elusive items. You can use the "Stocking the Shelves" list (pages 31–39) as a starting point, and add any other items that you use regularly. Begin with the obvious, and jot down other things as you think of them.

· · ·

Fine-Tuning the List

If you want, you can include every unique item. If you use several different brands, types, forms, or

sizes of a product, you can note these particulars next to each item. For example, you might specify 60-watt, 100-watt, and 3-way light bulbs, and you could include every brand of cereal your family eats. Make the list as general or as specific as you like. This is not an exercise in exhaustion. It's a tool to help you stay in control of your kitchen.

Once you've finished making your list, compare the things you have on hand with what you've written down, and add to your shopping list accordingly. It's always smart to have extras of critical items, according to the amount of storage space you have available. Many times you

GROCERY LIST

PRODUCE	BREAD & BAKED GOODS	COOKIES & CRACKERS	CANNED VEGETABLES, FRUITS, MEATS, & SOUPS
	CEREALS & JUICES	MEAT, FISH, & POULTRY	
	COFFEE & TEA	DELI & COLD CUTS	
PASTA, RICE, GRAINS, & BEANS	STAPLES, MIXES, HERBS, & SPICES	PICKLES, OLIVES, & CONDIMENTS	HOUSEHOLD & PET SUPPLIES
FROZEN FOODS	DAIRY & EGGS	CHEESE & REFRIGERATOR CASE	PAPER GOODS & PLASTICS
CLEANING SUPPLIES	CHIPS & SNACKS	SOFT DRINKS	MISCELLANEOUS

can cut costs by buying in quantity. However, sometimes things deteriorate before you get around to using them, so be practical. Don't go overboard. It is comforting to know, though, that even as you're squeezing out the last glob of toothpaste, there's a brand-new tube waiting on the shelf.

Of course, this "Sears Catalog" isn't something you'll turn to each time you make out your grocery list, but that's not to say it isn't valuable. Every so often it's helpful to do a mini-inventory, since we use up things that we forget to replenish from time to time. And whenever inventory time rolls around, it's good to have the right tool for the job. Every couple of months, take a tour through your kitchen cabinets, pantry, refrigerator, and freezer, as well as your bathroom cabinets, the laundry area, and wherever you keep your cleaning and household supplies. Make notes of any needed items, and check expiration dates on foods, so you can plan to use up anything that's about to go over the hill.

■ ■ ■

Where Do I Keep All That Stuff?

As you arrange things on your pantry shelves, remember that similar items don't necessarily have to be kept together. For example, you could keep a canister of flour on your kitchen counter and stash an un-

opened five-pound sack in your pantry. What about toilet paper? Perhaps you'll have several extra rolls in the bathroom, an unopened package in the hall closet, and if you have a large family and shop at a warehouse club, maybe a whole case of it in your garage. If you're short on kitchen space, you might want to stash a carton or basket in an out-of-the-way place, filled with some of the extra things that won't fit in your pantry.

■ ■ ■

Take a Tip from Noah

Noah had the right idea—loading up the ark two-by-two. The amount of storage space you have

will determine how many things you can fit into your own personal ark. But it's important to have a backup supply of items that are essential to your well-being: at least one unopened package of every critical item. As soon as you open the backup supply, write the item down on your list. Don't wait until you've used it all up. To compose your list, mentally rehearse your normal activities and the situations you might encounter in an average day: fixing breakfast, packing lunches, bathing and dressing, cleaning house, doing laundry, cooking dinner, feeding the dog, plus emergency situations, such as getting through a storm, or nursing a cold or the flu. It's distressing

NOAH'S TOP-FORTY LIST

Besides those animals, here are some things that Noah might want to round up two-by-two for his ark today.

- Allergy and Cold Medicine
- All-Purpose Cleaner
- Aspirin/Substitute
- Batteries
- Bread
- Butter/Margarine
- Cereal
- Cheese
- Chicken, Canned
- Chicken Broth
- Coffee
- Crackers
- Deodorant
- Detergent
- Dishwasher Powder
- Eggs
- Feminine Hygiene Products
- Glass Cleaner
- Honey
- Juice
- Ketchup
- Kleenex
- Light Bulbs
- Lunch Meats
- Mayonnaise
- Milk
- Mustard
- Noodles and Pasta
- Paper Towels
- Pasta Sauce
- Peanut Butter
- Pet Food and Supplies
- Rice
- Shampoo
- Snack Foods (Chips, Snack Bars, Cookies, etc.)
- Soap
- Soft Drinks
- Soup, Canned
- Toilet Paper
- Toothpaste

to realize that you're out of aspirin, Kleenex, chicken noodle soup, crackers, and ginger ale when the room is spinning and your temperature is 102°. It's even worse when you have to bundle up a sick child who's too young to stay home alone, to accompany you on an emergency mission to the store. Once you've determined all the different things you can't live without, make a list. Check your supply of these items frequently, just in case you've used the last of something important, and you forgot to write it on your shopping list. Your list may be longer or shorter than Noah's List, but you can refer to it for ideas to help you get started.

■ ■ ■
Don't Shop 'til You Drop!

Experts estimate that the average home contains more than 300,000 items. (The report did not indicate whether this figure was calculated before or after a streamlining marathon.) It's quite a challenge to keep up with this seemingly endless array of supplies. Just after you've poured a bowl of cereal is not the best time to realize that there's no milk! Running out of just one of life's little necessities at an inopportune time is at best inconvenient. It could also cause an unpleasant chain reaction, by delaying you further when you're already in a hurry. By planning ahead, you'll be more likely to have what you need

when you need it, and the peace of mind that brings is priceless. Like a good scout, you'll appreciate the benefits of being prepared!

■ ■ ■
Ways to Save at the Supermarket

Regardless of the size of your food budget, you'll want to get the biggest bang for the buck when it comes to buying groceries. Following are some ways to conserve your food dollar, and help it stretch just a little further.

■ Keep a well-stocked pantry so that you can avoid unscheduled trips to the store.

■ Buy a freezer and learn to use it for all it's worth.

■ The Grocery List: Don't leave home without it!

■ Periodically stock up on frozen foods, nonperishables, cleaning supplies, and paper products at a warehouse club or discount store.

■ Choose fresh produce in season, and take advantage of local farmers' markets, co-ops and truck stands.

■ Local newspapers usually feature supermarket specials in the food section on the same day each week. Look through the ads for sales and coupons. Those editions are also likely to have recipes and special food features.

■ Clip coupons only for the items you already use or seriously want to try. Don't be seduced into buying something you don't need, just because you have a coupon for it.

■ If you do use coupons, keep them organized in your purse, and check them periodically for expiration dates.

■ Even with the savings that a coupon provides, the store brand may still be less expensive, so be sure to compare prices.

■ If you go grocery shopping no more often than once a week, you'll save time, energy, and money. Remember that the money you're likely to spend at the supermarket increases proportionally with the amount of time you spend there. That's one reason it's a good idea to shop alone if you possibly can. And in case you haven't figured it out yet, that's why they always seem to be rearranging things on the shelves. Naturally, they say it's to make shopping more convenient for you. If you believe that, I have a bridge I want to sell you.

■ Whenever possible, avoid shopping for groceries during the busiest times of the day.

■ Avoid shopping for groceries when you're hungry, angry, or depressed.

■ Unless it's absolutely necessary, don't shop at more than one grocery store each week.

■ Determine a reasonable limit to spend on groceries, and stick to it.

■ Large chain stores frequently feature their own brands, which can save you money. Often there is little difference between the private-label products and so-called "premium" brands, especially for things like tomato sauce. Many times large chain stores (both grocery and drug) have arrangements with manufacturers to put their store label on packages of exactly the same premium-brand product. So when I find a store-brand label that closely resembles that of a premium brand, I usually try it once just to check it out. I've rarely been disappointed.

- Choose generic brands, if you know the quality is acceptable. Here are some items that are likely to be about as good as their premium-priced counterparts: cooking oils, vinegar, dried fruits, juices, honey, extracts and flavorings, herbs, spices, nonfat powdered milk, baking soda, cornstarch, sugar, salt, and flour.

- While shopping, watch for unadvertised specials and markdowns. Many times packaged meat and poultry is marked down because it must be sold that day or pulled from the shelves. The meat is perfectly good, and you can take it home and use it that day or put it in the freezer.

- Learn to make wise choices when it comes to convenience foods. Some, such as chocolate cake mix and frozen orange juice, might actually be less expensive than preparing the same food from scratch. Others can be quite expensive, and are sometimes even inferior in quality.

- Pay attention to the unit-pricing information attached to the shelves. If

---

ABOUT YOUR STOVE AND OVEN...

- An ounce of prevention is worth a pound of cure when it comes to keeping the cooktop and oven clean. When cooking messy foods on top of the stove, use a splatter screen. (It's a piece of wire mesh about the size of a large skillet, with a long handle, and looks sort of like a giant fly swatter. You can find these in variety and specialty cookware stores.) Or use an aluminum 3-panel folding screen around whatever is cooking.

- Glass cleaner and paper towels are very efficient for wiping off glass surfaces on cooktops and ovens. They don't leave streaks, as dish towels often do. (Incidentally, be sure not to launder your dish towels with fabric softener. It makes them less absorbent.)

- When baking messy things that might bubble up and spill over (such as fruit pies), catch the spills by setting a piece of foil on the rack beneath the food. Fold up the edges to form a shallow lip to keep the spills from running off and dripping on the bottom of the oven. If something makes a mess in spite of your efforts, be sure to wipe it up promptly. Otherwise, you'll be greeted by clouds of smoke the next time you turn on the oven. (Naturally, this is most likely to occur when you're having company.)

- Put a stale piece of bread in the roasting pan underneath the rack that the meat rests on, to absorb grease as it drips off a roast. This will help cut down on spattering.

- When things do create a mess, the sooner you wipe them up, the better. The more you accomplish on an as-you-go basis, the less of a production the cleanup job will be.

---

these prices aren't displayed at your supermarket, use a pocket calculator when you shop. A larger size isn't necessarily a better value. Sometimes the smaller size is on sale, as is often the case with soft drinks. In particular, examine the pricing of "giant" sizes, which can by tricky. Unless these packages are labeled "economy," as in "Giant Economy Size," the smaller size might actually be a better buy. Likewise, compare prices for different sizes of products that are packaged in multiples (paper towels in the single-roll, 3-pack, or 12-pack, or soft drinks in the 6-pack versus the 12-pack).

- When comparing the price per pound of different fresh foods, take into account the amount of waste: peels, seeds, trimmings, bones, etc.

- Buy only as much as you can use or freeze promptly.

- Learn to use leftovers creatively.

- Avoid impulse purchases.

- Be open to suggestions. Allow enough flexibility in your menus to take advantage of unadvertised specials.

- If what you need isn't available, be willing to substitute something that would work just as well in its place.

- Write a check or pay cash for groceries. Put the credit card away.

- Take advantage of supermarket memberships that entitle registered shoppers to further discounts, over and above the normal specials.

- Drink more water and fewer soft drinks.

...
Unpacking the Trunk

Hauling in ten bags of groceries is tiring enough in itself. But there are miles to go before you sleep. The food has to be put away (some of it even has to be washed), and there's the ubiquitous evening meal to prepare. A little planning simplifies things a lot.

- At the supermarket, have all the refrigerated and frozen foods bagged together.

- Plan a simple dinner on the day you go grocery shopping. A meal pulled from the freezer, or something waiting in the slow cooker would be ideal. If you plan your menus in advance, this is simple enough to arrange, especially if you do your grocery shopping on the same day each week.

- As mentioned before, clean out the refrigerator before you go on your shopping expedition. Better yet, clean one refrigerator shelf or bin each evening while you're doing the dinner dishes. That way, you won't have to face a refrigerator full of leftovers and unidentified remains.

- Unpack and put away the groceries in steps. Instead of running around the kitchen stashing things willy-nilly, try this: (1) Put away everything that needs to be frozen or refrigerated right away: ice cream, milk, meats, etc. (This is easier to do if it was bagged separately at the supermarket.) (2) Fill the sink with cold water. (3) Set all the grocery sacks on the floor, and clear off as much counter space as possible. (4) Set one sack at a time on the counter, and as you unpack it, put any fresh produce that needs to be washed into the sink. Arrange the other groceries on the counter in groups, based on their final destination: canned foods, paper goods, cleaning products, etc. (5) After you've emptied all the sacks, then put everything away, one group at a time. (6) Finish washing the fresh produce that's in the sink and put it away. (7) Wipe off the counters, put away the sacks, and you're done.

...
Now You're Cooking!

It's almost time to start fixing dinner. But before you put on your apron, roll up your sleeves, and turn on the stove, remember that the last section of this book (pages 317–404) contains a sizeable collection of reference material to answer any food-related questions you might have. And here are a few more general tips for getting good results:

- Read the recipe carefully, all the way through. Be sure you have all the ingredients and the necessary equipment, and that you understand any special terms in the instructions.

- If you need a particular ingredient that you don't have on hand, refer to the Food Substitutions section (pages 393–398) to see if there's something else that you can use in its place.

- If you don't have exactly the right size pan, refer to the list of Container Capacities (pages 399–400) to determine if you have another pan that might work just as well.

- If you don't understand the terms described in a recipe, refer to the Food Terms section (pages 359–376).

- Occasionally, certain ingredients like butter or cream cheese need to be brought to room temperature, or they need to stand for a period of time before they're used in a recipe. Be sure to allow adequate time for this. In a pinch, some things can be softened in the microwave, but don't leave them in there too long.

- Sometimes foods have to simmer or chill for a while before they're ready. Don't overlook these instructions when calculating the total time a recipe will take to prepare.

- Read and measure carefully, using standard measuring cups and spoons. Although measuring spoons can be used to measure small quantities of either liquid or dry ingredients, there are different types of cups that are used for

wet and dry ingredients. Containers for measuring liquids come in 1-, 2-, and 4-cup sizes, with measurements marked on the side of the cup and a pouring spout on the lip. The liquid is poured into the container, and the measurement is checked by holding the cup at eye level. Cups for measuring dry ingredients come in sets of ¼-, ⅓-, ½-, and 1-cup sizes. The dry ingredient is spooned lightly into the cup until the cup is overfilled, and then the excess is leveled off with a knife. Brown sugar and shortening are packed firmly into the cup and then leveled off with a knife. (I prefer shortening that comes in stick form, with measurements marked on the wrapper, similar to butter. It's easier just to slice off the desired amount.)

■ Measure all the dry ingredients before the wet ingredients, so you won't have to rinse and dry the spoons between measurings.

■ Don't hold measuring cups and spoons directly over your mixing bowl when measuring ingredients into them. Something could easily spill or gush out of a container into the cup or spoon, and ruin what's in the bowl.

■ Remember that *1 cup of chopped parsley* is not the same amount as *1 cup of parsley, chopped.* (The former indicates that the parsley is chopped and then measured, and is a larger quantity than the latter, which calls for measuring the parsley first and then chopping it.) Pay attention to the exact wording of each recipe.

ABOUT YOUR FREEZER...

■ Having a freezer full of food doesn't do you much good if you have no idea what's inside. Keep a list of your inventory. The most convenient way to do this is with a small spiral or looseleaf notebook that you keep close to the freezer. Start a new page for each heading of foods that you might store in the freezer, such as:

■ Uncooked Meats	■ Prepared Fish	■ Baked Goods
■ Uncooked Poultry	■ Casseroles	■ Ice Cream and Yogurt
■ Uncooked Fish	■ Vegetables	■ Desserts
■ Prepared Meats	■ Fruits	■ Bread and Rolls
■ Prepared Poultry	■ Juices	■ Snack Foods

Now draw four columns down each page: a narrow one at the left for "Date Frozen," a wide one in the center for "Food Description," and then two more narrow ones at the right for "Amount" or "Number of Servings," and "Use by This Date." Take an inventory of your freezer and make an entry for each item. (For example, if you have two containers of spaghetti sauce, list each one separately.) Add new foods to the list as you put them in your freezer. Cross off foods as you use them up. Check your list from time to time to see if there's anything that needs to be used up soon. Refer to the Food Storage section (pages 343–358) to see how long various foods keep.

■ If your freezer came with a use and care booklet, read it. It might also offer tips on wrapping foods properly for the freezer, and it might give additional information about which foods are good candidates for freezing.

■ Take advantage of every opportunity when cooking foods that freeze well (spaghetti sauce, casseroles, etc.) to make extra for the freezer. A freezer that's well stocked with prepared foods is one of the biggest kitchen time-savers you can have.

■ Prepare and freeze your own convenience foods: chopped onions, grated cheese, chicken broth, etc.

■ Stock up on things like ground beef when it's on sale. Freeze it immediately in ½- or 1-pound packages, or whatever quantities are convenient for you to use at one time.

■ When pork tenderloin is on special, buy several packages. Then repackage them with 1 tenderloin per package.

■ Wrap food tightly and securely before freezing, to avoid freezer burn and resulting deterioration.

■ When adding unfrozen food to the freezer, only add 3 pounds at a time for every cubic foot of freezer capacity. Don't add any more until that food is frozen solid. This allows things to freeze quickly, retarding the rate of bacterial growth.

■ When freezing casseroles, first line the dish with heavy-duty foil. Then arrange the food in the casserole. Wrap the foil around the food and freeze solid. Then remove the "foil brick," label it, slip it in a plastic bag, and replace it in the freezer.

■ Don't start experimenting until you feel quite familiar with a recipe. And never experiment with the proportions in recipes for cooked candy. That's asking for trouble! Remember that recipes involve more than just taste. They often involve chemistry and physics as well!

- If a recipe calls for several cups or spoonfuls of an ingredient to be added a little at a time (4 cups flour, 6 tablespoons oil, etc.), measure the entire quantity into a separate container first, counting out loud so that you won't forget how many you've added. Don't trust your memory. If the phone rings while you're measuring, first finish counting out the amount. Then you won't need to ask yourself, "Was that the third cup or the fourth cup of flour that I just added?" When you finish measuring, add the total amount to the recipe, a little at a time, or in the manner that the recipe specifies.

- Leave the recipe in plain view as you prepare it. No matter how many times you've made something, especially if the list of ingredients is long, it's a good idea to check to be sure you've added everything and haven't skipped a step. Cookbook stands make it easy to see the recipe without the book taking up too much counter space. They're sold in many cookware shops. If you buy one, make sure it's substantial enough to hold a large cookbook.

- Before you begin preparing a recipe, assemble all the ingredients on the counter to one side of the container you'll be using for mixing. As you add an ingredient to the recipe, move it to the other side of the bowl, to avoid accidentally adding something twice.

- Use a container large enough to hold all the ingredients. Be sure to allow room for expansion when mixing or pouring ingredients into any container that you'll be cooking the food in. I still remember my horror the first time I made blueberry muffins. I wanted nice, fat muffins, so I disregarded the instructions to "fill the muffin cups two-thirds full"! This advice is also important to avoid an erupting volcano when cooking candy or pasta. It's usually better to use a container that's slightly too large than one that's too small.

■ ■ ■

Is It Soup Yet?

Here are some helpful tips for managing your time as you're getting meals to the table:

- Get into the habit of starting dinner preparation with an empty dishwasher, so you can load it as you go. This will save you lots of frustration. If you think you're tired before dinner, how do you think you'll feel after it's over? You know you'll want to get the dishes done as quickly as possible, so you can turn into a couch potato. If the dishwasher is full of dirty dishes, you'll either have to wash a lot of things by hand, or you'll have to scrape the dishes and stack them, only to face them first thing in the morning. That's not a pretty sight to wake up to.

- Before you begin to cook, fill the sink with hot, soapy water. Drop in anything that might need to soak or be washed by hand, as well as the pots and pans as you mess them up.

- Clean up things as you go, wiping off counters and putting away ingredients as soon as you've finished using them. This may sound like a directive from Mary Poppins, but we're talking about tiny jobs that only take a matter of seconds. If you'll practice this for a while, pretty soon it will become a habit. Every chore you can get out of the way while you're preparing a meal means one less thing you'll have to deal with after the meal is over. Besides, the less clutter and confusion you have around you as you're cooking, the less likely you'll be to make mistakes or have accidents.

- If you need to put something in the refrigerator to chill, such as a congealed salad, be sure to make room for it before you prepare the recipe, so you won't have to slosh it around trying to fit it in.

- I've said it before, and I'll say it again: Get into the habit of preparing extra quantities of foods that keep or freeze well. It's just as easy to make a double recipe of chili or spaghetti sauce as it is to fix a smaller batch. You won't mess up any more pots and pans preparing two casseroles than you would fixing just one. Serve

one for dinner, and wrap one for the freezer. However, be careful doubling recipes for baked goods. Sometimes the results can be unpredictable.

■ Guests aren't guinea pigs, so don't try out new recipes on them. Never ever. When you're having company, you don't need to deal with any unpleasant surprises. Always practice something at least once for yourself or for your family. This is important for several reasons: (1) to be certain you know what you're doing; (2) to verify that the recipe looks and tastes the way you think it's supposed to; (3) to be sure you know how long it takes to prepare it; and (4) to give you confidence and peace of mind. Sometimes a recipe that sounds simple can take longer to prepare than you think. For example, a big tray of fresh veggies and dip sounds easy, until you realize how long it takes to wash, trim, peel, and cut up all of them. Conversely, don't be intimidated by a recipe that has a long list of ingredients. For example, some soups that might appear difficult to prepare can really be quite simple.

■ Before you begin preparing the meal, set the table, pour the drinks, and put the salt and pepper and any condiments you intend to serve with the meal on the table. Although you can do these things during little breaks while you're waiting for food to cook, it's nice to have them all taken care of, so that when the last dish is prepared, you're certain that

---

ABOUT YOUR DISHWASHER...

■ For some reason, many people procrastinate about emptying the dishwasher. That's probably because it's usually crammed so full that unloading it is a major ordeal. You might want to try running it more often. For most families, twice a day is sufficient. You'll be amazed how much time you'll save by washing smaller, more frequent loads of dishes. Dishes will get cleaner because more water can reach them, and it's not such a hassle to empty it. That means you'll be less likely to drag your feet about doing it, so it won't become a bottleneck!

■ Try to have a regular time for unloading the dishwasher. Maybe in the morning while you wait for the coffee to brew, and again before you start cooking dinner.

■ Measure the correct amount of dishwasher detergent into the cup. Too much can make your dishes look like they have the measles. Too little, and they won't get clean.

■ For spot-free dishes, try one of the products designed for this purpose: either the liquid that's emptied into the special dispenser, or the little basket that snaps onto the top rack.

■ Be sure not to block the water source as you load the dishwasher.

■ Carefully position items that are likely to collect water (such as bowls and glasses), so that they won't turn over when the water hits them.

■ If your dishwasher doesn't have a special basket for tiny items that are likely to get lost, you can often find them in houseware catalogs. They're quite handy, and can keep your dishwasher from getting jammed or clogged up.

---

there's nothing to keep you from sitting down to dinner immediately.

■ Try to plan no more than one dish per meal that requires a lot of last-minute attention. Anything that has to be stirred constantly falls into this category. Trying to do two things at once is asking for trouble.

■ ■ ■

The Mop-Up Operation

Think how overwhelmed a 3-year-old gets when he's had a friend over to play, and it's time to put away all the toys. No matter who's cleaning up, it's so much less confusing when you have a system. The key

here is having a focal point. After dinner, focus on just one type of operation or area at a time. It's easier and much more effective. Use the following "focal points" as guidelines:

■ Try to create as much visual order as possible by corralling the dinner mess into as small a space as possible. Focus on the eating area first. Clear the table, wipe it off, and straighten the chairs.

■ Next, put away leftovers and anything that needs to be refrigerated or frozen. The longer food is left at room temperature, the more likely it is to spoil. The rule of thumb is that perishable foods should not be left out for longer than two hours, total. That includes the time they stay on the counter while you eat dinner, plus any subsequent trips they make out of the refrigerator. (Remember this the next time you're tempted to leave the jar of mayonnaise out on the counter until after you eat your sandwich.)

- Look for stray cartons, boxes, bottles, jars, and packages next. Put them back where they belong.

- Throw away trash and dispose of recyclable items.

- Scrape the plates.

- If you have a dishwasher, load it in this order: plates, utensils, glasses, cups or mugs, and finally, whatever else will fit. Take care not to block the water flow. When you're unloading it, it's a good idea to pull out the lower rack and empty it first. That way, if something on the top rack has tipped over and is filled with water, it won't splash on the clean dishes on the lower rack. Incidentally, lots of things can be washed in a dishwasher that you might not have thought of (baseball caps, for example).

- Clean out one shelf or bin of the refrigerator. It will only take a minute or two. Wipe off sticky jars, throw away moldy oldies, and clean off the shelf. To save refrigerator space, transfer leftovers to smaller containers if possible, and put the old containers in the dishwasher or sink.

- You may still have to wash some things by hand. If so, go to the next step. Otherwise, skip the next step.

- Hopefully, you've already filled the sink with hot, soapy water, as mentioned earlier. Now clear and wipe off the counter on the side of the sink that has the dish drainer. If you don't have a dish drainer, lay a clean dish towel on the counter. (If you're right-handed, this will probably be on the right side of the sink.) Put all the dirty dishes that didn't go into the dishwasher on the opposite side of sink. First wash and rinse anything that was soaking while you fixed dinner. Then wash the rest of the dishes in this order: glassware, plates, serving dishes, and utensils. Wash pots and pans last of all, since they're likely to be messier. Rinse things as you go, and set them in the drainer or on the dish towel. When you've finished, dry the dishes and put them away. Or spread a clean dish towel over them and leave them to drain overnight.

- Now think about tomorrow's breakfast. Measure coffee and water into the coffeemaker. Set it on an automatic timer if you like. If necessary, make up more orange juice, or move a can of concentrate from the freezer to the refrigerator to thaw overnight. Check to be sure there's plenty of milk, cereal, bread, fruit, or whatever you plan to serve for breakfast. If you're low on milk, in an emergency you can reconstitute some instant dry milk and refrigerate it overnight.

- If you need to pack lunches for tomorrow, do it now.

- Consider your dinner plans for tomorrow night. If the meat or anything else needs to be defrosted, move it from the freezer into the refrigerator.

- Wipe off the countertops and any appliances that you used. Turn on the dishwasher.

- Wipe up any spills on the floor with a spray bottle of all-purpose cleaner and some paper towels, or use a sponge set aside just for that purpose.

- Sweep the floor or use an electric broom (one of my favorite appliances).

- Replace your dirty dish cloth and towel with fresh ones, empty the trash, hang up your apron, turn off the light, and go put your feet up. You deserve a break!

■ ■ ■
The Hostess with the Mostest

I've known great hostesses who weren't too swift in the cooking department, and great cooks who weren't very good hostesses. I've also known people who were both and neither. But if I had to choose the one whose home I'd rather be a guest in, I'd go for the great hostess over the gourmet cook.

Some people make you feel welcome and at ease from the moment you set foot in their home. You're confident that they're really glad you came, and that even if they did go to some trouble, they enjoyed it. Others convince you by their body language that your visit has put them into a tailspin, and they make you nervous with their incessant fretting over details. Instead of sitting down to chat with you, they hop up and down like a jack in the box. You wish they'd just relax and phone for a pizza.

I think one secret of being a good hostess is getting your mind off yourself and onto your guests, focusing on how you can make them feel comfortable and welcome. Enjoy your company, instead of worrying that they're undercover agents, secretly grading you on your cooking or housekeeping skills. Like most things, being able to do this requires some advance planning. Don't choose a menu that requires too much last-minute preparation. A delicious casserole like lasagne, that can be prepared (or even frozen) ahead of time is ideal, along with a crisp green salad and some crusty bread. Don't fuss with an elaborate homemade concoction for dessert, either. If you want to serve a fancy dessert, order something from a specialty shop or bakery. Otherwise, serve something simple, like ice cream, fresh fruit, and cookies.

Good entertaining doesn't have to be elaborate, but it does need to be well thought out. Planning is critical. Simpler is better for everyone concerned—for the hostess as well as for the guests. Plan to serve something you're comfortable with, and don't bite off more than you can chew. Although your home should be reason-

ably clean and tidy, if you wait until the photographers from *Architectural Digest* are on their way over, you'll never have company. If you remember that the purpose of entertaining is to enhance relationships—not show off—you'll be well on your way to becoming a successful hostess.

Most of your entertaining will probably be for small groups of guests. But occasionally, you'll entertain for larger numbers. When you entertain on a grander scale, it takes even more planning. With holiday meals, you can learn from year to year and fine-tune your skills. Be sure to refer to the extensive tips on preparing, serv-

ing, and cleaning up after holiday dinners (beginning in the sidebars on page 130). When you prepare a large or complicated meal, writing down your plans helps you remember everything. As you do, you'll be forced to think through all the specifics that you might otherwise overlook. Then save these plans, the same way you save your menus. As the years go by, you'll have a wealth of valuable experience, resources, and information to draw on and to pass along.

While you're planning, don't forget about other details besides food. Having a party that includes more guests than usual might necessitate

SAVING TIME IN THE KITCHEN

- Prepare several days' worth of salad ingredients at a time and refrigerate them in a plastic container or zip bag. Then all you have to do is take out what you need and toss it with dressing at the last minute. Stretch the salad by using up whatever leftovers you have on hand.

- Serve homemade soups once a week. They're not difficult to make, and generate several days' worth of delicious leftovers. Chilled soups like gazpacho don't even have to be heated!

- Use a food processor to slice, chop, or shred big batches of onions, cabbage, carrots, and cheese. They'll be ready when you need them.

- Prepare congealed salads, which last for several days in the refrigerator. Leftover cranberry salad, as well as some other dense congealed fruit salads, can be remolded by softening in the microwave and chilling again in a smaller container.

- Keep several cans of vegetables and fruits chilling in the refrigerator for a quick side dish. Arrange whole green beans, asparagus spears, or grapefruit sections on a bed of lettuce and top with a little dressing.

- Cook batches of chicken breasts and freeze the meat to use in recipes calling for cooked chicken.

- Always cook more rice than you can use for a single meal.

- Whenever you make casseroles—especially vegetables—always prepare extras for the freezer. Those that freeze well include squash, spinach, broccoli, and twice-baked potatoes.

renting some extra glassware or dishes. When this is the case, don't try to squeeze by with the minimum number. Always pad your estimates to allow for the unexpected. At the last minute, you might end up with an extra guest or two. Maybe someone will drop a fork or plate, and you'll need some spares. It's always better to have a few too many plates or a little leftover food than it is to come up short in either department. Also consider some of the other logistics:

- Where will your guests put their coats? If you're short on closet space, you may need to have them put their things on the bed. If that's the case, be sure the bedroom is tidy.

- What if the weather is messy: Do you have a mat for guests to wipe their feet, as well as a place to stash wet umbrellas and perhaps even muddy boots?

- Do you have fresh soap, plenty of hand towels, and extra tissue in the powder room? Think of the things you'd like to find in someone else's powder room if you were a guest, and include them if possible.

- Don't forget an attractive centerpiece. If you don't have a permanent arrangement on your table, you can use something like a basket of colorful vegetables (red and yellow peppers, artichokes, eggplant, tomatoes, and squash) that have been washed and polished with a little vegetable oil. A mound of lemons, limes, or oranges on a pretty blue and white plate looks lovely. When you see something pretty in a magazine—especially if it's simple to create—save the picture and use it for inspiration.

■ ■ ■

Parting Words

The book you're holding has been compiled from years of reading, study, and personal experience. But it will become even more valuable to you as you add your own special notes in the sidebars. Scan the weekly food section in your newspaper for ideas. Study other cookbooks for charts, tips, menus, and recipes. Cut out pictures and articles from magazines. Pay close attention when you're a guest in someone else's home. Always be watching and learning. Copy your ideas down, so they'll be there where you can find them.

Managing a home, and particularly a kitchen, involves constant adaptation and adjustment. It's sort of like learning to ride a bicycle, and the beginning stages can be a little wobbly. It seems as though it's easier for some people to get the hang of it than it is for others. Just as there are natural-born athletes, there also seem to be people who waltz through the kitchen effortlessly, with style and grace. At the other end of the spectrum are those who stumble around as if they're blindfolded and have one hand tied behind their back. But no matter how awkward these skills may be to master, try not to get discouraged. Your abilities will improve with experience, and the job gets easier the longer you do it.

The irony of it all is that as you get older, you amass a wealth of experience, and you begin to fine-tune your craft to the point that it's fairly simple. If you have little ones underfoot, it will be even more challenging for you. Know that this, too, will pass.

You've been entrusted with an awesome responsibility. No matter what anyone might say to the contrary, the job of running a home and managing a kitchen has far more important implications than just making beds, doing laundry, and slinging hash. You're creating a springboard for your family that will launch them to greater heights than could ever have been possible without your loving care. I wish you all the best, and I hope that you'll derive great satisfaction from creating a home that provides your family sanctuary from the cares of the world. As the old saying goes, "The kitchen is the heart of the home." So from my heart to yours, God bless you as you look after the ones you love.

Suggested Menus

The recipes listed in these menus are included in the Recipe section of this book. Convenience foods may be substituted as desired.

■

Chicken Quesadillas (page 135)
Pineapple and Avocado Salsa
(page 135)
Green Salad

■

Baked Ham (page 120)
Southern-Style Green Beans (page 212)
with New Potatoes
Molded Pineapple Salad (page 247)
Dinner Rolls

■

Tortilla Soup (page 93)
Ham Sandwiches
Grapefruit Sections and
Avocado Slices

■

Spaghetti with Meat Sauce
(page 173)
Green Salad
Garlic Bread

THE RIGHT TIME FOR THE JOB

Kitchen jobs don't always have to be done at a conventional time. Here's a thought to ponder: Although the hour before dinner seems like a high-speed chase, once the family disappears after dinner, things quiet down considerably. That's when you're not as likely to be under the gun, and you can move in slow motion. Pour yourself a cup of herbal tea, put on some relaxing music, and shift gears. Now's a good time to think about tomorrow's breakfast and dinner, when you're not rushing. If you take just a few steps in that direction, you'll alleviate some of the rush tomorrow. Save the more labor-intensive jobs for the weekend, when you're more likely to have a larger block of time. When you really have to get the kitchen messed up, go all out. Instead of spending an hour making a jumbo mess, spend 2 or 3 hours, prepare lots more food, and still have only one mess to clean up.

WAYS TO DOVETAIL KITCHEN CHORES

■ While bread is heating in the toaster oven, set the dinner plates on top of it to warm.

■ While you're waiting for water to boil, pasta to cook, or vegetables to steam, fill the water glasses and set them on the table.

■ While food is browning on the stove, assemble the salad without dressing and set it in the refrigerator to chill.

■ Before the timer goes off on the stove, load the dishwasher and tackle any dishes that need to be washed by hand.

■

Planked Salmon (page 146)
Couscous (page 182)
Stir-Fried Asparagus (page 190)
Dill Bread (page 263)

■

Tacos (page 113)
Lettuce, Tomatoes, Cheese, Olives,
and Avocados

■

Grilled Flank Steak (page 108)
Baked Potatoes (page 223)
Caesar Salad (page 241)
Hard Rolls

■

Southwestern Corn Chowder
(page 89)
BLT Sandwiches (page 96)
Melon Slices

■

Linguine with Ham Sauce (page 165)
Green Salad
Sourdough Rolls

■

Barbecued Chicken (page 127)
Mashed Potatoes (page 225)
Green Beans with
Honey Mustard Horseradish Sauce
(page 252)
Sliced Tomatoes
Garlic Bread

■

Roast Turkey Breast (page 142)
Sausage Dressing (page 184)
Green Beans with Cream Cheese
Sauce (page 213)
Cranberry Relish (page 242)
Dinner Rolls

Stuffed Pasta Shells (page 172)
Green Salad
Garlic Bread
■
Roast Chicken (page 136)
Wild Rice (page 177)
Oven-Steamed Asparagus (page 189)
Pears and Cottage Cheese
Dinner Rolls
■
Oriental Chicken Salad (page 140)
Pineapple Slices
Sourdough Rolls
■
Hamburgers (page 98)
Corn on the Cob (page 207)
Lettuce and Sliced Tomatoes
Potato Chips
■
Salmon Croquettes (page 147)
Corn and Rice Casserole (page 208)
Creamy Cole Slaw (page 202)
Sourdough Rolls
■
Texas-Style Chili (page 110)
Green Salad
Tortilla Chips
■
Chicken with Lime Butter (page 130)
Rice Pilaf with Almonds (page 178)
Summer Squash (page 231)
Spinach Salad (page 228)
Dinner Rolls
■
Roast Pork Tenderloin (page 117)
Noodles with Sour Cream
(page 169)
Steamed Broccoli (page 197)
Carrot and Raisin Salad (page 204)
Sourdough Rolls

Baked Lasagne (page 164)
Green Salad
Garlic Bread
■
Tomato Florentine Soup (page 93)
Puffed Cheese Sandwiches
(page 99)
Sliced Pineapple
■
Quick Black Beans and Rice
(page 192)
Green Salad
Tex-Mex Cornbread (page 262)
■
Ground Beef and Macaroni
(page 112)
Green Bean Salad (page 213)
Hard Rolls
■
Barbecued Brisket (page 103)
Baked Beans (page 193)
Creamy Cole Slaw (page 202)
Corn Light Bread (page 262)
■
Chicken and Rice (page 135)
Steamed Broccoli (page 197)
Fruit Salad (page 244)
Sourdough Rolls
■
Cream of Mushroom Soup
with Rice (page 90)
Tuna Salad Sandwiches (page 100)
Apple Slices
■
Ground Beef Stroganoff (page 112)
Baby Salad Greens with Apples
(page 240)
Sourdough Rolls

Grilled Kielbasa Sausage (page 120)
Twice-Baked Potatoes (page 223)
Red, White, and Green Bean Salad
(page 213)
Baked Apples (page 238)
Sourdough Rolls
■
French Bread Pizza (page 97)
Green Salad
■
Meatloaf (page 113)
Macaroni and Cheese (page 166)
Lemon Buttered Carrots
(page 203)
Beet Salad (page 197)
Dinner Rolls
■
Stir-Fried Pork Teriyaki (page 116)
Rice
French Green Peas (page 220)
Pineapple Slices
Dinner Rolls
■
Vegetable Beef Soup (page 94)
Pineapple Slices and
Cottage Cheese
Corn Light Bread (page 262)

Ham Pizza Deluxe (page 98)
Green Salad

■

Gazpacho (page 91)
Egg Salad Sandwiches (page 97)
Oven-Steamed Asparagus
(page 189)

■

Maryland Chicken (page 131)
Noodle Ring (page 168)
French Green Peas (page 220)
Dill Carrots (page 204)
Dinner Rolls

■

Roast Pork Tenderloin (page 117)
Cheese Grits (page 183)
Wilted Spinach Salad (page 228)
Baked Apricots (page 240)
Dinner Rolls

■

Breaded Pork Chops (page 118)
Brown Rice (page 177)
Spinach Salad (page 228)
Escalloped Apples (page 238)
Sourdough Rolls

■

Bacon and Leek Quiche (page 157)
Double Hearts Vinaigrette Salad
(page 244)
Baked Peaches (page 246)
Dinner Rolls

■

Chicken Tetrazzini (page 138)
Green Salad
French Bread

■

Baked Fish (page 145)
Tabbouleh (page 183)
Asparagus Vinaigrette (page 190)
Baked Tomatoes (page 236)
Sourdough Rolls

■

Ground Beef and Noodles (page 111)
Green Beans Amandine (page 212)
Sourdough Rolls

■

Baked Ham (page 120)
Macaroni and Cheese (page 166)
Steamed Broccoli (page 197)
Sliced Tomatoes
Dinner Rolls

■

Beef Stroganoff (page 109)
Rice
Romaine Salad with Mandarin
Oranges (page 247)
Sourdough Rolls

■

Old-Fashioned Pot Roast with
Roast Potatoes and Carrots
(page 104)
Green Beans with Honey Mustard
Sauce (page 212)
Dinner Rolls

■

Chicken and Dressing (page 130)
Rice
French Green Peas (page 220)
Cranberry Sauce
Dinner Rolls

■

Minute Steaks (page 107)
Mashed Potatoes (page 225)
Green Salad
Sliced Pickled Beets
Dinner Rolls

■

Grilled Fish (page 146)
Corn on the Cob (page 207)
Spinach Rockefeller (page 229)
Sliced Tomatoes
Dill Bread (page 263)

■

Fried Chicken (page 128)
Mashed Potatoes (page 225)
Steamed Green Beans (page 211)
Fruit Salad (page 244)
Dinner Rolls

■

Baked Potato Soup (page 91)
Ham Sandwiches
Green Salad

■

Chicken Parmesan (page 133)
Buttered Noodles
Spinach Salad (page 228)
Roasted Roma Tomatoes (page 235)
Dinner Rolls

■

Mostaccioli with Ham
and Tomato Sauce (page 168)
Green Salad
Garlic Bread

■

Southwestern Chicken (page 137)
Mexican Rice (page 180)
Shredded Lettuce with
Guacamole Dip (page 78)
Tex-Mex Cornbread (page 262)

Beverages and Appetizers

BEVERAGES
...

HOW TO MAKE
A POT OF TEA
...

Because the tea that's used to make tea bags has been chopped more finely than the tea that's packaged loose, it tends to becomes stale more quickly.

■ Pour plenty of fresh, cold water into a teakettle or saucepan, cover it, and bring the water to a boil.

■ When the water comes to a boil, pour a little into the teapot and let it stand until the teapot is warm. Then empty the teapot.

■ Now measure the tea into the teapot. For each cup of tea, use 1 teaspoon loose tea. A tea bag is enough to make 2 cups of tea. For iced tea, make the tea slightly stronger, since ice will dilute the tea.

■ To the teapot, add ¾ cup of rapidly boiling water for each cup of tea that you want to make, and put the lid on the teapot.

■ Allow the tea to steep for 3–5 minutes. Steeping the tea longer than that can cause it to become bitter.

■ Press the tea bags to remove the excess liquid, and remove them from the pot. If you used loose tea instead of tea bags, strain the tea into another warmed pot, or strain it directly into the cups that it will be served in.

TEA FOR A CROWD
...

Servings	Tea	Water
25	6–7 tablespoons	1¼ gallons
50	¾–1 cup	2½ gallons
75	1½ cups	4 gallons
100	2 cups	5 gallons

ICED TEA
...

8 tea bags
1 quart boiling water
1 quart cold water

Place tea bags in a saucepan or teapot and add 1 quart boiling water. Cover and steep for 5 minutes. Remove tea bags, pressing out excess liquid. Pour tea into a 2-quart container. Add 1 quart cold water and chill. Serve over ice with sugar and lemon, if desired. MAKES 2 QUARTS.

Note: To make refrigerator tea, place tea bags in a 2-quart container and add 2 quarts cold water. Cover and refrigerate for 8 hours. Remove tea bags, pressing out excess liquid.

TEA PUNCH
■ ■ ■

This is refreshing on a hot summer afternoon, and is the perfect thing to offer friends who drop in.

8 tea bags
1 quart boiling water
2 cups sugar
1 (12-ounce) can frozen lemonade concentrate
1 (12-ounce) can frozen orange juice concentrate
2–3 drops cinnamon oil (available at most pharmacies)
cold water
mint sprigs (optional)

Place tea bags in a saucepan or teapot and add 1 quart boiling water. Cover and steep for 5 minutes. Remove tea bags, pressing out excess liquid. Pour tea into a gallon container. Add sugar, lemonade, orange juice, and cinnamon oil. Stir to dissolve. Add enough cold water to make 1 gallon of tea. Chill and serve over ice, with a sprig of mint if desired.

MAKES 1 GALLON.

INSTANT SPICED TEA MIX
■ ■ ■

This recipe has been around as long as I can remember. It's nice to keep in a jar close to the stove to fix a quick treat on a cold day.

1 (9-ounce) jar Tang (1⅓ cups)
⅓ cup instant tea with lemon
½ cup sugar
½ teaspoon cinnamon
¼ teaspoon ground cloves
dash salt

Combine all ingredients in a container with a tightly-fitting cover, and shake to blend thoroughly. To prepare, spoon 1 rounded tablespoon of the mix into a mug and add 1 cup boiling water. Stir to dissolve.

MAKES 24 (8-OUNCE) SERVINGS.

HOW TO MAKE A POT OF COFFEE
■ ■ ■

■ Start with a clean coffeemaker. Oils build up over time, making the coffee taste bitter. Besides washing the coffeemaker each day, it's good to give it a special cleaning once a month. Run a solution of commercial cleaner through it, or use 2 tablespoons vinegar to 1 quart water. Then run fresh water through the coffeemaker for two cycles before using it again.

■ Use fresh coffee. Store it in an airtight container. Ground coffee keeps in the refrigerator for up to 2 weeks. Whole beans keep in the freezer for up to 3 months.

■ Don't add the last of a package of coffee grounds to a fresh container.

(continued)

Different Roasts for Different Folks

Darker roasts have less caffeine.

American (Regular): Medium roast.

European: A blend of two-thirds dark roast plus one-third medium roast.

French (Heavy): Dark roast. This makes a rich, strong brew.

Italian: Extra-dark roast (the strongest of all), used to make espresso.

Viennese: A blend of two-thirds medium roast plus one-third dark roast.

Popular Coffee Drinks

Café au lait: Equal parts of strong coffee and scalded milk mixed together.

Café con Canela: A cup of strong coffee plus 1 ounce coffee liqueur and 1 teaspoon vanilla extract, topped with whipped cream.

Café latte: One part espresso plus 3–4 parts of hot, foamy steamed milk. Sometimes it is served over ice.

Café macchiato: Espresso topped with 1–2 tablespoons of foamy, steamed milk.

Café mocha: Espresso plus chocolate syrup and foamy, steamed milk.

Cappuccino: Half a cup of hot espresso, topped with equal parts of steamed milk and milk foam. It may be sweetened with sugar and sprinkled with cinnamon or cocoa powder.

Demitasse: Double-strength coffee, served in small cups.

Espresso: Extra-strong coffee, brewed from specially roasted and ground beans. It is processed by forcing steaming water through the grounds.

Irish coffee: A cup of strong coffee mixed with 1 ounce of Irish whiskey and a touch of sugar, topped with whipped cream.

■ Use the correct grind, depending on which type of coffeemaker you have: drip, percolator, etc.

■ Use the right size pot. Always prepare at least ¾ of the capacity of the coffeemaker. (For an 8-cup capacity coffeemaker, prepare at least 6 cups.) If you frequently need to prepare less, buy a smaller coffeemaker.

■ Insert a clean filter, and measure the coffee accurately. A medium brew calls for a rounded tablespoon of ground coffee for each 6-ounce cup. Use a little more or less, to suit your taste. Never reuse grounds.

■ Decaf is slightly weaker, so use a little more coffee than you would normally use to make regular coffee.

■ Start with cold, fresh tap water, which tastes fresher than hot tap water. If your tap water has an off-taste, so will the coffee, so use bottled water instead.

■ Never reheat coffee or allow it to boil, since it will taste bitter.

■ Coffee is best when served within an hour of the time it's made. To keep it longer, transfer it to a carafe or thermos to preserve its flavor.

Coffee for a Crowd

■■■

Servings	Coffee	Water
12	¼ pound	3 quarts
25	½ pound	1½ gallons
50	1 pound	3 gallons
75	1½ pounds	4½ gallons
100	2 pounds	6 gallons

Instant Café au Lait Mix

■■■

¼ cup instant coffee
½ cup sugar
½ cup nondairy powdered coffee creamer

Combine all ingredients in a container with a tightly-fitting cover. Shake to blend thoroughly. To prepare, spoon 2 rounded teaspoons of mix into a cup, add ¾ cup boiling water, and stir.

MAKES 30 (6-OUNCE) SERVINGS.

Instant Swiss Mocha Mix

■■■

¼ cup instant coffee
1 cup instant cocoa mix

Combine all ingredients in a container with a tightly-fitting cover. Shake to blend thoroughly. To prepare, spoon 2 rounded teaspoons of mix into a cup, add ¾ cup boiling water, and stir.

MAKES 30 (6-OUNCE) SERVINGS.

INSTANT COCOA MIX
■ ■ ■

2 1/4 cups nonfat dry milk
1/3 cup unsweetened cocoa
1/4 cup sugar
1/2 teaspoon cinnamon
1/4 teaspoon nutmeg

Combine all ingredients in a container with a tightly-fitting cover. Shake to blend thoroughly. To prepare, spoon 2 heaping teaspoons of mix into a cup, add 3/4 cup boiling water, and stir. For mocha cocoa, add 1/2 teaspoon instant coffee to each serving.

MAKES 40–50 (6-OUNCE) SERVINGS.

OLD-FASHIONED COCOA
■ ■ ■

This brings back memories of children coming in from playing in the snow with red cheeks, wet boots, and soaking mittens.

1/4 cup unsweetened cocoa
1/2 cup sugar
dash salt
1/3 cup hot water
4 cups milk
1 teaspoon vanilla extract
marshmallows (optional)

Combine cocoa, sugar, and salt in a medium saucepan. Whisk in the hot water and bring to a boil over medium heat, stirring constantly. Boil and stir for 2 more minutes. Stir in milk and continue stirring and heating until steaming hot, but not boiling. Remove from heat and stir in vanilla extract. If desired, add marshmallows before serving.

MAKES 4 (8-OUNCE) SERVINGS.

MICROWAVE COCOA
■ ■ ■

1 tablespoon sugar
1 heaping teaspoon unsweetened cocoa
dash salt
1 cup milk

In a microwave-safe mug, combine sugar, cocoa, and salt. Add 1 tablespoon of the milk and stir until smooth. Stir in the remaining milk and microwave on full power for 1–1 1/2 minutes. Stir to blend.

MAKES 1 (8-OUNCE) SERVING.

LEMONADE
■ ■ ■

1/3 cup sugar (or 8 packets Equal)
1/4 cup hot water
juice of 2 lemons (4–6 tablespoons)
1 quart cold water

Combine sugar and hot water and stir until sugar is dissolved. Stir in lemon juice and cold water. Serve over ice.

MAKES ABOUT 1 QUART.

LIMEADE
■ ■ ■

1/3 cup sugar (or 8 packets Equal)
1/4 cup hot water
juice of 2 limes (3–4 tablespoons)
1 quart cold water

Combine sugar and hot water and stir until sugar is dissolved. Stir in lime juice and cold water. Serve over ice.

MAKES ABOUT 1 QUART.

N·O·T·E·S

SPICED CIDER

▪▪▪

Keep this simmering on the stove on cold, snowy weekends. It smells and tastes wonderful.

1/2 gallon apple cider
1 cup orange juice
1/4 cup lemon juice
1/2 cup brown sugar
1/2 teaspoon whole cloves
3 sticks cinnamon

Combine all ingredients in a large saucepan or kettle and bring to a boil, stirring until brown sugar is dissolved. Reduce heat and simmer uncovered for 10–15 minutes. Remove cloves and cinnamon, and pour into mugs.

MAKES ABOUT 2 QUARTS.

PERCOLATOR PUNCH

▪▪▪

This is easy to serve at get-togethers when it's cold outside. Not only does it taste delicious, but it fills the house with a spicy aroma. It can be assembled ahead of time and turned on half an hour before the guests arrive.

3 cups pineapple juice
3 cups cranberry juice
1 1/2 cups water
1/3 cup brown sugar
1/8 teaspoon salt
1 1/2 teaspoons whole cloves
1 whole cinnamon stick

Combine pineapple juice, cranberry juice, water, brown sugar, and salt in a large (party-size) automatic percolator. Place cloves and cinnamon stick in percolator basket and perk. If made in advance, remove basket before reheating. Serve in mugs.

MAKES ABOUT 2 QUARTS.

CITRUS PUNCH

▪▪▪

2 cups sugar
6 1/2 cups water, divided use
1 (12-ounce) can frozen orange juice concentrate, thawed
1 (46-ounce) can pineapple juice
2/3 cup lemon juice
1 quart ginger ale

Dissolve sugar in 1 cup of the water over low heat. Remove from heat and combine with remaining 5 1/2 cups water, orange juice, pineapple juice, and lemon juice. Stir well and chill. Add ginger ale just before serving.

MAKES ABOUT 1 GALLON.

RASPBERRY FIZZ

▪▪▪

1 (64-ounce) bottle cran-raspberry juice cocktail
1 (12-ounce) can frozen orange juice concentrate, thawed
3/4 cup lemon juice
48 ounces ginger ale, chilled
24 ounces club soda, chilled

Combine cran-raspberry juice, orange juice concentrate, and lemon juice. Chill. To serve, mix with ginger ale and club soda, and pour over ice.

MAKES ABOUT 5 QUARTS.

Note: Make up the mix ahead of time, if desired, and store in a clean gallon jug.

BLOODY MARYS

■ ■ ■

1 (46-ounce) can tomato juice
2 (10½-ounce) cans beef broth
3 tablespoons lemon juice
3 tablespoons Worcestershire sauce
1 teaspoon salt
2 tablespoons sugar
6 dashes Tabasco sauce
dash seasoned pepper
vodka
lime wedges or celery sticks

Combine all ingredients except vodka and lime or celery, and chill. When ready to serve, put ice into each glass and pour 1 jigger of vodka into each glass. Add Bloody Mary mix and garnish with lime wedge or celery stick.
MAKES ABOUT 2 QUARTS MIX.

Note: Make up mix ahead of time and let it chill in the refrigerator. Without the vodka, the mix can also be used as a base for tomato aspic. Or serve without the vodka, garnished with a slice of lemon.

CITRUS WINE COOLER

■ ■ ■

2 cups orange juice
1 (6-ounce) can frozen lemonade
   concentrate, thawed
1 cup Cointreau or Triple Sec
1 (25.4-ounce) bottle dry white
   wine, chilled
1 quart club soda, chilled
orange slices

Mix orange juice, lemonade concentrate, Cointreau or Triple Sec, and wine in a punch bowl. Stir in club soda and serve over crushed ice. Garnish with orange slices.
MAKES 14 (6-OUNCE) SERVINGS.

FROZEN DAIQUIRIS

■ ■ ■

1 (6-ounce) can frozen limeade
   concentrate
¾ cup light rum
2 cups crushed ice

Pour limeade and rum into blender. Buzz for a few seconds to mix. Add crushed ice and blend on high speed for about a minute, or until smooth.

Note: For fruit-flavored daiquiris, add 1½ cups fresh or frozen fruit, such as strawberries, peaches, or bananas. Add sugar to taste.
MAKES 4 (6-OUNCE) SERVINGS.

About Frozen Drinks: Be sure that your ice is fresh and clean, and that it has been stored away from strong-smelling foods. Since ice absorbs odors readily, it can impart an objectionable flavor to whatever it's mixed with. To crush ice, place cubes in a heavy plastic zip bag and wrap in a dish towel. Use a hammer or a meat mallet to pound until crushed.

N·O·T·E·S

CHEESE AND FRUIT TRAY

When company's coming, an assortment of cheese, fruit, and crackers is a simple, versatile solution to the problem of what to serve before dinner.

The cheese and fruit tray can be simple or elaborate. Plan to have at least three cheese selections, and allow about 2 ounces of cheese per person.

Start with a mild cheese, such as Gouda. Add a block of Gruyère or Jarlsberg, and a softer cheese, such as a round of Boursin, a wedge of Brie, a cheese ball, or a crock of cheese spread. After choosing the cheeses, arrange them on the tray in a loose triangle.

Add a fruit for color and texture: clusters of grapes or bunches of dried apricots. Granny Smith is a good variety for apple wedges. Dip the slices into a solution of water and lemon juice or Fruit Fresh to keep them from turning brown.

Finish off the tray with some crackers to fill in the bare spots. Water biscuits or Bremner Wafers are attractive for the cheeses, but if you serve a spread, be sure to offer something firm enough to stand up to it without crumbling.

Set out a cheese knife or spreader for each cheese, and place a stack of cocktail napkins close by. Small hors d'oeuvre plates or bread and butter plates would be nice, if you have them.

VEGGIES AND DIP

When choosing raw vegetables, called *crudités*, select an assortment of colors and shapes, and arrange them around a dip, perhaps served in a hollowed-out red cabbage or other natural bowl. You might want to try broccoli or cauliflower florets, slices of yellow squash or zucchini, sticks of carrot, celery, or jícama, and whole raw mushrooms, radishes, or snow peas.

SANGRÍA
■■■

2 oranges
1 lemon
1 lime
1 (1.5-liter) bottle red wine
⅓ cup brandy
¼ cup sugar
1 (12-ounce) bottle club soda
fresh peach or apple slices
  (optional)

Wash oranges, lemon, and lime, and slice thin. Place in a large plastic or glass pitcher and pour wine and brandy over it. Stir in sugar, cover, and refrigerate overnight. When ready to serve, stir again. Then stir in club soda. Put ice into serving glasses and add sangría. If desired, fresh peach or apple slices can be added as garnish.
MAKES ABOUT 2 QUARTS.

FROZEN MARGARITAS
■■■

1 (6-ounce) can frozen limeade
  concentrate
¾ cup tequila
¼ cup Triple Sec
2 cups crushed ice

Pour limeade, tequila, and Triple Sec into blender and buzz for a few sec-

onds to mix. Add crushed ice and blend on high speed for a minute, or until smooth. If necessary, stop the blender intermittently to stir down the contents, so that the ice is well incorporated.
MAKES 5 (6-OUNCE) SERVINGS.

Variation: Blend in 1½ cups sliced strawberries, peaches, or bananas, plus sugar to taste. (Fruit may be fresh or frozen.) If desired, add a drop of food coloring.

MARGARITAS BY THE PITCHER
■■■

3 cups unsweetened lime juice
1¼ cups superfine sugar
3 cups tequila
⅓ cup Triple Sec
¼ cup salt
1 lime, cut into wedges

Pour lime juice into a large pitcher and stir in sugar. Let stand, stirring occasionally, until sugar is completely dissolved. Stir in tequila and Triple Sec. Add ice cubes, stir, and set aside. Salt rims of glasses. (See below.) Stir pitcher of Margaritas once more and pour into prepared glasses.
MAKES ABOUT 1½ QUARTS.

How to Salt the Rims of Glasses:
Place ¼ cup salt in a saucer or small bowl. Rub the rim of each glass thoroughly with a wedge of lemon or lime and then dip the edge of the glass into the salt, rotating the it slightly to coat the rim with salt.

APPETIZERS

■■■

ARTICHOKE BACON DIP

■■■

1 (14-ounce) can artichoke hearts
½ pound bacon, cooked and
*   crumbled*
½ cup chopped celery
½ cup mayonnaise
salt and pepper

Drain and chop artichoke hearts. Combine with bacon, celery, and mayonnaise, and season to taste with salt and pepper. Spread on crackers or Crostini Crisps (page 78). Or use as a stuffing for fresh tomatoes. Can also be used as a sandwich filling.

MAKES ABOUT 2½ CUPS.

ARTICHOKE PARMESAN DIP

■■■

Warning: This is addictive!

OVEN: 350°

1 cup mayonnaise
1 cup grated Parmesan cheese
⅛ teaspoon garlic powder
1½ tablespoons lemon juice
2 (14-ounce) cans artichoke hearts,
*   drained and chopped*
cayenne
paprika

Mix mayonnaise, Parmesan cheese, garlic powder, and lemon juice. Fold in artichoke hearts and season to taste with cayenne. Spread in a greased 1½-quart baking dish and sprinkle with paprika. Bake for 20–30 minutes, or until bubbly. Serve with small crackers.

MAKES ABOUT 4 CUPS.

ASPARAGUS ROLLERS

■■■

OVEN: 400°

24 slices sandwich bread
½ cup butter, softened
1 (8-ounce) package cream cheese
4 ounces softened blue cheese
24 spears asparagus (partially
*   cooked fresh or frozen, well*
*   drained)*
½ cup butter, melted

Trim crusts from bread and flatten each slice with a rolling pin. Mix butter with cheeses and spread on bread. Top each slice with an asparagus spear. Roll bread around asparagus, securing with a toothpick. Dip in melted butter and cut each roll into fourths. Freeze pieces on a cookie sheet. When frozen, transfer to a plastic bag and store in freezer until ready to prepare. To prepare, bake frozen rollers on cookie sheet for 15 minutes.

MAKES 8 DOZEN.

CHEESE STRAWS
■ ■ ■

OVEN: 350°

2 cups (8 ounces) shredded sharp
*   Cheddar cheese*
½ cup butter, softened
1½ cups flour
1 teaspoon baking powder
1 teaspoon salt
¼ teaspoon cayenne

Using an electric mixer or a food processor, cream cheese with butter. Blend in flour, baking powder, salt, and cayenne. Transfer to a cookie press and squeeze strips onto an ungreased cookie sheet. (A star-shaped disc makes pretty straws.) Bake for 15–20 minutes. While still warm, cut into 2″–3″ pieces, but leave on cookie sheet until cool. Remove and store in an airtight tin. These stay fresh for several weeks. They can also be frozen for longer periods of time.

MAKES 6 DOZEN.

CHEESE TORTA
■ ■ ■

8 ounces cream cheese
4 ounces mild goat cheese
1 cup fresh spinach leaves, washed,
*   dried, and loosely packed*
¾ cup flat-leaf parsley
¼ cup fresh basil leaves
1 teaspoon minced garlic
¼ cup olive oil
¼ cup chopped pine nuts
1 cup grated Parmesan cheese
¼ cup slivered sun-dried tomatoes,
*   packed in oil, drained and*
*   patted dry*

Bring cream cheese and goat cheese to room temperature. Blend in a small bowl and set aside. Place spinach, parsley, basil, and garlic in a food processor. Turn on, drizzle in oil, and process until smooth. Place pine nuts and Parmesan cheese in a medium bowl and stir in spinach mixture. Use 2 sheets of plastic wrap, each about 15″ long, placed crosswise in a "+," to line a 5½″ x 2½″ loaf pan. Allow extra wrap to extend evenly over sides. Spoon a third of cheese mixture into loaf pan; spread evenly. Add half of spinach mixture; spread evenly. Arrange half of tomatoes next. Spread on another third of cheese mixture, then remaining spinach mixture and tomatoes. Spread remaining cheese mixture on top. Fold plastic wrap over torta. Refrigerate overnight. Remove from refrigerator and unmold onto serving plate 30 minutes before serving. Serve with crisp crackers or Crostini Crisps (page 78).

MAKES 6–8 SERVINGS.

SNACK MIX

■■■

OVEN: 250°

1/2 cup butter
1 1/4 teaspoons seasoned salt
1/4 teaspoon garlic powder
2 tablespoons Worcestershire sauce
2 2/3 cups Corn Chex cereal
2 2/3 cups Rice Chex cereal
2 2/3 cups Wheat Chex cereal
1 cup salted mixed nuts
1 cup honey roasted peanuts
1 cup pretzels
1 cup Ritz Bits crackers

Melt butter in a large roasting pan. Stir in seasoned salt, garlic powder, and Worcestershire sauce. Add cereals, nuts, pretzels, and Ritz Bits, mixing until everything is coated with butter mixture. Bake for 1 hour, stirring every 15 minutes. Cool and store in a container with a tight-fitting lid.
MAKES 12 CUPS.

CHILI CON QUESO

■■■

This is the same dip I remember my mother fixing years ago. You can add a pound of cooked and crumbled sausage if you like.

1 (10-ounce) can Ro-Tel diced
   tomatoes and chiles (see Special
   Ingredients, page 68)
1 pound Velveeta cheese, diced
tortilla chips

Pour undrained tomatoes and chiles into a medium-size microwave-safe dish. Add cheese. Microwave on high for 3 minutes and stir. Microwave for 2–3 more minutes, or until all the cheese is melted, and stir again. Serve with tortilla chips. If desired, arrange tortilla chips on microwave-proof serving plate and spoon Chili con Queso over them. Add various toppings to create nachos. Heat briefly in microwave.
MAKES 3 1/2 CUPS.

CHIPPED BEEF DIP

■■■

OVEN: 350°

1 (8-ounce) package cream cheese,
   softened
1/2 cup sour cream
2 tablespoons milk
1/2 teaspoon Worcestershire sauce
1 teaspoon finely chopped onion
1 (2 1/2-ounce) jar dried beef
1/2 cup chopped pecans

Blend the cream cheese with the sour cream and milk. Stir in the Worcestershire sauce and onion. Chop and add the dried beef. Place in a small greased baking dish or pie plate, and sprinkle the pecans on top. Bake for 20 minutes. Serve with sturdy chips or crackers.
MAKES ABOUT 2 1/2 CUPS.

VARIETIES OF CHEESE
(CONTINUED)

Camembert cheese—A soft-ripened French cheese similar to Brie, with a gray rind and slightly bitter flavor.

Cantal—A French cheese made from cow's milk, with a smooth texture and a flavor similar to Cheddar cheese.

Cheddar cheese—A popular semifirm cheese made from cow's milk. Its color varies from an almost pure white to a deep golden-orange. Available in different flavors, ranging from mild to sharp. Often covered with wax.

Cheshire cheese—A semifirm English cheese that comes in three varieties. The young varieties, pale yellow and apricot-colored, are mild and taste somewhat like Cheddar. The blue-veined variety tastes more like Stilton.

Chèvre cheese—A pure white cheese made of goat's milk, with a tangy flavor and soft texture. Some varieties are covered with a thin layer of ground cinders, which are edible. **Montrachet** is one variety of chèvre. When chèvre gets old, it becomes sour, and should be discarded.

Colby cheese—A mild, semifirm type of Cheddar cheese.

Cream cheese—A soft, uncured cheese made from milk and/or cream.

Danbo cheese—A Danish cheese similar to Swiss, sold with a yellow or red wax covering. It tastes somewhat nutty, and has a firm texture.

Devonshire cheese—A soft, creamy English cheese made of Devonshire cream.

(continued)

CLAM DIP
■■■

1 (8-ounce) package cream cheese, softened
1 teaspoon Worcestershire sauce
1 teaspoon lemon juice
1 (7½-ounce) can minced clams, drained

Blend cream cheese with Worcestershire sauce and lemon juice. Fold in minced clams. Serve with chips or crackers.

MAKES ABOUT 2 CUPS.

CROSTINI CRISPS
■■■

OVEN: 425°

1 thin loaf French bread
olive oil

Slice bread thinly or have it done at the supermarket. Arrange on greased cookie sheets. Spray or brush on olive oil. Bake for about 5 minutes: just long enough to get crisp, but not too brown. Serve with any spread or pâté.

MAKES ABOUT 2 DOZEN, DEPENDING ON SIZE OF BREAD LOAF.

DILL DIP
■■■

⅔ cup mayonnaise
⅔ cup sour cream
1 tablespoon grated onion
1 teaspoon dill weed
½ teaspoon onion salt
½ teaspoon celery salt
1 teaspoon parsley flakes

Combine all ingredients. Chill. Serve with raw vegetables.

MAKES ABOUT 1⅓ CUPS.

GUACAMOLE DIP
■■■

2 ripe avocados
½ tablespoon lime or lemon juice
½ small onion, finely chopped
½ teaspoon seasoned salt
4 dashes Tabasco sauce
1 tablespoon mayonnaise (about)

Peel and mash avocados with a fork, allowing for a slightly lumpy texture. Blend in remaining ingredients, using enough mayonnaise to achieve the desired consistency. Spoon into a refrigerator container and press plastic wrap onto surface of the dip, to reduce air contact and help prevent darkening. Cover and refrigerate. Serve as a dip, or mounded on shredded lettuce as a salad.

MAKES ABOUT 1½ CUPS.

HORSERADISH DIP
■ ■ ■

1 cup mayonnaise
1½ cups chili sauce
1 small onion, grated
1½ tablespoons horseradish
2 teaspoons dry mustard
dash Tabasco sauce

Combine all ingredients and chill.
Serve with shrimp or raw veggies.
Keeps for weeks in refrigerator.
MAKES ABOUT 1¾ CUPS.

"I just hate
health food."

—Julia Child

LOW-FAT DIP
■ ■ ■

2 cups (16 ounces) plain low-fat
   yogurt
1 bunch green onions, chopped
½ teaspoon dill weed
¼ teaspoon garlic powder
Tabasco sauce

Mix all ingredients in a bowl or
blender, using as much Tabasco sauce
as desired. Chill for several hours before serving. Serve with raw vegetables, or use as a topping for baked
potatoes.
MAKES 2 CUPS.

NACHO LAYERED DIP
■ ■ ■

1 (16-ounce) can refried beans
1 (8-ounce) carton sour cream
2 tablespoons taco seasoning mix
   (about ½ of a 1¼-ounce
   package)
1–2 medium avocados, diced
1 tablespoon lemon juice
¼ cup bottled taco sauce
1 (4½-ounce) can chopped ripe
   olives, drained
2 medium tomatoes, diced
1½ cups (6 ounces) shredded
   Monterey Jack cheese
tortilla chips

Spread refried beans into a 10" pie pan
or a 2-quart shallow pan. Use a dish
that's attractive enough for serving.
Mix sour cream with taco seasoning
mix and spread over refried beans. Toss
diced avocados with lemon juice and
taco sauce and arrange them evenly
over the sour cream mixture. Make
layers of the remaining ingredients, except for the tortilla chips, in the order
listed. Serve with tortilla chips.
MAKES 6–8 SERVINGS.

N·O·T·E·S

VARIETIES OF CHEESE
(CONTINUED)

Double-cream cheese—An enriched cheese made from cow's milk, that contains at least 60 percent milk fat.

Edam cheese—A mild, semifirm Dutch cheese, similar to Gouda, and shaped like a ball, with a waxy red or yellow rind.

Emmentaler cheese—A light golden Swiss cheese made from cow's milk, with large holes and a light brown rind. Its flavor is somewhat nutty and slightly sweet.

Farmer cheese—A fresh cheese similar to cottage cheese.

Feta cheese—A white, crumbly Greek cheese with a tangy flavor.

Fontina cheese—A pale yellow, mild Italian cheese with a semifirm, buttery texture and tiny holes.

Gloucester—A hard, mellow English cheese, similar in flavor to Cheshire and Cheddar.

Gorgonzola cheese—An Italian blue-veined cheese with a firm but crumbly texture.

Gouda cheese—A mellow, semisoft Dutch cheese, similar to Edam, covered with a red rind.

Gruyère cheese—A Swiss-type cheese with a semifirm texture and a creamy, delicate taste.

Havarti cheese—A mild, tangy, semisoft Danish cheese with small holes.

Jarlsberg cheese—A mild, buttery, semifirm Norwegian cheese with small holes and a yellow wax rind.

(continued)

NUTS AND BOLTS
■■■

OVEN: 250°

4 cups Rice Chex cereal
4 cups bite-size shredded wheat
1 cup salted peanuts
1 (9-ounce) package pretzel sticks
1 cup pecan pieces
1 cup butter, melted
2 tablespoons Worcestershire sauce
2 tablespoons garlic salt
2 teaspoons curry powder

Mix all ingredients in a large bowl. Spread on cookie sheets and bake for 2 hours. Cool and store in a tightly covered container.

MAKES 14 CUPS.

PRALINE PECANS
■■■

OVEN: 250°

1 egg white
1/2 cup sugar
1/2 teaspoon salt
1/4 teaspoon cinnamon
1/4 teaspoon ground cloves
1/4 teaspoon nutmeg
1 pound pecan halves

Beat egg white until frothy. Beat in sugar, salt, and spices. Add pecans and stir to coat well with mixture. Spray 2 cookie sheets with non-stick spray and spread pecan halves evenly over sheets, so that they're not in clumps. Bake for 1 hour. Allow to cool and store in tins.

MAKES ABOUT 4 CUPS.

SPICY PECANS
■■■

OVEN: 325°

1/2 cup butter
1/2 teaspoon Tabasco sauce
1 teaspoon Worcestershire sauce
1 tablespoon onion salt
1 pound pecan halves

Melt butter in a large saucepan. Stir in Tabasco sauce, Worcestershire sauce, and onion salt. Add pecans and toss to coat with butter mixture. Pour into a 10" x 15" jelly roll pan and spread mixture into a single layer. Bake for 20 minutes, stirring twice. Remove from oven and cool. Store in an airtight container.

MAKES 4 CUPS.

MINI PIZZAS
■■■

OVEN: 350°

1 pound hot bulk sausage
1 pound ground beef
1 pound Velveeta cheese
1 teaspoon dried basil
2 tablespoons parsley flakes
1 teaspoon oregano
1 teaspoon garlic salt
2 loaves party-size rye bread
1 (16-ounce) jar pizza sauce or pasta sauce (optional)

Brown sausage and beef in a skillet and drain well. Cut Velveeta into cubes and microwave in a large microwave-safe dish until cheese is melted, stirring from time to time.

Add cooked meats, basil, parsley flakes, oregano, and garlic salt to cheese. Stir to mix well. Spread bread slices with mixture and arrange on cookie sheets. Freeze until hard. Then remove from cookie sheets and store in plastic zip bags in freezer until needed. To cook, transfer as many pieces as needed to a cookie sheet. If desired, spoon about 1 teaspoon pizza or pasta sauce on each one. Bake frozen pizzas for about 10 minutes, or until bubbly.

MAKES ABOUT 5 DOZEN.

Potato Skins
■ ■ ■

This is a hearty snack. Add a salad to turn it into a light supper.

OVEN: 425°/BROIL

6 medium baking potatoes
salt
vegetable oil for frying
1½ cups (6 ounces) shredded
    Cheddar cheese
½ pound bacon, cooked and
    crumbled
sour cream

Bake potatoes at 425° for 1–1¼ hours, or until done. Cut in half lengthwise and scoop out most of the potato, leaving about ½" thickness of potato on the skin. (Unused potato can be sea-

soned for mashed potatoes, and served at another time.) Sprinkle with salt. Refrigerate until about 15 minutes before serving. Then pour oil ¾" deep into a heavy skillet and fry the potato pieces, skin side down, until the skins are crisp and golden. Sprinkle with the cheese and bacon, and run under the broiler until the cheese is melted. Serve with sour cream.

MAKES 1 DOZEN.

Sausage Appetizers
■ ■ ■

OVEN: 375°

1 (8-ounce) package butterflake
    refrigerator rolls
½ pound hot sausage, cooked,
    crumbled, and drained
2 eggs, lightly beaten
1 (8-ounce) carton cottage cheese
1 tablespoon snipped chives
freshly ground pepper
¼ cup grated Parmesan cheese

Grease miniature muffin tins. Separate each roll into 8 layers. Fit each piece into a muffin cup, and spoon about 1 teaspoon of the sausage into each one. Mix the eggs, cottage cheese, and chives in a blender. Spoon into a mixing bowl and season with pepper. Stir in the Parmesan cheese, and spoon a dab of the cheese mixture over the sausage in each muffin cup. Bake for 20 minutes, or until the filling is lightly browned. These can be made ahead and frozen in plastic zip bags, either before or after baking.

MAKES 4 DOZEN.

VARIETIES OF CHEESE
(CONTINUED)

Leicester—A mellow, crumbly English cheese with a flavor similar to Cheddar. Its unique texture and smooth melting ability make it ideal for cheese sauce.

Liederkranz cheese—A soft-ripened American cheese.

Limburger cheese—A soft-ripened fermented cheese with a very strong flavor.

Mascarpone cheese—A soft Italian cheese similar to ricotta.

Monterey Jack cheese—Also called "Jack" cheese, a semisoft, mild cheese, similar in flavor to Muenster. Often used in Southwestern cuisine.

Mozzarella cheese—A specially processed white Italian cheese with a mild flavor and a rubbery texture. Fresh mozzarella has a softer texture, a more delicate flavor, and a much shorter shelf life than other types of Mozzarella. Buffalo mozzarella is a type of fresh mozzarella made with buffalo milk.

Muenster cheese—A soft-ripened mild cheese, pale gold in color, usually with an edible orange rind.

Neufchâtel—A soft, unripened cheese made from cow's milk. As it ripens, it becomes firmer and the flavor becomes more pungent. American neufchâtel cheese is a type of cream cheese.

Parmesan cheese—This cheese is also called Parmigiano-Reggiano. It is a firm Italian cheese, and is most often grated and used as an ingredient or a topping. Occasionally served as a dessert cheese.

Pont l'Évêque cheese—A soft French cheese with a strong flavor.

(continued)

SAUSAGE AND CHEESE BALLS
■ ■ ■

OVEN: 350°

1 pound hot sausage, uncooked
4 cups (1 pound) shredded sharp Cheddar cheese
4 cups Bisquick

Combine all ingredients and roll into small balls. Bake for 15 minutes.
MAKES 5–6 DOZEN.

SMOKED SALMON
■ ■ ■

Mix equal parts softened cream cheese and mayonnaise and spread on slices of party-size pumpernickel bread. Top with a thin slice of smoked salmon and garnish with a sprig of fresh dill. Arrange on a serving tray, cover with plastic wrap, and refrigerate for up to 2 hours.

SPINACH DIP
■ ■ ■

1 (10-ounce) package frozen chopped spinach, thawed and drained
1 (8-ounce) can water chestnuts, drained and chopped
3 green onions, chopped
1 1/2 tablespoons lemon juice
1 (1.4-ounce) package Knorr vegetable soup mix (see Special Ingredients, page 68)
1 (8-ounce) carton sour cream
1 cup mayonnaise

In a medium bowl, combine spinach with water chestnuts, green onions, and lemon juice. Mix well. Blend the vegetable soup mix with the sour cream and mayonnaise. Add this to the spinach mixture. Refrigerate for several hours or overnight. Serve in a hollowed-out head of red cabbage, surrounded with crackers or raw vegetables.
MAKES ABOUT 4 CUPS.

Note: When selecting raw vegetables, choose a nice assortment of colors and shapes, cut into easy-to-manage sizes.

JALAPEÑO SPINACH DIP
■ ■ ■

OVEN: 350°

2–3 jalapeño peppers
1 medium onion
2 tablespoons vegetable oil
1 (4-ounce) can chopped green chiles, undrained
1 (14 1/2-ounce) can diced tomatoes, undrained
1 1/2 tablespoons red wine vinegar
1 (8-ounce) package cream cheese, cubed
1 (10-ounce) package frozen chopped spinach, thawed and well drained
1 cup half and half
3 cups (12 ounces) shredded Monterey Jack cheese
tortilla chips
salt
Knorr Aromat seasoning (see Special Ingredients, page 68)
paprika

Remove stems from jalapeños and cut the jalapeños in half lengthwise. Scrape out seeds and discard. Cut each piece in half and chop fine. Peel and chop onion. Heat oil in large, deep skillet over medium heat and add jalapeños and onion. Sauté until onion is soft. Stir in green chiles and tomatoes, and cook for 2 more minutes. Stir in vinegar and cubed cream cheese, cooking and stirring until cream cheese is blended with other ingredients. Stir in spinach, half and half, and Monterey Jack cheese. Season to taste with salt and Knorr seasoning. Pour into a greased 2-quart baking dish and sprinkle with paprika. Bake for 30 minutes. Serve with tortilla chips. Can be frozen, thawed, and reheated in microwave.

MAKES 8–12 SERVINGS.

SPINACH QUICHE BITES
■■■

OVEN: 350°

1 (8-ounce) can refrigerated
    crescent rolls
1 (8-ounce) package shredded
    Swiss or Monterey Jack cheese
1/2 cup grated Parmesan cheese
3 tablespoons flour
1 1/4 cups milk
4 eggs, beaten slightly
1/4 teaspoon salt
1/8 teaspoon pepper
1/8 teaspoon nutmeg
1 (10-ounce) package frozen
    chopped spinach, cooked and
    drained

Press the entire sheet of crescent roll dough into a greased 13" x 9" x 2" pan, allowing it to come up the sides 1/4" to form a crust. In a large bowl,

toss the cheeses with the flour. Mix in the milk, eggs, salt, pepper, and nutmeg, and then fold in the spinach. Pour into the prepared crust and bake for 50 minutes. Allow to cool and then cut into small squares. Serve immediately or freeze. To reheat frozen squares, place in a preheated 400° oven for 15–20 minutes.

MAKES ABOUT 3 DOZEN.

TOMATO TART
■■■

OVEN: 400°

pie crust for single-crust pie
1 tablespoon flour
2 cups (8 ounces) shredded
    mozzarella cheese
5–6 tablespoons chopped fresh
    basil (or one 3/4-ounce package),
    divided use
4 firm ripe Roma tomatoes,
    washed, seeded, and sliced
    about 1/4" thick
salt and pepper
2 tablespoons olive oil

Sprinkle pie crust with flour and spread flour around with your hand. Lay pie crust, flour-side-down, in an 8" or 9" tart pan with a removable bottom. Gently press crust around

(continued)

sides of pan, so that edges of crust conform to the fluted edges of the pan. (It might not come all the way up the sides of the pan.) Moisten your finger with water and press any cracks gently to seal. Prick bottom of crust with a fork and bake for 8–10 minutes. Remove from oven and sprinkle cheese into crust, spreading it evenly. Sprinkle all but 1 tablespoon of the fresh basil evenly over the cheese. Place 1 tomato slice in the center of the tart and then place concentric circles of tomato slices around it, so that they touch each other. Cut any remaining tomato slices in half and arrange them around the outside of the tart, filling in as much of the remaining space as possible. Sprinkle tart with salt and pepper and drizzle olive oil evenly on top. Place tart in the center of the oven and lay a piece of foil on the rack underneath it to catch any olive oil that might leak out of the tart pan. Bake for 30–40 more minutes, or until tomato slices just barely begin to brown around the edges. Remove from oven and sprinkle with remaining fresh basil. Remove tart ring, taking care not to get burned. Slide tart from flat bottom of tart pan onto a serving plate, using a spatula to keep tart from breaking. Cut into wedges and serve warm or at room temperature. Excellent either as a first course or as a side dish. Also good with cooked bacon sprinkled on top before serving. The tart can be prepared in a slightly smaller pan if desired.

MAKES 8 SERVINGS.

ZUCCHINI PIE
...

OVEN: 350°

3 cups very thinly sliced unpeeled zucchini (4–5 small ones)
1 medium onion, chopped
5 eggs
1/2 cup vegetable oil
1 cup Bisquick
2/3 cup grated Parmesan cheese
1/2 teaspoon salt
dash pepper
1/8 teaspoon garlic powder
3 tablespoons parsley flakes
1/2 teaspoon oregano

Arrange zucchini in a greased, rectangular 2-quart baking dish. Scatter chopped onion on top. Beat eggs with oil. Blend in Bisquick, Parmesan cheese, salt, pepper, garlic powder, parsley flakes, and oregano. Pour over zucchini and bake for 25–30 minutes, or until set. Cut into bite-size squares to serve.

MAKES ABOUT 20 (2") SQUARES.

> *"The first zucchini
> I ever saw I killed it
> with a hoe."*
>
> —John Gould

Soups and Sandwiches

SOUPS
···

BLACK BEAN SOUP
···

2 cups dried black beans
8 cups cold water
3 medium onions, chopped
4 tablespoons butter
⅛ teaspoon garlic powder
2 bay leaves
2 tablespoons parsley
1 ham bone
½ teaspoon salt
freshly ground black pepper
⅔ cup dry sherry
crumbled bacon, chopped green onions, or sour cream (optional)

Place beans in a soup kettle, cover with water, and soak overnight. Drain beans and fill kettle with 8 cups cold water. Bring to a boil, cover, and reduce heat to simmer. Meanwhile, sauté onions in butter and add to beans, along with garlic powder, bay leaves, parsley, ham bone, salt, and pepper. Cover and cook over low heat for about 3 hours, or until beans are soft. Add more water if necessary. Remove ham bone and cut meat into small pieces. Return meat to kettle and add sherry. Continue cooking until hot, adjusting seasonings if necessary. Remove bay leaves and serve. If desired, top with crumbled bacon, chopped green onions, or a dollop of sour cream.

MAKES 6–8 SERVINGS.

MIXED BEAN SOUP
···

3 cups dried mixed beans
2 tablespoons salt
2 quarts water
1 meaty ham bone (cooked) with about ½ pound meat
1 large onion, chopped
1 (28-ounce) can diced tomatoes, undrained
juice of 1 lemon (2–3 tablespoons)
⅛ teaspoon garlic powder
3 tablespoons ham flavor base (optional)
Tabasco sauce

Place beans in a large saucepan and cover with 2″ of cold water. Stir in salt and bring to a boil. Reduce heat, cover, and simmer for 2 minutes. Remove beans from heat and let stand for 1 hour, covered. Meanwhile, pour the 2 quarts water into a soup kettle and add ham bone. (Ham bone can be frozen.) Bring to a boil. Then reduce heat, cover, and simmer while beans are standing. After beans have stood for an hour, drain water from beans. Remove ham bone from soup kettle, leaving water in kettle. Remove meat from bone; chop meat or pull it into shreds, and return it to the soup kettle. Add drained beans and bring to a boil. Reduce heat, cover, and simmer for 2½–3 hours. Add remaining ingredients and Tabasco sauce to taste, and simmer for 30–45 more minutes, or until beans are tender. If desired, add salt to taste.

MAKES 10–12 SERVINGS.

WHITE BEAN SOUP
■ ■ ■

1 pound dried Great Northern
    (white) beans
1 meaty ham bone
2½ quarts water
1 large onion, chopped
2 tablespoons cooking oil
2 teaspoons salt
½ teaspoon pepper
½ teaspoon garlic salt
Tabasco sauce

Wash and sort beans; place in a bowl, add enough cold water to cover them, and soak for 1 hour. Then put ham bone in a large kettle and add 2½ quarts water. Bring to a boil, cover, reduce heat, and simmer for 1 hour. Remove ham bone from kettle and cut meat from bone into bite-size pieces. Return meat to kettle. Sauté onion in oil and add to ham. Drain off water that beans have been soaking in and

add beans to kettle, along with salt, pepper, and garlic salt. Cover and continue to simmer for 2 more hours, or until beans crush easily against side of kettle with a heavy spoon. If necessary, add a little more water. When beans are tender, crush enough of them against the side of the kettle to thicken soup to desired consistency. Season to taste with Tabasco sauce.

MAKES 8 SERVINGS.

BEER CHEESE SOUP
■ ■ ■

10 tablespoons butter
½ cup finely chopped onion
½ cup finely chopped carrot
⅔ cup flour
1 (14-ounce) can chicken broth
1 (12-ounce) can evaporated milk
8 ounces Velveeta cheese, cubed
1 (12-ounce) can beer
12 drops Tabasco sauce
1½ teaspoons Worcestershire
    sauce
salt and pepper

Melt butter in a large saucepan over medium heat. Add onion and carrot, and cook for about 5 minutes, or until tender. Whisk in flour and stir until well blended. Slowly add chicken broth and milk, stirring with a whisk until smooth and thickened. Add cheese and stir until cheese is melted. Stir in beer, Tabasco sauce, Worcestershire sauce, and salt and pepper to taste. Bring almost to the boiling point, stirring constantly.

MAKES 4 SERVINGS.

BROWN STOCK

Save bones in the freezer until you have enough to make stock. This stock can be frozen for several months. Pour into freezer containers, or ladle into ice cube trays, freeze, and pop the cubes into a plastic zip bag to use as needed.

5–6 pounds meaty beef or veal bones
2 onions, peeled and quartered
2 cloves garlic, cut into large pieces
5–6 quarts cold water
2 small carrots, cut into chunks
2 ribs celery, cut into chunks
1 (6-ounce) can tomato paste
5–6 sprigs parsley
1/2 bay leaf
1 sprig fresh thyme or pinch dried thyme
6 peppercorns
2 teaspoons salt

Arrange bones, onions, and garlic in a roasting pan in a single layer, and roast at 425° for 30–45 minutes, or until well browned. Transfer to a large soup kettle, discarding any accumulated fat. Pour a cup or two of the water into the roasting pan and stir well to dislodge the crusted juices. Add this to the soup kettle, along with the remaining water and the other ingredients. If the water does not cover the ingredients by about 2", add more. Bring to a boil, reduce heat, and allow to simmer for several minutes, skimming off the scum as it rises to the surface. Cover the kettle loosely, with the cover slightly ajar so steam can escape. Simmer for 4–5 hours or more, if you have time, skimming off the scum as necessary. If the stock cooks down so that the ingredients are exposed, add a little more water. Strain stock into another pot and discard the other ingredients. Refrigerate until the fat congeals on top. Remove and discard fat. Since stock will be slightly congealed, it may be necessary to reheat it before pouring it into storage containers.

MAKES 2½–3 QUARTS.

CHICKEN SOUP
■■■

I remember years ago when I had the flu and thought I'd never get well. A dear friend brought this soup over, and in large measure I attribute my recovery to it!

1 whole chicken (about 3 pounds)
3 quarts water
2 medium onions, quartered
4 ribs celery, cut in chunks
5 whole garlic cloves, peeled
6 medium carrots, cut in chunks
2 teaspoons peppercorns
1 bunch fresh parsley
1 tablespoon chicken flavor base
salt (optional)
chicken bouillon cubes (optional)
4 cups cooked rice

Remove giblets and discard. Place chicken in a large soup kettle, cutting up if necessary, and add water. Add all remaining ingredients except salt, chicken bouillon, and rice, and bring almost to a boil. Reduce heat, cover partially, and simmer for 2 hours. Strain broth into another large pot. Remove white meat from bones, cut up into chunks, and add to broth. Discard remaining chicken and vegetables. Adjust seasonings to taste, adding salt if necessary. If the flavor isn't quite robust enough, add several chicken bouillon cubes. Ladle soup into serving bowls and spoon about ⅓ cup of cooked rice on top of each serving.

MAKES 10–12 SERVINGS.

Note: Always keep chicken soup just at a simmer, and never let it come to a boil, or it will become bitter.

CREAM OF CHICKEN SOUP WITH CHEESE
■■■

7 tablespoons butter, divided use
6 tablespoons flour
1 (14½-ounce) can chicken broth
2½ cups milk
2 teaspoons Worcestershire sauce
½ teaspoon salt
Tabasco sauce
3 cups (12 ounces) shredded Monterey Jack cheese
½ pound fresh mushrooms, sliced
1 (10-ounce) can white chicken, drained
dill weed

Melt 6 tablespoons of the butter in a large saucepan. Stir in flour. Cook and stir over medium-low heat for 3–5 minutes. Slowly blend in chicken broth and milk, cooking and stirring until thickened. Add Worcestershire sauce, salt, Tabasco sauce to taste, and cheese, and stir until cheese is completely melted and soup is smooth. Sauté mushrooms in the remaining 1 tablespoon of butter in a small skillet and add to soup. Break up chicken with a fork and add to soup. Continue cooking until soup is hot. Sprinkle with dill weed before serving.

MAKES 6 SERVINGS.

Note: If desired, omit cheese and/or mushrooms.

SOUTHWESTERN CORN CHOWDER
■ ■ ■

Bottled salsa makes this soup so easy to prepare. I like the kind with black beans and white corn.

8 slices bacon, diced
1 medium onion, chopped
4 tablespoons butter
4 tablespoons flour
2 (14½-ounce) cans chicken broth
1 (26-ounce) jar salsa
1 (16-ounce) package frozen white corn, thawed
2 cups milk
salt and pepper
Tabasco sauce
2 tablespoons dry sherry
shredded cheese for topping

Cook bacon in a skillet over medium heat until crisp. Drain on paper towels. Add onion to drippings and sauté until tender, about 5 minutes. Add butter and stir until melted. Sprinkle with flour and cook and stir for 1 more minute. Slowly stir in broth, salsa, and corn. Bring to a boil, reduce heat, cover, and simmer for 20 minutes. Stir in milk and continue cooking until hot. Season to taste with salt, pepper, and Tabasco sauce. Stir in sherry, pour into soup bowls, and top with bacon and shredded cheese.

MAKES 6 HEARTY SERVINGS.

Note: If you're in a hurry, omit the bacon and sauté the onion in a little vegetable oil. If you have real bacon bits on hand, sprinkle a few on top of each serving.

BASIC CREAM SOUP
■ ■ ■

½ cup butter
1 small onion, chopped
2 tablespoons flour
2 cups fresh sliced or chopped vegetables or 2 cups sliced or chopped cooked poultry or seafood or 2 (10-ounce) packages frozen chopped vegetables, thawed
2 (14½-ounce) cans chicken broth
½ teaspoon sugar
1 teaspoon dried herbs (basil, dill, thyme, parsley, mint, or whatever complements the vegetables) or 1 tablespoon fresh minced herbs
½ teaspoon salt (or more, to taste)
¼ teaspoon pepper
1½ tablespoons lemon juice
1 cup half and half
½–1 cup cooked rice (optional)
6 thin slices lemon (optional)

Melt butter in a soup kettle, add onion, and cook over low heat for about 10 minutes, or until onion is soft. Whisk in flour and cook, stirring, for 3–5 minutes, or until the foaming of the flour has subsided. Stir in vegetables (or poultry or seafood), chicken broth, sugar, herbs, salt, and pepper. Cover and simmer for 15 minutes. If using vegetables, you may pour part or all of the soup into a blender and purée. (You may have to do this in several batches.) Return soup to saucepan and stir in lemon

(continued)

juice, half and half, and rice, if desired. Taste soup to determine if it needs more salt or herbs. Continue cooking until it is piping hot, but not do not let it boil. Serve hot or chilled. If desired, garnish each serving with a thin slice of lemon.

MAKES 6 SERVINGS.

GREEK LEMON SOUP

■ ■ ■

6 cups chicken broth
½ cup uncooked long-grain
*   white rice*
3 eggs
¼ cup lemon juice
2 tablespoons minced fresh parsley

In a large saucepan, bring chicken broth to a boil. Stir in rice and reduce heat. Cover and simmer for 15–20 minutes, or until rice is done. Beat eggs until foamy and beat in lemon juice. Ladle a little of the broth into the eggs, stirring constantly until well mixed. Keep adding broth to the eggs, a little at a time, until the egg mixture is steaming. Then pour it back into the soup. Continue simmering the soup until heated through. Ladle into serving bowls and garnish with minced parsley.

MAKES 4 SERVINGS.

CREAM OF MUSHROOM SOUP WITH RICE

■ ■ ■

8 tablespoons butter, divided use
1 pound fresh mushrooms, sliced
2 (14½-ounce) cans chicken broth
6 tablespoons flour
2 cups milk or half and half
1 tablespoon parsley flakes
2 tablespoons dry sherry
1 teaspoon lemon juice
½ teaspoon Knorr Aromat
*   seasoning (see Special*
*   Ingredients, page 68)*
salt and pepper
Tabasco sauce
3 cups cooked rice
sour cream

Melt 2 tablespoons of the butter in a skillet. Add mushrooms and sauté for 2–3 minutes. Slowly add chicken broth. Cover and simmer for 15 minutes. Meanwhile, in a soup kettle, melt the remaining 6 tablespoons of butter and stir in flour. Cook and stir over low heat for 3–5 minutes. Slowly stir in milk or half and half, parsley flakes, sherry, lemon juice, and Knorr seasoning. Cook and stir until thickened. Season to taste with salt, pepper, and Tabasco sauce. Add mushroom mixture and rice, and stir until blended. Serve hot with a dollop of sour cream.

MAKES 6 SERVINGS.

BAKED POTATO SOUP

■ ■ ■

OVEN: 425°

6 medium baking potatoes
    (about 2 pounds)
¾ cup butter
¾ cup flour
4 cups milk
2 (14-ounce) cans chicken broth
½ bunch green onions, sliced
1½ cups (6 ounces) shredded
    Cheddar cheese
1 (8-ounce) carton sour cream
¾ teaspoon salt
½ teaspoon pepper
1 teaspoon dill weed
6 slices bacon, cooked and
    crumbled
chopped fresh parsley

Scrub potatoes well, pat dry, prick with a fork, and bake for 1–1¼ hours. Cut in half lengthwise and set aside to cool. In a large saucepan or kettle, melt butter. Whisk in flour and continue to cook and stir until smooth. Gradually add milk and chicken broth, stirring constantly until thickened. Scoop out all but two of the potato halves into the soup mixture, discarding peels. Mash and blend with the soup mixture. Add green onions, cheese, sour cream, salt, pepper, and dill weed. Stir until mixture is fairly smooth. Chop the remaining two potato halves, skin included, and stir into the soup. Simmer for about 10 more minutes, or until the cheese is completely melted and the soup is heated through. Ladle soup into individual bowls and top with crumbled bacon and fresh chopped parsley.

MAKES 6 SERVINGS.

GAZPACHO

■ ■ ■

1 (46-ounce) can tomato juice
2 (10½-ounce) cans beef broth
1 tablespoon soy sauce
1 tablespoon Worcestershire sauce
2 tablespoons vinegar
1 tablespoon lemon juice
¼ cup salad oil
⅛ teaspoon garlic powder
½ tablespoon salt
2 tablespoons sugar
Tabasco sauce
1 (28-ounce) can diced tomatoes,
    undrained
1 (3.8-ounce) can sliced ripe olives,
    drained
1 (14-ounce) can artichoke hearts,
    drained and quartered
2 cucumbers, peeled, seeded, and
    chopped

In a gallon container, mix tomato juice, beef broth, soy sauce, Worcestershire sauce, vinegar, lemon juice, salad oil, garlic powder, salt, and sugar. Season to taste with Tabasco sauce. Stir in tomatoes, olives, artichoke hearts, and cucumbers. Chill for several hours. Soup is even better the second day.

MAKES 16 SERVINGS.

N·O·T·E·S

FRENCH ONION SOUP
■ ■ ■

OVEN: 400°

4 large onions (about 2 pounds), thinly sliced

6 tablespoons butter, divided use

½ teaspoon salt (if using homemade stock; less if using canned broth)

½ teaspoon sugar

2 tablespoons flour

6 (10½-ounce) cans beef broth or 2 quarts Brown Stock (page 88)

½ cup white wine

6 slices French bread, toasted

¾ cup grated Parmesan cheese

1½ cups (6 ounces) shredded Swiss cheese

Cook onions slowly in 4 tablespoons of the butter for about 10 minutes, or until soft. Blend in salt (if desired) and sugar, and brown onions slowly for 20–30 more minutes. Blend in flour and cook for 2–3 more minutes. Add beef broth and wine, and bring back to a simmer. Cover loosely, leaving lid slightly ajar so that steam can escape. Cook for another hour, adding a little more water if soup becomes too thick. Place soup in a large ovenproof bowl or divide among 6 individual bowls. Top with French bread and sprinkle with cheeses. Dot with the remaining 2 tablespoons butter and heat in the oven until cheese and butter are melted.
MAKES 6 SERVINGS.

CREAM OF TOMATO SOUP
■ ■ ■

5 tablespoons butter

1 carrot, chopped very fine

¼ medium onion, chopped fine

¼ cup flour

2 cups milk

1 tablespoon tomato paste

1 (28-ounce) can diced tomatoes, undrained

¼ teaspoon salt

¼ teaspoon pepper

1½ teaspoons dried dill weed

1½ teaspoons dried basil

2 teaspoons Worcestershire sauce

¼ teaspoon baking soda

1 tablespoon lemon juice

Tabasco sauce

Melt butter in a large, heavy saucepan and add carrot and onion. Sauté until soft. Stir in flour. Cook and stir for about 5 more minutes. Gradually add milk and stir until soup is smooth. Blend in tomato paste, stirring until smooth. Stir in tomatoes, salt, pepper, dill weed, basil, Worcestershire sauce, and baking soda. Stir in lemon juice and add Tabasco sauce to taste. Keep stirring until soup is piping hot.
MAKES 3–4 SERVINGS.

Note: Adding the tomato paste and tomatoes after the milk makes the soup less likely to curdle. The soda counteracts some of the acidity, also reducing the likelihood of curdling. However if you add too much soda, the soup will have a bland flavor. If this happens, add a little more lemon juice and taste for seasoning.

TOMATO FLORENTINE SOUP
■ ■ ■

4 tablespoons butter
1/2 cup chopped onion (preferably
   Vidalia)
2 (10½-ounce) cans beef broth
3 cups water
1 (10-ounce) package frozen chopped
   spinach, thawed and drained
2 (14½-ounce) cans diced
   tomatoes, undrained
1 (15-ounce) can tomato sauce
1 (6-ounce) can tomato paste
1/4 teaspoon MSG
2 teaspoons sugar
1/2 teaspoon dried basil
1½ teaspoons Worcestershire sauce
1½ teaspoons lemon juice
dash Tabasco sauce
3 cups egg noodles, small shell
   pasta, or other small pasta, or
   7–8 ounces dry pasta

In a large saucepan, melt butter and
sauté onion over medium heat until
soft. Add beef broth and water, and
bring to a boil. Add spinach and return to a boil, stirring often. Reduce
heat to simmer. Add tomatoes, tomato
sauce, tomato paste, MSG, sugar,
basil, Worcestershire sauce, lemon
juice, and Tabasco sauce. Simmer uncovered for 20 minutes. Add pasta and
continue simmering for 10 more minutes, or until pasta is cooked al dente.
Serve hot. For a heartier soup, add
cooked diced chicken or ham.

MAKES 8 SERVINGS.

Note: Sometimes the spinach is
slightly bitter, so taste the soup for
seasoning, and add a little more
sugar if necessary.

TORTILLA SOUP
■ ■ ■

My husband, Jack, says that of all the
soups I make, this is his favorite!

2 tablespoons oil, plus additional
   for frying tortillas
2 tablespoons butter
1/2 cup chopped onion
1 teaspoon minced garlic
1/3 cup cornmeal or flour
3 (14½-ounce) cans chicken broth
   or 6 cups Chicken Stock
   (page 86)
1 (10-ounce) can Ro-Tel diced
   tomatoes and chiles, undrained
   (see Special Ingredients, page
   68), or 1 (12-ounce) jar salsa
1/2 teaspoon salt
1 teaspoon cumin
1 teaspoon chili powder
1 teaspoon Worcestershire sauce
2 cups chopped cooked chicken
   (about 2 large breast halves,
   cooked) or 2 (10-ounce) cans
   white chicken, drained and
   chopped
5 (6") corn tortillas
2 teaspoons lime juice
2 tablespoons snipped cilantro
   (optional)
1 small avocado, pitted, peeled,
   and diced
1 cup (4 ounces) shredded
   Monterey Jack cheese
1 lime, cut into wedges

Measure oil and butter into a soup
kettle and heat over medium heat
until butter is melted. Add onion and
garlic. Sauté over medium heat until
onion is soft. Sprinkle cornmeal or
flour over onion and stir in well. Add

(continued)

N·O·T·E·S

one can of the chicken broth and stir until mixture is fairly smooth. Stir in remaining chicken broth and canned tomatoes and chiles, salt, cumin, chili powder, Worcestershire sauce, and chicken. Simmer for 15–20 minutes, or until slightly thickened. Meanwhile, cut tortillas in half, then cut crosswise into ½″ strips. Heat a skillet over medium-high heat and add ½″ of oil. Add half of the tortilla strips and stir-fry for 1–2 minutes, or until crisp and lightly browned. Remove with a slotted spoon and drain on paper towels. Repeat with remaining tortilla strips. Add half of the fried tortilla strips to the soup and simmer for 10 minutes. Stir in lime juice. Ladle soup into bowls and top with cilantro (optional), remaining tortilla strips, diced avocado, and shredded cheese. Add a wedge of lime on the side.

MAKES 4 SERVINGS.

WILD RICE SOUP WITH TURKEY

■ ■ ■

Here's what to do with that leftover Thanksgiving turkey!

1 meaty carcass from leftover turkey (chicken can be substituted)

2 quarts water

1 (6-ounce) box Uncle Ben's Long Grain and Wild Rice

Put turkey or chicken carcass in a large soup kettle. Add water and bring just to a boil. Reduce heat to simmer and cover. Cook for 1 hour, or until meat falls off bones. Strain broth, meat, and

bones into another kettle or large saucepan. Cut meat into bite-size pieces and add to strained broth. Stir in rice mix. Cover and simmer gently for about 30 more minutes.

MAKES 6 SERVINGS.

VEGETABLE BEEF SOUP

■ ■ ■

1½ pounds ground beef or cut-up stew meat (or leftover roast)

3½ quarts water

1 (6.1-ounce) package Soup Starter Ground Beef Vegetable Soup Mix

1 (1.4-ounce) package Knorr Vegetable Soup Mix (see Special Ingredients, page 68)

1 (16-ounce) bag frozen mixed soup vegetables (use flavor packet if included in bag)

2 (28-ounce) cans diced tomatoes (undrained)

1 (15-ounce) can tomato sauce

1 (10½-ounce) can beef broth

1 tablespoon Worcestershire sauce

½ cup red wine

1 teaspoon salt

½ teaspoon MSG

1 tablespoon sugar

Tabasco sauce

1 (8-ounce) package Rice-a-Roni Beef Flavor Rice Mix

Brown meat in a skillet over medium heat. Using a slotted spoon, transfer meat to a large stockpot and add water. Stir in Soup Starter mix, Knorr Vegetable Soup Mix, and frozen mixed vegetables. (If a seasoning packet is included with the frozen vegetables, add that also.) Add tomatoes, tomato sauce, beef broth, Worcestershire sauce, and wine, and stir to blend. Add salt, MSG, and sugar, and season to taste with Tabasco sauce. Simmer uncovered for 1½–2 hours, skimming the fat off the top as necessary. Add rice mix and cook for 30 more minutes.

MAKES 7 QUARTS.

VICHYSSOISE
■ ■ ■

4 leeks
1 medium onion
2 tablespoons butter
5 medium potatoes (1–1½
    pounds), peeled and sliced
4 cups chicken broth
1 teaspoon salt
¼ teaspoon white pepper
dash Tabasco sauce
2 cups milk
2 cups half and half
1 (8-ounce) carton sour cream
chopped chives

Wash leeks well, discarding most of green part. Slice leeks and onion very thin and sauté over medium heat in butter until golden. Add potatoes, chicken broth, salt, pepper, and Tabasco sauce. Simmer for 45 minutes. Process in food processor or blender until smooth. Return to heat and stir in milk and half and half. Adjust seasonings if necessary. Cook until thickened slightly and then remove from heat. If desired, serve soup hot at this point and garnish with a dollop of sour cream. Or for a more traditional pre-sentation, chill for at least 2 hours; stir in sour cream and chill again. Garnish each serving with chopped chives.

MAKES 8 SERVINGS.

QUICK VICHYSSOISE
■ ■ ■

¼ small onion
1 (16-ounce) carton sour cream
2 (10¾-ounce) cans cream of
    potato soup
2 (14½-ounce) cans chicken broth
salt and pepper
Tabasco sauce
chopped chives

Place onion and sour cream in a food processor and pulse until onion is chopped. Add potato soup and chicken broth and pulse until creamy. Season to taste with salt, pepper, and Tabasco sauce. Chill. Garnish with chives and serve cold.

MAKES 8 SERVINGS.

SANDWICHES
∎∎∎

FILLING A SANDWICH

Here are some ideas for creating your own special "Dagwood"!

Main Event:
- American Cheese
- Anchovies
- Bacon
- Barbecue
- Blue Cheese
- Bologna
- Boursin Cheese
- Cheddar Cheese
- Cheese Sauce
- Chicken
- Chicken Salad
- Chili
- Corn Dogs
- Corned Beef
- Crabmeat
- Cream Cheese
- Eggs
- Egg Salad
- Fish Sticks
- Gouda Cheese
- Ham
- Hamburgers
- Ham Salad
- Hot Dogs
- Knackwurst
- Meatloaf
- Monterrey Jack
- Mozzarella Cheese
- Muenster Cheese
- Pastrami
- Peanut Butter
- Pepper Beef
- Philly Steak
- Pimiento Cheese
- Pot Roast
- Roast Beef
- Salami
- Salmon
- Sausage
- Shrimp Salad
- Sloppy Joes
- Swiss Cheese
- Tuna Salad
- Turkey

Extras:
- Applesauce
- Apple Slices
- Artichoke Hearts
- Avocados
- Bananas
- Beets
- Celery
- Chives
- Chutney
- Cucumbers
- Guacamole
- Lettuce
- Mushrooms
- Olives
- Onions
- Parsley
- Peanuts
- Pecans
- Peppers
- Pickles
- Pineapple
- Pine Nuts
- Raisins
- Scallions
- Slaw
- Sprouts
- Sunflower Seeds
- Tomatoes
- Walnuts
- Watercress

BLT SANDWICHES
∎∎∎

6–8 slices bacon
4 slices bread
mayonnaise
lettuce leaves
tomato slices
salt and pepper

Cook bacon in a skillet over medium heat until done on both sides (see page 98). Drain bacon on paper towels. Spread bread with mayonnaise. Arrange 3–4 slices of bacon on each of 2 bread slices. Place lettuce leaves on top of bacon and add tomato slices. Sprinkle with salt and pepper and add remaining slices of bread.

MAKES 2 SERVINGS.

Variation: Add sliced avocados, alfalfa sprouts, or Monterey Jack cheese.

CHICKEN SALAD SPREAD
∎∎∎

2 (5-ounce) cans premium white chicken, drained
1¹/₂ tablespoons lime juice (juice of 1 lime)
2 ounces pecan pieces, broken
2 teaspoons dried dill weed
¹/₃ cup mayonnaise
salt and pepper

Empty the cans of chicken into a small mixing bowl, and break up the chunks with a fork. Sprinkle lime juice over the chicken. If using a fresh lime, scrape the wedges on the edge of the bowl to extract as much of the pulp as possible. Add pecans, dill, and mayonnaise, and stir to blend. Season to taste with salt and pepper, and refrigerate. Delicious on a sandwich or stuffed in a fresh tomato.

MAKES ABOUT 1½ CUPS.

CREAMED CHIPPED BEEF
∎∎∎

6 tablespoons butter
6 tablespoons flour
3 cups milk
2 (2¹/₂-ounce) jars dried beef or 1 (8-ounce) package vacuum-packed shaved beef
2 teaspoons Worcestershire sauce
salt and pepper
toast, waffles, or biscuits
4–6 hard-cooked eggs, sliced (optional)

Melt butter in a large saucepan over medium heat. Whisk in flour, and cook and stir for 3–5 minutes, or until it starts to turn golden. Add milk slowly, stirring as it thickens. Tear beef into bite-size pieces and add to sauce. Stir in Worcestershire sauce and season to taste with salt and pepper. Spoon over toast, waffles, or split biscuits. If desired, top with slices of warm hard-cooked eggs.

MAKES 4–6 SERVINGS.

Egg Salad Spread

∎∎∎

8 hard-cooked eggs, chopped
1/3 cup mayonnaise
1 tablespoon Dijon mustard
2 teaspoons cider vinegar
2 tablespoons pickle relish
salt and pepper

Mix eggs with mayonnaise, mustard, vinegar, and relish. Season to taste with salt and pepper, and refrigerate.
MAKES ABOUT 2 CUPS.

Note: If desired, add 8 slices bacon, cooked and crumbled, or 1 cup ground ham to egg salad.

French Bread Pizza

∎∎∎

OVEN: 375°

4 individual loaves French bread, split in half (can substitute English muffins)
1 (6-ounce) can tomato paste
2 cups (8 ounces) shredded mozzarella cheese
1 (3½-ounce) package pepperoni slices

Spread bread with tomato paste. Sprinkle with cheese and top with several slices of pepperoni. Bake for about 15 minutes, or until bubbly. Freeze extras.
MAKES 8 SERVINGS.

Hint: To remove excess fat from pepperoni slices before cooking, place in pie pan and pour boiling water over them. Let stand for 5 minutes, remove pepperoni with slotted spoon, and drain on paper towels.

Grilled Cheese Sandwiches

∎∎∎

When I was in college, I went out of town to be in a wedding, and stayed with a friend during the festivities. Her mother made these sandwiches for us late one night after we returned from the rehearsal dinner. Her special secret ingredient was the Worcestershire sauce.

2 tablespoons butter
½ teaspoon Worcestershire sauce
4 ounces sliced or shredded cheese
4 slices bread

Melt butter in a large skillet over medium heat and stir in Worcestershire sauce. Divide cheese between each of 2 bread slices. Top with the remaining 2 slices of bread. Place in the skillet and cook until bread is browned on the bottom. Turn with a pancake turner and brown the other side, sliding the bread around in the skillet to absorb the butter. As cheese melts, press gently on bread with the back of the pancake turner. Remove as soon as both sides of bread are browned and cheese is melted.
MAKES 2 SERVINGS.

HOW TO COOK BACON

Remove as many strips from the package as desired, but don't separate them. Place the slab in a cold skillet and turn the heat to medium. As the skillet heats and the fat melts, use tongs to move the slab around the skillet to distribute the grease. Then turn it over and peel the top strip off the slab. Place it towards the outside of the skillet, leaving the slab in the middle. Keep turning the slab over and over, peeling off the top strip of bacon each time, until all the strips are separated. Turn bacon frequently until it is cooked to the desired degree of doneness. Drain on paper towels.

HOW TO COOK HOT DOGS

Hot dogs, as sold, are fully cooked, and only need to be heated. Here's how:

To Boil:

Fill a saucepan half-full with water and bring to a boil. Slip hot dogs into the water and cover. Remove pan from heat and let hot dogs stand for 6–8 minutes.

To Microwave:

Place one hot dog in a bun and wrap in a paper towel. Heat on high for 30 seconds. More hot dogs take longer.

To Cook in a Skillet:

Spray a skillet with non-stick spray and heat it until a few drops of water sizzle. Split hot dogs lengthwise almost all the way through, leaving the halves still attached (like an open book), or leave hot dogs whole. Cook over medium heat for 6–8 minutes, turning frequently.

Toasted Buns:

Split buns almost all the way through, open like a book, and spread with a little butter. Brown lightly under the broiler or in a toaster oven.

HAMBURGERS
***

1¼ pounds ground chuck
1 egg
2 teaspoons Worcestershire sauce
¾ teaspoon salt
¼ teaspoon pepper
softened butter
4 buns

Mix ground chuck with egg, Worcestershire sauce, salt, and pepper. Form into 4 patties about ¾" thick and about 4" in diameter. Cook on a grill for about 5–6 minutes on each side, or in a skillet for about 4–5 minutes on each side. (Ground beef should never be cooked rare. It should be cooked at least medium, which will appear light pink in the center and brown towards the outside.) While the hamburgers are cooking, butter the buns. When you turn the hamburgers, run the buns under the broiler or put them in the toaster oven. Watch them closely, and remove them as soon as they are lightly browned.

MAKES 4 SERVINGS.

HAM PIZZA DELUXE
***

OVEN: 425°

1 (10-ounce) can Pillsbury
*   refrigerated pizza dough*
¾ cup pizza sauce
2 cups (8 ounces) shredded cheese
1 cup chopped cooked ham
1 (4½-ounce) jar sliced
*   mushrooms, drained*
1 (2¼-ounce) can sliced ripe
*   olives, drained*
4 artichoke hearts, drained and
*   chopped*

Spray a 13" x 9" x 2" baking dish with non-stick spray. Unroll pizza dough and press into pan, pressing it just slightly up the edges of the pan to form a shallow lip. Bake crust for 5–7 minutes before filling. Remove from oven and place pan on a heavy dish towel to protect countertop. Spread pizza sauce over crust and sprinkle on cheese evenly. Scatter chopped ham over cheese and sprinkle on sliced mushrooms, sliced olives, and chopped artichoke hearts. Return to oven and bake for about 15 more minutes, or until cheese is bubbly and just beginning to turn golden. Cut into squares.

MAKES 16 (3¼" X 2¼") SQUARES.

Note: If desired, substitute an already-prepared packaged pizza crust for the pizza dough.

PIMIENTO CHEESE SPREAD
■ ■ ■

4 cups (1 pound) shredded Colby
   or Cheddar cheese
1 (4-ounce) jar diced pimientos
1/2 – 3/4 cup mayonnaise
1 tablespoon Worcestershire sauce
garlic salt
Tabasco sauce

Mix shredded cheese with drained
pimientos. Add enough mayonnaise
to bind ingredients together. Season
with Worcestershire sauce, garlic salt,
and Tabasco sauce. Refrigerate.

MAKES ABOUT 2½ CUPS.

PUFFED CHEESE SANDWICHES
■ ■ ■

OVEN: 350°

2 eggs
1 cup butter, softened
1 teaspoon onion salt
1/2 teaspoon garlic salt
1 teaspoon Worcestershire sauce
3 cups (12 ounces) shredded
   Cheddar or Colby cheese
24 slices Pepperidge Farm
   sandwich bread, crusts trimmed
paprika

Using a food processor or electric
mixer, beat eggs. Blend in butter,
onion salt, garlic salt, and Worcestershire sauce. Add cheese and beat until
smooth. Spread 12 slices of bread with
half of cheese mixture and arrange on
2 lightly greased baking sheets. Lay
the other 12 slices of bread on top and
"frost" with remaining cheese mixture. Cut each sandwich into 3 strips
or 4 small squares or triangles and gently pull apart so that they aren't touching each other. Sprinkle with paprika
and bake for 15 minutes. (Do not let
them get too brown.)

MAKES ABOUT 3 DOZEN.

Note: These freeze well, and can be
reheated after thawing. They're wonderful to serve as appetizers.

PITA POCKETS
■ ■ ■

OVEN: 350°

2 pounds pork sausage
1 tablespoon butter
1 large onion, chopped
1 package (6 slices) pita bread
1/4 cup soy sauce
1 (15-ounce) can tomato sauce
1½ cups (6 ounces) shredded
   mozzarella cheese

Brown and crumble sausage in a large
skillet over medium heat. Drain on
paper towels. Pour grease out of skillet and wipe with paper towels. Melt
butter in same skillet and sauté onion
over medium heat. Meanwhile, slice
each round of pita bread in half crosswise, place on cookie sheet, and heat
in oven for about 5 minutes. Add
sausage to onion and stir in soy sauce
and tomato sauce. Heat until bubbly.
Remove pita bread from the oven and
stuff with meat mixture. Top with
mozzarella cheese and serve.

MAKES 6 SERVINGS.

N·O·T·E·S

TUNA SALAD SPREAD
■■■

2 (6½-ounce) cans albacore tuna,
  drained
4 hard-cooked eggs, chopped
½ cup pickle relish
1 apple, cored but not peeled,
  diced
3 ribs celery, diced
½ cup mayonnaise
1 tablespoon lemon juice
salt and pepper

In a mixing bowl, break up tuna
with a fork. Add hard-cooked eggs,
pickle relish, apple, and celery, and
toss well. Whisk mayonnaise with
lemon juice and add to tuna. Mix
well. Season to taste with salt and
pepper, and refrigerate.
MAKES ABOUT 4 CUPS.

TUNA MELT
■■■

OVEN: BROIL OR TOP-BROWN

4 slices bread, toasted
mayonnaise
Tuna Salad Spread (see preceding
  recipe)
2 slices cheese (any kind)

Spread all of the toasted bread with
mayonnaise and top 2 slices with a
scoop of tuna salad, spreading it to
the edges of the bread. Place these 2
slices on a cookie sheet and top
each with a slice of cheese: Cheddar, Swiss, American, or whatever
you like. Place in a preheated broiler
or toaster oven and heat until the
cheese melts, or for about a minute.
(It may not take quite that long, so
watch to be sure the cheese doesn't
burn.) Remove from oven and top
with the remaining 2 slices of bread.
MAKES 2 SERVINGS.

Meats

MEATS

...

BEEF

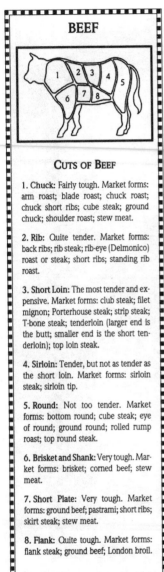

CUTS OF BEEF

1. Chuck: Fairly tough. Market forms: arm roast; blade roast; chuck roast; chuck short ribs; cube steak; ground chuck; shoulder roast; stew meat.

2. Rib: Quite tender. Market forms: back ribs; rib steak; rib-eye (Delmonico) roast or steak; short ribs; standing rib roast.

3. Short Loin: The most tender and expensive. Market forms: club steak; filet mignon; Porterhouse steak; strip steak; T-bone steak; tenderloin (larger end is the butt; smaller end is the short tenderloin); top loin steak.

4. Sirloin: Tender, but not as tender as the short loin. Market forms: sirloin steak; sirloin tip.

5. Round: Not too tender. Market forms: bottom round; cube steak; eye of round; ground round; rolled rump roast; top round steak.

6. Brisket and Shank: Very tough. Market forms: brisket; corned beef; stew meat.

7. Short Plate: Very tough. Market forms: ground beef; pastrami; short ribs; skirt steak; stew meat.

8. Flank: Quite tough. Market forms: flank steak; ground beef; London broil.

TRY A LITTLE TENDERNESS

...

Here are some clues to unraveling the mysteries of tender meat:

■ Tenderness is directly related to the part of the animal meat comes from. The more exercise an area gets, the tougher it is, but also the more flavorful. Ligaments and tendons are composed of connective tissue that should be trimmed away before the meat is cooked. Other connective tissue, made up of collagen, can be broken down using one or a combination of several different methods:

Mechanical Methods: Grinding the meat, pounding it with a mallet, scoring it lightly with a sharp knife, or running it through some sort of mechanical tenderizing machine (as is done for cube steaks) will sever some of the connective tissue.

Chemical Methods: Applying a powdered meat tenderizer or marinating the meat in an acid-based marinade (which can include vinegar, citrus juice, or wine) will help soften or eat away some of the tough fibers. Marinating tends to be more effective for a thinner cut of meat, such as a flank steak, than for a more massive cut, such as a roast. Care should be taken, though, not to overtenderize the meat, or it can become mushy.

Cooking Methods: Cooking tougher cuts of meat very slowly with steam or liquid (such as by pot roasting, braising, or stewing) breaks down some of the connective tissue into gelatin and water. Since the more tender portions of meat lack much of this connective tissue, they're better candidates for cooking methods that use dry heat, such as roasting, broiling, or grilling.

■ Tenderness is related to an animal's age. The older an animal gets, the tougher its connective tissues become. For example, beef tends to be less tender than veal.

■ Cooking temperature also affects tenderness. Here's an analogy to help explain why. If you put a cotton sweater in the dryer and set it on "high-heavy" instead of "low-delicate," it comes out two sizes smaller and stiff as a board. The same thing happens to meat that's cooked at too high a temperature: It shrivels up and gets tough. Although a tender piece of meat, such as tenderloin, can be cooked at a higher temperature, the same treatment ruins a beef brisket.

■ The thickness and the direction meat is sliced after it's cooked also affect its tenderness. Imagine that the meat is a pair of corduroy pants hanging on a hanger, with the fibers running up and down, like the cords in the fabric. Instead of cutting it into lengthwise strips, you should carve it as though you're cutting off its hem, slicing it across the grain. This way, you'll sever more of that connective tissue, allowing your knife to do the work instead of your teeth.

- Meat should always be brought to room temperature before cooking.

- Internal temperature of meat increases 5°–10° after it is removed from heat. During this time, cover roasts loosely with foil and let stand for about 15 minutes before carving. Letting meat stand after it's cooked allows the juices to become redistributed through the meat, thereby increasing its tenderness.

BEEF
■■■

Allow 24 hours for marinating beef, or up to 2 days for tough cuts.

BARBECUED BRISKET
■■■

OVEN: 225°

3 pounds beef brisket
2 tablespoons oil
1 (12-ounce) can cola
¹/₂ cup barbecue sauce, plus additional for serving
dash Liquid Smoke (optional)
garlic salt

Rinse brisket and pat dry with paper towels. Heat oil in a Dutch oven over medium-high heat. Add brisket and turn to brown well on all sides. Mix cola with barbecue sauce and a dash of Liquid Smoke, if desired. Pour over meat. Sprinkle with garlic salt and cover tightly. Place in oven and cook for about 3 hours, or until meat reaches an internal temperature of 145°. Remove from oven and let stand for 10–15 minutes. Transfer the meat to a large cutting board and slice it or pull it apart. Serve with barbecue sauce.

MAKES 5–6 SERVINGS.

CHUCK ROAST
■■■

OVEN: 225°

²/₃ cup flour
¹/₂ teaspoon salt
¹/₂ teaspoon pepper
3–4 pounds boneless top blade chuck roast
¹/₄ cup oil
¹/₂ cup water

Mix flour with salt and pepper. Dredge roast in seasoned flour. Heat oil in a Dutch oven on top of the stove over medium-high heat. Add roast and brown on all sides. Carefully add water, cover tightly, and transfer to the oven. Cook for 3–4 hours, or until meat reaches an internal temperature of 170°–175°. It may be necessary to add a little more water from time to time, as the meat cooks, to keep it from sticking to the pan. Remove meat from oven and let it stand for 10–15 minutes. Transfer it to a cutting board and slice.

MAKES 6 SERVINGS.

N·O·T·E·S

BEEF ROASTING GUIDELINES

Small roasts take more time per pound to cook, and larger ones take less time per pound. Test for doneness with a meat thermometer.

Eye of Round (boneless): For medium-rare, cook a 2–3-pound roast at 325° for 20–22 minutes per pound. Remove from oven when internal temperature is 135°.

Rib-Eye Roast (boneless): For medium-rare, cook a 4–6-pound roast at 350° for 22–26 minutes per pound. Remove from oven when internal temperature is 135°. For medium, cook for 25–30 minutes per pound. Remove from oven when internal temperature is 150°.

Rib Roast (bone-in): For medium-rare, cook a 4–6-pound roast at 350° for 22–26 minutes per pound. Remove from oven when internal temperature is 135°. For medium, cook for 27–34 minutes per pound. Remove from oven when internal temperature is 150°.

Sirloin Tip Roast (boneless): For medium-rare, cook a 2½–4-pound roast at 325° for 30–35 minutes per pound. Remove from oven when internal temperature is 140°. For medium, cook for 35–40 minutes per pound. Remove when internal temperature is 155°.

Tenderloin (boneless): For medium-rare, cook a 3–6-pound tenderloin at 400° for 10–11 minutes per pound. Remove from oven when internal temperature is 135°. For medium, cook for 12–13 minutes per pound. Remove when internal temperature is 140°.

Top Round Roast (boneless): Begin at 250°, and increase to 500° for final 15 minutes. For medium-rare, cook a 3–4-pound roast for 20–22 minutes per pound. Remove from oven when internal temperature is 130°. For medium, cook for 22–24 minutes per pound. Remove when internal temperature is 135°.

MARINATED CHUCK ROAST

■ ■ ■

OVEN: 250°/500°

3–4 pounds boneless chuck roast
meat tenderizer
2 tablespoons butter
1 tablespoon sesame seeds
1 large onion, chopped
½ cup strong coffee
½ cup soy sauce
1 tablespoon Worcestershire sauce
1 tablespoon vinegar
2 tablespoons oil

Place roast in a non-reactive pan and sprinkle with meat tenderizer. Melt butter in a skillet, add sesame seeds, and brown. Add chopped onion and cook until tender. Add coffee, soy sauce, Worcestershire sauce, and vinegar. Pour mixture over roast, cover, and refrigerate overnight, turning several times. Remove meat from refrigerator. Drain and discard marinade and let meat stand at room temperature for 30 minutes. Heat oil in a Dutch oven over medium-high heat. Add roast and turn to brown on all sides. Place in a preheated 250° oven and cook uncovered for about an hour. Check internal temperature and continue cooking until temperature reaches 110°. Then turn up oven to 500° and cook until internal temperature reaches 140°. Remove from oven, cover loosely with a sheet of foil, and let stand for 10–15 minutes before serving.

MAKES 6–8 SERVINGS.

SLOW COOKER POT ROAST

■ ■ ■

4–6 carrots, peeled and cut up
4–6 potatoes, quartered
1–2 onions, peeled and quartered
3 pounds rump roast
1 (1-ounce) package dried onion soup mix
1 (10¾-ounce) can cream of mushroom soup, undiluted

Arrange vegetables in a slow cooker. Place meat on top of vegetables and sprinkle onion soup mix over meat. Pour cream of mushroom soup into a bowl and stir until smooth. Spoon over meat and cover. Cook until tender. This should take 4–6 hours on high, or 8–10 hours on low.

MAKES 6 SERVINGS.

OLD-FASHIONED POT ROAST

■ ■ ■

OVEN: 225°

3–4 pounds boneless top blade chuck roast
⅔ cup flour
3 tablespoons oil
1 cup water or wine
¼ cup horseradish
salt and pepper
3–4 medium onions
6–8 medium carrots
6–8 ribs celery
6–8 small baking potatoes

Dredge meat in flour, coating well on all sides. Heat oil over medium-high heat in a Dutch oven. Brown meat in oil on all sides. Add water or wine and heat until liquid simmers. Remove pan from heat and spread horseradish on roast. Sprinkle with salt and pepper. Cover tightly and put in oven. Peel and quarter onions and carrots. Wash celery, trim off leaves and ends, and cut into chunks about 4" long. Save the leaves. Peel potatoes, cut in half lengthwise, and then cut each half into 2 or 3 chunks. Put all the vegetables and the celery leaves into a large bowl, cover with water, and set aside. When the roast has cooked for 2 hours, remove it from the oven. Drain water from vegetables. Place carrots and potatoes in the pan around roast, and then add onions and celery, including the leaves. If necessary, add a little more liquid to the pan, to keep meat from sticking. Cover the pan again and return to oven for 1–2 more hours, or until meat reaches an internal temperature of 170°–175°. When done, remove celery leaves. Allow to stand for 15 minutes before carving. To serve, place meat in center of serving platter and surround it with the cooked vegetables.

MAKES 6–8 SERVINGS.

"Roast beef, medium, is not only a food. It is a philosophy."

—Edna Ferber

GRILLED BEEF TENDERLOIN

■ ■ ■

Beef tenderloin is simple and elegant to serve as the main course for a dinner party. Or it can be served buffet-style with yeast rolls and Horseradish Sauce (page 253). If you prefer to cook it in the oven, use the recipe for Classic Beef Tenderloin (page 106). Take care not to overcook it.

GRILL: MEDIUM

3 pounds beef tenderloin
4–6 tablespoons Dijon mustard
garlic salt
6–8 slices bacon, uncooked

Rinse tenderloin and pat dry with paper towels. Spread with Dijon mustard and sprinkle with garlic salt. Cover and refrigerate for several hours. Remove from refrigerator 30 minutes before cooking. Wrap bacon around tenderloin and secure with toothpicks. Grill over medium coals for 15 minutes, and turn with tongs. Grill for another 15 minutes, and check temperature. Internal temperature should read 125°–130° for medium-rare, and 135°–140° for medium. Remove from grill, place on a heated platter, and lay a piece of foil over the tenderloin. Allow to stand for 15 minutes before carving. (Temperature will continue to rise about 5°–10° while meat is standing.) If desired, tenderloin can be cut into 1" steaks and grilled for about 5–6 minutes per side, for medium-rare.

MAKES 8 SERVINGS.

N·O·T·E·S

BEEF GRILLING GUIDELINES

Filet Mignon: (1″ thick) Set grill 2″–3″ from coals. For medium-rare, cook for 5–6 minutes on each side. Internal temperature should be 145°. For medium, cook for 6–7 minutes on each side. Internal temperature should be 160°.

Flank Steak: (1–1½ pounds) Set grill 2″–3″ from coals. For medium-rare, cook for 6 minutes on each side. Internal temperature should be 145°. For medium, cook for 7–8 minutes on each side. Internal temperature should be 160°.

Ground Beef: (½″–¾″ thick) Set grill 3″–4″ from coals. For medium, cook for 4–6 minutes on each side. Internal temperature should be 160°. For medium-well, internal temperature should be 170°.

Rib-Eye Steak: (¾″–1″ thick) Set grill 2″–4″ from coals. For medium-rare, cook for 4–5 minutes on each side. Internal temperature should be 145°. For medium, cook for about 6 minutes on each side. Internal temperature should be 160°.

Shish Kebabs: (1″ cubes) Set grill 3″–4″ from coals. For medium-rare, cook for 4 minutes on each side. Internal temperature should be 145°. For medium, cook for 5–6 minutes on each side. Internal temperature should be 160°.

Sirloin Steak (boneless): (¾″–1″ thick) Set grill 2″–4″ from coals. For medium-rare, cook for 6 minutes on each side. Internal temperature should be 145°. For medium, cook for 7–8 minutes on each side. Internal temperature should be 160°.

T-Bone or Porterhouse Steak: (1″ thick) Set grill 3″–4″ from coals. For medium-rare, cook for 5 minutes on each side. Internal temperature should be 145°. For medium, cook for 7 minutes on each side. Internal temperature should be 160°.

CLASSIC BEEF TENDERLOIN
■■■

OVEN: 400°

3 pounds beef tenderloin
½ cup Italian dressing
½ cup red wine
½ cup teriyaki sauce or teriyaki-style marinade
2 tablespoons Worcestershire sauce
2 teaspoons lemon pepper
chopped fresh parsley (optional)

Rinse meat, pat dry, and place in a heavy plastic bag. Mix Italian dressing, wine, teriyaki sauce or marinade, Worcestershire sauce, and lemon pepper. Pour mixture over meat. Seal bag and place in a container about the size of the tenderloin. Refrigerate for several hours or overnight, turning bag several times. Remove meat from refrigerator 30 minutes before cooking and drain off marinade. Place an empty roasting pan in the oven to heat for 15 minutes. Remove the hot roasting pan from the oven, set it on a heatproof surface, and place tenderloin in pan. Place meat in the oven and cook for about 30 minutes. Check the internal temperature at the center of the meat. Continue cooking for 10–15 more minutes, or until thermometer registers 130° for medium-rare, or 140° for medium. Remove meat from the oven, cover loosely with a piece of foil, and allow to stand for 10–20 minutes. (The internal temperature of the meat will continue to rise 5°–10° during this time.) To cook a whole beef tender-

loin (about 4–6 pounds), double the amount of marinade and cook for about 40–60 minutes, for medium-rare. A 1–1½ pound piece of tenderloin needs just half as much marinade, but takes about the same length of time to cook. Slice about ¾″ thick. If desired, garnish with parsley and serve with Horseradish Sauce (page 253).

MAKES 8 SERVINGS.

STANDING RIB ROAST
■■■

OVEN: 550°/350°

4–6 pounds standing rib roast
garlic salt
freshly ground black pepper
2 cups red wine (optional)

Remove roast from refrigerator 30–45 minutes before cooking. Sprinkle generously with garlic salt and pepper. Place rib-side-down (fat-side-up) in a roasting pan. Pour red wine around the roast if desired. Place in a preheated 550° oven. Close oven door and immediately reduce heat to 350°. Check temperature after 1¾ hours, and continue cooking until internal temperature is 135°, for medium-rare (22–26 minutes per pound).

MAKES 8 SERVINGS.

Note: Roast beef is delicious with Horseradish Sauce (page 253). For a real treat, serve with Yorkshire Pudding (page 183) and Creamed Spinach (page 228).

FILET MIGNON
■ ■ ■

GRILL: MEDIUM-HOT

1½ pounds beef tenderloin
4 strips bacon
Dijon mustard

Have butcher cut beef from the wide (butt) end of the tenderloin and slice into 4 equal filets, about 1" thick. Or select 4 individual filets, about 6 ounces each. Wrap a slice of bacon around each one, securing with three toothpicks. Spread top side liberally with Dijon mustard and allow to stand at room temperature while grill is heating. Grill for about 5–6 minutes on each side for medium-rare.

MAKES 4 SERVINGS.

MINUTE STEAKS
■ ■ ■

4 minute steaks, 6–8 ounces each
1 cup flour
salt and pepper
meat tenderizer
2 tablespoons butter
2 tablespoons oil

Dredge minute steaks in flour and sprinkle with salt, pepper, and meat tenderizer. Heat a large skillet over medium heat. Add butter and oil. Add steaks and pan-fry for 3–5 minutes on each side, or until nicely browned and cooked to desired degree of doneness.

MAKES 4 SERVINGS.

Note: For a real down-home indulgence, serve with Cream Gravy (page 251) and Mashed Potatoes (page 225).

BEEF FAJITAS
■ ■ ■

GRILL: MEDIUM-HOT
OVEN: 350°

1½ pounds flank or skirt steak
1 cup picante sauce
1 cup Italian dressing
2 tablespoons lemon juice
2 tablespoons chopped green onions
1 teaspoon garlic powder
1 teaspoon pepper
1 teaspoon celery salt
8 large flour tortillas (about 8½")
bottled salsa
guacamole or diced avocados
chopped tomatoes
shredded cheese
sour cream

Remove any fat from meat, rinse, and wipe dry with paper towels. Place in a shallow non-reactive pan. Combine picante sauce, Italian dressing, lemon juice, green onions, garlic powder, pepper, and celery salt. Pour over meat and cover. Refrigerate overnight, turning meat several times. Remove meat from refrigerator and allow to stand at room temperature for 30 minutes. Drain marinade and grill meat over medium heat for about 7–9 minutes on a side, for medium-rare. Allow to stand for 10 minutes before carving. Meanwhile, wrap tortillas in foil and heat for about 10 minutes in oven. Then slice meat thinly across the grain and serve with heated tortillas, salsa, guacamole or diced avocados, chopped tomatoes, shredded cheese, and sour cream.

MAKES 4 SERVINGS.

N·O·T·E·S

GRILLED FLANK STEAK

▪▪▪

GRILL: MEDIUM-HOT

1½ pounds flank steak
marinade (see below)
meat tenderizer

Rinse steak, pat dry with paper towels, and place in a non-reactive pan. Prepare one of the following marinades, and pour it over the steak.

Italian Dressing Marinade:
1 (8-ounce) bottle Italian dressing

Lime Marinade:
1 (10½-ounce) can beef broth
⅓ cup soy sauce
1½ teaspoons seasoned salt
½ teaspoon instant minced onion
3 tablespoons lime juice (juice of 2 limes)
2 tablespoons brown sugar

Honey Soy Marinade:
¾ cup oil
¼ cup soy sauce
½ cup honey
2 tablespoons Dijon mustard
½ teaspoon instant minced onion
⅛ teaspoon garlic powder
¼ teaspoon ginger

Turn steak over in the pan so that both sides are coated with marinade. Sprinkle with meat tenderizer and pierce with a sharp fork several times at intervals. Cover with foil or plastic wrap and marinate overnight in refrigerator, turning occasionally. Remove from refrigerator 30 minutes before grilling. Grill over medium-high heat for about 6 minutes on each side, for medium-rare. When done, place meat on a large cutting board and carve across grain into thin strips.

MAKES 4 SERVINGS.

ROAST BEEF HASH

▪▪▪

3 tablespoons vegetable oil
1 medium onion, chopped
3 cups chopped cooked lean beef
3 cups frozen diced hash-brown potatoes, thawed
½ teaspoon minced garlic
1 teaspoon Worcestershire sauce
½ teaspoon salt
¼ teaspoon pepper
2 teaspoons parsley flakes
ketchup or chili sauce

Heat oil in a large skillet and add onion. Cook and stir over medium heat until onion is soft. Add beef, potatoes, garlic, Worcestershire sauce, salt, pepper, and parsley flakes. Stir and press mixture gently and evenly around skillet. Brown on one side for about 5–7 minutes and turn. Brown on other side for about 5–7 more minutes. Serve with ketchup or chili sauce.

MAKES 4 SERVINGS.

STIR-FRIED BEEF AND BROCCOLI

■■■

1½ pounds flank steak
⅔ cup Italian dressing
1 (1-ounce) package Kikkoman
   Stir-Fry Seasoning Mix
2 tablespoons water
3 tablespoons oil (peanut is best)
3 cups broccoli florets
1 (8-ounce) can sliced water
   chestnuts, drained
1 onion, sliced and separated
4 ounces fresh mushrooms, sliced
4 cups cooked rice

Slice steak across grain into thin strips (easier if steak has been placed in freezer for 30–45 minutes first). Put in a non-reactive dish, toss with dressing, and let stand at room temperature for 30 minutes. Combine seasoning mix with water and set aside. Heat oil in a large skillet or wok over medium-high heat. Drain meat, add to skillet, and stir-fry for 1–2 minutes, or until meat is seared. Remove meat from skillet and add broccoli, water chestnuts, and onion to the pan. Stir-fry for 2 minutes, or until vegetables are crisp-tender. Add mushrooms and cook for another minute. Return meat to skillet and add seasoning mix sauce. Cook and stir until sauce is thickened and vegetables are glazed. Serve over cooked rice.
MAKES 4–6 SERVINGS.

Note: The supermarket salad bar is a good place to buy vegetables for stir-fry. You can buy exactly the quantities you need, with no waste.

BEEF STROGANOFF

■■■

This is perfect for a buffet dinner. Serve with a big bowl of rice, a tossed green salad, and a basket of hard rolls. It can be prepared ahead of time, up to the point just before adding the seasoned sour cream. Then it can be frozen in a heavy plastic zip bag. The day before serving, transfer it from the freezer to the refrigerator to thaw. About an hour before serving, take it out of the refrigerator. If it's still quite cold, heat it in the microwave for several minutes until you can stir it easily. Then transfer it to a large saucepan and warm it over low heat on the stove. While the meat is warming, blend the flour, salt, caraway seeds, and nutmeg with the sour cream. Stir into the meat and continue heating until it's piping hot, stirring occasionally.

1½ pounds tender, lean beef
   (see Note)
3 tablespoons oil
3 tablespoons butter
1 medium onion, chopped
12 ounces fresh mushrooms, sliced
1 (10½-ounce) can beef broth
¼ cup flour
1 teaspoon salt
½ teaspoon caraway seeds
⅛ teaspoon nutmeg
2 (8-ounce) cartons sour cream
cooked rice or noodles

Cut meat into thin strips, about 2"–3" long, and set aside. Heat oil and butter

(continued)

N·O·T·E·S

in a large skillet or Dutch oven over medium heat. Add onion and mushrooms, and cook until soft. Add meat and cook for about 10 more minutes, or until meat loses its red color. Stir in beef broth, turn down heat, and simmer for 30 more minutes. Make seasoned sour cream by whisking together flour, salt, caraway seeds, nutmeg, and sour cream. Add this mixture to the skillet and cook over low heat until sauce thickens. Do not allow it to boil. Serve over cooked rice or noodles.

MAKES 6–8 SERVINGS.

Note: If using a cut of beef that's not too tender, marinate it overnight first, using a mild-flavored marinade or Italian dressing. Or, if desired, leftover cooked meat (such as flank steak) can be used. To avoid overcooking it (and thereby causing it to be tough), add it after stirring in the beef broth. Proceed with the recipe from there.

GROUND BEEF

■■■

Texas-Style Chili

■■■

2 pounds coarsely-ground chuck
1 (8-ounce) can tomato sauce
2¼ cups water, divided use
1½ teaspoons salt
⅛ teaspoon garlic powder
½ cup chili powder
1½ tablespoons instant onion flakes
2½ teaspoons cumin
1 teaspoon oregano
1 teaspoon paprika
1½ teaspoons cayenne (use less if you're timid!)
1½ tablespoons masa harina (Mexican corn flour) (if not available, substitute plain cornmeal)
1 (15-ounce) can red kidney beans, drained
1 (15-ounce) can diced tomatoes, undrained

Brown meat in a Dutch oven. Drain grease. Add tomato sauce and 2 cups of the water and stir. Stir in salt, garlic powder, chili powder, onion flakes, cumin, oregano, paprika, and cayenne. Cover and simmer for 30 minutes, stirring occasionally. Mix masa harina or cornmeal with remaining ¼ cup water to make a paste. Add to the chili, and stir in drained kidney beans and undrained tomatoes. Cook for another 15 minutes.

MAKES 6 SERVINGS.

BEEF ENCHILADAS
■ ■ ■

I grew up in Texas, and I cut my teeth on rolled-up tortillas. My mother often served enchiladas at informal dinner parties. I remember riding with her to Luna's Tortilla Factory, where she bought tortillas to make these. She served them with a salad loaded with sliced avocados. When her head was turned, I'd dip into the salad bowl to snatch as many avocados as I could.

OVEN: 350°

2 cups chili, without beans (use
    canned chili or see page 110)
3/4 cup water
vegetable oil
8 corn tortillas
1 cup (4 ounces) shredded
    Cheddar cheese
1 1/2 cups chopped onions
1 (8-ounce) carton sour cream
1 cup (4 ounces) shredded
    Monterey Jack cheese

In a medium saucepan, dilute chili with 3/4 cup water. Simmer for 20 minutes. Heat 1/2" oil in a small skillet, and dip tortillas one by one into the oil for about 5–10 seconds on each side, or just until they soften. Drain on paper towels. Stir Cheddar cheese into chili. Add onions. Spoon 1/4–1/3 cup chili mixture into the middle of each tortilla and roll up. Lay enchiladas seam-side-down, next to each other, in a greased rectangular baking dish. Pour remaining chili over enchiladas. Cover with foil and bake for 30 minutes. Uncover and spread sour cream and Monterey Jack cheese evenly on top. Bake uncovered for 5–10 more minutes, or until cheese melts.

MAKES 4 SERVINGS.

GROUND BEEF AND NOODLES
■ ■ ■

OVEN: 350°

8 ounces uncooked noodles
2 tablespoons butter
1 1/2 pounds ground chuck
1/4 cup chopped onion
1 (15-ounce) can tomato sauce
1 teaspoon salt
1/4 teaspoon garlic salt
1/8 teaspoon pepper
1 (8-ounce) package cream cheese,
    softened
1 (8-ounce) carton cottage cheese
1/2 cup sour cream
1 cup (4 ounces) shredded
    Cheddar cheese

Cook noodles according to package directions. Drain them and return them to the pan, and toss with butter. Set aside. Brown ground chuck in a skillet, crumbling it as it cooks. Drain fat and add onion, tomato sauce, salt, garlic salt, and pepper. Simmer for 5 minutes. Mix cream cheese, cottage cheese, and sour cream with noodles. Spoon half of noodle and cheese mixture into a greased 2-quart baking dish. Add half of meat mixture. Repeat layers and top with shredded cheese. Bake for about 30 minutes, or until bubbly.

MAKES 6–8 SERVINGS.

GROUND BEEF AND MACARONI
■■■

When I met my husband, Jack, he was a hungry bachelor with a freezer full of Stouffer's Macaroni and Beef with Tomatoes. I knew that I'd be wise to learn how to make this hearty skillet dish.

1 tablespoon butter
1 (4¹/₂-ounce) can sliced mushrooms, drained
¹/₂ medium onion, chopped
¹/₈ teaspoon garlic powder
1 pound ground chuck
1 (10¹/₂-ounce) can beef broth
¹/₂ teaspoon salt
¹/₄ teaspoon pepper
6 ounces uncooked macaroni
1 (8-ounce) can tomato sauce
¹/₄ cup taco sauce
1 (14¹/₂-ounce) can diced tomatoes, undrained

Melt butter in a large skillet. Stir in drained mushrooms, onion, and garlic powder, and cook until onion is soft. Add ground chuck and brown. Stir in beef broth, salt, and pepper. Stir in macaroni, tomato sauce, taco sauce, and undrained tomatoes. Cover and cook over low heat for 15–20 minutes, or until macaroni is tender.

MAKES 4 SERVINGS.

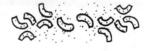

GROUND BEEF STROGANOFF
■■■

If you're in the mood for Beef Stroganoff (page 109), but you only have a pound of ground beef to work with, this is a close second. I remember being amazed the first time I made it and discovered that the noodles didn't have to be cooked first.

1 pound ground chuck
2 tablespoons butter
1 (6-ounce) jar sliced mushrooms, drained
1 tablespoon instant minced onion
¹/₈ teaspoon garlic powder
3 tablespoons lemon juice
3 tablespoons sherry
1 (10¹/₂-ounce) can beef broth
¹/₂ cup water
¹/₂ teaspoon salt
¹/₄ teaspoon pepper
8 ounces medium noodles, uncooked
1 (8-ounce) carton sour cream
chopped parsley

Brown ground chuck in a large skillet. Spoon off grease. Stir in butter, mushrooms, onion, and garlic powder, and cook until butter is melted. Mix in lemon juice, sherry, beef broth, water, salt, and pepper. Simmer for 5–10 minutes uncovered. Stir in uncooked noodles and cover. Simmer for about 15 more minutes, or until noodles are tender. Add a little more water if it seems too dry. Stir in sour cream and heat slowly, but do not boil. Sprinkle with chopped parsley and serve.

MAKES 4 SERVINGS.

MEATLOAF OR MEATBALLS
■■■

OVEN: 350°

½ teaspoon salt
¼ teaspoon pepper
1 teaspoon prepared mustard
½ teaspoon Worcestershire sauce
3 dashes Tabasco sauce
1 egg, slightly beaten
1 (8-ounce) can tomato sauce
¼ cup chopped onion
1¼ pounds ground chuck
1½ cups herb-seasoned stuffing mix

Mix salt, pepper, mustard, Worcestershire sauce, Tabasco sauce, egg, and tomato sauce. Stir in onion. Work in ground chuck, mixing well. Finally, work in stuffing mix. Do not overmix, or it will have a dense texture.

To Prepare Meatloaf: Press the mixture into a lightly greased 9″ x 5″ x 3″ loaf pan. Or turn it out onto a sheet of waxed paper, shape it into a loaf, and transfer it to a lightly greased shallow baking pan. Bake either one for about 1–1¼ hours, or until meatloaf reaches an internal temperature of 170°.

MAKES 4–6 SERVINGS.

Note: Individual loaves can be cooked in lightly greased muffin tins or custard cups for about 45 minutes.

To Prepare Meatballs: Shape mixture into meatballs about the size of golf balls (or smaller, for cocktail meatballs), and cook over medium heat in a skillet that has been sprayed with non-stick spray. Turn the meatballs as they cook, so that all sides are nicely browned. Cooked meatballs can be frozen on a cookie sheet, and transferred to a plastic zip bag once they're frozen.

MAKES ABOUT 2 DOZEN LARGE MEATBALLS.

TACOS
■■■

This is our customary Friday night dinner when we're at home. It's wonderfully predictable!

OVEN: 350°

1¼ pounds ground chuck
1 (1¼-ounce) package taco seasoning
¾ cup water
¼ cup bottled taco sauce, plus additional for serving
8 taco shells
1½ cups (6 ounces) shredded Cheddar cheese
2 cups chopped lettuce
4 Roma tomatoes, chopped
1 (2¼-ounce) can sliced ripe olives
1 avocado, diced
sour cream

In a large skillet, brown ground chuck and drain grease. Add taco seasoning, water, and ¼ cup taco sauce. Simmer meat sauce uncovered for 10 minutes. Meanwhile, heat taco shells in oven for 5 minutes. Serve meat sauce with bowls of shredded cheese,

(continued)

VEAL

CUTS OF VEAL

1. Shoulder: Though not as tough a portion as beef shoulder (chuck), nevertheless it's not very tender. Market forms: arm roast; arm steak; blade roast; blade steak; ground veal; shoulder arm roast; shoulder eye roast; stew meat.

2. Rib: A tender, flavorful portion. Market forms: crown roast; rib roast; rib chop; short ribs.

3. Loin: The most tender portion. Market forms: butterfly chop; cube steak; kidney chop; loin chop; loin roast; top loin chop; sirloin chop; sirloin roast.

4. Leg: A flavorful portion. Market forms: cutlets; rolled cutlets; round roast; round steak; rump roast; scallops; top round steak.

5. Shank: The most flavorful portion. Market forms: osso buco; shank; shank cross cuts.

6. Breast: A tough and rather fatty portion. Market forms: breast roast; riblets; stuffed breast; stuffed chops.

lettuce, tomatoes, sliced olives, diced avocado, sour cream, and additional taco sauce.

MAKES 8 TACOS.

Note: For **Taco Salad**, prepare meat sauce as directed. Combine lettuce, tomatoes, olives, and avocado in a salad bowl and toss. Spoon meat sauce on top, and sprinkle with cheese and corn chips. Serve with taco sauce.

VEAL
■ ■ ■

If marinating veal, allow 6–24 hours. Keep it moist and don't overcook it, since it can dry out quite easily.

VEAL AND MUSHROOMS
■ ■ ■

1½ pounds veal scallops
½ teaspoon onion salt
⅛ teaspoon pepper
4 tablespoons butter
½ pound fresh mushrooms, sliced
1 (10½-ounce) can beef broth
1 teaspoon minced chives
lemon slices

Pound veal scallops to ¼" thick. Sprinkle with onion salt and pepper. Heat butter in a large skillet over medium heat, and sauté veal quickly until barely browned on both sides. Do not overcook! Remove to a warm plate. Add mushrooms to skillet, and a little more butter, if necessary, and sauté quickly. Add beef broth and simmer for 3–5 minutes. Return veal to skil-

let and heat until the sauce bubbles again. Add chives and garnish with lemon slices.

MAKES 4–6 SERVINGS.

BREADED VEAL CUTLETS
■ ■ ■

OVEN: 350°

1 pound veal cutlets
1 cup plus 3 tablespoons flour, divided use
½ teaspoon salt
¼ teaspoon pepper
1 egg
1 tablespoon water
1 cup fine cracker crumbs
2 tablespoons butter
2 tablespoons oil
2 cups milk

Pound veal about ¼" thick. Set out 3 shallow bowls. In one, mix 1 cup of the flour with the salt and pepper. In the second, beat the egg with the water. Put the fine cracker crumbs into the third bowl. One at a time, dredge cutlets in seasoned flour, dip in beaten egg, and coat with cracker crumbs. Set them on a plate. Heat butter and oil over medium heat in a large skillet and brown veal quickly on both sides. Remove veal from skillet and spoon out all but 3 tablespoons of the drippings. Add remaining 3 tablespoons flour to skillet, stirring with a whisk, and slowly whisk in milk. Cook and stir gravy until it thickens. Pour gravy into a shallow baking dish large enough to hold all 4 of the cutlets, and arrange cutlets on top. Cover and bake for about 30 minutes.

MAKES 4 SERVINGS.

VEAL PARMESAN
■ ■ ■

2 eggs
2 tablespoons water
2 teaspoons lemon juice
3/4 cup flour
1/2 cup grated Parmesan cheese
1/2 teaspoon salt
1/2 teaspoon pepper
2 tablespoons chopped fresh basil
    or 2 teaspoons dried basil
1 tablespoon chopped fresh parsley
    or 1 teaspoon dried parsley
8 tablespoons butter, divided use
1/2 pound fresh mushrooms, sliced
12 ounces uncooked angel hair
    pasta
1 pound veal scallops, sliced thin
    and pounded less than 1/4" thick
    (pieces about 3"–4")
2 tablespoons olive oil
2 lemons, sliced very thin

Set out 2 small bowls. In 1 bowl, beat eggs with water and lemon juice. In the other bowl, mix flour, Parmesan cheese, salt, pepper, basil, and parsley. Melt 2 tablespoons of the butter in a small skillet and add sliced mushrooms. Cook and stir over medium heat for 3–5 minutes. Remove from heat, cover, and keep warm. Meanwhile, cook pasta al dente, according to package directions. Drain and toss with 4 tablespoons of the butter. Cover and keep warm. One by one, dip veal scallops into beaten eggs and then dredge in seasoned flour. Preheat a large skillet over medium heat and add remaining 2 tablespoons butter and olive oil. Stir until butter is melted. Sauté veal for about 2 minutes on each side, or just until delicately browned. Serve over angel hair pasta. Spoon sautéed mushrooms on top and garnish with lemon slices.

MAKES 4 SERVINGS.

VEAL PICCATA
■ ■ ■

1 pound veal scallops (medallions),
    sliced thin and pounded less
    than 1/4" thick (pieces about
    3"–4")
1/4 cup flour
salt and pepper
2 tablespoons butter
2 tablespoons olive oil
2 tablespoons lemon juice
1/4 cup white wine
fresh parsley
2 lemons, sliced very thin

Lightly flour veal on both sides and season with salt and pepper. In a large heavy skillet, heat butter and olive oil over medium heat until it bubbles. Add veal and sauté for 2 minutes on each side. When veal is nearly cooked, sprinkle with lemon juice. Remove from pan and keep warm. Add wine to pan and deglaze over high heat, stirring constantly. Reduce liquid to about 3 tablespoons. Pour over veal and garnish with parsley and lemon slices.

MAKES 4 SERVINGS.

N·O·T·E·S

PORK

CUTS OF PORK

1. Shoulder Butt (Blade Shoulder): Flavorful but fatty. Market forms: blade roast; blade steak; Boston butt roast; cube steak; shoulder roll.

2. Arm (Picnic) Shoulder: Flavorful. Market forms: arm roast; ground pork; ham hocks; link sausage; picnic ham; roll (bulk) sausage.

3. Loin: Very tender. Market forms: back ribs; blade chop; blade roast; butterfly chop; Canadian bacon; center-cut chop; center loin roast; center rib roast; country-style ribs; crown roast; cube steak; loin chop; loin roast; rib chop; sirloin chop; tenderloin.

4. Leg (Ham): Very lean and flavorful, but not too tender. Market forms: ham. On a ham, the butt section (sometimes called the rump) is meatier, and the shank section has more bone. However, the shank section is easier to carve.

5. Side: Flavorful but very fatty. Market forms: bacon; salt pork; spareribs.

PORK
■ ■ ■

If marinating pork, allow 12–24 hours. Sometimes pork is overcooked because of fear of **trichinosis**. Trichinae, which cause trichinosis, are killed at 137°, and to allow a margin for safety, it is recommended that pork be cooked to an internal temperature of at least 150°. It is not necessary to cook pork to a higher temperature for safety reasons, although some people prefer it for reasons of taste.

STIR-FRIED PORK TERIYAKI
■ ■ ■

1 1/2 pounds pork tenderloin
1/3 cup teriyaki sauce
1/3 cup pineapple juice
1 tablespoon honey
1 tablespoon oil
1/8 teaspoon garlic powder

Cut meat into bite-size pieces. Mix remaining ingredients and pour over meat in a non-reactive bowl. Cover and let stand at room temperature for about 30 minutes. Spray a skillet with non-stick spray, and heat over medium temperature. Transfer meat and a little of the marinade to skillet. Cook for about 5 minutes, stirring to brown meat on all sides. Reduce heat and simmer for about 10–15 more minutes, adding a little more marinade from time to time to keep meat from drying out. Serve over rice.
MAKES 4–6 SERVINGS.

MARINATED PORK LOIN
■ ■ ■

OVEN: 325°

3 pounds boneless rolled center-cut pork loin roast
1/2 cup lemon juice
1/2 cup frozen orange juice concentrate, thawed
1/4 cup vegetable oil
1 teaspoon dried rosemary, crushed
1/4 teaspoon nutmeg
1/4 teaspoon ground cloves
1/2 teaspoon salt
1/2 teaspoon pepper

Rinse roast, pat dry with paper towels, and place in a plastic zip bag. Mix remaining ingredients and pour over roast. Seal bag and place in a pan close to the size of the roast. Refrigerate overnight, turning several times to distribute marinade over meat. Remove from refrigerator and allow to stand for 30 minutes before cooking. Place in a roasting pan with marinade and roast uncovered for about 1 1/4 hours, basting with pan juices. Check internal temperature. Continue cooking until meat thermometer registers 155°. Place on a warm platter and allow to stand for 15–20 minutes before carving.
MAKES 6 SERVINGS.

"Never eat anything that you can't lift."

—Miss Piggy

ROAST PORK TENDERLOIN
...

OVEN: 425°

1½ pounds pork tenderloin
(often sold in vacuum-sealed
packages weighing about
1½ pounds, with 2 tenderloins
in each package)
½ cup teriyaki-style marinade
½ cup wine (any kind)
2 tablespoons Dijon mustard

Rinse tenderloins, pat dry with paper towels, and place in a non-reactive pan. Mix teriyaki-style marinade with wine and pour over the tenderloins. Spread top of the tenderloins liberally with Dijon mustard, using a little more if desired. Cover meat and let stand at room temperature for 30 minutes. Spray a roasting pan with non-stick spray or line it with foil and lay tenderloins in pan, discarding the marinade. Roast for about 20–30 minutes, and then check the internal temperature. Turn tenderloins over and continue cooking until meat thermometer registers 160°. Cooking time will vary slightly, depending on the size and shape of the tenderloins. Lay a piece of foil over meat and allow to stand for about 15 minutes after removing from oven, before slicing.
MAKES 4 SERVINGS.

Note: Pork tenderloin is easy to cook on the grill if desired. Allow about 25 minutes, and cook to an internal temperature of 160°.

STUFFED PORK TENDERLOIN
...

This makes an elegant and fairly simple dish for company. The tenderloins can be stuffed early that morning or the night before. Serve with wild rice, a green salad, Baked Apricots (page 240), and crusty bread.

OVEN: 350°

4 pork tenderloins, weighing a
total of about 3 pounds (often
sold in vacuum-sealed packages
weighing about 1½ pounds, with
2 tenderloins in each package)
seasoned salt and pepper
1 (8-ounce) package herb-seasoned
stuffing mix
4 tablespoons butter, melted
1½ cups apple juice, divided use
¾ cup chicken broth
1 Granny Smith apple, unpeeled,
cored, and chopped
½ cup pecan pieces
6–8 strips bacon

Rinse meat and pat dry with paper towels. Cut each tenderloin lengthwise almost all the way through. Spread each one open like a book and press down on the pieces to flatten them. Sprinkle all of them generously with seasoned salt and pepper, and set aside. In a medium bowl, toss stuffing mix with melted butter, ½ cup of the apple juice, chicken broth, chopped apple, and pecan pieces. Lay two of the flattened tenderloins in a

(continued)

PORK ROASTING GUIDELINES

Smaller roasts take more time per pound, and larger ones take less time per pound. Check doneness with a meat thermometer.

Boston Butt (boneless): For well done, cook a 3–4-pound roast at 325° for 40–45 minutes per pound. Remove from oven when internal temperature is 165°.

Ham (canned, boneless, fully cooked): Reheat at 325°. Heat a 3-pound ham 21–23 minutes per pound. Remove from oven when internal temperature is 135°.

Ham (cured, bone-in, half): For medium, cook a 6–7-pound ham at 325° for 22–24 minutes per pound. Remove from oven when internal temperature is 155°.

Ham (cured, bone-in, whole): For medium, cook a 12–14-pound ham at 325° for 18–20 minutes per pound. Remove from oven when internal temperature is 155°.

Ham (cured, boneless, whole): For medium, cook a 7–10-pound ham at 325° for 18–20 minutes per pound. Remove from oven when internal temperature is 155°.

Loin Roast (bone-in): For medium, cook a 3–5-pound roast at 325° for 20–25 minutes per pound. Remove from oven when internal temperature is 155°.

Loin Roast (boneless): For medium, cook a 2–4-pound roast at 325° for 20–25 minutes per pound. Remove from oven when internal temperature is 155°.

Ribs: Cook at 325° for about 1½–2 hours, or until tender.

Tenderloin (boneless): Cook at 425°. For medium, cook a ½–1½-pound tenderloin for 20–30 minutes, total. Remove from oven when internal temperature is 155°.

greased roasting pan, cut sides up, and spread the stuffing mixture over the meat, dividing it equally between the two pieces. Spread stuffing as thickly as possible and press it down. (Any stuffing left over can be baked separately in a small uncovered baking dish.) Lay the other flattened tenderloins on top of the ones in the pan, cut sides down, as though you were making a sandwich. (Although the tenderloins can be tied to secure them, this is not necessary. If this is desired, however, it will be easier to accomplish if the tenderloins are filled with the stuffing and tied before placing them in the pan.) Pour the remaining apple juice over the meat. Cover each piece with strips of bacon, running from side to side across the meat, and tuck the ends of the bacon under the meat. (This will keep the meat from drying out as it cooks.) Roast uncovered for 45 minutes, and check internal temperature. Continue cooking until meat thermometer registers 160°, perhaps for another 15 minutes. Remove meat from oven and allow to stand for about 10 minutes before carving. Bacon slices can be removed before serving.

MAKES 8–10 SERVINGS.

BARBECUED PORK SHOULDER
■■■

OVEN: 400°/300°

*3–4 pounds boneless rolled Boston
   butt shoulder roast*
Dijon mustard
barbecue sauce

Cover the roast liberally with Dijon mustard. Place on a rack in a roasting pan, cover, and cook at 400° for 30 minutes. Then lower the heat to 300° and continue cooking for 4–5 hours. Remove from oven and let stand for 15 minutes. Remove the meat from the pan to a large cutting board. Pull it apart, cutting where necessary. Arrange meat on a serving platter, drizzle barbecue sauce over meat, and serve.

MAKES 6 SERVINGS.

BREADED PORK CHOPS
■■■

OVEN: 375°

1 cup flour
½ teaspoon salt
¼ teaspoon pepper
1 egg
2 tablespoons water
1 cup fine cracker crumbs
4–6 medium pork chops
3 tablespoons oil

Set out 3 bowls about the size of one of the pork chops. In one of the bowls, mix the flour with the salt and pepper. In the second bowl, beat the egg with the water. Put the fine cracker crumbs into the third bowl. One at a time, dredge the pork chops in the seasoned flour, dip in the beaten egg, and coat with the cracker crumbs. Set them on a plate. Pour oil into a shallow baking dish and turn dish from side to side to spread oil so that it covers the bottom of the dish. Add chops, being sure they don't touch each other. Bake uncovered for 20 minutes and turn. Continue cooking for 20–30 more minutes, depending on the thickness of the chops. When internal temperature reaches 160°, chops will be done.

MAKES 4 SERVINGS.

GLAZED PORK CHOPS
■■■

4 thick loin pork chops
1/2 cup flour
salt and pepper
1 tablespoon butter
2 tablespoons oil
3/4 cup white wine
1/4 cup crabapple jelly, apricot
    preserves, or orange marmalade

Dredge chops in flour. Season with salt and pepper. Heat butter and oil in a large skillet and brown chops slowly on both sides. In a small saucepan, mix wine with jelly, preserves, or marmalade, heating and stirring to mix. Pour sauce over chops and cover skillet. Reduce heat to low and cook for 20–30 minutes, or until chops are tender. Remove cover and turn up heat slightly. Cook for about 10 more minutes, spooning glaze over chops as it bubbles, to coat them.

MAKES 4 SERVINGS.

BARBECUED RIBS
■■■

GRILL: LOW HEAT

3 cups ketchup
1/2 cup brown sugar
1/2 cup molasses
1/4 cup prepared mustard
2 tablespoons vinegar
2 tablespoons Liquid Smoke
2 tablespoons Worcestershire sauce
1/8 teaspoon cayenne
4 pounds pork back ribs
1/2 teaspoon garlic salt
1/4 teaspoon pepper

In a mixing bowl, combine ketchup, brown sugar, molasses, mustard, vinegar, Liquid Smoke, Worcestershire sauce, and cayenne. Pour half into a serving bowl, to be served at the table with the ribs. Set the rest aside. Cut ribs into serving-size pieces and place in a Dutch oven. Cover with water and add garlic salt and pepper. Bring to a boil. Cover, reduce heat, and simmer for 30 minutes. Drain well. Place ribs on grill, 5 inches from heat, over slow coals. Cook for 45 minutes, or until done, turning frequently. Baste ribs generously with the sauce in the mixing bowl during last 15 minutes. Serve remaining sauce on the side.

MAKES 4 SERVINGS.

N·O·T·E·S

BAKED HAM
■ ■ ■

OVEN: 325°

1 (6–8-pound) ham half, bone in (butt end)
whole cloves
1½ cups orange juice
¼ cup brown sugar
1 tablespoon honey
½ teaspoon cinnamon
¼ teaspoon nutmeg
1 teaspoon dry mustard

Score top of ham in a diamond pattern, sticking cloves at points of diamonds. Combine the remaining ingredients and pour over ham. Lay a "tent" of foil over the ham and bake for about 2½ hours, or until ham reaches an internal temperature of 165°. Baste with pan juices from time to time. Allow ham to stand on a heated platter for 15–20 minutes before carving.

MAKES 8–12 SERVINGS.

GRILLED KIELBASA
SAUSAGE
■ ■ ■

GRILL: LOW HEAT

1 pound smoked Kielbasa sausage
hot mustard

Prick the sausage a few times and cut into several pieces about 4"–6" long. Heat for about 5 minutes over low coals on the grill, or in a covered skillet to which a little water has been added. Serve with hot mustard.

MAKES 3–4 SERVINGS.

CREAMED HAM
AND ASPARAGUS
■ ■ ■

1 (10-ounce) package frozen cut asparagus
6 tablespoons butter
6 tablespoons flour
1 cup half and half
2 cups milk
salt and pepper
1 pound cooked ham, cubed
1 (4-ounce) can sliced mushrooms, drained

Cook asparagus until barely tender, drain, and set aside. In a medium saucepan, melt butter and add flour, stirring and cooking over low heat for 3–5 minutes, or until it begins to turn golden. Slowly add half and half and milk, stirring as it thickens. Season to taste with salt and pepper. Fold in ham, asparagus, and mushrooms. Cook slowly until well heated. Serve over cooked noodles, rice, or pasta.

MAKES 4–6 SERVINGS.

Note: This is attractive served in a Noodle Ring (page 168). A nice garnish would include quartered tomatoes, ripe olives, and sprigs of parsley.

HAM AND CORN CASSEROLE

∎ ∎ ∎

The first time I made this, I threw it together for friends who had dropped by for a late-afternoon visit. When dinnertime rolled around, we were having so much fun that we wouldn't let them go home. Since I had to dream up something to feed them, I concocted this. Thankfully, I had a some cooked ham in the refrigerator.

OVEN: 350°

1²/₃ cups water
4 tablespoons butter
1 (5-ounce) package yellow rice mix
1 pound boneless cooked ham, diced
1 (8-ounce) carton sour cream
1 (4-ounce) jar diced pimientos, drained, or ½ roasted red pepper, diced
1 (10-ounce) package frozen white corn, thawed
1 cup (4 ounces) shredded sharp Cheddar cheese, divided use

In a medium saucepan, bring water and butter to boil and stir in rice. Cover, reduce heat, and simmer for 20 minutes. When rice is done, transfer to large mixing bowl and stir in diced ham, sour cream, pimientos, corn, and ¾ cup of the cheese. Spoon into a greased 2-quart baking dish and sprinkle remaining cheese on top. Bake uncovered for about 30 minutes, or until bubbly.

MAKES 4–6 SERVINGS.

HAM AND MACARONI

∎ ∎ ∎

OVEN: 375°

12 ounces macaroni, cooked
8 tablespoons butter, divided use
4 tablespoons flour
1 cup milk
salt and pepper
1 pound boneless cooked ham, cubed
2 cups (8 ounces) shredded Cheddar cheese, divided use
½ cup crushed herb-seasoned stuffing mix

Place cooked macaroni in a large mixing bowl. Toss with 2 tablespoons of the butter and set aside. Melt 4 tablespoons of the butter in a small saucepan. Stir in flour. Cook and stir with a whisk for 3–5 minutes. Add milk gradually, stirring until sauce is thickened. Season to taste with salt and pepper. Stir sauce into macaroni and add ham and 1½ cups of the cheese. Spoon into a greased 2-quart baking dish. Melt remaining 2 tablespoons butter and toss with crushed stuffing mix and remaining ½ cup cheese. Sprinkle on top and bake for 30 minutes.

MAKES 6 SERVINGS.

Note: I buy packages of ham chunks from a shop nearby that specializes in spiral-cut hams. Besides the whole hams and chunks, they also sell slices and bones. I keep some of each in the freezer. Having the ham chunks ready makes this dish a cinch to prepare.

N·O·T·E·S

LAMB

CUTS OF LAMB

1. Shoulder: This is not a very tender portion. Market forms: shoulder roast; blade chop; arm chop; neck slice.

2. Rib: A tender, juicy portion. Market forms: rib chop; rack of lamb; rib roast; crown roast.

3. Loin: A very tender portion. Market forms: loin chop; loin roast; double loin chop; saddle of lamb.

4. Leg: A flavorful portion. Market forms: leg of lamb; sirloin chop; sirloin roast; hind shank.

5. Foreshank: A flavorful, although not very tender, and fairly fatty portion. Market forms: shank.

6. Breast: A flavorful, but very bony portion. Market forms: boneless rolled breast; spareribs; riblets.

SCALLOPED HAM AND POTATOES

■■■

OVEN: 375°

1 (10¾-ounce) can cream of
   celery soup
½ cup milk
1 teaspoon salt
¼ teaspoon pepper
1 tablespoon Dijon mustard
3 cups thinly sliced peeled potatoes
1½ cups cooked ham, diced
½ cup thinly sliced onion
½ cup (2 ounces) shredded
   Cheddar cheese
paprika

In a small mixing bowl, combine soup, milk, salt, pepper, and mustard. Set aside. Place a layer of potatoes in a greased 2-quart baking dish. Add a layer of ham, then a layer of onion, and repeat layers until all the potatoes, ham, and onion have been used. Pour soup mixture over all and cover. Bake for 1 hour. Uncover and top with cheese. Sprinkle with paprika and continue cooking uncovered for 15–20 more minutes, or until the cheese is melted and bubbly.

MAKES 4 SERVINGS.

HAM AND WILD RICE CASSEROLE

■■■

OVEN: 350°

1 (6-ounce) package long-grain
   and wild rice mix
1 (10-ounce) package frozen
   chopped broccoli
3 cups cubed cooked ham
1 (4-ounce) can sliced mushrooms,
   drained
1 (8-ounce) can sliced water
   chestnuts, drained
1 cup (4 ounces) shredded
   Cheddar cheese
1 (10¾-ounce) can cream of
   mushroom soup
1 cup mayonnaise
2 teaspoons prepared mustard
1 teaspoon curry powder
¼ cup grated Parmesan cheese
12 crushed Ritz crackers
2 tablespoons butter, melted

Prepare packages of wild rice mix and broccoli according to package directions. Butter a 13" x 9" x 2" baking dish and spoon in rice, spreading evenly in baking dish. Top with broccoli. In a mixing bowl, toss ham with mushrooms, water chestnuts, and shredded cheese. Stir in cream of mushroom soup, mayonnaise, mustard, and curry powder. Spread ham mixture evenly over broccoli. Toss Parmesan cheese with crushed Ritz crackers and melted butter. Sprinkle over ham and bake for 50–60 minutes, or until bubbly.

MAKES 8 SERVINGS.

LAMB

■ ■ ■

MARINATED LEG OF LAMB

■ ■ ■

The first time I prepared this was just after Jack and I were married. My parents came for a visit, and I wanted to impress them. I decided this would do the job. The leftovers are wonderful to use in Shepherd's Pie (see next recipe).

OVEN: 325°

*1 (6-pound) leg of lamb, boned,
    rolled, and tied (by butcher)
4 cloves garlic, cut into slivers
1/2 cup red wine
1 1/2 cups olive oil
1 tablespoon chopped fresh
    rosemary, or 1 teaspoon dried
    rosemary
1/2 teaspoon salt*

With a sharp knife, pierce lamb all over and insert garlic. Place in a large, zip-top plastic bag. Mix remaining ingredients and pour over lamb. Close bag and set it in a pan. Refrigerate for 1–2 days, turning lamb several times. To cook, remove lamb from marinade, reserving marinade, and place on a greased rack in a roasting pan. Pour marinade over lamb and place in oven. Roast for about 2 hours, or until meat thermometer reads 140° for rare, 160° for medium, or 170° for well done. Baste with pan juices several times during cooking. Allow lamb to stand for 15 minutes before carving. Serve with mint jelly, hot pepper jelly, or Dijon mustard.

MAKES 6–8 SERVINGS.

SHEPHERD'S PIE

■ ■ ■

I never think of this dish that I don't remember the neighbors who lived next door to us the first few years that Jack and I were married. On a hot Saturday night early in August, they invited us over for a supper of Shepherd's Pie. I was eight months pregnant and quite relieved that I had escaped from having to cook dinner. We got home about eleven-thirty, and as soon as Jack and I crawled into bed I noticed that I was feeling a little funny. Pretty soon I realized what was happening. I woke Jack up and told him to get the stopwatch. You guessed it. Adam arrived the next day just one minute before noon. We've always attributed his early arrival to the Shepherd's Pie!

OVEN: 350°

*4 tablespoons butter, divided use
1 pound ground lamb or cooked
    lamb, cut into bite-size pieces
1 1/2 teaspoons minced garlic
1/2 teaspoon salt
1 teaspoon dried rosemary
1 tablespoon Worcestershire sauce
1/4 cup finely chopped onion
1/2 cup chopped or diced carrot
1 tablespoon flour
3/4 cup beef broth
2 tablespoons wine (any kind)
2 1/2 cups leftover mashed potatoes
    or prepared instant potatoes*

Melt 2 tablespoons of the butter in a large skillet over medium heat. Add lamb, breaking into chunks if necessary. Stir in garlic and cook until lamb

N·O·T·E·S

is well browned, for 6–8 minutes for uncooked lamb, or for less time if using cooked lamb. Sprinkle with salt and rosemary, and stir in Worcestershire sauce. Remove meat from skillet with a slotted spoon and set aside. Drain grease and add remaining 2 tablespoons butter. When it melts, add onion and carrot and cook until carrot is soft, for about 5 more minutes. Sprinkle flour over vegetables and stir well. Stir in beef broth and wine. Cook and stir for about 5 more minutes, until gravy is slightly thickened. Return lamb to the skillet and cook until heated, for about 5 more minutes. Spoon lamb mixture into a greased 2-quart baking dish and spread mashed potatoes evenly on top. Bake for 30–40 minutes, or until heated through. To brown the potatoes, place under broiler for 2–3 minutes.

MAKES 4 SERVINGS.

PAN-FRIED LAMB CHOPS
■ ■ ■

OVEN: 325°

2 tablespoons oil
8 loin lamb chops
salt and pepper
mint jelly

Heat oil in a skillet over medium heat and brown chops on both sides. Reduce heat and cook for about 10 more minutes, or until light pink in center. Season to taste with salt and pepper and serve with mint jelly.

MAKES 4 SERVINGS.

BROILED LAMB CHOPS
■ ■ ■

OVEN: BROIL

8 loin lamb chops, 1″ thick, about 2 pounds total
3 tablespoons Worcestershire sauce
3 tablespoons lemon juice
2 tablespoons oil
butter or Dill Lemon Butter (page 251) (optional)
mint jelly (optional)

Place lamb chops in a shallow non-reactive pan. Combine Worcestershire sauce and lemon juice, and pour over chops, turning to coat both sides of the chops with the marinade. Cover and allow to stand at room temperature for 30 minutes. Remove the chops from the marinade and brush both sides of the chops with oil. Place the chops on a greased rack in a roasting pan. Set the pan in a preheated oven, about 4″ from the broiling element. Broil for about 5 minutes, and turn the chops with tongs. Continue broiling for 3–5 more minutes. The chops will be rare when the internal temperature reaches 140°, medium at 160°, and well done at 170°. If desired, dot the chops with butter or Dill Lemon Butter before serving, or serve with mint jelly.

MAKES 4 SERVINGS.

Chicken and Poultry

CHICKEN AND POULTRY
...

CHICKEN
...

APRICOT CHICKEN
...

1 egg
2 tablespoons water
1/2 cup flour
salt and pepper
4 boneless chicken breast halves
2 tablespoons butter
2 tablespoons cooking oil
1/4 cup white wine
1/3 cup water
1/3 cup apricot preserves
1 teaspoon Chinese five-spice powder

In a shallow bowl, beat egg with 2 tablespoons water. Mix flour, salt, and pepper in another shallow bowl. Dip chicken in egg and coat with flour mixture. Melt butter and oil in a large skillet over medium heat and sauté chicken breasts, browning well on both sides. Reduce heat and cook until chicken is tender. Remove chicken from skillet and spoon off oil. Add white wine to skillet and stir to deglaze pan. Mix 1/3 cup water with apricot preserves and Chinese five-spice powder, and stir into skillet. Cook and stir until heated; then add chicken to skillet. Spoon apricot glaze over chicken and cook until chicken is heated through.
MAKES 4 SERVINGS.

BACON-WRAPPED CHICKEN
...

OVEN: 275°

1 (2 1/2-ounce) jar dried beef
6 slices bacon
6 boneless chicken breast halves
1 (8-ounce) carton sour cream
1 (10 3/4-ounce) can cream of chicken soup

Chop dried beef finely and spread evenly over the bottom of a greased 2-quart baking dish. Wrap a slice of bacon around each chicken breast and secure with toothpicks. Arrange chicken breasts on the beef. Mix sour cream with soup and pour over chicken. Cover and bake for 2–2 1/2 hours.
MAKES 6 SERVINGS.

SLOW COOKER CHICKEN
...

1 whole chicken (3 pounds)
seasoned salt
pepper
4 medium potatoes
4 carrots
1 medium onion

Remove package of giblets from chicken and discard. Rinse chicken and pat dry. Season chicken inside and out with seasoned salt and pepper. Spray slow cooker with non-stick spray and add chicken. Cover and cook on low heat for 4 hours. Peel potatoes, carrots, and onion and cut into quarters. Add to slow cooker and replace cover. Continue cooking for 2 more hours on high heat, or for 4 hours on low heat.

MAKES 4 SERVINGS.

BARBECUED CHICKEN
■ ■ ■

OVEN: 325°, OR
GRILL: MEDIUM-LOW (ABOUT 325°)

4 chicken breast halves
bottled barbecue sauce

Marinate chicken in barbecue sauce in a non-reactive dish in the refrigerator for several hours. Then drain.

To Cook in Oven: Line a baking dish with foil and arrange chicken breasts in dish. Cover with foil and bake for 1–1½ hours. Makes 4 servings.

To Grill: Place on a double thickness of heavy-duty foil, rolling up the edges to form a lip. Lay on preheated grill and close lid. Baste several times with more barbecue sauce. After 30–35 minutes, punch several holes in the foil with a sharp long-tined fork, so that the juices and sauce can drip down on the coals and smoke. Continue cooking for about 10–15 more minutes, or until chicken is done.

MAKES 4 SERVINGS.

DIJON CHICKEN BREASTS
■ ■ ■

OVEN: 350°

½ cup Dijon mustard
½ cup sour cream
4 chicken breast halves
1 cup crushed herb-seasoned
*   stuffing mix*

Mix mustard and sour cream. Dip chicken breasts into sour cream mixture and roll in stuffing mix. Place chicken in a greased baking dish and bake for 45–60 minutes.

MAKES 4 SERVINGS.

GRILLED CHICKEN
■ ■ ■

GRILL: LOW

2 chickens, quartered, or 8 chicken
*   breast halves*
seasoned pepper
½ cup butter
2 teaspoons Worcestershire sauce
2 dashes Tabasco sauce
2 tablespoons lemon juice
½ teaspoon garlic salt
1 (12-ounce) can lemon-lime soda

Sprinkle chickens with pepper and let stand at room temperature for 30 minutes. Melt butter, add remaining ingredients, and set aside. Grill chicken over a low fire for about an hour, turning and basting often with lemon-lime soda mixture. Baste again after removing from grill.

MAKES 8 SERVINGS.

N·O·T·E·S

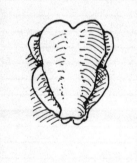
CHICKEN FAJITAS

■■■

GRILL: MEDIUM
OVEN: 350° (TO HEAT TORTILLAS)

*4 large boneless chicken breast
 halves*
1 cup picante sauce
1 cup Italian dressing
2 tablespoons lemon juice
2 tablespoons chopped green onions
1 teaspoon garlic powder
1 teaspoon pepper
1 teaspoon celery salt
8 (8½") flour tortillas
salsa
guacamole
chopped tomatoes
shredded Monterey Jack cheese
sour cream

Place chicken in a shallow dish. Combine picante sauce, Italian dressing, lemon juice, onions, garlic powder, pepper, and celery salt. Pour over chicken and cover. Refrigerate for several hours, turning several times. Allow chicken to stand at room temperature for 30 minutes before cooking. Drain marinade and grill chicken for about 5–8 minutes on each side, or until done. (Cooking time will vary, depending on size and thickness of chicken breasts.) While chicken is cooking, wrap tortillas in foil and heat in oven for about 10 minutes. Slice grilled chicken into strips and serve buffet-style with tortillas and bowls of salsa, guacamole, chopped tomatoes, shredded cheese, and sour cream.

MAKES 4 SERVINGS.

FRIED CHICKEN

■■■

If you've read *Fried Green Tomatoes* or watched the movie, you know that one of the secrets to a happy marriage is knowing how to fry chicken.

ELECTRIC SKILLET: 350°

*1 quart buttermilk (fresh or
 reconstituted from powder)*
1 cut-up chicken
2 cups flour
salt and pepper
2 teaspoons baking powder
1 teaspoon paprika
3 cups solid shortening
1 cup vegetable oil

Pour buttermilk over chicken and refrigerate for several hours. In a deep bowl, mix flour, salt, pepper, baking powder, and paprika. Drain chicken and place in bowl with flour mixture, one piece at a time. Work flour into each piece well. There's no effective way to do this without rolling up your sleeves and getting your hands a little messy! Let chicken stand at room temperature for 30 minutes and then coat with flour mixture again. If at all possible, use an electric skillet to cook the chicken, since this will enable you to keep the oil at a constant temperature. This is essential for crispy chicken. Heat shortening and oil to 350°. Add chicken, dark meat first, skin side down. Do not crowd the chicken in the pan. None of the pieces should touch each other. Don't add too many pieces at one time, either, as this lowers the temperature of the oil, and that's what causes the chicken to become greasy. Turn each piece after it is browned (about 10–15 minutes) and continue cooking until done. Drain on paper towels. Serve with hot biscuits and Cream Gravy (page 250) for a real Southern treat!

MAKES 4 SERVINGS.

FRIED CHICKEN FINGERS

■■■

ELECTRIC SKILLET: 350°

2 eggs, separated
1 (12-ounce) can beer
1 tablespoon butter, melted
1 teaspoon dry mustard
1/4 teaspoon salt
1/2 teaspoon pepper
1 1/2 cups flour, plus additional flour
    for dredging chicken
6 boneless chicken breast halves
1 pound solid shortening

Beat egg yolks with beer and butter. Add dry mustard, salt, and pepper. Mix in 1 1/2 cups flour, a little at a time. Beat egg whites until stiff and fold into batter. Cut each chicken breast into 4 strips. In electric skillet, heat shortening to 350°. Dredge chicken in flour and dip in batter. Add only a few pieces of chicken to skillet at a time, allowing oil to return to 350° before adding more. Fry until golden on all sides. Drain on paper towels.

MAKES 4–6 SERVINGS.

CHICKEN AND DUMPLINGS

■■■

6 cups water
1 carrot, cut up
1 rib celery, cut up
4 chicken breast halves
salt and pepper
parsley flakes
3 chicken bouillon cubes
4 tablespoons butter
1/4 cup flour
1 (10-ounce) can refrigerated
    biscuits

Place water, carrot, and celery in a medium saucepan and bring to a boil. Add chicken and cover. Reduce heat and simmer for 45 minutes. Remove chicken, cut it up, and set aside. Strain broth and season with salt, pepper, and parsley flakes to taste. Add bouillon cubes and simmer uncovered until broth is reduced to 4 cups. Melt butter in large saucepan and stir in flour. Cook over low heat for 5 minutes. Add broth and stir until smooth and thickened. Cut each biscuit into 4 pieces and drop into simmering gravy. Cook for 10 minutes and then add cut-up chicken.

MAKES 4 SERVINGS.

N·O·T·E·S

CHICKEN AND DRESSING

∎ ∎ ∎

OVEN: 350°

3 cups diced cooked chicken
1 (8-ounce) package herb-seasoned stuffing mix
1/2 cup butter, melted
1 cup chicken broth
2 (10 3/4-ounce) cans cream of chicken soup
1 (8-ounce) carton sour cream

Spread half of chicken in a greased 3-quart baking dish. Toss stuffing mix with butter and stir in broth, soup, and sour cream. Spread half of stuffing mixture over chicken. Add remaining chicken and top with remaining stuffing mixture. Bake for about 45 minutes, or until bubbly.

MAKES 8 SERVINGS.

CHICKEN WITH LIME BUTTER

∎ ∎ ∎

6 boneless chicken breast halves
1 cup flour
1/2 teaspoon salt
2 tablespoons oil
1 1/2 tablespoons lime juice (substitute lemon juice if desired)
6 tablespoons butter
1/2 teaspoon dried dill weed
1/2 teaspoon chopped chives

Dredge chicken in flour mixed with salt. In a large skillet, heat oil over medium heat and cook chicken for 5–8 minutes per side, or until tender and browned on both sides. Arrange on platter and keep warm. Spoon oil from skillet and add lime juice. Cook over low heat until lime juice bubbles. Add butter, cooking and stirring with wire whisk until butter becomes opaque and forms a creamy sauce. Stir in dill weed and chopped chives. Spoon sauce over chicken and serve.

MAKES 6 SERVINGS.

KING RANCH CHICKEN

∎ ∎ ∎

OVEN: 350°

1 (9-ounce) bag tortilla chips
1 onion, chopped
2 tablespoons butter
2 tablespoons picante sauce or salsa
2 (10 3/4-ounce) cans cream of chicken soup
1 (12-ounce) can evaporated milk
1 (4-ounce) can mild green chiles, drained
3 cups diced cooked chicken
2 cups (8 ounces) shredded Colby cheese

Crumble tortilla chips slightly and place half of them in a greased 3-quart baking dish. Sauté onion in butter and blend in picante sauce or salsa, soup, and evaporated milk. Stir in green chiles and chicken. Spoon half of mixture over tortilla chips. Sprinkle with remaining tortilla chips and add remaining chicken mixture. Top with cheese and bake for 30 minutes.

MAKES 6–8 SERVINGS.

CHICKEN ENCHILADAS
...

OVEN: 325°

6 cups water
4 large chicken breast halves
2 tablespoons butter
1 cup chopped onion
1 clove garlic, minced
1 (16-ounce) can diced tomatoes,
    undrained
1 (8-ounce) can tomato sauce
1 (4-ounce) can green chiles
1 teaspoon cumin
1/2 teaspoon oregano
1/2 teaspoon salt
3 cups (12 ounces) shredded
    Monterey Jack cheese, divided use
1 1/2 cups sour cream, divided use
oil for heating tortillas
12 (6"–8") corn tortillas

Bring water to a boil and add chicken. Reduce heat, cover, and simmer for about 45 minutes, or until done. While chicken is cooking, prepare enchilada sauce. Melt butter in a large skillet and add onion and garlic. Sauté for 3–5 minutes. Stir in undrained tomatoes and tomato sauce. Drain green chiles and add to sauce. Stir in cumin, oregano, and salt, and simmer for about 30 minutes. When chicken is done, drain it and remove skin. Pull meat from bones and chop or shred. Ladle all but 1/2 cup of the sauce into a large mixing bowl. Stir in chicken, 2 cups of the cheese, and 1 cup of the sour cream. Heat 1/2" oil in a small skillet. To make each enchilada, first dip a tortilla in the hot oil for a few seconds on each side to soften. Then dip tortilla into the sauce in the skillet. Place on a plate and spoon about 1/2 cup of the chicken mixture on each tortilla, roll up, and place seam-side-down in a greased 3-quart baking dish. Line the enchiladas up side by side so that they're touching each other. Pour the remaining sauce from the skillet over the enchiladas and bake for 20 minutes. Spread the remaining sour cream and cheese on top. Bake for 10 more minutes. If desired, serve with guacamole.

MAKES 4–6 SERVINGS.

MARYLAND CHICKEN
...

OVEN: 350°

4 chicken breast halves
1/2 cup flour
salt and pepper
2 eggs
2 tablespoons water
1 cup crushed herb-seasoned
    stuffing mix
butter
1/4 cup dry sherry (optional)
parsley flakes

Dredge chicken in flour seasoned with salt and pepper. Beat eggs with water. Then dip chicken in eggs, and roll in crushed stuffing mix. Place in a shallow baking dish and dot with butter. Drizzle sherry over the chicken, if desired, and sprinkle with parsley flakes. Bake for 45–55 minutes.

MAKES 4 SERVINGS.

N·O·T·E·S

CHICKEN MARSALA
■ ■ ■

OVEN: 325°

6 chicken breast halves
1 teaspoon seasoned salt
paprika
6 tablespoons butter, divided use
1 (10½-ounce) can beef broth
½ cup Marsala (or substitute dry sherry)
8 ounces fresh mushrooms, sliced
2 (14-ounce) cans artichoke hearts, drained and quartered

Sprinkle chicken with seasoned salt and paprika. Place in baking pan, skin-side-up. Melt 4 tablespoons of the butter and combine with beef broth. Pour over chicken and bake for 45 minutes, spooning pan juices over chicken several times. Add Marsala and continue cooking for 15–20 more minutes, basting once more. About 5 minutes before serving, sauté mushrooms in remaining 2 tablespoons butter. Transfer chicken breasts from roasting pan to heated platter and add pan drippings to skillet with mushrooms. Add artichoke hearts and heat thoroughly. Pour sauce over chicken and serve.

MAKES 6 SERVINGS.

> *"...laughter is the best seasoning there is."*
>
> —Barbara Kafka

CHICKEN WITH MUSHROOMS
■ ■ ■

6 tablespoons butter, divided use
1¼ pounds chicken tenders
8 ounces fresh mushrooms, sliced
2 ounces slivered almonds
2 tablespoons flour
1 (14½-ounce) can chicken broth
salt and pepper
8 ounces egg noodles, cooked

Melt 4 tablespoons of the butter in a large skillet. Sauté chicken in butter. Remove from skillet and keep warm. Add mushrooms to skillet and sauté for 3–5 minutes. Add almonds, cooking and stirring as almonds brown. Remove from heat. Melt remaining 2 tablespoons butter in a medium saucepan. Add flour and blend, stirring for 3–5 minutes, or until butter barely begins to brown. Add chicken broth slowly and stir until sauce thickens. Season with salt and pepper. Return chicken to skillet and add sauce. Place over medium-low heat. Stir to coat chicken and mushrooms with sauce, heat through, and serve over noodles.

MAKES 4 SERVINGS.

ORIENTAL CHICKEN

■ ■ ■

OVEN: 350°

2 cups brown sugar
1/3 cup soy sauce
1/2 cup pineapple juice
6 chicken breast halves
6 tablespoons sesame seeds

Mix brown sugar, soy sauce, and pineapple juice in a shallow non-reactive pan. Marinate chicken in soy sauce mixture for at least 6 hours, turning once. Remove chicken from marinade and arrange chicken in greased baking dish, skin-side-down. Bake for 30 minutes and turn. Sprinkle with sesame seeds and continue baking for 20–30 more minutes.

MAKES 6 SERVINGS.

CHICKEN PARMESAN

■ ■ ■

OVEN: 350°

1 cup crushed herb-seasoned
     stuffing mix
1/2 cup grated Parmesan cheese
1/4 cup parsley flakes
1/8 teaspoon garlic powder
4 chicken breast halves
1/2 cup butter, melted

Mix crushed stuffing mix, Parmesan cheese, parsley flakes, and garlic powder in a large bowl. Dip chicken in melted butter and roll in crumb mixture, pressing crumbs into chicken well. Place on a greased cookie sheet or shallow baking pan, skin-side-up.

For a thicker breading, sprinkle leftover crumbs over the top and then drizzle with butter. Bake for 45 minutes to an hour, depending on size of the chicken breasts.

MAKES 4 SERVINGS.

CHICKEN PARMIGIANA

■ ■ ■

OVEN: 350°

6 boneless chicken breast halves
3/4 cup flour
salt and pepper
3/4 cup oil
3/4 cup meatless pasta sauce
1/3 cup grated Parmesan cheese
2 ounces shredded mozzarella
     cheese

Dredge chicken in flour seasoned with salt and pepper, and sauté in oil for about 5 minutes on each side, or until evenly browned. Place in a greased 2-quart baking dish and spoon pasta sauce over chicken. Sprinkle with Parmesan cheese and bake for about 20–30 minutes. Sprinkle mozzarella cheese on chicken breasts, dividing equally among all 6 pieces. Continue cooking for about 5 more minutes, or until cheese is melted.

MAKES 6 SERVINGS.

TIPS FOR HOLIDAY DINNERS

- The most important thing you can do is plan ahead. Every detail you think through ahead of time will translate into greater peace of mind for you during the meal. When you know things are under control, you're much more likely to be able to relax and enjoy yourself.

- Don't just think your plans through; write them down. This detail will help you feel more in control, and will add immensely to your peace of mind!

- No detail is too small to include in your plans. It's usually those little things, like not being able to find the candles, or discovering that you're out of coffee or ice, that can cause such hassles during busy times.

- Make a time chart to work by. Write down when you plan to sit down at the table, and work backwards from there.

- Allow time for unexpected events, plus time for getting dressed. Don't schedule yourself too tightly. Unexpected things always come up. It's such a luxury not to be in a hurry, and planning ahead helps this happen for you.

- Once you plan ahead, try to do as much as possible ahead of time. Collect recipes that can be prepared ahead of time and refrigerated or frozen. Stock up on staples in advance. Every step you can do in advance is one less hassle you have to deal with at "rush hour." Holidays are not pop quizzes. We know they're coming far in advance, so why let them catch us unprepared?

- Don't let your carefully engineered plans get swept into the trash! Save your notes and add to them each year. Remember, the holidays will be back next year, same time, same station. You'll be so glad to have all that information you thought you'd remember but didn't.

(continued)

CHICKEN PICCATA
■ ■ ■

4 boneless chicken breast halves
1/3 cup flour
1/4 teaspoon salt
1/4 teaspoon pepper
4 tablespoons butter
1 tablespoon olive oil
4 tablespoons white wine or sherry
3 tablespoons lemon juice
8 thin lemon slices
4 tablespoons chopped fresh parsley

Place chicken breasts between 2 pieces of waxed paper and pound them until they're about 1/4" thick. Dredge in flour and sprinkle both sides with salt and pepper. In a large skillet, heat butter and olive oil together until the butter is melted and bubbly. Add the chicken breasts and cook for 3–5 minutes, or until delicately browned on the bottom. Turn and brown the other side for another 3–5 minutes. Remove chicken from the skillet and place on a warm platter. Lay a piece of foil over the chicken to keep it warm while preparing the sauce. Add white wine or sherry to the skillet and stir, scraping the bottom of the skillet to loosen any small bits of chicken left in the pan. Add lemon juice, stir until sauce is slightly thickened, and spoon sauce over chicken. Garnish with lemon slices and sprinkle chopped fresh parsley on top.

MAKES 4 SERVINGS.

CHICKEN POT PIE
■ ■ ■

OVEN: 375°

6 tablespoons butter, divided use
1 (8-ounce) can crescent roll dough
3 (5-ounce) cans premium white chicken
1 (10-ounce) package frozen mixed vegetables, thawed
1 (4-ounce) can mushrooms, drained
1/2 cup flour
1 (14 1/2-ounce) can chicken broth
1 cup milk
salt and pepper

Melt 2 tablespoons of the butter and pour into a 2-quart rectangular baking dish, turning to coat pan. Unroll can of crescent rolls and spread the whole rectangle of dough into the pan. Drain chicken and break into small pieces with a fork. Spread the chicken over the roll dough, layer thawed frozen vegetables over the chicken, and layer mushrooms over the vegetables. Melt the remaining 4 tablespoons butter in a medium saucepan. Add the flour and blend, cooking and stirring for 3–5 minutes, or until butter barely begins to brown. Slowly add chicken broth and milk. Heat and stir until sauce thickens. Season with salt and pepper. Pour sauce on top and bake for 30–40 minutes.

MAKES 4–6 SERVINGS.

CHICKEN QUESADILLAS
■■■

1 (5-ounce) can white chicken
1 (16-ounce) jar chunky salsa,
    divided use
1 ripe avocado, peeled and diced
1 (8-ounce) can crushed pineapple,
    drained
juice of 1 lime
8 (8½") flour tortillas
2 cups (8 ounces) shredded
    Monterey Jack cheese
3 tablespoons butter
3 tablespoons oil
sour cream

Drain chicken well, put in a small bowl, and break up into small chunks. Add 2–3 tablespoons of the salsa to chicken, mix well, and set aside. To make **Pineapple and Avocado Salsa**, pour remaining salsa into a medium bowl. Gently stir in diced avocado, crushed pineapple, and lime juice. Set salsa aside. Lay 4 of the tortillas on a work surface and divide the cheese equally among them, spreading it almost to the edges. Spoon the chicken mixture onto the cheese, dividing it equally. Top with the remaining tortillas. Melt butter in a small saucepan and stir in oil. Brush some of the butter mixture on a griddle. (A skillet can be used, but you can only cook 1 quesadilla at a time.) Carefully place the quesadillas on the griddle and brush some more of the butter mixture on top. Cook until the bottom tortilla turns golden-brown. Then carefully flip the que-

sadillas, as you would turn grilled cheese sandwiches. This is easier to do if you have 2 pancake turners, using one on the top and one on the bottom, so that the filling doesn't slip out of the quesadilla. Cook until the other side is nicely browned and the cheese is melted. Remove from heat and keep warm until all the quesadillas are prepared. Then place one quesadilla on each serving plate. Cut into quarters and pull the wedges apart slightly. Spoon a mound of salsa in the center and top with a dollop of sour cream.
MAKES 4 MEAL-SIZE SERVINGS.

Note: Quesadillas can be filled with a variety of good things. Try yellow rice with chopped artichoke hearts and green onions. Or black beans, yellow rice, corn, and chopped Roma tomatoes. Experiment with leftovers.

CHICKEN AND RICE
■■■

OVEN: 275°

2 (10¾-ounce) cans cream of
    chicken soup
1 cup uncooked rice (not instant)
salt and pepper
6 chicken breast halves
¼ cup butter, melted

Combine soup with rice, salt, and pepper, and spread in a greased 2-quart baking dish. Lay chicken on top and drizzle with melted butter. Season with more salt and pepper and cover with foil. Bake for 2 hours.
MAKES 6 SERVINGS.

CHICKEN ROSEMARY

■ ■ ■

OVEN: 350°

4 chicken breast halves
2 tablespoons butter, softened
2 tablespoons chopped fresh rosemary
salt and pepper

Rinse chicken and pat dry with paper towels. Spread butter over the skin side of chicken breasts and sprinkle with rosemary, salt, and pepper. Spray a 3-quart rectangular baking dish with non-stick spray and arrange chicken breasts skin-side-up in the dish. Bake for 45-55 minutes, or until done.

MAKES 4 SERVINGS.

SOUR CREAM CHICKEN

■ ■ ■

4 tablespoons butter
4 chicken breast halves
1 (8-ounce) carton sour cream
½ cup white wine
1 bunch green onions, chopped
1 (8-ounce) can sliced mushrooms, undrained
salt and pepper

Melt butter in a large skillet and add chicken. Brown for 5–8 minutes on each side and remove from skillet. Whisk sour cream and wine into pan drippings and add green onions and mushrooms. Return chicken to skillet and sprinkle with salt and pepper. Cover, reduce heat, and simmer for about 30 minutes. Serve with rice.

MAKES 4 SERVINGS.

ROAST CHICKEN

■ ■ ■

OVEN: 375°

1 whole chicken (3 pounds)
softened butter
salt and pepper
2 tablespoons chopped fresh herbs (rosemary, parsley, etc.)
1 lemon

Remove packet of giblets from the chicken cavity. They can be used to make giblet gravy (page 251), if desired. Rinse chicken well inside and out, and pat dry with paper towels. Rub chicken with butter and sprinkle generously with salt and pepper inside and out. Put some of the chopped herbs inside the chicken cavity, and sprinkle the rest over the outside. Cut the lemon in half and place inside the chicken cavity. Do not truss the chicken. It slows the cooking process of the inner thigh—the area that takes the longest to cook! If you feel you must tie the legs together, do so loosely. If desired, use an oven browning bag, following instructions on the package. However, this shouldn't be necessary. Roast for 50 minutes, and then check internal temperature at the inside of the thigh. Continue cooking until thermometer registers 175°. (Temperature of breast might be slightly higher.) Remove from oven and let stand for 15 minutes before carving.

MAKES 4 SERVINGS.

SOUTHWESTERN CHICKEN
■ ■ ■

1/2 cup taco sauce
1/4 cup Dijon mustard
2 tablespoons lime juice
6 boneless chicken breast halves
2 tablespoons butter
6 tablespoons plain yogurt or sour cream
6 lime slices
chopped cilantro (optional)

Mix taco sauce, mustard, and lime juice. Add chicken and turn to coat both sides. Cover and refrigerate for at least 30 minutes. Remove from refrigerator 30 minutes before cooking. Melt butter in a large skillet. Remove chicken from marinade and brown in skillet for 5–8 minutes on each side. Add marinade and cook for 5 more minutes, or until chicken is tender. Remove chicken to a warm platter and continue cooking marinade until thickened. Pour over chicken. Top each serving with 1 tablespoon yogurt or sour cream, and garnish with lime and cilantro, if desired.

MAKES 6 SERVINGS.

CHICKEN STIR-FRY
■ ■ ■

1 (1 1/2-ounce) envelope Kikkoman Teriyaki Sauce Mix
1/2 cup water
4 boneless chicken breast halves
oil for stir-frying
1 medium onion, sliced
1 bunch broccoli, cut up
1 (8-ounce) can sliced water chestnuts
1 (8-ounce) can sliced mushrooms, drained
1 (10 1/2-ounce) can condensed beef broth (as much as needed)
teriyaki sauce (bottled)

Dissolve teriyaki sauce mix in water. Place chicken in a non-reactive dish and pour sauce over it. Cover and refrigerate for several hours, turning several times. Reserving marinade, remove chicken and cut into chunks or strips. Heat oil in a wok or a very large skillet and sauté chicken. Remove from pan and add onion, cooking until softened. Add broccoli and reserved marinade and stir-fry until barely tender. Add water chestnuts and mushrooms. Return chicken to the pan and add enough condensed beef broth to moisten it well. Add bottled teriyaki sauce to taste and heat through. Serve over cooked rice.

MAKES 4–6 SERVINGS.

N·O·T·E·S

TIPS FOR HOLIDAY DINNERS
(CONTINUED)

- Big holiday meals are a prime opportunity for silverware to get thrown away accidentally. Keep a dishpan filled with hot soapy water just for silverware, as plates are being cleared from the table. Then use a rubber spatula to scrape plates.

- Fill the sink with hot soapy water and slip the empty serving pieces in there to soak. You can even use an extra dishpan filled with hot soapy water at a secondary location just to soak dishes until you can load them into the dishwasher.

- Be sure to have plenty of trash bags. Holidays always generate more trash than usual.

- Several days after the big event, have a "debriefing" session on paper. Jot down things you could do next time to simplify. Make notes of anything you could have done ahead of time. These notes will be priceless later on. The more you document, the easier it will be next time. And there will be a next time!

- During this debriefing session, ask yourself, "Did I have too much or too little of anything? Was anything a disaster? What was the favorite item? Was anything more work than it was worth? Were there any bottlenecks?" Ask your family for their input.

- Once you get a menu fine-tuned, you can even go so far as to make out a shopping list that you can use each year.

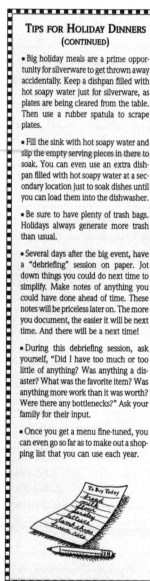

CHICKEN TACOS
■■■

OVEN: 350°

1 tablespoon butter
¼ cup chopped onion
3 cups chopped cooked chicken
1 cup sour cream
2 teaspoons Mexican seasoning
¼ teaspoon Tabasco sauce
¼ teaspoon salt
12 taco shells or flour tortillas
shredded Monterey Jack cheese
shredded lettuce
chopped tomatoes
diced avocados
taco sauce

Melt butter in a large skillet and sauté onion until soft. Reduce heat and stir in chicken, sour cream, Mexican seasoning, Tabasco sauce, and salt. Cook until hot. Heat taco shells on a cookie sheet for 5 minutes or wrap flour tortillas in foil and heat for 10 minutes. Then fill with the chicken mixture, shredded cheese, and lettuce. Top with chopped tomatoes and diced avocados and serve with taco sauce.
MAKES 4–6 SERVINGS.

CHICKEN TETRAZZINI
■■■

OVEN: 350°

1 quart chicken broth
8 ounces spaghetti, broken up
6 tablespoons butter
6 tablespoons flour
1 cup half and half
¼ teaspoon salt
⅛ teaspoon pepper
8 chicken breast halves, cooked, boned, and diced
1 (6-ounce) can sliced mushrooms, drained
2 cups (8 ounces) shredded Cheddar, Colby, or Monterey Jack cheese
paprika

Bring chicken broth to a boil in a large saucepan. Add spaghetti and cook for 8 minutes. Remove from heat, leaving spaghetti in broth. In a small saucepan, melt butter, stir in flour, and cook for 3–5 minutes. Slowly add half and half and season with salt and pepper. Ladle about a cup of the hot chicken broth (that the spaghetti was cooked in) into the cream sauce, and stir to blend until smooth. Then stir all of the cream sauce back into the large saucepan of broth and spaghetti. Cook and stir until thickened. Stir in diced chicken, mushrooms, and half of the cheese. Pour into a greased 3-quart baking dish and top with the remaining cheese. Sprinkle with paprika and bake uncovered for about 30 minutes, or until bubbly.
MAKES 8–10 SERVINGS.

Chicken and Wild Rice

■■■

OVEN: 275°

3 (10¾-ounce) cans condensed
    soup: any combination of cream
    of celery, cream of chicken,
    and/or cream of mushroom
1 (4-ounce) can sliced mushrooms,
    drained
1 (6-ounce) box wild rice mix
½ cup uncooked white rice
    (not instant)
salt and pepper
8 chicken breast halves
½ cup butter, melted

Combine soups with mushrooms, wild rice mix (both rice and seasoning packets), and white rice. Season with salt and pepper. Spread into greased 3-quart baking dish. Dip chicken pieces in melted butter and lay on top of rice mixture. Drizzle remaining butter on top, sprinkle again with salt and pepper, and cover with foil. Cook for 2 hours.

MAKES 8 SERVINGS.

CHICKEN SALADS

■■■

Chicken Salad with Grapes

■■■

3 cups cooked diced chicken
    breasts
1½ cups seedless green grapes,
    halved
1 (8-ounce) can sliced water
    chestnuts, drained
6 ounces slivered almonds, toasted
1½ cups diced celery
1½ cups mayonnaise
4 tablespoons lemon juice
1½ teaspoons dry mustard
salt and pepper
lettuce leaves
paprika

In a large mixing bowl, toss chicken with grapes, water chestnuts, almonds, and celery. In a small mixing bowl, blend mayonnaise with lemon juice and dry mustard. Season with salt and pepper, and fold into chicken mixture. Serve on lettuce leaves and sprinkle with paprika.

MAKES 6–8 SERVINGS.

Note: If desired, this salad can be presented in other ways:

■ Cut a cantaloupe in half and remove seeds. Then slice into thin rings and remove rind. Spoon a mound of chicken salad into the center of each ring and garnish with a sprig of mint.

(continued)

HEATING SMOKED TURKEY

(1) Preheat oven to 300°.

(2) Place thawed turkey in an extra-large browning bag. Do not add flour, as the package directions state.

(3) Make 6 slits in bag, set turkey in a roasting pan, and put it in the oven.

(4) Set a pan of water under or alongside the turkey and heat turkey for 6 minutes per pound. Remove turkey from oven and let stand for 15 minutes before carving.

TURKEY GUIDELINES

• To allow for leftovers, buy 1–1½ pounds whole turkey per person.

• Allow adequate time for thawing in refrigerator: 1½–2 days for under 8 pounds; 2–2½ days for 8–12 pounds; 3 days for 12–16 pounds; 3½–4 days for 16–20 pounds; and 4–4½ days for 20–24 pounds.

• Place raw turkey on a nonporous surface, and not on a wooden cutting board.

• Use paper towels to dry turkey and wipe up juices before cooking.

• Never stuff turkey in advance. Always wait and stuff turkey immediately before cooking.

• Wash hands and all work surfaces with hot, soapy water after handling raw turkey.

• Salmonella bacteria are most prevalent on poultry skin. Heat kills salmonella. So the safest oven cooking temperature is no lower than 325°.

• Always remove stuffing from turkey and store it separately.

• Store turkey (and all cooked foods) within 2 hours after cooking.

• For questions about preparing holiday turkey, call the USDA Meat and Poultry Hotline at (800) 535-4555.

• Leaving the leaves attached, cut a fresh pineapple lengthwise into quarters. Separate the pulp from the skin, cut it into chunks, and arrange it to one side, perhaps with several strawberries. Spoon chicken salad over the pineapple shell.

ORIENTAL CHICKEN SALAD
•••

With a head of cabbage in the refrigerator, this salad can be prepared with things from the pantry. I make it often in the summer, especially on nights when Jack plays tennis. He likes it best when the ramen noodles are warm.

4 tablespoons sugar
1 teaspoon pepper
2 teaspoons MSG
2 teaspoons salt
2 tablespoons sesame oil
6 tablespoons vegetable oil
1 tablespoon teriyaki sauce
6 tablespoons vinegar
1 head cabbage, shredded
3 (5-ounce) cans premium white chicken, drained and chopped, or 1½ cups chopped cooked chicken breasts (about 1 pound)
3 (3-ounce) packages chicken-flavored ramen noodle soup mix
4 cups boiling water
2 tablespoons butter
4 tablespoons sesame seeds
4 tablespoons slivered almonds

In a large mixing bowl, blend sugar, pepper, MSG, salt, sesame oil, vegetable oil, teriyaki sauce, and vinegar.

Add cabbage and chicken, and toss well. Break ramen noodles into pieces and cook in 4 cups boiling water for 3 minutes. Drain and mix with contents of seasoning packets that come with the noodles. Add noodles to salad. Melt butter in a small skillet and toast sesame seeds and almonds for 3–5 minutes. Mix with salad. Serve warm or chilled.

MAKES 10–12 SERVINGS.

CHICKEN AND WILD RICE SALAD
•••

1 (5-ounce) box brown and wild rice mix
1 (14-ounce) can artichoke hearts, drained and quartered
3 cups diced cooked chicken breasts
½ cup chopped celery
1 (8-ounce) can sliced water chestnuts, drained
½ cup creamy Italian dressing
⅔ cup mayonnaise
2 tablespoons lemon juice
3 tablespoons chopped fresh parsley
salt and pepper
lettuce leaves

Prepare wild rice mix according to package directions, omitting butter and using only 1⅓ cups water. While it cooks, combine artichoke hearts and diced chicken in a large mixing bowl and toss with celery and water chestnuts. In a small mixing bowl, whisk together Italian dressing, mayonnaise,

and lemon juice. Pour over chicken mixture, sprinkle with parsley, and toss to mix well. Add cooked wild rice mix and toss again. Season to taste with salt and pepper. Serve on lettuce leaves.
MAKES 8 SERVINGS.

CHICKEN PASTA SALAD
■■■

1 (10.4-ounce) box Kraft Classic Ranch pasta salad
1 (5-ounce) can premium white chicken, drained and chopped
1 (14-ounce) can artichoke hearts, drained and quartered
1 (2¼-ounce) can sliced ripe olives, drained
2 tomatoes, coarsely diced

Prepare pasta salad according to package directions. Stir in chicken, artichoke hearts, olives, and tomatoes. Refrigerate or serve immediately.
MAKES 4 SERVINGS.

TURKEY
■■■

ABOUT TURKEY
■■■

Frequently, turkey is wrapped in plastic and frozen. Unless the package directions indicate otherwise, follow these guidelines. The easiest method for thawing a turkey is in the refrigerator.

Best: If you have adequate time to thaw it in the refrigerator, this is the safest way: Leave turkey in the plastic wrapper and place in a baking pan to catch drips. Put it in the refrigerator and leave it there to thaw. Allow approximately 2–3 days for a turkey breast, or about 1 day for every 4 pounds. If it still isn't completely thawed on the morning you want to prepare it, finish thawing with the next method.

Acceptable: If you must cook it the next day: Leave turkey in plastic wrapper. Be sure that the packaging is not torn or punctured. Put it in a large, deep pan, or place it in the sink, and cover with cold water. Change the water every hour. This can take 3–7 hours, depending on the size of the turkey. Do not leave the turkey overnight in the sink in cold water. Put it in a pan in the refrigerator, still packaged in its original plastic wrapper. The next day, prepare the turkey (rub with butter, salt, etc.), and roast it according to the timetable printed on the wrapper.

In a Pinch: If you want to cook it right away: Unwrap turkey; place on rack in shallow roasting pan and cook at 325° for 1 hour. Remove turkey from oven and take neck, giblets, and anything else packed inside turkey from both the neck cavity and the body cavity. (These need to be cooked right away.) Prepare the turkey (rub with butter, salt, etc.); return it to the oven, and roast according to timetable printed on the wrapper. Cook the stuffing separately.

N·O·T·E·S

ROAST TURKEY BREAST
...

OVEN: 450°/350°

*6–8 pounds frozen turkey breast,
thawed in refrigerator (Norbest,
if available) (see Special
Ingredients, page 68)*
melted butter or vegetable oil
seasoned salt
black pepper

Remove thawed turkey breast from refrigerator. Allow to stand at room temperature for 30–45 minutes. Remove wrapper, rinse turkey breast thoroughly inside and out, and pat dry. Line a heavy roasting pan with heavy-duty foil. Place a rack on the foil and brush the rack with oil. Brush turkey with melted butter or oil inside and out and sprinkle liberally with seasoned salt and pepper. Place turkey breast on the rack in the pan. Make a "tent" of foil over the turkey and place in a preheated 450° oven. Cook for 30 minutes and then reduce heat to 350°. Continue cooking for the length of time specified on the package, usually for a total of 3–4 hours. (It may take longer, if turkey wasn't completely thawed.) When the internal temperature reaches about 160°, remove foil, to allow skin to brown. When the internal temperature reaches 170°–175°, remove turkey from the oven. Before carving, let stand for 15 minutes after removing from the oven.

MAKES 6–8 SERVINGS.

ROAST TURKEY
...

OVEN: 325°

turkey (thawed)
butter or vegetable oil
salt and pepper
oven browning bag

Remove thawed turkey from refrigerator and remove packet of giblets from inside the turkey. Use to make Giblet Gravy (page 251). Allow turkey to stand at room temperature for 30–45 minutes. Rinse and pat dry. Rub turkey with butter or oil and season with salt and pepper inside and out. Prepare an oven browning bag according to package directions. Place turkey inside bag and roast according to the timetable printed on the turkey wrapper, or until turkey thigh reaches an internal temperature of 170°– 175°. (Allow about 2–3 hours for 4–8 pounds; 3½–4 hours for 8–12 pounds; 4–5 hours for 12–16 pounds; 5–6 hours for 16–20 pounds; and 6–7 hours for 20–24 pounds. If the turkey is not completely thawed, it will take longer.) If turkey gets done a few minutes early, turn off the oven and lay a piece of foil over the turkey. After removing turkey from the oven, let it stand for 15 minutes before carving. If turkey is stuffed, the stuffing needs to reach an internal temperature of 160°.

*"A good cook is
never without
friends."*

—H. Jackson Brown

Fish and Seafood

FISH AND SEAFOOD

■ ■ ■

FISH

■ ■ ■

BUTTERMILK-FRIED FISH

■ ■ ■

ELECTRIC SKILLET: 350°

1 1/2 pounds fish fillets
2 cups buttermilk
1 1/2 cups Bisquick
salt and pepper
vegetable oil

Soak fish in buttermilk for 30 minutes. Mix Bisquick with salt and pepper and dredge fish fillets in it. Pour oil into an electric skillet to a depth of 3" and heat to 350°. Fry fish in oil, adding a few fillets at a time. Cook until golden brown on both sides.

MAKES 4 SERVINGS.

PAN-FRIED FISH

■ ■ ■

1 1/2 pounds fish fillets: catfish, snapper, or flounder (fresh; not previously frozen)
1/2 cup milk
pepper
1 cup Ritz cracker crumbs
3 tablespoons oil
3 tablespoons butter

Rinse fish and pat dry. Dip in milk and season with pepper. Roll fillets in Ritz cracker crumbs and lay them on a plate. Heat oil and butter in a large, heavy skillet over medium-high heat. Roll the fillets once more in the cracker crumbs. Cook fillets in skillet, being careful not to crowd them. Brown on both sides, cooking until fish is opaque and flaky.

MAKES 4 SERVINGS.

BEER-BATTER-FRIED FISH

■ ■ ■

ELECTRIC SKILLET: 350°

1 1/2 pounds fish fillets
1 1/4 cups Bisquick, divided use
1/2 teaspoon salt
1 egg, beaten
1/2 cup beer
vegetable oil

Dredge fish in 1/4 cup of the Bisquick and set aside. Combine remaining 1 cup Bisquick with salt, egg, and beer. Mix until smooth. Pour oil into electric skillet to a depth of 3" and heat to 350°. Dip each fish fillet into beer batter. Fry fish in oil, turning until golden brown on both sides.

MAKES 4 SERVINGS.

BLACKENED FISH

■ ■ ■

1½ pounds fish fillets
½ cup milk
blackened fish seasoning
3 tablespoons cooking oil
3 tablespoons butter

Soak fish in milk for 15–20 minutes. Drain and season both sides liberally with blackened fish seasoning. Heat oil and butter in a large skillet (preferably cast-iron) over high heat and sauté fillets until fish is no longer opaque, about 5 minutes on each side.

MAKES 4 SERVINGS.

BAKED FISH

■ ■ ■

OVEN: 425°

1½ pounds fish fillets or steaks
½ teaspoon salt
¼ teaspoon pepper
2 tablespoons minced parsley
¼ cup white wine
¼ cup crushed herb-seasoned
    stuffing mix
3 tablespoons butter, melted

Rinse fish, pat dry, and place in a greased baking dish. Sprinkle with salt, pepper, and parsley. Carefully add wine and sprinkle crushed stuffing mix on top. Drizzle with melted butter and bake for 15–20 minutes, or until crumbs are browned and fish flakes easily with a fork.

MAKES 4 SERVINGS.

BAKED FISH
IN SOUR CREAM

■ ■ ■

OVEN: 350°

1½ pounds fish fillets
½ cup butter, melted
1 tablespoon white wine
1 tablespoon lemon juice
¼ teaspoon onion juice
1 teaspoon dill weed
1 (8-ounce) carton sour cream
¼ cup dried bread crumbs or
    crushed herb-seasoned
    stuffing mix
2 tablespoons grated Parmesan
    cheese

Rinse fish fillets, pat dry, and set aside. Mix butter, wine, lemon juice, and onion juice. Dip fish in butter mixture and arrange in a greased baking dish. Drizzle remaining butter mixture over the fish and sprinkle with dill. Spread sour cream over fish. Combine bread crumbs or stuffing mix with Parmesan cheese and sprinkle over fish. Bake for 25–30 minutes, or until fish is flaky.

MAKES 4 SERVINGS.

N·O·T·E·S

HANDLING FISH AND SEAFOOD

- When you buy fish, slip it into a plastic bag to keep juices from coming into contact with your other groceries.

- Fish is extremely perishable, and ideally should be kept on crushed ice. Because it's cold-blooded, organisms particular to fish that cause spoilage can sometimes survive at even 40°.

- Store fish in the coldest part of the refrigerator for no more than a day, or freeze it immediately. Freezing doesn't prevent spoilage; it only slows it down. It's better to buy commercially frozen fish than it is to freeze it yourself.

- Fish should be rinsed thoroughly and dried with paper towels before storing. Line a container with paper towels and lay rinsed fish on the towels. Cover container with plastic wrap, and if possible, set the container on a pan of crushed ice in the refrigerator.

PREPARING FISH AND SEAFOOD

- Buy whatever is freshest, and choose the recipe accordingly. Try to be flexible, so that you can take advantage of whatever looks best at the market.

- It only takes 30–45 minutes to marinate fish.

- The only safe way to thaw fish and seafood is in the refrigerator. Allow sufficient time, and thaw it in milk for a better flavor.

- If you're not sure how long to cook fish, use this rule of thumb: Cook it at about 425°–450° for 10 minutes per inch of thickness at the thickest part, or for up to 20 minutes if it's frozen. Usually, it takes longer to bake fish in the oven than it does to poach it or fry it.

- When fish is done, it will be opaque, it will not cling to its bones, and the flesh will flake easily with a fork.

GRILLED FISH

GRILL: MEDIUM-HOT

1½ pounds fish fillets: orange roughy, trout, or salmon
4 tablespoons butter
2 tablespoons lime juice
1 teaspoon Worcestershire sauce
¼ teaspoon Liquid Smoke
parsley flakes
dill weed

Lay fish fillets in a disposable foil pan or on several thicknesses of heavy-duty foil, with the edges folded up to make a lip. Heat butter, lime juice, Worcestershire sauce, and Liquid Smoke in a small saucepan, and stir until butter is melted. Pour over fish and turn to coat both sides. Sprinkle with parsley flakes and dill, and place on grill. Lower the lid and cook fish for 10–15 minutes, depending on the size of the fillets. Fish is done when it is opaque and flakes easily with a fork.

MAKES 4 SERVINGS.

PLANKED SALMON

OVEN: 350° (NOT PREHEATED)

2–3 tablespoons oil, divided use
1 salmon fillet (2½–3 pounds) or 8 pieces salmon fillet, about 6 ounces each
salt and pepper
fresh dill or parsley
lemon or lime wedges

Brush about 1 tablespoon of the oil on the surface of a cedar plank (see Note), and place in a cold oven. Turn temperature to 350° and heat plank for 15 minutes. Meanwhile, remove pin bones from salmon: With the fillet skin side down, run your thumb down the center of the fillet, pressing slightly. You'll feel the pin bones, if any, protruding like thick splinters. They're very easy to remove if you use a pair of needle nose pliers. When you've removed the pin bones, brush the salmon with the remaining oil. Sprinkle with salt and pepper. Using oven mitts or hot pads, remove the plank from the oven and set it on a heatproof surface. Lay salmon on the hot plank, skin side down, and return to oven. Cook for about 35–40 minutes, or until internal temperature registers 135°–140°. (It takes longer to cook fish on a cedar plank than in a baking dish.) Sprinkle with fresh dill or parsley, and serve on the plank, garnished with lemon or lime wedges. Serve with Clarified Butter (page 252), Dill Sauce (page 251), or Dill Lemon Butter (page 251).

MAKES 8 SERVINGS.

Note: Cedar planks and accessories can be ordered from Chinook Planks in Seattle, Washington. Their toll-free number is (800) 765-4408.

SALMON CROQUETTES

■ ■ ■

OVEN: 350° (OR COOK IN SKILLET)

1 (6-ounce) can pink salmon
  (skinless and boneless, if
  available)
1½ cups Ritz cracker crumbs
  (36 crackers), divided use
1 tablespoon lemon juice
1 egg, beaten
2 tablespoons mayonnaise
½ teaspoon dill weed
6 shots Tabasco sauce
2–3 green onions, chopped
  (white part only)
vegetable oil (for cooking croquettes
  in a skillet or for greasing baking
  dish)

Drain salmon and put into a medium mixing bowl. Pick out any bones and skin. Put 1 cup of the cracker crumbs into a shallow bowl. Break up salmon with a fork and stir in lemon juice, beaten egg, mayonnaise, dill weed, Tabasco sauce, green onions, and remaining ½ cup cracker crumbs. Mix gently and shape into 4–6 patties. (The patties will be very moist.) Dip each patty into the 1 cup of cracker crumbs in the bowl, coating both sides thoroughly. Heat a little oil in a skillet and cook patties until lightly browned on one side. Turn carefully and cook until other side is golden brown. Or bake in a greased baking dish at 350°, turning halfway through cooking. Serve with Cocktail Sauce (page 250), tartar sauce, or Cayenne Mayonnaise (page 253).

MAKES 2–3 SERVINGS.

*"Fish, to taste right,
must swim
three times—
in water,
in butter,
and in wine."*

—Old Polish Proverb

SWORDFISH AND ARTICHOKE HEARTS

■ ■ ■

OVEN: 400°

4 swordfish steaks
3 tablespoons lime juice (juice of 2
  limes)
¼ cup oil
freshly ground black pepper
1 (14-ounce) can artichoke hearts,
  drained
½ cup mayonnaise
½ cup grated Parmesan cheese

Arrange swordfish steaks in a nonreactive baking dish. Mix lime juice with oil and pour over fish, turning to coat both sides. Sprinkle with pepper, cover, and refrigerate for 1 hour. Chop artichoke hearts and combine with mayonnaise and Parmesan cheese. Remove fish from refrigerator, spread with artichoke mixture, and bake for 20–25 minutes.

MAKES 4 SERVINGS.

N·O·T·E·S

TYPES OF FISH

With so many different varieties of fish, it's difficult to break them down into neat categories. It seems that the only thing they all have in common is that they live in water. First, there's the continental divide that separates fish, which have fins, from shellfish, which have shells. But that's only the beginning.

Fish with fins can be further subdivided, according to what type of water—fresh or salt—they call home. And yet some saltwater fish, such as salmon, retreat to fresh water to spawn, while some freshwater fish—eels, for example—venture out into the ocean to do likewise. Saltwater fish tend to be sturdier than their cousins from the streams. Freshwater fish are even more fragile once their scales have been removed. Experts warn, with the growing safety concerns over inland waterways, that no one eat more than ½ pound of freshwater fish per week. They further advise that pregnant and nursing women avoid freshwater fish entirely.

Then there's the issue of shape: round versus flat. Round fish, such as salmon and swordfish, begin life with a fairly round or oval shape, and stay that way as they mature. They have an eye on each side of the body, and they swim in a vertical position, with the dorsal fin pointing upward. But flatfish, such as flounder, Dover sole, and turbot, are different. In their early stages of development, flatfish look similar to round fish. But then they begin to flatten out and swim on their side. As this change takes place, the eye on the bottom side shifts around to the top side.

Still another line of demarcation is between lean fish, such as snapper, which have a milder flavor, and oily fish, such as tuna, which taste a little stronger. This distinction affects the type of recipe that's the most suitable choice for each.

TUNA NOODLE CASSEROLE
■■■

OVEN: 350°

4 tablespoons butter
5 tablespoons flour
2 cups milk
3 dashes Tabasco sauce
salt and pepper
2 (6½-ounce) cans albacore tuna, drained and flaked
8 ounces uncooked egg noodles
1 cup (4 ounces) shredded Cheddar cheese

Melt butter in a large saucepan. Stir in flour and cook over medium heat until butter begins to turn golden. Stir in milk and Tabasco sauce. Cook and stir until thickened. Season with salt and pepper. Stir tuna into sauce. Slightly undercook noodles, drain, and stir into tuna. Pour into a greased 2-quart baking dish, sprinkle with cheese, and bake for 30 minutes.

MAKES 6 SERVINGS.

SEAFOOD
■■■

BOILED SHRIMP
■■■

4 quarts water
1 package crab boil
1 lemon, sliced
1 onion, diced
1 cup salt
5 pounds shrimp in shell

Measure water into a stock pot or large kettle. Put crab boil, lemon, and onion in a square of cheesecloth and tie with kitchen twine. Add salt and bag of seasonings to water. Bring to a boil and add shrimp. Return to a boil and cook for 5 minutes. Remove from heat and let stand for 10–15 minutes. Drain shrimp and serve.

MAKES 10–12 SERVINGS.

SHRIMP SCAMPI
■■■

1 tablespoon minced garlic
4 sprigs parsley, chopped
¾ cup butter, melted
2 pounds fresh shrimp, peeled and deveined
¼ cup white wine
2 tablespoons lemon juice
salt and pepper

In a large skillet, sauté garlic and parsley in butter over medium heat for 2 minutes. Reduce heat to low and add shrimp. Cook for about 5 minutes, stirring frequently. Remove shrimp from pan with a slotted spoon to a serving dish, and keep warm. Leave butter in skillet and add wine, lemon juice, and salt and pepper to taste. Simmer for 2 minutes. Pour butter mixture over shrimp and serve immediately.

MAKES 4 SERVINGS.

BARBECUED SHRIMP
■■■

My mother had a friend who was traveling to New Orleans by plane. Her seat mate asked her what her favorite restaurant in New Orleans was. When she replied, "Manale's," she hit the jackpot. It turned out that her seat mate's family owned the restaurant, and she gave her this recipe!

GRILL: MEDIUM-HOT (OR BROILER)

2 pounds whole shrimp in shell
1 cup butter, melted
2 tablespoons lemon juice
2 cloves garlic, pressed
3 tablespoons white wine
¼ cup olive oil or salad oil
pepper

This can be prepared on a grill or under the broiler. Preheat one or the other. Place unpeeled shrimp in a colander and rinse well with cold water. Shake the colander to drain the shrimp well. Prepare sauce by mixing butter, lemon juice, garlic, white wine, and oil together in a small saucepan. Spread shrimp in a single layer in a large broiling pan. (A deep disposable aluminum pan makes cleanup very simple.) Pour sauce over shrimp and sprinkle very liberally with pepper. (You can't use too much!) Place pan on a grill or under the broiler. Close the lid if using a grill. Cook for about 7 minutes and then flip shrimp over. Sprinkle again generously with pepper, and cook for about 7 more minutes.

MAKES 4 SERVINGS.

Note: This is one of those meals that gets pretty messy. We call them "dish towel dinners." I keep a stack of clean dish towels in a basket on my kitchen counter, and we reach for a handful of them whenever I fix this!

CRAB CAKES
■■■

2 (6-ounce) cans lump crabmeat, drained
16 Ritz crackers, crushed, divided use
1 egg
1 tablespoon mayonnaise
¼ teaspoon salt
¼ teaspoon Dijon mustard
1½ teaspoons parsley flakes
½ teaspoon dried dill weed
¼ teaspoon cayenne
dash Tabasco sauce
½ teaspoon white pepper
oil for frying

Place crabmeat in a medium bowl and break up slightly with a fork. Gently

(continued)

N·O·T·E·S

MARKET FORMS

- **Whole** or **Round:** This describes fish exactly as they're taken from the water.

- **Drawn:** This describes whole fish with the entrails removed.

- **Dressed:** This describes drawn fish with the gills, fins, and scales removed.

- **Pan-dressed:** This describes dressed fish minus the tails, and usually minus the heads, unless the fish are quite small.

- **Steaks:** These are portions of larger fish that are cut in a cross section, with a distinctive horseshoe shape.

- **Fillets:** These are pieces cut from the sides of the fish, from which the bones have been removed.

- **Butterfly Fillets:** This describes pan-dressed fish with both sides attached at the center, and opened like a book.

POPULAR VARIETIES OF FISH

Saltwater Fish: Anchovies, Cod, Flounder, Grouper, Haddock, Halibut, Herring, Mackerel, Mahi Mahi, Monkfish, Orange Roughy, Pompano, Redfish, Red Snapper, Salmon, Sea Bass, Sea Trout, Sole, Swordfish, Tuna, and Turbot

Freshwater Fish: Bass, Carp, Catfish, Crappie, Perch, Pike, Sturgeon, Trout, and Whitefish

GUIDE TO FROZEN FISH

Fresh: Fish that was never frozen.

Flash-frozen: Fish that is frozen within hours of being caught.

Fresh-frozen: Fish that is frozen while it's very fresh, but not quite as soon after being caught as if it were flash-frozen.

Glazed: Fish that has been processed by freezing, then dipping in water, and then freezing a second time, to produce an icy, protective glaze.

mix 2 tablespoons of the cracker crumbs with crabmeat. Place remaining crumbs in a small dish and set aside. In a small bowl, beat egg with mayonnaise, salt, Dijon mustard, parsley flakes, dill weed, cayenne, Tabasco sauce, and white pepper. Gently blend egg mixture with crabmeat. Form into patties about the size of sausage patties and dip in the remaining cracker crumbs to coat both sides. Heat oil in skillet and sauté crab cakes until golden brown on one side. Turn gently and continue cooking until the other side is brown. Serve with Cocktail Sauce (page 250), tartar sauce, Cayenne Mayonnaise (page 253), or Dill Sauce (page 251).

MAKES 3–4 SERVINGS.

TUNA SALAD WITH WATER CHESTNUTS
■■■

2 (6½-ounce) cans albacore tuna, drained

1½ tablespoons lime juice (juice of 1 lime)

2 ounces slivered almonds

2 teaspoons dried dill weed

1 (8-ounce) can sliced water chestnuts, drained

1 (2¼-ounce) can sliced ripe olives, drained

½ cup mayonnaise

In a mixing bowl, break up tuna with a fork. Sprinkle lime juice over the tuna. If using a fresh lime, scrape wedges on the edge of the bowl to extract as much pulp as possible. Add

slivered almonds, dill weed, water chestnuts, ripe olives, and mayonnaise. Mix well. Can be used as a sandwich filling, or to stuff fresh tomatoes or cantaloupe.

MAKES 4–6 SERVINGS.

"He was a bold man that first ate an oyster."

—Jonathan Swift

TUNA AND RICE SALAD
■■■

2 (6½-ounce) cans albacore tuna, drained

1½ tablespoons lime juice (juice of 1 lime)

1 (2¼-ounce) can sliced ripe olives, drained

1 (14-ounce) can artichoke hearts, drained and quartered

2 cups cooked rice

½ cup mayonnaise

2 teaspoons dried dill weed

In a mixing bowl, break up tuna with a fork. Sprinkle lime juice over the tuna. If using a fresh lime, scrape wedges on the edge of the bowl to extract as much pulp as possible. Stir. Fold in olives, artichoke hearts, and rice. Add mayonnaise and stir in dill weed.

MAKES 4–6 SERVINGS.

Eggs, Quiches, and Soufflés

EGGS, QUICHES, AND SOUFFLÉS

...

EGG SIZES

Most cookbooks call for large eggs. The size of an egg is determined by the weight per dozen eggs. The "ten cents" rule suggests that if the next larger size is less than 10 cents more per dozen, it is a better buy. Here are the five standard egg sizes and their weights per dozen:

Jumbo................................30 ounces
Extra-Large.........................27 ounces
Large.................................24 ounces
Medium.............................21 ounces
Small.................................18 ounces

HOW TO SEPARATE EGGS

1. To separate eggs, set out 2 bowls, a cup, and as many eggs as you want to separate.

2. Gently rap the "equator" of 1 egg on the side of the cup. Immediately turn egg upright over the cup, holding the bottom of the egg with one hand. (A cup is used in case an egg yolk breaks and runs into the white.)

3. Place your other hand on top of the egg, and gently lift off the top, as if it were hinged like a box, allowing the egg white to spill over the shell and fall into the cup.

4. Carefully transfer egg yolk back and forth from one half of the shell to the other, allowing all of the egg white to fall into the cup. (A little egg white will still cling to the yolk, which is fine. Just don't allow any yolk to get into the white.) Be careful not to puncture the yolk with the shell, causing it to run.

5. Put the egg yolk into one of the bowls, and pour the egg white into the other bowl. Repeat the process with each egg.

6. If you accidentally drop a small bit of shell into the bowl, use a larger piece of egg shell as a scoop to remove it.

EGGS

...

SOFT-COOKED AND HARD-COOKED EGGS

...

Boiling eggs makes them tough. Cook them this way instead:

1. To reduce the chance of cracked shells, let eggs stand at room temperature for an hour before cooking. If you can't wait for an hour, place eggs in a bowl, cover with hot tap water, and let stand for several minutes.

2. Place eggs in a saucepan that's large enough to hold them in a single layer.

3. Add cold water so that eggs are covered with water, plus 1 inch. Do not cover the pan yet.

4. Heat the water over medium-high heat until it just simmers, but does not boil. You will see tiny bubbles around the outside edge of the water, but no bubbles rising from the center. This will take about 10 minutes.

If you're uncertain as to exactly when water "simmers," use a thermometer to learn which signs to look for. When the water temperature reaches 185°–195°, the water is the right temperature to cook eggs.

5. Remove the pan from the heat. Cover and allow to stand for the length of time indicated in the following chart, depending on what size eggs you are cooking, and what degree of firmness you want.

Firm white and soft yolk: The yolk will be so soft that the egg will be almost impossible to peel. It will need to be served in an egg cup, with the top tapped off with a knife, or removed with an "egg guillotine."

Cook a medium egg..... 2½ minutes
Cook a large egg .... 3 minutes
Cook an extra-large egg .. 3½ minutes
Cook a jumbo egg........ 4 minutes

Firm white and semisoft yolk:
Cook a medium egg..... 3½ minutes
Cook a large egg .... 4 minutes
Cook an extra-large egg .. 4½ minutes
Cook a jumbo egg........ 5 minutes

Firm white and medium yolk:
Cook a medium egg..... 5½ minutes
Cook a large egg .... 6 minutes
Cook an extra-large egg .. 6½ minutes
Cook a jumbo egg........ 7 minutes

Firm white and firm yolk:

Cook a medium egg. . . . . . 12 minutes
Cook a large egg . . . . 13 minutes
Cook an extra-large egg . . . 14 minutes
Cook a jumbo egg . . . . 15 minutes

6. Now set the pan in the sink and run cold water over the eggs to stop the cooking process.

7. If you're not going to use hard-cooked eggs right away, mark them with a pencil, so you can tell the cooked ones from the uncooked ones. You can refrigerate them for up to a week. If you forget to mark them, and you aren't sure whether they're hard-cooked or not, spin them on the counter. A hard-cooked egg will spin, and a raw egg will just wobble.

SCRAMBLED EGGS
■ ■ ■

1. For each serving, break 2 eggs into a bowl and beat them with 1 teaspoon water, milk, or cream. Add salt and pepper to taste.

2. Place 1 tablespoon butter in a small skillet; turn heat to medium.

3. When butter is melted, gently pour beaten eggs into skillet and reduce heat to medium-low.

4. As eggs cook, stir gently, using a spatula to "pull" cooked eggs from the outside of the pan towards the center, and turning the pan so that the uncooked eggs run towards the sides.

5. When eggs are cooked almost to desired doneness, remove from heat. They will set a little more even off the heat. The longer the eggs cook, the drier they become. They should be removed from heat when they are still a little glossy.

6. Transfer the eggs to a warm plate.

POACHED EGGS
■ ■ ■

To Poach Eggs Using an Egg Poacher

1. Spray egg cups of poacher with non-stick spray or put 1 teaspoon butter in each cup.

2. Pour an inch of water into the bottom section of the pan, and bring it to a boil over high heat.

3. Crack eggs, one at a time, into a small bowl or cup (being careful not to break yolk), and transfer each egg into one of the cups of the egg poacher. (It's easier to break eggs into a bowl than it is to break them neatly into the cup of the egg poacher. Hence, this extra step.)

4. Carefully place egg cups over boiling water.

5. Cover pan, reduce heat to low, and simmer eggs for 3–5 minutes. Whites should be firm. Yolks can be checked for doneness by pressing them gently with the back of a spoon.

OMELET FOR ONE

Before preparing the omelet, set a serving plate in a 200° oven, or on top of a toaster oven set to 350°. The plate will be warm when the omelet is done.

3 eggs
2 teaspoons water
¼ teaspoon salt
⅛ teaspoon pepper
1 tablespoon butter
3–4 tablespoons filling: diced ham, sliced green onion, cooked and crumbled bacon, shredded cheese, sliced sautéed mushrooms, chopped parsley or dill, sliced ripe olives, snipped chives, diced tomato, sour cream, salsa, or chopped pepper

Break eggs into a small mixing bowl and add water, salt, and pepper. Beat with a whisk or fork until yolks and whites are well mixed. In a 6"–8" skillet, heat butter over medium heat until it melts, foams, and the foam starts to subside.

Pour eggs into the skillet all at once. As soon as the edges begin to set, lift them up with a spatula, turning the pan slightly so that the unset egg runs underneath. To keep eggs from sticking, give the pan a gentle shake from time to time.

Once the eggs are set (but the top is still shiny and moist), run the spatula around the pan to loosen the omelet, and remove the pan from the heat.

Let the omelet stand for a few seconds, and add the filling in one of several ways: (a) Sprinkle it evenly over the whole omelet and fold it either in half or in thirds; (b) sprinkle it over half of the omelet and fold it in half; (c) sprinkle it down the center of the omelet and fold it in thirds, turning each side over the center; (d) fold the omelet as desired and spoon the filling on top.

Serve immediately on the heated plate.

To Poach Eggs Using Custard Cups

1. Put 1 teaspoon butter in each cup, or spray well with non-stick spray.

2. Pour about an inch of water into a saucepan and set the custard cups in the pan. Bring the water just to a simmer.

3. When the water simmers, crack each egg, one at a time, into a small bowl, taking care not to break yolk. Transfer each egg into a custard cup.

4. Cover pan, reduce heat to low, and simmer eggs for 3–5 minutes. Whites should be firm. Yolks can be checked for doneness by pressing them gently with the back of a spoon.

To Poach Eggs Without an Egg Poacher

1. To help eggs retain their shape, first heat-treat them. Bring a pan of water to a boil. Use enough to cover eggs by 1". Gently spoon the uncracked eggs into pan. Wait 8 seconds from the time you put the first egg in, and then remove them in the same order that you put them into the pan.

2. After removing heat-treated eggs, add 1 teaspoon white vinegar or lemon juice per egg, to keep white from separating.

3. Bring water to a boil over high heat, and reduce heat so that water just simmers. Bubbles should form at the bottom of the pan.

4. One at a time, break eggs into a small

bowl or saucer and slide them into the water. Be careful not to break yolks.

5. For soft yolks, simmer eggs for 3–5 minutes. Firm yolks take 7–10 minutes. Remove eggs with a slotted spoon and drain on a paper towel.

6. Eggs can be poached up to a day ahead, refrigerated, and reheated. To reheat, spoon cooked eggs into very hot tap water and let stand for 5–10 minutes.

FRIED EGGS
###

1. Place ½ tablespoon butter in a small skillet and turn heat to medium.

2. Break an egg into a small bowl.

3. When butter is melted, transfer egg to skillet and cook over medium to medium-low heat until the white of the egg is opaque.

4. For sunny-side-up, do not turn the egg, but keep cooking it until the yolk is as done as you like.

5. For over-easy, turn the egg over in the pan carefully as soon as the white is opaque, and continue cooking until the yolk is as done as you like.

6. Remove from pan with a spatula.

CREAMED EGGS

■■■

4 tablespoons butter
¼ cup flour
½ teaspoon salt
2 cups milk
1 teaspoon Worcestershire sauce
*8 hard-cooked eggs, peeled and
    sliced*

In a medium saucepan, melt butter and whisk in flour and salt. Cook and stir for 3–5 minutes, or until it barely turns golden. Add milk slowly, stirring constantly. Cook and stir until smooth and thickened. Add Worcestershire sauce, fold in eggs, and cook until eggs are hot. Serve over toast or biscuits.

MAKES 4 SERVINGS.

STUFFED EGGS

■■■

8 hard-cooked eggs, peeled
2 tablespoons mayonnaise
½ teaspoon dry mustard
1 tablespoon cider vinegar
1 tablespoon Durkee's dressing
¼ teaspoon salt
pepper
dash Tabasco sauce
1 tablespoon pickle relish
paprika

Slice eggs lengthwise. Carefully remove yolks and put in a mixing bowl. Reserve the best-looking 12 white halves. If desired, the remaining 4 white halves can be chopped and added to the stuffing mixture, or they can be used for another purpose. Mash egg yolks with a fork. Blend in mayonnaise, dry mustard, vinegar, Durkee's dressing, salt, pepper to taste, Tabasco sauce, and pickle relish. Mix until smooth. Mound egg yolk mixture into egg whites and sprinkle with paprika. Cover with plastic wrap and refrigerate.

MAKES 12 EGG HALVES.

SAUSAGE AND EGG CASSEROLE

■■■

OVEN: 350°

*10 slices bread, trimmed of crusts
    and cubed*
*1 pound bulk sausage, cooked,
    drained, and crumbled*
10 eggs, beaten
1 cup milk
1 cup half and half
1 teaspoon salt
¼ teaspoon pepper
1 teaspoon dry mustard
*2 cups (8 ounces) shredded
    Cheddar cheese, divided use*

Grease a 3-quart baking dish. Line with bread and sausage. Mix eggs, milk, half and half, salt, pepper, dry mustard, and 1 cup of the cheese. Pour over eggs and top with remaining 1 cup cheese. Cover and refrigerate overnight. Remove from refrigerator 45 minutes before baking. Bake for 45 minutes, or until cheese is bubbly.

MAKES 10–12 SERVINGS.

EGG FACTS

- There is no nutritional difference between brown eggs and white eggs. And they behave exactly the same way when they are cooked.

- Store eggs in the refrigerator with the small end of the eggs pointing down. It's best to store them in the original carton.

- To tell how fresh an egg is, place it in cold water. Fresh eggs sink to the bottom and lay horizontally. Older eggs tilt up at about a 45° angle. Even older eggs stand upright. Discard any eggs that float.

- The fresher an egg is, the heavier it will feel for its size. As an egg ages, it begins to lose moisture, so it feels lighter and sloshes around more in its shell.

- If you're not sure if an egg is raw or hard-cooked, spin it on the counter. If it's raw, it will just wobble around. If it's hard-cooked, it will spin without wobbling, since its center of gravity is stable.

- Eggs should be at room temperature before beating them, to provide the greatest volume. They should also be at room temperature when they are incorporated into butter and sugar.

- Although egg whites will yield more volume if you allow them to reach room temperature first, cold eggs are easier to separate. So separate eggs while they're cold, and then allow them to reach room temperature.

- If you don't have time to allow eggs to come to room temperature naturally, you can place eggs that are still in their shells in a bowl of hot tap water for a few minutes.

- Very fresh eggs are best for most uses. However, they're quite difficult to peel. If you plan to cook them in the shell, it's best to use eggs that are a week or so old, so they'll be easier to peel.

(continued)

EGGS BENEDICT
■ ■ ■

6 slices Canadian bacon, cooked
3 English muffins, split, buttered, and toasted
6 eggs, poached (pages 153–154)
salt
white pepper
³/4 cup Hollandaise Sauce (page 252)

Place a slice of Canadian bacon on each toasted English muffin half and top with a poached egg. Season with salt and white pepper and cover with Hollandaise Sauce.

MAKES 6 SERVINGS.

BRUNCH EGGS
■ ■ ■

OVEN: 350°

16 eggs, hard-cooked
6 tablespoons butter
6 tablespoons flour
2 cups milk
2 tablespoons Worcestershire sauce
2 tablespoons soy sauce
¹/2 teaspoon dry mustard
salt and pepper

Peel eggs and chop very fine or put through a potato ricer. Melt butter in a large saucepan over low heat and stir in flour. Cook and stir for 3–5 minutes. Add milk and cook until thickened. Add remaining ingredients, seasoning to taste with salt and pepper. Blend sauce with eggs and turn into a greased 3-quart baking

dish. Bake for 30 minutes, or until set and golden brown.

MAKES 10–12 SERVINGS.

EGGS AND ENGLISH MUFFINS
■ ■ ■

6 eggs
1 tablespoon milk
¹/2 teaspoon salt
¹/2 teaspoon pepper
1 tablespoon butter
2 English muffins, split and toasted
¹/2 cup (2 ounces) shredded cheese
8 slices bacon, cooked and crumbled

Beat eggs with milk, salt, and pepper. Melt butter in a skillet and pour in eggs. Cook and stir until lightly scrambled (see page 153). Remove from heat and divide among the muffin halves. Sprinkle with cheese and top with crumbled bacon.

MAKES 4 SERVINGS.

QUICHES
■ ■ ■

When making quiche, always bake the pie crust before filling it, to prevent a soggy crust. Fit pastry into the pie or quiche pan and lay a sheet of buttered aluminum foil on top, buttered side down. Fill with a layer of pie weights, uncooked rice, or dried beans, and bake at 425° for about 10 minutes. Take pastry out of the oven and remove foil and weights. Then fill with ingredients and proceed with recipe. It's sometimes risky to use a tart pan with a removable bottom to make a quiche, since the liquid ingredients might seep through the bottom, creating quite a mess!

BACON AND LEEK QUICHE
■ ■ ■

OVEN: 425°/400°

1 pie crust for 9" pie
6–8 slices bacon, cut into 1" pieces
1 bunch leeks (2–3 medium) or
   2 small sweet onions
¹/₄ cup snipped flat-leaf parsley
3 eggs
1 cup half and half
¹/₂ teaspoon salt
¹/₄ teaspoon pepper
¹/₈ teaspoon nutmeg

Fit crust into a 9" quiche pan or pie pan. (If using packaged pie crust, follow package directions.) Prick crust with a fork and bake at 425° for 10 minutes. Remove from oven. Reduce temperature to 400°. Sauté bacon until crisp. Remove from skillet, reserving bacon drippings in skillet, and drain bacon on paper towels. If using onions, cut in half lengthwise, peel, and slice thinly. If using leeks, cut to 6". Discard dark green upper part of leaves. Cut off stem end next to roots and discard. Slice leeks in half lengthwise and hold under cold running water, fanning out leaves to be sure all sand and dirt are removed. Pat dry and slice thinly crosswise. Sauté leeks

or onions in bacon drippings until soft. Remove from skillet with a slotted spoon and transfer to the baked pastry shell. Sprinkle bacon and parsley over leeks. In a small bowl, beat eggs with half and half and blend in salt, pepper, and nutmeg. Pour into pie pan or quiche pan and bake for 30 minutes, or until set in center. Let stand for 10 minutes before cutting.
MAKES 6 SERVINGS.

BRUNCH QUICHE
■ ■ ■

OVEN: 350°

1 pound sausage, cooked
1 bunch green onions
1 cup (4 ounces) shredded
   Cheddar cheese
1¹/₂ cups milk
1 cup Bisquick
³/₄ cup sour cream
3 eggs
salt and pepper

Spread sausage in a shallow 2-quart baking dish. Sprinkle on onions and cheese. Mix milk, Bisquick, sour cream, and eggs in a blender and pour over the top. Sprinkle with salt and pepper and bake for 35–45 minutes, or until set in center. Let stand for 10 minutes before cutting.
MAKES 4–6 SERVINGS.

EGG FACTS
(CONTINUED)

- To simplify peeling eggs cooked in the shell, pierce the shell with a push pin before cooking. Not only does it help to prevent the egg from cracking during cooking, but it lets in just enough water to help the shell separate more easily from the egg.

- It's easier to peel hard-cooked eggs if you start at the large end of the egg. Tap it on the edge of the sink, and peel it under cold running water.

- Commercially packaged eggs have a protective coating on them, so don't wash them before storing. It's best to store eggs in the original carton.

- Check the date on the egg carton. If there are two dates, the first one is the processing date, and the later one is the last date the eggs may be legally sold. Eggs usually keep under refrigeration for about 3–4 weeks after purchase.

- Give the eggs a visual once-over before buying them. If they appear to be free of cracks, "wiggle" each egg in its individual slot. If the shell has a crack that's not readily visible, any leaks will cause it to stick to the carton. Don't buy cracked raw eggs, because they may carry salmonella bacteria. If the egg sticks to the carton after you get it home, you can loosen it without breaking it by wetting the carton and gently turning the egg until it comes free.

- If you crack a raw egg while you're handling it, cook it right away, to destroy any harmful bacteria introduced by cracks. **Salmonella** is destroyed by cooking eggs to 140° for 3 minutes.

- To prevent plastic wrap from sticking to a plate of stuffed eggs, stand toothpicks up in several of the eggs around the outer rim of the plate, and lay the plastic wrap over the eggs like a tent.

HAM AND BROCCOLI QUICHE
■ ■ ■

OVEN: 350°

4 eggs
1 cup half and half
½ teaspoon dry mustard
⅛ teaspoon pepper
1 cup cubed cooked ham
1½ cups (6 ounces) shredded
Monterey Jack or Swiss cheese
1 (10-ounce) box frozen chopped broccoli, thawed and drained
1 prebaked pie crust for 9" pie
1 tablespoon flour

Beat eggs with half and half, dry mustard, and pepper. Set aside. Layer ham, cheese, and broccoli in the pie crust. Sprinkle with flour and pour egg mixture over it. Bake for 45–50 minutes, or until set in center. Let stand for 10 minutes before cutting.
MAKES 6 SERVINGS.

QUICHE LORRAINE
■ ■ ■

OVEN: 425°/325°

2 cups (8 ounces) shredded Monterey Jack or Swiss cheese
1 tablespoon flour
1 (3-ounce) can real bacon bits
1 prebaked pie crust for 9" pie
4 eggs
1 cup half and half
nutmeg

In a mixing bowl, toss cheese with flour and bacon bits. Spoon into the prebaked pie crust. Beat eggs with half and half and pour over cheese mixture. Sprinkle with nutmeg and bake at 425° for 20 minutes. Reduce heat to 325° and bake for another 30 minutes, or until set in center. Let stand for 10 minutes before cutting.
MAKES 6 SERVINGS.

SPINACH QUICHE
■ ■ ■

OVEN: 325°

1 pound fresh mushrooms, sliced
4 tablespoons butter
2 prebaked pie crusts for 9" pies
4 eggs
2 cups half and half
3 tablespoons flour
4 cups (1 pound) shredded Monterey Jack cheese
¼ teaspoon salt
⅛ teaspoon pepper
1 (10-ounce) package frozen chopped spinach, thawed and well drained

Sauté mushrooms in butter and arrange in the pie shells. Beat eggs with half and half and flour, and stir in remaining ingredients. Ladle over

the mushrooms, dividing the amount equally. Bake for 45–50 minutes, or until set in center. Let stand for 10 minutes before cutting.
MAKES 12 SERVINGS.

TEX-MEX QUICHE
■■■

OVEN: 375°

1 cup (4 ounces) shredded Monterey Jack cheese
¹/₄ cup finely chopped onion
8 slices bacon, crisply cooked and crumbled
1 (4-ounce) can mild green chiles, drained and diced
1 prebaked pie crust for 9" pie
4 eggs, lightly beaten
¹/₂ cup half and half
¹/₄ teaspoon salt
¹/₈ teaspoon pepper
1¹/₂ tablespoons butter, melted

Layer cheese, onion, bacon, and chiles in the baked pie crust. Mix remaining ingredients and pour into pie shell. Bake for 45 minutes, or until set in center. Let stand for 10 minutes before cutting.
MAKES 6 SERVINGS.

SOUFFLÉS
■■■

BASIC SOUFFLÉ
■■■

OVEN: 375°

Ingredients for 1¹/₂-Quart Soufflé:
2¹/₂ tablespoons butter
3 tablespoons flour
1 cup milk or broth
4 egg yolks
³/₄ cup flavor ingredients (cheese, vegetables, etc.)
5 egg whites
¹/₈ teaspoon cream of tartar

Ingredients for 2-Quart Soufflé:
3¹/₂ tablespoons butter
4¹/₂ tablespoons flour
1¹/₂ cups milk or broth
6 egg yolks
1¹/₄ cups flavor ingredients (cheese, vegetables, etc.)
7–8 egg whites
¹/₈ teaspoon cream of tartar

Method: Melt butter in heavy saucepan. When butter is hot and foaming, remove from heat and blend in flour. Return to heat and cook and stir over low heat for 3–5 minutes. It should have a faint nutty aroma. (This

(continued)

_____
_____
_____
_____
_____
_____
_____
_____
_____
_____
_____
_____
_____
_____
_____
_____
_____
_____
_____
_____
_____
_____
_____
_____
_____
_____
_____
_____
_____
_____
_____
_____
_____
_____
_____
_____

is very important. The flour must cook before adding the milk, or else the soufflé will have a pasty taste.) Add milk or broth slowly, stirring constantly, and continue to cook until sauce is smooth and thickened. Remove from heat and beat in egg yolks one at a time. Stir in flavor ingredients. Beat egg whites until foamy and add cream of tartar. Continue to beat until egg whites stand in soft peaks. Stir about 1 cup of the egg whites into the warm sauce. Pour sauce back over the rest of the egg whites and fold in gently. (Do not attempt to mix completely, or too much air will escape from the egg whites, causing a less puffy soufflé.) Carefully spoon soufflé mixture into a greased soufflé dish, and place on the center rack of a preheated oven. Bake for about 30 minutes, or until the soufflé is puffed and the top is lightly browned. Serve immediately.

THE 1½-QUART SOUFFLÉ MAKES 4–6 SERVINGS, AND THE 2-QUART SOUFFLÉ MAKES 6–8 SERVINGS.

MOCK CHEESE SOUFFLÉ
■ ■ ■

OVEN: 325°

3½ tablespoons butter, softened, divided use

6 slices white bread

2 cups (8 ounces) shredded Cheddar cheese

1 teaspoon salt

1 teaspoon dry mustard

dash garlic powder

dash Worcestershire sauce

4 eggs

2½ cups milk

Butter a 1½-quart soufflé dish with ½ tablespoon of the butter. Remove crusts from bread and spread with remaining 3 tablespoons butter. Cut bread into large cubes and spread in the soufflé dish. Combine cheese with salt, dry mustard, garlic powder, and Worcestershire sauce, and pour over bread. Beat together eggs and milk and pour over cheese. Cover and refrigerate for at least 8 hours, or overnight. Remove from refrigerator 1 hour before baking. Place soufflé dish in pan of hot water and bake for 1¼ hours.

MAKES 4–6 SERVINGS.

Pasta and Pasta Sauces

PASTA AND PASTA SAUCES

∎∎∎

- Use a large pot and at least a gallon of water per pound of pasta. To keep pasta from sticking, add 2 tablespoons oil and 1½ teaspoons salt per gallon of water. Never cook more than 2 pounds of pasta in one pot.

- Add pasta to the water slowly, so that water keeps boiling. Stir it as you add the pasta, to keep it from clumping together. Don't cover the pot.

- To add long pasta strands to the pot, grasp the end of a bunch and lower it into the water, pushing it against the side of the pot as it softens, until all the pasta is submerged.

- Fresh pasta cooks quite a bit faster than dried pasta.

- Pasta should be firm when you bite into it, neither flabby nor hard; hence, the expression *al dente*, literally, "to the tooth." When a strand is cut, if the center is hard and white, or if it tastes like flour, it is not done. Pasta made with semolina (durum) flour does not absorb as much water, so it is superior to pasta made with softer types of wheat flour.

- Slightly undercook any pasta that is to be used in a casserole.

- Drain pasta as soon as it's done. If it's to be served hot, don't rinse it, unless it needs to be cooled enough to handle. Otherwise, rinse in cold water. Toss a little butter, oil, or salad dressing with it, to keep it from sticking together while it's refrigerated.

- To keep pasta warm before serving, drain it and return it to the pot. Stir in some soft butter, cover the pot, and place it on the stove over very low heat, or set it in a 175° oven for no more than 30 minutes.

- To reheat pasta without sauce, cover with boiling water and let stand for 2 minutes. Drain immediately.

LOTS OF PASTABILITIES

∎∎∎

Years ago, before pasta became such a trendy item in American cuisine, relatively little grocery shelf space was allocated to it. There was only a modest assortment of noodles and a few packages of spaghetti. Kraft had a monopoly on macaroni and cheese. Chef Boy-R-Dee was the king of canned pasta, and all my neighborhood school friends were well acquainted with him. To find much more of a selection than that, you had to pack the family in the car and head for an Italian restaurant. Nowadays, the selection at supermarkets is staggering. Besides the more familiar varieties, now there are novelty shapes: tiny likenesses of everything from Elvis Presley's guitar to Elton John's glasses. Pasta is popping up everywhere!

Since the basic ingredients in different types of pasta don't vary much, all plain pasta tastes very similar. As long as you're careful not to overcook it, the real challenge in preparing pasta is choosing the best sauce and other ingredients to complement it.

Although tiny strands of capelli d'angelo are perfect with a delicate sauce of olive oil and pesto, who would think of serving hefty lasagne noodles with that same simple dressing? Little tubes like penne and mostaccioli beg for a sauce of just the right consistency to fill up some of their hollow places. And a dish of fat conchiglioni demands a nice, textured cheese stuffing, plus perhaps a tomato sauce as well. With so many choices of pasta, the possibilities of combinations are endless.

When you prepare it, though, you need to remember four things:

1. Don't overcook pasta. It should be cooked just until it gives a slight resistance when you bite into it, or *al dente*. That's Italian for *to the tooth*. The pasta won't feel the least bit brittle, and it won't taste like flour. If you were to cut a strand in half, you wouldn't see a characteristic white streak at the center, indicating uncooked flour. Experienced cooks can almost recognize whether or not pasta is cooked al dente just by looking at it.

2. Drain pasta thoroughly, so that water doesn't dilute the sauce.

3. Match pasta with the type of sauce that will enhance its own particular personality.

4. Serve pasta on heated plates, so that the pasta doesn't cool off before it can be enjoyed. If you start warming the serving dishes before you begin to cook the pasta, they'll be ready when the pasta is done. You can do this in any one of three ways:

(1) Set them on top of a heated toaster oven while the pasta cooks. This is very convenient if you're already heating bread in the toaster oven. (2) Place the plates in a warm oven for a few minutes. (3) For a last-minute heating, pour some of the boiling water that the pasta was cooked in into the dishes, and let it stand while you're draining the pasta. Then pour the water out and add the pasta.

ANGEL HAIR PASTA WITH HAM AND ARTICHOKES
■ ■ ■

2 tablespoons butter
1 pound cooked ham, diced
1 (14-ounce) can artichoke hearts, drained and quartered
1 (2¼-ounce) can sliced ripe olives
2 (26-ounce) jars tomato basil pasta sauce
2 (9-ounce) packages fresh angel hair pasta
grated Parmesan cheese

Melt butter in a large saucepan and add ham. Sauté ham for 3–5 minutes. Stir in artichoke hearts and continue cooking for 5 more minutes. Add olives and pasta sauce and simmer for about 20 minutes to blend flavors, stirring occasionally. Cook pasta according to package directions and drain. Arrange pasta on individual serving dishes and spoon sauce over it. Sprinkle with Parmesan cheese and serve immediately.

MAKES 6 SERVINGS.

FETTUCCINE ALFREDO
■ ■ ■

1 cup heavy cream, divided use
8 ounces fettuccine noodles
½ cup butter
¾ cup freshly grated Parmesan cheese
1 teaspoon white pepper
nutmeg

Warm cream in a microwave-safe glass measuring cup in the microwave and set aside. Cook fettuccine in boiling salted water for 7–8 minutes, or according to package directions. While it's cooking, melt butter in a medium saucepan and add ½ cup of the cream. Mix and simmer for 1 minute to thicken. Remove from heat. When fettuccine is cooked al dente, drain, add to butter mixture, and toss to coat noodles. Add remaining ½ cup cream, Parmesan cheese, and white pepper to taste. Transfer to a heated serving dish and sprinkle lightly with nutmeg.

MAKES 4 SERVINGS.

BAKED LASAGNE
•••

OVEN: 375°

2 pounds ground chuck

3½ tablespoons parsley flakes, divided use

1 tablespoon dried basil

3½ teaspoons salt, divided use

1 (29-ounce) can tomato sauce

1 (12-ounce) can tomato paste

1½ teaspoons Worcestershire sauce

1 tablespoon sugar

1 (10-ounce) package lasagne, uncooked

1 (24-ounce) carton cottage cheese

2 eggs, beaten

½ teaspoon pepper

¾ cup grated Parmesan cheese

1 pound sliced or shredded mozzarella cheese

Brown meat in a large, deep skillet, spooning off fat as it cooks. Add 1½ tablespoons of the parsley, the basil, 1½ teaspoons of the salt, the tomato sauce, tomato paste, Worcestershire sauce, and sugar. Simmer uncovered for 30–45 minutes, stirring occasionally. Meanwhile, slightly undercook lasagne, drain, and lay flat on waxed paper. Mix cottage cheese, remaining 2 tablespoons parsley, eggs, remaining 2 teaspoons salt, pepper, and Parmesan cheese. Place half of the noodles in a 13" x 9" x 2" baking dish. Spread half of the cottage cheese mixture on top. Spoon half of the meat sauce over the cottage cheese mixture. Layer half of the mozzarella cheese over the meat sauce. Repeat layers. Bake uncovered for 30 minutes. Then cover with a piece of foil and let stand at room temperature for 15 minutes before cutting.

MAKES 8 SERVINGS.

LINGUINE FLORENTINE
•••

10 tablespoons butter

10 tablespoons flour

6 cups chicken broth

2½ cups heavy cream

2 cups (8 ounces) shredded Gruyère or Muenster cheese

salt and pepper

nutmeg

Tabasco sauce

1 (10-ounce) box frozen chopped spinach, cooked and well drained

1½ pounds diced cooked chicken

1½ pounds linguine, cooked and drained

Melt butter in a heavy saucepan. Add flour and cook for 3–5 minutes, stirring as it turns golden. Add broth and stir until thickened. Add cream and cheese, stirring until cheese melts. Season to taste with salt, pepper, nutmeg, and Tabasco sauce. Add well-drained spinach and chicken, and stir to mix. Continue cooking until spinach and chicken are heated through. Serve over linguine.

MAKES 10–12 SERVINGS.

LINGUINE WITH HAM SAUCE

■ ■ ■

1 (26-ounce) jar pasta sauce
1 (8-ounce) can tomato sauce
8 ounces diced cooked ham
4 artichoke hearts, quartered
1 (2¼-ounce) can sliced ripe
    olives, drained
8 ounces uncooked linguine
grated Parmesan cheese

In a medium-size, heavy saucepan, stir together pasta sauce and tomato sauce. Stir in ham, artichoke hearts, and ripe olives. Bring to a simmer over medium-low heat. Allow to simmer uncovered while cooking linguine according to package directions. When linguine is cooked al dente, drain and transfer to serving dishes. Spoon sauce over linguine and top with Parmesan cheese.

MAKES 3–4 SERVINGS.

LINGUINE WITH SHRIMP

■ ■ ■

1 (14-ounce) package frozen
    peeled shrimp
2 tablespoons butter
¼ teaspoon garlic powder
1 (26-ounce) jar pasta sauce
12 ounces uncooked linguine
freshly grated Parmesan cheese

Thaw shrimp according to package directions and drain well. Melt butter in a large skillet and add garlic powder. Stir in shrimp and cook until shrimp is opaque. Stir in pasta sauce and reduce heat to simmer. Cook linguine according to package directions and drain. Spoon onto warm plates and top with shrimp in pasta sauce. Serve with freshly grated Parmesan cheese.

MAKES 4 SERVINGS.

MACARONI SALAD

■ ■ ■

8 ounces elbow macaroni, cooked
    and drained
1 cup diced celery
½ cup chopped green onions
⅓ cup minced sweet pepper
1 cup mayonnaise
2 tablespoons vinegar
2 teaspoons prepared mustard
1 teaspoon salt
⅛ teaspoon pepper

In a large bowl, toss cooked macaroni with celery, green onions, and sweet pepper. In a small bowl, whisk together remaining ingredients. Toss this dressing with the macaroni mixture and adjust seasoning if necessary. Cover and refrigerate for several hours. Remove salad from the refrigerator about 15 minutes before serving, to take the chill off. To expand this side dish into a main-dish salad, add cooked diced ham, chicken, or tuna and top with grated Parmesan cheese.

MAKES 6 SERVINGS.

N·O·T·E·S

VARIETIES OF PASTA RIBBONS AND STRANDS

One serving of uncooked spaghetti held in a bunch is about the diameter of a penny.

Bavettine: very narrow linguine

Bucatini: slightly larger in diameter than spaghetti, but hollow

Capelli d'Angelo: (angel's hair) the thinnest, most delicate pasta strands

Capellini: strands slightly thicker than angel's hair

Fedelini: very fine spaghetti

Fettucce: fettuccine about ½" wide

Fettuccelle: fettuccine about ⅛" wide

Fettuccine: ("little ribbons") about ⅜" wide

Fusilli: strands of spiraled spaghetti from 1½"–12" long

Gemelli: ("twins") pairs of strands of hollow spaghetti about 1½" long, twisted together

Lasagne: 1½"–2" wide; edges are flat or ruffled

Linguine: ("little tongues") very narrow ribbons; also called flat spaghetti

Mafalde: very wide noodles with ruffled edges, somewhat like narrow lasagne

Margherite: ("daisies") narrow, flat noodles with one ruffled side

Noodles: vary in width, with medium noodles measuring about ½"

Pappardelle: flat noodles with ruffled edges, about ⅝" wide

Perciatelli: hollow pasta about twice the diameter of spaghetti

Spaghetti: ("strings") the thickest of all the types of pasta strands

Spaghettini: very thin spaghetti, but thicker than vermicelli

Tagliarini: long, narrow noodles, usually less than ⅛" wide, and paper-thin

Tagliatelle: about ¼" wide (northern Italian name for fettuccine)

Trenete: narrow noodles similar to tagliatelle, but thicker and narrower

Vermicelli: ("little worms") thinner than spaghettini

MACARONI AND CHEESE
■ ■ ■

OVEN: 350°

8 ounces elbow macaroni (about 2 cups uncooked)

6 tablespoons butter

¼ cup flour

2¾ cups milk

2 teaspoons Worcestershire sauce

½ teaspoon salt

⅛ teaspoon pepper

½ teaspoon dry mustard

1½ cups (6 ounces) shredded Cheddar cheese

1 cup (4 ounces) shredded Monterey Jack cheese

¾ cup grated Parmesan cheese

Cook macaroni according to package directions. Drain and set aside. Melt butter in a large, heavy saucepan and stir in flour. Cook and stir until butter just begins to turn golden, for about 3–5 minutes. Slowly add milk, and continue to cook and stir until sauce begins to thicken. Stir in Worcestershire sauce, salt, pepper, and dry mustard, and fold in Cheddar and Monterey Jack cheeses. Fold mac-

aroni into sauce and mix gently until it is well coated with sauce. Pour into a well-greased 3–quart baking dish. Sprinkle Parmesan cheese on top. Bake for 30 minutes.

MAKES 6 SERVINGS.

MANICOTTI WITH CREAM SAUCE
■ ■ ■

OVEN: 350°

4 tablespoons butter

3 tablespoons flour

3 cups milk

1 teaspoon salt, divided use

white pepper

⅔ cup grated Parmesan cheese, divided use

2 eggs

1 (8-ounce) carton ricotta cheese

1 (8-ounce) carton cottage cheese

1 (10-ounce) package frozen chopped spinach, cooked and well drained

12 manicotti, slightly undercooked

In a medium saucepan, melt butter and stir in flour. Cook and stir for 3–5 minutes. Add milk slowly, and stir until slightly thickened. Stir in ½ teaspoon of the salt, white pepper to taste, and ⅓ cup of the Parmesan cheese. Set the cream sauce aside. In a medium bowl, beat the eggs slightly, and stir in ricotta cheese, cottage cheese, remaining ⅓ cup Parmesan cheese, remaining ½ teaspoon salt, and the well-drained spinach. Spread ½ cup of the cream sauce in a greased 13" x 9" x 2" baking dish. Stuff each manicotti shell with about ¼ cup of the spinach-cheese filling, and lay them side by side in the baking dish. Spoon about 3 tablespoons cream sauce over each filled manicotti shell. Bake for about 20 minutes, or until hot and bubbly.

MAKES 12 MANICOTTI, OR 4–6 SERVINGS.

> *"Eat plenty of garlic. This guarantees you twelve hours of sleep—alone— every night."*
>
> —Chris Chase

MARINARA SAUCE
■ ■ ■

1 teaspoon minced garlic
2 tablespoons olive oil
1 (8-ounce) can tomato sauce
1 (6-ounce) can tomato paste
1½ cups water
1 (15½-ounce) can diced tomatoes
1 teaspoon sugar
½ teaspoon salt
2 teaspoons oregano
1 teaspoon dried basil
1 tablespoon parsley flakes
⅛ teaspoon pepper
pinch nutmeg

Sauté garlic in olive oil in a large skillet for 1–2 minutes. Add remaining ingredients and mix well. Bring just to the boiling point. Reduce heat, cover, and simmer for 1 hour.

MAKES 4 CUPS SAUCE.

MOSTACCIOLI WITH CREAM SAUCE
■ ■ ■

OVEN: 350°

1 pound mostaccioli, uncooked
4 cups milk
1 cup heavy cream
8 tablespoons butter, divided use
1½ cups grated Parmesan cheese, divided use

Cook mostaccioli in boiling salted water for 5 minutes, or for only half as long as package directions specify. Drain and set aside. In a large, heavy 6-quart saucepan, combine milk with cream. Remove 1 cup of the milk mixture and set it aside. Warm remaining milk mixture over medium heat, and add the mostaccioli to the saucepan. Cook gently until mostaccioli is firm-tender, and almost all of the liquid is absorbed. Dot 4 tablespoons of the butter in a 3-quart rectangular baking dish, and sprinkle ½ cup of the cheese over the butter. Spread half of the cooked mostaccioli mixture over the cheese. Sprinkle another ½ cup of the cheese over the mostaccioli in the baking dish, and then add the remaining mostaccioli. Pour the reserved 1 cup of milk mixture over the mostaccioli and top with remaining ½ cup cheese. Dot remaining 4 tablespoons butter over the cheese and bake uncovered until bubbly, for about 30 minutes. Let stand for 10 minutes before serving.

MAKES 10–12 SERVINGS.

N·O·T·E·S

VARIETIES OF SPECIAL PASTA SHAPES

Acini di Pepe: tiny "peppercorns" often used in soups

Agnolotti: crescent-shaped stuffed pasta, like miniature turnovers

Cappelletti: ("little hats") ring-shaped stuffed pasta

Cavatelli: small shells with rippled edges

Conchiglie: ("seashells") resemble conch shells

Conchigliette: tiny conchiglie shells

Conchiglioni: large conchiglie shells

Farfalle: ("butterflies") about 1½" long with fluted edges

Farfalline: tiny farfalle

Gnocchi: ("dumplings") solid pasta, usually shaped like small balls

Lumache: ("snails") pasta shells larger than conchiglie, usually stuffed

Orecchiette: ("little ears") small, round, flat pasta

Orzo: (barley pasta) rice or oval-shaped

Pansotti: ("pot bellied") triangular-shaped, stuffed pasta pillows with pinked edges, similar to ravioli

Pastina: ("tiny dough") generic name for small pasta shapes, such as orzo

Quadrettini: small flat pasta squares

Radiatore: ("little radiators") small, shaped pasta with ruffled edges, about 1" long and ½" in diameter

Ravioli: 1"–2" filled squares, with straight or pinked edges

Raviolini: small ravioli

Riso: ("rice") tiny pasta similar to orzo, shaped like rice

Rotelle: ("little wheels") small, round pasta with spokes and a grooved rim

Rotini: little corkscrews about 1½" long

Semi de melone: ("melon seeds") small, flat pasta resembling melon seeds

Stelle: ("stars") small, flat, star shapes

Stellini: ("small stars") a miniature version of stelle

Tortellini: ("little twists") similar to cappelletti; stuffed pasta

Tortelloni: larger tortellini

Tripolini: small bow ties

MOSTACCIOLI WITH HAM AND TOMATO SAUCE

∎∎∎

6 tablespoons butter
¾ pound cooked ham, ground
1½ teaspoons minced garlic
1 (28-ounce) can diced tomatoes, undrained
1 (8-ounce) can tomato sauce
2 teaspoons dried basil
8 ounces mostaccioli, cooked and drained
1 cup grated Parmesan cheese

Melt butter in a large saucepan over low heat. Add ham and garlic, and cook for 10 minutes, stirring occasionally. Stir in tomatoes, tomato sauce, and basil. Bring to a boil. Reduce heat, cover, and simmer for 45 minutes, stirring occasionally. Toss with mostaccioli and sprinkle with Parmesan cheese.

MAKES 4–6 SERVINGS.

NOODLES AMANDINE

∎∎∎

1 pound uncooked egg noodles
¾ cup butter
6 ounces slivered almonds
¾ teaspoon salt
white pepper
⅓ cup poppy seeds
milk (optional)

Cook noodles according to package directions. Meanwhile, melt butter in a heavy skillet and add almonds. Cook until almonds are golden, and stir in salt, white pepper to taste, and poppy seeds. Drain noodles, return to saucepan, and toss with butter, almonds, and poppy seeds. Add a little milk if necessary, and heat through.

MAKES 6–8 SERVINGS.

NOODLE RING

∎∎∎

My mother often made this for company. She always served it with Creamed Ham and Asparagus (page 120) and garnished it with ripe olives and quartered tomatoes. I've always loved noodles, and this is delicious!

OVEN: 350°

8 ounces uncooked egg noodles
1 (4-ounce) jar Kraft Old English cheese
1 cup milk
2 tablespoons butter, melted
1 teaspoon salt
½ teaspoon paprika
4 eggs, separated

Cook noodles al dente. Meanwhile, melt cheese in milk in a large saucepan over medium-low heat. Stir in butter, salt, and paprika. Drain noodles, add to saucepan, and stir well. Let stand in saucepan. Beat egg yolks and whites separately. Stir beaten yolks into noodle mixture and fold in stiffly beaten whites. Butter a 1½-quart ring mold heavily and pour in noodle mixture. Set mold in a pan with ½" hot water in it. Bake for 45 minutes. When done, run a knife around the edges and turn noodle ring onto serving plate.

MAKES 4–6 SERVINGS.

NOODLES WITH CREAM CHEESE
■ ■ ■

OVEN: 325°

1 pound uncooked egg noodles
¾ cup butter, melted
1 (8-ounce) package cream cheese, cut into chunks
½ cup half and half
salt and pepper
⅓ cup minced parsley

Cook noodles according to package directions and drain. Return to saucepan and toss with butter and cream cheese. Stir in half and half and cook over low heat until cheese melts, stirring frequently. Season with salt and pepper, and add parsley. Pour into a greased 2-quart baking dish and cover with foil. Bake for about 15–20 minutes, or until hot and bubbly.
MAKES 8 SERVINGS.

NOODLES WITH MOZZARELLA
■ ■ ■

OVEN: 350°

1 pound uncooked egg noodles
4 tablespoons butter, melted
salt and pepper
1 cup grated Parmesan cheese
1 cup half and half
2 cups (8 ounces) shredded mozzarella cheese

Cook noodles according to package directions. Drain and return to pan. Stir in butter and season with salt and pepper to taste. Toss with Parmesan cheese. Spoon into a greased 2-quart baking dish and pour half and half over noodles. Top with mozzarella cheese and bake for about 30 minutes, or until hot and bubbly.
MAKES 6–8 SERVINGS.

NOODLES PARMESANO
■ ■ ■

1 pound uncooked egg noodles
⅔ cup half and half
½ cup butter, melted
¾ cup grated Parmesan cheese

Cook noodles al dente. Drain and return to pan. Toss with half and half, melted butter, and Parmesan cheese. Cook until hot. Serve immediately.
MAKES 6–8 SERVINGS.

NOODLES WITH SOUR CREAM
■ ■ ■

OVEN: 325°

8 ounces uncooked noodles
1 (8-ounce) carton sour cream
¾ cup grated Parmesan cheese, divided use

Cook noodles according to package directions and drain. Toss with sour cream and ¼ cup of the Parmesan cheese. Pour into a greased 1½-quart baking dish and sprinkle with remaining ½ cup Parmesan cheese. Bake for about 30 minutes, or until hot and bubbly.
MAKES 4 SERVINGS.

N·O·T·E·S

_____
_____
_____
_____
_____
_____
_____
_____
_____
_____
_____
_____
_____
_____
_____
_____
_____
_____
_____
_____
_____
_____
_____
_____
_____
_____
_____
_____
_____
_____
_____

COOKING DRIED PASTA

Check pasta after the length of time given below, and continue cooking until al dente.

Acini di Pepe	9 minutes
Agnolotti	7 minutes
Bucatini	12 minutes
Cannelloni	7 minutes
Capelli d'Angelo	2 minutes
Capellini	3 minutes
Cavatappi	8 minutes
Conchiglie	10 minutes
Conchiglioni	12 minutes
Ditali	8 minutes
Farfalle	9 minutes
Farfalline	6 minutes
Fettuccelle	9 minutes
Fettuccine	6 minutes
Fusilli	10 minutes
Gemelli	12 minutes
Gnocchi	10 minutes
Lasagne	8 minutes
Linguine	6 minutes
Macaroni	8 minutes
Manicotti	7 minutes
Mostaccioli	9 minutes
Noodles	5 minutes
Orzo	7 minutes
Pappardelle	6 minutes
Penne	9 minutes
Perciatelli	11 minutes
Pipe Rigate	7 minutes
Radiatore	5 minutes
Ravioli	7 minutes
Rigatoni	10 minutes
Riso	11 minutes
Rotelle	8 minutes
Rotini	8 minutes
Spaghetti	10 minutes
Spaghettini	8 minutes
Spirali	10 minutes
Stellini	7 minutes
Tagliatelle	6 minutes
Tortellini	10 minutes
Tortelloni	12 minutes
Vermicelli	4 minutes
Ziti	9 minutes

PASTA GOURMET
■■■

This recipe takes quite a bit of time to prepare, but it's absolutely delicious, and can be made ahead of time and frozen. It's perfect for a brunch or dinner buffet. Serve with Romaine Salad with Mandarin Oranges (page 247) and some crusty bread.

OVEN: 350°

1 cup plus 1 tablespoon butter, divided use
4 pounds boneless chicken breasts
2/3 cup Madeira or sherry
1/2 cup plus 1 tablespoon flour
6 cups chicken broth
2 1/4 cups heavy cream
2 cups (8 ounces) shredded Gruyère cheese
salt and white pepper
nutmeg
10 dashes Tabasco sauce
1 1/4 pounds uncooked small or medium shell pasta
12 ounces sliced country ham or baked ham
15 Greek olives, slivered
grated Parmesan cheese
paprika

Using 2 heavy skillets, place 1/4 cup of the butter in each skillet and melt over medium heat. Add 2 pounds of the chicken to each skillet and cook for 10 minutes. Reduce heat, turn chicken, and cook for 5-10 more minutes. Add 1/3 cup of the Madeira or sherry to each skillet and cook for 5 more minutes. Turn off heat and remove chicken from the skillets, reserving pan juices.

In a very large, heavy saucepan melt remaining 9 tablespoons butter over medium-low heat and blend in flour. Cook the roux for 3-5 minutes, or until it just begins to turn golden. Slowly blend in chicken broth and continue cooking and stirring until it thickens. Stir in heavy cream, reserved pan juices, and Gruyère cheese, and blend thoroughly. Season with salt and white pepper to taste, nutmeg, and Tabasco sauce.

Cook shell pasta al dente. Drain and arrange in 2 greased 2-quart baking dishes. Lightly fry ham slices and cut into julienne. Cut chicken into julienne and mix with ham. Toss slivered Greek olives with ham and chicken and stir into the sauce. Mix well and pour the sauce over pasta, dividing equally. Sprinkle with Parmesan cheese and paprika to taste. Bake for 35-45 minutes, or until lightly browned and bubbly.

MAKES 16 SERVINGS.

PASTA CARBONARA
■■■

1/2 pound bacon, cut into 1" pieces
12 ounces fettuccine, linguine, spaghetti, or penne, uncooked
1/4 cup heavy cream
4 tablespoons butter
1 cup egg substitute
1 cup grated Parmesan cheese
1/4 cup chopped parsley
freshly ground black pepper

Sauté bacon until crisp and drain on paper towels. Cook pasta in a large saucepan or kettle. While pasta cooks, heat cream and butter over low heat until butter is melted. When pasta is cooked al dente, drain and put back into the saucepan. Add egg substitute and toss well. Add cream and butter and toss well. Add cooked bacon, Parmesan cheese, parsley, and pepper, and toss once more. Serve immediately.

MAKES 4 SERVINGS.

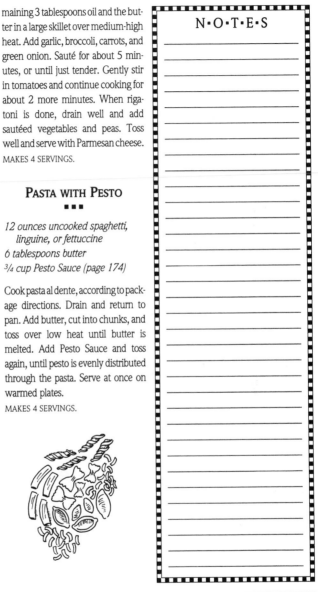

PASTA PRIMAVERA
■ ■ ■

4 quarts water
1½ teaspoons salt
5 tablespoons oil, divided use
12 ounces uncooked rigatoni
1 tablespoon butter
1 teaspoon minced garlic
1 cup broccoli florets
½ cup shredded carrots
1 green onion, trimmed and chopped
2 large tomatoes, seeded and chopped (or substitute 4–6 Roma tomatoes)
½ cup frozen green peas, thawed
grated Parmesan cheese

Pour water into a large heavy pot (at least 8-quart size) and add salt and 2 tablespoons of the oil. Bring to a boil. Add rigatoni and boil uncovered for 10 minutes, or until rigatoni is al dente. While rigatoni is cooking, heat re-

maining 3 tablespoons oil and the butter in a large skillet over medium-high heat. Add garlic, broccoli, carrots, and green onion. Sauté for about 5 minutes, or until just tender. Gently stir in tomatoes and continue cooking for about 2 more minutes. When rigatoni is done, drain well and add sautéed vegetables and peas. Toss well and serve with Parmesan cheese.

MAKES 4 SERVINGS.

PASTA WITH PESTO
■ ■ ■

12 ounces uncooked spaghetti, linguine, or fettuccine
6 tablespoons butter
¾ cup Pesto Sauce (page 174)

Cook pasta al dente, according to package directions. Drain and return to pan. Add butter, cut into chunks, and toss over low heat until butter is melted. Add Pesto Sauce and toss again, until pesto is evenly distributed through the pasta. Serve at once on warmed plates.

MAKES 4 SERVINGS.

STUFFED PASTA SHELLS

■ ■ ■

OVEN: 350°

1 (12-ounce) box jumbo pasta
   shells (36 shells), uncooked
3 eggs
2 tablespoons parsley flakes
1 tablespoon dried basil
1 teaspoon salt
½ teaspoon pepper
1 cup (4 ounces) shredded
   Monterey Jack cheese
1 cup (4 ounces) shredded
   mozzarella cheese
½ cup grated Parmesan cheese, plus
   additional cheese for topping
1 (16-ounce) carton ricotta cheese
1 (16-ounce) carton cottage cheese
1 (26-ounce) jar marinara sauce or
   pasta sauce

Cook pasta shells according to package directions, but undercook
slightly. Meanwhile, beat eggs and
add parsley flakes, basil, salt, and pepper. Stir in Monterey Jack, mozzarella, Parmesan, ricotta, and cottage
cheeses. When pasta shells are cooked
al dente, drain and rinse in cold water.
Spray 2 (2-quart) rectangular baking
dishes with non-stick spray. Spoon
about ½ cup of the marinara sauce
or pasta sauce into each baking dish
and spread to cover the bottom. Stuff
each shell with cheese mixture (full,
but not overstuffed). Lay shells open-
side-up in baking dishes (18 shells per
dish). Spoon a little marinara sauce or
spaghetti sauce over the center of each
shell. (It may not be necessary to use
the entire jar of sauce.) Cover with
foil and bake for 35 minutes. Remove
foil, sprinkle with Parmesan cheese,
and bake for 10 more minutes.
MAKES 8–12 SERVINGS.

PASTA SALAD WITH TUNA

■ ■ ■

3 cups cooked rotini or other
   shaped pasta
2 cups fresh broccoli florets
6 Roma tomatoes, cut into wedges
1 (2¼-ounce) can sliced ripe
   olives, drained
1 (6½-ounce) can albacore tuna,
   drained and flaked
¼ cup vinegar
¼ cup lemon juice
⅓ cup olive oil
1 tablespoon Dijon mustard
½ teaspoon pepper

Toss pasta with broccoli, tomato
wedges, olives, and tuna. In a jar,
combine vinegar, lemon juice, olive
oil, mustard, and pepper. Shake vigorously to blend. Pour over pasta
mixture and toss well. Cover and refrigerate for at least 2 hours before
serving.
MAKES 4 SERVINGS.

SPAGHETTI WITH MEAT SAUCE

■ ■ ■

This is a favorite of my husband, Jack. In addition to being a great spaghetti sauce, you can also use the sauce to make Baked Lasagne (page 164). When I make it, I often double the quantity and freeze it in plastic zip bags, with just enough in a bag for one dinner. With this in the freezer, a great dinner is so easy to get on the table in very little time! The recipe is foolproof, unless you drop the pot when you carry it from the stove to the counter.

1½ pounds ground chuck
½ pound bulk sausage or Italian sausage
2 (14½-ounce) cans tomato sauce
1 (12-ounce) can tomato paste
1½ tablespoons parsley flakes
1 tablespoon dried basil
½ teaspoon salt
⅛ teaspoon garlic powder
½ tablespoon Worcestershire sauce
1 tablespoon sugar
1 (10½-ounce) can beef broth
1 pound uncooked thin spaghetti

Brown meats and spoon off excess fat. Stir in tomato sauce, tomato paste, parsley flakes, basil, salt, garlic powder, Worcestershire sauce, sugar, and beef broth. Simmer uncovered for about 45 minutes. (Flavor improves with freezing.) Serve over thin spaghetti, cooked al dente.

MAKES 2 QUARTS MEAT SAUCE, OR 6–8 SERVINGS.

"Everything you see, I owe to spaghetti."

—Sophia Loren

PASTA SALAD WITH CHEESE

■ ■ ■

1 pound fresh Roma or cherry tomatoes
½ cup olive oil
½ teaspoon dried basil or 1½ teaspoons chopped fresh basil
1 (2¼-ounce) can sliced ripe olives, drained
¼ cup grated Parmesan cheese
salt and pepper
1 (8-ounce) package small pasta shells
2 cups (8 ounces) shredded mozzarella cheese

Wash tomatoes, cut them in half, and scoop out seeds. Cut tomatoes into narrow strips and toss with olive oil. Add basil, ripe olives, and Parmesan cheese. Season to taste with salt and pepper. Toss, cover, and refrigerate for at least 2 hours. Before serving, cook pasta al dente. Drain pasta and toss with mozzarella cheese. Add the tomato mixture and toss again. Serve immediately.

MAKES 4 SERVINGS.

N·O·T·E·S

PESTO SAUCE

···

¾ cup olive oil
2 cups fresh basil leaves, stems
    removed
½ cup fresh parsley
½ cup freshly grated Parmesan
    cheese
1 teaspoon minced garlic
2 tablespoons pine nuts (see Note)
½ teaspoon salt
pepper
1–2 teaspoons hot water (as
    needed)

Place all ingredients except hot water in a food processor and process with metal blade for about 45 seconds. If desired, thin with hot water. Cover and refrigerate, or freeze in ice cube trays. After freezing, pop out cubes and store in the freezer in a plastic bag.
MAKES 1½ CUPS SAUCE.

Note: If desired, use **Toasted Pine Nuts:** Place pine nuts in a shallow pan and bake for 3–5 minutes at 350°. To prepare **Spinach Pesto,** substitute spinach leaves for the basil leaves, and add 1 teaspoon dried basil.

**"Woe to the cook
whose sauce
has no sting."**

—Geoffrey Chaucer

BAKED ZITI

···

OVEN: 350°

2 pounds ground chuck
1 pound bulk sausage
1 (26-ounce) jar pasta sauce
½ teaspoon dried basil
¼ teaspoon oregano
¼ teaspoon dried rosemary
¼ teaspoon garlic powder
1 pound uncooked ziti
3 cups (12 ounces) shredded
    mozzarella cheese
¾ cup grated Parmesan cheese

Brown ground chuck and sausage in a large skillet over medium heat, crumbling it as it cooks. Drain grease from skillet and stir in pasta sauce, basil, oregano, rosemary, and garlic powder. Reduce heat to low and let it simmer. Meanwhile, slightly undercook ziti and drain. Spoon half of ziti into a greased 3-quart baking dish and pour half of meat sauce over it. Sprinkle half of mozzarella cheese on top, and then half of Parmesan cheese. Repeat layers of ziti, meat sauce, and cheeses. Bake for 30–45 minutes, or until bubbly.
MAKES 8 SERVINGS.

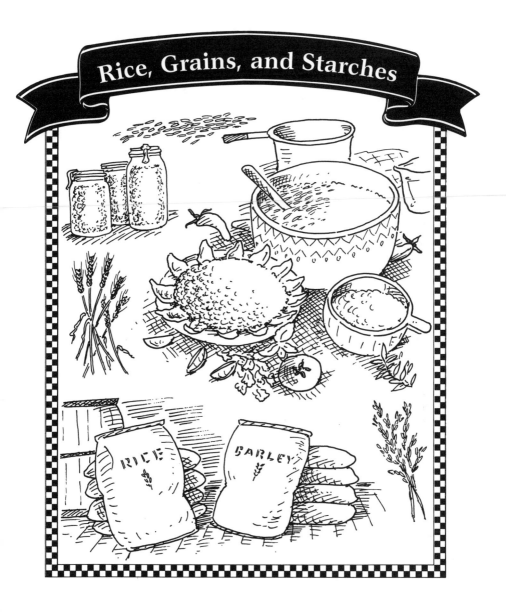

Rice, Grains, and Starches

RICE, GRAINS, AND STARCHES
■■■

▪▪▪▪▪▪▪▪▪▪▪▪▪▪▪▪▪

PREPARING RICE

Rice is one of the most versatile foods on the planet. It can be served hot or cold, all by itself, or mixed with various kinds of ingredients, from meats to seafoods to vegetables. It can be a foundation for creamy foods, such as Beef Stroganoff (page 109), or it can be mounded on top of a hearty bowl of gumbo or bean soup. It can even show up on the dessert table! Since it's so easy to prepare, you don't need to resort to the instant variety, which lacks character. Always cook a little extra, since it's so convenient to have on hand. Here are some tips for preparing it:

▪ Don't stir rice while it's cooking. It causes the outer covering of the grains to break, and it results in sticky, starchy rice. Wait until it's done, and then fluff it up with a fork.

▪ Rice doesn't need to be washed before cooking. That practice goes back to the days when rice sat around in big open bags at the general store, and was often dirty. However if you prefer to rinse it, you can do so with only a slight loss in nutritional value.

▪ Long-grain rice produces fluffy, individual grains. It's good for casseroles, rice pilaf, and salads.

▪ Aromatic rice (including basmati, popcorn, and Texmati) is superb as a side dish, since its flavor and fragrance are so pleasant.

▪ Short-grain rice is stickier than long-grain rice. It's good for stir-fry, risotto, and rice pudding, or whenever you want a creamy or sticky texture.

▪ Wild rice has a unique texture and flavor. Because it's somewhat nutty and crunchy, it's delicious in salads, and it mixes well with long-grain rice. It also makes a good ingredient for stuffings.

RICE
■■■

RICE IS NICE!
■■■

There's a world of good eating in the grain kingdom, and it's as close as the nearest supermarket. Years ago, just about the only kind of rice you could find in the supermarket was the familiar orange and white box of Uncle Ben's converted rice. These days, we're becoming much more sophisticated in our love affair with rice. We have short grain, medium grain, and long grain; we have white rice, brown rice, and yellow rice; and we have many ethnic varieties as well. We can buy flavored rice mixes in so many varieties that we could have a different kind every day for a month. What other food is so versatile? It appears on our menu in every course from soup to dessert. And besides rice, there are many other grains as well: bulgur, couscous (which is actually a type of pasta, and not really a grain, although it's treated as one), kasha, millet, and quinoa. With so many different ethnic influences on our cuisine, we're learning much from other cultures about their particular favorites, and now it seems as though we're incorporating them into our menus as if they were our own.

HOW TO MOLD RICE IN A RING
■■■

Mix about 6 cups of cooked rice with 4 tablespoons of melted butter and pack firmly into a well-greased 1½-quart ring mold. (Use more or less rice, depending on the size of the ring mold.) Place mold in a roasting pan with 1" of hot water and heat at 350° for about 15 minutes. Invert the mold onto a serving plate, the same way you'd turn out a molded salad. The ring can be filled with vegetables or creamed chicken or seafood.

HOW TO COOK RICE
■■■

Rice can be cooked in several different ways. Cooking it on the stove in water or broth is the most frequently used method. It can also be sautéed before the liquid is added, in which case it is called *pilaf.* And it can be cooked covered in the oven for about half an hour, whether or not it has been sautéed first. The oven method is much more convenient if you're cooking a large amount, and is simple to do if you're already using the oven to cook something else.

Arborio Rice (Short Grain):
Measure 1½ cups water and ½ teaspoon salt into a saucepan. Bring to a boil and stir in 1 cup rice. Reduce heat, cover, and simmer for 10 minutes.
MAKES 2 CUPS.

Aromatic Rice (Basmati, Texmati):
Measure 1¾ cups water, ½ teaspoon salt, 1 tablespoon butter, and 1 cup rice into a saucepan. Bring to a boil. Reduce heat, cover, and simmer for 15–20 minutes.
MAKES 3 CUPS.

Brown Rice (Instant):
Measure 1¼ cups water, ½ teaspoon salt, and 1 tablespoon butter into a saucepan. Bring to a boil and stir in 1 cup rice. Reduce heat, cover, and simmer for 10 minutes.
MAKES 2 CUPS.

Brown Rice (Regular, Long Grain):
Measure 2¾ cups water, ½ teaspoon salt, 1 tablespoon butter, and 1 cup rice into saucepan. Bring to a boil. Reduce heat, cover, and simmer for 45–50 minutes.
MAKES 4 CUPS.

Jasmine Rice:
Measure 1¾ cups water, ½ teaspoon salt, 1 tablespoon butter, and 1 cup rice into a saucepan. Bring to a boil. Reduce heat, cover, and simmer for 15–20 minutes.
MAKES 3 CUPS.

Popcorn Rice:
Measure 2 cups water, ½ teaspoon salt, 1 tablespoon butter, and 1 cup rice into a saucepan. Bring to a boil. Reduce heat, cover, and simmer for 15–20 minutes.
MAKES 3 CUPS.

White Rice (Converted):
Measure 2½ cups water, ½ teaspoon salt, and 1 tablespoon butter into a saucepan. Bring to a boil. Stir in 1 cup rice. Reduce heat, cover, and simmer for 20–25 minutes.
MAKES 3–4 CUPS.

White Rice (Instant):
Measure 1 cup water, ½ teaspoon salt, and 1 tablespoon butter into a saucepan. Bring to a boil and stir in 1 cup rice. Cover and remove from heat. Let stand covered for 5 minutes.
MAKES 2 CUPS.

White Rice (Regular, Long Grain):
Measure 2 cups water, ½ teaspoon salt, 1 tablespoon butter, and 1 cup rice into a saucepan. Bring to a boil. Reduce heat, cover, and simmer for 15 minutes.
MAKES 3 CUPS.

Wild Rice:
Measure 2½ cups water, ½ teaspoon salt, 1 tablespoon butter, and 1 cup rice into a saucepan. Bring to a boil. Reduce heat, cover, and simmer for 40–50 minutes.
MAKES 3 CUPS.

N·O·T·E·S

RICE PILAF
■ ■ ■

4 tablespoons butter
1 small onion, chopped
(about ½ cup)
1½ cups uncooked rice
3 bouillon cubes (chicken or beef)
3 cups boiling water
½ teaspoon salt

Melt butter in a medium saucepan over medium-low heat. Add onion and cook for 2–3 minutes, or until onion is soft. Stir in rice and sauté for about 3 more minutes, or until rice turns light golden. Meanwhile, dissolve bouillon cubes in boiling water. Stir into rice mixture and add salt. Bring back to a boil, reduce heat, cover, and cook for about 20 minutes without stirring. Remove cover, stir, and leave on low heat for 3–5 more minutes, or until rice has absorbed all the liquid. Fluff up with a fork.

MAKES 6 SERVINGS.

Variation #1: Substitute ½ cup vermicelli, broken into small pieces, for ½ cup of the rice, and cook as directed above.

Variation #2: Substitute 8 ounces of fresh sliced mushrooms for the onion, and sauté in the butter until soft.

Variation #3: Add 2 tablespoons fresh chopped parsley or basil to the rice after it is cooked.

Variation #4: Stir in 1 tablespoon curry powder while sautéing onions. Then stir in ¼ cup raisins and ¼ cup walnuts during last 5 minutes of cooking.

RICE PILAF WITH ALMONDS
■ ■ ■

OVEN: 350°

1½ cups long-grain rice
6 tablespoons butter
1 (4-ounce) package slivered almonds
salt and pepper
2 (10½-ounce) cans beef broth
1 cup water

Brown rice in a skillet with butter. Stir in almonds, and add salt and pepper to taste. Place in a greased 1½-quart baking dish and pour in broth and water. Stir and cover. Bake for 45 minutes.

MAKES 4–6 SERVINGS.

RICE WITH BROCCOLI AND CHEESE
■ ■ ■

OVEN: 350°

1 medium onion, chopped
3 tablespoons butter
1 cup milk
1 (10¾-ounce) can cream of chicken soup
1 (8-ounce) jar Cheez Whiz
1 (10-ounce) package frozen chopped broccoli, thawed
2 cups cooked rice
salt and pepper

Sauté onion in butter for 3–5 minutes. Stir in milk, soup, and Cheez Whiz. Simmer until cheese is melted, and stir in well-drained broccoli. Fold in rice, and season to taste with salt and pepper. Transfer to a greased 2-quart baking dish and bake for 35–40 minutes.

MAKES 6 SERVINGS.

FRIED RICE
■ ■ ■

For each serving, scramble an egg, cut it into small bits, and set aside. Heat a little oil in the skillet and add a cup of cold rice and several tablespoons of leftover vegetables, meat, poultry, or seafood. Stir-fry for 3–5 minutes, add cooked egg to heat it up, and serve.

GREEN RICE
■ ■ ■

OVEN: 350°

1 (10-ounce) package frozen
   chopped broccoli
½ cup chopped onion
2 tablespoons butter
2 cups cooked rice
1 (10¾-ounce) can cream of
   mushroom soup
½ cup crushed Ritz crackers (about
   12 crackers)

Thaw and crumble broccoli, but do not cook. Sauté onion in butter until soft. Stir in rice, soup, and broccoli. Spoon into a greased 1½-quart baking dish and top with crushed crackers. Bake for 30 minutes.
MAKES 6 SERVINGS.

BROWN RICE SALAD
■ ■ ■

1 (5-ounce) box brown and wild
   rice mix
1 (14-ounce) can artichoke hearts,
   drained and quartered
1½ tablespoons Italian dressing
½ cup mayonnaise
1 (8-ounce) can sliced water
   chestnuts, drained
½ cup chopped fresh parsley
1 (2¼-ounce) can sliced ripe
   olives, drained
cayenne
salt and pepper
lemon juice

Cook rice according to package directions, using only 1⅓ cups water. Set aside. In a large bowl, toss artichoke hearts with Italian dressing and mayonnaise. Mix in rice, water chestnuts, parsley, and olives. Season to taste with cayenne, salt, pepper, and lemon juice. Refrigerate for several hours.
MAKES 6–8 SERVINGS.

Note: You can add tuna, shrimp, or diced chicken to this salad.

How to Cook Kasha

Measure 2 cups water, chicken broth, or a combination of the two, and ½ teaspoon salt into a saucepan and bring to a boil. Slowly stir in 1 cup kasha and 1 tablespoon olive oil, and reduce heat to low. Cover and simmer for 12–15 minutes. Remove from heat and let stand covered for 5–10 minutes. Fluff up with a fork before serving. Makes 3 cups.

How to Cook Cracked Wheat

Measure 2¼ cups water and ½ teaspoon salt into a saucepan. Stir in 1 cup cracked wheat and bring to a boil. Reduce heat to low. Cover and simmer for 40 minutes. Makes 3 cups.

How to Cook Bulgur

Coarse-Grain Bulgur:
Measure 6 cups water and 1 teaspoon salt into a saucepan and bring to a boil. Slowly stir in 1 cup bulgur and reduce heat to low. Simmer uncovered for 12–14 minutes. Remove from heat and let stand for 5 minutes. Pour bulgur into a sieve and drain for 5–10 minutes. Fluff up with a fork before serving. Makes 3 cups.

Fine- or Medium-Grain Bulgur:
Place 1 cup bulgur in a medium bowl. Pour 3 cups boiling water over bulgur and stir in ½ teaspoon salt. Let stand for 40–50 minutes. Then pour bulgur into a colander with small holes, or a sieve, and drain for 5–10 minutes. Fluff up with a fork before serving. Makes 3 cups.

Rice with Mushrooms

■■■

OVEN: 350°

1 (10½-ounce) can beef broth
⅔ cup water
½ teaspoon salt
2 tablespoons butter
1 cup uncooked long-grain rice
1 (4-ounce) can sliced mushrooms, drained

Pour beef broth, water, salt, and butter into a medium saucepan and heat to boiling. Put uncooked rice and drained mushrooms into a 1½-quart baking dish and pour in beef broth mixture. Stir, cover, and bake for about 45 minutes, or until rice has absorbed liquid.

MAKES 4 SERVINGS.

Rice Monterey

■■■

OVEN: 350°

3⅓ cups water
1½ teaspoons salt
1½ tablespoons butter
1½ cups long grain white rice
1½ cups sour cream
1 (4-ounce) can chopped mild green chiles, drained
1½ cups (6 ounces) shredded Monterey Jack cheese, divided use
paprika

Bring water to a boil in a medium saucepan. Add salt, butter, and rice. Cover, reduce heat, and cook for 20 minutes, or until the water is ab-

sorbed. Grease a 2-quart baking dish and spoon in a third of the cooked rice. Spread on a third of the sour cream, a third of the green chiles, and ½ cup of the cheese. Repeat layers, finishing with the cheese. Sprinkle with paprika and bake for 30 minutes.

MAKES 8 SERVINGS.

Mexican Rice

■■■

OVEN: 350°

4 tablespoons butter
1 bunch green onions, chopped
3 cups cooked white rice
1 (8-ounce) carton sour cream
¾ teaspoon salt
½ teaspoon pepper
1 (4-ounce) can chopped green chiles, undrained
1 cup (4 ounces) shredded sharp Cheddar or Monterey Jack cheese

Melt butter in a skillet and add green onions. Sauté for 2–3 minutes and remove from heat. In a medium bowl, toss onions with rice, sour cream, salt, pepper, green chiles, and cheese. Spread in a greased 2-quart baking dish, and bake for 30 minutes, or until piping hot.

MAKES 6–8 SERVINGS.

ORANGE PECAN RICE
...

OVEN: 350°

1 1/4 cups water
3/4 cup orange juice
1 teaspoon salt
2 tablespoons butter
3/4 cup uncooked long-grain rice
1/2 cup pecan pieces
1 tablespoon grated orange peel

Pour water, orange juice, salt, and butter into a medium saucepan and heat to boiling. Mix uncooked rice with pecan pieces and orange peel in a 1 1/2-quart baking dish and pour in orange juice mixture. Stir, cover, and bake for about 45 minutes, or until rice has absorbed liquid.

MAKES 4 SERVINGS.

RICE WITH PEAS
...

1 (10-ounce) package frozen green peas
1/4 cup chopped onion
6 tablespoons butter, divided use
2 tablespoons chopped parsley
1 cup uncooked white long grain rice
1 (14 1/2-ounce) can chicken broth, plus water to make 2 cups liquid
1 teaspoon salt

Cook peas according to package directions, until just barely done. Drain and set aside. Sauté onion in 4 tablespoons of the butter for about 5 minutes. Add parsley and rice and sauté for 5 more minutes, stirring occasionally. Add chicken broth, water, and salt, and bring to a boil. Cover, reduce heat, and simmer for 15 more minutes, or until rice has absorbed the liquid. Add peas and remaining 2 tablespoons butter, and heat until butter is melted and peas are hot.

MAKES 6 SERVINGS.

RICE SOUFFLÉ
...

OVEN: 350°

2 cups milk
2 tablespoons butter
1/2 cup (2 ounces) shredded Cheddar cheese
1 1/2 cups cooked rice
1/2 teaspoon salt
2 eggs
paprika

Heat milk in a large saucepan and add butter and cheese. Cook and stir until cheese is melted. Add rice and salt. Beat eggs and fold into rice mixture. Mix thoroughly and pour into a greased 1 1/2-quart baking dish. Sprinkle with paprika and bake for 30 minutes.

MAKES 6 SERVINGS.

N·O·T·E·S

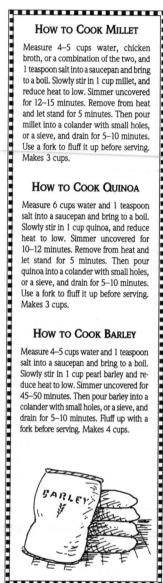

How to Cook Millet

Measure 4–5 cups water, chicken broth, or a combination of the two, and 1 teaspoon salt into a saucepan and bring to a boil. Slowly stir in 1 cup millet, and reduce heat to low. Simmer uncovered for 12–15 minutes. Remove from heat and let stand for 5 minutes. Then pour millet into a colander with small holes, or a sieve, and drain for 5–10 minutes. Use a fork to fluff it up before serving. Makes 3 cups.

How to Cook Quinoa

Measure 6 cups water and 1 teaspoon salt into a saucepan and bring to a boil. Slowly stir in 1 cup quinoa, and reduce heat to low. Simmer uncovered for 10–12 minutes. Remove from heat and let stand for 5 minutes. Then pour quinoa into a colander with small holes, or a sieve, and drain for 5–10 minutes. Use a fork to fluff it up before serving. Makes 3 cups.

How to Cook Barley

Measure 4–5 cups water and 1 teaspoon salt into a saucepan and bring to a boil. Slowly stir in 1 cup pearl barley and reduce heat to low. Simmer uncovered for 45–50 minutes. Then pour barley into a colander with small holes, or a sieve, and drain for 5–10 minutes. Fluff up with a fork before serving. Makes 4 cups.

OTHER GRAINS, CEREALS, AND STARCHES

■■■

Couscous

■■■

1 1/2 cups water, chicken broth, or a combination of the two
2 1/2 tablespoons butter
1/4 teaspoon salt
1 tablespoon chicken stock base
1 cup couscous
1/2 cup raisins (optional)

Bring water or broth, butter, salt, and chicken stock base to a boil. Stir in couscous. Cover, reduce heat, and simmer for 1 minute. Stir again and add raisins if desired. Cover and remove from heat. Let stand for about 5 minutes, or until all liquid is absorbed. Fluff up with a fork and serve.

MAKES 4–6 SERVINGS.

Spoon Bread

■■■

OVEN: 400°

2 cups half and half
1 cup milk
1 1/4 cups cornmeal
3 eggs
1 teaspoon salt
1 3/4 teaspoons baking powder
4 tablespoons butter, melted, plus additional butter for serving

Bring half and half and milk to a boil in a large, heavy saucepan. Very slowly, add cornmeal while stirring constantly with a wire whisk. Keep stirring until mixture is thick. Remove from heat. Break eggs into a large mixing bowl and beat with an electric mixer for 2 minutes on high speed. Add salt and baking powder, and beat in cornmeal mixture, a spoonful at a time. Pour butter into a 1 1/2-quart baking dish, turn to coat, and then pour butter back into the cornmeal mixture. Beat on medium speed for 10 more minutes, scraping sides of bowl frequently. Pour into baking dish and bake for 25 minutes. Serve hot with additional butter.

MAKES 6 SERVINGS.

Polenta

■■■

3 tablespoons butter, plus melted butter for serving
1/2 cup finely chopped onions
3 1/2 cups milk, chicken broth, or water
1 teaspoon salt
1 cup yellow cornmeal
3 tablespoons grated Parmesan cheese

Heat butter in a large saucepan and add onions. Cook and stir over medium heat for about 5 minutes, or until onions are soft. Add milk, broth, or water, and salt, and bring just to a boil. Add cornmeal, stirring constantly as mixture thickens. Continue to cook and stir over low heat for about 20–25 more minutes, or until very thick. Stir in Parmesan cheese and serve with melted butter.

MAKES 4 SERVINGS.

YORKSHIRE PUDDING

■■■

OVEN: 425°

1 cup flour
1/2 teaspoon salt
1 cup milk
2 eggs
1/2 cup hot roast beef drippings

Beat together flour, salt, milk, and eggs with a whisk or rotary beater until smooth. Heat a 9" x 9" x 2" pan in oven. Add drippings to pan and pour batter over drippings. Bake for 35 minutes. Cut into squares to serve.

MAKES 6–8 SERVINGS.

TABBOULEH

■■■

1 heaping cup bulgur
3 cups boiling water
1/2 teaspoon salt
1/2 cup lemon juice
2/3 cup olive oil, divided use
1 1/2 cups chopped fresh
  flat-leaf parsley
1 bunch green onions
1/4 cup dried mint (or 1 cup fresh)
4 tomatoes, seeded
1 cucumber, peeled and seeded
dash garlic powder
1 teaspoon pepper

Rinse bulgur in a colander and transfer to a large bowl. Add water and salt. Let stand for 45 minutes. Spoon back into colander to drain for 5–10 minutes, and fluff up with a fork. Put it back into bowl and add lemon juice and 1/3 cup of the olive oil. Chop pars-ley with onions, mint, tomatoes, and cucumber. Toss in a small bowl with remaining 1/3 cup olive oil. Stir into bulgur. Season with garlic powder, pepper, and more salt if desired. Cover and let stand for 30 more minutes. Serve immediately or refrigerate. Let come to room temperature before serving.

MAKES 6–8 SERVINGS.

CHEESE GRITS

■■■

Traditional breakfasts in the South always include this dish.

OVEN: 350°

6 cups water
1 1/2 teaspoons salt
6 tablespoons butter
1 1/2 cups quick grits (not "instant")
1 (6-ounce) roll jalapeño cheese
3 cups (12 ounces) shredded
  Cheddar cheese, divided use
1/4 cup half and half
1/4 teaspoon pepper
1 tablespoon Worcestershire sauce
Tabasco sauce

Bring water, salt, and butter to a boil. Add grits. Cook for 5 minutes, stirring occasionally. Cut jalapeño cheese into chunks and add with 2 cups of the shredded cheese. Stir until melted. Stir in half and half, pepper, Worcestershire, and Tabasco sauce to taste. Pour into a greased 2-quart baking dish and top with remaining 1 cup shredded cheese. Bake for 45 minutes to an hour.

MAKES 8–12 SERVINGS.

CORNBREAD DRESSING
■■■

OVEN: 375°

4 cups crumbled cornbread or
   1 (8-ounce) package cornbread
   stuffing mix
½ cup chopped celery
½ cup chopped onion
2 eggs, beaten
1 cup turkey or chicken broth
1 cup turkey drippings (or ¾ cup
   additional broth plus ¼ cup
   melted butter)
1 tablespoon sugar

Mix cornbread with celery and onion in a large bowl. Stir in eggs, broth, drippings, and sugar. Pour into a greased 2-quart baking dish and bake for 20 minutes, until it is set but not dry.

MAKES 6 SERVINGS.

SAUSAGE DRESSING
■■■

OVEN: 350°

2 (8-ounce) packages herb-
   seasoned stuffing mix
1 (14½-ounce) can chicken broth,
   plus water to make 2 cups liquid
1 cup butter, melted
1 pound hot bulk sausage, cooked,
   crumbled, and drained
½ pound sliced mushrooms,
   sautéed

Pour stuffing mix into a large bowl. Add chicken broth, water, and melted butter. Stir in cooked sausage and mushrooms. Stuff inside turkey, or turn into a greased 3-quart baking dish and bake for 30 minutes.

MAKES 10–12 SERVINGS.

OYSTER DRESSING
■■■

OVEN: 350°

3 pints raw oysters with their liquid
2 tablespoons oil
1 loaf stale French bread
1 bunch green onions
1 medium onion
3 cloves garlic
4 tablespoons butter, divided use
2 tablespoons chopped fresh
   parsley (or 2 teaspoons dried)
2 eggs, beaten

Drain oysters into a colander placed over a large mixing bowl, saving liquid in the bowl. Heat oil in a large skillet and add oysters. Cook over low heat until edges begin to curl. Pour oysters back into the colander and drain again, saving liquid. Transfer oysters to a cutting board. Tear bread into chunks and add to the oyster liquid, tossing bread so that all of it is exposed to the liquid. When bread is soft, squeeze it and place it on the cutting board with the oysters. Chop bread and oysters into small pieces and transfer to the mixing bowl. Chop all onions and garlic. Melt 1 tablespoon of the butter in the skillet the oysters were cooked in, and sauté onions and garlic until soft. Toss with oysters and bread. Stir in parsley and eggs. Melt remaining 3 tablespoons butter in the same skillet and add oyster mixture. Cook over low heat for 10 minutes, stirring constantly. Transfer to a greased 3-quart baking dish. Cover and bake for 30 minutes.

MAKES 8–10 SERVINGS.

Vegetables

VEGETABLES
•••

SELECTING
FRESH VEGETABLES
•••

For detailed information about selecting and storing fresh produce, refer to the Food Facts section (pages 319–342).

For top quality and value, always choose fresh vegetables when they're at their seasonal peak. And for the best possible flavor during the warmer months, buy them from a farmer's market or roadside stand whenever they're available. (I probably should have a bumper sticker that reads, "Warning: I Brake for Truck Stands!") As far as I'm concerned, it's hard to beat a sack of vine-ripe Bradley tomatoes and Silver Queen corn from a roadside stand on a sweltering day in July. Thankfully, though there are many varieties of produce that are available year round, with little variation in quality from one season to the next. Some are imported after the domestic growing season. Others are held in cold storage during the off-season, and brought to market as needed. Commercially frozen produce, picked at the peak of freshness and flash-frozen, is an excellent choice whenever a particular favorite is not available fresh. And what would we do without the convenience of tomatoes and other canned vegetables in the pantry!

PREPARING
FRESH VEGETABLES
•••

All fresh vegetables need to be cleaned before they're prepared, although this cleaning can take a variety of forms. Whereas sturdy potatoes require a good scrubbing with a stiff brush, more delicate mushrooms need just a gentle wiping with a damp cloth. Many vegetables, such as spinach and leeks, are loaded with dirt and grit, and need to be rinsed thoroughly in several changes of cold water. After cleaning, many vegetables require a little trimming, peeling, or scraping as well. Getting to the edible part of some vegetables, such as artichokes, is even more complicated, since they need considerable grooming before they're cooked. If a special technique is required to prepare a particular vegetable, it will be indicated in each recipe as needed.

COOKING
FRESH VEGETABLES
•••

Many fresh vegetables are often enjoyed raw. Others can be served either raw or cooked. Some, such as asparagus, are best when they're cooked until they're tender but still slightly crisp. And finally, there are vegetables such as artichokes, that are almost inedible unless they're cooked thoroughly. Although cooking can destroy some of the nutrients in many vegetables, it can actually enhance the nutritional value of others, such as carrots. Since there's such a wide variety of cooking techniques, each recipe in this chapter offers specific recommendations for ways to produce the most delicious results. Many vegetables can be cooked using a variety of methods, such as steaming, baking, boiling, sautéing, or grilling. Experiment to see which methods you prefer for your favorite vegetables.

ARTICHOKES
■ ■ ■

How to Prepare: Trim off the top and stem, and pull off the outer leaves at the base of the stem. Then snip off the thorny leaf tips and rub the cut edges with lemon to prevent darkening.

How to Remove the Choke: The small, fuzzy choke at the center, and the cluster of thin, purple-tipped sharp leaves, can be removed either before or after cooking, although this is usually done after cooking. To do so, spread the outer leaves gently, pull out the tiny thistle-like leaves, and scrape out the fuzzy fibers with a spoon.

How to Tell When Done: Artichokes are done when the stem end can be pierced easily with a knife, and a center leaf pulls out easily.

How to Eat: Pull off the leaves one by one, dipping the base of each leaf in sauce. Bite down on the base of the leaf, pulling it through your teeth to scrape off the tender pulp. Then discard what's left of the leaf, laying it to one side of your plate. Work your way around the artichoke until you've finished all the leaves. If the choke has not already been removed, scrape it out with a spoon and set it to one side with the discarded leaves. Then cut the bottom into bite-size pieces with a knife and fork. Spear them with a fork, dip them in sauce, and enjoy.

STEAMED ARTICHOKES
■ ■ ■

Prepare artichokes as described at left. Pour 1" of water into a saucepan just large enough to hold the artichokes upright snugly, and add ¼ teaspoon salt for each artichoke. Add 1 teaspoon lemon juice and about 1 tablespoon oil for each artichoke. Stand artichokes upright in the saucepan and bring the water to a boil. Reduce heat, cover, and cook for 30–40 minutes. Artichokes are done when the stem end can be pierced easily with a knife, and a center leaf pulls out easily. Carefully remove them from the pan with tongs, and turn them upside down in a colander to drain well in the sink. Remove the chokes (see left). Serve hot with lemon butter or Hollandaise Sauce (page 252), or chill and serve with Mayonnaise (page 253) or Basic Vinaigrette (page 256).

N·O·T·E·S

ARTICHOKE HEARTS WITH MUSHROOMS

● ● ●

OVEN: 350°

2 (14-ounce) cans artichoke hearts
6 tablespoons butter
1 pound fresh mushrooms, sliced
1 (8-ounce) carton sour cream
1 teaspoon Worcestershire sauce
1 tablespoon snipped fresh parsley
dried bread crumbs

Drain artichoke hearts and squeeze them gently over the sink to remove excess liquid. Quarter and place in a greased 1½-quart baking dish. Melt butter in a skillet and sauté mushrooms for 6–8 minutes. Remove mushrooms from skillet with a slotted spoon, reserving butter, and scatter over the artichoke hearts in the baking dish. Add sour cream to the butter in the skillet and blend with a whisk. Stir in Worcestershire sauce and parsley. Pour over artichoke hearts and mushrooms and sprinkle with dried bread crumbs. Bake for about 30 minutes, or until bubbly.

MAKES 6 SERVINGS.

STUFFED ARTICHOKE HEARTS

● ● ●

OVEN: 350°

3 tablespoons butter
¼ cup minced onion
1 (10-ounce) package frozen chopped spinach, cooked and drained
¼ cup sour cream
½ teaspoon salt
¼ teaspoon pepper
dash cayenne
½ cup grated Parmesan cheese, divided use
2 (14-ounce) cans artichoke hearts, drained thoroughly

Melt butter in a skillet and sauté onion for 5 minutes, or until soft. Stir in spinach, sour cream, salt, pepper, cayenne, and 2 tablespoons of the Parmesan cheese. Gently squeeze artichoke hearts upside down over the sink to remove any excess liquid. Spread leaves of each artichoke heart and stuff with spinach mixture. Set artichoke hearts upright in a well-greased shallow baking dish, fitting them in snugly so that they won't topple over. Sprinkle remaining Parmesan cheese over the top and bake for 20 minutes.

MAKES 6–8 SERVINGS.

ASPARAGUS

■ ■ ■

How to Prepare: Snap off the tough part of the stem. Peel remaining stem end only if quite thick.

How to Boil: Pour about ½" of water into a large skillet, add 1 teaspoon salt, and bring water to a boil. Slide asparagus into water. Cook uncovered for 3–5 minutes, timing from when water comes to a boil the second time.

How to Steam: Pour about 1" of water into a large saucepan and set a steamer basket in place. Lay asparagus spears in the basket and bring water to a boil. Cover and steam for about 3–5 minutes, depending on the thickness of the asparagus spears.

How to Sauté: Slice asparagus spears diagonally into pieces about 1½" long. For each pound of asparagus, melt about 2 tablespoons of butter in a skillet. Add asparagus and cook for about 3–5 minutes.

How to Tell When Done: Asparagus should be cooked just until it's crisp-tender: not too soft, and not too crunchy.

How to Eat: In most instances, it's acceptable to use your fingers to pick up firm, whole asparagus spears that are cooked without a drippy sauce. However, this isn't a good idea at a formal dinner. If in doubt, remember that it's always considered proper to eat asparagus with a fork, cutting pieces with a knife if necessary.

OVEN-STEAMED ASPARAGUS

■ ■ ■

I learned to fix fresh asparagus this way many years ago, and I've never gone back to the traditional way of steaming it.

OVEN: 325°

1½ pounds fresh asparagus
salt
3 tablespoons butter

Wash asparagus and snap off tough stem ends. Line a cookie sheet with foil, arrange the asparagus, and sprinkle with salt. Dot with butter and cover with another piece of foil. Roll up the edges of the foil, sealing like an envelope. Bake for 10–15 minutes, or until crisp-tender. Pencil-thin asparagus might cook in less time. Do not overcook. Open the foil, transfer the asparagus to a serving dish, and pour the butter sauce over the top of it.

MAKES 4 SERVINGS.

CHILLED ASPARAGUS WITH LEMON MAYONNAISE

■ ■ ■

2 (10½-ounce) cans asparagus
spears or 1½ pounds fresh
asparagus, trimmed and cooked
Lemon Mayonnaise (page 253)
dash dill weed

Chill asparagus spears. Spoon Lemon Mayonnaise over asparagus and sprinkle with dill weed.

MAKES 4 SERVINGS.

N·O·T·E·S

ASPARAGUS WITH HORSERADISH
■■■

*1½ pounds fresh asparagus or
2 (10-ounce) boxes frozen
asparagus spears
1 cup sour cream
2 tablespoons horseradish
2 teaspoons sugar
dash seasoned salt
¾ cup crushed herb-seasoned
stuffing mix
1 tablespoon butter, melted*

Steam fresh asparagus for 3–5 minutes, until crisp-tender, or prepare according to recipe for Oven-Steamed Asparagus (page 189). If using frozen asparagus, cook according to package directions. Transfer to a serving dish and keep warm. Mix sour cream with horseradish, sugar, and salt. Warm sauce over low heat and pour over asparagus. Toss crushed stuffing mix with melted butter and sprinkle it on top.
MAKES 4 SERVINGS.

> *"The most remarkable thing about my mother is that for thirty years she served the family nothing but leftovers. The original meal has never been found."*
>
> —Calvin Trillin

STIR-FRIED ASPARAGUS
■■■

*1½ pounds fresh asparagus
1½ tablespoons oil
1½ tablespoons butter
1 teaspoon minced garlic
salt and pepper*

Prepare asparagus for cooking by washing and snapping off tough portion of stems. Cut asparagus spears on the diagonal into pieces about 1½" long. Measure oil and butter into a skillet and heat until butter is completely melted. Add asparagus and stir-fry for about 2 minutes. Add garlic, sprinkle with salt and pepper, and continue cooking for another minute or two, or until asparagus is crisp-tender.
MAKES 4 SERVINGS.

ASPARAGUS VINAIGRETTE
■■■

*1½ pounds fresh asparagus
3 tablespoons salad oil
¼ cup chopped fresh parsley
2 tablespoons chopped chives
3 tablespoons vinegar
½ teaspoon salt
⅛ teaspoon pepper
1 tablespoon sugar*

Steam asparagus for 3–5 minutes, until crisp-tender, or prepare according to recipe for Oven-Steamed Asparagus (page 189). Blend remaining ingredients together and pour over asparagus. Chill for several hours.
MAKES 4 SERVINGS.

BEANS

■ ■ ■

How to Prepare Fresh Beans with Inedible Pods: Hold the bean in one hand and pop open the pod by pressing the seam near the stem end with your thumb. Run your thumbnail down the seam, pulling it apart, and pop out the beans. If necessary, remove the seed pod covering as well.

How to Prepare Dried Beans: Dried beans should be soaked and boiled before cooking. The preferred method is the slow method. However, the fast method is a fair substitute. Lima beans need to be removed from the pods, and then washed and drained.

Slow Soaking Method: Rinse and sort beans. Place in a heavy saucepan and add enough water to cover by at least 2". Let soak for 8–24 hours. Drain and rinse beans. Return to heavy saucepan and add enough water to cover by at least 2". Bring to a boil and boil uncovered for 2 minutes. Then drain beans and proceed with desired recipe.

Fast Soaking Method: Rinse and sort beans. Place in a heavy saucepan and add enough water to cover by at least 2". Bring to a boil and boil uncovered for 2 minutes. Remove from heat, cover, and let stand for 1 hour. Then drain beans and proceed with desired recipe.

How to Tell When Done: All types of beans should be cooked until completely tender.

CUBAN-STYLE BLACK BEANS

■ ■ ■

My father worked with an airline, which provided us with marvelous travel opportunities. Before the days of Fidel Castro, we visited Havana regularly. The station manager there frequently invited us to his home for a traditional Cuban dinner, which always included black beans and rice.

1 pound dried black beans
2 quarts water
1/4 cup salad oil
1 large onion, chopped
1 clove garlic, minced
1/4 cup cider vinegar
1/4 cup sherry
1/2 teaspoon cumin
1/2 teaspoon oregano
1/2 teaspoon salt
3–4 dashes Tabasco sauce
1/2 pound bacon, uncooked and diced

Wash, sort, and soak beans (see instructions at left). Drain and place in a large saucepan and add water. Heat oil in a skillet and sauté onion and garlic until soft. Add to beans. Simmer for about 3 hours, covered, or until beans are soft. Add vinegar, sherry, cumin, oregano, salt, Tabasco sauce, and bacon. Cover and cook for another hour. To thicken beans, mash some with the back of a large spoon against the side of the saucepan and stir to blend.

MAKES 4–6 SERVINGS.

N·O·T·E·S

QUICK BLACK BEANS AND RICE
■ ■ ■

When you're in the mood for black beans and rice and don't have time to make the slow version, this is a good substitute. It's easy to prepare at a moment's notice, if you keep a well-stocked pantry and refrigerator.

2 (15-ounce) cans black beans, undrained
1 large onion, chopped
3 tablespoons olive oil
⅛ teaspoon garlic powder
2 tablespoons cider vinegar
2 tablespoons lemon juice
2 tablespoons sherry
½ teaspoon cumin
½ teaspoon oregano
½ teaspoon salt
3–4 dashes Tabasco sauce
½ pound cooked bacon, ham, or Kielbasa sausage, diced
4 cups hot cooked rice
4 green onions, chopped

In a heavy saucepan, heat beans over medium-low heat. In a small skillet, sauté onion in oil until soft, and add to beans. Add garlic powder, vinegar, lemon juice, sherry, cumin, oregano, salt, Tabasco sauce, and diced meat. Cook until piping hot. To thicken beans, mash some with the back of a large spoon against the side of the saucepan and then stir. Ladle beans into serving bowls and add a generous spoonful of rice. Top with chopped green onions.

MAKES 4–6 SERVINGS.

BLACK BEANS AND YELLOW RICE
■ ■ ■

1 (5-ounce) package Mahatma yellow rice
1 (15-ounce) can black beans
1 (10-ounce) package frozen white corn, thawed
1 bunch green onions (white parts), chopped
2 tablespoons Italian dressing
2 tablespoons cider vinegar
2 tablespoons lemon juice
1 tablespoon sherry
½ teaspoon cumin
½ teaspoon oregano
½ teaspoon garlic salt
¼ teaspoon salt
3–4 Roma tomatoes, diced

Cook rice according to package directions. While it cooks, drain beans, rinse well in a colander, and put them in a mixing bowl. Add corn and green onions and toss. Mix together Italian dressing, vinegar, lemon juice, sherry, cumin, oregano, garlic salt, and salt, and toss with bean mixture. When rice is done, toss it with the bean mixture. Fold in tomatoes and serve warm or chilled.

MAKES 5–6 SERVINGS.

MARINATED BLACK BEANS
■ ■ ■

1/3 cup red wine vinegar
1/3 cup olive oil
3/4 teaspoon salt
1/2 teaspoon pepper
2 cloves garlic, crushed
3 (15-ounce) cans black beans,
    drained and rinsed
1 (10-ounce) package frozen white
    corn, thawed
1 sweet red pepper, seeded and
    chopped
1 red onion, chopped
lettuce leaves
2 large ripe tomatoes, seeded and
    chopped
fresh snipped parsley

Whisk together vinegar, olive oil, salt, pepper, and garlic. Let stand for 30 minutes and whisk again. In a large bowl, combine black beans with corn, red pepper, and onion. Add dressing and mix gently to coat beans. Cover and refrigerate overnight. Serve on lettuce leaves and top with chopped tomatoes and parsley.

MAKES 10–12 SERVINGS.

BAKED BEANS
■ ■ ■

OVEN: 300°

1 pound great Northern or navy
    beans
1 teaspoon salt
1/2 cup diced salt pork
1/2 cup chopped onion
1/2 cup brown sugar
2 tablespoons ketchup
1 teaspoon prepared mustard
2 cups hot water
4 tablespoons butter
6 slices bacon

Wash and sort beans. Soak using either method (see beginning of Beans section, page 191). Drain and place beans in a large pot and cover with 2" of boiling water. Add salt and cover. Cook for 2½ hours over low heat. Drain again. Spoon beans into a greased 2½-quart baking dish. Add salt pork and onion. Mix brown sugar, ketchup, mustard, and 2 cups hot water. Pour over beans and dot with butter. Lay bacon slices on top and cover with foil. Bake for 2–3 hours.

MAKES 10–12 SERVINGS.

N·O·T·E·S

N·O·T·E·S

_____
_____
_____
_____
_____
_____
_____
_____
_____
_____
_____
_____
_____
_____
_____
_____
_____
_____
_____
_____
_____
_____
_____
_____
_____
_____
_____
_____
_____

EASY BAKED BEANS
■■■

OVEN: 350°

6 slices bacon
1/2 cup brown sugar
1/2 cup barbecue sauce
1 teaspoon Dijon mustard
1 teaspoon Worcestershire sauce
1/4 cup lemon juice
2 (20 1/4-ounce) cans Big John's
   Beans 'n Fixins

Cook bacon until crisp; crumble and set aside. Open the small cans of topping that are packaged with the beans. Spoon into a large bowl. Add brown sugar, barbecue sauce, mustard, Worcestershire sauce, and lemon juice, and mix well. Stir in beans and pour into a 2-quart baking dish. Top with crumbled bacon and cook uncovered for 1 1/2 hours.
MAKES 6–8 SERVINGS.

LIMA BEANS WITH DILL
■■■

3 (10-ounce) packages frozen
   lima beans
4 tablespoons butter, melted
2 teaspoons dill weed
1/2 teaspoon salt

Cook lima beans according to package directions. Drain well and return to saucepan. Add butter, dill weed, and salt. Toss together and serve.
MAKES 8 SERVINGS.

LIMA BEAN CASSEROLE
■■■

OVEN: 375°

2 (10-ounce) packages frozen
   lima beans
8 slices bacon, diced
1 medium onion, chopped
1 (8-ounce) carton sour cream
1/2 teaspoon salt
1 teaspoon sugar
2 teaspoons horseradish
2 teaspoons parsley flakes
1/8 teaspoon garlic powder
3/4 cup crushed herb-seasoned
   stuffing mix
2 tablespoons butter, melted
dash paprika

Cook lima beans according to package directions and set aside. Cook bacon and drain, reserving 2 tablespoons drippings. Sauté onion in reserved bacon drippings and stir in sour cream, salt, sugar, horseradish, parsley flakes, and garlic powder. Add beans and bacon and pour into a greased 1 1/2-quart baking dish. Combine stuffing mix with butter and scatter on top. Sprinkle with paprika, and bake for 30–45 minutes, or until piping hot.
MAKES 6 SERVINGS.

RED BEANS AND RICE

∎∎∎

In Louisiana, this is a traditional dish for Monday night supper.

1 pound dried red beans
2 quarts water
1 pound smoked link sausage, cut into 1" pieces
½ pound ham, cubed
1 large onion, chopped
1 clove garlic, crushed
1 (16-ounce) can tomatoes, undrained
1 teaspoon salt
pepper to taste
Tabasco sauce to taste
8 cups hot cooked rice

Wash, sort, and soak beans (see beginning of Beans section, page 191). Drain and place beans in a heavy saucepan and add water. Add sausage, ham, onion, and garlic, and bring beans to a boil. Reduce heat, cover, and simmer for 1½–2 hours, or until beans are almost tender. Add tomatoes, salt, pepper, and Tabasco sauce. Continue cooking, uncovered, until beans are tender. (If necessary, add a little more water to keep beans from sticking.) Serve over hot rice.

MAKES 8 SERVINGS.

WHITE BEANS

∎∎∎

1 pound great Northern or navy beans
2 quarts water
1 medium onion, chopped
1 clove garlic, minced
¼ cup vegetable oil
1 meaty ham bone (should have at least ½ pound meat)
1 teaspoon salt
½ teaspoon pepper
Tabasco sauce

Wash and sort beans. Soak using either method (see beginning of Beans section, page 191). Drain and place beans in a heavy saucepan and add water. Sauté onion and garlic in oil until soft, and add to beans. Add meaty ham bone, and turn heat to low. Cover and cook for about 3 hours, or until beans are soft. Season with salt, pepper, and Tabasco sauce to taste, and cook for another 30 minutes. Serve with cornbread and sliced onions.

MAKES 6 SERVINGS.

BEETS

■ ■ ■

How to Prepare: Trim off all but 1″ of top and most of root. Take care not to puncture skin, or beets will bleed.

How to Boil: Cook beets in boiling, salted water to cover. They'll cook faster if the saucepan is covered. Small beets should be done in 30–45 minutes, but large ones can take up to twice that long. After cooking, drain and plunge into cold water. Peel them when they're cool enough to handle.

How to Tell When Done: Beets are done when tender.

BAKED BEETS

■ ■ ■

OVEN: 400°

2 pounds small fresh beets
4 tablespoons butter
1 tablespoon cider vinegar
2 tablespoons grated orange peel
1 teaspoon caraway seeds
salt and pepper
1 teaspoon snipped chives

Prepare beets for cooking (see above), and arrange in a shallow baking pan. Add just enough water to cover the bottom of the pan. Cover and bake for 1 hour, or until beets are tender enough to be pierced easily with a sharp knife. Remove from oven and allow to stand until they are cool enough to handle. Peel and slice thinly or cut into quarters. Melt butter in a large skillet and add beets.

Toss gently to cover with butter, and add vinegar, orange peel, and caraway seeds. Season to taste with salt and pepper. Cook and stir gently for about 5 more minutes, or until thoroughly heated. Arrange in serving dish and sprinkle with chives.
MAKES 6 SERVINGS.

BEETS WITH HORSERADISH

■ ■ ■

2 (16-ounce) cans whole baby beets
1/4 cup horseradish
1/4 cup sugar
1/4 cup cider vinegar
salt and pepper

Drain beets, reserving juice. Heat juice with horseradish, sugar, and vinegar. Season with salt and pepper and pour over beets. Refrigerate until chilled.
MAKES 6 SERVINGS.

BEETS WITH SOUR CREAM

■ ■ ■

1/2 cup sour cream
2 tablespoons cider vinegar
1 1/2 teaspoons sugar
1 teaspoon salt
1 teaspoon onion juice
dash cayenne
2 (16-ounce) cans sliced beets, drained

Mix together all ingredients except beets. Fold in beets gently. Chill.
MAKES 6 SERVINGS.

HARVARD BEETS
...

½ cup sugar
2 teaspoons cornstarch
½ cup cider vinegar
1 (16-ounce) can sliced beets,
  drained
2 tablespoons butter

Mix sugar, cornstarch, and vinegar together in a saucepan, and boil for 5 minutes. Add beets and stir in butter, cooking over low heat until butter melts. Turn off burner, cover, and let stand for 30 minutes. Turn heat back on low, and warm before serving.
MAKES 3–4 SERVINGS.

BEET SALAD
...

2 (16-ounce) cans whole beets
2 teaspoons sugar
⅓ cup mayonnaise
dash onion salt
dash pepper
1 tablespoon vinegar
1 tablespoon lemon juice
lettuce leaves

Drain beets and shred. Spoon shredded beets into a colander and gently press out all the excess juice. Transfer to a mixing bowl and add sugar, mayonnaise, onion salt, pepper, vinegar, and lemon juice. Mix well. Add a little more mayonnaise if desired. Spoon onto lettuce leaves.
MAKES 4–6 SERVINGS.

BROCCOLI
...

If you dislike broccoli, it's probably because you've only had it when it's been overcooked. The sad result is a limp, strong-smelling disaster. When broccoli is cooked properly—just until it's crisp-tender—you just may change the way you feel about it!

How to Prepare: First, trim off the woody base of the stalk. Next, cut the broccoli into spears, or cut off the florets with a sharp knife. Finally, peel away the tough skin from the lower part of the stalk with a vegetable peeler or sharp paring knife. The stalk can then be cut in half lengthwise and sliced thinly, or cut into julienne.

How to Steam: Pour about 1″ of water into a large saucepan and set a steamer basket in place. Add broccoli and bring water to a boil. Cover, reduce heat, and steam for about 5–6 minutes. If you intend to cook the broccoli further, such as in a stir-fry recipe, steam it only for 3–4 minutes.

How to Tell When Done: Broccoli is done when stems are crisp-tender.

"I'm the President of the United States, and if I don't want to eat my broccoli, no one can make me!"

—George Bush

N·O·T·E·S

BROCCOLI WITH CREAM CHEESE

■■■

OVEN: 350°

3 tablespoons butter
3 tablespoons flour
1¼ cups milk
1 (8-ounce) package cream cheese, cut into chunks
3 (10-ounce) packages frozen chopped broccoli, thawed and drained
15 Ritz crackers, crushed

Melt butter in a large saucepan and stir in flour. Cook and stir over medium-low heat for 3–5 minutes. Slowly add milk and cook and stir until sauce thickens. Add cream cheese, stirring as it melts. Fold in broccoli and mix well. Pour into a greased 2-quart baking dish and sprinkle crushed crackers on top. Bake for 30 minutes.
MAKES 8–10 SERVINGS.

BROCCOLI WITH BACON AND WALNUTS

■■■

6 slices bacon
2 pounds fresh broccoli
¾ cup chopped walnuts
¼ cup chopped green onions

Cook bacon in a skillet until crisp. Remove from skillet, reserving 2 tablespoons of the drippings, and drain on paper towels. Then crumble it and set it aside. Wash broccoli, trimming off leaves and tough ends. Cut apart into spears and steam in a large saucepan until just tender, for about 5–6 minutes. While broccoli is cooking, sauté walnuts in bacon drippings, stirring constantly for about 3 minutes. As soon as broccoli is done, drain it and arrange it on a serving dish. Spoon sauce over broccoli, sprinkle with bacon, and serve.
MAKES 6 SERVINGS.

BROCCOLI CRUNCH CASSEROLE

■■■

OVEN: 350°

1 (10¾-ounce) can cream of mushroom soup
1 cup mayonnaise
1 cup (4 ounces) shredded Cheddar cheese
1 medium onion, chopped
salt and pepper
2 (10-ounce) packages frozen chopped broccoli, thawed and drained
2 eggs, beaten
2 cups herb-seasoned stuffing mix
4 tablespoons butter, melted

Combine soup, mayonnaise, cheese, and onion. Season with salt and pepper. Add broccoli and fold in eggs. Place in a greased 2-quart baking dish. Combine stuffing mix with butter, and scatter on top. Bake for about 45 minutes.
MAKES 6–8 SERVINGS.

BROCCOLI WITH LIME SAUCE
■■■

1 bunch fresh broccoli
½ cup mayonnaise
½ cup sour cream
1½ tablespoons lime juice (juice of
   1 lime)
1 teaspoon grated lime peel
½ teaspoon horseradish
½ teaspoon Dijon mustard
¼ teaspoon salt

Cut broccoli into spears and steam for 5–6 minutes, or until crisp-tender. Chill. Mix remaining ingredients and chill separately. To serve, arrange broccoli on a serving plate and spoon sauce over it.
MAKES 4 SERVINGS.

MARINATED BROCCOLI
■■■

2 bunches fresh broccoli
1 cup cider vinegar
1½ cups vegetable oil
1 tablespoon sugar
1 tablespoon dill weed
2 teaspoons MSG
1 teaspoon salt
1 teaspoon pepper
1 teaspoon garlic salt
1 pint cherry tomatoes, halved

Cut broccoli into spears and steam for 5–6 minutes. Mix vinegar, oil, sugar, dill weed, MSG, salt, pepper, and garlic salt. Add broccoli and toss well. Add tomatoes and toss again. Place in a large plastic zip bag. Chill overnight, turning several times. Drain and serve.
MAKES 8 SERVINGS.

BROCCOLI AND RICE
■■■

OVEN: 350°

2 (10-ounce) packages frozen
   chopped broccoli
1 medium onion, chopped
4 tablespoons butter
1 (10¾-ounce) can cream of
   chicken soup
1 cup milk
1 teaspoon salt
½ teaspoon pepper
4 cups cooked rice
1 (8-ounce) can sliced water
   chestnuts, drained
2 cups (8 ounces) shredded Colby
   cheese, divided use

Cook broccoli according to package directions and drain. Sauté onion in butter until soft. Stir in soup, milk, salt, and pepper. Fold in broccoli, rice, and water chestnuts. Mix in 1 cup of the cheese and pour into a greased 3-quart baking dish. Top with remaining 1 cup cheese and bake for 30 minutes.
MAKES 6–8 SERVINGS.

N·O·T·E·S

_____

_____

_____

_____

_____

_____

_____

_____

_____

_____

_____

_____

_____

_____

_____

_____

_____

_____

_____

_____

_____

_____

_____

_____

_____

_____

_____

_____

BROCCOLI IN SOUR CREAM SAUCE
■ ■ ■

OVEN: 350°

3 (10-ounce) packages frozen
  broccoli spears, thawed
1 (8-ounce) can sliced water
  chestnuts, drained
2 (8-ounce) cartons sour cream
1 cup mayonnaise
1/2 cup grated Parmesan cheese

Arrange broccoli in a greased 2½-quart baking dish. Top with water chestnuts. Blend sour cream with mayonnaise and spread on top. Sprinkle with Parmesan cheese and bake for 20–30 minutes.

MAKES 8–10 SERVINGS.

BROCCOLI SUPREME
■ ■ ■

OVEN: 350°

2 (10-ounce) packages frozen
  chopped broccoli, thawed
1 (14-ounce) can artichoke hearts,
  drained and quartered
1 (10³/4-ounce) can cream of
  mushroom soup
1/2 cup mayonnaise
2 eggs, slightly beaten
1 teaspoon lemon juice
1 teaspoon Worcestershire sauce
1/4 teaspoon garlic salt
1 cup (4 ounces) shredded
  Cheddar cheese
1/2 cup bread crumbs
4 tablespoons butter, melted

Drain broccoli well; set aside. Place artichoke hearts in a greased 2-quart baking dish. Mix soup, mayonnaise, eggs, lemon juice, Worcestershire sauce, and garlic salt. Stir in broccoli and pour over artichoke hearts. Sprinkle with cheese and bread crumbs and drizzle butter on top. Bake for 30 minutes.

MAKES 6–8 SERVINGS.

CABBAGE
■ ■ ■

How to Prepare: Cut cabbage into quarters lengthwise. Cut a V-shaped notch in each quarter to remove core. Cut into wedges or shred, as desired.

How to Boil: Pour about 1" of water into a large saucepan and add 1 teaspoon salt and 2 tablespoons lemon juice or white vinegar. Bring water to a boil and add shredded cabbage or cabbage cut into wedges. Cover, reduce heat, and simmer cabbage until it is crisp-tender. Shredded cabbage should take about 5 minutes, and cabbage wedges should be done in about 10 minutes.

How to Steam: Pour about 1" of water into a large saucepan and set a steamer basket in place. Add shredded cabbage or cabbage wedges and bring water to a boil. Cover, reduce heat, and steam until crisp-tender. Shredded cabbage should take about 5 minutes, and cabbage wedges should be done in about 10 minutes.

How to Tell When Done: Cabbage should be cooked just until it is crisp-tender.

Note: Shredded cabbage to be used for slaw will keep for several days in the refrigerator, if it is stored in a plastic zip bag separately from dressing.

SOUR CREAM CABBAGE
■ ■ ■

OVEN: 350°

1 medium head cabbage
2¹/₂ cups water
1 teaspoon salt
1 (8-ounce) carton sour cream
3 tablespoons butter, melted, divided use
1 tablespoon sugar
1 tablespoon white vinegar
1 teaspoon Knorr Aromat Seasoning (see Special Ingredients, page 68)
¹/₂ teaspoon cracked pepper
¹/₂ cup crushed herb-seasoned stuffing mix

Wash, core, and coarsely chop cabbage. Place in a large saucepan and add water and salt. Bring to a boil and boil for 5 minutes. Drain. Spoon cabbage into a greased 2-quart baking dish. Combine sour cream, 2 tablespoons of the butter, the sugar, vinegar, Knorr seasoning, and pepper. Mix with cabbage. Toss crushed stuffing mix with remaining 1 tablespoon butter, and sprinkle over cabbage. Bake for 20–25 minutes, or until hot.

MAKES 4–6 SERVINGS.

SWEET AND SOUR CABBAGE
■ ■ ■

5 cups shredded cabbage
4 slices bacon, diced
2 tablespoons flour
2 tablespoons brown sugar
¹/₃ cup vinegar
¹/₂ cup water
salt and pepper
1 small onion, sliced thin

Boil cabbage in about 1″ of water for 5 minutes. (See instructions on page 200.) Drain. Fry bacon in a skillet and remove from pan with slotted spoon. Blend flour and brown sugar into bacon drippings. Add vinegar, ¹/₂ cup water, and salt and pepper to taste. Cook over low heat until thickened. Stir in onion, bacon, and cabbage, and heat through.

MAKES 4–6 SERVINGS.

GRILLED CABBAGE
■ ■ ■

GRILL: MEDIUM HOT

1 medium head cabbage
¹/₂ teaspoon salt
¹/₄ teaspoon pepper
¹/₄ cup half and half
4 tablespoons butter

Cut cabbage into slivers. Place in a large bowl and toss with salt and pepper. Cut 4 sheets of aluminum foil about 1 foot square each. Lay each sheet shiny-

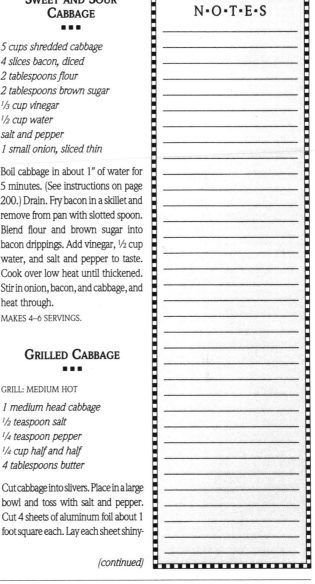

N·O·T·E·S

(continued)

_____
_____
_____
_____
_____
_____
_____
_____
_____
_____
_____
_____
_____
_____
_____
_____
_____
_____
_____
_____
_____
_____
_____
_____
_____
_____
_____
_____

side-down and spray the dull side with non-stick spray. Divide cabbage into 4 portions, placing an equal amount on each piece of foil. Drizzle about 1 tablespoon of half and half on each portion and dot with butter. Fold foil around cabbage to make a packet, and grill for 12–15 minutes. Serve in foil packet or transfer to a serving dish, saving all the creamy juices.

MAKES 4 SERVINGS.

"Cabbage: A familiar kitchen-garden vegetable about as large and wise as a man's head."

—Ambrose Bierce

SWEET AND SOUR COLE SLAW
■ ■ ■

1 large head cabbage
1 cup sugar
1 cup vinegar
³/₄ cup vegetable oil
1 teaspoon dry mustard
1 teaspoon salt
1 teaspoon celery seed
pepper

Shred cabbage finely and place in a large bowl. In a saucepan, mix sugar, vinegar, oil, dry mustard, salt, celery seed, and pepper to taste. Heat and stir until sugar is dissolved. Cool and toss with cabbage. Refrigerate for several hours before serving. Keeps very well.

MAKES 8–10 SERVINGS.

CREAMY COLE SLAW
■ ■ ■

Slaw tends to become juicier after standing, so be sure to use a light hand when adding the dressing. You probably won't need to add as much as you might think. If you add too much dressing, slaw will become soupy. When I make slaw, I like to store the shredded cabbage and carrots separately from the dressing in the refrigerator, until just before I'm ready to prepare the slaw. I keep the shredded cabbage and carrots in a plastic zip bag, and I store the dressing in a jar or bottle. The cabbage seems to keep much better that way, and there's no chance of it becoming soupy. I can toss together as many servings as I need, and the rest stays fresh.

1 medium head cabbage
¹/₂ pound carrots, shredded
1 (8-ounce) carton sour cream
1 cup mayonnaise
1 (1-ounce) package ranch
    dressing mix
2 tablespoons sugar
¹/₃ cup vinegar
¹/₄ teaspoon salt
1 teaspoon pepper
2 teaspoons celery seed

Shred cabbage and carrots. Blend the remaining ingredients together to make the dressing. Add the dressing to the slaw, a little at a time, tossing to mix well. Use only as much dressing as necessary. (Some dressing will probably be left over.) Store in refrigerator.

MAKES 6–8 SERVINGS.

CARROTS

■■■

How to Prepare: Remove tops and peel carrots with a vegetable peeler. Remove the core of large, tough carrots. Slice into medallions or cut in half lengthwise. Then cut halves into strips, and cut strips into dice.

How to Boil: Pour about 1" of water into a saucepan and add 1 teaspoon salt and 1 teaspoon sugar. Bring water to a boil and add carrots. Shredded carrots will cook in about 5 minutes. Sliced or cut-up carrots will take 10–15 minutes. Whole carrots will cook in 15–20 minutes.

How to Steam: Pour about 1"of water into a saucepan and set a steamer basket in place. Add carrots and bring water to a boil. Cover and reduce heat. Shredded carrots will cook in 3–4 minutes. Sliced or cut-up carrots will take 8–10 minutes. Whole carrots will cook in 12-15 minutes.

How to Tell When Done: Carrots should be cooked until crisp-tender.

ALMOND CARROTS

■■■

¹/₄ cup slivered almonds
5 tablespoons butter, divided use
1 pound carrots, coarsely grated
1 teaspoon sugar
2 tablespoons lemon juice
1 tablespoon snipped parsley
2 tablespoons chicken broth

Sauté almonds in 1 tablespoon of the butter and set aside. Mix carrots in a saucepan with remaining 4 tablespoons butter, sugar, lemon juice, parsley, and chicken broth. Cover tightly and simmer until tender, for about 10 minutes. Toss with almonds and serve.

MAKES 3–4 SERVINGS.

LEMON BUTTERED CARROTS

■■■

1 pound baby carrots
¹/₄ cup water
¹/₂ teaspoon salt
2 tablespoons butter
1 teaspoon paprika
1 tablespoon lemon juice

Rinse carrots and cut into quarters lengthwise, to make thin strips. Place in a saucepan with remaining ingredients and cover. Steam over low heat until carrots are just barely tender, for about 8–10 minutes. Serve with pan juices.

MAKES 3–4 SERVINGS.

CARROT AND RAISIN SALAD
■■■

1 pound carrots
1 cup seedless raisins
1 (8-ounce) can crushed pineapple
1/2 teaspoon salt
1 cup chopped pecans
1 cup mayonnaise

Peel and grate carrots. Toss with raisins. Drain pineapple, reserving juice, and add to carrots. Add salt, pecans, and mayonnaise and toss. If desired, thin with a little of the reserved pineapple juice. Chill before serving.

MAKES 4 SERVINGS.

DILL CARROTS
■■■

This is an easy dish to fix for a picnic.

2 pounds baby carrots
1 cup any combination of salad
    dressings
1/2 teaspoon salt
1 teaspoon pepper
2 teaspoons dill seed
2 teaspoons parsley flakes
lettuce leaves

Cut carrots into quarters lengthwise. Steam until barely crisp-tender, for about 8–10 minutes. Drain and set aside. Mix salad dressing, salt, pepper, dill seed, and parsley flakes. Pour over carrots and stir to mix well. Refrigerate for at least 4 hours, stirring from time to time. Drain and serve on lettuce leaves.

MAKES 6–8 SERVINGS.

GLAZED CARROTS
■■■

2 pounds carrots
salt
1/2 cup butter, melted
1/4 cup honey
1 teaspoon vinegar
1 tablespoon chopped mint leaves

Peel carrots and slice. Steam until barely tender, for about 8–10 minutes. Drain and add salt to taste. Return to saucepan and add butter, honey, vinegar, and mint leaves. Cook over medium heat until sauce thickens to form a glaze over the carrots.

MAKES 6–8 SERVINGS.

SWEET AND SOUR CARROTS
■■■

1 pound baby carrots
1 1/2 tablespoons butter
1/4 teaspoon MSG
1/4 cup cider vinegar
1/3 cup sugar
1 tablespoon honey

Cut carrots into quarters lengthwise. Steam for 8–10 minutes, or until barely crisp-tender. Drain carrots, return them to the pan, and add remaining ingredients. Cook over low heat until heated through. Serve hot.

MAKES 3–4 SERVINGS.

CARROTS IN TOMATO MARINADE

∎∎∎

2 pounds carrots, peeled and
   sliced
1 medium sweet onion, sliced
½ cup oil
¾ cup cider vinegar
1 teaspoon Worcestershire sauce
1 (10¾-ounce) can tomato soup
1 cup sugar
1 teaspoon Dijon mustard
salt and pepper

Steam carrots until barely crisp-tender, for about 8–10 minutes. Cool and drain. Layer carrots and onion in a 2-quart baking dish. Combine remaining ingredients in a saucepan and heat, stirring until blended. Pour over carrots and onion. Cover and refrigerate for at least 24 hours.

MAKES 6–8 SERVINGS.

CAULIFLOWER

∎∎∎

How to Prepare: Trim off the stem and remove the green outer leaves. Then cut florets off the core with a sharp knife.

How to Steam: Pour 1" of water into a saucepan and set a steamer basket in place. Add cauliflower and bring water to a boil. Cover, reduce heat, and cook until tender. Whole cauliflower should take 15–20 minutes, and florets should take 5–7 minutes.

How to Tell When Done: Cauliflower should be cooked until tender.

CAULIFLOWER WITH CHEESE SAUCE

∎∎∎

1 head cauliflower
2 tablespoons butter
2 tablespoons flour
1 cup milk
½ teaspoon salt
¾ cup (3 ounces) shredded
   Cheddar cheese

Separate cauliflower into florets. Then make cheese sauce: Melt butter in a medium saucepan and whisk in flour. Cook and stir over medium heat for 3–5 minutes, and slowly add milk. Cook and stir until thickened. Add salt and cheese. Reduce heat and stir until cheese is melted. While cheese is melting, steam cauliflower for 5–7 minutes, or until tender. Place cauliflower in a serving dish and spoon sauce over it.

MAKES 4 SERVINGS.

N·O·T·E·S

CAULIFLOWER WITH PEAS
■ ■ ■

½ cup water
1 (10-ounce) package frozen
  cauliflower
1 (10-ounce) package frozen
  green peas
½ teaspoon salt
1 cucumber, peeled and diced
¼ cup ranch dressing
¼ cup sour cream
½ teaspoon dill weed

Pour water into a saucepan and insert steamer basket. Add cauliflower and peas and sprinkle with salt. Cover and steam for about 5 minutes. Transfer cauliflower and peas to a bowl and add cucumber, ranch dressing, sour cream, and dill weed. Toss well and serve warm or chilled.
MAKES 4 SERVINGS.

CELERY
■ ■ ■

How to Prepare: Cut off the root end and wash the ribs. Then slice the ribs crosswise or make several lengthwise slices and cut into dice.

CELERY CASSEROLE
■ ■ ■

4 cups sliced celery
¼ cup slivered almonds
1 (8-ounce) can sliced water
  chestnuts, drained
1 (4-ounce) can sliced mushrooms,
  drained
6 tablespoons butter, melted,
  divided use
3 tablespoons flour
½ cup half and half
1 cup chicken broth
½ cup crushed herb-seasoned
  stuffing mix
½ cup grated Parmesan cheese

Cook celery in boiling salted water for 5 minutes. Drain and mix with almonds, water chestnuts, and mushrooms. Whisk 5 tablespoons of the butter in a saucepan with the flour. Cook and stir for 3–5 minutes. Stir in half and half and chicken broth, and cook until thickened. Fold in celery and pour into a greased 2-quart baking dish. Toss stuffing mix with remaining 1 tablespoon butter and sprinkle over celery. Top with Parmesan cheese. Bake for about 20 minutes, or until bubbly.
MAKES 6–8 SERVINGS.

STUFFED CELERY
■ ■ ■

Wash and chill celery. Stuff it with any of the following: bacon and horseradish dip; cream cheese mixed with chopped olives and pimientos; peanut butter; pimiento cheese spread; tuna salad.

CORN
■ ■ ■

How to Prepare: Remove the husks, snap off the stems, and remove the silks under running water. To cut kernels off the cob, hold the ear of corn upright in a shallow pan and cut the kernels off, 3 or 4 rows at a time. For cream-style corn, cut the outer half of the kernels off the cob. Then scrape the cob with the dull side of a knife.

How to Tell When Done: Corn should be cooked without salt until tender. Corn becomes tough when it is overcooked.

CORN ON THE COB
■ ■ ■

Put about 3 quarts of water into a large kettle. Add 2 tablespoons sugar, bring water to a boil, and add shucked corn. When water returns to a boil, cook corn uncovered for about 5 more minutes, or until tender. (Fresh-picked corn might take less time; older corn might take slightly longer.) Remove with tongs and serve with melted butter, salt, and pepper. For a real treat, sprinkle a little Parmesan cheese on it. (Never add salt until after corn is cooked. Adding it earlier will toughen the corn.) Cooked corn can be left in the hot water for about 15 minutes. Leftover cooked corn on the cob can be cut from the cob and refrigerated for later use.

CORN FRITTERS
■ ■ ■

1½ cups flour
1½ teaspoons baking powder
¾ teaspoon salt
1 egg
⅔ cup milk
1 (12-ounce) can cream-style corn
vegetable oil for frying

Mix flour with baking powder and salt. Beat egg with milk and add gradually to flour mixture. Stir in corn and mix well. Drop by tablespoonfuls into deep hot oil. Cook for 2–5 minutes, until fritters are browned.
MAKES 4–6 SERVINGS.

CREAMED CORN
■ ■ ■

¼ pound bacon, diced
½ medium onion, chopped
1 teaspoon sugar
1 (8-ounce) carton sour cream
1 (16-ounce) package frozen white corn, cooked
salt and pepper

Fry bacon with onion. As soon as bacon is done, pour off drippings and stir in sugar and sour cream. Fold in corn and season with salt and pepper. Continue cooking until hot.
MAKES 4 SERVINGS.

_____
_____
_____
_____
_____
_____
_____
_____
_____
_____
_____
_____
_____
_____
_____
_____
_____
_____
_____
_____
_____
_____
_____
_____
_____
_____
_____
_____
_____
_____
_____

FRIED CORN
■ ■ ■

12 ears corn
4 tablespoons butter
3 tablespoons bacon drippings
1 tablespoon flour
1½ tablespoons sugar
salt and pepper

Shuck corn and cut kernels off the cob, as for cream-style corn (see page 207). Melt butter and bacon drippings in a large, heavy skillet. Stir in corn and cook over medium-high heat for 5 minutes, stirring constantly. Stir in flour and sugar and reduce heat to low. Cover and cook for about 30 more minutes, stirring occasionally. Add salt and plenty of pepper before serving. A little hot water can be added during cooking, if necessary, to keep corn from drying out or sticking to the pan.

MAKES 6 SERVINGS.

CORN PUDDING
■ ■ ■

OVEN: 350°

3 eggs
3 tablespoons flour
½ teaspoon salt
1 tablespoon sugar
1½ tablespoons butter, melted
2 (12-ounce) cans white corn
1½ cups milk or half and half

Beat eggs and blend in flour, salt, sugar, and butter. Stir in corn and milk or half and half. Pour into a greased 1½-quart baking dish and set it inside a larger pan. Pour hot water into the larger pan so that it comes halfway up the outside of the dish that the corn is in. Bake for about an hour, or until pudding is set.

MAKES 6 SERVINGS.

CORN AND RICE CASSEROLE
■ ■ ■

OVEN: 350°

3⅓ cups water
½ cup butter
2 (5-ounce) packages Mahatma
  Yellow Rice Mix
2 (4-ounce) jars diced pimientos,
  drained
1 (8-ounce) carton sour cream
1 (10½-ounce) can cream of
  mushroom soup
1 (16-ounce) package frozen white
  corn
2 cups (8 ounces) shredded sharp
  Cheddar cheese, divided use

In a large saucepan, bring water and butter to a boil and stir in rice. Cover, reduce heat, and simmer for 20 minutes. Stir in pimientos, sour cream, soup, corn, and 1½ cups of the cheese. Spoon into a greased 3-quart baking dish and sprinkle with remaining ½ cup cheese. Bake uncovered for about 30 minutes, or until bubbly.

MAKES 8–12 SERVINGS.

Succotash
■■■

6 slices bacon, cut into 1" pieces
1 small yellow onion, chopped
1 (10-ounce) package frozen baby
   lima beans, thawed
1 (10-ounce) package frozen white
   corn, thawed
1 (14½-ounce) can diced
   tomatoes, drained
salt and pepper

Sauté bacon in a large skillet. Remove from pan with a slotted spoon, drain, and set aside. Add onion to skillet and cook for about 5 minutes, or until onion is soft. Spoon off grease and stir in lima beans and corn. Cook over medium-low heat until hot. Stir in tomatoes. Continue cooking until tomatoes are hot. Season with salt and pepper. Serve topped with crumbled bacon.
MAKES 6 SERVINGS.

CUCUMBERS
■■■

How to Prepare: Peel cucumbers and remove ends, which tend to be bitter. Slice crosswise into medallions or cut in half lengthwise and scrape out the seeds with a spoon. Then slice crosswise, or make several lengthwise slices and cut into dice.

Cucumbers in Sour Cream
■■■

2 cucumbers
1 onion, thinly sliced
½ cup sour cream
2 tablespoons vinegar
2 tablespoons water
1 teaspoon salt
½ teaspoon pepper
4 teaspoons dill weed

Wash and dry cucumbers and score sides with a fork. Slice thinly and mix with onion. Mix sour cream with vinegar, water, salt, pepper, and dill. Toss with cucumbers and chill.
MAKES 4 SERVINGS.

Stuffed Cucumbers
■■■

3 cucumbers
bottled French dressing
1 (3-ounce) package cream cheese,
   softened
¼ cup half and half
1 tablespoon prepared horseradish
1 (3-ounce) can real bacon bits
6 Boston lettuce leaves

Peel cucumbers and cut in half lengthwise. Scoop out seeds and cut in thirds crosswise. Marinate in French dressing for at least an hour. Mash cream cheese and blend in half and half. Stir in horseradish and bacon. Drain cucumbers and stuff with cream cheese filling. Serve 3 pieces per person on a bed of lettuce.
MAKES 6 SERVINGS.

N·O·T·E·S

_____
_____
_____
_____
_____
_____
_____
_____
_____
_____
_____
_____
_____
_____
_____
_____
_____
_____
_____
_____
_____
_____
_____
_____
_____
_____
_____
_____
_____
_____
_____
_____
_____

CUCUMBERS AND ONIONS
■■■

3 cucumbers
1 sweet onion, thinly sliced
1 cup Italian dressing
2 tablespoons sugar
freshly ground pepper

Peel cucumbers and slice thinly. Mix with onion. Toss with Italian dressing and sugar. Sprinkle heavily with pepper and chill.

MAKES 6 SERVINGS.

EGGPLANT
■■■

How to Prepare: Trim off the stem. Peel eggplant only if the skin is tough. (If eggplant is very small, it does not need to be peeled.) Then cut eggplant into crosswise slices. If desired, cut the slices into cubes.

How to Boil: Pour about 1" of water into a saucepan and add 1 teaspoon salt. Bring water to a boil and add sliced or cubed eggplant. Cover and cook for 5–8 minutes.

How to Steam: Pour about 1" of water into a saucepan and set a steamer basket in place. Add eggplant and bring water to a boil. Cover, reduce heat, and cook for 5–7 minutes.

How to Sauté: Melt 3–4 tablespoons butter in a large skillet and sauté eggplant for 5–10 minutes.

How to Tell When Done: Eggplant should be cooked until it is tender.

EGGPLANT PARMESAN
■■■

OVEN: 350°

2 tablespoons tomato paste
4 cups diced fresh tomatoes
½ cup olive or vegetable oil, divided use
1 teaspoon sugar
1½ teaspoons salt
¼ teaspoon pepper
1 clove garlic, minced
1½ pounds eggplant
2 cups herb-seasoned stuffing mix
2 tablespoons butter, melted
2 tablespoons chopped parsley
½ cup grated Parmesan cheese
1 cup (4 ounces) shredded mozzarella cheese

Mix tomato paste with tomatoes, 2 tablespoons of the oil, the sugar, salt, pepper, and garlic. Simmer in a medium saucepan for 15 minutes to thicken, and remove it from the heat. Peel the eggplant and slice it ½" thick. Heat the remaining 6 tablespoons of oil in a skillet over medium heat, and brown the eggplant slices on both sides. Grease a 2-quart baking dish and line it with the eggplant slices. Toss the stuffing mix with the melted butter and combine it with parsley and Parmesan cheese. Sprinkle half of the mixture over the eggplant and cover it with the tomato mixture. Add the remaining stuffing mixture and top with mozzarella cheese. Bake for 30 minutes. Serve hot.

MAKES 8 SERVINGS.

FRIED EGGPLANT
■ ■ ■

1 medium eggplant (about 1¼ pounds)

lemon juice

1 egg

2 tablespoons milk

½ teaspoon salt

¼ teaspoon pepper

2 cups dried bread crumbs

3 tablespoons grated Parmesan cheese

½ cup vegetable oil

Peel eggplant, slice it ¼" thick, and sprinkle with lemon juice. Beat egg and add milk, salt, and pepper. In another dish, mix bread crumbs with Parmesan cheese. Dip eggplant slices into egg batter and then dredge in bread crumb mixture. Heat oil in a skillet, and fry eggplant until browned on bottom and slightly transparent. Turn and brown on the other side.

MAKES 4 SERVINGS.

BAKED EGGPLANT
■ ■ ■

OVEN: 375°

1 small eggplant (8–10 ounces)

softened butter

grated Parmesan cheese

seasoned bread crumbs

Cut eggplant in half but do not peel. Using a sharp knife, cut around inside edges to free eggplant from sides of peel. Then score pulp into bite-size sections. Rub with softened butter and sprinkle generously with Parmesan cheese and seasoned bread crumbs. Place in a greased shallow baking dish and bake for 30–45 minutes.

MAKES 2 SERVINGS.

GREEN BEANS
■ ■ ■

How to Prepare: After washing, snap off one end, pulling the tip down the bean to remove the string. Repeat with the other tip. If desired, snap beans into pieces, or cut french-style into thin slivers.

How to Boil: For each pound of beans, pour about 3 quarts of water into a very large saucepan and add 1½ teaspoons salt. Bring water to a boil and add green beans. Boil uncovered for 10–12 minutes.

How to Steam: Pour about 1" of water into a saucepan and set a steamer

(continued)

basket in place. Add green beans and bring water to a boil. Cover, reduce heat, and cook for 10–12 minutes.

How to Tell When Done: Green beans should be cooked until crisp-tender.

SOUTHERN-STYLE GREEN BEANS
■■■

*1/4 pound bacon, ham hock, or
    salt pork*
1 quart water
2 chicken bouillon cubes
1 1/2 pounds fresh green beans
*1 pound new potatoes, scrubbed
    and cut in half (optional)*
1 small onion, peeled and quartered
2 teaspoons sugar
salt and pepper

Cut up bacon, ham hock, or salt pork, and put in a large saucepan with water and bouillon cubes. Bring to a boil, cover, reduce heat, and cook for about 30 minutes. Wash and trim beans, snap into 3" pieces, and add to saucepan. If desired, add new potatoes. Add onion, sugar, salt, and pepper to taste. Stir, cover, and continue cooking for about 30 more minutes, or until tender. Old-fashioned Southern green beans are cooked for several hours.
MAKES 4–6 SERVINGS.

GREEN BEANS WITH HONEY MUSTARD SAUCE
■■■

*2 (15-ounce) cans vertical pack
    whole green beans, chilled,
    or 2 pounds fresh green
    beans, steamed*
6 Boston lettuce leaves
*Honey Mustard Horseradish Sauce
    (page 252)*
pimiento strips (optional)

Drain beans. Arrange on lettuce leaves. Spoon Honey Mustard Horseradish Sauce over each serving. If desired, garnish with pimiento strips.
MAKES 6 SERVINGS.

GREEN BEANS AMANDINE
■■■

*2 pounds green beans, trimmed, or
    2 (15-ounce) cans, drained*
8 slices bacon, diced
1/2 cup chopped onion
1/3 cup vinegar
salt and pepper
1/4 cup toasted almonds

Steam beans until crisp-tender and set aside. Sauté bacon, remove from pan, and drain on paper towels. Sauté onion in bacon drippings and stir in beans, vinegar, and salt and pepper to taste. Continue cooking until beans are heated through. Pour into serving dish and sprinkle with bacon and almonds.
MAKES 6 SERVINGS.

Variation: To make **Sweet and Sour Green Beans**, omit almonds and add 2 teaspoons sugar.

GREEN BEANS WITH CREAM CHEESE SAUCE
■ ■ ■

2 pounds green beans, trimmed, or
  2 (15-ounce) cans, drained
3/4 cup milk
1 (8-ounce) package cream cheese
1/2 teaspoon salt
1/2 teaspoon garlic salt
1/2 cup grated Parmesan cheese

Steam beans for 10–12 minutes, or until crisp-tender. Set aside. Heat milk in a medium saucepan. Cut cream cheese into chunks and add to milk, stirring until cream cheese melts. Add salt, garlic salt, and Parmesan cheese. Stir in green beans and serve.

MAKES 6 SERVINGS.

GREEN BEANS IN SOUR CREAM
■ ■ ■

1 (8-ounce) carton sour cream
1–2 tablespoons horseradish
1/2 teaspoon Worcestershire sauce
2 (15-ounce) cans whole green
  beans, or 2 pounds fresh green
  beans, steamed
salt and pepper
garlic salt
2 hard-cooked eggs, chopped

In a large bowl, mix sour cream, horseradish, and Worcestershire sauce. Toss with beans and season to taste with salt, pepper, and garlic salt. Cover and chill for several hours. Before serving, spoon beans into serving dish and sprinkle chopped eggs on top.

MAKES 6 SERVINGS.

GREEN BEAN SALAD
■ ■ ■

2 (16-ounce) cans cut green beans,
  drained
1 (16-ounce) can wax beans,
  drained
1 (16-ounce) can kidney beans,
  drained and rinsed
1 red Bermuda onion, sliced
1/2 cup sugar
1/2 cup vegetable oil
2/3 cup vinegar
1/2 teaspoon Worcestershire sauce
dash Tabasco sauce
1 teaspoon salt
1/8 teaspoon pepper

Mix beans in a large bowl with onion. Blend remaining ingredients and toss with beans. Cover and chill for at least 4 hours, stirring from time to time.

MAKES 10–12 SERVINGS.

RED, WHITE, AND GREEN BEAN SALAD
■ ■ ■

On a recent Fourth of July, some friends invited us to join them for a block party. This was no ordinary neighborhood get-together, with several hundred in attendance. The Nashville Symphony played "The Stars and Stripes Forever," someone read the opening paragraphs of the Declaration of Independence, and everyone brought something to eat, which was judged in a contest. This recipe won a red ribbon! Predictably,

(continued)

N·O·T·E·S

N·O·T·E·S

_____
_____
_____
_____
_____
_____
_____
_____
_____
_____
_____
_____
_____
_____
_____
_____
_____
_____
_____
_____
_____
_____
_____
_____
_____
_____
_____
_____
_____
_____

the blue ribbon was awarded to a guest who brought a chocolate dessert. Afterwards, I remarked to our hostess that if I had known there was going to be a contest, I would have brought a pan of Brownies with Amaretto Frosting (page 290).

2 (16-ounce) cans cut green beans, drained
1 (16-ounce) can kidney beans, drained and rinsed
1 (16-ounce) package frozen tiny green peas, thawed
1 (16-ounce) package frozen white corn, thawed
1 (16-ounce) can julienned beets, drained and rinsed well
2 Vidalia onions, sliced
1 cup sugar
1 cup vegetable oil
1 1/3 cups vinegar
1 teaspoon Worcestershire sauce
dash Tabasco sauce
2 teaspoons salt
1/2 teaspoon pepper

Mix beans, peas, corn, beets, and onions in a large bowl. Whisk together remaining ingredients and toss with bean mixture. Cover and chill for at least 4 hours, stirring from time to time. Better the second day.

MAKES 16–20 SERVINGS.

> ## "There is no such thing as a little garlic."
>
> —Anonymous

MUSHROOMS
■ ■ ■

How to Prepare: Clean caps with a damp cloth or soft brush. Do not soak them in water. Remove the stems at the base. Holding each mushroom gill-side-down on a cutting board, slice it evenly to thickness desired.

How to Sauté: For a pound of mushrooms, melt 4 tablespoons butter in a large skillet. Add whole button mushrooms or sliced mushrooms and sauté for 3–5 minutes, or until tender.

How to Steam: Pour about 1" of water into a saucepan and set a steamer basket in place. Add mushrooms and bring water to a boil. Cover, reduce heat, and cook for 6–8 minutes.

How to Tell When Done: Mushrooms should be cooked until tender.

BAKED MUSHROOMS
■ ■ ■

OVEN: 400°

1 pound fresh mushrooms
1/2 cup olive oil
1/4 cup lemon juice
1/2 teaspoon dried basil
1/4 teaspoon salt
1/2 teaspoon pepper
dash Tabasco sauce
1/2 teaspoon minced garlic

Clean mushrooms and trim bottoms. Set aside. Whisk together olive oil, lemon juice, basil, salt, pepper, Tabasco sauce, and minced garlic.

Add mushrooms and stir to coat well. Marinate for 30 minutes, stirring several times. Transfer to a baking dish and bake for 15 minutes uncovered, or until mushrooms are tender. Serve with pan juices.

MAKES 4 SERVINGS.

STEAMED MUSHROOMS
■■■

OVEN: 400°

1 pound medium-size fresh mushrooms
1 teaspoon seasoned salt
1/4 teaspoon paprika
1/8 teaspoon pepper
4 tablespoons butter, melted
2 tablespoons dry sherry
1/4 cup chopped fresh parsley

Wash mushrooms, trim stems, and cut in half. Place on a large sheet of heavy foil and sprinkle with seasoned salt, paprika, and pepper. Mix melted butter and sherry and drizzle on top. Sprinkle with parsley. Fold foil over mushrooms to form a packet, and fold edges shut. Place foil packet on a cookie sheet and bake for 20 minutes.

MAKES 4–6 SERVINGS.

SAUTÉED MUSHROOMS
■■■

1 pound fresh mushrooms
4 tablespoons butter
salt and pepper
lemon juice

Wash mushrooms and cut off just the tips of the stems. (Remove entire stems only if soft or woody.) If the mushrooms are quite mixed in size, leave the small ones whole and slice or quarter the larger ones. Otherwise, slice all the mushrooms and sauté in butter for about 3–5 minutes, or until tender. Season with salt, pepper, and a few drops of lemon juice.

MAKES 4 SERVINGS.

MUSHROOMS WITH SOUR CREAM
■■■

OVEN: 400°

2 tablespoons butter
2 pounds mushrooms, sliced
2 teaspoons lemon juice
2/3 cup sour cream
1/2 teaspoon salt
1/4 teaspoon pepper
2 tablespoons flour
1/4 cup fresh chopped parsley
1 1/2 cups (6 ounces) shredded Swiss or Monterey Jack cheese

Melt butter in a large skillet and sauté mushrooms for 3–5 minutes, or until tender. Transfer mushrooms to a medium bowl and sprinkle with lemon juice. In a small bowl, mix sour cream, salt, pepper, and flour. Add to mushrooms and toss well. Transfer to a greased 2-quart baking dish. Sprinkle with parsley and cheese and bake for 10–15 minutes, or until cheese melts and mushrooms are heated thoroughly.

MAKES 8 SERVINGS.

MARINATED MUSHROOMS
■■■

1 pound fresh mushrooms
1/3 cup white wine vinegar
1/3 cup salad oil
1/2 bunch green onions, chopped
2 tablespoons chopped fresh parsley
1/2 teaspoon salt
1/2 teaspoon dry mustard
1/2 teaspoon dried basil
1/8 teaspoon pepper

Wash mushrooms and pat dry. Remove and discard stems. Combine remaining ingredients and add mushrooms. Toss gently to coat well. Cover and refrigerate for 4–6 hours.
MAKES 4 SERVINGS.

STUFFED MUSHROOMS
■■■

OVEN: 350°

2 pounds medium-size fresh
   mushrooms, all as close as
   possible to same size
1 (8-ounce) package cream cheese,
   softened
1/4 cup grated Parmesan cheese
1 (0.7-ounce) envelope Italian
   dressing mix
paprika

Wash mushrooms. Remove and discard stems. Blend cream cheese with Parmesan cheese and Italian dressing mix. Stuff mixture into mushroom caps, and arrange in a well-greased baking dish. Sprinkle lightly with paprika and bake for about 15 minutes.
MAKES 8–10 SERVINGS.

OKRA
■■■

How to Prepare: Trim the tip off each pod and slice off the stem. Cut into slices if desired.

How to Boil: Pour about 1" of water into a saucepan and add 1 teaspoon salt. Bring to a boil and add okra. Cover, reduce heat, and simmer for about 10 minutes.

How to Steam: Pour about 1" of water into a saucepan and set a steamer basket in place. Add okra and bring water to a boil. Cover, reduce heat, and cook for about 6–8 minutes.

How to Tell When Done: Okra should be cooked until tender.

BATTER-FRIED OKRA
■■■

1 tablespoon butter
1 pound fresh okra, sliced
1 cup flour
1/2 teaspoon salt
2 teaspoons baking powder
1 egg, beaten
1/2 cup half and half
vegetable oil for frying

Melt butter in a skillet and add okra. Sauté until light brown and drain on paper towels. Combine flour with salt and baking powder, and mix with egg and half and half. Dip okra into batter, remove with a slotted spoon, and fry in vegetable oil at 375° until crusty. Drain on paper towels.
MAKES 4 SERVINGS.

FRENCH-FRIED OKRA
■ ■ ■

ELECTRIC SKILLET: 375°

2 eggs
½ cup buttermilk
1 pound fresh okra, sliced
½ cup self-rising flour
½ cup self-rising cornmeal
½ teaspoon pepper
4 cups vegetable oil for frying

Beat eggs with buttermilk. Stir in okra and set aside for 10 minutes, to allow okra to soak. Mix flour with cornmeal and pepper. Remove okra from the buttermilk mixture with a slotted spoon, a few pieces at a time, and dredge it in the flour mixture. Fry it in oil at 375° until golden brown on all sides. Drain on paper towels.
MAKES 4 SERVINGS.

OKRA AND TOMATOES
■ ■ ■

1 tablespoon butter
1 tablespoon oil
1 pound fresh okra, cut into ½"
    slices
1 medium onion, chopped
1 (16-ounce) can diced tomatoes,
    undrained
salt and pepper

Heat butter and oil in a large skillet until butter is melted. Add okra and onion to skillet, and sauté until okra is browned. Add tomatoes and salt and pepper to taste. Cover, reduce heat, and cook slowly for about 15 minutes, adding a little water if necessary to keep

from sticking. Remove cover and cook for another 5 minutes, or until tender.
MAKES 4 SERVINGS.

ONIONS
■ ■ ■

I used to dislike the strong flavor of onions so much that when a recipe called for them, I simply left them out. Then I discovered Vidalias. What a world of difference there is! Now I've discovered Bland Farms frozen chopped Vidalias in my supermarket, and I've joined the onion fan club. Some people avoid eating onions for fear of getting "onion breath." The National Onion Association recommends three solutions: (1) Rinse your mouth with equal parts of lemon juice and water. (2) Chew a piece of citrus peel to sweeten the breath. (3) Eat a sprig or two of parsley.

How to Prepare Dry Onions: Peel and trim off the stem end, leaving the root end intact. Cut the onion in half from stem end to root end. Lay the cut sides face-down on a cutting board. Make lengthwise cuts ⅛"–¼" apart, being careful not to cut through the root end. Make crosswise slices ⅛"–¼" apart. Because onions are formed in concentric layers, the slices will fall apart naturally into diced pieces.

How to Prepare Green Onions: Cut off the root fibers and remove tough outer layers. Remove as much of the green tops as desired, and slice.

N·O·T·E·S

CARAMELIZED ONIONS

∎∎∎

OVEN: 425°

2 pounds sweet onions (Vidalia or Walla Walla)
2 tablespoons brown sugar
1 teaspoon salt
1/4 teaspoon pepper
1/4 teaspoon garlic powder
1/2 cup white wine

Peel onions and cut into very thin lengthwise wedges, like a lemon. Spread in a greased 2-quart baking dish. Mix brown sugar, salt, pepper, and garlic powder, and sprinkle over onions. Add wine and bake for 25 minutes. Turn onions over with a pancake turner, and return to oven to bake for another 25 minutes, or until onions are golden brown and tender.

MAKES 4 SERVINGS.

ROASTED VIDALIA ONIONS

∎∎∎

OVEN: 350°

4 medium Vidalia onions
salt and pepper
4 tablespoons butter

Remove the stems and the dry outer skins from the onions. Remove the cores almost to the bottom, leaving a cavity about 1″ in diameter. (Do not go all the way through to the bottom of the onion when removing the core.) Sprinkle with salt and pepper and stuff 1 tablespoon butter into each cavity. Wrap each onion in a foil square, bringing the corners up around the onion and twisting the tops closed. Place in a shallow baking dish and bake for about an hour, depending on the size of the onions. (Small onions might take a little less time.) Unwrap the tops of the foil wrappers for the last 10 minutes of cooking.

MAKES 4 SERVINGS.

ONIONS PARMESAN

∎∎∎

OVEN: 350°

6 medium sweet onions
1/2 cup butter
1/2 teaspoon MSG
1 teaspoon sugar
1/2 teaspoon salt
1/2 teaspoon pepper
1/2 cup white wine
1/2 cup grated Parmesan cheese

Slice onions into 1/2″ thick slices and separate into rings. Sauté in butter for 5–8 minutes. Sprinkle with MSG, sugar, salt, and pepper. Stir in wine and cook for 2–3 more minutes. Transfer to a 1 1/2-quart baking dish and sprinkle with Parmesan cheese. Bake for 30 minutes.

MAKES 6 SERVINGS.

FRIED ONION RINGS
■ ■ ■

ELECTRIC SKILLET: 375°

1 large Bermuda onion
1 cup flour
1½ teaspoons salt
1½ teaspoons baking powder
1 egg, separated
⅔ cup milk
1 tablespoon vegetable oil
solid shortening for frying

Slice onion crosswise into slices about ¼" thick and separate slices into rings. Cover with cold water and let stand for about 30 minutes. Drain on paper towels. Sift together flour, salt, and baking powder into a medium bowl, and set aside. In a small bowl, beat egg yolk with milk and oil. Stir into flour mixture. Beat egg white until soft peaks form, and fold into batter. Melt about 1" of shortening in an electric skillet and heat to 375°. Dip onion rings into batter, remove with a slotted spoon, and fry in shortening, several at a time, until golden brown, turning as necessary. Drain on paper towels.

MAKES 4 SERVINGS.

PEAS
■ ■ ■

How to Prepare: To shell peas, hold them in one hand and pop open the pod by pressing the seam near the stem end with your thumb. Run your thumbnail down the seam, pulling it apart, and pop out the peas. To remove the strings, cut or snap off one tip without severing the string. Pull it down the pod to remove the string. Repeat on the other end.

How to Boil Dried Black-eyed Peas: Place in a saucepan and add several cups of cold water, or enough to cover the peas. Bring to a boil, and boil uncovered for 2 minutes. Reduce heat, cover, and simmer for 1–1½ hours, or until tender.

How to Boil Green Peas: Pour about 1" of water into a saucepan and add 1 teaspoon salt and 1 teaspoon sugar. Bring water to a boil and add green peas. Boil uncovered for about 5 minutes. Then cover, reduce heat, and continue cooking for about 5 more minutes, or until tender.

How to Steam: Pour about 1" of water into a saucepan and set a steamer basket in place. Add green peas and bring water to a boil. Cover, reduce heat, and cook for 10–12 minutes.

How to Tell When Done: Green peas and black-eyed peas should be cooked until tender.

N·O·T·E·S

N·O·T·E·S

BLACK-EYED PEAS WITH BACON

■ ■ ■

6 slices bacon, diced
1 onion, chopped
2 (16-ounce) cans black-eyed peas
1/8 teaspoon garlic powder
1/4 teaspoon salt
1/2 teaspoon crushed red pepper

In a large skillet, fry bacon until crisp. Remove with a slotted spoon and drain on paper towels. Add onion to skillet and sauté until onion is tender. Add undrained black-eyed peas, garlic powder, salt, and red pepper, and heat thoroughly. Sprinkle with bacon and serve.

MAKES 6 SERVINGS.

HOPPING JOHN

■ ■ ■

4 slices bacon, diced
1/2 cup chopped onion
1 (16-ounce) can black-eyed peas
1 cup cooked rice
salt and pepper
Tabasco sauce

Cook bacon in a skillet until crisp. Remove and drain on paper towels. Add onion to skillet and sauté until soft. Stir in undrained black-eyed peas and rice and season with salt, pepper, and Tabasco sauce. Heat thoroughly, sprinkle with bacon, and serve.

MAKES 4 SERVINGS.

BLACK-EYED PEA SALSA

■ ■ ■

2 (16-ounce) cans black-eyed peas, drained and rinsed
2 bunches green onions, sliced on diagonal
2 jalapeño peppers, seeded and finely diced
1 red pepper, diced
1/4 cup chopped fresh parsley
2/3 cup olive oil
5 tablespoons wine vinegar
1 large shallot, minced
3 tablespoons grainy mustard
salt and pepper

Combine black-eyed peas, green onions, jalapeño peppers, red pepper, and parsley in a large bowl. Mix remaining ingredients and pour over black-eyed peas. Toss and season to taste. Chill overnight in refrigerator. Toss again before serving.

MAKES 6–8 SERVINGS.

FRENCH GREEN PEAS

■ ■ ■

4 large lettuce leaves
2 (10-ounce) packages frozen green peas
1 1/2 teaspoons sugar
1/2 teaspoon salt
pepper to taste
1 bunch green onions, sliced thin
4 tablespoons butter

Place 2 lettuce leaves in a large saucepan. Add peas, and sprinkle with sugar, salt, and pepper to taste. Sprinkle green onions over peas and dot with butter. Lay the remaining leaves of lettuce on top, cover, and cook over medium-low heat for 8–10 minutes, or until tender. Discard lettuce leaves before serving.

MAKES 4–6 SERVINGS.

GREEN PEAS AND MUSHROOMS
■ ■ ■

OVEN: 350°

2 (10-ounce) packages frozen green
   peas
5 tablespoons butter, divided use
1 (4-ounce) can sliced mushrooms,
   drained
1 (8-ounce) carton sour cream
1 1/2 teaspoons sugar
1/2 teaspoon salt
dash pepper
1 (2-ounce) package slivered
   almonds

Thaw peas. Place in a saucepan and add 4 tablespoons of the butter. Cook over low heat until butter melts. Toss with mushrooms and stir in sour cream. Season with sugar, salt, and pepper and transfer to a baking dish. Melt remaining 1 tablespoon butter in a small skillet and add almonds. Stir to coat almonds with butter, and cook over medium-low heat until butter begins to turn golden. Pour almonds and butter on top of peas. Cover loosely with foil and bake for 20 minutes.

MAKES 6 SERVINGS.

GREEN PEAS AND CORN IN SOUR CREAM
■ ■ ■

1 small onion, minced
1 tablespoon chopped fresh parsley
3 tablespoons butter
2 (10-ounce) packages frozen green
   peas, thawed
1 (10-ounce) package frozen white
   corn, thawed
salt and pepper
1/2 cup sour cream
1 teaspoon lemon juice

Sauté onion and parsley in butter over medium-low heat until tender. Add peas and corn. Season to taste with salt and pepper. Add sour cream and lemon juice, and continue cooking until heated through.

MAKES 8 SERVINGS.

GREEN PEA SALAD
■ ■ ■

2 (16-ounce) packages frozen
   green peas, thawed
6 slices bacon, cooked and
   crumbled
6 green onions, sliced
1/2 cup mayonnaise
1/2 cup sour cream
1/2 teaspoon salt
2 hard-cooked eggs, chopped

Combine peas, bacon, and onions in a medium bowl. Mix mayonnaise with sour cream and salt. Toss with green peas. Transfer to a serving dish and top with hard-cooked eggs.

MAKES 6–8 SERVINGS.

N·O·T·E·S

SUGAR SNAPS AND SNOW PEAS
■ ■ ■

1/2 pound sugar snap peas
1/2 pound snow peas
2 tablespoons butter
1 teaspoon sugar
1/2 teaspoon salt
1 tablespoon chopped fresh mint
1/2 teaspoon grated lemon zest

Pour 4" of water into a large saucepan. Bring to a boil and add sugar snaps and snow peas. Boil for 3 minutes, or until barely tender. Drain and plunge into ice water. In a large skillet, melt butter over medium heat. Stir in sugar and add sugar snaps and snow peas. Cook just long enough to heat well, stirring to coat with butter. Stir in salt, mint, and lemon zest, and serve immediately.

MAKES 4 SERVINGS.

POTATOES
■ ■ ■

How to Prepare: Cooked potatoes can be eaten with the skin, but they may be peeled if desired. To do so, use a vegetable peeler, rinsing the potatoes under running water as you peel them. If any eyes remain, cut them out with the tip of a paring knife. Slice or cut up the potatoes as desired.

How to Bake: Pierce potatoes in several places with a sharp fork to allow steam to escape. If desired, rub with a little oil or shortening. Bake russet potatoes at 425° for 1–1 1/4 hours, or until they are soft when squeezed gently. (Red potatoes and new potatoes are more often boiled.) If necessary, potatoes can be baked as slowly as 325°, but the cooking time will need to be increased to about 1 1/2 hours or more. It takes about 4 minutes to cook an average baking potato in a microwave oven on full power.

How to Boil: Peel potatoes, cut out blemishes, eyes, and any greenish spots, and cut into quarters or smaller pieces. (New potatoes can be left whole and unpeeled, if desired.) Place in a saucepan, add 1 teaspoon salt, and add water to cover. Bring to a boil, cover, reduce heat, and boil gently for 20–35 minutes, or until tender when pierced with a sharp fork. Cooking time will vary, depending on the size of the potato pieces. When done, drain water, return potatoes to pan, and set over low heat for 2–3 minutes, shaking pan slightly so water will evaporate from potatoes.

How to Tell When Done: Potatoes are done when they can be pierced easily with a sharp fork.

BAKED POTATOES

···

OVEN: 425°

6 russet potatoes
vegetable oil or shortening

Scrub potatoes and dry thoroughly. Rub with oil or shortening, and pierce with a sharp fork. For soft-skinned potatoes, wrap in foil. For crisper skin, leave off the foil. Bake for 1–1¼ hours, or until potatoes feel soft when squeezed.

MAKES 6 SERVINGS.

TWICE-BAKED POTATOES

···

OVEN: 425°/375°

12 russet potatoes
1 cup butter, softened
1 (8-ounce) carton sour cream
1 (8-ounce) carton French onion dip
1 (8-ounce) package cream cheese
½ teaspoon salt
½ teaspoon pepper
Knorr Aromat seasoning (see
    Special Ingredients, page 68)
2 cups (8 ounces) shredded
    Cheddar cheese

Scrub potatoes, prick with a fork, and bake for 1–1¼ hours, or until done. Cool slightly and cut in half lengthwise. Carefully scoop out potatoes into a large bowl, leaving a shell about ¼" thick. Set 16 of the nicest-looking shells aside, and discard the others. Add butter, sour cream, onion dip, cream cheese, salt, pepper, and Knorr seasoning to taste. Mash until fairly smooth. Stuff the potato mixture back into the shells and top with a sprinkling of shredded cheese. At this point, potatoes can be frozen if desired. Place them on a cookie sheet and freeze for about an hour, or until firm. Then place the potatoes in plastic zip bags and return to the freezer. Thaw potatoes before baking. Arrange stuffed potatoes in a greased baking dish and return to a 375° oven for 30–45 minutes, or until cheese is melted and potatoes are piping hot.

MAKES 16 SERVINGS.

Note: Instead of stuffing potatoes into shells, they can be served as a casserole. Spoon into a greased 4-quart baking dish and dot with 2 tablespoons butter. Sprinkle with paprika and bake for 30 minutes.

STEAK HOUSE POTATOES

···

OVEN: 425°

6 russet potatoes
2 egg whites, beaten slightly
sea salt

Scrub potatoes and dry thoroughly. Brush with egg whites and roll in sea salt. Pierce in several places with a sharp fork. Bake for 1–1¼ hours, or until potatoes feel soft when squeezed.

MAKES 6 SERVINGS.

N·O·T·E·S

COTTAGE FRIES
■■■

4 tablespoons bacon drippings or
*   vegetable oil*
1 medium onion, chopped
4 cups cooked or canned white
*   potatoes, sliced*
salt and pepper

Heat bacon drippings or oil in a heavy skillet and add onion. Cook until onion is soft, and add potatoes. Cook for 5–10 minutes, or until a crispy coating has formed. Turn with a pancake turner, and cook until the other side is browned. Season to taste with salt and pepper.

MAKES 4–6 SERVINGS.

POTATO PANCAKES
■■■

leftover mashed potatoes
flour
beaten egg
crushed Ritz cracker crumbs
butter

Form potatoes into patties and coat with flour. Use a pancake turner to lower potato patties into beaten egg, and then coat with cracker crumbs on both sides. Melt butter in a skillet and brown patties for about 2 minutes on each side.

NUMBER OF SERVINGS VARIES.

NEW POTATOES
IN PARSLEY BUTTER
■■■

2 pounds red new potatoes
4 tablespoons butter
salt and pepper
2 tablespoons chopped fresh
*   parsley or 2 teaspoons flakes*

Wash potatoes and peel a strip from around the center of each one. Place in a saucepan and cover with cold water. Boil for 25 minutes, or until tender. Drain. Melt butter in the saucepan and add potatoes. Season with salt and pepper and stir in parsley, turning potatoes to coat well.

MAKES 6 SERVINGS.

Note: If desired, substitute canned new potatoes. There's no need to boil them. Just heat potatoes with other ingredients and serve.

RANCH ROASTED POTATOES
■■■

OVEN: 450°

¼ cup oil
2 pounds red potatoes
1 (1-ounce) package ranch
*   dressing mix*

Pour oil into a 9" x 13" baking dish and heat in the oven for 5 minutes. Meanwhile, scrub potatoes, cut into quarters, and toss with ranch dressing mix. Spread in baking dish, return to oven, and cook for 30–35 minutes, shaking dish occasionally.

MAKES 6 SERVINGS.

MASHED POTATOES
■ ■ ■

6 medium russet potatoes
1/2 cup butter, plus additional
    butter for topping, if desired
3/4 cup milk or half and half
salt and pepper
Knorr Aromat seasoning (see
    Special Ingredients, page 68)

Peel potatoes and cut into quarters. Place in a large saucepan and add cold water to cover. Bring to a boil and cover. Reduce heat to simmer and cook for about 15–20 minutes, or until they are tender and can be easily pierced with a fork. Drain potatoes and return to the saucepan. Mash the potatoes several times to break them up. (A potato masher with a round waffle bottom is preferable to the kind with a zigzag wire bottom.) Don't use an electric mixer unless you don't have a potato masher. These are supposed to be mashed potatoes, not whipped potatoes. Cut butter into chunks and add to potatoes, mashing until potatoes are free of large lumps. Now add the milk or half and half slowly, mashing as you go. You may need to use a little more or less milk or half and half, depending on how creamy or stiff you like your mashed potatoes. Keep mashing until they're as smooth and fluffy as you like, and then season to taste with salt, pepper, and Knorr seasoning. (This seasoning is sometimes difficult to find, but adds a rich, delicious flavor to lots of foods—especially potatoes and yellow squash. It tastes like well-seasoned chicken stock.) Put potatoes in a serving dish and add more butter on top, if desired.

MAKES 6 SERVINGS.

SMASHED POTATOES
■ ■ ■

2–3 pounds red potatoes, unpeeled
1/2 cup milk
2 tablespoons butter, softened
1 teaspoon salt
1/2 teaspoon pepper
1/3 cup sour cream
2 tablespoons chopped fresh
    parsley
2 tablespoons chopped green
    onions

Scrub potatoes well and cut in half. Place in a large saucepan and cover with cold water. Bring to a boil and cook for about 15–20 minutes, or until they are tender and can be easily pierced with a fork. Drain water from potatoes and return them to the saucepan. Add milk and mash just slightly. Turn heat to low and add butter, salt, and pepper. Mash just a little more, but leave them slightly lumpy. Stir in sour cream, and add a little more salt and pepper if desired. Stir in parsley and green onions and serve.

MAKES 4–6 SERVINGS.

N·O·T·E·S

_____

_____

_____

_____

_____

_____

_____

_____

_____

_____

_____

_____

_____

_____

_____

_____

_____

_____

_____

_____

_____

_____

_____

_____

_____

_____

_____

_____

_____

_____

POTATOES AU GRATIN
■ ■ ■

OVEN: 375°

5 tablespoons butter, divided use
3 tablespoons flour
2 cups milk or half and half
2 cups (8 ounces) shredded
   Cheddar cheese, divided use
6 russet potatoes (about 2
   pounds), peeled and sliced
   about 1/8" thick
salt and pepper
nutmeg
6 Ritz crackers, crushed

Melt 4 tablespoons of the butter in a medium saucepan. Whisk in flour. Cook and stir over low heat for 3–5 minutes. Slowly add milk or half and half, stirring constantly until sauce is thickened. Add 1 1/2 cups of the cheese and stir until cheese is melted. Spread a very thin layer of sauce in a greased 2-quart baking dish. Arrange half of the potato slices in the dish, and sprinkle with salt, pepper, and nutmeg. Spoon half of the remaining cheese sauce on top, and then add the remaining potatoes and cheese sauce. Bake uncovered for 1 hour. Toss remaining 1/2 cup shredded cheese with cracker crumbs, and scatter over potatoes. Dot with remaining 1 tablespoon butter. Bake for about 15–20 more minutes.

MAKES 6 SERVINGS.

POTATO SALAD
■ ■ ■

3 pounds red potatoes
1 (8-ounce) carton sour cream
2 cups mayonnaise
1 (1-ounce) package ranch
   dressing mix
1 tablespoon horseradish
1/3 cup parsley flakes
4 hard-cooked eggs, sliced
fresh sprigs of parsley
sliced ripe olives
4 slices bacon, cooked and
   crumbled
paprika

Select regularly shaped potatoes. Scrub, cut in half, and peel only where necessary. Put in a large saucepan, cover with cold water, and bring to a boil. Cover, reduce heat, and cook for 15–20 minutes, or until tender, but firm enough to slice neatly. Drain, cover with cold water, and set aside. Mix sour cream and mayonnaise with ranch dressing mix. Add horseradish and parsley flakes. Spread a thin layer of dressing in a 3-quart serving dish. Slice potatoes about 1/4" thick and arrange a layer in the serving dish. Spread with a little dressing. Repeat layers of potatoes and dressing until all potatoes are used. Spread remaining dressing on top. Arrange egg slices in the center, with parsley and ripe olives in clusters around the outside. Crumble bacon around the egg slices. Sprinkle lightly with paprika. Cover and refrigerate.

MAKES 8–10 SERVINGS.

SCALLOPED POTATOES
■■■

OVEN: 350°

5 tablespoons butter, divided use
1 medium yellow onion, peeled
*   and chopped coarsely*
3 tablespoons flour
2 cups milk
1 teaspoon salt
¼ teaspoon pepper
1 teaspoon dill weed
6 russet potatoes (about 2 pounds),
*   peeled and sliced ¼" thick*

Melt 1 tablespoon of the butter in a small skillet, and sauté onion over medium heat until soft. Set aside. Melt 3 tablespoons of the butter in a medium saucepan. Stir in flour with a whisk. Cook and stir over low heat for 3–5 minutes. Slowly add milk, stirring until sauce is thickened. Stir in salt, pepper, and dill weed. Arrange half of the potato slices in a greased 2-quart baking dish. Scatter on half of the onions and spoon half of the sauce on top. Add layers of remaining potatoes, onions, and sauce. Dot with remaining 1 tablespoon butter. Cover and bake for 1 hour. Uncover and bake for about 20–30 more minutes, or until potatoes are tender.
MAKES 6 SERVINGS.

SPINACH
■■■

How to Prepare: Swish the leaves around in a sink full of cold water. Press the leaves down several times in the water in a pumping motion, to dislodge sand. Change water several times, repeating the process. Shake the excess water off the leaves or dry them in a salad spinner. To remove the stems, fold each leaf in half like a book, with the stem and center rib where the spine of the book would be. Hold the leaf closed with one hand, and grasp the stem with the other hand, pulling it toward the leaf, and away at an angle, removing the stem and the center rib. Then tear the spinach leaves into pieces if desired.

How to Steam: Place freshly washed spinach leaves in a saucepan, with only the water that clings to the leaves after washing. Cover and cook until tender, for 3–10 minutes.

How to Tell When Done: Spinach is done when the leaves are wilted but still bright in color.

"Part of the secret of success in life is to eat what you like and let the food fight it out inside."

—**Mark Twain**

N·O·T·E·S

SPINACH SALAD

■ ■ ■

2 pounds fresh spinach
1/2 pound fresh mushrooms, sliced
1 red onion, sliced thin
6 hard-cooked eggs, chopped
1/2 pound bacon, cooked and
    crumbled
1 1/2 cups (6 ounces) shredded
    Swiss cheese
Sweet and Sour Dressing #1
    (page 255)

Wash spinach well and remove stems.
Tear into bite-size pieces. Combine
with mushrooms, onion, eggs, bacon,
and cheese. Toss with dressing.
MAKES 6 SERVINGS.

WILTED SPINACH SALAD

■ ■ ■

1 pound fresh spinach
4 slices uncooked bacon, diced
2 teaspoons brown sugar
1/4 cup sliced green onions
1/4 teaspoon salt
1 1/2 tablespoons vinegar
1/8 teaspoon dry mustard
dash paprika

Wash spinach and tear coarsely into a
salad bowl. Cook bacon just until crisp.
Remove bacon from skillet with a slotted spoon, drain on paper towels, and
set aside. Reduce heat and add remaining ingredients. Bring just to a boil
and remove from heat. Pour over
spinach and toss. Top with bacon.
MAKES 3-4 SERVINGS.

SPINACH WITH ARTICHOKE HEARTS

■ ■ ■

OVEN: 350°

1 medium onion, chopped
1/2 cup butter
1 (14-ounce) can artichoke hearts,
    drained and quartered
2 (8-ounce) cartons sour cream
2 (10-ounce) packages frozen
    chopped spinach, thawed and
    well drained
salt and pepper
garlic salt
1/2 cup grated Parmesan cheese

Sauté onion in butter in a large skillet. Add artichoke hearts and sour
cream and mix well. Fold in spinach
and season with salt, pepper, and garlic salt. Spoon into a greased 2-quart
baking dish and sprinkle with Parmesan cheese. Bake for 30 minutes.
MAKES 6-8 SERVINGS.

CREAMED SPINACH

■ ■ ■

OVEN: 350°

2 (10-ounce) packages frozen
    chopped spinach, thawed
1/2 lemon
3 tablespoons butter
2 tablespoons flour
1 cup half and half
salt and pepper
nutmeg (freshly grated if possible)
dash cayenne

Drain spinach very well by pressing
all the moisture out in a colander.

Transfer spinach to a mixing bowl, squeeze lemon over spinach, and toss to mix well. Set aside. In a large saucepan, melt butter and stir in flour with a whisk. Cook and stir for 3–5 minutes, until butter just begins to turn golden. Slowly whisk in half and half. Cook and stir until sauce is thickened. Stir in spinach and season to taste with salt, pepper, nutmeg, and cayenne. Cook over low heat until heated through.

MAKES 6 SERVINGS.

SPINACH CASSEROLE WITH CREAM CHEESE
■ ■ ■

OVEN: 350°

2 (10-ounce) packages frozen
    chopped spinach, thawed
1 (8-ounce) package cream cheese,
    softened
1/2 cup butter, melted, divided use
1 (8-ounce) package herb-seasoned
    stuffing mix

Drain spinach very well by pressing all the moisture out in a colander. Transfer spinach to a mixing bowl. Add cream cheese and 1/4 cup of the butter and mix well. Sprinkle half of the stuffing mix into a greased 1 1/2-quart baking dish. Spoon spinach mixture over it and top with remaining stuffing mix. Drizzle remaining 1/4 cup butter on top and bake for 30 minutes.

MAKES 6 SERVINGS.

SPINACH ROCKEFELLER
■ ■ ■

This recipe can also be used as a stuffing for baked tomatoes.

OVEN: 350°

4 (10-ounce) packages frozen
    chopped spinach, thawed
3/4 cup butter
1 (8-ounce) carton sour cream
2 tablespoons vinegar
1/2 teaspoon Worcestershire sauce
1 (3-ounce) package cream cheese
1 (6-ounce) roll jalapeño cheese
salt and pepper
garlic salt
8 slices bacon, cooked and crumbled

Drain spinach well in a colander and press out excess moisture with the back of a spoon. Put it in a very large saucepan and add butter, cooking over low heat until butter melts. Stir in sour cream, vinegar, and Worcestershire sauce. Cut cream cheese and jalapeño cheese into chunks and stir into spinach. Cook until cheeses melt. Season to taste with salt, pepper, and garlic salt. Transfer to a greased 3-quart baking dish and top with bacon. Bake for 30 minutes, or until piping hot.

MAKES 12 SERVINGS.

> *"How can you govern a country which has 246 varieties of cheese?"*
>
> —Charles DeGaulle

N·O·T·E·S

_____
_____
_____
_____
_____
_____
_____
_____
_____
_____
_____
_____
_____
_____
_____
_____
_____
_____
_____
_____
_____
_____
_____
_____
_____
_____
_____
_____
_____
_____
_____
_____

SQUASH

...

How to Prepare Summer Squash:
Wash squash but do not pare, since
the skin is edible. Trim off the stem
and blossom ends, and cut away any
blemishes. Then cut squash in half
lengthwise, or slice lengthwise or
crosswise, as desired.

How to Prepare Winter Squash:
Wash squash and cut in half lengthwise. Remove seeds and stringy fibers.
Unless the cooked squash is to be
served in the rind, remove it. Cut
squash into cubes if desired.

How to Boil Summer Squash: Pour
1" of water into a saucepan and add
1 teaspoon salt. Bring to a boil and add
sliced squash. Cover, reduce heat, and
simmer until tender. Slices take about
6–9 minutes, and cubes 5–7 minutes.

How to Boil Winter Squash: Pour
about 1" of water into a saucepan and
add 1 teaspoon salt. Bring to a boil
and add sliced or cubed squash.
Cover, reduce heat, and boil gently
for 15–20 minutes, or until tender.

How to Steam Summer Squash:
Pour about 1" of water into a saucepan
and set a steamer basket in place. Add
squash and bring water to a boil.
Cover, reduce heat, and cook for
about 5–7 minutes.

How to Steam Winter Squash: Pour
about 1" of water into a saucepan and
set a steamer basket in place. Add

squash and bring water to a boil.
Cover, reduce heat, and cook until
tender. Slices should take about
12–15 minutes, and cubes about 7–10
minutes.

How to Bake Winter Squash: Cut
in half lengthwise and scrape out
seeds and fibers. Sprinkle with salt and
pepper, and dot with butter. Wrap
each piece in aluminum foil and set
in a baking dish, cut side up. Bake at
375° for 45 minutes, or until tender,
and easily pierced with a fork.

How to Tell When Done: Squash
should be cooked until fork-tender.

BAKED ACORN SQUASH

...

OVEN: 375°

3 medium acorn squash
6 tablespoons butter, softened
salt
6 teaspoons brown sugar
6 teaspoons honey
nutmeg

Wash squash and cut in half lengthwise. Scoop out seeds and fibrous
membranes. Rub the inside of each
half with 1 tablespoon butter, and salt
lightly. Add 1 teaspoon brown sugar
and 1 teaspoon honey to each half and
sprinkle with nutmeg. Pour a little
water into a 3-quart baking dish (to
keep squash from sticking) and arrange
squash in baking dish. Bake for about
45 minutes, or until squash is tender.
MAKES 6 SERVINGS.

SUMMER SQUASH

■ ■ ■

2 pounds yellow crookneck squash
4 tablespoons butter
1/2 small onion, chopped
salt and pepper
Knorr Aromat Seasoning (see
    Special Ingredients, page 68)

Scrub squash and trim off ends and
any bruised spots. Slice thinly and
steam for about 8–10 minutes, or
until tender. Drain in a colander,
pressing out as much liquid as possible with the back of a large spoon.
Melt butter in a large saucepan and
add onion. Cook for 5 minutes. Return drained squash to saucepan and
mix well with butter and onion. Season well with salt, pepper, and Knorr
seasoning. Add a little more butter if
desired, and continue cooking until
squash is heated through.
MAKES 4 SERVINGS.

STUFFED SQUASH

■ ■ ■

OVEN: 350°

6 small yellow squash
4 tablespoons butter, divided use
1 small yellow onion, chopped
salt and pepper
8 Ritz crackers, crushed
1/2 cup (2 ounces) shredded
    Cheddar cheese

Wash squash and trim off ends. Place
in a steamer basket over boiling water
and cover. Steam for 7–8 minutes, or
until tender. Then cut squash in half

lengthwise. Heat 2 tablespoons of the
butter in a skillet and add onion. Sauté
for 5 minutes, or until onion is soft.
Meanwhile, scoop pulp out of squash
into a bowl, being careful not to break
the skin. Set squash shells aside. Season pulp with salt and pepper, and toss
with crackers. Stir into skillet, coating
well with butter. Stuff pulp back into
the shells, and arrange in a well-greased
baking dish. Top with a little shredded
cheese and dot with remaining 2 tablespoons butter. Bake for about 10–15
minutes, or until cheese is melted.
MAKES 4 SERVINGS.

CRUNCHY SQUASH
CASSEROLE

■ ■ ■

OVEN: 350°

1 cup water
1 teaspoon sugar
1 chicken bouillon cube
2 pounds yellow squash, sliced
3/4 cup butter, divided use
1 medium onion, chopped
1 (8-ounce) carton sour cream
1 (10 3/4-ounce) can cream of
    chicken soup
1 (8-ounce) can sliced water
    chestnuts, drained and
    chopped
1 (8-ounce) package herb-seasoned
    stuffing mix

Bring water to a boil in a large
saucepan. Add sugar and bouillon cube
and stir to dissolve. Add squash. Cover,
reduce heat, and cook until tender.

(continued)

Drain squash in a colander and set aside. In the same saucepan, melt ½ cup of the butter. Add onion and cook until soft. While squash is still in the colander, use the back of a spoon to press excess moisture out of the squash. Transfer it to the saucepan and stir in sour cream, soup, and water chestnuts. Melt remaining ¼ cup butter and toss with stuffing mix. Pour all but 1 cup of the stuffing mix into a greased 2-quart baking dish. Spread squash mixture over stuffing mix, and sprinkle remaining 1 cup stuffing mix on top. Bake for 30–45 minutes, or until bubbly and hot.

MAKES 8 SERVINGS.

SQUASH AU GRATIN
■■■

OVEN: 375°

3 pounds yellow squash
½ cup butter, melted, divided use
½ cup chopped onion
½ teaspoon salt
¼ teaspoon pepper
2 teaspoons sugar
2 eggs, beaten
12 Ritz crackers, crushed

Scrub and slice squash. Steam for 5–7 minutes, or until tender. Drain well and mash. Add ¼ cup of the butter, the onion, salt, pepper, sugar, and eggs, and mix well. Spoon into a greased 1½-quart baking dish and top with crackers. Drizzle remaining ¼ cup butter on top and bake for 1 hour.

MAKES 6 SERVINGS.

SWEET POTATOES
■■■

How to Prepare: Scrub sweet potatoes well and leave them whole if baking. Quarter them or cut them into large pieces if boiling. Sweet potatoes are easier to peel after cooking.

How to Boil: Pour about 1″ of water into a saucepan and add 1 teaspoon salt. Bring water to a boil and add peeled and quartered sweet potatoes. Cover, reduce heat, and boil gently for 30–35 minutes, or until tender.

How to Steam: Pour about 1″ of water into a saucepan and set a steamer basket in place. Add peeled and quartered sweet potatoes and bring water to a boil. Cover, reduce heat, and cook for 25–30 minutes, or until tender.

How to Bake: Scrub sweet potatoes and prick with a fork to allow steam to escape. Place on a foil-lined baking sheet and bake at 400° for 45–55 minutes, or until tender. Because sweet potatoes contain a fairly high amount of natural sugar, they are likely to ooze some of this sugar when pricked with a fork and baked. For that reason, a foil-lined pan will make cleaning up easier. Sweet potatoes can be baked at a lower temperature, but they will take longer to cook.

How to Tell When Done: Sweet potatoes are done when they can be pierced easily with a fork.

BAKED SWEET POTATOES

■ ■ ■

OVEN: 400°

4 medium sweet potatoes
butter
salt and pepper
maple syrup (optional)

Scrub sweet potatoes and dry. Pierce each potato with a fork several times and place on a greased foil-lined baking sheet. Bake for about 45–55 minutes, or until potatoes are soft when squeezed. Make an "x" in the top of each potato and squeeze from the ends to plump them up. Stuff with butter and sprinkle with salt and pepper. Serve with maple syrup if desired.
MAKES 4 SERVINGS.

BAKED ORANGE SWEET POTATOES

■ ■ ■

OVEN: 400°

6 medium sweet potatoes
⅔ cup sugar
1 tablespoon cornstarch
1 teaspoon salt
½ teaspoon grated orange peel
1 cup orange juice
3 tablespoons butter

Peel sweet potatoes. Cut in half lengthwise and then again crosswise. Arrange in a greased 2-quart baking dish. In a small saucepan, mix together sugar, cornstarch, salt, and orange peel. Stir in orange juice. Bring to a boil, stirring constantly. Cook for 1 minute. Pour over sweet potatoes and dot with butter. Cover with foil and bake for 1 hour, basting with pan juices occasionally.
MAKES 6 SERVINGS.

ROASTED SWEET POTATOES

■ ■ ■

OVEN: 375°

2 medium sweet potatoes
2–3 tablespoons oil
½ teaspoon minced garlic
½ teaspoon salt
¼ teaspoon pepper
1 lime, cut into wedges

Peel sweet potatoes and cut in half lengthwise. Turn cut sides down on a cutting board and cut into ¾"-thick slices. Pour oil into a shallow baking dish and stir in garlic. Add sweet potatoes and toss to coat both sides. Sprinkle with salt and pepper and roast uncovered for 20 minutes. Turn with a pancake turner and roast for 15–20 more minutes, or until tender. Arrange on a serving plate and serve with wedges of fresh lime.
MAKES 4 SERVINGS.

AMARETTO SWEET POTATOES
■ ■ ■

OVEN: 350°

½ cup butter
2 (29-ounce) cans cut yams or
  sweet potatoes (unsweetened),
  drained, or 3 pounds fresh
  sweet potatoes, cooked
¼ cup honey
¼ cup orange juice
¼ cup Amaretto
½ teaspoon cinnamon
¼ teaspoon nutmeg
½ teaspoon salt
⅛ teaspoon MSG
dash pepper
½ teaspoon vanilla extract
fresh mint leaves (optional)

In a large saucepan, melt butter over low heat. Add sweet potatoes, honey, orange juice, Amaretto, cinnamon, nutmeg, salt, MSG, pepper, and vanilla extract. Mash with a potato masher until free of lumps and well mixed. Transfer to a greased 2½-quart baking dish and bake for 30 minutes, or until piping hot. Garnish with fresh mint leaves if desired.

MAKES 8 SERVINGS.

Note: This is a part of our traditional Thanksgiving dinner menu. Since I make Cranberry Salad (page 243) as well, I always have extra scooped-out orange shells left over. So instead of baking the sweet potatoes as a casserole, I stuff the sweet potato mixture into the orange shells. Then I arrange them in a well-greased 2-quart rectangular baking dish, so that the orange shells touch each other and don't topple over. I dot them with butter, sprinkle slivered almonds over them, and bake them as above. When they come out of the oven, I garnish each one with a couple of mint leaves.

SWEET POTATO SOUFFLÉ
■ ■ ■

OVEN: 350°

2 (16-ounce) cans sweet potatoes,
  drained
½ teaspoon salt
6 tablespoons butter, softened,
  divided use
1 teaspoon vanilla extract
½ cup maple syrup
2 eggs
½ cup milk
1 cup brown sugar
1 cup chopped pecans
⅓ cup flour

Mash sweet potatoes together with salt, 4 tablespoons of the butter, vanilla extract, maple syrup, eggs, and milk. Pour into a greased, shallow 3-quart baking dish. Combine brown sugar with pecans, remaining 2 tablespoons butter, and flour. Sprinkle over sweet potatoes and bake for 30–35 minutes, or until top is browned and crunchy.

MAKES 6–8 SERVINGS.

TOMATOES

■■■

In the winter, when most of the decent tomatoes are probably south of the equator, don't forget the Roma tomato. Although it's no substitute for summer tomatoes, at least it will get you through the winter. And remember, the quickest way to ruin a good tomato is to put it in the refrigerator!

How to Peel: Cut a cone-shaped plug out of the top of the tomato, to remove the stem end. Then peel it in one of two ways: (1) Trim the base and peel the tomato with a vegetable peeler, using a sawing motion. (2) Cut an X at the base of the tomato and lower it into boiling water for 15–20 seconds. Then drain and cool the tomato, and strip off the skin in sections, from the points of the X that you cut in the base.

How to Prepare: Cut the tomato in half crosswise, and squeeze gently to remove the seeds. Then cut it into wedges or dice it, as desired.

FRIED GREEN TOMATOES

■■■

3 large green tomatoes
1 cup white cornmeal
3 tablespoons flour
1 teaspoon salt
¼ teaspoon pepper
½ cup buttermilk
oil or bacon grease

Wash tomatoes, slice off ends, slice crosswise about ¼″ thick, and soak in ice water for about an hour. Drain well. Mix cornmeal with flour, salt, and pepper in a shallow bowl. Measure buttermilk into another shallow bowl. Heat oil or bacon drippings in a skillet over medium heat. Coat tomato slices with buttermilk and then dip in cornmeal. Turn to coat both sides well. Transfer tomato slices to skillet and fry until golden brown on both sides. Drain on paper towels.

MAKES 4 SERVINGS.

ROASTED ROMA TOMATOES

■■■

OVEN: 325°

6 firm Roma tomatoes
2 tablespoons olive oil
salt and pepper
2 tablespoons chopped fresh basil
2 tablespoons grated Parmesan
   cheese

Wash tomatoes and trim off ends. Cut in half lengthwise and arrange in a greased shallow baking dish. Drizzle with oil and sprinkle with salt and pepper. Bake tomatoes for about 20 minutes. Toss basil with Parmesan cheese and sprinkle on tomatoes. Bake for 5 more minutes.

MAKES 4 SERVINGS.

N·O·T·E·S

BAKED TOMATOES

•••

OVEN: 350°

4 medium-size firm tomatoes
butter
Dijon mustard
salt and pepper
¹/₃ cup dried bread crumbs
¹/₃ cup grated Parmesan cheese

Trim tops off tomatoes and scoop out seeds. Place cut-side-down on paper towels to drain for 15 minutes. Stuff slivers of butter into cavities of tomatoes and spread with Dijon mustard. Sprinkle with salt and pepper. Mix bread crumbs and Parmesan cheese and sprinkle on tomatoes. Place in a greased baking dish and bake for about 15 minutes.

MAKES 4 SERVINGS.

ZUCCHINI

•••

How to Prepare: Wash the zucchini, but do not pare it, since the skin is edible. Trim off the stem and blossom ends, and cut away any blemishes. Then cut it in half lengthwise or slice it lengthwise or crosswise, as desired.

How to Boil: Pour about 1" of water into a saucepan and add 1 teaspoon salt. Bring water to a boil and add sliced or cubed zucchini. Cover, reduce heat, and boil gently until tender. Slices should take about 6–9 minutes, and cubes about 5–7 minutes.

How to Steam: Pour about 1"of water into a saucepan and set a steamer basket in place. Add zucchini and bring water to a boil. Cover, reduce heat, and cook for about 5–7 minutes.

How to Tell When Done: Zucchini should be cooked until fork-tender.

ZUCCHINI AND BACON

•••

OVEN: 350°

6 slices bacon, diced
1 cup chopped onion
3¹/₂ cups sliced zucchini
1 (8-ounce) can tomato sauce
³/₄ teaspoon salt
¹/₄ teaspoon pepper
15 crushed Ritz crackers
¹/₂ cup grated Parmesan cheese

Fry bacon slightly in a large skillet. Add onion and cook until soft. Stir in zucchini and tomato sauce, and season with salt and pepper. Pour into a greased 2-quart baking dish and sprinkle with crushed crackers and Parmesan cheese. Cover and cook for about 30 minutes.

MAKES 6 SERVINGS.

Salads and Side Dishes

SALADS AND SIDE DISHES
■■■

SEARCHING FOR SALADS
■■■

Although this chapter contains many delicious green salads and other side dishes, the preceding Vegetables chapter is the place to find even more salads listed by vegetable, including Potato Salad and Spinach Salad.

BAKED APPLES
■■■

OVEN: 375°

6 medium baking apples (see pages 319–320)
boiling water
³/₄ cup brown sugar
¹/₈ teaspoon cinnamon
¹/₈ teaspoon ground ginger (optional)
3 tablespoons butter
1 cup raisins
1 cup pecans, chopped

Wash and core apples, leaving ½″ core at base. Put in a baking dish so apples are close together. Cover bottom of baking dish with boiling water. Mix together brown sugar, cinnamon, and ginger (optional). Fill center of each apple with 2 tablespoons of the brown sugar mixture and ½ tablespoon butter. Cover and bake for about 45 minutes, or until apples are tender, basting occasionally with pan juices. Remove carefully from pan to a serving dish. Pour remaining liquid from the baking dish into a saucepan and add raisins and nuts. Boil the syrup gently until it thickens. Spoon syrup over apples and serve.

MAKES 6 SERVINGS.

ESCALLOPED APPLES
■■■

6–8 cooking apples (see pages 319–320)
¹/₂ cup water
2 tablespoons butter
2 tablespoons flour
1 tablespoon lemon juice
¹/₂ cup sugar (or more to taste, depending on flavor of apples)
1 teaspoon cinnamon
pinch salt
dash nutmeg (optional)

Core apples, peel them, and cut into wedges. Cut each wedge in half. Put apples in a saucepan with ½ cup water. Cover and cook gently until tender, for 15–20 minutes. In another saucepan, melt butter. Stir in flour and cook over low heat for 3–5 minutes. Add apples and stir in lemon juice, sugar, cinnamon, and salt. If desired, add a dash of nutmeg before serving.

MAKES 6–8 SERVINGS.

APPLESAUCE

■ ■ ■

*6–8 cooking apples, cored, peeled,
and sliced (see pages 319–320)*
¼ cup water
1 teaspoon cinnamon
½ cup sugar
2 tablespoons brown sugar
lemon juice (optional)

Put apples and water in a saucepan. Simmer for 15–20 minutes, or until tender. Remove from heat. Mash apples slightly and stir in cinnamon and sugars, adding more sugar if necessary. If apples are lacking in flavor, add a little lemon juice. For smooth applesauce, put through a food mill. Serve warm or chilled.

MAKES 6–8 SERVINGS.

FRIED APPLES

■ ■ ■

4 strips bacon, diced
*5–6 cooking apples, cored and
sliced (see pages 319–320)*
¾ cup sugar
1 tablespoon lemon juice
few slivers lemon peel
½ teaspoon ground cloves
½ teaspoon nutmeg
½ teaspoon cinnamon
½ cup water

Fry bacon and set aside, reserving drippings. Add apples to bacon drippings and stir to coat each piece with drippings. Add sugar, lemon juice, and lemon peel, and stir to blend. Sprinkle with cloves, nutmeg, and cinnamon. Add the reserved bacon and water. Cover and cook over medium-low heat for about 10 minutes, or until apples are softened. Reduce heat and simmer for another 10 minutes. If necessary, add a little more water to keep apples from sticking. When done, they should be golden with a dark caramel coating.

MAKES 6 SERVINGS.

STEWED APPLES

■ ■ ■

*2 pounds tart cooking apples,
cored and peeled (see pages
319–320)*
2 tablespoons butter
½ cup sugar
1 stick cinnamon
4 whole cloves
*1 cup water or wine, or a
combination of the two*
1 lemon

Cut apples into thick slices and sauté in butter in a large skillet for about 5 minutes. Stir in sugar, cinnamon, and cloves. Add water or wine or a combination of the two. Wash lemon and grate the peel. Cut lemon in half and squeeze the juice into a small cup. Add lemon peel and strained lemon juice to the water or wine. Bring just to a boil and then reduce heat. Simmer for 8–10 minutes, or until apples can be pierced easily with a fork.

MAKES 6 SERVINGS.

N·O·T·E·S

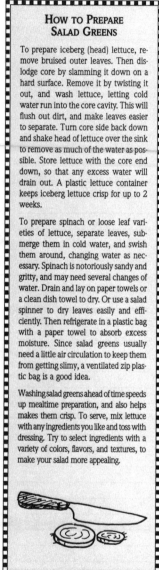

HOW TO PREPARE SALAD GREENS

To prepare iceberg (head) lettuce, remove bruised outer leaves. Then dislodge core by slamming it down on a hard surface. Remove it by twisting it out, and wash lettuce, letting cold water run into the core cavity. This will flush out dirt, and make leaves easier to separate. Turn core side back down and shake head of lettuce over the sink to remove as much of the water as possible. Store lettuce with the core end down, so that any excess water will drain out. A plastic lettuce container keeps iceberg lettuce crisp for up to 2 weeks.

To prepare spinach or loose leaf varieties of lettuce, separate leaves, submerge them in cold water, and swish them around, changing water as necessary. Spinach is notoriously sandy and gritty, and may need several changes of water. Drain and lay on paper towels or a clean dish towel to dry. Or use a salad spinner to dry leaves easily and efficiently. Then refrigerate in a plastic bag with a paper towel to absorb excess moisture. Since salad greens usually need a little air circulation to keep them from getting slimy, a ventilated zip plastic bag is a good idea.

Washing salad greens ahead of time speeds up mealtime preparation, and also helps makes them crisp. To serve, mix lettuce with any ingredients you like and toss with dressing. Try to select ingredients with a variety of colors, flavors, and textures, to make your salad more appealing.

APPLE WALDORF SALAD

•••

3 cups cored, unpeeled diced apples
2 teaspoons lemon juice
¾ cup diced celery
½ cup raisins
½ cup broken pecans or walnuts
¼ teaspoon salt
¾ cup mayonnaise

Toss apples with lemon juice. Add celery, raisins, and nuts. Sprinkle with salt and fold in mayonnaise.
MAKES 4–6 SERVINGS.

BAKED APRICOTS

•••

OVEN: 300°

2 (17-ounce) cans apricot halves, drained
1 cup brown sugar
8 ounces Ritz crackers (2 rolls)
12 tablespoons butter
1 (16-ounce) can tart cherries, drained

Grease a 3-quart baking dish. Line it with 1 can of the apricot halves and sprinkle ¼ cup of the brown sugar over them. Add 2 ounces (half a roll) of crumbled Ritz crackers and dot with 3 tablespoons of the butter, cut into chunks. Next, add half the cherries, followed by another ¼ cup of the brown sugar, half a roll of the crumbled Ritz crackers, and 3 tablespoons of the butter. Make another layer with the second can of apricot

halves, ¼ cup of of the brown sugar, half a roll of the crumbled Ritz crackers, and 3 tablespoons of the butter. Finish with the remaining cherries, brown sugar, crumbled Ritz crackers, and butter. Bake uncovered for 1 hour.
MAKES 8 SERVINGS.

BABY SALAD GREENS WITH APPLES

•••

6 ounces mixed baby salad greens (mesclun)
1 Granny Smith apple
2 tablespoons lemon juice
2 ounces walnut pieces
2 ounces blue cheese, crumbled
Walnut Vinaigrette (page 256)

Arrange salad greens in 4 individual bowls. Wash, core, and slice apple thinly, and place in a small dish. Sprinkle with lemon juice and toss to mix well. Arrange apple slices over greens, and scatter walnut pieces and blue cheese on top. Drizzle with Walnut Vinaigrette.
MAKES 4 SERVINGS.

BROILED BANANAS
WITH HONEY

■ ■ ■

6 bananas, split lengthwise
2 tablespoons honey
2 tablespoons lime juice
cinnamon

Arrange banana halves cut-side-up in a large shallow baking dish. Sprinkle ½ teaspoon honey and ½ teaspoon lime juice over each half. Sprinkle with cinnamon and broil 4" from heat for 3–4 minutes, or until tender.
MAKES 6 SERVINGS.

BAKED BANANAS

■ ■ ■

OVEN: 350°

4 medium bananas, slightly underripe
4 tablespoons butter
¼ cup brown sugar
salt
cinnamon
nutmeg

Peel bananas, split lengthwise, and cut in two crosswise. Arrange in a shallow baking dish. Melt butter in a small saucepan and stir in sugar.

Pour over bananas and bake for 15–20 minutes, or until bananas are soft and pale golden. Sprinkle with a dash of salt, cinnamon, and nutmeg before serving.
MAKES 4 SERVINGS

CAESAR SALAD

■ ■ ■

1 egg
⅓ cup Caesar Dressing (page 250), divided use
1 large head romaine lettuce
1 cup garlic croutons
¼ cup grated Parmesan cheese

Bring a small saucepan of water to a simmer. Carefully lower the egg on a slotted spoon into the water and leave it for exactly 1 minute. Then remove the egg and break it into a large wooden salad bowl. Add about half of the dressing and whisk it well with the egg. Tear the lettuce into bite-size pieces and add to the salad bowl with the remaining dressing, tossing well. Top with croutons and Parmesan cheese. Toss once more and serve immediately.
MAKES 4 SERVINGS.

N·O·T·E·S

CLUB SALAD

■ ■ ■

1 head iceberg lettuce, cored, washed, and chilled
1/2 cup Thousand Island Dressing (page 255)
6 slices bacon, cooked and crumbled
2 hard-cooked eggs, chopped

Cut lettuce into 8 wedges. Place 2 wedges on each salad plate and spoon dressing over lettuce. (Use more or less to taste.) Sprinkle with crumbled bacon and chopped egg.
MAKES 4 SERVINGS.

COBB SALAD

■ ■ ■

1 large head iceberg lettuce, washed and torn into pieces
2/3 cup Basic Vinaigrette (page 256)
3 ounces blue cheese, crumbled
1 tomato, peeled and diced
1 avocado, peeled and diced
2 hard-cooked eggs
8 slices bacon, cooked and crumbled
1 1/2 cups diced cooked chicken

In a large, shallow bowl, toss lettuce with dressing. Mound blue cheese in the center of lettuce, and arrange other ingredients in separate wedges on top of lettuce, like a pinwheel. Bring to the table for presentation, and then toss again and serve.
MAKES 4–6 SERVINGS.

CRANBERRY RELISH

■ ■ ■

1 3/4 cups water
1 cup sugar
2 tablespoons corn syrup
1 medium onion (mild or sweet), chopped
1 tablespoon minced garlic
2 teaspoons cinnamon
3/4 teaspoon ground cloves
1/2 teaspoon salt
1/2 cup cider vinegar
1/4 teaspoon cayenne
2 (6-ounce) bags dried cranberries (sometimes called "craisins")
1 cup raisins
1 Granny Smith apple, cored but not peeled, chopped
1/2 teaspoon ground ginger
1/2 cup light brown sugar

Mix water, sugar, corn syrup, onion, garlic, cinnamon, cloves, salt, vinegar, and cayenne in a large saucepan. Bring to a boil over medium-high heat, stirring constantly. Reduce heat and simmer uncovered for 5 minutes. Add cranberries and simmer for 15 more minutes. Add raisins, apple, ginger, and brown sugar. Simmer uncovered, stirring occasionally, for 15 more minutes. Pour into a refrigerator-safe container and cool for 15 minutes. Then refrigerate for at least 2 hours before serving, to allow flavors to blend. Serve warm or at room temperature. Keeps well in the refrigerator.
MAKES ABOUT 4 CUPS.

> *"Strange to see how a good dinner and feasting reconcile everybody."*
>
> —Samuel Pepys

CRANBERRY SALAD
■ ■ ■

This has been a part of our Thanksgiving dinner since the first year Jack and I were married, and it always gets rave reviews.

1 (12-ounce) bag cranberries
4 navel oranges, one unpeeled
1 (15¼-ounce) can crushed
    pineapple, packed in juice
2 cups sugar
½ cup fruit juice: orange, apple,
    pineapple, or cranberry
3 envelopes unflavored gelatin
6–8 ounces pecans
sprigs of parsley for garnish
mayonnaise (optional)

Wash cranberries, discarding bad ones, and chop in a food processor, using metal blade. Spoon into a large mixing bowl. Peel 3 of the 4 oranges and cut all of the oranges into quarters. Chop in a food processor and add to berries. Drain juice from pineapple and reserve. Add crushed pineapple to mixing bowl. Stir in sugar and mix well. Pour reserved pineapple juice and ½ cup additional fruit juice into a small saucepan. Whisk in gelatin. Stir over low heat just until gelatin is dissolved. (Caution: Do not turn your back on it while it's heating! It can boil very quickly, which will cause it to lose its ability to jell.) Add gelatin mixture to fruit and stir in pecans. Pour into a well-greased 3-quart mold (such as a Bundt pan) and chill until set. Unmold salad onto a serving dish and garnish with parsley sprigs. Serve with mayonnaise if desired.

MAKES 16–20 SERVINGS.

Note: Without the gelatin, this makes a delicious cranberry relish that keeps well in the refrigerator. It's also thick enough to mold a second time. Warm the leftovers in the microwave just until softened. Then pour into a smaller mold and refrigerate until set.

CUCUMBER SALAD
■ ■ ■

1 (3-ounce) package lime gelatin
1⅓ cups boiling water
3 tablespoons lemon juice
½ teaspoon salt
1 (8-ounce) carton cottage cheese
½ cup mayonnaise
1 tablespoon onion juice
1 cup peeled, seeded, chopped
    cucumber
1 teaspoon prepared horseradish
1 cup slivered almonds

Dissolve gelatin in 1⅓ cups boiling water. Add lemon juice and salt and chill until thickened but not set. Fold in remaining ingredients. Pour into a 1½-quart mold and chill until set.

MAKES 8 SERVINGS.

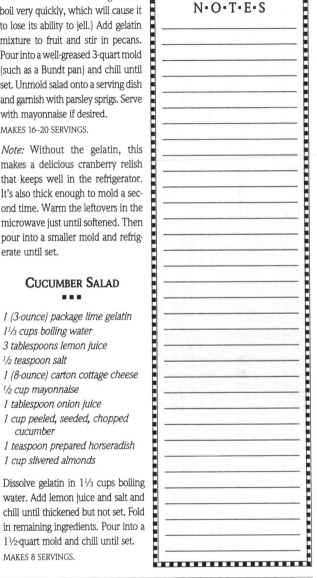

N·O·T·E·S

How to Prepare Citrus Fruits

Oranges, Grapefruit, and Tangerines

1. To juice any citrus fruit, wash it, cut in half, and squeeze or use a reamer.

2. To peel, slice off ends with a serrated knife and cut rind off in a spiral. (Tangerines usually have loose skin, and can be peeled by hand.)

3. To section, hold peeled fruit in one hand and slice fruit away from membranes on each side.

Preparing Tropical Fruits

Figs: Wash gently. Eat out of hand, cut in half lengthwise, or slice.

Kiwi fruit: After washing, eat out of hand. Or cut in half and separate skin from pulp with a spoon. Then slice as desired.

Mangoes: Cut in half lengthwise and remove seed. Then cut flesh into cubes without cutting through skin. Finally, turn skin inside out to pop cubes away, and slice them away from the skin.

Pineapple: Slice off both ends and stand fruit up on a cutting board. Slice away skin in downward strokes with a sharp knife, and cut into slices or chunks as desired.

Or cut pineapple into quarters lengthwise, with or without top. Then slice away core, separate pulp from skin, and cut into chunks.

Double Hearts Vinaigrette Salad
■■■

1 (14-ounce) can hearts of palm, drained
1 (14-ounce) can artichoke hearts, drained
1 (16-ounce) bottle Italian dressing
4 large Boston lettuce leaves
4 hard-cooked eggs, quartered
2 medium tomatoes, quartered
12 ripe olives, pitted

Cut hearts of palm into lengthwise sticks about the thickness of a pencil. Quarter artichoke hearts. Put into separate shallow containers and pour 1 cup of the Italian dressing over each. Cover and refrigerate for several hours. When ready to serve, drain and arrange each portion on a lettuce leaf. Garnish with eggs, tomatoes, and olives.

MAKES 4 SERVINGS.

Fruit Salad
■■■

Use ripe, fresh fruits in any combination and quantity: apples, oranges, kiwi fruit, blueberries, plums, nectarines, grapes, bananas, peaches, melon, cherries, raspberries, and strawberries. Cut up fruit and toss with lemon juice. Serve with Poppy Seed Dressing (page 254).

Baked Curried Fruit
■■■

OVEN: 350°

1 (24-ounce) can or jar applesauce
1/2 teaspoon cinnamon
1/2 teaspoon nutmeg
1 (15 1/4-ounce) can pineapple chunks packed in juice (reserve juice)
1 (6-ounce) jar red maraschino cherries
1 (16-ounce) can peach halves
1 (16-ounce) can pear halves
1 (16-ounce) can apricot halves
3 bananas, peeled and sliced
2 tablespoons butter
2 tablespoons cornstarch
4 teaspoons curry powder
1/2 cup dry sherry

Mix applesauce, cinnamon, and nutmeg. Drain pineapple, reserving juice, and stir into applesauce. Drain cherries, peaches, pears, and apricots and add to applesauce. Pour into a buttered 3-quart baking dish and top with bananas. In a small saucepan, melt butter and stir in cornstarch and curry powder. Cook and stir over low heat for 3–5 minutes. Blend in 1/2 cup of the reserved pineapple juice and sherry, and heat until thickened. Pour over fruit and bake for 30–45 minutes, or until bubbly.

MAKES 10–12 SERVINGS.

GRAPEFRUIT AND AVOCADO SALAD
■ ■ ■

1 (16-ounce) can grapefruit
    sections
lettuce leaves
1 ripe avocado
Kraft Casino French dressing

Mound grapefruit sections on lettuce leaves. Surround with avocado slices and drizzle with French dressing.

MAKES 3–4 SERVINGS.

BROILED GRAPEFRUIT HALVES
■ ■ ■

OVEN: BROIL

4 grapefruit halves
4 teaspoons cinnamon-sugar
    mixture (see Note page 264)
4 teaspoons honey
4 teaspoons melted butter
4 maraschino cherries

Cut around the edges of each grapefruit section, leaving the sections in the shell. Sprinkle each grapefruit half with 1 teaspoon cinnamon-sugar mixture. Drizzle 1 teaspoon honey and 1 teaspoon melted butter over each grapefruit half. Broil for 5–7 minutes. Place a cherry in the center of each half and serve.

MAKES 4 SERVINGS.

LAYERED SALAD
■ ■ ■

1 medium head lettuce, torn up
1/2 pound spinach leaves, washed
    well and torn into pieces
2 green onions, thinly sliced
1 cucumber, peeled and sliced
1 (10-ounce) package frozen
    green peas
2 medium tomatoes, diced
1 (14-ounce) can artichoke hearts,
    drained and quartered
1 cup mayonnaise
1 (8-ounce) carton sour cream
4 hard-cooked eggs, quartered
6 slices bacon, cooked and
    crumbled
1 (2 1/4-ounce) can sliced ripe
    olives, drained

Arrange lettuce, spinach, onions, cucumber, peas, tomatoes, and artichoke hearts in layers in a large salad bowl. Blend mayonnaise with sour cream and spread on top. Arrange egg quarters around the outside. Sprinkle bacon inside the eggs, and put olives in the center. Cover and refrigerate. Serve without tossing.

MAKES 12 SERVINGS.

BAKED PEACHES
■ ■ ■

OVEN: 350°

8 peach halves (fresh or canned)
2 tablespoons lemon juice
1 tablespoon butter, melted
2 tablespoons brown sugar
cinnamon

Arrange peach halves, cut-side-up, in a greased 1½-quart baking dish. Mix lemon juice, melted butter, and brown sugar and spoon over peaches. Sprinkle with cinnamon and bake for 20–30 minutes.

MAKES 4 SERVINGS.

BAKED PEARS
■ ■ ■

OVEN: 350°

8 pear halves (canned)
¼ cup mint jelly
¼ cup water
½ cup chopped pecans

Arrange pear halves cut-side-up in a greased 1½-quart baking dish. Melt mint jelly in ¼ cup water over low heat and drizzle over pears. Put 1 tablespoon of the pecans in the center of each pear and bake for 20–30 minutes.

MAKES 4 SERVINGS.

BREAD AND BUTTER PICKLES
■ ■ ■

5 pounds sugar
1 pint white vinegar
1 (1¾-ounce) box pickling spice
2 gallons whole sour pickles

Mix sugar with vinegar in a large saucepan and cook over low heat, stirring constantly, until sugar dissolves. Remove from heat, let cool to room temperature, and stir in pickling spice. Drain pickles, and slice to desired thickness. Transfer to a nonreactive container that holds a little over 2 gallons. Cover the pickles with ice cubes and fill the container with cold water. Let stand for 1 hour, and then drain off the water. If the container that the pickles have been standing in has a tight-fitting lid, leave them in that container. Otherwise, wash the gallon jars that the pickles came in and transfer the pickles back into those jars. Pour the vinegar mixture over the pickles (dividing it evenly, if you're using 2 containers). Stir gently to distribute the vinegar mixture and cover the container(s). Let the pickles stand for a week, stirring them gently several times each day. Sometimes the shape of the container makes it difficult to stir the pickles without breaking or mashing them. If this is the case, then be sure the lid(s) are secured snugly and just turn the container(s) upside down. Turn them back over once or twice each day. At

the end of the week, pack the pick-les and juice into wide-mouth jars. Re-frigeration makes the pickles crisper.
MAKES 8 QUARTS.

MOLDED PINEAPPLE SALAD
■ ■ ■

1 (3-ounce) box lemon gelatin
1 (3-ounce) box lime gelatin
2 cups boiling water
1 cup mayonnaise
1/2 cup milk
1/4 cup horseradish
1 (16-ounce) carton cottage cheese
1 (20-ounce) can crushed pineapple, packed in juice, undrained

In a large bowl, mix lemon and lime gelatin together and add boiling water. Stir to dissolve. Stir in may-onnaise and milk. Fold in horserad-ish, cottage cheese, and crushed pineapple, and mix with a rotary beater or wire whisk. Pour into a well-greased 3-quart rectangular pan and chill until firm.
MAKES 12 SERVINGS.

SCALLOPED PINEAPPLE
■ ■ ■

OVEN: 350°

1/2 cup butter, softened
1 cup sugar
4 eggs, beaten
1 (20-ounce) can crushed pineapple, undrained
6 slices bread

Cream butter with sugar. Add eggs and pineapple. Trim crusts from bread, cut into cubes, and fold into pineap-ple mixture. Pour into a greased 1 1/2-quart baking dish. Refrigerate for about an hour to allow bread to absorb some of the liquid. Then bake for 1 hour.
MAKES 6 SERVINGS.

ROMAINE SALAD WITH MANDARIN ORANGES
■ ■ ■

1 head romaine lettuce
1 small Bermuda onion
1 (11-ounce) can mandarin oranges, drained
1/2 cup vegetable oil
1/4 cup orange juice
2 tablespoons cider vinegar
1 1/2 teaspoons sugar
salt and pepper
1 cup croutons

Wash lettuce and tear up in a salad bowl. Slice onion and add with or-anges. Whisk together oil, orange juice, vinegar, sugar, and salt and pep-per. Pour over salad and toss. Add croutons and toss again.
MAKES 4 SERVINGS.

N·O·T·E·S

SWEET AND SOUR ROMAINE SALAD

■ ■ ■

Dressing:

¼ cup chopped onion
1 cup vegetable oil
¾ cup sugar
¼ cup cider vinegar
⅓ cup ketchup
2 tablespoons Worcestershire
    sauce
½ teaspoon salt

Salad:

1 (14-ounce) can artichoke hearts,
    drained
2 avocados
1 (11-ounce) can mandarin
    oranges, drained
1 large head romaine lettuce
½ red onion, sliced thinly and
    separated into rings

Measure dressing ingredients into the work bowl of a food processor or blender and blend for 1–2 minutes, or until thoroughly mixed. Transfer to a covered container and refrigerate.

At least several hours before serving the salad, and as early as that morning, prepare the vegetables: quarter artichoke hearts and cut avocados into chunks. Then place these in a container with a cover and add mandarin oranges. Pour dressing on top and toss gently to mix. Cover and refrigerate. To serve, break lettuce into a salad bowl and add onion slices. Add the marinated artichoke hearts, avocados, and mandarin oranges with dressing, and toss well.

MAKES 6 SERVINGS.

TOMATO ASPIC

■ ■ ■

1 (10½-ounce) can beef bouillon
3 envelopes unflavored gelatin
3 (12-ounce) cans tomato juice
2 tablespoons lemon juice
1½ tablespoons Worcestershire
    sauce
½ teaspoon salt
1 tablespoon sugar
Tabasco sauce
1 (14-ounce) can artichoke hearts,
    drained and quartered
lettuce leaves
mayonnaise
dill weed

Pour beef bouillon into a small saucepan and sprinkle gelatin on top to soften. Heat over low heat to dissolve, stirring constantly, but do not boil. In a medium bowl, combine tomato juice, lemon juice, Worcestershire sauce, salt, sugar, and Tabasco sauce to taste. Stir in beef bouillon. Pour carefully into a well-greased shallow 2-quart baking dish, ring mold, or gelatin mold. Chill until thickened but not set. Arrange quartered artichoke hearts in mold and chill until firm. Cut into portions and serve on lettuce leaves with a dollop of mayonnaise and a sprinkle of dill weed.

MAKES 6–8 SERVINGS.

Note: Individual gelatin molds may be used, if desired. These single servings make an attractive base for chicken salad or any type of seafood salad. This type of luncheon dish is good with cheese straws.

Sauces and Salad Dressings

SAUCES AND SALAD DRESSINGS
...

BÉCHAMEL (WHITE) SAUCE

Béchamel, known in French cuisine as one of the *mother* sauces, can be prepared in varying thicknesses. The sauce below is a simplified version of the traditional sauce, which calls for the milk to be simmered for about 20 minutes with an *onion piquet* before being added to the butter and flour "roux." (An onion piquet is a peeled onion with a bay leaf attached to it, using a clove as a push pin.)

All variations make about 1 cup of sauce.

Thin Sauce: *for thin cream soups*
Melt 1 tablespoon butter in a heavy saucepan and blend in 1 tablespoon flour and ¼ teaspoon salt. Cook and stir over low heat for 3–5 minutes, or until it barely begins to turn golden. Add 1 cup milk slowly, stirring constantly. Continue cooking until smooth and thickened.

Medium Sauce: *standard white sauce*
Melt 2 tablespoons butter in a heavy saucepan and blend in 2 tablespoons flour and ¼ teaspoon salt. Cook and stir over low heat for 3–5 minutes, or until it barely begins to turn golden. Add 1 cup milk slowly, stirring constantly. Continue cooking until smooth and thickened.

Thick Sauce: *for soufflés*
Melt 3 tablespoons butter in a heavy saucepan and blend in 3 tablespoons flour and ¼ teaspoon salt. Cook and stir over low heat for 3–5 minutes, or until it barely begins to turn golden. Add 1 cup milk slowly, stirring constantly. Continue cooking until smooth and thickened.

Heavy Sauce: *for binding croquettes*
Melt 4 tablespoons butter in a heavy saucepan and blend in 4 tablespoons flour and ¼ teaspoon salt. Cook and stir over low heat for 3–5 minutes, or until it barely begins to turn golden. Add 1 cup milk slowly, stirring constantly. Continue cooking until smooth and thickened.

BUTTERMILK DRESSING
...

½ cup buttermilk
½ cup mayonnaise
2 teaspoons salt
¼ teaspoon Worcestershire sauce
dash paprika

Mix all ingredients thoroughly. Use as a salad dressing or for cole slaw.
MAKES 1 CUP.

CAESAR DRESSING
...

1 tablespoon red wine vinegar
1 tablespoon balsamic vinegar
1 tablespoon lemon juice
1 tablespoon Worcestershire sauce
1 teaspoon Dijon mustard
1 teaspoon anchovy paste (or less, to taste)
½ teaspoon salt
freshly ground black pepper
¾ cup olive oil
3 cloves garlic, peeled

In a small bowl, whisk together both vinegars, lemon juice, Worcestershire sauce, mustard, anchovy paste, salt, and pepper. Gradually drizzle in olive oil, whisking vigorously until all oil is incorporated. Transfer to a covered container and add garlic. Shake and let stand for 30 minutes. Shake again and remove garlic cloves.
MAKES 1 CUP.

COCKTAIL SAUCE
...

2 (12-ounce) bottles seafood cocktail sauce
2 teaspoons prepared horseradish
2 teaspoons lemon juice
¼ teaspoon Worcestershire sauce
⅛ teaspoon soy sauce
5 shots Tabasco sauce

Combine ingredients and refrigerate. Essential with cold shrimp, and delicious with other seafood as well.
MAKES 1½ CUPS.

CREAM GRAVY
...

6 tablespoons pan drippings from fried chicken, etc.
6 tablespoons flour
3 cups milk
½ teaspoon salt
¼ teaspoon pepper

In the same skillet in which meat has been cooked, blend pan drippings with flour. Cook and stir for 3–5 minutes, scraping up all the crunchy little bits of chicken, pork chops, or chicken-fried steak that remain on the bottom of the pan. Slowly stir in milk and cook and stir as gravy thickens. Season with salt and pepper.
MAKES ABOUT 3 CUPS.

DILL SAUCE

■ ■ ■

1 cup mayonnaise
1 tablespoon Dijon mustard
3 tablespoons chopped fresh dill or
*   1 tablespoon dried dill weed*

Blend together mayonnaise, mustard, and fresh dill or dried dill weed. Refrigerate. Wonderful with salmon and other types of fish and seafood.

MAKES ABOUT 1 CUP.

DILL LEMON BUTTER

■ ■ ■

½ cup butter, softened
2 tablespoons snipped fresh dill
2 tablespoons snipped flat-leaf
*   parsley*
2 teaspoons minced fresh chives
1 tablespoon lemon juice
3 dashes Tabasco sauce

Blend all ingredients together and taste for seasoning. Spoon mixture onto a piece of foil and roll into a log about 6″ long. Twist ends of foil to seal, and refrigerate for about 2 hours, or until firm. (Can be frozen for up to 1 month.) To serve, unwrap and slice into serving portions. Makes enough for about 12 patties ½″ thick.

MAKES ABOUT ¾ CUP.

FRENCH DRESSING

■ ■ ■

¼ cup tomato sauce
⅓ cup red wine vinegar
1 cup salad oil
1 tablespoon sugar
1 teaspoon salt
1 teaspoon dried basil
1 teaspoon Worcestershire sauce
¼ teaspoon dry mustard
¼ teaspoon pepper
⅛ teaspoon Tabasco sauce
⅛ teaspoon garlic powder

Combine all ingredients in a blender or mix with a whisk. Blend until smooth. Transfer to a covered container and refrigerate.

MAKES 1⅔ CUPS.

GIBLET GRAVY

■ ■ ■

giblets from chicken or turkey,
*   washed*
4 cups cold water
4 tablespoons butter
4 tablespoons flour
2 cups pan drippings or chicken
*   broth*
½ cup milk or half and half
½ teaspoon salt
½ teaspoon pepper
2 hard-cooked eggs, chopped

Remove liver from package of giblets and refrigerate. Place giblets in saucepan, cover with 4 cups cold water, and bring to a boil. Reduce heat and

(continued)

BÉARNAISE SAUCE

Use recipe for Hollandaise Sauce (at right), omitting lemon juice. Instead, simmer ¼ cup tarragon vinegar until it is reduced to 2 tablespoons, and blend it into sauce.

BROWN SAUCE

Use exactly the same proportions of butter, flour, salt, and liquid as called for in medium Béchamel Sauce (page 250), substituting beef broth for the milk. Melt butter in a heavy saucepan and blend in flour and salt. Cook and stir over low heat for 3–5 minutes, or until it barely begins to turn golden. Add beef broth slowly, stirring constantly. Continue cooking until smooth and thickened. To give the sauce a rich color, add a dash of Kitchen Bouquet.
MAKES ABOUT 1 CUP.

BORDELAISE SAUCE

Chop the white parts of 8 green onions and place in a small saucepan with ½ cup red wine. Simmer until wine is reduced to ¼ cup, and add to 1 cup of Brown Sauce.

CLARIFIED BUTTER

Cut 1 cup (2 sticks) unsalted butter into chunks and place in a small, heavy saucepan. Melt it over low heat until it begins to bubble. Let it simmer for about 2 minutes. During this time you'll hear it "crackle." When it almost stops crackling, the butter will be clarified. Remove from heat and let stand for 5–10 minutes, so milk solids can settle to the bottom. Pour off the clarified butter into a tightly covered container, and discard the milk solids. Clarified butter keeps for a month or more in the refrigerator, and it can be frozen. This is good for sautéing, since it has a higher smoke point than butter, which means that it doesn't burn as quickly as butter.
MAKES ⅔ CUP.

simmer for about an hour. Now add the liver and simmer for another 30 minutes. Drain in a colander, allow to cool, chop, and set aside. Melt butter in a heavy saucepan and stir in flour. Cook and stir for 3–5 minutes, or until butter barely begins to turn golden. Slowly stir in drippings or chicken broth and milk or half and half. Continue cooking and stirring until thickened. Season with salt and pepper. Stir in hard-cooked eggs and chopped giblets and serve.
MAKES 3 CUPS.

HERB DRESSING
###

½ cup salad oil
3 tablespoons wine vinegar
⅛ teaspoon powdered thyme
⅛ teaspoon powdered marjoram
¼ teaspoon dried basil
1 tablespoon minced onion
1 tablespoon water
½ teaspoon salt
1 tablespoon chopped fresh parsley

Combine ingredients in a blender and blend for 30 seconds.
MAKES ⅔ CUP.

"Without butter, without eggs, there is no reason to come to France."

—**Paul Bocuse**

HOLLANDAISE SAUCE
###

3 eggs
2 tablespoons lemon juice
¼ teaspoon cayenne
½ cup butter, melted and hot

Fill a saucepan two-thirds full of water and bring to a boil. With a large spoon, gently lower eggs into boiling water and leave for exactly 1 minute. Remove from heat and run cold water over eggs. Then separate eggs, discarding whites. Put egg yolks, lemon juice, and cayenne into blender. Blend briefly. With the blender running, gradually add hot melted butter in a thin, steady stream, mixing until sauce is smooth and thickened. Reheat leftover sauce over boiling water.
MAKES ¾ CUP.

HONEY MUSTARD HORSERADISH SAUCE
###

½ cup mayonnaise
1 tablespoon Dijon mustard
1 tablespoon honey
1 tablespoon vinegar
1–2 tablespoons horseradish
dash Tabasco sauce

Mix ingredients and refrigerate. Wonderful over chilled vegetables.
MAKES ¾ CUP.

HORSERADISH SAUCE

■ ■ ■

1 cup mayonnaise
¼ cup horseradish
¼ cup lemon juice
2 teaspoons grated lemon peel
⅛ teaspoon cayenne
1 cup heavy cream, whipped

Mix mayonnaise with horseradish, lemon juice, lemon peel, and cayenne. Fold in whipped cream. Chill for at least an hour. Wonderful with beef.

MAKES 3½ CUPS.

MAYONNAISE

■ ■ ■

2 eggs
2 tablespoons lemon juice
1 teaspoon dry mustard
½ teaspoon salt
¼ teaspoon paprika
dash cayenne
1 cup vegetable oil

Fill a saucepan two-thirds full of water and bring to a boil. With a large spoon, gently lower eggs into the water and leave for exactly 1 minute. Remove the pan from the heat and run cold water over the eggs. Then separate the eggs, discarding the whites. Put egg yolks, lemon juice, dry mustard, salt, paprika, and cayenne into a blender or food processor. Blend for 5–10 seconds on high speed. With the motor running, slowly add oil in a fine stream. As soon as mayonnaise is thick and smooth, turn off the motor. Transfer mayonnaise to a covered container and refrigerate.

MAKES 1¼ CUPS.

Variation #1: To make **Cayenne Mayonnaise**, blend 1 cup mayonnaise with 1 teaspoon cayenne, 1 tablespoon balsamic vinegar, and 1 tablespoon sherry. Wonderful with crab cakes.

Variation #2: To make **Lemon Mayonnaise**, blend 1 cup mayonnaise with 1 tablespoon lemon juice, 2 teaspoons Dijon mustard, and 1 teaspoon paprika. Good with chilled asparagus.

MUSTARD MAYONNAISE DRESSING

■ ■ ■

1 cup mayonnaise
3 tablespoons Dijon mustard
3 tablespoons lemon juice
2 teaspoons Worcestershire sauce

Mix ingredients together in a mixing bowl with a whisk. Refrigerate in a covered container.

MAKES 1⅓ CUPS.

CHEESE SAUCE

Stir ½ cup shredded Cheddar cheese into 1 cup Béchamel Sauce (page 250). Heat just until cheese is melted. Cooking longer than that causes cheese to become stringy.

CURRY SAUCE

Stir ½ teaspoon curry powder and a pinch of ground ginger into 1 cup Béchamel Sauce (page 250).

MALTAISE SAUCE

Make Hollandaise Sauce (page 252), substituting 2 tablespoons orange juice for the lemon juice.

MORNAY SAUCE

Stir ¼ cup grated Parmesan cheese and a pinch of freshly ground nutmeg into 1 cup Béchamel Sauce (page 250). Heat just until cheese is melted.

MOUSSELINE SAUCE

Mix equal amounts of Hollandaise Sauce (page 252) and whipped cream.

MUSTARD SAUCE

Stir 1 tablespoon Dijon mustard into 1 cup of Béchamel Sauce (page 250).

VELOUTÉ SAUCE

Substitute chicken or veal stock for the milk in Béchamel Sauce (page 250). Cook exactly as for Béchamel Sauce.

POPPY SEED DRESSING
■ ■ ■

2 teaspoons poppy seeds
½ cup sugar
1 teaspoon paprika
1 teaspoon dry mustard
¼ teaspoon salt
½ cup honey
6 tablespoons vinegar
1 teaspoon onion juice
3 tablespoons lemon juice
1 cup vegetable oil

Put poppy seeds in a cup and add cold water to cover. Soak for about 2 hours. Drain on paper towels. In a blender, mix sugar, paprika, dry mustard, and salt. Blend in honey, vinegar, onion juice, and lemon juice. Blend in oil very slowly, pouring it in a thin, steady stream. Add poppy seeds, blend very briefly, and chill.
MAKES 2½ CUPS.

RÉMOULADE SAUCE
■ ■ ■

¾ cup ketchup
2 tablespoons chili sauce
2 tablespoons mayonnaise
1 hard-cooked egg, chopped
1 tablespoon pickle relish
1½ teaspoons vinegar
1½ teaspoons horseradish
1 teaspoon lemon juice
salt and pepper

Mix ingredients together and chill. Serve with seafood or salad.
MAKES 1½ CUPS.

SOUR CREAM DRESSING
■ ■ ■

1 (8-ounce) carton sour cream
½ cup mayonnaise
2 tablespoons lemon juice
1 teaspoon dill weed

In a small mixing bowl, blend together all ingredients with a whisk. Cover and refrigerate.
MAKES 1½ CUPS.

> *"There is no sauce in the world like hunger."*
>
> —Miguel de Cervantes

SWEET AND SOUR SAUCE
■ ■ ■

1 cup sugar
1½ cups water
3 tablespoons oil
½ teaspoon MSG
⅔ cup malt vinegar
4 tablespoons cornstarch
½ teaspoon salt
¼ cup soy sauce
½ cup chopped onion
½ teaspoon ground ginger
¼ cup ketchup

Mix all ingredients except ketchup in a saucepan. Bring to a boil over medium heat. Boil for 1 minute, remove from heat, and stir in ketchup.
MAKES 3 CUPS.

SWEET AND SOUR DRESSING #1

■ ■ ■

½ cup vegetable oil
1 tablespoon soy sauce
¾ cup chili sauce
¾ cup red wine vinegar
½ cup sugar

Put all ingredients in a jar. Cover and shake well. Refrigerate.
MAKES 2¼ CUPS.

SWEET AND SOUR DRESSING #2

■ ■ ■

¼ cup chopped onion
1 cup vegetable oil
¾ cup sugar
¼ cup cider vinegar
⅓ cup ketchup
2 tablespoons Worcestershire sauce
½ teaspoon salt

Blend all ingredients in a food processor or a blender for 1–2 minutes. Cover and refrigerate.
MAKES 2 CUPS.

THOUSAND ISLAND DRESSING

■ ■ ■

1¼ cups mayonnaise
¼ cup chili sauce
1 small onion, peeled and quartered
1 teaspoon salt
1 teaspoon paprika
dash pepper
2 hard-cooked eggs, quartered
2 tablespoons sweet pickle relish

Put mayonnaise, chili sauce, onion, salt, paprika, and pepper in a blender or a food processor and blend briefly until the onion is chopped. Add hard-cooked eggs and pulse to chop. Transfer to a covered container, stir in pickle relish, and refrigerate.
MAKES 2½ CUPS.

MOCK TURKEY GRAVY

■ ■ ■

If you don't have any giblets, try this gravy for Thanksgiving dinner.

4 tablespoons butter
¼ cup flour
1 (14½-ounce) can chicken broth
3 tablespoons white wine or water
1 teaspoon Kitchen Bouquet
1 teaspoon Worcestershire sauce
1 teaspoon chicken stock base
salt and pepper

In a medium saucepan, melt butter, stir in flour, and cook and stir over low heat for 3–5 minutes. Add broth

(continued)

N·O·T·E·S

and wine or water and stir as it thickens. Blend in Kitchen Bouquet, Worcestershire sauce, and chicken stock base, and season to taste with salt and pepper.

MAKES 2 CUPS.

BASIC VINAIGRETTE
■ ■ ■

3 tablespoons white wine vinegar
1 tablespoon balsamic vinegar
2 tablespoons Dijon mustard
½ teaspoon salt
¼ teaspoon pepper
¾ cup vegetable oil
¼ cup olive oil

In a medium bowl, whisk together vinegars, mustard, salt, and pepper. Combine oils in a measuring cup and add slowly, beating constantly with a whisk. Refrigerate until needed. Shake well before using.

MAKES 1¼ CUPS.

"People who loathe the idea of a salad are very like those who claim not to like perfume: they just haven't met the right one."

—**Miriam Polunin**

CREAMY VINAIGRETTE
■ ■ ■

2 teaspoons salt
1 teaspoon white pepper
½ teaspoon cracked black pepper
¼ teaspoon sugar
½ teaspoon dry mustard
1½ tablespoons lemon juice
1 garlic clove, pressed
5 tablespoons wine vinegar
½ cup vegetable oil
2 tablespoons olive oil
¼ cup egg substitute
½ cup half and half

Blend ingredients in a blender or food processor. Store in refrigerator.

MAKES 2 CUPS.

WALNUT VINAIGRETTE
■ ■ ■

2 tablespoons white vinegar
2 tablespoons white wine
2 tablespoons Dijon mustard
¼ teaspoon sugar
½ teaspoon salt
¼ teaspoon pepper
¾ cup vegetable oil
¼ cup walnut oil

In a medium bowl, whisk together vinegar, wine, mustard, sugar, salt, and pepper. Combine oils in a measuring cup and add slowly, beating constantly with a whisk. Transfer to a glass jar or bottle and refrigerate until needed. Shake well before using.

MAKES 1¼ CUPS.

Breads

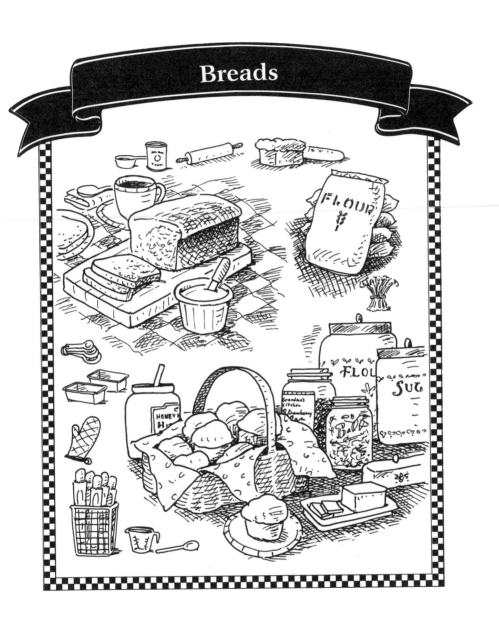

BREADS

...

APRICOT NUT BREAD

...

OVEN: 325°

2 cups chopped dried apricots
1 cup boiling water
4 tablespoons butter
1½ cups sugar
2 eggs
3 cups flour
2 teaspoons baking powder
½ teaspoon salt
1 cup chopped pecans

Put apricots in a small bowl and cover with boiling water. Let stand for 15 minutes. Meanwhile, cream butter and sugar together. Beat in eggs and blend in apricot mixture. Mix in flour, baking powder, and salt. Fold in pecans and pour into a greased and floured 9" x 5" x 3" loaf pan. Bake for 45–50 minutes, or until a toothpick inserted in the center comes out clean.

MAKES 1 LOAF.

BANANA NUT BREAD

...

OVEN: 350°

1 cup butter, softened
1½ cups sugar
2 eggs
½ teaspoon lemon juice
4 ripe bananas, mashed
1 teaspoon vanilla extract
¼ cup buttermilk
2 cups flour
1½ teaspoons baking soda
1 teaspoon salt
1 cup chopped pecans or walnuts

Cream butter and sugar and beat in eggs. Blend in lemon juice, bananas, vanilla extract, and buttermilk. Sift together flour, baking soda, and salt, and stir into banana mixture. Add nuts, and divide batter between 2 greased and floured 9" x 5" x 3" loaf pans. Bake for 45–50 minutes, or until a toothpick inserted in the center comes out clean.

MAKES 2 LOAVES.

BEER BISCUITS
■ ■ ■

OVEN: 400°

1 cup Bisquick
1 tablespoon sugar
*½ cup regular (not light) beer, at
   room temperature*

Stir ingredients together and spoon
into well-greased muffin tins, dividing the batter evenly. Let rise for 30
minutes and then bake for 10 minutes.

MAKES 1 DOZEN.

BEER MUFFINS
■ ■ ■

OVEN: 350°

3 cups flour
5 teaspoons baking powder
½ teaspoon salt
3 tablespoons sugar
*12 ounces regular (not light) beer,
   at room temperature*
4 tablespoons butter, melted

Combine flour, baking powder, salt,
and sugar in a large mixing bowl. Stir
in beer and spoon into greased standard-size muffin tins, dividing the batter evenly. Brush tops with melted
butter and bake for 15–20 minutes.

MAKES 1 DOZEN.

BLUEBERRY MUFFINS
■ ■ ■

OVEN: 425°

1 egg
1 cup milk
4 tablespoons butter, melted
2 cups flour
⅓ cup sugar
1 tablespoon baking powder
½ teaspoon salt
1 cup blueberries, drained

In a large mixing bowl, blend egg
with milk and melted butter. In another mixing bowl, sift together flour,
sugar, baking powder, and salt. Combine flour mixture with egg mixture
and fold in blueberries. Line muffin
cups with paper liners or grease the
muffin cups well. Spoon batter into
muffin cups, filling two-thirds full,
and dividing the batter evenly. Bake
for about 20 minutes, or until lightly
browned.

MAKES 1 DOZEN.

• Punching down: Once dough has risen sufficiently, you need to compress it again so that you can roll it out or shape it. Make a fist with your hand and press down into the center of the dough. Now fold the puffy sides in towards the center and flip the dough over in the bowl, pressing it down again with your fist.

• Shaping bread or rolls: Once the dough is punched down, it's ready to be shaped according to the directions in the recipe. (Also see the sidebar sections on "A Dozen Roll Shapes, pages 262 and 264.") After shaping, dough is usually covered lightly again with a clean dish towel, and set in a warm place, away from drafts, to rise a second time.

• Testing after second rising: Usually, yeast dough needs to rise twice: once in the bowl, and a second time after it's shaped. To see if it's ready to be baked, gently press dough in an inconspicuous place to see if it springs back. If it does, leave it to rise a little longer. If it doesn't spring back, it's ready to be baked.

• Testing for doneness: After a loaf of bread has baked long enough, it should pull away from the sides of the pan. Once it does, thump it lightly. It should sound hollow. When you tap the bottom of the loaf pan, it should have a hollow sound as well.

• Reheating an unsliced loaf of bread: Preheat oven to 400°. Place an already-baked unsliced loaf of bread on a baking sheet and warm it in the oven, uncovered, for about 5–10 minutes. If you like, you can sprinkle a few drops of water on top of the loaf before you put it in the oven.

BRAN MUFFINS
■ ■ ■

OVEN: 400°

3 cups 100% bran cereal
1 cup boiling water
2 cups buttermilk
½ cup shortening
1½ cups sugar
2 eggs, beaten
2½ cups flour
2½ teaspoons baking soda
½ teaspoon salt

Measure cereal into a medium bowl and stir in 1 cup boiling water and the buttermilk. Set aside. Cream shortening and sugar together and add eggs. Stir in buttermilk mixture. Sift flour with baking soda and salt, and add to cereal mixture. Cover and refrigerate for up to 6 weeks. To prepare, pour into greased muffin tins, ⅔ full. Bake for 15–20 minutes, until muffins are no longer shiny on top.

MAKES 2 QUARTS BATTER; ENOUGH FOR ABOUT 2½–3 DOZEN MUFFINS.

BUTTERMILK BISCUITS
■ ■ ■

OVEN: 450°

2 cups flour, plus additional flour
for rolling out biscuits
1 teaspoon sugar
1 tablespoon baking powder
¼ teaspoon baking soda
1 teaspoon salt
½ cup shortening
¾ cup buttermilk

Place flour, sugar, baking powder, baking soda, and salt in the bowl of a food processor, and pulse to mix. Add shortening, cut into ½" chunks. (I prefer Crisco sticks, since they're so easy to measure and handle.) Pulse 15–20 times, or until shortening is evenly incorporated into dry ingredients, and mixture has the texture of coarse meal. Then remove top of food processor and drizzle buttermilk evenly over flour mixture. Replace top and pulse several times, just until the milk is mixed in and mixture forms small clumps. Let dough stand for 2–3 minutes. Meanwhile, put a little flour in a small bowl so it will be easy to scoop up as you work, whenever you need to sprinkle flour on the dough, the rolling pin, the board, the biscuit cutter, or your hands. Sprinkle some flour onto the work surface, and using a rubber spatula, scrape the dough from the food processor onto the work surface. Sprinkle a little flour on top of the dough and on your hands, and knead the dough 8–10 times, turning it a quarter turn each time. It will still be fairly moist. Form the dough into a flat ball and wrap it in waxed paper or plastic wrap. Refrigerate for 20 minutes, or for up to 2 hours. If desired, pinch dough off and shape biscuits by hand. Or turn dough out onto a floured surface and roll it or pat it into a circle or rectangle about ¾" thick. Dip a 2½" biscuit cutter into flour, and then press it firmly into dough. Don't twist cutter; just press it straight down. Dip cutter in flour between biscuits. After you've cut out 4–5 biscuits, place them in a greased 8- or 9-inch layer cake pan. Arrange biscuits in it so that they touch each other, beginning with one in the center. (If biscuits do not touch, they won't rise as high.) Gather leftover scraps into a ball and pat or roll it out again. Keep this up until you've used all the dough. Bake biscuits for 9–12 minutes, or until lightly browned.

MAKES 8–10 BISCUITS.

CHEESE BISCUITS
■ ■ ■

OVEN: 450°

2¼ cups Bisquick
⅔ cup milk
¾ cup shredded cheese
1 teaspoon parsley flakes
4 tablespoons butter, melted
¼ teaspoon garlic powder

Blend Bisquick and milk in a mixing bowl and stir in cheese and parsley flakes. Mix for about 30 seconds. For each biscuit, measure 2–3 tablespoons batter and drop it in mounds onto an ungreased baking sheet, 2" apart. Bake for 8–10 minutes. Stir butter and garlic powder together in a small dish and brush on biscuits as soon as they come out of the oven.

MAKES 8–10 BISCUITS.

Note: To make plain biscuits, omit cheese and parsley. (Garlic butter is optional.) Either drop, as above, or turn dough onto a work surface dusted with Bisquick, and roll out ½" thick. Cut out with 2½" biscuit cutter.

CARROT NUT BREAD
■ ■ ■

OVEN: 350°

1 cup grated carrots
1 cup sugar
½ cup vegetable oil
1½ cups flour
2 teaspoons baking powder
½ teaspoon baking soda
½ teaspoon salt
1 teaspoon cinnamon
2 eggs
1 cup chopped pecans

Mix together carrots, sugar, oil, flour, baking powder, baking soda, salt, and cinnamon. Beat in eggs one at a time and stir in pecans. Pour into a greased and floured 9" x 5" x 3" loaf pan and bake for 55–60 minutes.

MAKES 1 LOAF.

N·O·T·E·S

A Dozen Roll Shapes

• **Clothespin Crullers:** Grease old-fashioned wooden clothespins. Roll dough into a 12" wide rectangle, less than 1/2" thick. Brush with melted butter. Cut into strips 1/2" wide. Twist dough slightly and wrap in a spiral around clothespins, so that edges barely touch. Let rise again and bake as directed. After baking, give each clothespin a twist and pull on the wider end, removing the clothespin from the cruller. Fill with jelly or fruit filling.

• **Cloverleaf Rolls:** Roll dough into 1" balls. Place 3 balls in each cup of a greased standard-size muffin pan. Let rise again and bake as directed.

• **Coils:** Roll dough into a 12" wide rectangle, less than 1/2" thick. Brush with melted butter. Cut into 1/2" wide strips. Roll each strip into a rope. Twist slightly. Place one end on a greased baking sheet. Wind into a circle, tucking end under coil. Let rise again and bake as directed.

• **Crescent Rolls:** Roll dough 1/4" thick into a 12" circle. Cut each circle into 12 wedges. Roll up tightly from wide end to point. Place with points down on greased baking sheets. Curve ends slightly to form crescents. Let rise again and bake as directed.

• **Fan Tans:** Roll dough into a 9" wide rectangle, 1/8" thick. Brush with melted or softened butter. Cut 1 1/2" wide strips from rectangle, and stack 6 strips on top of each other. Cut each stack into 6 (1 1/2") pieces. Place in greased standard-size muffin pan cups, with each stack standing on its edges. Let rise again and bake as directed.

• **Figure Eights:** Roll dough into a 12" wide rectangle, less than 1/2" thick. Brush with melted butter. Cut into strips 1/2" wide. Roll each strip into a figure eight. Pinch ends together and place on a greased baking sheet. Let rise again and bake as directed.

(continued)

Cheese Bread
■ ■ ■

OVEN: 375°

1 1/2 cups Bisquick
1 cup (4 ounces) shredded
  Cheddar cheese
1 tablespoon poppy seeds
1/2 cup milk
1 egg, beaten
1/4 cup shortening, melted

Place Bisquick in a bowl and stir in cheese and poppy seeds. Mix in milk, egg, and shortening, and stir until dry ingredients are moistened. Spoon into a greased and floured 9"x5"x3" loaf pan and spread batter evenly. Bake for 25–30 minutes, or until lightly browned.
MAKES 1 LOAF.

Corn Light Bread
■ ■ ■

OVEN: 350°

2 cups self-rising cornmeal
1/2 cup flour
3/4 cup sugar
2 cups buttermilk
4 slices bacon, cooked and
  crumbled (optional)
3 tablespoons bacon drippings
  or vegetable oil

Mix all ingredients together. Pour into a greased 9" x 5" x 3" loaf pan. Bake for 1 hour. This bread doesn't get very brown, so be sure not to overcook. It will pull away from the sides of the pan when it's done. Freezes well.
MAKES 1 LOAF.

Tex-Mex Cornbread
■ ■ ■

OVEN: 350°

2 eggs, beaten
1 (8-ounce) carton sour cream
1 (16-ounce) can cream-style corn
1/2 cup oil
1 cup (4 ounces) shredded
  Cheddar cheese
3 tablespoons chopped onion
1 (4-ounce) can chopped green
  chiles
3 tablespoons chopped red pepper
1 1/2 cups cornmeal
2 1/2 teaspoons baking powder
1 teaspoon salt

Mix eggs, sour cream, corn, oil, cheese, onion, chiles, and red pepper. Mix cornmeal with baking powder and salt and add to sour cream mixture. Pour into a greased 13" x 9" x 2" pan and bake for 45 minutes.
MAKES 8–12 SERVINGS.

Corn Pancakes
■ ■ ■

1 (7 1/2-ounce) box yellow corn
  muffin mix
1/2 cup milk
4 tablespoons sour cream
1 (8 1/2-ounce) can cream style corn
cooking oil

Empty corn muffin mix into a medium bowl and break up lumps with a fork. Add milk and sour cream gradually and stir with whisk until batter is smooth. Stir in corn. Heat a large skillet or griddle over medium heat and brush on a little oil. When a drop of water sizzles in the skillet, drop in mounds of batter, using ¼ cup batter for each pancake. As soon as pancakes are browned on one side, flip them over and continue cooking until done. Remove pancakes from the skillet and keep them warm until all the pancakes are cooked.

MAKES 10–12 PANCAKES.

CRANBERRY BREAD
■ ■ ■

OVEN: 350°

3 cups flour
1 cup sugar
1½ teaspoons baking powder
½ teaspoon baking soda
4 tablespoons butter, softened
¾ cup orange juice
1 egg, beaten
1 tablespoon grated orange peel
½ cup chopped pecans
1 cup chopped cranberries

Measure flour, sugar, baking powder, and baking soda into the work bowl

of a food processor. Add butter and process until mixture resembles fine crumbs. Transfer to a mixing bowl and stir in orange juice and egg. Fold in orange peel, pecans, and cranberries. Spread into a greased 9" x 5" x 3" loaf pan and bake for about 1 hour, or until a toothpick inserted in the center comes out clean.

MAKES 1 LOAF.

DILL BREAD
■ ■ ■

OVEN: 350°

3 cups self-rising flour
3 tablespoons sugar
2 tablespoons dried parsley flakes
1½ teaspoons dill weed
1 (12-ounce) can beer (not light)
4 tablespoons butter, melted

Combine flour, sugar, parsley flakes, and dill weed in a large bowl. Blend in beer. Spoon into a greased 9" x 5" x 3" loaf pan and bake for 30 minutes. Remove from the oven, pour melted butter on top, and return to the oven. Bake for 20–30 more minutes, or until top is lightly browned. Remove from the oven and let cool in the pan before turning out.

MAKES 1 LOAF.

N·O·T·E·S

- **Flowers:** Roll into balls. Place 1 ball in the center of each greased 8″ round baking pan, surrounded by 8 more balls. Brush with melted butter. Let rise again as directed. Just before baking, use scissors to make 6 snips in each ball, ¾″ deep, in a sunburst shape around the perimeter of roll. Bake as directed.

- **Knots:** Roll dough into a 12″ wide rectangle, less than ½″ thick. Brush with melted butter and fold in half. Cut into strips ½″ wide and 6″ long. Twist slightly and tie loose knot in center of each rope. Place on a greased baking sheet. Let rise again and bake as directed.

- **Pan Rolls:** Roll into balls. Place 1 ball in the center of each greased 8″ round baking pan, surrounded by 8 more balls. Brush with melted butter. Let rise again and bake as directed.

- **Parker House Rolls:** Roll out dough to ½″ thick. Cut with a biscuit cutter. Dip circles in melted butter and fold in half. (Be sure butter has cooled to lukewarm.) Let rise again and bake as directed.

- **Rosettes:** Roll dough into a 12″ wide rectangle, less than ½″ thick. Brush with melted butter. Cut into ½″ wide strips. Roll each strip into a rope, twisting slightly. Tie a loose knot in the center of each rope. Bring the bottom end up and tuck it into the center of the roll. Wrap the top end around and tuck it under the roll. Let rise again and bake as directed.

- **Twists:** Roll dough into a 12″ wide rectangle, less than ½″ thick. Brush with melted butter. Cut into ½″ wide strips. Form each strip into a figure eight and pinch ends together. Then twist each figure eight one or two more times in the center. Place on a greased baking sheet. Let rise again and bake as directed.

FRENCH TOAST
···

6 slices day-old bread
6 eggs
½ cup milk
2 tablespoons cinnamon-sugar mixture (see Note)
⅛ teaspoon nutmeg
½ teaspoon vanilla extract
butter
powdered sugar
maple syrup

Arrange bread in a 3-quart rectangular baking dish so that there is no overlap. Beat eggs with milk, cinnamon-sugar, nutmeg, and vanilla extract. Pour over bread and let stand for a little while to absorb egg mixture. (It can be covered and refrigerated overnight, if desired.) When ready to cook, grease a skillet or griddle with butter. Gently place bread in the heated skillet or griddle, being careful not to crowd slices. Brown on both sides, cut in half diagonally, and dust with powdered sugar before serving with warm maple syrup.

MAKES 3–4 SERVINGS.

Note: To make **Cinnamon-Sugar Mixture**, which can be used for cinnamon toast as well, pour 2 cups sugar into a jar with a tight-fitting lid. Add ¼ cup cinnamon and shake well to blend, turning the jar as you shake it, so that cinnamon is distributed evenly.

PRALINE FRENCH TOAST
···

This is good for holiday breakfasts, since it can be prepared the night before.

OVEN: 350°

2 (6¼-ounce) packages Pepperidge Farm Butter Crescent Rolls (12 rolls in all)
8 eggs
¾ cup milk
1¾ cups half and half
2 tablespoons sugar
1 teaspoon vanilla extract
½ teaspoon cinnamon
1 cup butter
1 cup brown sugar
2 tablespoons maple syrup
1 cup pecan halves or pieces

Slice crescent rolls in half (as though you were going to make a sandwich) and arrange the pieces cut-side-down in 2 rectangular baking dishes, 12 halves per dish. Beat eggs with milk, half and half, sugar, vanilla extract, and cinnamon. Pour mixture over rolls, dividing equally between the 2 baking dishes. Cover and refrigerate overnight. When ready to bake, melt butter in a small saucepan and stir in brown sugar and maple syrup. Heat until brown sugar is melted, and stir in pecans. Spoon dabs of the mixture over crescent rolls and bake for 40–45 minutes. Serve hot, as sticky buns.

MAKES 6–8 SERVINGS.

GARLIC BREAD
■ ■ ■

OVEN: 425°

1 loaf French bread
¹/₂ cup butter, melted
1 tablespoon parsley flakes
*2 tablespoons grated Parmesan
    cheese*
¹/₈ teaspoon garlic powder

Slice bread diagonally, leaving slices attached at bottom. Blend remaining ingredients and brush between slices of bread. If any butter is left, brush it over the top of bread as well. Wrap loaf in foil and bake for 10–12 minutes.

Note: To make **Garlic Rolls,** substitute a package of French rolls, cut in half, for the loaf of French bread. Do not wrap rolls in foil before baking.
MAKES 5–6 SERVINGS.

HUSH PUPPIES
■ ■ ■

ELECTRIC SKILLET: 375°

2 cups cornmeal
2 tablespoons flour
1 tablespoon baking powder
1¹/₂ teaspoons baking soda
1 teaspoon salt
dash cayenne
¹/₃ cup chopped onion
1 egg
2 cups buttermilk
vegetable oil

Mix cornmeal, flour, baking powder, baking soda, salt, and cayenne in a large bowl. Stir in onion. Beat egg and buttermilk in a small bowl. Blend buttermilk mixture into dry ingredients. Heat about 2″ of oil to 375° in an electric skillet. Drop spoonfuls of batter into oil and fry for 2–3 minutes, turning so that hush puppies become golden brown on all sides. Drain on paper towels.
MAKES 8 SERVINGS.

LEMON BREAD
■ ■ ■

OVEN: 350°

Bread:
¹/₂ cup butter
1 cup sugar
2 eggs
1¹/₂ cups flour
¹/₄ teaspoon salt
¹/₄ teaspoon baking soda
¹/₂ cup buttermilk
1 teaspoon grated lemon peel
¹/₂ cup chopped pecans

Glaze:
¹/₂ cup powdered sugar
¹/₃ cup lemon juice

Cream together butter and sugar. Beat in eggs. Sift together flour, salt, and soda. Add dry ingredients to butter and sugar mixture alternately with buttermilk, mixing well. Fold in lemon peel and pecans. Pour into a greased 9″ x 5″ x 3″ loaf pan and bake for 1 hour. As soon as it comes out of the oven, mix powdered sugar with lemon juice and pour over bread while it's hot.
MAKES 1 LOAF.

N·O·T·E·S

QUICK PANCAKES

2 cups Bisquick
1 cup milk (increase up to 1 1/2 cups
   for thinner pancakes)
2 eggs

Stir all ingredients together in a mixing bowl, adding a little more milk for thinner pancakes. Grease a skillet or griddle and preheat over medium-high heat. (The skillet is hot enough when a drop of water sizzles and dances.) Using a 2-tablespoon coffee measure, ladle heaping scoops of batter onto a skillet or a griddle, being careful not to let pancakes run together. When bubbles rise to the top and break, use a pancake turner to lift an edge gently. If pancake is brown enough, flip and cook briefly on the other side. Keep cooked pancakes warm in the oven or toaster oven while remaining pancakes cook. Serve with melted butter and warm maple syrup. If desired, add a mashed ripe banana to the batter.

MAKES 12–15 PANCAKES.

QUICK WAFFLES

1 egg
1 1/3 cups milk
2 tablespoons vegetable oil
2 cups Bisquick

Spray a waffle iron with non-stick spray and preheat. Beat egg and milk together and mix in oil. Stir in Bisquick. For a standard waffle iron, pour in about 1 cup batter and spread evenly with a knife. Cook for about 5–8 minutes, or until waffle iron no longer steams and waffle is done. Keep warm while preparing remaining waffles. Serve with melted butter and warm maple syrup.

MAKES 12 (4") WAFFLES.

Note: If you store batter overnight in the refrigerator, stir in a teaspoon of baking powder just before cooking.

MONKEY BREAD
■ ■ ■

OVEN: 350°

4 (10-ounce) cans refrigerator
   biscuits
1 cup sugar
1 1/2 tablespoons cinnamon
3/4 cup chopped pecans
1/2 cup butter
1 cup brown sugar

Remove biscuits from cans and cut into quarters. Mix sugar and cinnamon in a plastic bag and add biscuit pieces, 6–8 pieces at a time, and shake well to coat with cinnamon-sugar mixture. Grease a tube pan or Bundt pan well and place a layer of biscuits in the pan. Sprinkle on some chopped pecans, and repeat layers of biscuits and pecans until all are used. Melt butter in a small saucepan and stir in brown sugar. Cook and stir over low heat until sugar is dissolved. Drizzle over the biscuits in the pan and bake for about 30 minutes, or until lightly browned. Let biscuits stand in the pan for 15 minutes after removing from the oven. Then turn out onto a serving plate.

MAKES 16 SERVINGS.

"Bread that must be sliced with an axe is bread that is too nourishing."

—Fran Lebowitz

PANCAKES
■ ■ ■

1 1/2 cups flour
1 teaspoon salt
3 tablespoons sugar
1 3/4 teaspoons baking powder
2 eggs
3 tablespoons butter, melted
1 cup milk
1 ripe banana, mashed (optional)

Sift together flour, salt, sugar, and baking powder. Beat eggs slightly and beat in melted butter and milk. Blend egg mixture with flour mixture, but do not overbeat. To make thinner pancakes, add a little more milk. If desired, stir in a mashed banana. Grease a skillet or griddle and preheat over medium-high heat. (The skillet is hot enough when a drop of water sizzles and dances.) Use a 2-tablespoon coffee measure to ladle batter onto skillet or griddle, being careful not to let pancakes run together. When bubbles rise to the top and break, use a pancake turner to lift an edge gently. If pancakes are brown enough, flip them and cook them briefly on the other side. (The second side never takes as long as the first.) Keep the cooked pancakes warm in the oven while you cook the remaining pancakes. Serve with melted butter and warm maple syrup.

MAKES 12–14 PANCAKES.

POPPY SEED BREAD
■ ■ ■

OVEN: 325°

Batter:
3 cups less 2 tablespoons
   self-rising flour
2$^1/_3$ cups sugar
3 eggs
1$^1/_2$ cups milk
1$^1/_8$ cups vegetable oil
1$^1/_2$ teaspoons vanilla extract
1$^1/_2$ teaspoons almond extract
1$^1/_2$ teaspoons butter flavoring
2 tablespoons poppy seeds

Glaze:
$^3/_4$ cup sugar
$^1/_4$ cup orange juice
$^1/_2$ teaspoon vanilla extract
$^1/_2$ teaspoon almond extract
$^1/_2$ teaspoon butter flavoring

Mix all batter ingredients together with an electric mixer. (Batter will be thin.) Grease and flour 2 (9" x 5" x 3") loaf pans and divide batter evenly between them. Bake for 50–60 minutes. Remove from oven and cool for 15 minutes. While bread is cooling, prepare the glaze. Blend all glaze ingredients together and pour over 2 loaves of bread, which have cooled for 15 minutes. Allow glaze to cool completely before removing loaves from pans. Freezes well.

MAKES 2 LOAVES.

POPOVERS
■ ■ ■

OVEN: 450°/350°

3 tablespoons butter, softened,
   divided use
1 cup milk
2 eggs, at room temperature
1 cup flour
$^1/_4$ teaspoon salt

Use 2 tablespoons of the butter to grease 6 custard cups. Melt remaining 1 tablespoon butter in a small saucepan and stir in milk. Warm milk slightly. Beat eggs in a mixing bowl and whisk in flour and salt. Add milk mixture to egg and flour mixture and stir until somewhat (but not completely) smooth. Fill each custard cup halfway with batter and put in a 450° oven. Bake for 20 minutes and reduce heat to 350°. Don't open oven door while they're cooking. Bake for 20 more minutes. Remove from custard cups and serve immediately.

MAKES 6 POPOVERS.

_____
_____
_____
_____
_____
_____
_____
_____
_____
_____
_____
_____
_____
_____
_____
_____
_____
_____
_____
_____
_____
_____
_____
_____
_____
_____
_____
_____
_____
_____
_____
_____
_____

PUMPKIN BREAD
■ ■ ■

OVEN: 350°

3½ cups sifted flour
2 teaspoons baking soda
1½ teaspoons salt
1 teaspoon baking powder
2 teaspoons cinnamon
2 teaspoons nutmeg
1 teaspoon allspice (optional)
½ teaspoon ground cloves
3 cups sugar
⅔ cup water
1 cup oil
5 eggs, beaten
1 (16-ounce) can pumpkin
1 cup chopped pecans

In a large bowl, mix together flour, baking soda, salt, baking powder, cinnamon, nutmeg, allspice (optional), cloves, and sugar. Blend in water and oil and mix in eggs. Blend in pumpkin and stir in pecans. Pour into 2 greased 9" x 5" x 3" loaf pans or 3 greased 8" x 4" x 2" loaf pans and bake for 1 hour, or until a toothpick inserted in center comes out clean.
MAKES 2 OR 3 LOAVES.

REFRIGERATOR ROLLS
■ ■ ■

The first time I made these rolls was right after Jack and I were married. It was the night before Thanksgiving, and my parents had come for a visit. I was so excited to have pulled this off! As soon as the rolls were done, we stood in the kitchen with a stick of butter and a squeeze bottle of honey, stuffing ourselves with these delicious homemade treats!

OVEN: 375°

¼ cup lukewarm (105°–115°) water
2 packages dry rapid-rise yeast
1 cup milk
¾ cup shortening
1 cup mashed potatoes (instant or regular)
½ cup sugar
1½ teaspoons salt
2 eggs, beaten
5 cups flour, plus additional if needed
non-stick spray
1 cup butter, melted

Measure ¼ cup lukewarm water into a small bowl and sprinkle yeast on top. Stir until yeast is dissolved. Set aside. Scald milk in a small saucepan. Add shortening and stir until dissolved. Pour milk mixture into a large mixing bowl and let cool to lukewarm (105°–115°). Stir yeast mixture into milk mixture. Add mashed potatoes and stir with a whisk until mixture is smooth. Stir in sugar, salt, and eggs.

Mix in flour, about ½ cup at a time, to make a stiff dough. As the dough begins to stiffen, you'll need to switch from a whisk to a wooden spoon. You may need to add up to ¼ cup more flour, until dough pulls away from the sides of the bowl. Spray another mixing bowl with non-stick spray and transfer the dough into the greased bowl. Spray the dough with non-stick spray and cover with plastic wrap. Refrigerate for several hours.

To prepare rolls, divide dough into fourths and roll each fourth into a 9" x 12" rectangle about ¼" thick. Cut out dough with a biscuit cutter. Dip each roll into melted butter and fold in half. (Butter should not be hotter than lukewarm, or it will kill the yeast, and the rolls will not rise successfully.) Arrange each dozen rolls in a greased 9" pie pan, with 2 in the center and 10 in a circle, touching each other. Let rise a second time at room temperature, away from drafts, for 2 hours. Bake for about 15 minutes. Watch rolls closely to be sure they don't get too brown. If you plan to serve the rolls at a later time, bake for only about 10 minutes. Rolls can be covered and frozen at this point. Then allow rolls to thaw, and bake them at 375° for about 5 more minutes before serving. Dough will keep in refrigerator for 4–5 days, and can be used as needed. Reheat fully-baked rolls in foil at 375° for 5–10 minutes. MAKES 4 DOZEN.

SOUR CREAM COFFEE CAKE
▪▪▪

OVEN: 350°

1 cup butter
2 cups sugar
2 eggs
1 (8-ounce) carton sour cream
½ teaspoon vanilla extract
1¾ cups flour
1 teaspoon baking powder
¼ teaspoon salt
½ cup chopped pecans
2 teaspoons cinnamon
¼ cup brown sugar

In an electric mixer, cream together butter and sugar. Beat in eggs and turn speed to low. Blend in sour cream, vanilla extract, flour, baking powder, and salt. Spoon half of the batter into a greased and floured 10" angel food cake pan or Bundt pan. Mix pecans, cinnamon, and brown sugar together in a small bowl, and spread over the batter in the pan. Spread remaining batter on top. With a knife, make a few swirls or zigzags in the batter, just to mix in the nuts slightly. Bake for 1 hour. MAKES 12 SERVINGS.

STRAWBERRY BREAD

■■■

OVEN: 350°

3 cups flour
2 cups sugar
1 tablespoon cinnamon
1 teaspoon baking soda
1 teaspoon salt
1 cup vegetable oil
4 eggs, beaten
2 (10-ounce) packages frozen
    strawberries, thawed and
    crushed
1¼ cups chopped pecans

Measure flour, sugar, cinnamon, baking soda, and salt into a large bowl. Mix in oil and eggs. Fold in strawberries and pecans. Grease and flour 2 (9" x 5" x 3") loaf pans and divide batter evenly between them. Bake for 1 hour and 15 minutes. Cool before cutting.

MAKES 2 (9" X 5" X 3") LOAVES.

WAFFLES

■■■

2 eggs
2 cups milk
2 cups flour
6 tablespoons vegetable oil
1 teaspoon salt
1 teaspoon sugar
2 teaspoons baking powder

Spray waffle iron with non-stick spray and preheat. Beat eggs and milk together and mix in flour, oil, salt, sugar, and baking powder. For a standard size waffle, use about 1 cup batter, and spread evenly with a knife. Cook for 5–7 minutes per waffle, or until done. Keep warm in the oven while preparing remaining waffles. Serve with melted butter and maple syrup.

Note: If waffle batter is stored overnight in the refrigerator, stir in another teaspoon of baking powder just before cooking.

MAKES 4 SERVINGS.

ZUCCHINI PINEAPPLE BREAD

■■■

OVEN: 325°

3 eggs, beaten
2 cups sugar
1 cup oil
3 teaspoons vanilla extract
2 cups grated zucchini
3 cups flour
1 teaspoon baking soda
1 tablespoon cinnamon
1 teaspoon salt
½ teaspoon baking powder
1 cup chopped pecans
1 (8-ounce) can crushed pineapple,
    drained

Mix eggs, sugar, oil, and vanilla extract, and beat well. Mix in remaining ingredients. Pour into 2 greased and floured 8" x 4" x 2" loaf pans and bake for an hour, or until a toothpick inserted in the center comes out clean.

MAKES 2 LOAVES.

Cakes and Frostings

CAKES AND FROSTINGS

■■■

<table>
</table>

TIPS FOR BETTER CAKES AND FROSTING

- To prepare the pan, choose one: (1) Using a small piece of waxed paper, spread about 1 tablespoon shortening or softened butter around the bottom and sides of the pan. Or brush vegetable oil around the pan. When greasing a tube pan or Bundt pan, take extra care to grease the part of the pan where the tube attaches to the pan. Then sprinkle about 1 tablespoon flour into the pan and shake it around, turning the pan so that the bottom and sides are coated with flour. Finally, turn the pan upside down over the sink and tap it lightly to shake out the excess flour. (2) Line the bottom of the pan with a paper towel or a piece of parchment paper cut to fit. Then spray the sides of the pan with non-stick spray that contains flour, such as Baker's Joy.

- To test for doneness, choose one: (1) Check cake after minimum baking time has elapsed. It should spring back when touched lightly, and pull away from the sides of the pan slightly. (2) Insert a toothpick into the center of the cake. If toothpick comes out clean, the cake is done.

- To make a cake mix taste more like homemade, add 1 teaspoon vanilla extract and one more egg than the package directions call for.

- To help stabilize an oversize or multi-layer cake, add 1/4 cup flour per package of white cake mix. Also, reduce baking temperature from 350° to 325°.

- Never fill a cake pan more than two thirds full, and spread the batter in the pan evenly, using a spatula if necessary. Tap the pan on the counter to knock out any large air bubbles.

- Place pans in the center of the oven.

- To create more evenly baked layers, look in cookware stores for strips that wrap around layer cake pans and attach with Velcro.

(continued)

CAKES

■■■

AMARETTO CAKE

■■■

OVEN: 325°

1 1/2 cups chopped toasted almonds, divided use

1 (18 1/2-ounce) box butter recipe yellow cake mix

1 (3.4-ounce) package instant vanilla pudding mix

4 eggs

1/2 cup vegetable oil

1/2 cup water

1/2 cup Amaretto

1 teaspoon almond extract

Glaze:

1/2 cup sugar

1/4 cup water

2 tablespoons butter

1/4 cup Amaretto

1/2 teaspoon almond extract

Sprinkle 1 cup of the almonds into a greased and floured 10" Bundt pan. Combine cake mix, pudding mix, eggs, oil, water, Amaretto, and almond extract. Beat on low speed to moisten; then beat on medium speed for 4 minutes. Stir in remaining 1/2 cup almonds. Pour batter into pan and bake for 1 hour, or until done. Cool cake in pan for 15 minutes. Then remove from pan and cool completely. To make glaze, combine sugar, water,

and butter in a small saucepan and bring to a boil. Reduce heat and boil gently for 5 minutes. Then cool for 15 minutes. Stir in Amaretto and almond extract. Punch holes in the cooled cake with an ice pick and slowly spoon glaze over the cake, allowing cake to absorb the glaze.

MAKES 12 SERVINGS.

ANGEL FOOD CAKE

■■■

OVEN: 375°

1 cup flour

1 1/2 cups sugar, divided use

12 eggs, at room temperature

1 1/2 teaspoons cream of tartar

1/4 teaspoon salt

1 tablespoon vanilla extract

1/2 teaspoon almond extract

Mix flour with 3/4 cup of the sugar in a small bowl, and set aside. To separate the eggs, set out 1 large, very clean bowl for whites, a small bowl for yolks, and a cup. (There should be absolutely no oily residue on either the large bowl or on the beaters, since that would prevent the egg whites from beating up properly.) One by one, crack each egg on the side of the cup and break shell open, allowing white to fall into the cup. Put yolks into small bowl. After checking to be sure that no tiny pieces of egg yolk have fallen into the egg white in the cup, transfer it to the large bowl. (A cup is used in case an egg yolk breaks and runs into the white. This way, you won't ruin whole batch of whites.) If a bit of yolk does get into the white, use a piece of egg shell to scoop it out. Once all the egg whites are in the bowl, refrigerate or freeze the egg yolks for another use. With an electric mixer at medium speed, beat the egg whites until they are foamy. Sprinkle the cream of tartar and salt on the egg whites as the mixer is running, and continue to beat the egg whites until they form soft peaks. With the mixer still running, add remaining ¾ cup sugar, a few tablespoons at a time, and continue beating until mixture holds stiff but not dry peaks. Then add vanilla and almond extracts, beating only until well mixed. Turn off mixer, remove bowl, and using a rubber spatula, gently fold in the flour mixture, sifting it over the egg whites in 4 batches. Spread batter evenly into an ungreased 10" tube pan. Cut through the batter with a knife to release any large air bubbles. Then drop the pan onto the counter several times, from about 8", further releasing any air bubbles. Bake for 30–35 minutes, or just until done. The top will be toasty brown and will spring back when pressed gently with your finger, and a toothpick inserted into the cake will come out clean. Immediately invert the pan, resting the center tube on a funnel or on the neck of a bottle. Allow the cake to cool upside down for several hours. When it is completely cooled, run a sharp knife around the outside of the pan and around the center tube, to free cake from the pan. Rap the pan gently on the counter, and then remove the cake from the pan.

MAKES 12 SERVINGS.

ANGEL FOOD ICE CREAM CAKE
■ ■ ■

1 prepared angel food cake (round, full size)
6 tablespoons Amaretto
2 quarts ice cream, softened (same or different flavors)
1 pint very cold heavy cream
4 tablespoons powdered sugar

Slice cake into 3 layers. Place bottom layer on a large sheet of heavy foil. Sprinkle on 2 tablespoons of Amaretto and spread on 1 quart of the ice cream. Add second cake layer, 2 more tablespoons Amaretto, and remaining ice cream. Place third cake layer on top and sprinkle on remaining Amaretto. Whip cream until stiff and blend in powdered sugar. Frost cake with whipped cream mixture and set in freezer. When solid, wrap foil around cake. Serve frozen.

MAKES 12 SERVINGS.

N·O·T·E·S

- After removing the cake from the oven, cool it on a rack for the length of time specified in the recipe. If no time is given, let it cool for about 15 minutes.

- Before removing the cake from the pan, run a knife around the outside of the pan to loosen the sides. Then, using a clean dish towel, gently pat the cake down to keep it from "mounding" in the center.

- For a professional-looking layer cake, "peel" the crust off the top of each layer before frosting the cake. Here's how to do it: As soon as you remove the cake from the oven, cover the top of each layer with waxed paper and press down gently so that waxed paper adheres to the top of the cake, which will be slightly moist. Let cake cool in the pan, and then remove the waxed paper to peel off the crust before turning the cake out of the pan.

- Before frosting a cake, freeze cake layers if possible. Frozen cake layers are much easier to frost than those at room temperature. If you don't have time to freeze them completely, even a short time in the freezer will help to firm them up and make them easier to frost.

- After removing cake from the freezer, use a small serrated knife to trim off any "overhang" from the top of each layer. This will make the sides of the frosted layer cake look smoother and prettier.

- To frost a cake, first brush off any loose crumbs. Next, apply frosting to the top of the layer, and then apply it to the sides. Add the next layer and repeat.

- After applying frosting to the entire cake, dip a flat metal spatula into hot water and use it to smooth the frosting before applying any decoration.

APPLE KUCHEN
■■■

OVEN: 350°

3/4 cup sugar
1/3 cup butter
1 egg
1 1/2 cups flour
2 teaspoons baking powder
1/2 teaspoon salt
1/2 teaspoon nutmeg
1/2 cup half and half
2 Granny Smith apples
1 1/2 cups cranberries or blueberries
4 tablespoons sugar
2 teaspoons cinnamon
heavy cream, softly whipped

Cream together sugar, butter, and egg, and beat until fluffy. In a separate bowl, combine flour, baking powder, salt, and nutmeg. Add dry ingredients and half and half alternately to sugar and butter mixture, stirring until just mixed. Spoon batter into a greased deep 9" pie pan. Core and slice apples. Press them into batter in a starburst pattern around the outside edge, with peel facing up and cut side facing down. Press cranberries or blueberries into center of batter. Mix sugar with cinnamon and sprinkle over all. Bake for 45 minutes, or until a toothpick inserted into center comes out clean. Serve with whipped cream.

MAKES 8 SERVINGS.

CAKE MAKE-OVER
■■■

Turn a plain frosted cake into a work of art with inexpensive flowers from the supermarket. Rinse them in cool water and let them dry. Then snip the stems short and arrange the flowers on top of the cake. Finish your design with a few sprigs of greenery.

CARROT CAKE
■■■

OVEN: 350°

2 cups flour
2 teaspoons baking soda
1 teaspoon salt
2 teaspoons cinnamon
1/2 teaspoon nutmeg
2 cups sugar
1 1/2 cups vegetable oil
4 eggs
3 cups raw grated carrots
 (about 1 pound)

Sift flour, baking soda, salt, cinnamon, and nutmeg into a large bowl. Stir in sugar and mix in oil. Beat in eggs one at a time. Mix in carrots. Pour into 3 greased and floured 9" cake pans. Bake for 25–30 minutes, or until cake pulls away from sides of pan slightly. Frost with Cream Cheese Frosting (page 286).

MAKES 12–16 SERVINGS.

CHEESECAKE

■ ■ ■

OVEN: 425°

Crust:

24 graham crackers, crushed
(2½" squares)
⅓ cup powdered sugar
½ cup butter, melted

Cake:

3 (8-ounce) packages cream
cheese, well softened
1 scant cup sugar
4 eggs plus 1 additional egg yolk
1½ tablespoons vanilla extract
2 teaspoons lemon juice
1 (8-ounce) carton sour cream
cinnamon

To make crust, combine graham cracker crumbs with powdered sugar and stir in melted butter. Press mixture evenly into the bottom of an 8" springform pan. Set aside. To make cake, use an electric mixer to combine cream cheese with sugar, and beat until smooth and creamy. One at a time, beat in eggs and egg yolk. Stir in vanilla extract, lemon juice, and sour cream, and beat again until mixture is very smooth. Spread cream cheese mixture over graham cracker crust. Sprinkle very lightly with cinnamon and bake for 35 minutes. Turn off oven and leave cheesecake in the oven for 30 more minutes. Remove from oven and let cool. Then refrigerate overnight before serving.

MAKES 12 SERVINGS.

Note: If desired, spread 1 (21-ounce) can fruit pie filling (cherry, blueberry, etc.) on top of cheesecake. Or, instead of using fruit filling as a topping, substitute chocolate shavings, chocolate syrup, raspberry sauce, etc.

CHOCOLATE BUTTERMILK CAKE

■ ■ ■

OVEN: 350°

½ cup butter, softened
2 cups sugar
2 eggs
6 tablespoons cocoa
2 cups flour
½ teaspoon baking powder
1 teaspoon baking soda
⅔ cup buttermilk
1 cup boiling water
1 teaspoon vanilla extract

Cream butter with sugar. Beat in eggs. Mix in cocoa. Mix flour with baking powder and baking soda and add to butter and sugar mixture alternately with buttermilk. Mix in 1 cup boiling water and vanilla extract. Pour into 2 greased and floured 9" layer pans or a 13" x 9" x 2" pan and bake for 30–35 minutes.

MAKES 12–16 SERVINGS.

"There is a simple memory aid that you can use to determine whether it is the correct time to order chocolate dishes: any month whose name contains the letter A, E, or U is the proper time for chocolate."

—Sandra Boynton

CHOCOLATE MARBLE CAKE

■ ■ ■

OVEN: 350°

1 (18½-ounce) box butter recipe yellow cake mix
1 (3.4-ounce) package instant vanilla pudding mix
½ cup vegetable oil
1 (8-ounce) carton sour cream
4 eggs
1 teaspoon vanilla extract
⅔ cup chocolate syrup
½ cup semisweet chocolate morsels

Combine cake mix, pudding mix, oil, sour cream, eggs, and vanilla extract. Beat for 2 minutes. Pour a third of the batter into a greased and floured tube pan or Bundt pan. Transfer half of the remaining batter to a small mixing bowl and blend in chocolate syrup and chocolate morsels. Spread this mixture over the first layer. Pour the remaining batter on top. Use a knife to make zigzags in the batter, so that the layers swirl together just slightly. Bake for 45–50 minutes. Cool for 25 minutes before removing from the pan. Top with Basic Glaze (page 286).

MAKES 12–16 SERVINGS.

CHOCOLATE POUND CAKE

■ ■ ■

OVEN: 350°

1 cup butter
½ cup shortening
3 cups sugar
5 eggs
3 cups flour
½ cup cocoa
½ teaspoon baking powder
1¼ cups milk
1½ teaspoons vanilla extract

Put butter, shortening, and sugar into a large bowl. Cream together with an electric mixer at high speed until light and fluffy. Reduce speed to medium and beat in eggs, one at a time. Sift together flour, cocoa, and baking powder, and add to butter mixture alternately with milk. Mix in vanilla extract, and pour into a greased and floured tube pan or Bundt pan. Bake for 1½ hours, or until a toothpick inserted into cake comes out clean.

Allow cake to cool on a wire rack for 15 minutes before removing from pan. Frost with Chocolate Butter Cream Frosting (page 284).

MAKES 12–16 SERVINGS.

HERSHEY BAR CAKE
■■■

OVEN: 350°

6 (1.55-ounce) Hershey milk
    chocolate bars
1 cup butter, softened
1¼ cups sugar
4 eggs
2½ cups flour
¼ teaspoon baking soda
pinch salt
1 cup buttermilk (can use
    reconstituted)
½ cup chocolate syrup
2 teaspoons vanilla extract

Grease and flour a 3-quart Bundt pan. Break Hershey bars into pieces and set aside. In a large bowl, use an electric mixer to cream butter with sugar, beating until fluffy. Beat in eggs, one at a time. Add chocolate pieces and beat well. In a medium bowl, stir together flour, baking soda, and salt. Alternately beat flour mixture and buttermilk into batter, blending well. Pour batter into prepared pan and bake for 1 hour and 15 minutes, or until toothpick inserted in center comes out clean. Cool for 10 minutes in the pan. Remove from pan and allow to cool completely on wire rack. Drizzle Vanilla Glaze (page 286) over cake.

MAKES 12 SERVINGS.

COCONUT CAKE
■■■

OVEN: 375°

1 (18½-ounce) box butter recipe
    yellow cake mix
⅔ cup water
½ cup butter, softened
3 eggs
2 cups sugar
¾ cup milk
¼ cup rum
1 (9-ounce) carton Cool Whip
¼ cup coconut liqueur
1 (6-ounce) package shredded
    coconut

Blend cake mix, water, butter, and eggs. Beat for 2 minutes. Spread in a greased and floured 13″ x 9″ x 2″ pan and bake for 35–40 minutes. About 10 minutes before cake is done, mix sugar, milk, and rum in a medium saucepan. Bring to a boil and boil gently for 1–2 minutes. Remove cake from the oven, leave it in the pan, and punch holes in it with an ice pick. Pour sugar mixture over it and let the cake cool at room temperature for 1 hour. Mix Cool Whip with coconut liqueur and spread over the cake. Sprinkle coconut on top and refrigerate.

MAKES 15–18 SERVINGS.

How Long Should I Bake the Cake?

Square Layers:

8".................................... 27–32 min.

Round Layers:

6".................................... 35–45 min.
8".................................... 32–37 min.
9".................................... 27–32 min.
10"................................... 45–55 min.
12"................................... 45–55 min.
14"................................... 45–55 min.
16"................................... 45–55 min.

Rectangular Pans:

9" x 13" x 2".................... 30–35 min.
10½" x 15½" x 1".......... 19–24 min.
11" x 15" x 2"................. 45–55 min.
12" x 17" x 1"................. 35–45 min.
12" x 18" x 2"................. 37–47 min.
18" x 24" x 2"................. 43–53 min.

Cupcakes:

12 cupcakes .... 18–23 min.
24 cupcakes................... 18–23 min.

How Much Will My Cake Pan Hold?

■ To determine the capacity of a cake pan, fill it with water to the level that you would normally add batter. Then pour the water into a measuring cup to see how much batter the pan will hold.

■ Rectangular Pan Volume = length × width × depth

■ Round Pan Volume = 3.14 × radius × depth

■ Volume of standard measuring cup = about 14 cubic inches

■ Each package of white cake mix yields 5½ cups batter

■ Rule of Thumb: Allow about ¼ cup batter for each cupcake

CREAM CHEESE COCONUT CAKE

■ ■ ■

OVEN: 350°

1 (18½-ounce) box butter recipe yellow cake mix

½ cup butter, softened

3 eggs, divided use

1 cup shredded coconut

1 cup chopped pecans

1 (1-pound) box powdered sugar (about 4¼ cups sifted)

1 (8-ounce) package cream cheese, softened

1 tablespoon vanilla extract

Combine cake mix with butter, 2 of the eggs, coconut, and pecans. Beat until well blended. Spread in a greased and floured 13" x 9" x 2" pan. Beat powdered sugar with cream cheese, and beat in the remaining egg and the vanilla extract. Spread over bottom layer. Bake for 30 minutes. Let cool, and then refrigerate before cutting.

MAKES 12–18 SERVINGS.

CRUMB CAKE

■ ■ ■

OVEN: 350°

¾ cup butter, divided use

2½ cups flour, divided use

½ cup brown sugar

½ cup broken pecans

2 teaspoons baking powder

½ teaspoon baking soda

½ teaspoon salt

1 (8-ounce) package cream cheese, softened

1¼ cups sugar

2 eggs

1 teaspoon vanilla extract

½ cup milk

Measure ¼ cup of the butter, ½ cup of the flour, and the brown sugar into a small bowl and cut together with knives until mixture is crumbly. Stir in pecans and set aside. Sift together the remaining 2 cups flour, the baking powder, baking soda, and salt. In a large bowl, cream together the remaining ½ cup butter and the cream cheese. Gradually beat in sugar, eggs, and vanilla extract. Add dry ingredients alternately with milk. Pour batter into a greased 13" x 9" x 2" pan, and sprinkle nut mixture on top. Bake for 35–45 minutes.

MAKES 12 SERVINGS.

> *"When you become a good cook, you become a good craftsman, first. You repeat and repeat and repeat until your hands know how to move without thinking about it."*
>
> —Jacques Pepin

HUMMINGBIRD CAKE
■■■

OVEN: 350°

3 cups flour
2 cups sugar
1 teaspoon salt
1 teaspoon baking soda
1 teaspoon cinnamon
3 eggs, beaten
1½ cups vegetable oil
1½ teaspoons vanilla extract
1 (8-ounce) can crushed pineapple
2 cups chopped bananas
2 cups chopped pecans,
   divided use

Combine flour, sugar, salt, baking soda, and cinnamon. Add eggs and oil and stir until moist, but do not beat. Stir in vanilla extract, undrained pineapple, bananas, and 1 cup of the pecans. Spoon batter into 3 greased and floured 9" layer cake pans. Bake for 25–30 minutes. Cool for 10 minutes before removing from pans. Fill and frost with Cream Cheese Frosting (page 286). Top with remaining 1 cup pecans.
MAKES 12–16 SERVINGS.

ITALIAN CREAM CAKE
■■■

OVEN: 350°

½ cup butter
½ cup shortening
2 cups sugar
5 eggs, separated
2 cups flour
¼ teaspoon salt
1 teaspoon baking soda
1 cup buttermilk
1 teaspoon vanilla extract
1 cup shredded coconut
2 cups chopped pecans,
   divided use

Cream together butter, shortening, and sugar. Beat in egg yolks. Sift together flour, salt, and baking soda, and add alternately with buttermilk. Add vanilla extract and stir in coconut and 1 cup of the pecans. Beat egg whites until soft peaks form and fold into batter. Pour into 3 greased and floured 9" layer cake pans and bake for 25 minutes. Fill and frost with Cream Cheese Frosting (page 286). Sprinkle the remaining 1 cup pecans on top.
MAKES 12–16 SERVINGS.

JAM CAKE
• • •

OVEN: 300°

1 cup butter, softened
2 cups brown sugar
3 eggs, separated
1 cup jam (any flavor)
1 cup raisins
¾ cup chopped pecans
3¾ cups flour, divided use
1 tablespoon cocoa
1 teaspoon cinnamon
1 teaspoon ground cloves
2 teaspoons baking soda
2 cups buttermilk (can use reconstituted)

Cream together butter and sugar, and beat in egg yolks. Fold in jam. Mix raisins and pecans with ¼ cup of the flour. Sift the remaining 3½ cups flour with cocoa, cinnamon, and cloves. Stir baking soda into buttermilk and add to jam mixture alternately with flour mixture, beginning with flour. Stir in raisin mixture. Beat egg whites until stiff and fold in. Pour into a greased and floured 10" tube pan or Bundt pan and bake for 1½ hours, or until cake pulls away from the sides of the pan. Cool cake for 10 minutes before removing from the pan. Frost with Caramel Frosting (page 286).

MAKES 12–16 SERVINGS.

LEMON SPONGE CAKE
• • •

OVEN: 325°

6 eggs, at room temperature, separated
½ teaspoon cream of tartar
½ teaspoon salt
1 cup sugar, divided use
2 tablespoons water
1 tablespoon lemon juice
2 teaspoons lemon peel
1 teaspoon vanilla extract
1 cup flour

With solid shortening, grease only the bottom of a 10" tube pan and dust with flour. Set aside. Using an electric mixer, beat egg whites with cream of tartar and salt until soft peaks form. Beat in ½ cup of the sugar, 2 tablespoons at a time, and continue beating until stiff peaks form. Set aside. In a large mixing bowl, beat egg yolks until thick and lemon-colored. Gradually beat in remaining ½ cup sugar, 1 tablespoon at a time. Combine water with lemon juice, lemon peel, and vanilla extract, and mix into egg yolks. Using a rubber spatula, gently fold in flour, sifting it over egg yolks gradually. Then fold in egg whites.

Spread the batter evenly into the prepared tube pan. Cut through batter with a knife to release any large air bubbles. Bake for 1 hour, or until just done. Top will spring back when pressed gently with your finger, and a toothpick inserted into the cake will come out clean. Immediately invert pan, resting the center tube on a funnel or on the neck of a bottle. Allow the cake to cool upside down for several hours. When completely cooled, run a sharp knife around the outside of the pan and around the center tube to free the cake from the pan, and remove the cake from the pan.
MAKES 12 SERVINGS.

LEMON POUND CAKE
■ ■ ■

OVEN: 350°

1 (18½-ounce) box lemon
   cake mix
1 (3-ounce) package lemon gelatin
¾ cup apricot nectar
¾ cup vegetable oil
5 eggs
1 teaspoon lemon extract

Mix cake mix with lemon gelatin, apricot nectar, oil, eggs, and lemon extract. Beat with an electric mixer at medium speed for 2 minutes. Grease and flour a 10″ fluted or plain tube pan and pour in cake batter. Bake for 1 hour. Cool for 25 minutes before removing cake from the pan. Top with Citrus Glaze (page 286).
MAKES 12 SERVINGS.

PINEAPPLE CAKE
■ ■ ■

OVEN: 375°

1 (18½-ounce) box butter recipe
   yellow cake mix
⅔ cup water
½ cup butter, softened
3 eggs
1 (15¼-ounce) can crushed
   pineapple, undrained
1 cup sugar
1 (3.4-ounce) package instant
   vanilla pudding mix
2 cups cold milk
1 (9-ounce) carton Cool Whip
1 (6-ounce) package shredded
   coconut

Combine cake mix, water, butter, and eggs. Beat for 2 minutes. Spread into a greased and floured 13″ x 9″ x 2″ pan and bake for 35–40 minutes. About 10 minutes before cake is done, mix pineapple with sugar in a medium saucepan. Bring to a boil and boil gently for 5 minutes. Remove cake from the oven, leave in the pan, and punch holes in it with an ice pick. Pour pineapple mixture over it and cool for 1 hour. Combine pudding mix with cold milk, and beat for 2 minutes. Refrigerate for 5 minutes to thicken pudding slightly; spread on cake. Spread Cool Whip over the pudding and sprinkle coconut on top. Refrigerate. (Tastes even better the next day.)
MAKES 15–18 SERVINGS.

N·O·T·E·S

FROSTING FOR DECORATING

If you have enough leftover frosting, and want to use it to decorate a cake, you'll need to thicken it slightly. Otherwise, it's likely to spread out and lose its shape. First, use as much of the frosting as necessary to frost and fill the cake. Then add more powdered sugar to the remaining frosting, beating it in about 1/4 cup at a time, until the remaining frosting is thick enough to use for decorating. Add a few drops of food coloring to the frosting, if desired. To make several different colors, divide the frosting into small bowls and tint each one a different color. Any leftover frosting can be frozen in a plastic zip bag to use later on for decorating.

BUTTER CREAM FROSTING

1/2 cup butter, softened
1 1/2 teaspoons vanilla extract
1/8 teaspoon salt
3 1/2 cups powdered sugar, divided use
2 tablespoons milk or cream, plus
    additional 1 tablespoon (optional)

Cream together butter, vanilla extract, and salt. Gradually beat in 1 cup of the powdered sugar. Add 2 tablespoons of the milk or cream and remaining powdered sugar, and beat until frosting has a smooth consistency. Add remaining 1 tablespoon milk or cream only if necessary to achieve desired consistency. (If you add too much, the frosting will slide off the cake.)

MAKES ENOUGH TO FROST A 2-LAYER CAKE.

Note: If you intend to add any kind of cake decoration (writing, piping, flowers, etc.), you will need more frosting than a single recipe makes. Double this recipe in order to have plenty of frosting for both the cake and the decoration.

PETIT FOURS
■ ■ ■

OVEN: 350°

1 (18 1/2-ounce) box white cake mix
1/4 cup flour (regular or self-rising)
3 egg whites
1 1/4 cups water
1/3 cup vegetable oil
1/3 teaspoon vanilla extract
1/3 teaspoon lemon extract
1/3 teaspoon orange extract

Grease and flour sides of a 13" x 9" x 2" pan or spray with a non-stick spray with flour added, such as Baker's Joy. Then line bottom of pan with a paper towel or parchment paper cut to fit.

Sift dry cake mix together with flour into a large mixing bowl. (This extra flour will firm up the cake, making the petit fours easier to cut and handle.) Blend this dry mixture with egg whites, water, oil, and vanilla, lemon, and orange extracts for about 30 seconds on low speed of electric mixer, or until moistened. Increase speed to medium, and beat for 2 more minutes. Pour batter into the prepared pan and bake for 30–35 minutes. Cake is done when toothpick inserted into the center comes out clean.

As soon as cake is removed from the oven, slide a knife around the edges of the pan to release the cake. Then cover the surface of the cake with waxed paper and press down gently so that the waxed paper adheres to the cake. Let the cake cool in the pan with waxed paper on it. Then remove waxed paper so that you "peel" off the top crust of the cake. Carefully turn cake out of the pan onto a cooling rack and peel off the paper that you lined the pan with. Put cake in the freezer on the rack. When the cake is very firm, remove from freezer. While cake is still frozen, carefully trim off 1/2" from each of the 4 edges of the cake, so that cake measures 12" x 8", with all the outside crust trimmed off. Use a ruler as a straight edge to help you cut straight. Then use ruler as a guide to cut cake into 2" squares. Frost with Fondant Frosting (page 287).

MAKES 2 DOZEN.

POPPY SEED CAKE
■ ■ ■

OVEN: 350°

1 (18 1/2-ounce) box butter recipe
*   yellow cake mix*
1 (3-ounce) package instant vanilla
*   pudding mix*
1 cup water
1/2 cup butter, softened
5 eggs
2 tablespoons poppy seeds
1/2 teaspoon cinnamon
1 teaspoon vanilla extract
1 teaspoon almond extract

Mix all ingredients and beat for 2 minutes. Pour into a greased and floured 10" Bundt pan and bake for 45–55 minutes. Cool for 25 minutes. Remove from pan and top with Basic Glaze (page 286).

MAKES 12 SERVINGS.

SOUR CREAM POUND CAKE
■ ■ ■

OVEN: 325°

1 cup butter, softened
3 cups sugar
6 eggs
2 tablespoons vanilla extract
1 teaspoon lemon extract
1 teaspoon almond extract
3 cups flour
¼ teaspoon baking soda
½ teaspoon mace (optional)
1 (8-ounce) carton sour cream

Cream together butter and sugar, and beat until fluffy. Beat in eggs, one at a time. Add vanilla, lemon, and almond extracts. Sift flour with baking soda and mace (optional), and add alternately with sour cream. Pour into a greased and floured 10″ tube pan or Bundt pan and bake for 1½ hours.
MAKES 16–20 SERVINGS.

OLD-FASHIONED POUND CAKE
■ ■ ■

OVEN: 325°/350°

1 cup butter, softened
½ cup shortening
3 cups sugar
4 eggs
3 cups flour
1 teaspoon baking powder
½ teaspoon mace (optional)
pinch salt
1 cup milk
1½ teaspoons vanilla extract

Cream together butter, shortening, and sugar. Beat until fluffy. Beat in eggs one at a time. Sift flour with baking powder, mace (optional), and salt, and add alternately with milk. Add vanilla extract. Pour into a greased and floured 10″ tube pan and bake for 1½ hours at 325°. Increase heat to 350° and continue baking for 15 more minutes.
MAKES 16–20 SERVINGS.

N·O·T·E·S

BUTTER CREAM FROSTING VARIATIONS

For these variations, prepare Butter Cream Frosting (page 282) with the following changes:

Almond Butter Cream Frosting: Reduce vanilla extract to 1 teaspoon, and add ½ teaspoon almond extract.

Chocolate Butter Cream Frosting: Add ½ cup cocoa.

Coffee Butter Cream Frosting: Add 2 teaspoons instant coffee, dissolved in 1 teaspoon boiling water.

Lemon Butter Cream Frosting: Substitute an equal amount of lemon juice for the milk or cream, and add 1 tablespoon grated lemon peel.

Liqueur Butter Cream Frosting: Substitute 1 tablespoon brandy or any flavor of liqueur (coconut, etc.) for 1 tablespoon of the milk or cream.

Maple Butter Cream Frosting: Substitute ¼ cup maple syrup for the milk and add ¼ cup chopped nuts.

Mocha Butter Cream Frosting: Add ¼ cup cocoa and 1 teaspoon instant coffee granules.

Orange Butter Cream Frosting: Substitute an equal amount of orange juice for the milk, and add 2 teaspoons grated orange peel.

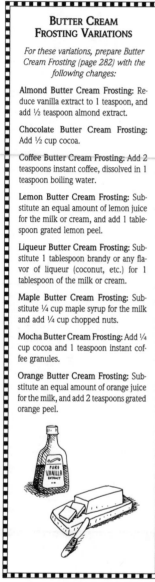

RUM CAKE
∎ ∎ ∎

OVEN: 375°

1 (18½-ounce) box butter recipe yellow cake mix
1 (3.4-ounce) package instant vanilla pudding mix
½ cup butter, softened
½ cup water
½ cup light rum
4 eggs
1 cup chopped pecans

Glaze:

1 cup sugar
½ cup butter
¼ cup water
¼ cup rum
1 teaspoon vanilla extract

Combine cake mix, pudding mix, butter, water, rum, and eggs. Beat for 4 minutes. Stir in pecans. Pour into a greased and floured 10" Bundt pan and bake for 45–50 minutes. About 10 minutes before cake is done, prepare glaze. Combine sugar, butter, water, rum, and vanilla extract in a saucepan and bring to a boil. Boil gently for 2 minutes. Remove cake from oven when done, leave in pan, punch holes in cake with an ice pick, and pour glaze over cake. Allow cake to cool completely before removing from pan.

MAKES 12 SERVINGS.

STRAWBERRY CAKE
∎ ∎ ∎

OVEN: 350°

1 (18½-ounce) box white cake mix
1 (3-ounce) package strawberry gelatin
1 cup vegetable oil
½ cup milk
4 eggs
1 (10-ounce) package frozen strawberries, thawed
1 cup shredded coconut
1 cup chopped pecans

Mix together cake mix and gelatin. Blend in oil and milk. Beat in eggs one at a time. Fold in thawed strawberries, coconut, and pecans. Pour into 3 greased and floured 8" layer cake pans and bake for 20–25 minutes. Fill and frost with Strawberry Frosting (page 288).

MAKES 12–16 SERVINGS.

"Baking is just like driving a car: you can read every manual you can get your hands on, but until you get in and do it, you won't really learn how."

—Marion Cunningham

SOCK IT TO ME CAKE
■■■

OVEN: 375°

1 (18½-ounce) box butter recipe
    yellow cake mix
½ cup granulated sugar
¾ cup vegetable oil
4 eggs
1 (8-ounce) carton sour cream
1 cup chopped pecans
2 tablespoons brown sugar
2 teaspoons cinnamon

In a large mixing bowl, blend cake
mix, granulated sugar, oil, eggs, and
sour cream. Beat for 2 minutes. In a
small mixing bowl, stir together
pecans, brown sugar, cinnamon, and
2 tablespoons of the cake batter.
Grease and flour a 10″ tube or Bundt
pan and pour half of the cake batter
into the pan. Spread on the nut filling and spread the remaining batter
evenly over the filling. Bake for 45–55
minutes. Cool for 25 minutes before
removing the cake from the pan. Top
with Basic Glaze (page 286).
MAKES 12–16 SERVINGS.

FROSTINGS
AND GLAZES
■■■

AMARETTO GLAZE
■■■

½ cup butter, melted
2 cups powdered sugar
3 tablespoons Amaretto

Mix butter, powdered sugar, and
Amaretto, and drizzle over cooled
cake. For thicker frosting, increase
powdered sugar up to 3½ cups and
increase Amaretto up to 4 tablespoons.
MAKES ENOUGH FOR A 10″ TUBE CAKE.

Variation: Chocolate Amaretto
Glaze: Add 4 tablespoons cocoa to
above recipe. For thicker frosting, increase cocoa up to 5 tablespoons.

BANANA FROSTING
■■■

½ cup butter, softened
1 teaspoon vanilla extract
⅛ teaspoon salt
3½ cups powdered sugar,
    divided use
2 tablespoons milk, plus additional
    1 tablespoon (optional)
3 tablespoons mashed banana
    (about ½ medium banana)
1 tablespoon lemon juice
½ cup chopped nuts (optional)

Cream together butter, vanilla extract, and salt. Gradually beat in 1 cup

(continued)

BASIC GLAZE

4 tablespoons butter
2 cups powdered sugar
2–3 tablespoons water or milk

Measure butter into a small bowl and melt in microwave. Mix in powdered sugar and water or milk, and beat until smooth. Drizzle over cooled cake.

MAKES ABOUT 1¼ CUPS GLAZE, OR ENOUGH TO GLAZE A 10″ TUBE CAKE OR BUNDT CAKE.

Note: Glaze can be tinted with a few drops of food coloring, if desired. If it is to be used as an icing for sweet rolls, or if it needs to be thicker, add a little more powdered sugar until it reaches desired consistency. To help maintain its consistency as you work with it, set the bowl of glaze into a larger pan of hot water, and stir it often.

BASIC GLAZE VARIATIONS

Almond Glaze: Add ¼ teaspoon almond extract to the basic recipe.

Brandy Glaze: Substitute brandy for the water or milk.

Citrus Glaze: Substitute lemon juice, orange juice, or lime juice for the water or milk. Add ½ teaspoon finely grated peel.

Creamy Glaze: Substitute heavy cream for the water or milk.

Rum Glaze: Substitute rum for the water or milk.

Vanilla Glaze: Add ½ teaspoon vanilla extract to the basic recipe.

of the powdered sugar. Add 2 tablespoons of the milk and the remaining 2½ cups powdered sugar, and beat until frosting has a smooth spreading consistency. Mix in banana and lemon juice. Thin frosting with remaining 1 tablespoon milk, only if necessary to achieve desired consistency. Stir in nuts, if desired.

MAKES ENOUGH TO FROST A 2-LAYER CAKE.

CARAMEL FROSTING
■ ■ ■

4 tablespoons butter
2 cups firmly packed brown sugar
½ cup granulated sugar
1 cup heavy cream
1 tablespoon vanilla extract

Mix butter, brown sugar, granulated sugar, and cream in a large, heavy saucepan. Stir over low heat until butter is melted and sugars are dissolved. Increase heat to medium and insert candy thermometer. Bring to a boil and cook until it reaches 234°–239° (soft-ball stage). Remove from heat, remove thermometer, and allow it to cool for 15 minutes. Stir in vanilla extract, and beat frosting until it loses its shine and becomes thick enough to spread. Although you may have to beat the frosting for up to 10 minutes, it can be done in stages, pausing to rest in between.

MAKES ENOUGH TO FROST A 2-LAYER CAKE.

CHOCOLATE FROSTING
■ ■ ■

½ cup cocoa
½ cup butter
½ cup evaporated milk
1¾ cups sugar
1 teaspoon vanilla extract
⅛ teaspoon salt

Mix cocoa, butter, evaporated milk, and sugar in a heavy saucepan and bring to a rolling boil. Boil for 2 minutes. Cool and beat with an electric mixer until creamy. Mix in vanilla extract and salt and spread on cake immediately, before frosting hardens.

MAKES ENOUGH TO FROST A 2-LAYER CAKE.

CREAM CHEESE FROSTING
■ ■ ■

1 (12-ounce) carton soft cream cheese
¾ cup butter, softened
4 teaspoons vanilla extract
6 cups powdered sugar

In an electric mixer, beat together cream cheese and butter. Mix in vanilla extract and beat in powdered sugar, 1 cup at a time.

MAKES ENOUGH TO FROST AND FILL A 3-LAYER CAKE.

FONDANT FROSTING

• • •

⅔ cup scalding hot tap water
⅓ cup solid shortening
½ cup light corn syrup
½ teaspoon vanilla extract
¼ teaspoon orange extract
¼ teaspoon lemon extract
2 (1-pound) boxes powdered sugar
    (about 8 cups)

Pour ⅔ cup scalding hot tap water over solid shortening in the top half of a double boiler. Add corn syrup and vanilla, orange, and lemon extracts. Mix well. Stir in 2 cups of the powdered sugar and mix well. Continue to add powdered sugar, 1 cup at a time, mixing well after each addition. Set aside. Pour about 1"–1½" of water in the bottom half of the double boiler. (Use just enough water so that when the top half of the double boiler is inserted, the water almost touches it.) Place the bottom half of the double boiler on the stove and bring water to a rapid boil. When water comes to a boil, remove it from the heat and set the top half of the double boiler over the bottom half. Beat the ingredients until the water in the bottom half of the double boiler has cooled to lukewarm.

To frost Petit Fours (page 282), place cake squares on a rack and pour the fondant over them. When fondant has cooled and set, you can remove the Petit Fours from the rack.

MAKES ENOUGH TO FROST 50
(2" SQUARE) PETIT FOURS.

MOCHA FROSTING

• • •

1 (1-pound) box powdered sugar
    (about 4¼ cups sifted)
5 tablespoons cocoa
4 tablespoons butter, melted
½ cup prepared coffee

Beat ingredients together and pour over sheet cake or brownies. Refrigerate cake or brownies for at least 4 hours before cutting.

MAKES ENOUGH TO FROST A
13" X 9" X 2" SHEET CAKE OR PAN
OF BROWNIES.

ROYAL ICING

• • •

3 egg whites
½ teaspoon cream of tartar
4–5 cups sifted powdered sugar
few drops water or lemon juice
    (optional)

Beat egg whites with cream of tartar until foamy. Gradually beat in 4 cups of the powdered sugar. Keep beating in more of the powdered sugar, a little at a time, until icing is the consistency you need. Beat on high speed for 5–8 minutes, or until icing is light and fluffy. If frosting gets too thick, add a few drops of water or lemon juice. If it's too thin, beat in a little more powdered sugar. Use it as it is, or divide the batch into several small bowls and tint each one with a different shade of food coloring.

MAKES 2½ CUPS.

(continued)

N·O·T·E·S

Note: Royal icing dries very hard, and is excellent for decorating cookies. It can also be used as "Baker's White Glue," to anchor decorations on cakes. Pipe it on from a pastry bag. It keeps for up to 2 weeks in the refrigerator, covered in an airtight container.

SEVEN-MINUTE FROSTING

■ ■ ■

3 egg whites
2¼ cups sugar
⅛ teaspoon salt
½ cup water
1 tablespoon light corn syrup
2 teaspoons vanilla extract

Beat egg whites until foamy. Combine with sugar, salt, water, and corn syrup in the top of a double boiler, and beat for 1 minute with a portable electric mixer. Place the top of the double boiler over boiling water and beat constantly at high speed for 7 minutes, or until stiff peaks form. Stir frosting up from the bottom and sides of the pan occasionally, so that all the frosting becomes smooth. Remove from heat and pour into a large mixing bowl. Add vanilla extract and beat for 1 more minute, or until frosting is thick enough to spread.

MAKES ENOUGH TO FROST A 2-LAYER CAKE.

STRAWBERRY FROSTING

■ ■ ■

½ cup butter, softened
1 (1-pound) box powdered sugar
  (about 4¼ cups sifted)
½ cup chopped pecans
1 (10-ounce) box frozen strawberries,
  thawed and drained
½ cup shredded coconut

Thoroughly cream together butter and sugar. Mix in pecans, strawberries, and coconut. Spread between layers and on top of cake, and let the frosting drizzle down the sides.

MAKES ENOUGH TO FROST 3 (8") LAYERS.

Cookies and Candy

COOKIES AND CANDY

■ ■ ■

BROWNIES WITH AMARETTO FROSTING

■ ■ ■

OVEN: 350°

Brownies:

1¼ cups butter

¾ cup cocoa

4 eggs

2 cups sugar

2 teaspoons vanilla extract

1 cup flour

½ teaspoon baking powder

¼ teaspoon salt

1½ cups chopped nuts

Amaretto Frosting:

½ cup butter

2¼ cups powdered sugar

¼ cup Amaretto

¼ cup cocoa

To make brownies, place butter in a small mixing bowl and microwave until melted. Then stir in cocoa with a whisk. Blend until smooth and set aside. In a large mixing bowl, beat eggs with a whisk. Beat in sugar and continue to beat until mixture is smooth and thick. Blend in chocolate mixture, vanilla extract, flour, baking powder, and salt, and beat with whisk until smooth. Stir in nuts and spread batter into a greased 10" x 15" x 2" (4-quart rectangular) pan, and bake for 30 minutes, or until firm. Or divide the batter between 2 greased 7" x 11" x 2" (2-quart rectangular) pans,

and bake for about 25 minutes. Do not overcook. To make frosting, place butter in a medium bowl and heat in the microwave until melted. Add powdered sugar alternately with Amaretto. Beat until smooth. Beat in cocoa. Spread frosting over brownies as soon as they come out of the oven. Spread frosting all the way to the edges. The heat from the brownies will cause the frosting to melt temporarily, and become smooth on top. It will set and stiffen somewhat as it cools, developing a slightly crunchy top. Allow brownies to cool thoroughly before cutting.

MAKES 24–35 BROWNIES.

BISCOTTI

■ ■ ■

OVEN: 325°

½ cup slivered almonds

⅓ cup butter, softened

¾ cup sugar

2 eggs

1 teaspoon vanilla extract

¼ teaspoon almond extract

2 teaspoons grated orange peel

2¼ cups flour

2 teaspoons baking powder

¼ teaspoon salt

⅛ teaspoon nutmeg

Put almonds into a shallow pan and bake for 10 minutes, or until lightly toasted. Remove from the oven and set aside. In a mixing bowl, cream butter with sugar and beat until fluffy. Beat in eggs one at a time. Mix in vanilla extract, almond extract, and orange peel. Combine flour, baking powder, salt, and nutmeg in another bowl, and add to butter mixture, stirring until well blended. Then mix in almonds. Divide dough in half on waxed paper and pat into 2 logs, each about 8" long. Place several inches apart on a greased baking sheet, and flatten slightly to a height of about 1". Bake for 20–25 minutes, or until golden brown. Remove from the oven, place on a rack, and let cool for 5 minutes. Then transfer to a cutting board and slice about ½" thick. Lay slices flat on a baking sheet and bake for 5 more minutes. Turn and bake for 5 minutes longer. Cool on wire racks and store in an airtight container.

MAKES ABOUT 3 DOZEN.

BUTTERSCOTCH BROWNIES
■ ■ ■

OVEN: 350°

1 (1-pound) box brown sugar
¾ cup butter
2 eggs
2 cups flour
2 teaspoons baking powder
½ teaspoon salt
1 teaspoon vanilla extract
1 cup chopped pecans

Melt brown sugar with butter in a saucepan, and then let cool. In a large mixing bowl, beat eggs. Beat in brown sugar mixture. Mix together flour, baking powder, salt, and vanilla extract. Blend into egg mixture and stir in pecans. Spread in a greased 13" x 9" x 2" pan and bake for 30 minutes. Allow to cool before cutting.

MAKES 24–28 BROWNIES.

BUTTER COOKIES
■ ■ ■

OVEN: 375°

1 cup butter
1½ cups sugar
1 egg
1 teaspoon vanilla extract
2½ cups flour
1 teaspoon baking soda
1 teaspoon cream of tartar
¼ teaspoon salt

Cream together butter and sugar thoroughly. Beat in egg and add vanilla extract. Sift together flour, baking soda, cream of tartar, and salt. Blend with butter and sugar mixture. Drop by teaspoonfuls onto ungreased cookie sheets. Bake for 8 minutes.

MAKES 5 DOZEN.

N·O·T·E·S

CARROT COOKIES

■■■

I remember my visits to see my grandmother, who made these cookies often, and left them to cool on the kitchen table. My cousins and I would sample them when she was looking the other way.

OVEN: 350°

Cookies:
3/4 cup butter
3/4 cup sugar
1 egg, beaten
3/4 cup mashed cooked carrots
    (can substitute junior baby food)
2 cups flour
1 teaspoon baking powder
3/4 teaspoon salt
1 teaspoon vanilla extract

Glaze:
3 cups powdered sugar
1/4 cup orange juice
1 teaspoon melted butter
1 teaspoon finely grated orange
    peel

To make cookie batter, cream together butter and sugar. Beat in egg and carrots. Mix in flour, baking powder, and salt. Add vanilla extract. Drop by teaspoonfuls onto ungreased cookie sheets and bake for 10 minutes. To make glaze, beat powdered sugar with orange juice. Stir in melted butter and orange peel, and mix until well blended. While warm, remove cookies from cookie sheet. Add glaze while cookies are still warm.

MAKES 3 DOZEN.

CHESS CAKE BARS

■■■

OVEN: 325°

1 (18 1/2-ounce) box butter recipe
    yellow cake mix
1/2 cup butter, softened
4 eggs, divided use
1 cup chopped pecans
1 (8-ounce) package cream cheese,
    softened
4 cups powdered sugar

Grease a 13" x 9" x 2" (3-quart rectangular) baking dish. Combine cake mix with butter, 1 of the eggs, and pecans. Press into the bottom of the pan. Beat the remaining 3 eggs with cream cheese, and beat in the powdered sugar. Spread the cream cheese mixture evenly on top of the cake mixture, and bake for 35–45 minutes. Allow to cool and cut into squares.

MAKES 24 SQUARES.

"Kissing don't last;
cookery do!"

—George Meredith

CHOCOLATE CHIP GINGER COOKIES
■■■

OVEN: 375°

1 cup butter, softened
1½ cups granulated brown sugar
1 egg
2 cups flour
1 teaspoon baking soda
½ teaspoon salt
2 teaspoons cinnamon
½ teaspoon nutmeg
1½ teaspoons ginger
1 teaspoon vanilla extract
1 (12-ounce) package semisweet
    chocolate morsels
1 cup chopped pecans
powdered sugar

Cream together butter and granulated brown sugar. Add egg and beat well. Mix together flour, baking soda, salt, cinnamon, nutmeg, and ginger. Add to butter mixture and mix well. Add vanilla extract and stir in chocolate morsels and pecans. Chill dough for several hours. (This is very important!) Then form into balls about 1½" in diameter and roll in powdered sugar. Put about 15 balls on each cookie sheet, in 3 rows of 5 each. Flatten them very slightly with the bottom of a glass which has been dipped in powdered sugar. Bake for 10 minutes.
MAKES 5 DOZEN.

CHOCOLATE CHIP TOLL HOUSE COOKIES
■■■

OVEN: 375°

2¼ cups flour
1 teaspoon baking soda
1 teaspoon salt
1 cup butter, softened
¾ cup granulated sugar
¾ cup packed brown sugar
1 teaspoon vanilla extract
2 eggs
2 (6-ounce) packages semisweet
    chocolate morsels
1 cup chopped pecans

Combine flour, baking soda, and salt in a small bowl, and set aside. In a large bowl, combine softened butter, granulated sugar, brown sugar, and vanilla extract. Beat until creamy. Beat in eggs. Gradually stir flour mixture into butter mixture. Stir in chocolate morsels and pecans. Drop by level tablespoonfuls onto ungreased cookie sheets and bake for 9–11 minutes.
MAKES 5 DOZEN.

N·O·T·E·S

TESTING CANDY FOR DONENESS

Test your candy thermometer for accuracy by holding it in boiling water. If it doesn't register 212°, adjust your cooking either higher or lower by that many degrees. You'll need to make adjustments for weather, as well. On clear, dry days, use the lower temperature in the following chart. On humid or rainy days, use the higher temperature in the range.

To use the cold water method, use a fresh cup of cold tap water each time you perform the test. First, remove candy from heat. Next, spoon about ½ teaspoon of hot candy into the cold water. Then pick up the drop of candy and roll it into a ball, if possible. The way the ball responds determines the candy's level of doneness.

Thread: 230°–234°: Candy forms a soft 2″ thread when dropped from a spoon.

Soft-Ball: 234°F–240°: Candy forms a soft ball, which flattens out when it is removed from the water.

Firm-Ball: 244°–248°: Candy rolls into a firm, but pliable ball.

Hard-Ball: 250°–265°: Candy rolls into a hard ball, which loses all its flexibility when it is removed from the water. It can then be rolled around on a plate.

Soft-Crack: 270°F– 290°: Candy separates into hard but pliable threads in water, which soften when candy is removed from water.

Hard-Crack: 300°–310°: Candy separates into brittle threads in water, which remain brittle when removed from water. They sound brittle when tapped against the side of the cup.

Caramelized: 310°– 321°: Sugar melts first, and then turns golden brown. When dropped into cold water, it will form a hard, brittle ball.

CREAM CHEESE COOKIES
■■■

OVEN: 375°

½ cup butter, softened
½ cup shortening
1 (3-ounce) package cream cheese, softened
1 cup sugar
1 egg, beaten
1 teaspoon vanilla extract
2½ cups flour
½ teaspoon nutmeg

Cream together butter, shortening, softened cream cheese, and sugar. Mix in egg and vanilla extract. Blend together flour and nutmeg, and add to other ingredients. Drop by teaspoonfuls onto ungreased cookie sheets. Bake for 15 minutes.

MAKES 2½ DOZEN.

FUDGE
■■■

9 (1.55-ounce) Hershey plain milk chocolate bars
2 (6-ounce) packages semisweet chocolate morsels
1 (16-ounce) jar marshmallow cream
1 tablespoon butter
1 teaspoon vanilla extract
4½ cups sugar
1 (12-ounce) can evaporated milk (not sweetened)
1 pound (4 cups) pecans, chopped

Break the Hershey bars into a 6- to 8-quart bowl. Add chocolate morsels, marshmallow cream, butter, and

vanilla extract. Stir and set aside. Measure sugar into a 4- to 6-quart saucepan. Stir in evaporated milk and bring to a boil over medium heat. Once it reaches a boil, begin timing it. Let it boil for 6 minutes, stirring constantly. Remove from heat and pour over the chocolate mixture. Stir until it's completely smooth, but do not beat it. Stir in pecans and spread fudge on a buttered cookie sheet or on a large buttered platter. Allow it to cool completely, for about 4–6 hours. Then cut into small squares and store in a tin or tightly covered container, separating layers of fudge with sheets of waxed paper.

MAKES ABOUT 6 POUNDS OF FUDGE.

LEMON BARS
■■■

OVEN: 350°

½ cup butter, softened
1 cup plus 3 tablespoons flour, divided use
¼ cup powdered sugar, plus additional for topping
3 eggs
3 tablespoons lemon juice
1 teaspoon grated lemon peel
¾ teaspoon baking powder
1½ cups granulated sugar

Combine butter, 1 cup of the flour, and ¼ cup powdered sugar in the bowl of a food processor. Process until mixture resembles fine crumbs.

Press into an 11" x 7" x 2" (2-quart rectangular) baking dish, and spread evenly to form a crust. Bake for 15 minutes. Beat eggs slightly and add lemon juice, lemon peel, the remaining 3 tablespoons flour, baking powder, and granulated sugar. Spread mixture over baked crust and bake for 25 more minutes. Cool, and then sprinkle with powdered sugar and cut into squares.

MAKES 24 SQUARES.

OATMEAL COOKIES
■■■

OVEN: 350°

1 cup butter
1 cup brown sugar
1 cup granulated sugar
2 eggs
1½ teaspoons vanilla extract
1½ cups flour
1 teaspoon baking soda
½ teaspoon salt
1 teaspoon cinnamon
¼ teaspoon nutmeg
3½ cups quick-cooking
  (not instant) oatmeal
½ cup chopped pecans
½ cup flaked coconut
1 cup raisins

Beat butter with brown sugar and granulated sugar until fluffy. Beat in eggs and vanilla extract. Sift flour with baking soda, salt, cinnamon, and nutmeg, and mix well with butter mixture. Stir together oatmeal, pecans, coconut, and raisins, and fold into cookie batter. Drop by rounded tablespoonfuls onto ungreased cookie sheets. Bake for 10 minutes. Cool for 1 minute on the cookie sheet, and remove to a wire rack.

MAKES 4 DOZEN.

PEANUT BRITTLE
■■■

½ cup light corn syrup
1 cup sugar
1 teaspoon water
1 cup unsalted peanuts (raw
  or roasted)
1 teaspoon baking soda
1 teaspoon vanilla extract
1 teaspoon butter
⅛ teaspoon salt

Mix corn syrup, sugar, and water in a 2-quart microwave-safe glass bowl or measuring pitcher. Cover with waxed paper or a paper towel to prevent spattering. Microwave on full power for 4 minutes. Remove from microwave carefully, using a pot holder. Stir in peanuts, replace paper on top, and cook for 4½–5 more minutes at high power, or until light brown. Remove, again being careful not to burn yourself, and stir in baking soda, vanilla extract, butter, and salt. Spread about ¼" thick on a well-buttered cookie sheet. (It will be an irregular shape, and will not cover the cookie sheet.) Allow to cool thoroughly. Then lift the cookie sheet about 12" off the counter and drop it, to break the peanut brittle into pieces. Store in a tin or other tightly closed container.

MAKES ABOUT 1½ POUNDS.

N·O·T·E·S

PEANUT BUTTER COOKIES
■ ■ ■

OVEN: 375°

1/2 cup butter
1/2 cup granulated sugar
1/2 cup packed brown sugar
1/2 teaspoon salt
1 egg
1/2 cup crunchy peanut butter
1/2 teaspoon vanilla extract
1 1/4 cups flour
1/2 teaspoon baking soda
1/2 teaspoon nutmeg
1/4 teaspoon ground cloves
1/2 teaspoon cinnamon

Cream butter with granulated sugar, brown sugar, and salt. Beat in egg and stir in peanut butter and vanilla extract. Sift together flour, baking soda, nutmeg, cloves, and cinnamon, and add to peanut butter mixture. Form into small balls and place on greased cookie sheets. Flatten slightly, making a crisscross pattern with the back of a fork. Bake for 10 minutes, or until golden brown.
MAKES 3 DOZEN.

PRALINES
■ ■ ■

I'll never think of pralines that I don't think of my mother. She reigned as the world class queen of praline cooks. Every Christmas she gave them for gifts to her best friends. Daddy and I would sneak as many as we could while she wasn't looking!

2 cups sugar
1/8 teaspoon salt
1 teaspoon baking soda
1 cup buttermilk (do not use reconstituted powder)
2 tablespoons butter
1 1/2 cups pecan halves
1 teaspoon vanilla extract

This candy requires your undivided attention, so before assembling the ingredients, lay a large sheet of waxed paper on the counter to drop the pralines onto. Combine sugar, salt, baking soda, and buttermilk in a 4-quart, heavy saucepan. Bring to a boil quickly, stirring constantly, until mixture turns a creamy beige (about 210°). Add butter and pecan halves and continue cooking over medium heat, stirring frequently with a wooden spoon, until it reaches the soft-ball stage (234°–240°). Remove from the heat and add vanilla extract. Beat candy with a wooden spoon until the mixture loses its gloss. Drop in mounds onto waxed paper, working fast, since the candy sets up very quickly. Allow to cool completely. Store candy in an airtight container.
MAKES 12–15 PRALINES.

RICE KRISPIES TREATS
■ ■ ■

4 tablespoons butter
1 (10½-ounce) bag Kraft miniature
    marshmallows (these must
    be fresh)
6 cups Kellogg's Rice Krispies
    cereal

Put butter and marshmallows in a
large, microwave-safe glass mixing
bowl. Microwave on high power for
2 minutes. Stir the mixture and microwave again for 1½–2 more minutes,
or until marshmallows are completely
melted. Stir in Rice Krispies, and
spoon mixture into a heavily greased
11" x 7" x 2" (2-quart rectangular) baking dish. Spray a piece of waxed paper
with non-stick cooking spray and lay
the paper, sprayed-side-down, over
the Rice Krispies treats. Press them
firmly and evenly into the pan. Let
the treats cool, and then cut into
squares.

MAKES 28 BARS.

SAND TARTS
■ ■ ■

OVEN: 325°

1 cup butter, softened
½ cup powdered sugar, plus
    additional for topping
2 cups flour
1 cup chopped pecans
1 teaspoon vanilla extract

Cream together softened butter and
sugar. Stir in flour, chopped pecans,
and vanilla extract. Shape into balls
or crescents, and bake on ungreased
cookie sheets for 20 minutes, or until
cookies are light brown. Roll cookies
in powdered sugar while they are still
warm.

MAKES 4 DOZEN.

SNICKERDOODLES
■ ■ ■

OVEN: 375°

½ cup butter, softened
⅔ cup sugar
1 egg
1½ cups flour
½ teaspoon baking soda
¼ teaspoon salt
½ teaspoon cream of tartar
1 teaspoon vanilla extract
2 tablespoons sugar
2 teaspoons cinnamon

Cream butter and sugar together.
Beat in egg. Sift flour with baking
soda, salt, and cream of tartar. Blend
into egg mixture. Stir in vanilla extract. Mix sugar and cinnamon in a
shallow bowl. Form cookie dough
into 1" balls and roll in cinnamon
and sugar mixture. Arrange balls
about 2" apart on greased cookie
sheets, and bake for 8–10 minutes.

MAKES 2–3 DOZEN.

N·O·T·E·S

SOUR CREAM COOKIES
■ ■ ■

When I was a child, my favorite baby-sitter was my godmother's mother. Everyone called her "Grammie." She always made a pot of hot tea after we finished dinner, and when she poured the tea into her cup, she used to call the tiny bubbles that floated in the teacup "money." She showed me how to use a teaspoon to "grab the money" before it floated away. She often brought these cookies when she came to stay with me, and we'd have several while we sat at the kitchen table and drank our hot tea after dinner.

OVEN: 375°

2 eggs
1¼ cups sugar
½ cup sour cream
⅓ cup butter, melted
1 teaspoon vanilla extract
2 cups flour
½ teaspoon baking soda
1 teaspoon nutmeg
½ teaspoon cinnamon
cinnamon-sugar for topping
   (see Note, page 264)

Beat eggs. Mix in sugar, sour cream, melted butter, and vanilla extract. Sift together flour, baking soda, nutmeg, and cinnamon, and add to eggs. Drop mixture by teaspoonfuls onto greased cookie sheets, placing the cookies about 1" apart. Sprinkle with cinnamon-sugar. Bake for 12–14 minutes.
MAKES 5 DOZEN.

SUGAR COOKIES
■ ■ ■

OVEN: 350°

1 cup butter, softened
2 cups sugar
2 eggs
2 tablespoons water or brandy
1 teaspoon vanilla extract
4 cups flour
½ teaspoon salt
1 teaspoon baking powder

Using an electric mixer, cream together butter and sugar. Beat in eggs, water or brandy, and vanilla extract. Sift together flour, salt, and baking powder. Add dry ingredients to butter mixture, a little at a time. Mix until well blended. Pat dough into 3 flat rounds, wrap in plastic wrap, and refrigerate for at least 1 hour. Dust a board with a mixture of half sugar and half flour, and work with 1 flat round of dough at a time. Roll out to about ⅛" thickness, and cut out with cookie cutters. Use a metal pancake turner or wide spatula to lift shapes onto lightly greased cookie sheets, dusting off excess flour with a pastry brush. Bake for 8–10 minutes, but do not allow cookies to brown. Cool on racks before icing. Frost with Royal Icing (page 287).
MAKES 5–6 DOZEN.

Pies and Cobblers

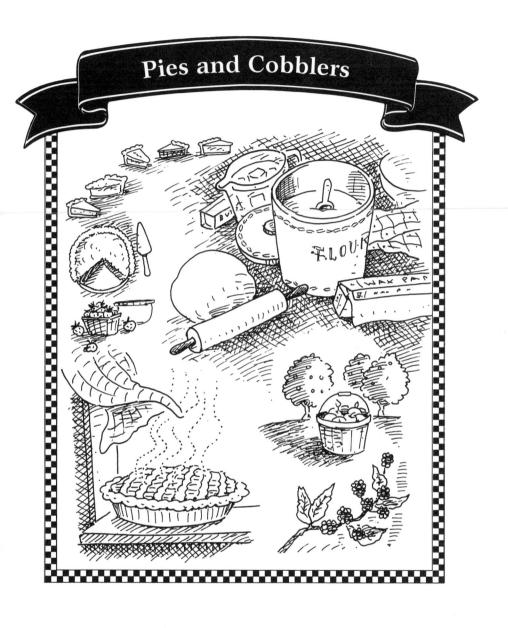

PIES AND COBBLERS
...

BASIC FOOD PROCESSOR PIE CRUST

OVEN: 425° (FOR BAKED CRUST)

1¼ cups flour
½ teaspoon salt
3 tablespoons very cold butter
2 tablespoons very cold shortening
¼ cup ice water

Put flour and salt in the bowl of a food processor. Pulse 1–2 times to blend. Add butter and shortening, cut into small chunks. Pulse 4–5 times, until mixture resembles coarse meal. Sprinkle on 1½ tablespoons of the water and pulse twice. Repeat with another 1½ tablespoons of the water. Finally, pulse in the last 1 tablespoon of water. Do not overmix, or dough will become tough. Form dough into a ball and wrap in plastic. Handle it as little as possible. Refrigerate for 30–45 minutes before rolling out. Do not double this recipe. If a double crust is needed, make the recipe twice.

MAKES 1 SINGLE CRUST FOR A 9" OR 10" PIE.

To bake pastry unfilled, roll out and fit into pan. Trim and finish edges (crimp or flute) and prick bottom and sides with a fork. Lay a circle of parchment or foil (shiny-side-down) on the bottom and fill with rice, dried beans, or pie weights. (These can be used over and over. Keep in a jar between uses.) Bake for 8–10 minutes. Carefully remove paper and rice, beans, or pie weights. Bake for 8–10 more minutes, or until golden brown. Allow crust to cool before filling, unless recipe states otherwise.

Cheese Pastry: Add ½ cup shredded cheese before adding water.

Nut Pastry: Add ¼ cup ground nuts before adding water.

Spice Pastry: Add ¼ teaspoon each of cinnamon, cloves, and allspice, plus a pinch of nutmeg, before adding water.

APPLE PIE
...

OVEN: 425°

pie crust for double-crust pie
6 cups sliced, peeled Granny Smith apples
6 tablespoons flour
1 cup sugar
¼ teaspoon cinnamon
¼ teaspoon nutmeg
⅛ teaspoon salt
1 teaspoon lemon juice
1½ tablespoons butter
2 tablespoons cream

Line a 9" pie pan with bottom crust. Mix apples with flour, sugar, cinnamon, nutmeg, salt, and lemon juice. Spoon into the bottom crust and dot with butter. Place top crust over apples, crimping edges of top and bottom crusts together, and cut vents in top crust. Or make a lattice top crust. Brush top with cream and bake for about 45 minutes, or until crust is nicely browned.

MAKES 6–8 SERVINGS.

*"An apple pie
without some cheese
is like a kiss
without a squeeze."*

—**Old Proverb**

BLACKBERRY PIE
...

Oh, how Jack loves this pie! We used to have gas stove with a pilot light under the burners. We'd set the pie on the back of the stove where it would stay warm, just in case someone came into the kitchen late at night for a midnight snack.

OVEN: 425°

pie crust for double-crust pie
3 cups fresh (or frozen, thawed) blackberries
1¼ cups sugar
3 tablespoons quick-cooking tapioca
1 teaspoon grated lemon peel
6 tablespoons butter, divided use

Line a 9" pie pan with bottom crust. Rinse berries and drain. Mix sugar, tapioca, and lemon peel. Toss mixture with berries. Spoon into pie pan. Dot 4 tablespoons of the butter on top of berries and cover with top crust. Crimp edges of top and bottom crusts together, and cut vents in top crust. Or make a lattice top crust. Dot remaining 2 tablespoons butter on top. Blackberries are very juicy, so lay a piece of foil on the rack under the pie to catch juicy drips. Bake for 45–50 minutes, or until crust is nicely browned.

MAKES 6–8 SERVINGS.

BLUEBERRY PIE
■ ■ ■

OVEN: 400°

pie crust for double-crust pie
1 cup sugar
3 tablespoons quick-cooking tapioca
1/2 teaspoon cinnamon
4 cups blueberries, washed and
    drained
4 tablespoons butter
1 tablespoon lemon juice
Whipped Cream (page 312)

Line a 9″ pie pan with one of the crusts, according to package directions. Mix sugar with tapioca and cinnamon. Toss with blueberries, and pour into the bottom pie crust. Dot with butter and sprinkle with lemon juice. Place top crust over berries, crimping edges of top and bottom crusts together, and cut vents in top crust. Or make a lattice top crust. Bake for 45 minutes, or until crust is nicely browned. Serve with whipped cream.

MAKES 6–8 SERVINGS.

BUTTERSCOTCH PIE
■ ■ ■

OVEN: 350°

3 eggs, separated
1/2 teaspoon salt
1 1/2 cups milk
4 tablespoons butter
6 tablespoons granulated sugar,
    divided use
1/4 cup flour
1 cup dark brown sugar
1 teaspoon vanilla extract
1 Graham Cracker Pie Crust
    (page 304)

Beat egg yolks slightly and combine in a heavy saucepan with salt, milk, and butter. Add 2 tablespoons of the granulated sugar, and the flour and brown sugar. Cook over low heat for about 15 minutes, or until thickened, stirring constantly. Cool and add vanilla extract. Pour into pie crust and set aside. Beat egg whites until stiff, and gradually beat in the remaining 4 tablespoons granulated sugar, 1 tablespoon at a time. Spread meringue over pie, being careful to spread it all the way to the edges of the crust. Bake for 15-20 minutes, or until meringue is golden brown.

MAKES 6–8 SERVINGS.

N·O·T·E·S

CHOCOLATE PIE CRUST

OVEN: 350°

*1½ cups chocolate wafer crumbs
(28–30 cookies)*
4 tablespoons butter, softened
2 tablespoons sugar

Blend all ingredients and press firmly into bottom and sides of pie pan. Bake for 8–10 minutes. Cool before filling.

MAKES A SINGLE CRUST FOR A 9" PIE.

COCONUT PIE CRUST

OVEN: 300°

½ cup butter, melted
2 cups flaked coconut

Combine butter and coconut and press evenly into pie pan. Bake for 20–30 minutes, or until crust is golden. Allow to cool before filling.

MAKES A SINGLE CRUST FOR A 9" PIE.

CREAM CHEESE PASTRY

OVEN: 425°

1 cup butter, softened
1 (8-ounce) package cream cheese, softened
¼ cup heavy cream
2½ cups flour

Cream together butter and cream cheese. Add cream, beating until smooth. Add flour in 3 batches, blending well after each addition. Shape into 2 balls and wrap in plastic wrap. Refrigerate for at least an hour. To bake pastry before filling, roll out and fit into pie pan. Trim and finish the edges and prick bottom and sides with a fork. Lay a circle of parchment or foil (shiny-side-down) on the bottom, and fill with uncooked rice or pie weights. Bake for 8–10 minutes. Carefully lift out paper and rice or weights. Bake for 8–10 more minutes, or until golden. Cool before filling, unless recipe states otherwise.

MAKES A DOUBLE CRUST FOR A 9" PIE.

CHERRY COBBLER
■ ■ ■

OVEN: 375°

4 tablespoons butter, softened
1 cup sugar, divided use
1 cup flour
2 teaspoons baking powder
½ cup milk
1 (29-ounce) can pitted sour cherries

Cream butter and ½ cup of the sugar together. Add flour, baking powder, and milk, and mix well. Pour into a greased 8" square pan, and spread evenly. Drain juice from cherries into a bowl, and pour cherries over batter. Add remaining ½ cup of sugar to cherry juice, and pour mixture over cherries. Bake for 1 hour.

MAKES 6–8 SERVINGS.

CHOCOLATE ALMOND PIE
■ ■ ■

OVEN: 300°

1 (2-ounce) package slivered almonds
1 tablespoon butter, melted
4 (1.45-ounce) Hershey milk chocolate bars with almonds
3 cups fresh miniature marshmallows
¼ cup milk
½ pint heavy cream, whipped, plus additional for topping
2 tablespoons Amaretto
1 Graham Cracker Pie Crust (page 304)
shaved chocolate

Spread almonds on a cookie sheet and drizzle with the melted butter. Bake for 8–10 minutes and set aside. Place Hershey bars, marshmallows, and milk in a heavy saucepan over low heat, and cook until completely melted, stirring constantly. Pour chocolate mixture into a bowl and place in the freezer for about 10 minutes to chill. Remove chocolate mixture from the freezer and fold in almonds, whipped cream, and Amaretto. Pour into the pie crust, spread evenly, and cover carefully with plastic wrap. Refrigerate for several hours before serving. Serve with a dollop of whipped cream and shaved chocolate on top.

MAKES 6–8 SERVINGS.

CHOCOLATE CHESS PIE
■ ■ ■

OVEN: 400°/300°

4 tablespoons butter, melted
1½ cups sugar
pinch salt
3 tablespoons cocoa
2 eggs, lightly beaten
½ cup evaporated milk
1 teaspoon vanilla extract
1 unbaked 9" pie crust

Mix melted butter, sugar, salt, cocoa, eggs, evaporated milk, and vanilla extract together. Pour into unbaked pie crust, and bake at 400° for 10 minutes. Reduce heat to 300° and continue baking for 25 more minutes, or until filling is set.

MAKES 6–8 SERVINGS.

CHOCOLATE FUDGE PIE
■ ■ ■

OVEN: 350°

10 tablespoons butter
6 tablespoons cocoa
2 eggs
1 cup sugar
1 teaspoon vanilla extract
½ cup flour
¼ teaspoon baking powder
⅛ teaspoon salt
¾ cup chopped nuts

Melt butter in a heavy saucepan. Remove from heat. Add cocoa and beat until smooth. In a large mixing bowl, beat eggs and gradually beat in sugar, until mixture is thick. Stir in chocolate mixture and add vanilla extract. Stir in flour, baking powder, and salt, and beat until smooth. Stir in nuts, and spread filling into a greased 9" or 10" pie pan. Bake for 35–40 minutes, or until filling is firmly set. Allow to cool thoroughly before cutting. Serve with ice cream.

MAKES 8 SERVINGS.

CHOCOLATE MERINGUE PIE
■ ■ ■

OVEN: 325°

1¾ cups sugar, divided use
⅓ cup flour
¼ cup cocoa
2 cups milk
2 tablespoons melted butter
4 eggs, separated
1 baked 9" pie crust
4 egg whites
½ teaspoon cream of tartar
½ cup sugar

Measure 1¼ cups of the sugar, the flour, and the cocoa into a large, heavy saucepan. Measure milk into a medium bowl, and add melted butter and egg yolks. Beat until well blended. Gradually add milk mixture to cocoa mixture in saucepan, stirring until smooth. Cook over medium heat for about 10 minutes, stirring constantly, until thick and bubbly. Spread in baked pie crust and set aside. In a medium mixing bowl, combine egg whites with cream of tartar. Beat at high speed with an electric mixer until foamy. Beat in remaining ½ cup sugar, 1 tablespoon at a time. Continue beating until sugar is dissolved and egg whites hold stiff peaks. This should take 2–4 minutes. Gently spread meringue over pie, taking care to spread it to the edge of crust to seal. Bake for 25 minutes, or until meringue is golden brown.

MAKES 8 SERVINGS.

N·O·T·E·S

GINGERSNAP PIE CRUST

OVEN: 350°

1½ cups gingersnap crumbs
(23–24 cookies)
4 tablespoons butter, softened

Blend crumbs and butter together and press firmly into bottom and sides of pie pan. Bake for 8–10 minutes. Cool before filling.

MAKES A SINGLE CRUST FOR A 9" PIE.

GRAHAM CRACKER PIE CRUST

OVEN: 350°

1½ cups graham cracker crumbs
(22–23 squares)
⅓ cup butter, softened
¼ cup sugar

Blend all ingredients together and press firmly into bottom and sides of pie pan. Bake for 8–10 minutes. Cool before filling.

MAKES A SINGLE CRUST FOR A 9" PIE.

MERINGUE PIE SHELL

OVEN: 250°

4 egg whites
¼ teaspoon cream of tartar
¾ cup sugar

Beat egg whites until frothy. Beat in cream of tartar. Beat in sugar very gradually, and continue beating until stiff peaks form when beaters are lifted from egg whites. Grease a 9" pie pan with shortening, and lightly dust it with flour. Spoon the egg white mixture into pie pan and use a rubber spatula to spread it evenly over bottom and sides of pan. Bake for 1¼ hours. Remove pie crust from oven and test for doneness. If crust is still soft, continue baking a little longer.

MAKES A SINGLE CRUST FOR A 9" PIE.

COFFEE PIE

■ ■ ■

OVEN: 300°

1 (2-ounce) package slivered almonds
1 tablespoon butter, melted
20 large marshmallows or 2 cups miniature marshmallows
1 cup strong coffee
½ pint heavy cream, whipped
1 baked 9" pie crust

Spread almonds on a cookie sheet and drizzle with the melted butter. Bake for 8–10 minutes and set aside. Put marshmallows in a saucepan and add coffee. Place over low heat and cook until marshmallows are melted. Allow to cool, and then fold in whipped cream. Pour mixture into pie crust and spread evenly. Sprinkle almonds on top and refrigerate.

MAKES 6–8 SERVINGS.

CUSTARD PIE

■ ■ ■

OVEN: 450°/325°

1 unbaked 9" pie crust
3 eggs
¾ cup sugar
½ teaspoon salt
1 cup milk
1 cup half and half
1½ teaspoons vanilla extract
½ teaspoon nutmeg

Bake pie crust for 10 minutes at 450°. Remove from oven and turn down to 325°. In a medium mixing bowl, beat eggs. Add sugar and salt, and beat again. Scald milk and half and half, and add slowly to egg mixture, mixing well. Add vanilla extract, and pour into partially baked pie crust. Sprinkle nutmeg on top, and bake at 325° for 30 minutes, or until a knife inserted 2" from the center comes out clean. Allow to cool before slicing.

MAKES 6–8 SERVINGS.

ICE CREAM PIE

■ ■ ■

1 Chocolate Pie Crust (page 302)
1 quart vanilla ice cream, softened
raspberry preserves

Fill pie crust with softened ice cream. Return to freezer until firm. Heat raspberry preserves and spoon over slices of pie before serving.

MAKES 6–8 SERVINGS.

LEMON CREAM CHEESE PIE

■ ■ ■

1 (8-ounce) package cream cheese, softened
2 cups milk
1 (3.4-ounce) package instant lemon pudding mix
1 Graham Cracker Pie Crust (see sidebar at left)

Combine cream cheese with ½ cup of the milk, and beat until smooth. Add remaining milk and pudding mix, and beat until smooth. Pour filling into crust, and refrigerate for at least an hour before serving.

MAKES 6–8 SERVINGS.

LEMON CHESS PIE

∎ ∎ ∎

This pie makes a command performance at our Thanksgiving dinner table every year.

OVEN: 375°

1/2 cup butter, softened
1 1/2 cups sugar
3 eggs
1 heaping tablespoon cornmeal
1 1/2 tablespoons lemon juice
1 tablespoon vanilla extract
1/8 teaspoon nutmeg
1 unbaked 9" pie crust

Cream butter and sugar together and beat in eggs. Mix in cornmeal, lemon juice, vanilla extract, and nutmeg. Pour into pie crust and bake for 45–50 minutes, or until knife inserted 2" from center comes out clean.

MAKES 6–8 SERVINGS.

LEMON MERINGUE PIE #1

∎ ∎ ∎

When I was in college, I used to make this pie for my boyfriends.

OVEN: 300°

1 (14-ounce) can sweetened
    condensed milk
4 eggs, separated
juice of 3 lemons (about 1/2 cup)
1 Graham Cracker Pie Crust
    (see sidebar at left)
1/4 cup sugar

Beat sweetened condensed milk with egg yolks and lemon juice. Pour into prepared pie crust. Beat egg whites until they form stiff peaks. Add sugar, 1 tablespoon at a time, beating well after each addition. Spread meringue over pie and bake for about 30 minutes, or until meringue is pale golden.

MAKES 6–8 SERVINGS.

LEMON MERINGUE PIE #2

∎ ∎ ∎

OVEN: 350°

1 1/3 cups sugar, divided use
3 tablespoons cornstarch
1 1/2 cups cold water or milk
4 eggs, separated
grated peel and juice of 2 lemons
1 tablespoon butter
1 baked 9" pie crust

Place 1 cup of the sugar and the cornstarch in a 2-quart saucepan, and gradually whisk in water, stirring until smooth. Add egg yolks and cook over medium heat until mixture boils, stirring constantly. Boil and stir for 1 minute. Remove from heat and add lemon peel, lemon juice, and butter, stirring until butter is melted. Let cool, spread into baked pie crust, and set aside. With an electric mixer, beat egg whites until soft peaks form. Gradually beat in remaining 1/3 cup sugar until stiff peaks form. Spread meringue over pie, beginning at the edges, and working to the center. Bake for 15–20 minutes, or until meringue is lightly browned. Cool before cutting.

MAKES 6–8 SERVINGS.

N·O·T·E·S

NUT CRUMB PIE CRUST

OVEN: 350°

1 cup Ritz cracker crumbs
   (24 crackers)
1/2 cup finely chopped nuts
1/3 cup butter, softened
1/4 cup sugar

Blend all ingredients together and press firmly into bottom and sides of a 9" pie pan. Bake for 8–10 minutes. Cool before filling.

MAKES A SINGLE CRUST FOR A 9" PIE.

OREO COOKIE PIE CRUST

OVEN: 350°

14 Oreo cookies, crushed
4 tablespoons butter, softened

Blend cookie crumbs and butter together and press firmly into bottom and sides of a 9" pie pan. Bake for 8–10 minutes. Cool before filling.

MAKES A SINGLE CRUST FOR A 9" PIE.

VANILLA WAFER PIE CRUST

OVEN: 350°

1 1/2 cups vanilla wafer crumbs
   (28–30 cookies)
4 tablespoons butter, softened
2 tablespoons sugar

Blend all ingredients together and press firmly into bottom and sides of a 9" pie pan. Bake for 8–10 minutes. Cool before filling.

MAKES A SINGLE CRUST FOR A 9" PIE.

KEY LIME PIE
■ ■ ■

OVEN: 300°

6 eggs, separated
1 (14-ounce) can sweetened
   condensed milk
1/2 cup fresh lime juice (key lime
   juice, if available)
1 baked 9" pie crust
1/4 cup sugar

Beat egg yolks and mix with condensed milk. Add lime juice and blend well. Pour into baked pie crust. Beat egg whites until stiff. Beat in sugar gradually, 1 tablespoon at a time. Spread meringue on pie, spreading all the way to edges to seal. Bake for about 30 minutes, or until meringue is pale golden.

MAKES 6–8 SERVINGS.

PEACH COBBLER
■ ■ ■

OVEN: 350°

6 tablespoons butter
3/4 cup flour
2 cups sugar, divided use
2 teaspoons baking powder
1/8 teaspoon salt
3/4 cup milk
2 cups sliced fresh or frozen peaches
ice cream for topping

Melt butter in a 1 1/2-quart baking dish. In a mixing bowl, mix flour, 1 cup of the sugar, baking powder, salt, and milk. Gently pour batter into baking dish without stirring. Combine peaches with remaining 1 cup sugar and gently pour on top of batter without stirring. Bake for about 30 minutes, or until lightly browned. Crust will rise to the top. Serve warm with ice cream.

MAKES 6–8 SERVINGS.

PEACH CRUNCH PIE
■ ■ ■

OVEN: 400°

3/4 cup sugar
3 tablespoons quick-cooking
   tapioca
1/2 teaspoon cinnamon
1/4 teaspoon nutmeg
1/2 teaspoon salt
5 cups sliced peaches
1 tablespoon lemon juice
1 cup flour
1/2 cup brown sugar
1/2 cup plus 2 tablespoons butter,
   softened, divided use
1/2 cup chopped pecans
1 unbaked 9" pie crust

Mix sugar, tapioca, cinnamon, nutmeg, and salt. Add peaches and toss to coat well with sugar mixture. Stir in lemon juice and set aside. Combine flour, brown sugar, and 1/2 cup of the butter. Mix until crumbly. Stir in pecans. Pour peach mixture into pie crust and dot with the remaining 2 tablespoons butter. Sprinkle brown sugar topping mixture evenly over the peaches. Lay a piece of foil on top of pie to keep it from browning too quickly. Bake for 25 minutes. Remove foil and bake for another 15 minutes.

MAKES 6–8 SERVINGS.

OLD-FASHIONED PEACH PIE

■ ■ ■

OVEN: 425°

pie crust for double-crust pie
4 cups fresh (or frozen, thawed)
*   peach slices*
½ cup granulated sugar
⅓ cup brown sugar
3 tablespoons quick-cooking tapioca
½ teaspoon cinnamon
¼ teaspoon nutmeg
½ teaspoon grated lemon peel
dash salt
4 tablespoons butter

Line a 9″–10″ pie pan with bottom crust. Mix peaches with granulated sugar, brown sugar, tapioca, cinnamon, nutmeg, lemon peel, and salt. Pour into pie crust and dot with butter. Add top crust, crimping edges of top and bottom crusts together, and cut vents in top crust. Or make a lattice top crust. Bake for 1–1¼ hours.
MAKES 6–8 SERVINGS.

PECAN PIE

■ ■ ■

OVEN: 350°/250°

3 eggs
1 cup sugar
1 tablespoon flour
¾ cup corn syrup
3 tablespoons butter, melted
1 teaspoon vanilla extract
1 cup pecan halves
1 unbaked 9″ pie crust

Beat eggs in mixing bowl. Add sugar, flour, corn syrup, melted butter, and vanilla extract, mixing well. Arrange pecans in pie crust, and pour in egg mixture. Bake at 350° for 10 minutes. Then reduce heat to 250° and continue baking for another 1¼ hours, or until knife inserted close to center comes out clean.
MAKES 6–8 SERVINGS.

PECAN TARTS

■ ■ ■

OVEN: 350°/250°

1 (3-ounce) package cream cheese,
*   softened*
6 tablespoons butter, softened,
*   divided use*
1 cup flour
2 eggs
1 cup brown sugar
dash salt
2 teaspoons vanilla extract
1 cup coarsely broken pecans

Blend cream cheese and 4 tablespoons of the butter together and add flour. Roll pastry into a ball and wrap in plastic wrap. Refrigerate for an hour. Then shape the dough into 24 balls, about 1″ in diameter. Place balls into ungreased miniature muffin tins and press them down to shape them into tart shells. Beat eggs with the remaining 2 tablespoons butter, brown sugar, salt, and vanilla extract. Mix in pecans and put about 1 tablespoon of the filling into each tart shell. Bake at 350° for 15–20 minutes. Reduce heat to 250° and bake for 15–20 more minutes, or until tarts are light brown.
MAKES 2 DOZEN MINIATURE TARTS.

N·O·T·E·S

PUMPKIN PIE
...

OVEN: 425°/350°

2 eggs
3/4 cup sugar
1 teaspoon cinnamon
1/4 teaspoon ground cloves
1/2 teaspoon nutmeg
1/2 teaspoon ground ginger
1/2 teaspoon salt
1 1/2 cups (12-ounce can)
    evaporated milk
1 (15–16-ounce) can pumpkin
1 unbaked 9" deep-dish pie crust

In a large bowl, beat eggs lightly and mix in sugar, cinnamon, cloves, nutmeg, ginger, and salt. Stir in evaporated milk and pumpkin, and mix until smooth. Pour into pie crust and bake at 425° for 15 minutes. Reduce temperature to 350° and continue baking for 45–50 more minutes, or until knife inserted near center comes out clean.
MAKES 6–8 SERVINGS.

STRAWBERRY PIE
...

1 1/4 cups sugar, divided use
3 tablespoons cornstarch
4 tablespoons strawberry gelatin
1 cup boiling water
1 pint strawberries, washed,
    capped (stems removed), and
    halved
1 baked 9" pie crust
1/2 pint whipping cream

In a saucepan combine 1 cup of the the sugar, cornstarch, and gelatin. Add boiling water and stir to dissolve. Bring to a boil and remove from heat. Refrigerate until thick. Add strawberries, and pour filling into pie crust. Whip cream, beat in remaining 1/4 cup sugar, and spread over pie. Refrigerate.
MAKES 6–8 SERVINGS.

SWEET POTATO PIE
...

OVEN: 425°/325°

4 tablespoons butter, softened
1/2 cup brown sugar
1 cup cooked or canned sweet
    potatoes, mashed
3 eggs, slightly beaten
1/3 cup corn syrup
1/3 cup milk
1/2 teaspoon salt
1 teaspoon vanilla extract
1 unbaked 9" pie crust

Cream together butter and brown sugar until fluffy. Add mashed sweet potatoes and eggs and mix well. Mix in corn syrup, milk, salt, and vanilla extract, and pour filling into pie crust. Bake at 425° for 10 minutes. Turn oven down to 325° and bake for another 35–45 minutes, or until knife inserted near center comes out clean. Cool before cutting.
MAKES 6–8 SERVINGS.

Desserts and Dessert Sauces

DESSERTS AND DESSERT SAUCES

...

HOT FUDGE SAUCE

¹/₂ cup granulated sugar
³/₄ cup dark brown sugar
¹/₂ cup cocoa
pinch salt
1 (5-ounce) can evaporated milk
¹/₃ cup light corn syrup
¹/₃ cup butter
1 teaspoon vanilla extract

Mix both sugars, cocoa, and salt in a medium saucepan. Whisk in milk and corn syrup. Cook over medium heat, stirring constantly, until sauce boils. Boil for 1 minute, stirring constantly. Remove from heat and stir in butter and vanilla extract. Serve immediately, or refrigerate in a covered container. Reheat in microwave.

MAKES 1¾ CUPS.

VANILLA CUSTARD SAUCE

2 cups heavy cream
¹/₂ cup sugar
4 egg yolks
1 tablespoon flour
4 teaspoons vanilla extract
¹/₄ teaspoon salt
2 scoops vanilla ice cream

Bring cream and sugar just to a boil in a medium saucepan over medium heat. Remove from heat. In a small bowl, beat egg yolks with flour, vanilla extract, and salt. Ladle about ¼ cup of the cream mixture into the egg mixture, stirring with a whisk. Then add ¼ cup more, still stirring constantly. (This heats up the eggs gradually, so they won't curdle.) Now pour the heated egg mixture back into the cream mixture, stirring constantly. Place saucepan back over low heat and cook, stirring constantly, until mixture thickens. Remove from heat and add ice cream, stirring sauce until ice cream is melted. Strain and serve warm or chilled. Refrigerate leftover sauce and reheat in microwave.

MAKES ABOUT 3 CUPS.

APPLE CRISP

...

OVEN: 350°

1 (20-ounce) can sliced apples
¹/₂ teaspoon cinnamon
¹/₂ teaspoon nutmeg
¹/₄ cup water
1¹/₄ cups brown sugar
¹/₂ cup butter
¹/₂ cup flour

Drain apples and place in a 1-quart baking dish. Sprinkle cinnamon, nutmeg, and water on top. Cream brown sugar with butter and cut in flour. Mix until crumbly. Spread mixture over apples and bake for 30 minutes.

MAKES 4–6 SERVINGS.

BANANAS FOSTER

...

4 small firm bananas
1 tablespoon lemon juice
6 tablespoons butter
¹/₂ cup packed brown sugar
¹/₂ teaspoon cinnamon
2 tablespoons banana liqueur
¹/₄ cup rum
1 quart vanilla ice cream

Peel bananas, split lengthwise, and cut in half crosswise. Sprinkle with lemon juice. In a large skillet, melt butter over low heat. Add brown sugar, and stir until dissolved. Add bananas, and cook until barely tender, turning gently to coat with syrup. Sprinkle with cinnamon, and add banana liqueur and rum. Continue cooking until sauce is thoroughly warmed. Ignite sauce and spoon flaming mixture over bananas until flame goes out. Serve over ice cream.

MAKES 4 SERVINGS.

BANANA PUDDING

...

OVEN: 425°

4 eggs, divided use
³/₄ cup sugar, divided use
3 tablespoons flour
2 cups milk
¹/₂ teaspoon vanilla extract
1 (9-ounce) box vanilla wafers
4–5 ripe bananas, sliced

Separate 3 of the eggs and set aside. Mix ½ cup of the sugar and the flour in top of a double boiler. With a whisk, mix in the whole egg, the 3 egg yolks, and the milk. Cook over boiling water, stirring constantly, until thickened. Remove from heat and stir in vanilla extract. Spread a fourth of the pudding in a 1½-quart baking dish and cover with a layer of vanilla wafers and a layer of bananas. Make 2 more layers of pudding, wafers, and bananas. Spread remaining pudding on top. With an electric mixer, beat the reserved egg whites until soft peaks form. Gradually beat in the remaining ¼ cup sugar, until egg whites stand in stiff peaks. Smooth over the pudding, spreading all the way to the edges, and bake for 5 minutes, or until topping is lightly browned.

MAKES 8 SERVINGS.

*"A good bread
pudding always
makes my
tongue smile."*

—H. Jackson Brown

BREAD PUDDING
■ ■ ■

OVEN: 425°/350°

1 (6¾-ounce) package Pepperidge
  Farm Butter Crescent Rolls
5 tablespoons unsalted butter,
  melted
4 eggs
2⅔ cups milk
⅔ cup sugar
2 teaspoons vanilla extract
¼ teaspoon cinnamon
¼ teaspoon nutmeg
⅔ cup raisins

Cut rolls into 1½" chunks. Place in an 8" square cake pan, and bake at 425°

for 8–10 minutes, so that bread is lightly toasted but not too brown. Remove from oven and reduce temperature to 350°. Drizzle bread with melted butter, toss to coat well, and set aside. In a medium mixing bowl, beat eggs with milk, sugar, vanilla extract, cinnamon, and nutmeg. Pour mixture over bread, and scatter raisins evenly on top. Bake for about 45 minutes, or until pudding is set. Serve warm with Vanilla Custard Sauce (page 310). Refrigerate leftovers and reheat in microwave.

MAKES 8–9 SERVINGS.

CHOCOLATE
POTS DE CRÈME
■ ■ ■

1 (10–12-ounce) package
  chocolate morsels (semisweet
  or mint chocolate)
⅓ cup sugar
2 eggs
1 teaspoon vanilla extract
pinch salt
1 cup milk
whipped cream for topping
fresh mint leaves (optional)

Put chocolate morsels, sugar, eggs, and vanilla extract in a blender. Add a pinch of salt. Scald milk, and add to blender. Blend for 1–2 minutes. Pour into individual pots de crème or small dessert dishes and chill. Top with whipped cream before serving. If desired, garnish with fresh mint leaves.

MAKES 4 SERVINGS.

N·O·T·E·S

LEMON SAUCE

½ cup sugar
2 tablespoons cornstarch
¾ cup water
2 tablespoons butter
¼ cup lemon juice
1 tablespoon grated lemon peel

Mix sugar and cornstarch in a medium saucepan. Add water gradually, and bring to a boil over medium heat, stirring constantly as mixture thickens. Boil for 1 minute. Remove from heat, add butter, and stir until melted. Stir in lemon juice and lemon peel. Serve warm. Refrigerate leftovers in a covered container.

MAKES 1¼ CUPS.

RASPBERRY SAUCE

1 (10-ounce) package frozen
*   raspberries, with juice, thawed*
1 (12-ounce) jar seedless raspberry jam
½ cup sugar
3 tablespoons cornstarch

Place raspberries in a medium saucepan. Stir in raspberry jam, sugar, and cornstarch. Cook over low heat, stirring constantly, until sauce is thickened and smooth. Strain and serve warm or chilled. Store in a covered container in the refrigerator for up to 1 month.

MAKES 1½ CUPS.

WHIPPED CREAM

½ pint heavy cream
1 tablespoon sugar
1 teaspoon vanilla extract
1 tablespoon brandy or liqueur
*   (optional)*

Chill cream, mixing bowl, and beaters for at least 30 minutes. Then pour cream into bowl and beat on high speed for 1 minute. Gradually add sugar, vanilla, and brandy, if desired, beating continuously, for 2–3 more minutes, or until soft peaks form when beaters are lifted. Don't beat too long, or it will turn to butter!

MAKES 2 CUPS.

BAKED CUSTARD
###

OVEN: 325°

3¾ cups milk, cream, or
*   combination of the two*
1⅛ cups sugar (white or brown)
⅛ teaspoon salt
8 eggs, beaten
1 tablespoon vanilla extract
nutmeg

Beat together milk (or milk and cream), sugar, salt, eggs, and vanilla extract. Pour into 11 custard cups. Sprinkle on nutmeg and set cups in a 4-quart rectangular pan, with 4 cups on the outside rows, and 3 cups down the center. Pour 1" of hot water into the pan, taking care not to get it into the custard cups. Bake for 1¼ hours, or until knife inserted in center comes out clean.

MAKES 11 SERVINGS.

Note: The reason for the odd number of servings is because that's how many custard cups will fit in a 4-quart rectangular pan, with 4 on the outside rows and 3 in the center.

CARAMEL CUSTARD (FLAN)
###

My father charted airline routes in Central and South America in the late 1940s, and I traveled there often as a small child, sometimes staying in Lima, Peru, for months at a time. This dessert was a classic finish for a Latin American dinner.

OVEN: 300°

Caramel:
½ cup sugar
¼ cup water

Custard:
5 eggs
⅓ cup sugar
⅛ teaspoon salt
1 cup heavy cream
1½ cups milk
1 teaspoon vanilla extract

To make the caramel, measure ½ cup sugar into a large saucepan or skillet.

Stir in ¼ cup water, and cook over low heat, stirring just until sugar is dissolved. When sugar is dissolved, stop stirring immediately. Turn up the heat to medium, and let sugar syrup turn a light golden brown. If it boils, that's fine. Just don't stir it. This should take about 8–10 minutes. When sugar syrup is a light golden brown, remove it from heat. Carefully pour it into 6 custard cups, dividing it evenly among them. Or pour into a 1-quart mold or soufflé dish. Rotate the dish(es) to coat the bottom evenly with the syrup. Set aside. To make the custard, beat eggs with sugar and salt in a medium bowl. Add cream, milk, and vanilla extract and stir with a whisk to blend. Pour into custard cups and set cups in a rectangular baking pan. Pour about 1" of hot water into baking pan, being careful not to get hot water into custard cups. Bake for 1¼ hours, or until knife inserted in center comes out clean. Cool to room temperature, and then refrigerate for several hours. To serve, loosen edges with a sharp knife and unmold custard onto serving dish(es). The caramel in the bottom will form a sauce over the custard when it is unmolded.

MAKES 6 SERVINGS.

FROZEN LEMON DESSERT
■■■

OVEN: 350°

Crust:
1½ cups vanilla wafer crumbs
   (28–30 cookies)
2 tablespoons sugar
¼ cup butter, melted

Mix wafer crumbs with sugar and toss to coat with butter. Press firmly into the bottom of an 8" or 9" springform pan. Bake for 10 minutes, and then set it aside to cool while preparing filling.

Filling:
4 (5-ounce) cans evaporated milk
   (not sweetened)
1¼ cups sugar
¾ cup lemon juice
1 tablespoon grated lemon rind
fresh mint leaves (optional)

Put cans of milk, a mixing bowl, and beaters into the freezer to chill for 20–30 minutes. Then pour milk into the bowl, and whip it into soft peaks. Beat in sugar gradually. Add lemon juice and lemon rind. Pour into the prepared crust and freeze for at least 3 hours. Remove the springform and cut dessert into wedges. To serve, top with whipped cream and garnish with fresh mint leaves, if desired.

MAKES 6–8 SERVINGS.

"Clever food is not appreciated at Christmas. It makes the little ones cry and the old ones nervous."

—Oliver Wendell Holmes, Sr.

DESSERT IDEAS WITH ICE CREAM

Here are some quick desserts you can put together with ice cream.

Cantaloupe Rings: Cut a cantaloupe in half, scoop out seeds, slice into rings, and remove rind. For each dessert, place a ring on a dessert plate and put a scoop of chocolate mint chip ice cream in the center. Spoon a little Hot Fudge Sauce (page 310) on top and garnish with a sprig of mint.

Ice Cream Balls: Scoop ice cream into balls and roll in toasted coconut, chopped toasted almonds, pecans, or crushed cookies. Return to freezer until ready to serve. Place in a dessert dish or champagne saucer and spoon your favorite dessert sauce over it. Try vanilla ice cream rolled in chopped pecans with Butterscotch Sauce (page 316); coconut ice cream rolled in toasted coconut with Rum Sauce (page 316); chocolate ice cream rolled in crushed chocolate wafers with Raspberry Sauce (page 312).

Ice Cream and Liqueur: Pour 1½ ounces (3 tablespoons) of liqueur over ice cream, and add a topping. Try these combinations:

- Crème de menthe with a sprig of mint.

- Amaretto with toasted almonds.

- Godiva liqueur with a few fresh raspberries.

- Galliano with sliced strawberries and a sprig of mint.

- Grand Marnier or Cointreau with a few mandarin orange slices.

- Coconut liqueur with toasted coconut.

- Crème de cacao with chocolate shavings.

- Crème d'ananas or light rum and a spoonful of crushed pineapple.

- Brandy with a few fresh peach slices.

FRUIT CRISP
•••

OVEN: 400°

4 cups fresh, frozen, or canned fruit
⅓ cup water or fruit juice
½ cup butter, softened
1 cup sugar
1 cup self-rising flour

Pour fruit into a greased 2-quart baking dish (such as an 8" square cake pan). Add water or fruit juice and stir. Bake for about 10 minutes, or until fruit is hot. Cream together butter and sugar, and cut in flour until mixture is crumbly. Sprinkle on top of fruit and return to oven. Bake on top shelf of oven for 25–30 more minutes, or until top is browned.

MAKES 8 SERVINGS.

MERINGUE SHELLS
•••

OVEN: 250°

6 egg whites, at room temperature
½ teaspoon salt
½ teaspoon cream of tartar
1 (1-pound) box powdered sugar (about 3¾ cups unsifted)
1 teaspoon vanilla extract or ½ teaspoon almond extract

Using an electric mixer, beat egg whites until foamy. Mix in salt and cream of tartar. Add powdered sugar, about a tablespoon at a time, beating constantly. This may take 15 minutes. Add vanilla or almond extract. Beat until stiff. Drop mixture by heaping tablespoonfuls 3" apart onto cookie sheets lined with foil or parchment. With back of spoon, form shallow depression in center of each mound. (Meringues won't bake properly if shells are more than 2½" in diameter.) Bake for 1 hour. Don't open oven door! Turn off oven and leave meringues in oven for at least 4 hours or overnight. Then remove meringues and wrap them in an airtight container. Delicious filled with ice cream, fruit, or Raspberries in Cointreau (page 315).

MAKES 24 LARGE SHELLS.

MOCHA CREAM DESSERT
•••

1 heaping tablespoon instant coffee granules
1 cup boiling water
30 large marshmallows or 3 cups miniature marshmallows
1 cup heavy cream
1 teaspoon vanilla extract
whipped cream for topping
chocolate shavings for topping

In a medium saucepan, dissolve instant coffee in boiling water. Add marshmallows. Cook over low heat until they are dissolved. Stir in heavy cream (unwhipped) and vanilla extract. Pour into dessert dishes or parfait glasses and chill. Top with whipped cream and chocolate shavings.

MAKES 4–6 SERVINGS.

Long Island Peaches

■ ■ ■

One summer, Jack brought home a whole basket full of ripe peaches when he returned from a road trip to Georgia. This is what happened to most of them.

6 ripe peaches, peeled and sliced
2 teaspoons Fruit Fresh
½ cup sugar
2 tablespoons Amaretto
2 tablespoons rum
2 tablespoons Triple Sec
1 quart vanilla ice cream

Toss peaches with Fruit Fresh and sugar. Add Amaretto, rum, and Triple Sec. Stir to mix. Cover and let stand for about an hour to blend flavors. Spoon over vanilla ice cream.

MAKES 6 SERVINGS.

Raspberries in Cointreau

■ ■ ■

1 (10-ounce) package frozen raspberries
2 tablespoons sugar
½ cup Cointreau
½ pint heavy cream

Place raspberries in a bowl and sprinkle with sugar. Add Cointreau and stir. Cover and refrigerate for 2 hours. Stir again and drain juice, reserving it for later. Whip cream and fold into raspberries. Spoon into dessert glasses or Meringue Shells (page 314). Serve with juice in a small pitcher.

MAKES 4 SERVINGS.

Rice Pudding

■ ■ ■

This is a delicious comfort food, and a great way to use up leftover rice.

OVEN: 350°

2½ cups cold milk
¾ cup sugar
pinch salt
2 eggs
⅛ teaspoon nutmeg
⅛ teaspoon cinnamon
½ teaspoon vanilla extract
2 cups cooked rice
½ cup raisins

In a large mixing bowl, combine milk with sugar and salt. Beat in eggs, nutmeg, cinnamon, and vanilla extract. Fold in cooked rice and raisins and turn into a buttered 1½-quart baking dish. Place baking dish in a shallow pan of hot water, and carefully set pan in the oven. Bake for about 45 minutes, or until pudding is set.

MAKES 6 SERVINGS.

"Cooking is like love. It should be entered into with abandon or not at all."

—**Harriet Van Horne**

N·O·T·E·S

STRAWBERRY SHORTCAKE
•••

OVEN: 375°

1 pint fresh strawberries
6 tablespoons sugar, divided use
1 (10-ounce) can refrigerator biscuits
2 tablespoons butter, melted
1 cup sweetened whipped cream
(page 312)

Slice berries and add 2 tablespoons of the sugar. For each shortcake, press together 2 biscuits and flatten slightly. Put melted butter and remaining 4 tablespoons sugar into separate small bowls. Dip tops of biscuits into butter and then into sugar. Place on baking sheet sugar-side-up. Bake for 10 minutes. Cool and split. Place an unsugared half on each plate and spoon on strawberries. Add whipped cream and the sugared top of biscuit. Spoon on more berries and more whipped cream.
MAKES 5 SERVINGS.

TAPIOCA PUDDING
•••

2 cups milk
3 tablespoons quick-cooking tapioca
1/3 cup plus 1 tablespoon sugar,
divided use
1/8 teaspoon salt
2 eggs, separated
1 teaspoon vanilla extract

Mix milk, tapioca, 1/3 cup of the sugar, salt, and egg yolks in a microwave-safe glass 2-quart bowl. Let stand for 5 minutes, and then stir. Cook at 80 percent power in the microwave for 8–10 minutes. Stir in vanilla extract. Beat egg whites until foamy. Gradually add the remaining 1 tablespoon sugar, and keep beating until mixture forms soft peaks. Fold egg whites into pudding and spoon into dessert dishes.
MAKES 6 SERVINGS.

BUTTERSCOTCH SAUCE
•••

2/3 cup light corn syrup
1 1/4 cups brown sugar
1/4 cup butter
1/4 teaspoon salt
1 (5-ounce) can evaporated milk
2 tablespoons half and half

Measure corn syrup, brown sugar, butter, and salt into a heavy, medium size saucepan. Bring to a boil over medium heat. Reduce heat to medium-low and continue to boil and stir until thickened. Remove from heat, cool, and stir in evaporated milk and cream. Serve immediately, or refrigerate in a covered container.
MAKES 2 CUPS.

RUM SAUCE
•••

1/2 cup butter
1 cup brown sugar
4 tablespoons rum

Melt butter in a heavy saucepan and stir in brown sugar and rum. Cook and stir until sugar is dissolved. Serve warm.
MAKES 1 CUP.

Reference Section

Food Facts

■ ■ ■

HOW TO SELECT FRESH PRODUCE

■ ■ ■

APPLES

■ ■ ■

What to Look For ... apples that are firm and fragrant. Whatever variety, their color should be bright and glossy. They should be free of blemishes, soft spots, or bruises.

How Much to Allow ... 1 medium apple, or ⅓ pound per serving. One pound (3 medium apples) yields about 3 cups of unpeeled, diced or sliced apples, or about 2½ cups of peeled, diced or sliced apples. For a 9″ pie, you need 6 medium apples, or about 2 pounds.

How Long to Keep ... for 2–3 days at room temperature, or for 2–4 weeks in a plastic bag in the refrigerator. Apples give off a gas that turns carrots bitter, so they should be stored separately.

How to Prepare ... Wash and peel if desired. To remove the core, use a corer or cut into quarters and core. To prevent browning, cut with a stainless steel knife and dip cut slices into lemon juice or acidulated water.

Different Varieties and When to Buy ...

Baldwin: Tart-sweet, crisp, juicy; all-purpose cooking apple; stays firm. (November–April)

Cortland: Mildly tart, crisp, firm; doesn't brown after cutting; good for salad, and holds its shape when baked. (September–February)

Cox Pippin: Crisp, mild, juicy, firm, slightly acid; all-purpose, but best for eating out-of-hand. (September)

Crabapples: Sour, crisp; suitable only for cooking, and especially good for jelly. (September–November)

Fuji: Crisp, sweet, juicy; best for eating out-of-hand. (August–September)

Gala: Crisp, sweet-tart, firm; good for cooking, and excellent for eating out-of-hand. (August–September)

Golden Delicious: Sweet, mild, semifirm, crisp, juicy; versatile, all-purpose apple; excellent for pie; holds its shape well; excellent for salad, since it doesn't brown very quickly; a good dessert apple. (August–June, but best in the fall)

Granny Smith: Outstanding green apple; tart, firm, crisp, juicy; very good all-purpose apple, both for cooking and for eating out-of-hand. (November–July)

Gravenstein: Fairly tart, juicy, crisp; excellent for cooking, and superb for applesauce. Truly a summer apple. (July–September)

Grimes Golden: Juicy, mellow, sweet, crisp-tender, firm; best for salads and for eating out-of-hand. (October–February)

Ida Red: Sweet, spicy, crisp; excellent for eating out-of-hand; good for cooking. (October–November)

Jonathan: Tart, tender, very juicy; good for cider and applesauce, but poor for baking. (September– May, but best in the fall)

Macoun: Sweet-tart, crisp, juicy; excellent for eating out-of-hand; good for cooking. (October–November)

McIntosh: Sweet-tart, fragrant, very juicy; excellent for applesauce or salad, but gets mushy quickly, and shouldn't be cooked for as long as other varieties. (September–June, but best in the fall)

Newton Pippin: Slightly tart, firm, juicy; excellent for pie, applesauce, freezing, and baking. (September–June)

Northern Spy: Spicy, crisp, firm, sweet- tart, juicy; all-purpose apple. (October– November)

Paula Red: Mildly tart to sweet. (September)

Red Delicious: Considered the #1 eating apple in the United States. Mildly tart, juicy, firm, crisp; excellent for salads, and delicious sliced and served with cheese, but poor for baking and for other cooking purposes. (all year, but best in the fall)

Rhode Island Greening: Tart, crisp, juicy; excellent for cooking, but gets very soft; good for pie. (September–June, but best in the fall)

Rome Beauty: Slightly tart, firm; considered the favorite apple for baking, since it holds its shape well when cooked; also very good for freezing. (October–June)

Stayman: Spicy, winy, slightly tart, crisp, juicy; excellent for cooking, and especially for applesauce. (October–April, but best in the fall)

Winesap: Spicy, slightly tart, very juicy, firm, crisp; excellent for salad; good for applesauce and pies; tender but not mushy when cooked. (September–June, but best in the fall)

York (York Imperial): Tart, honey-flavored, firm, mildly crisp; best for cooking, pies, and baking, since the flavor is slightly bland. (September–November)

APRICOTS
■■■

What to Look For ... plump, firm, evenly golden fruit, with a rosy blush and a pleasant, floral fragrance. Avoid apricots that look dull, yellowish, or greenish, or those that are soft, mushy, bruised, shriveled, cracked, or hard.

How Much to Allow ... 1–2 average apricots, or 2–3 small ones per serving (or a little less than ¼ pound). A pound contains 8–12 average apricots, and yields about 2 cups of apricot slices or halves.

How Long to Keep ... at room temperature until ripe; then for 2–3 days in a plastic bag in the refrigerator.

How to Prepare ... Wash, cut in half, and remove the pit. No need to peel.

When to Buy ... June–August

ARTICHOKES
■■■

What to Look For ... compact, plump, heavy artichokes, with green, silky, tightly closed leaves. (The rounder the artichoke, the bigger the heart.) The leaves should squeak when pressed against each other. Brown leaves indicate old age, injury, or toughness. Check for worm injury at the base; it could indicate internal damage.

How Much to Allow ... 1 whole artichoke per serving as a first course; ½ of an artichoke per serving as an appetizer (stuffed); 1–2 artichoke bottoms per serving (stuffed); 3–5 artichoke hearts per serving.

How Long to Keep ... up to 1 week in a plastic bag in the refrigerator.

How to Prepare ... Wash under cold, running water. Using a serrated knife, cut off the stem flush with the base. Then cut about an inch off the top of the artichoke. Break off the small outside leaves close to the stem. With scissors, trim the thorny tips off the remaining leaves. Rub lemon juice over the cut surfaces, to prevent discoloration. The small, fuzzy choke at the center, and the cluster of thin, purple-tipped, sharp leaves can both be removed either before or after cooking. To do so, spread the outer leaves gently, pull out the tiny thistle-like leaves, and scrape the fuzzy fibers out with a spoon.

When to Buy ... November–March and June–October

ASPARAGUS
■ ■ ■

What to Look For ... bright green color (not dull khaki), firm, round, straight stalks 6″–8″ long. The tips should be compact, very tightly closed (not soggy or flabby) and perhaps tinged with lavender. The bases should be moist. Asparagus that is flat or angular is usually tough. Avoid asparagus with open tips, and stalks with vertical ridges. These are a sign of aging. The stalks become tough and stringy at the end of the season, so waste can be increased up to 50 percent. Stalks that are of uniform size cook more evenly.

How Much to Allow ... 5–6 large stalks, 7–10 medium stalks, or ⅓–½ pound of asparagus per serving. One pound (16–20 medium stalks) yields about 3 cups when trimmed and cut into 2″ lengths, and cooks down to about 2½ cups.

How Long to Keep ... for 4–5 days, with the bottoms of the stems first wrapped in damp paper towels, and then the whole package snugly wrapped in a plastic bag in the refrigerator.

How to Prepare ... Soak asparagus in cold water for several minutes, and then swish it around to remove any sand or dirt. Bend each stem gently to snap off the tough, woody portion at the lower end. (The stems should snap off naturally at the right place.) Discard the bases. If the stalks are quite thick, you can peel them with a vegetable peeler, removing the lower scales as well, where grit can hide.

When to Buy ... March–June and October–November

AVOCADOS
■ ■ ■

What to Look For ... heavy, firm avocados, just barely beginning to soften. California varieties are smaller. They have a dark, pebbly, alligator skin, a buttery taste, and make the best guacamole, since they have a higher fat content. They are also called "alligator pears." Florida varieties are smooth-skinned, larger, and brighter green. Ripe avocados yield to gentle pressure. Avoid avocados with bruises, cuts, or dark sunken spots, which indicate decay; light brown, irregular markings ("scabs") are only surface imperfections, and shouldn't affect the quality. Baby av-

ocados, also called cocktail avocados, are seedless or have a soft pit, which is edible.

How Much to Allow ... ¼–½ of an avocado per serving. One pound of avocados yields about 1½ cups of pulp. There is generally about 25 percent waste when an avocado is peeled and the pit is removed.

How Long to Keep ... at room temperature until ripe; then uncut in the refrigerator for 2–3 days. (They will be soft, but as long as they haven't been cut, they'll be fine for guacamole even after up to a week in the refrigerator.) To speed up the ripening process, store avocados in a loosely closed paper bag at room temperature, in order to confine the gases that help ripen the fruit.

How to Prepare ... Ripen at room temperature. (This can take 2–6 days.) Cut in half lengthwise, and remove the pit by rapping it with the blade of a sharp knife, and then twisting the knife until the pit pulls free. It is easiest to peel avocados if they are cut into quarters first. The skin can be removed readily when the fruit is ripe, by peeling it away from the top. Sprinkle or dip in lemon juice immediately, to prevent browning. If mashing, as for guacamole, store the mashed avocado in a container that allows as little of it as possible to be exposed to the air, since air contact is what causes browning. Press a film of plastic wrap over the top of the mashed avocado, and peel off the plastic wrap just before serving.

Different Varieties and When to Buy ...

California (Haas—dark-skinned to almost black) avocados: all year

Florida (Fuerta—bright green) avocados: July–February

BANANAS
■■■

What to Look For ... plump, firm bananas, of uniform color. Ripe ones are yellow (without green tips) and flecked with brown. Avoid bananas that are bruised or split. Bananas that look dull, regardless of color, were probably overchilled at some point, and will not ripen properly.

How Much to Allow ... 1 medium banana, or about ⅓ pound (weighed with peel) per serving. One pound (3 average bananas) yields 1½–2 cups mashed, or about 2 cups of sliced bananas. There is generally about 25 percent waste after peeling.

How Long to Keep ... at room temperature until ripe; then for 2–3 days in the refrigerator. The skin will darken, but the flesh will be fine. To hasten ripening, store bananas in a closed paper bag at room temperature.

How to Prepare ... Ripen at room temperature. (This might take 3–5 days.) Refrigeration causes the skin to turn brown. After peeling, dip the fruit in lemon juice to prevent darkening, unless serving immediately.

When to Buy ... all year

Different Varieties ...

Cavendish: the common yellow banana, speckled with brown.

Chicadita (Lady Finger): miniature banana; yellow and very sweet.

Lemon Banana: miniature banana; yellow, round, lemon-flavored.

Plantain: large banana, dark and bland in flavor.

Red Cuban: short, fat banana, with reddish-purple skin and dark, creamy flesh that's speckled with black; very intense flavor.

BEANS: CRANBERRY, FAVA, LIMA, AND BLACK-EYED PEAS
■■■

Cranberry Beans are often called "Shell Beans" or "Shellies."

Fava Beans are also called "Broad Beans."

What to Look For ... small, velvety, bright, shiny, fresh-looking pods. They should be plump and tightly closed. Avoid pods that are limp, flabby, spotted, or yellow, as well as those that have sunken areas.

How Much to Allow ... ¾ pound of beans in the pod, or ¼ pound of shelled beans per serving. One pound of beans in the pod yields ¾–1¾ cups of shelled beans, depending on the variety.

How Long to Keep ... for 1–2 days in a plastic bag in the refrigerator.

How to Prepare ... Remove peas from the pods. Wash, sort, and drain.

When to Buy ... March–August

BEANS: GREEN, WAX, AND ITALIAN
■■■

What to Look For ... slender, firm, straight, small, tender beans with barely visible seeds. Beans with large seeds will probably be tough and stringy. They should be crisp enough to break when bent at a 45° angle. They should be free of scars or blemishes, and the ends should not be shriveled.

How Much to Allow ... ¼–⅓ pound of green or wax beans per serving. One pound yields about 3 cups of cut beans.

How Long to Keep ... for 4–5 days in a plastic bag in the refrigerator.

How to Prepare ... Wash and drain. If beans have strings, remove them when snapping off the ends,

much as you would peel a banana. Remove any brown spots and leave the beans whole or cut into pieces.

Different Varieties and When to Buy ...

Green and wax beans: June–August (although usually available all year)

Italian beans: March–August

BEETS
···

What to Look For ... small, firm beets, 1½″–2″ in diameter, with a deep, rich color and uniform size. The skin should be smooth and unscarred. Any attached greens should be fresh—not yellowed or deteriorated. Avoid beets with bruises, blemishes, shriveling, or soft spots. Larger beets are not as tender as smaller ones.

How Much to Allow ... ⅓ pound (3–4 small beets) per serving. There are about 10 (2″) beets in a pound, or about 2 cups of sliced or diced beets.

How Long to Keep ... for 7–10 days in a plastic bag in the refrigerator, although greens keep for only a few days. Remove beet greens about 1″ above the roots as soon as you get them home.

How to Prepare ... Although beet greens should be removed, as described above, the roots should be left attached. Be careful not to cut or pierce the beets before cooking, as this will cause them to "bleed" when they

cook. Wash beets, scrubbing them well with a soft brush. Beets should be peeled only after cooking.

When to Buy ... June–September (although usually available all year)

BERRIES
···

What to Look For ... plump, shiny berries, of uniform color, that are fragrant and firm (not soft or mushy). Avoid berries that are dull, bruised, crushed, or moldy. Check the bottom of the container for signs of stickiness or leaking juice, which indicates damage. Berries with their caps still attached (except strawberries) are immature, and not as flavorful.

How Much to Allow ... about ¼ of a quart-size container, or about ¼ pound of berries per serving. One quart generally yields about 3½ cups of berries, and is enough to make a 9″ pie. A pint of strawberries yields about 1¾ cups sliced, or about 1¼ cups of puréed strawberries. A pound of dried currants yields about 3 cups of currants.

How Long to Keep ... most berries, for only 1–2 days in the refrigerator. Cranberries can be kept in the original plastic bag for up to a month in the refrigerator, or for up to a year in the freezer.

How to Prepare ... Refrigerate berries in the original carton. Before serving, remove any spoiled berries. Wash gently and drain well. To prepare cranberries, fill the sink with about 2″ of cold water. Empty the package of berries into the sink and swish them around gently. Pick up the berries, a handful at a time, discarding any that are bruised, soft, or badly discolored. Remove any remaining stems. Then put the good berries in a colander to drain.

Different Varieties and When to Buy ...

Blackberries: Glossy purple-black. (June–August)

Blueberries: Round, dusty blue; silvery bloom. (June–September)

Boysenberries: Larger cousin to dewberries. (July–August)

Cranberries: Should be hard and lustrous. (October–December)

Currants: Red, white, and black varieties. (June–August)

Dewberries: Glossy purple-black. (June–August)

Gooseberries: Silver-green; cousin to currants. (June–July)

Lingonberries: Red; similar to cranberries. (June–August)

Loganberries: Dark red. (May–August)

Raspberries: Very fragile; use quickly or purée. (June–August)

Strawberries: Bright red; caps should be attached. (April–August)

BROCCOLI

■■■

What to Look For ... tight, compact buds, dark to purplish-green; stalks should be firm, crisp, and moist. (Slender stalks will be more tender.) If buds have begun to turn yellow or flower, the broccoli is old.

How Much to Allow ... ⅓–½ pound of broccoli, or 3 stalks per serving. One bunch usually weighs about 1¼ pounds, and yields about 3 cups of cooked broccoli, or a little over 2 cups of florets.

How Long to Keep ... for 3–5 days in a plastic bag in the refrigerator.

How to Prepare ... Wash broccoli thoroughly under cold running water. If necessary, soak for half an hour in salted water to remove insects. Remove the large leaves, and the very end of the stem. Cut broccoli into serving-sized spears, or cut into smaller florets, as desired. Peel the stem with a vegetable peeler or sharp paring knife, and then cut it in half lengthwise. Then slice it into smaller pieces or cut it into julienne.

When to Buy ... October–May (although usually available all year)

BRUSSELS SPROUTS

■■■

What to Look For ... clean-looking, firm, crisp heads with tightly-clinging leaves that are bright or deep green. Sprouts should be of a uniform size. Avoid sprouts that look puffy, yellow, withered, or wilted. Sprouts with a smudged or dirty look have probably been infested by aphids (plant lice). Be sure to check for worm damage as well.

How Much to Allow ... ¼ pound of brussels sprouts per serving. Sometimes they're sold loose, but more often they're sold by the quart (which weighs about 1¼ pounds) or in smaller 10-ounce cartons.

How Long to Keep ... for 3–5 days in a plastic bag in the refrigerator.

How to Prepare ... Remove yellow outer leaves, and trim off a sliver of the bottom. (Don't remove too much, or it will cause the leaves to drop off.) Rinse well and drain. If necessary, soak sprouts for half an hour in salted water, to remove insects. Pierce the bottoms with a sharp knife, to allow for more even cooking.

When to Buy ... August–March

CABBAGE

■■■

What to Look For ... head cabbage that is solid, firm, and heavy for its size. All varieties should have bright, crisp leaves that are finely ribbed.

Avoid cabbage with bruised, yellowed, wilted, or discolored leaves. The stem should be cut close to the head. Holes indicate worm infestation.

How Much to Allow ... about ⅓ pound of cabbage per serving if cooked; less than that if served raw. A 1½-pound head yields 4–6 cups of shredded cabbage (before adding dressing). Shredded raw cabbage "weeps" when dressing is added, so add dressing to slaw sparingly.

How Long to Keep ... for 1–2 weeks (uncut) in a plastic bag in the refrigerator.

How to Prepare ... Rinse and remove any wilted or discolored leaves. Remove the core if you are going to shred or chop, as for slaw. (This is easier to do if the cabbage is first cut into quarters.) Leave the core attached if you plan to cook the cabbage in wedges, since it will hold them together. Just trim the bottom.

When to Buy ... March–June (although usually available all year)

CARROTS

■■■

What to Look For ... smooth, firm, crisp, straight, bright orange carrots. (Don't be fooled by an orange-striped

wrapper!) They shouldn't be longer than 6", or more than 1" in diameter at their widest point. Avoid carrots that are cracked, split, flabby, or big and woody-looking. If the greens are still attached, they should be fresh-looking, crisp, and unwilted. Smaller carrots are more tender than larger ones.

How Much to Allow ... about ¼–⅓ pound of carrots per serving. One pound (5–7 medium carrots, 12–14 small ones, or 2–3 dozen baby carrots) yields 2½–3 cups of shredded or sliced carrots, or 2½–2¾ cups of diced or cooked carrots.

How Long to Keep ... for 1–2 weeks in a plastic bag in the refrigerator. If the greens are still attached, remove them as soon as you get them home, since they draw moisture from the carrots.

How to Prepare ... Remove and discard the tops, including any leaves. Wash and peel with a vegetable peeler, or scrape with a knife. (Baby carrots only need to be washed; they do not require peeling.)

When to Buy ... all year

CAULIFLOWER
■ ■ ■

What to Look For ... heavy, compact, clean, creamy-white heads—not yellowed or brownish. The flower clusters should be tightly packed, and the leaves should be crisp, fresh, and green. The buds should be tightly closed, and should have a fine grain. Avoid cauliflower with smudges or dirty-looking spots, which indicate insect damage. Brown edges are a sign of old age.

How Much to Allow ... about ½–¾ pound of cauliflower (weighed before trimming) per cooked serving. An average head weighs 1¾–2¼ pounds, however 30–40 percent of that may be trimmed away.

How Long to Keep ... for 4–7 days in a plastic bag in the refrigerator.

How to Prepare ... Trim the tough part of the stalk and remove the leaves. Trim away any discolorations. Wash in cold running water. Cut into florets, leaving a portion of the center stalk attached to prevent crumbling. If preparing whole, remove the center stalk.

When to Buy ... September–December (but usually available all year)

CELERIAC
■ ■ ■

Also called "Celery Root" and "Knob Celery."

What to Look For ... firm, heavy, clean, crisp knobs about 2"–4" in diameter, with few scars or blemishes. Avoid larger ones, which can be soft and mushy at the center.

How Much to Allow ... 1 small knob or ½ of a large knob per serving.

How Long to Keep ... for 2–3 days in a plastic bag in the refrigerator.

How to Prepare ... Wash well, drain, and peel. Cut as desired.

When to Buy ... October–April

CELERY
■ ■ ■

What to Look For ... crisp, firm bunches, with fresh-looking leaves. The ribs should be straight and brittle enough to snap easily. Avoid celery that's cracked, bruised, yellowed, wilted, limp, or droopy.

How Much to Allow ... ¼ of a medium (1-pound) bunch per serving for cooked celery. One pound yields about 2 cups of diced or sliced raw celery; 3 average ribs yield about 1 cup of diced or sliced raw celery.

How Long to Keep ... for 1–2 weeks in a plastic bag in the refrigerator.

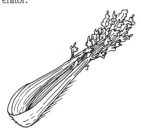

How to Prepare ... Cut off the root end and submerge the ribs in water. Swish the celery around to separate the ribs. Scrub with a brush, rinse, and drain. Remove the leaves, dried ends, and strings. The leaves may be used for soups.

When to Buy ... all year

CHERRIES
■ ■ ■

What to Look For ... firm, bright, plump, shiny, dry cherries. Sticky cherries are overripe. Once picked, cherries do not continue to ripen; they just decay. Avoid those with bruises, blemishes, or small brown spots.

How Much to Allow ... about ¼ pound per serving. One quart weighs about a pound and yields about 2 cups of pitted cherries.

How Long to Keep ... for 2–4 days in a plastic bag in the refrigerator.

How to Prepare ... Leave cherries in the original carton in the refrigerator until ready to use. Remove stems and sort, removing any decayed fruit. Rinse, drain well, and remove pits.

Different Varieties and
When to Buy ...

Sweet Cherries: Bing, Chapman, Lambert, Queen Anne, Republican, Royal Ann (Napoleon), Tartarian, Windsor: (May–September)

Sour Cherries: Early Richmond, English Morello, Montmorency: (June–August)

COCONUT
■ ■ ■

What to Look For ... well-rounded, heavy coconuts. The liquid should slosh when the coconut is shaken. Avoid coconuts that have soft or cracked shells. The eyes should not be wet or moldy.

How Much to Allow ... One average coconut yields about 3 cups of grated coconut.

How Long to Keep ... for 1 week at room temperature, and then for 3–4 weeks in the refrigerator uncut, or for 4–5 days after cutting.

How to Prepare ... Pierce coconut twice with an ice pick, and drain liquid. Place in a 400° oven for 15 minutes. Remove from the oven and use a hammer to crack the shell. Remove the meat with a sharp knife. The brown skin can be peeled with a vegetable peeler.

When to Buy ... all year

CORN
■ ■ ■

What to Look For ... blunt ear tips, and darkened, dry silks at the top. The husks should be fresh, tightly wrapped, and green. The stems should be moist, and not chalky or yellowed. The kernels should be

bright, plump, evenly arranged, and filled with milky juice. Very large kernels will have a woody texture, and very tiny kernels are immature and will lack flavor. Clear juice in the kernel means the corn is immature; lack of juice means it's old. The ears should be free of worms. Don't buy corn with the husks removed—it's likely to be tough.

How Much to Allow ... 1–2 ears per serving. Three medium ears weigh about a pound and yield about 1 cup of cut kernels.

How Long to Keep ... for no more than a day in the refrigerator. The sugar in the kernels begins to turn to starch as soon as the corn is picked, and even faster once the husks are removed. As the old saying goes, don't pick the corn until the water is boiling!

How to Prepare ... Just before cooking, remove the husks and silks. The silks can be removed more easily by holding the corn stem-side-down, and wiping downward with a damp paper towel or dish towel. Sometimes the silks are easier to remove if the corn is submerged in cool water. Cut off the stem, and snap off the tip of the ear. Break corn into pieces if desired.

When to Buy ... May–September

Different Varieties ... Yellow corn has larger kernels, while white corn, such as *Silver Queen*, has smaller, sweeter kernels. In varieties such as *Peaches and Cream*, identified as "supersweet," the sugar converts to starch more slowly, and the corn stays sweet and tender longer.

CUCUMBERS
■ ■ ■

What to Look For ... small, slender, dark green cucumbers that are well shaped and firm. Avoid those with shriveled skin, puffiness, dark or soft spots, or yellowing. Fat cucumbers are usually seedy and pithy.

How Much to Allow ... ½ of an average cucumber per serving. Two medium cucumbers weigh about a pound, and yield 2½–3 cups of peeled, seeded, and sliced cucumbers.

How Long to Keep ... for 4–5 days in the refrigerator, wrapped in plastic.

How to Prepare ... Wash, trim the ends, and peel if waxed. Or, if desired, the peel can be scored with a fork before slicing. To chop, first peel cucumbers and cut into quarters lengthwise. Scoop out the seeds with a sharp knife, and then chop or dice, as desired.

When to Buy ... May–August (although usually available all year)

EGGPLANT
■ ■ ■

What to Look For ... deep purple eggplant that's firm and heavy, with a glossy shine. The caps and stems should look fresh and green. When squeezed gently, eggplant should yield slightly. If it's too soft, it's old; if it's hard, it's immature. Avoid scarred, shriveled, soft, or flabby eggplant, or any with green or brown rust spots. Worm holes can be an indication of extensive internal damage. The best size is about 3″ in diameter and 6″ long. Plump, rounded eggplant tends to be slightly more juicy, and is better for baking and casseroles. Longer, more slender eggplant tends to be slightly drier, and is better for frying.

How Much to Allow ... ¼–⅓ of a medium eggplant, or 1–2 whole baby eggplants per serving. A baby eggplant weighs about ¼ pound. A medium eggplant weighs about 1¼ pounds, and yields about 3 cups of diced eggplant, which cooks down to about 2½ cups.

How Long to Keep ... for a day or two in a cool, dry place, or for 3–4 days in the vegetable crisper of the refrigerator.

How to Prepare ... Wash and trim the stem end. Peel eggplant if skin is tough. Dip the cut pieces in lemon juice to prevent darkening.

When to Buy ... July–September (although usually available all year)

ENDIVE
■ ■ ■

What to Look For ... *Belgian endive*, which looks like 5″–6″ torpedoes or fat cigars, should have very firm, crisp, tight-clinging leaves, with no brown spots or frayed brown edges. The tip should be pale yellow. *Curly endive* has ruffled, narrow leaves, and grows in loose heads. *Escarole* has curly or wavy leaves that are broader than curly endive. *Radicchio* resembles a small red cabbage, and has burgundy-colored leaves with white ribs. Whatever variety, the leaves should look fresh and crisp, without any signs of insect damage, blemishing, wilting, flabbiness, or discoloration.

How Much to Allow ... ½–1 of a head of most varieties as a salad serving; 1 head per serving for cooked Belgian endive.

How Long to Keep ... Belgian endive is very perishable, and keeps for no more than a day, wrapped in a damp paper towel and placed in a plastic bag in the refrigerator. Curly endive and escarole keep for 3–5 days, wrapped in a plastic bag in the refrigerator. Radicchio keeps for up to a week, wrapped in a plastic bag in the refrigerator.

How to Prepare ... Separate the leaves and wash thoroughly, changing the water several times to be sure all the dirt is removed. Drain well, using a salad spinner basket or paper towels. Crisp in the refrigerator in a perforated bag before serving.

When to Buy ... *Belgian endive:* October–May; *curly endive* and *escarole:* June–October; *radicchio:* December–April.

FENNEL
■ ■ ■

What to Look For ... clean, crisp, rounded bulbs with even, creamy white color and no signs of yellowing or browning. Fat bulbs are preferable to longer, thinner ones. If greens are attached to the bulb, they should have a bright, fresh appearance.

How Much to Allow ... ½ of a bulb per serving. A pound yields about 3 cups of sliced fennel.

How Long to Keep ... for 7–10 days in a plastic bag in the refrigerator.

How to Prepare ... Trim the base and the feathery stalks. Remove the tough outer ribs. Wash, cut in half, and remove the core. Slice as desired.

When to Buy ... September–March

FIGS
■ ■ ■

What to Look For ... soft-ripe, plump figs that are neither bruised nor broken. A sour or fermented smell indicates that they are overripe. There are three popular varieties: *Black Mission* figs are purplish-black and honey-flavored, with a thin skin and small seeds. *Calimyrna* figs are almost golden, with a rich flavor and large nutty seeds. *Kadota* figs are green and fragrant, with a light, sweet flavor. If you add figs to gelatin, the gelatin won't set properly.

How Much to Allow ... 3 figs or ¼ pound per serving. One pound contains about 12–16 medium figs, and yields about 2⅔ cups of chopped figs.

How Long to Keep ... for no more than 1–2 days in the refrigerator.

How to Prepare ... Gently rinse, drain, and remove the stem ends.

When to Buy ... June–October, except Calimyrna, which are available only in June

GARLIC
■ ■ ■

What to Look For ... clean, large, dry, firm, tight-skinned bulbs of garlic. Avoid garlic bulbs that are soft, sprouted, or spongy, or any bulbs whose outer skin is broken. Shriveled bulbs and brown spots indicate decay. If garlic is green, that indicates that it has gone bad.

How Much to Allow ... Garlic is most often used to flavor other foods. An average bulb has 8–15 cloves.

How Long to Keep ... for 2–3 weeks (unbroken) in a cool, dry place; for 3–10 days after breaking individual cloves from the bulb. Fresh chopped garlic and minced garlic are also available in jars. After opening, jars should be stored in the refrigerator, to be used as needed.

How to Prepare ... Separate as many cloves as needed. To separate all the cloves at once, strike a whole bulb of garlic with the heel of your hand. Peel the cloves by placing them on a cutting board and laying the flat side of a large knife on top of the clove. Strike the knife firmly with your fist. This will dislodge the peel, which can then be removed. After peeling, trim the root end, and sliver, chop, or mince the garlic as desired. The end of the garlic clove that is attached to the bulb (root end) has a stronger flavor than the rest of the garlic, so trim it off and discard it for a milder flavor.

When to Buy ... all year

GRAPEFRUIT
■ ■ ■

What to Look For ... firm grapefruit that is heavy for its size, with smooth,

thin skin. Avoid fruit with puffy or withered skin or soft spots. Grapefruit with a slightly pointed stem end usually has thicker skin and less juice.

How Much to Allow ... ½ of a medium grapefruit per serving. One medium grapefruit weighs about a pound, and yields ⅔–¾ cup of juice, or about 1¼ cups or 10–12 sections.

How Long to Keep ... for up to a week at room temperature, or for up to 2 weeks in the refrigerator.

How to Prepare ... Rinse and dry. To serve halves, cut in half crosswise, and cut sections away from the membranes with a small knife that has a serrated blade. To cut into sections or slices, first trim off the ends. Set one of the cut ends on a cutting board and carve away the peel in sections, cutting downward and curving around the fruit, as close as possible to the fruit. Then slice away the sections from the membrane, or cut into crosswise slices.

When to Buy ... Different varieties are available throughout the year.

GRAPES
■■■

What to Look For ... plump, ripe grapes, firmly attached to the stems in full bunches. Avoid grapes that are soft, mushy, withered, or moldy. Stems shouldn't be brown, shriveled, or decayed. Grapes should cling to their stems. If many grapes fall from the stem when a bunch is shaken ("shattering"), this indicates that the grapes aren't fresh. Green ("white") grapes will have a faint yellowish cast when they are ripe. Purple ("black") grapes should have a rich color, with no green cast.

How Much to Allow ... ¼–⅓ pound per serving. One pound of seedless grapes yields about 2½ cups of halves; a pound of grapes with seeds yields just over 2 cups of halves.

How Long to Keep ... for 3–5 days in a plastic bag in the refrigerator.

How to Prepare ... Refrigerate in the original container, or in a perforated plastic bag. Before serving, wash and drain well. Leave in clusters or remove the grapes from the stems and cut in half, removing the seeds if necessary.

Different Varieties and When to Buy ...

Cardinal: Red; large; juicy, sweet; some seeds. (May–July)

Concord: Purplish-black; round; tart; large seeds. (September–October)

Flame Tokay: Red; large; juicy, mildly sweet; with seeds. (September–November)

Perlette: Green; round; mildly sweet; seedless. (May–June)

Red Emperor: Light reddish-purple; large; juicy, crisp, bland; with seeds. (November–May)

Red Flame: Red: juicy, crisp, very sweet; seedless. (August–October)

Red Malaga: Pink to reddish-purple; crisp; very sweet. (August–November)

Ribier: Purplish-black; sweet-tart; some seeds. (July–February)

Thompson: Yellowish-green; oval; juicy, sweet; seedless. (July–January)

GREENS
■■■

What to Look For ... crisp, clean, bright green leaves that are free of bruises and insect injury. Avoid greens that are dry, flabby, yellowed, or wilted. The stems should not be woody.

How Much to Allow ... ⅓–½ pound per cooked serving.

How Long to Keep ... for 1–2 days in a plastic bag in the refrigerator.

How to Prepare ... Wash greens very thoroughly, using several changes of water if necessary. Thick, woody stems should be removed. Small leaves can be cooked whole, and larger ones can be cut or torn up.

Different Varieties and
When to Buy ...

Beet Greens: June–October

Collard Greens: June–March

Dandelion Greens: March–May

Kale: December–April

Mustard Greens: June–October

Turnip Greens: January–April

JÍCAMA
■ ■ ■

What to Look For ... firm, heavy flesh and unblemished skin.

How Much to Allow ... ¼ pound per serving.

How Long to Keep ... for 1–2 weeks in a plastic bag in the refrigerator.

How to Prepare ... Wash and dry. Peel and remove the white fibrous layer just under the skin.

When to Buy ... November–May

KIWI FRUIT
■ ■ ■

What to Look For ... firm, plump, light brown fruit that yields to gentle pressure, without any bruises or soft spots.

How Much to Allow ... one per serving.

How Long to Keep ... for 2 weeks in the refrigerator, after ripening. To hasten ripening, store kiwi fruit in a paper bag with an apple or banana.

How to Prepare ... Wash, peel if desired, and slice crosswise. The skin is edible.

When to Buy ... Domestic: October–March; Imported: all year

LEEKS
■ ■ ■

What to Look For ... crisp, white, straight stalks no more than 1½″ in diameter, with fresh-looking tops. Avoid those that look wilted or yellow. Smaller leeks are more tender.

How Much to Allow ... ½ pound, or ½ of an average bunch per serving. A bunch weighs about a pound, and yields about 2 cups of chopped raw leeks, which cook down in volume to about 1 cup.

How Long to Keep ... for 1–2 weeks in a plastic bag in the refrigerator.

How to Prepare ... Remove roots and the tough, upper part of the leaves, leaving the tender, white part of the bulb. Cut in half lengthwise. Fan out the leaves and hold them under cold running water, to remove all the embedded dirt.

When to Buy ... September–December and April–July

LEMONS
■ ■ ■

What to Look For ... firm, heavy, deep-yellow lemons, with smooth, thin skin. Avoid lemons with thick

or green-tinged skin, or any that are bruised or wrinkled.

How Much to Allow ... One pound of lemons (4–6 medium) yields ⅔–1 cup of juice. One medium lemon yields 2–3 tablespoons of juice, and 2–3 teaspoons of grated peel.

How Long to Keep ... for 2–3 weeks in a plastic bag in the refrigerator.

How to Prepare ... Wash and dry. Cut into slices or wedges as desired.

When to Buy ... all year

LETTUCE AND
SALAD GREENS
■ ■ ■

What to Look For ... fresh-smelling leaves. Iceberg lettuce should be tightly packed, heavy, and firm. The core should not smell bitter, and the base shouldn't be brown and moldy-looking. Avoid lettuce with soggy, wilted, or yellow leaves. If the outer leaves look rusty or brown-tipped, the inner ones are likely to look the same. Avoid lettuce whose base looks slimy, brown, or dried out.

How Much to Allow ... 1½ cups of torn lettuce per salad serving. One pound of iceberg lettuce yields 4–6 cups of shredded lettuce.

How Long to Keep ... most varieties, for up to 10 days in a plastic bag in the refrigerator; butterhead varieties, for 3–4 days in a plastic bag in the refrigerator.

How to Prepare ... Remove any bruised outer leaves. Wash the loose leaf varieties of lettuce in several changes of cold water. Drain and dry thoroughly, or use a salad spinner. Dislodge the core of iceberg lettuce by slamming it down on a hard surface, and twisting it out. Let cold water run into the core cavity to flush out dirt. Turn the core side back down, and shake it over the sink to remove as much water as possible. To keep salad greens from turning brown prematurely, store them in a ventilated plastic bag or lettuce container with a paper towel, to absorb excess moisture.

When to Buy ... Most varieties are available all year.

Different Varieties ...

Arugula (Rocket): small bunches of slender green leaves with a nutty, peppery, bittersweet flavor

Bibb (a variety of *Butterhead*): tiny, tender, crinkly heads with a delicate, mellow flavor

Boston (a variety of *Butterhead*): soft leaves with a smooth, buttery flavor

Chicory: coarse-textured leaves with a bitter flavor

Iceberg: round, compact, evenly-formed head with pale, crisp leaves and a fairly sweet, mild flavor

Leaf (Loose leaf): green or reddish-bronze leaves with a delicate, sweet flavor

Mâche (Lamb's Lettuce or Corn Salad): soft leaves with a mild, nutty flavor

Romaine (Cos): very crisp and crunchy leaves with a slightly nutty, tangy flavor

Sorrel (Dock): crisp leaves with a sour flavor

Watercress: small, crisp leaves with a tart, piquant, peppery flavor

LIMES
■ ■ ■

What to Look For ... firm, heavy, plump, dark green limes with thin skins. Small surface blemishes do not necessarily indicate poor quality; however, avoid limes that are pale, soft, shriveled, or wrinkled. Persian limes are similar in size and shape to lemons. Key limes are smaller and rounder.

How Much to Allow ... One pound of limes (6–8 medium) yields ½–¾ cup of juice. One medium lime yields

1–1½ tablespoons of juice, and about 1 teaspoon of grated peel.

How Long to Keep ... for 2–3 weeks in a plastic bag in the refrigerator.

How to Prepare ... Wash and dry. Cut in half, or into slices or wedges, as desired. For more juice, microwave for 10 seconds.

When to Buy ... all year

MANGOES
■ ■ ■

What to Look For ... firm but not hard mangoes that yield slightly to pressure. They should be clear in color, with no blemishes. The riper the mango, the more yellow-red the skin will be. Avoid mangoes with pitted or spotted skin.

How Much to Allow ... ½ of a small mango, or several slices of a large mango per serving.

How Long to Keep ... for 2–3 days in a plastic bag in the refrigerator.

How to Prepare ... Allow fruit to ripen until slightly soft. Then cut in half vertically and peel away the skin. Cut the flesh off the center stone in long, vertical slices. Be careful of the juice, which causes stains.

When to Buy ... May–September

MELONS

■■■

What to Look For ... firm, plump, heavy melons with a clean, smooth scar at the stem end (with no trace of the stem), indicating that melon has ripened on the vine. A deep, irregular scar, or part of a stem, indicates that it was harvested too early, and is likely to be tough and lacking in flavor. Ripe melons yield to slight pressure and give off a sweet fragrance at both the stem and blossom ends. Soft, sunken spots, whether or not accompanied by mold, indicate decay. If a melon is soft all over, or makes a sloshing sound when shaken, it's overripe. Larger melons usually offer better quality and value. *Cantaloupe* should have a yellowish cast under a thick, well-raised netting, and a fragrant smell. *Persian melon* should have a delicate netting and pale green rind. *Christmas melon* should have a rind with a yellowish cast. *Casaba melon* should look slightly wrinkled and the rind should be a smooth, yellow color. *Honeydew* should be creamy white, very pale green, or yellowish. The rind should feel velvety, not slick. Unlike cantaloupe, honeydew doesn't have a distinctive fragrance to indicate its sweetness. *Watermelon* has a characteristic light-colored patch on the underside, called the "ground spot." It should be yellowish or creamy, but not white. If purchasing watermelon cut, avoid any pieces with a hard, white streak at the center.

How Much to Allow ... about ¼–½ of a small melon, or several slices of a larger melon per serving.

How Long to Keep ... at room temperature until ripe, then most varieties for 3–5 days in the refrigerator. After cutting, wrap in plastic wrap.

How to Prepare ... Wash and dry. Melons with seeds at the center should be cut in half, and the seeds and fibers should be scraped out. Cut into portions, as desired. Melon can be served with or without the rind.

Different Varieties and When to Buy ...

Cantaloupe: Sweet, juicy, salmon-orange flesh. (May–November) Although we call this melon a *cantaloupe*, it is more correctly called a *muskmelon*.

Casaba: Very mild-flavored, creamy-colored flesh. (August–November)

Christmas: Sweet, yellow-green flesh. (November–December)

Crenshaw: Spicy-sweet, salmon-colored flesh. (July–October)

Honeydew: Juicy, sweet, pale green flesh. (June–November)

Persian: Sweet, salmon-colored flesh. (July–October)

Watermelon: Sweet, pinkish-red flesh. (June–September)

MUSHROOMS

■■■

What to Look For ... clean, snowy, plump, dry mushrooms. Caps should be tightly closed around the stems, hiding the gills (the fluted membranes between the caps and the stems). Avoid any that are soft, slimy, or discolored. Select larger mushrooms for stuffing.

How Much to Allow ... ¼–⅓ pound per serving. One pound (30–40 small mushrooms) yields 4–5 cups of sliced raw mushrooms, but cooks down to about 2 cups, since mushrooms have a high water content.

How Long to Keep ... for 2–3 days, refrigerated, with good air circulation. Wrap mushrooms in a paper bag or cardboard container. Do not wash before storing.

How to Prepare ... Trim the bottoms of the stems. Mushrooms absorb water readily, so wash them quickly in cold water and dry them well, or wipe them with a damp towel. If necessary, use a soft brush to clean them.

When to Buy ... November–April (although usually available all year)

NECTARINES

■■■

What to Look For ... smooth, shiny nectarines, with a rosy blush and no green at the stem end. They should be firm, but not hard. Avoid fruit that is spotted, cracked, or bruised. Ripe nectarines will be slightly soft along the "side seam." They should have a fresh, sweet, peachy fragrance.

How Much to Allow ... 1 per serving.

How Long to Keep ... at room temperature until ripe, then for 5–7 days in the refrigerator.

How to Prepare ... Wash nectarines, cut in half, and remove the pit. They do not need to be peeled. Dip the cut sides in lemon juice to prevent darkening.

When to Buy ... June–September

OKRA
■■■

What to Look For ... uniformly green, fresh, tender, crisp pods about 2"–3" long. Avoid okra that is soft, shriveled, punctured, or discolored.

How Much to Allow ... ¼–⅓ pound per serving.

How Long to Keep ... for 2–3 days in a plastic bag in the refrigerator.

How to Prepare ... Wash, trim the ends, and leave whole or slice.

When to Buy ... July–October

ONIONS: DRY
■■■

What to Look For ... onions that are clean, hard, and well shaped, with dry, papery skins, and a bright color. Avoid onions that are moist or soft at the neck, sprouting, hol-

low-feeling, or discolored. Onions with black spots or smudges are moldy. Avoid them as well. Most of the tear-producing gases in onions are at the root end, so cut off that end last when slicing or chopping onions. Remove lingering onion smells from your hands by rubbing them on a piece of stainless steel.

How Much to Allow ... ¼–⅓ pound per serving. A pound yields 2–2½ cups of chopped onions. A medium onion yields ½–¾ cup of chopped onions.

How Long to Keep ... for 2–3 weeks in a cool, dry place, or for 2–3 days in the refrigerator after cutting. Onions sprout sooner if they are kept near potatoes.

How to Prepare ... Cut off the stem end, peel, and rinse. Cut up, slice, or chop as desired. To reduce tears, remove the root end last, after slicing or chopping.

Different Varieties and When to Buy ...

Bermuda: March–June

Red, White, and Yellow: all year

Spanish: August–April

ONIONS: GREEN
■■■

Green Onions are also called "Scallions."

What to Look For ... crisp, tender scallions with necks that are light-colored for 2"–3" above the roots. The tops should be fresh and green. Yellowed or wilted tops indicate that onions are old and tough. The white part should have little or no bulb formation.

How Much to Allow ... ½ of a bunch (3 stalks) per serving.

How Long to Keep ... for 5–7 days in a plastic bag in the refrigerator.

How to Prepare ... Trim roots and any wilted part of the green tops. Use as much or as little of the green tops as desired.

When to Buy ... May–August (although usually available all year)

ORANGES
■■■

What to Look For ... heavy, smooth, thin-skinned oranges. The heavier the orange, the juicier it is likely to be. Avoid oranges with puffy skin or soft spots. Brown patches, called "russeting," are not signs of

inferiority, and are sometimes a signal of sweetness and juiciness. A greenish tinge is also acceptable, and does not indicate that the orange is unripe. (Sometimes oranges re-green after they are picked.) Pointed ends usually mean that the skin is thick and the orange is less juicy.

How Much to Allow ... 1 medium orange, or ⅓ pound per serving. One pound (3 medium oranges) yields ¾–1 cup of juice, or about 1 cup of sections. One medium orange yields ¼–⅓ cup of juice or ⅓ cup of sections, and 2 tablespoons of grated peel.

How Long to Keep ... for 3–5 days at cool room temperature, or for up to 3 weeks in the refrigerator.

How to Prepare ... Rinse and dry. To cut into sections or slices, first trim off the ends. Set one of the cut ends on a cutting board, and carve away the peel in sections, cutting downward and curving around the fruit, as close as possible to the fruit. Then slice away the sections from the membrane, or cut the orange into crosswise slices. A special fruit knife can be purchased that will allow you to scoop the pulp out of the halves of peel so that the shells can be used for stuffing with sweet potatoes, etc. This knife has a small, sharp notch for removing a thin sliver of peel around the orange's "equator." Its curved blade then enables you to loosen the peel from the pulp, and twist the two halves of peel away from the sections of the orange, exposing a whole, peeled orange.

Different Varieties and When to Buy ...

Blood: Thin skin and pinkish-red flesh, with a flavor that almost tastes like berries. (November–March)

Clementine: Honey-sweet. (November–January)

Hamlin: Fairly small; very good for juice; few or no seeds. (October–January)

Mandarin: Loose-skinned, mild, and sweet, with some seeds; Actually a member of the tangerine family. (January–May)

Navel: Sweet and juicy; seedless; best for eating out-of-hand; easy to peel and separate into sections. (November–June)

Parson Brown: Not always the best flavor, and heavily seeded; best for juice. (October–December)

Pineapple: Very juicy and fragrant, but with lots of seeds. (December–February)

Seville: Very sour, and too bitter to eat out-of-hand, but superb for making marmalade and candied peel. (January–February)

Temple: Sweet and juicy; good for eating out-of-hand and juicing; easy to section; actually a cross between an orange and a tangerine. (December–April)

Valencia: Coarse-grained, sweet, and very juicy; few seeds; good for eating out-of-hand, and considered to be the best variety for juicing. (January–November)

PAPAYA
■ ■ ■

What to Look For ... firm, symmetrical, yellow papaya that yields slightly to pressure. Avoid those that are mushy or that have dark spots. Dark green papaya is not likely to ripen properly. One that weighs 2–3 pounds is best. If you add papaya to gelatin, the gelatin won't set properly.

How Much to Allow ... ¼ pound per serving.

How Long to Keep ... at room temperature until ripe, then for 7–10 days in a plastic bag in the refrigerator.

How to Prepare ... Ripen at room temperature until almost completely yellow. Wash and cut in half lengthwise. Scrape out the seeds, and serve like cantaloupe. Peel if desired.

When to Buy ... all year

PARSLEY
■ ■ ■

What to Look For ... bright, green, fresh-looking leaves, without any yellowing or wilting.

How Much to Allow ... Parsley is most often used as a garnish or seasoning.

How Long to Keep ... for up to a week, wrapped first in dry paper towels to absorb moisture, and then in a plastic bag in the refrigerator.

How to Prepare ... Wash and drain well. Remove the tough stems and yellow leaves. Store like a bouquet in a jar of water in the refrigerator, and cover the top with a plastic bag. To use, cut into sprigs for garnish, or chop as desired.

When to Buy ... all year

Different Varieties ...

Curly Leaf: Common supermarket variety; best for garnishing, but somewhat sharp in flavor.

Flat Leaf (Italian): Best for seasoning, as its flavor is mellower than the curly leaf variety.

PARSNIPS
■ ■ ■

What to Look For ... small parsnips that are smooth, firm, and crisp. The color should be a uniform tan-yellow. Very large parsnips are likely to be woody and coarse-textured. Those with soft or shriveled roots will probably be tough and fibrous. Avoid parsnips that are limp, flabby, or split. Dark spots indicate that they might have been frozen; soft spots or gray spots are a sign of internal decay. There will be a lot of waste in the preparation of misshapen parsnips, so look for those that are well-shaped.

How Much to Allow ... ¼–⅓ pound per serving. A bunch weighs about a pound.

How Long to Keep ... for 7–10 days in a plastic bag in the refrigerator. Refrigeration helps to develop the sweetness of parsnips.

How to Prepare ... Scrub well, trim the ends, and peel. Cut or leave whole, as desired.

When to Buy ... October–January

PEACHES
■ ■ ■

What to Look For ... fragrant peaches that are firm but not hard, with a creamy color and a rosy blush. The amount of red blush does not indicate ripeness. There are two varieties: *clingstone,* whose flesh clings to the seed, and *freestone,* whose flesh releases the seed easily. Avoid any with bruises or brown decay spots. Green peaches will not ripen properly. A visible bruise on the surface warns of a large discoloration underneath.

How Much to Allow ... 1 medium peach, or ¼–⅓ pound per serving. One pound (3–4 medium peaches) yields 2 cups of sliced peaches. Two pounds (6–8 medium peaches) make a 9″ pie.

How Long to Keep ... at room temperature until ripe, then for 3–5 days in a plastic bag in the refrigerator. If you find a big basket full of already-ripe peaches at a roadside stand in the summer, go ahead and buy them. Prepare them as directed below, and store them in plastic zipper freezer bags.

How to Prepare ... To make it easier to remove the peel, first use a ladle to lower the peaches into boiling water for about 30 seconds. Plunge briefly into ice water, and then slip off the skin. Cut in half and remove the pits. Slice if desired, and drop into lemon juice or an ascorbic acid product, such as Fruit Fresh, to keep fruit from darkening.

When to Buy ... June–September

PEARS
■ ■ ■

What to Look For ... slightly underripe pears that are firm but not hard, and slightly soft at the stem end. Avoid any with cuts, bruises, soft spots, or discolorations.

How Much to Allow ... 1 medium pear, or ¼–⅓ pound per serving. One pound (3–4 medium pears) yields about 2 cups of sliced pears.

How Long to Keep ... for 7–10 days in the refrigerator, after ripening.

How to Prepare ... Wash and peel if desired. Cut into sections and remove the core, or serve whole.

Different Varieties and When to Buy ...

Anjou: Buttery, juicy, sweet, crisp; stores well; best for eating out-of-hand. (October–May)

Bartlett: Fine-textured, very smooth, sweet, juicy, all-purpose. (August–December)

Bosc: Sweet, not too juicy, but not as smooth as the Bartlett; all-purpose. (September–May)

Clapp Favorite: Fine, sweet, juicy; all-purpose. (August–November)

Comice: Very delicate, smooth, juicy, sweet; best for eating out-of-hand. (October–February)

Easter: Buttery texture; all-purpose. (February–April)

Gorham: Fine, smooth, sweet, juicy; best for eating out-of-hand. (August–November)

Hardy: Very soft. Also called *French Butter* pear; best for eating out-of-hand. (September–October)

Kieffer: Coarse, sandy flesh; best for canning. (September)

Seckel: Gritty, grainy texture; spicy, juicy; best for eating out-of-hand. (August–January)

Winter Nellis: Fine, buttery, spicy, rich; all-purpose. (October–April)

SHELL (ENGLISH) PEAS, SNOW PEAS, AND SUGAR SNAP PEAS
■ ■ ■

What to Look For ... velvety, bright green pods that are small and well-filled, but not bulging. Avoid pods that are withered, yellow, dried-out, damp, soggy, or mildewed. Snow peas will be slightly limp, but sugar snap peas should be crisp.

How Much to Allow ... ½ pound of shell peas in the pod per serving. One pound yields 1 cup of shelled peas. Allow ¼ pound of snow peas or sugar snap peas per serving.

How Long to Keep ... for 3–4 days in a plastic bag in the refrigerator.

How to Prepare ... Shell and rinse English peas. Wash snow peas and sugar snaps, remove the stem ends, and pull off the strings at the sides of the pods.

When to Buy ... April–August

PEPPERS: CHILE
■ ■ ■

What to Look For ... shiny, firm peppers with tight, uncracked skins.

How Much to Allow ... varies according to use.

How Long to Keep ... for up to 3 weeks in a paper bag in the refrigerator.

How to Prepare ... While handling peppers, wear rubber gloves, and be careful not to touch your eyes or tongue, as chile peppers can irritate the skin and cause severe discomfort. Wash hands well after handling peppers.

When to Buy ... all year

Different Varieties ...

Anaheim: medium green; 6″–8″ long and narrow; fairly mild

Ancho: (a dried *Poblano* pepper) dark brick red; 3″–4″ long; mild to hot; fairly sweet

Cayenne: bright red; 3″–5″ long and narrow; extremely hot

Cherry pepper: bright red; 1″–2″ in diameter; mild to medium hot; slightly sweet

Chipotle: a smoked *Jalapeño* pepper

Fresno: light green to bright red; short and similar in flavor to the *Jalapeño*

Güero: any of several varieties of yellow pepper, including the *Hungarian wax;* about 5″ long; pungent

Habanero: light green to bright orange; small and lantern-shaped; extremely hot

Jalapeño: dark green; about 2″ long; very hot; the seeds and veins are even hotter

Pasilla: very dark brown; 6″–8″ long; medium hot

Pepperoncini: bright red; 2″–3″ long; sweet-hot (often used in antipasto trays)

Poblano: very dark green; 4″–5″ long, and 2″–3″ in diameter, tapering to a point; mild to slightly hot; often stuffed

Serrano: bright green, turning to red as it matures; about 2″ long; very hot

PEPPERS: GREEN, RED, OR YELLOW BELL
■ ■ ■

What to Look For ... shiny, firm, thick-fleshed, deep green, bright red, bright yellow, or orange peppers. The leaf cup should be fresh and green, regardless of the color of the pepper. Choose well-shaped, unblemished, fresh-looking peppers with tight, shiny skins and firm flesh. Bleached or blackened spots indicate decay. Avoid peppers that are wrinkled, shriveled, withered, bruised, soft, pale, or limp. They should not have any soft spots.

How Much to Allow ... ½–1 large pepper per serving. One pound (3 large peppers) yields 3–4 cups of chopped peppers.

How Long to Keep ... for 4–5 days in a paper or plastic bag in the refrigerator.

How to Prepare ... Wash and leave whole, or cut in half lengthwise. Scoop out the seeds, core, and white membranes. To peel, cut in half, remove the seeds, and roast peppers cut-side-down in a 500° oven for 15–20 minutes, or until they are blackened and blistered. Then place them in a plastic bag to sweat for about 10–15 minutes. The skin should be loosened and easy to peel off by hand.

When to Buy ... all year

PERSIMMONS
■ ■ ■

What to Look For ... plump, glossy, bright-colored, firm-tender persimmons that are not mushy. The stem caps should be attached.

How Much to Allow ... 1 persimmon per serving.

How Long to Keep ... after ripening, for 1–2 days in the refrigerator.

How to Prepare ... Ripen at room temperature, or wrap in foil and freeze overnight. Remove the stem caps, cut as desired, and remove the seeds.

When to Buy ... October–February

PINEAPPLE
■ ■ ■

What to Look For ... fragrant, firm, heavy pineapple with flat eyes, bright color, and shiny skin. The richer gold the color, the better the pineapple will taste. Pineapple with pointed eyes and a dull color was harvested too soon and won't ripen properly. The center leaves should pull out easily. Avoid fruit that is soft, mushy, tinged with green, or that smells fermented. Dark areas at the base and around the eyes indicate decay. If one side is much lighter in color than the other, the fruit has been sunburned, and the flesh underneath the light area will be hard, dry, and pithy. If you add fresh or frozen pineapple to gelatin, the gelatin won't set properly. However, canned pineapple is fine to add to gelatin.

How Much to Allow ... ⅓ pound per serving. One medium pineapple weighs about 2 pounds and yields about 3 cups of chunks.

How Long to Keep ... After 1–2 days at room temperature, store for 3–5 days in a plastic bag in the refrigerator.

How to Prepare ... Cut off both ends, and then stand the pineapple upright on a cutting board. Slice off the peel in strips about 1½″ wide, with a downward sawing motion, moving around the pineapple until the peel is completely removed. Remove the eyes with the point of a sharp knife. Pineapple can be sliced and served with the core still in place, or the core can be removed first. (Gadgets for peeling and coring pineapple are available at some kitchen specialty stores.) Pineapple can also be cut into quarters or chunks, slicing lengthwise, and removing the core afterward. Pineapple "boats" can be made by cutting the fruit and leaves into lengthwise quarters. Then cut the pulp away from the rind.

When to Buy ... all year, but most plentiful March–June

PLUMS

•••

What to Look For ... plump plums that yield slightly to gentle pressure. Plums that are hard or shriveled are immature and won't ripen properly. Sunburned plums have brownish blotches, and are inferior.

How Much to Allow ... ¼ pound (1–2 plums) per serving. A pound yields about 2 cups of halved and pitted plums.

How Long to Keep ... at room temperature until ripe, then for 3–5 days in a plastic bag in the refrigerator.

How to Prepare ... Wash and serve whole, or cut in half and remove the pits.

Different Varieties and When to Buy ...

European (Damson, Greengage): Smaller and more tart. (May–September)

Japanese (Burbank, Duarte, Santa Rosa): Larger; sweeter. (August–October)

POMEGRANATES

•••

What to Look For ... medium-large fruit that is bright pink or red. It should be firm, but not hard, and shouldn't have any cracks or splits in the skin.

How Much to Allow ... ½ of a pomegranate per serving.

How Long to Keep ... for 2–3 weeks in the refrigerator. Seeds can be refrigerated for up to 2 weeks, or frozen for a year.

How to Prepare ... The seeds and bright red pulp are edible, but the yellowish membrane is very bitter. Wash the fruit and roll it around on a hard surface to release the juice (as you would a lemon or lime). Then pierce it carefully with a skewer, and suck out the juice. Or cut the fruit in half, and scoop out the seeds and their pulpy coating from the inedible light-colored membranes. Be careful, because the juice squirts and stains.

When to Buy ... September–January

POTATOES

•••

What to Look For ... firm, smooth, well-shaped potatoes, with shallow eyes and even color. Avoid any with cracks, withering, sprouts, or green discoloration.

How Much to Allow ... ⅓ pound per serving. One pound yields 1¾–2 cups of mashed potatoes, or 3 of cups cubed potatoes.

How Long to Keep ... for 2–3 weeks (new potatoes for 3–4 days), in a cool, dark, well-ventilated area. Do not refrigerate. Do not store with onions, as it causes the onions to sprout more quickly.

How to Prepare ... Scrub well or peel if desired. Drop cut potatoes into cold water to prevent darkening.

Different Varieties and When to Buy ... Most varieties are sold early as "new potatoes," and as mature potatoes later on.

Long white potatoes: Best for boiling. (May–September and December–March)

Red potatoes: Mainly used for boiling. (all year, but best in the spring)

Round white potatoes: Good for boiling, baking, and french fries. (all year)

Russet (Idaho) potatoes: All-purpose potatoes, perfect for baking. (all year)

PRICKLY PEARS

•••

What to Look For ... plump, unshriveled fruit, with few barbs. It should be shiny and firm, but not hard.

How Much to Allow ... 1 per serving.

How Long to Keep ... at room temperature until ripe, then for up to 3 days in the refrigerator.

How to Prepare ... Use pliers to pull out the sharp spines. Cut off the ends, and peel from top to bottom. Press the pulp through a sieve to remove the seeds.

When to Buy ... August–October

PUMPKIN
■ ■ ■

What to Look For ... small, heavy, firm, unblemished pumpkins, about 6"–7" in diameter, that are bright orange. Shape is unimportant.

How Much to Allow ... 1 pound per serving. One pound yields 1 cup of cooked and mashed pumpkin.

How Long to Keep ... for up to a month at room temperature, or for 2–3 months in the refrigerator.

How to Prepare ... Wash and cut off the top. Scoop out the seeds and membranes, and cut into sections. Remove the rind with a sharp knife.

When to Buy ... October

QUINCES
■ ■ ■

What to Look For ... fruit with a good yellow color that is as unblemished as possible.

How Much to Allow ... One pound (3 medium quinces) yields 1½ cups of chopped quinces.

How Long to Keep ... at room temperature until ripe, and then for 2–3 weeks in a plastic bag in the refrigerator.

How to Prepare ... Quince is prepared much as an apple or pear would be, by washing, quartering, and removing the core. It is quite tart, and is usually peeled and cooked.

When to Buy ... October–December

RADISHES
■ ■ ■

What to Look For ... firm, smooth, crisp radishes. Small cracks, bruises, or skinned areas aren't a serious drawback, but flabby, soft, or spongy radishes will be pithy. Avoid misshapen or withered ones. If the tops are still attached, they should be crisp and green. Remove the tops before storing, since they draw moisture from the radishes.

How Much to Allow ... ½ bunch or bag per serving.

How Long to Keep ... for 1–2 weeks in a plastic bag in the refrigerator.

How to Prepare ... Wash and remove the root and stem ends.

When to Buy ... May–July (although usually available all year)

RHUBARB
■ ■ ■

What to Look For ... deep red rhubarb with firm, crisp stalks. Stalks should be neither too thin nor too thick; oversize stalks tend to be tough and stringy.

How Much to Allow ... One pound (4–8 stalks) yields 2 cups of cut rhubarb. It takes 2½ pounds of rhubarb to make a 9" pie.

How Long to Keep ... for 3–5 days in a plastic bag in the refrigerator.

How to Prepare ... Leaves are poisonous, so be sure to remove any traces. Trim the roots and cut rhubarb into pieces as desired.

When to Buy ... February–July

RUTABAGAS
■ ■ ■

What to Look For ... firm, smooth rutabagas with no wrinkles, and few leaf scars around the crown. Avoid rutabagas with mold on the surface.

How Much to Allow ... ⅓–½ pound per serving. One pound yields 2–2½ cups of cut rutabagas. An average rutabaga weighs 2–3 pounds.

How Long to Keep ... for up to 1 week at cool room temperature, or for 1–2 weeks in a plastic bag in the refrigerator.

How to Prepare ... Peel the thick skin completely away, and rinse.

When to Buy ... October–January

SALSIFY
■ ■ ■

Also called "Oyster Plant."

What to Look For ... firm, unblemished, medium-length roots. Avoid salsify that looks shriveled.

How Much to Allow ... ⅓–½ pound per serving.

How Long to Keep ... for 1–2 weeks in a plastic bag in the refrigerator.

How to Prepare ... Wash well and trim roots and stems. Salsify can be peeled before or after boiling.) Drop cut pieces into cold water to prevent darkening.

When to Buy ... October–November

SHALLOTS
■ ■ ■

The shallot is a cousin of the onion and garlic, with a flavor that is more delicate than either.

What to Look For ... firm, dry shallots; not soft, sprouted, or spongy.

How Much to Allow ... 1 medium shallot weighs about ½ ounce and yields 1 tablespoon of minced shallots.

How Long to Keep ... for up to a month in a cool, well-ventilated place.

How to Prepare ... Remove the papery skin and trim away the roots. Chop or mince as desired.

When to Buy ... all year

SPINACH
■ ■ ■

What to Look For ... crisp, dark green leaves, with no signs of wilting, yellowing, browning, or slime. Leaves can be smooth or crinkly, depending on the variety. Spinach should look stocky, rather than straggly and spindly. It's better to buy fresh spinach loose, but if you buy it packaged, check to be sure that it's not wilted or slimy.

How Much to Allow ... ½–¾ pound per serving if it is to be cooked, or ¼ pound per raw serving. One pound yields 3–4 cups of raw leaves, or 1½ cups of cooked spinach.

How Long to Keep ... for 2–3 days in a plastic bag in the refrigerator.

How to Prepare ... Remove the tough stems and discard any bruised or damaged leaves. Wash very thoroughly in cold water. Swish the leaves around, and then press them down in the water, using a pumping motion, to dislodge all the dirt and sand. It will probably be necessary to change the water several times. Rinse thoroughly and drain. Spinach is notoriously sandy and dirty, so it may take several washings to get it completely cleaned. Otherwise, you may end up with a gritty salad!

When to Buy ... March–July (although usually available all year)

SQUASH:
SUMMER VARIETIES
■ ■ ■

Varieties include Yellow Crookneck, Yellow Straightneck, and Pattypan.

What to Look For ... squash that is small (crookneck or straightneck should be no more than 4"–6" long; pattypan should be no more than 3" in diameter). All varieties of summer squash should be tender and thin-skinned. The skin should be brightly colored and should pierce easily with a fingernail. Avoid any squash that is bruised, soft, or flabby.

How Much to Allow ... ½ pound per serving.

How Long to Keep ... for 5–7 days in a plastic bag in the refrigerator.

How to Prepare ... Wash or scrub well. Remove the stems and blossom ends, as well as any small blemishes. Slice or cut up as desired.

When to Buy ... April–September (although usually available all year)

SQUASH: WINTER VARIETIES
■ ■ ■

Varieties include Acorn, Buttercup, Butternut, Hubbard, Spaghetti, and Turban.

What to Look For ... firm, heavy squash with a hard, smooth, unblemished rind. Avoid squash with cracks, dried-up stems, or with watery or soft spots. Acorn squash should be dark green.

How Much to Allow ... ½ pound per serving. One pound yields about a cup of mashed squash.

How Long to Keep ... for 2 weeks or more, depending on the variety, in a cool, dark, well-ventilated place.

How to Prepare ... Wash and cut squash in half. Remove the seeds and fibers, and cut squash into portions. The rind may be removed before or after cooking, or the squash may be served with its rind, if desired.

When to Buy ... Most plentiful during the fall and winter months.

STAR FRUIT
■ ■ ■

Also called "Carambola."

What to Look For ... glossy, shiny, moist fruit with a golden-yellow color.

How Much to Allow ... depending on its size, about 1 fruit per person.

How Long to Keep ... at room temperature until ripe, then for up to a week in a plastic bag in the refrigerator.

How to Prepare ... Wash and slice. The peel is edible.

When to Buy ... August–February

SWEET POTATOES
■ ■ ■

What to Look For ... small, firm, heavy, well-shaped sweet potatoes of uniform rose to bronze color. They should have smooth skin, and they should taper at both ends. Avoid sweet potatoes that are extensively cracked, or any that are bruised, scarred, soft, shriveled, withered, or blackened.

How Much to Allow ... 1 medium sweet potato, or ⅓ pound per serving. One pound of sweet potatoes (3 medium) yields 1¾–2 cups of mashed sweet potatoes, or 3 cups of cubed sweet potatoes.

How Long to Keep ... for up to 2 weeks in a cool, dark, well-ventilated place.

How to Prepare ... Before cooking, scrub and peel, if desired. Drop cut pieces in cold water to prevent darkening.

When to Buy ... Different varieties are available throughout the year.

SWISS CHARD
■ ■ ■

What to Look For ... chard with crisp, green leaves and fleshy stalks. Avoid if the leaves are wilted, yellowed, or discolored.

How Much to Allow ... about ⅓ pound per serving. An average bunch weighs about a pound.

How Long to Keep ... for 2–3 days in a plastic bag in the refrigerator.

How to Prepare ... Wash and remove the leaves from the ribs. The ribs can be cut into smaller pieces. (They take longer to cook than the leaves.)

When to Buy ... June–October

TANGERINES
■ ■ ■

Also called "Mandarin Oranges."

What to Look For ... plump, heavy, bright, lustrous, firm tangerines. Skin is normally loose; however, any pronounced softening at the stem end is a sign of decay.

How Much to Allow ... 1 per serving.

How Long to Keep ... for 1–2 weeks at room temperature, or for up to a month in the refrigerator.

How to Prepare ... Wash and remove skins. They slip off easily.

When to Buy ... November–April

TOMATOES

...

What to Look For ... heavy, plump, smooth, firm tomatoes that yield to gentle pressure. The color should be bright, whether the tomatoes are red, yellow, or green. Scars, roughness, or well-healed cuts on the skin should not affect the internal quality. Avoid tomatoes that are mushy, light for their size, very hard, or that show evidence of worm holes or oozing.

How Much to Allow ... 1/3–1/2 pound per serving. One pound of tomatoes (3 medium globe tomatoes, 7–8 plum tomatoes, or about 30 cherry tomatoes) yields 1–1½ cups of raw pulp (after peeling and removing the seeds), which cooks down to about ¾ cup of pulp.

How Long to Keep ... ripen at room temperature, and then use within several days. Refrigeration destroys the flavor.

How to Prepare ... Wash and remove the core. Although the peel is edible, it's simple to remove it. First, use the point of a sharp knife to cut a small cone out of the top of the tomato, to remove the stem scar. Then use a sharp vegetable peeler and a sawing motion to remove the peel in strips. It sounds like a lot of work, but it makes all the difference in the quality of a stuffed tomato or a fresh tomato sandwich! If you have several tomatoes to peel, use this method: Make a small "x" at the bottom of each tomato with a sharp knife. Using a ladle, lower the tomatoes one by one into boiling water for 15 seconds. Remove them from the boiling water and plunge them into cold water. The skins will slip off easily.

When to Buy ... May–August (Hothouse tomatoes are usually available all year, but vine-ripened tomatoes taste much better.) Roma tomatoes are a suitable fresh-tasting alternative when vine-ripened tomatoes are out of season. The world's best tomatoes usually come from a truck stand or farmer's market, where they have escaped the refrigeration that ruins good tomatoes.

TURNIPS

...

What to Look For ... firm, smooth, heavy turnips, no larger than 2", with unblemished skin and few leaf scars or roots. If the greens are attached, they should be tender and crisp. Soft or shriveled turnips are likely to be tough and pithy, with a strong flavor.

How Much to Allow ... ¼ pound (1 medium turnip) per serving.

How Long to Keep ... for 5–7 days in the refrigerator.

How to Prepare ... Wash and remove the thick skin with a sharp knife.

When to Buy ... October–January (although usually available all year)

ZUCCHINI

...

What to Look For ... firm, heavy, small zucchini (no more than 7"–8" long), with tender, thin skin that pierces easily with a fingernail. Avoid zucchini that is cut, scraped, bruised, soft, or flabby.

How Much to Allow ... 1/3 pound (1 medium zucchini) per serving. One medium zucchini yields about 2 cups of slices, or about 1½ cups of shredded zucchini.

How Long to Keep ... for 3–4 days in a plastic bag in the refrigerator.

How to Prepare ... Wash or scrub well. Remove the ends and slice or cut as desired.

When to Buy ... May–September

Food Storage

■ ■ ■

AMI = "According to Manufacturer's Instructions"
AO = "After Opening"
ASD = "After Sell-By (or Use-By) Date"
NR = "Not Recommended"
USD = "Until Sell-By (or Use-By) Date"

PRODUCT	PANTRY	REFRIG.	FREEZER	COMMENTS
Almonds: In Shell	1 year	1 year	1 year	Store in plastic bag or tightly covered container.
Almonds: Shelled		9 months	1 year	Store in plastic bag or tightly covered container.
Apple Pie Filling	1 year			
Apple Pie Filling: AO		1–2 weeks		Cover tightly.
Apples: Canned	1 year			
Apples: Canned: AO		1–2 weeks		Cover tightly.
Apples: Fresh	2–3 days	2–4 weeks	10–12 months	Dry well before storing. Refrigerate in plastic.
Applesauce: Canned	1 year			
Applesauce: Canned: AO		1–2 weeks		Cover tightly.
Apricots: Canned	1 year			
Apricots: Canned: AO		3–5 days		Cover tightly.
Apricots: Fresh	Until Ripe	2–3 days	10–12 months	Refrigerate in plastic.
Arrowroot	1 year			
Artichoke Hearts: Canned	1 year			
Artichoke Hearts: Canned: AO		4 days		Cover tightly.
Artichokes: Fresh	1–2 days	1 week	6–8 months	Refrigerate in plastic.
Arugula		3 days	NR	Refrigerate in plastic.
Asian Pears	Until Ripe	2–4 weeks	10–12 months	Treat like apples.
Asparagus: Canned	6 months			
Asparagus: Canned: AO		2–3 days		Cover tightly.
Asparagus: Fresh		4–5 days	8–10 months	Before refrigerating, wrap cut ends in damp paper towels; then overwrap in plastic.

PRODUCT	PANTRY	REFRIG.	FREEZER	COMMENTS
Avocados	Until Ripe	2–3 days*	3–6 months	Refrigerate after ripe. *Will keep in refrigerator for up to 1 week after ripening if avocados are going to be mashed or puréed, but will not hold their shape for slicing.
Bacon: Canadian		3–4 days	1 month	Wrap in plastic; store in coldest part of refrigerator.
Bacon: Slab		2–3 weeks	NR	Wrap in plastic; store in coldest part of refrigerator.
Bacon: Sliced		1 week ASD	NR	Wrap in plastic; store in coldest part of refrigerator.
Baking Powder	18 months or USD			
Baking Powder: AO	3 months			To check for freshness, sprinkle a little of the baking powder on vinegar; if it foams, it's still good.
Baking Soda	2 years			
Baking Soda: AO	6 months			Cover tightly or store opened box in plastic bag.
Bananas: Whole	Until Ripe	2–3 days	3 months	Refrigerate only after fully ripened. Although skin will darken, fruit will be fine, especially for cooking.
Barbecue Sauce	12–18 months			
Barbecue Sauce: AO	1 month	1 year		Refrigerate after opening for longer storage.
Basil: Fresh		1–2 days		Wrap in plastic.
Beans: Cranberry: Fresh		1–2 days	10–12 months	Wrap in plastic.
Beans: Dried	1 year			Some varieties keep longer.
Beans: Fava: Fresh		1–2 days	10–12 months	Wrap in plastic.
Beans: Green: Canned	6 months			
Beans: Green: Canned: AO		3–4 days		Cover tightly.
Beans: Green: Fresh		4–5 days	10–12 months	Refrigerate in plastic. Wash just before using.
Beans: Italian		4–5 days	10–12 months	Wrap in plastic. Wash just before using.
Beans: Lima: Canned	1 year			
Beans: Lima: Canned: AO		2–3 days		Cover tightly.
Beans: Lima: Fresh		1–2 days	10–12 months	Refrigerate in plastic.
Beans: Wax		4–5 days	10–12 months	Refrigerate in plastic. Wash just before using.
Beef: Ground		1 day	2–4 months	Refrigerate in store wrap. Freeze in freezer wrap.
Beef Ribs, Roasts, and Steaks		3 days	6–12 months	Refrigerate in store wrap. Freeze in freezer wrap.
Beef Stew Meat		1–2 days	2–4 months	Refrigerate in store wrap. Freeze in freezer wrap.
Beets: Canned	6 months			
Beets: Canned: AO		1 week		Cover tightly.
Beets: Fresh	1 day	7–10 days	10–12 months	Remove leafy tops. Refrigerate in plastic.
Beets: Pickled	12–18 months			
Beets: Pickled: AO		1–2 weeks		Cover tightly.
Berries (Also see specific listings)		1–2 days		Do not wash before refrigerating.
Biscuit Mix	15 months			Cover tightly after opening.
Biscuit Mix: AO	USD			Seal or cover tightly.
Blackberries		1–2 days	10–12 months	Remove decayed fruit. Store uncovered, without washing. To avoid bruising, store in single layer.
Black-eyed Peas: Fresh		1–2 days	10–12 months	Refrigerate in plastic.
Blueberries		1–2 weeks	1 year	Sort and remove decayed fruit. Do not wash before storing. Cover with plastic; store in rigid container.
Bok Choy		3–4 days	10–12 months	Refrigerate in plastic.

PRODUCT	PANTRY	REFRIG.	FREEZER	COMMENTS
Bones, Meat		1–2 days	6 months	Wrap tightly.
Bouillon Cubes and Crystals	1 year			Cover tightly.
Brazil Nuts: In Shell		9 months	9 months	Store in plastic bag or tightly covered container.
Brazil Nuts: Shelled		9 months	9 months	Store in plastic bag or tightly covered container.
Bread Crumbs: Dried		6 months	1 year	Seal tightly in plastic bag.
Bread: French: Unsliced	2 days		3 months	Wrap in paper or freeze in plastic wrap.
Bread Mix	12–18 months			
Bread Mix: AO	USD			Seal or cover tightly.
Bread: Non-Yeast: Banana, etc.	2–4 days	4–7 days	3 months	Wrap tightly.
Bread: Pita	2–4 days	4–7 days	4 months	Wrap tightly.
Bread: Yeast: Sliced	2–4 days	4–7 days	4 months	Wrap tightly.
Bread: Yeast: Unsliced	5–7 days	1–2 weeks	6–9 months	Wrap tightly.
Broccoli		3–5 days	10–12 months	Refrigerate in perforated plastic.
Brownie Mix	12–18 months			
Brownie Mix: AO	USD			Seal or cover tightly.
Brussels Sprouts		3–5 days	10–12 months	Refrigerate in plastic.
Butter	1–3 days	2–3 weeks ASD	6–9 months	Cover or wrap tightly. Salted butter keeps longer than unsalted butter.
Butter: Clarified		3 months		Store in tightly covered container.
Buttermilk		1–2 weeks ASD	3 months	Store in closed container. After freezing, suitable only for cooking.
Cabbage: Chinese		4–5 days	10–12 months	Refrigerate in plastic.
Cabbage: Cut or Shredded		1–2 days	10–12 months	Refrigerate in plastic. Frozen cabbage loses its texture, and cannot be used for slaw.
Cabbage: Whole Head		1–2 weeks		Refrigerate unwashed, uncut cabbage in plastic.
Cake: Angel, Sponge, Frosted	2 days	3 days	2 months	Store in airtight container.
Cake: Butter Type	2 days	3 days	4–6 months	Store in airtight container.
Cake: Fruitcake	1 week	2 days	2 years	Store in airtight container.
Cake Mix	12–18 months			
Cake Mix: AO	USD			Seal or cover tightly.
Cake: Whipped-Cream Type		2 days		Store in airtight container.
Candy: Chocolate; Filled	3 months	3 months	1 year	Store in cool, dry place in airtight container.
Candy: Commercially Made	1 year	1 year	1 year	Refrigerate in hot, humid weather.
Candy: Homemade	1 month*	1 month	1 year	Store in airtight container. *Divinity only keeps for 2–3 days at room temperature.
Cantaloupe: Cut		1–2 days	10–12 months	Wrap cut pieces in plastic.
Cantaloupe: Whole	Until Ripe	3–5 days		Refrigerate after ripe.
Carrots		1–2 weeks	10–12 months	Remove leafy tops; store in plastic, away from apples.
Casaba Melon: Cut		2 days	10–12 months	Wrap cut pieces in plastic.
Casaba Melon: Whole	Until Ripe	7–10 days		Refrigerate after ripe.
Cashews: Shelled		6 months	9 months	Store in plastic bag or tightly covered container.
Casseroles			3–4 months	Freeze casseroles with meat no longer than 2–3 months.
Cauliflower		4–7 days	10–12 months	Refrigerate in plastic. Wash just before using.
Celeriac		2–3 days	NR	Wrap in plastic.

PRODUCT	PANTRY	REFRIG.	FREEZER	COMMENTS
Celery		1–2 weeks	10–12 months	Sprinkle with water and refrigerate in plastic.
Cereal: Instant Hot	1 year			
Cereal: Ready to Eat	6–12 months			
Cereal: Ready to Eat: AO	2–3 months			Refold package liner tightly or cover tightly.
Cheese: American		USD	NR	Store in original container or wrap tightly in plastic.
Cheese: Blue		2–4 weeks	6 months	Wrap in plastic or store in covered container.
Cheese: Boursin		1 week or USD	NR	Store in original packaging.
Cheese: Boursin: AO		2–3 days	NR	Wrap in plastic.
Cheese: Cold Pack		USD	6 months	Wrap tightly in plastic, or store in covered container.
Cheese: Cottage		1 week ASD	NR	Cover tightly.
Cheese: Cream or Neufchâtel		2 weeks ASD	NR	Wrap tightly in plastic or foil.
Cheese: Farmer's		2 weeks	6 months	Wrap tightly in plastic or foil.
Cheese: Feta		2–3 months	NR	Pack in salt water. To reduce saltiness, soak in milk.
Cheese: Firm: Cut: Cheddar, etc.		1–2 months		Wrap in plastic or foil. For longer storage, wrap first in cheesecloth soaked in vinegar.
Cheese: Firm: Sliced: Cheddar, etc.		2 weeks		Wrap tightly in plastic or foil.
Cheese: Firm: Whole: Cheddar, etc.		6–9 months	6–9 months	Cheese develops stronger flavor as it ages.
Cheese: Goat		7–10 days	NR	Wrap tightly or store in a jar. Fresh goat cheese keeps for several weeks, but flavor gets stronger.
Cheese: Hard: Grated: Parmesan, etc.		1 year		Store in original container or wrap tightly in plastic.
Cheese: Hard: Wedge: Parmesan, etc.		2–6 months	6 months	Wrap tightly in plastic or foil.
Cheese: Mozzarella: Dry		2–3 weeks	6 months	Wrap tightly in plastic or foil.
Cheese: Mozzarella: Fresh		2–3 days	NR	Wrap tightly in plastic or foil.
Cheese: Processed		USD		Store in original packaging.
Cheese: Processed: AO		3–4 weeks		Wrap tightly in plastic or foil.
Cheese: Ricotta		1 week ASD	6 months	Store in tightly covered container. Discard if it turns yellowish.
Cheese: Semisoft: Muenster, etc.		3–4 weeks	6 months	Wrap tightly in plastic. Freezing reduces quality of texture somewhat, but is still suitable for cooking.
Cheese: Soft: Brie, etc.: Wedge	Up to 12 hours	2–3 days	NR	Wrap tightly. Inside should be creamy-soft. If it has hard, white streaks, it's not ripe enough, and won't ripen properly. If it's runny, it's overripe and will probably taste bitter.
Cheese: Soft: Brie, etc.: Whole		2–3 days after ripe	NR	When purchased, should not smell like ammonia. Leave in original packaging until ready to serve. When ripe, should feel springy, not hard. Once cut, it will not ripen further.
Cheese Spread (Processed)	USD	USD		Store in original container.
Cheese Spread (Processed): AO		3–4 weeks		Wrap or cover tightly.
Cherries: Canned	1 year			
Cherries: Canned: AO		1 week		Cover tightly.
Cherries: Fresh	NR	2–4 days	10–12 months	Do not wash before refrigerating. Refrigerate in plastic. Remove pits before freezing.
Cherries: Maraschino	12–18 months			
Cherries: Maraschino: AO		6–12 months		Cover tightly.
Chestnuts: In Shell		4–6 months		Store in perforated plastic bag.

PRODUCT	PANTRY	REFRIG.	FREEZER	COMMENTS
Chestnuts: Shelled		4–5 days	9–12 months	Make an "x" on flat end of each shell. Then boil chestnuts for 15 minutes, drain, and peel. Store in airtight container.
Chicken: Canned	12–18 months			
Chicken: Canned: AO		2–3 days	2–3 months	Cover tightly.
Chicken: Cooked		2–3 days	3–4 months	Cover tightly.
Chicken: Parts		1–2 days	6 months	Wrap in plastic or foil.
Chicken: Rotisserie		3–4 days	4 months	Wrap in plastic or foil.
Chicken: Smoked		2–3 days	6 months	Wrap in plastic or foil.
Chicken: Whole		1–2 days	4 months	Wrap in plastic or foil.
Chicken Salad		2–3 days		Cover tightly.
Chicory		3–5 days	NR	Rinse; dry thoroughly. Store in plastic with a paper towel to absorb moisture. Store away from fresh fruits, especially apples, which will cause browning.
Chili Sauce	12–18 months			
Chili Sauce: AO	1 month	6 months		Refrigerate for longer storage.
Chips	2 months, or USD			
Chips: AO	1–2 weeks			Seal tightly or store in airtight container.
Chocolate Morsels	2 months			Store in plastic and keep cool.
Chocolate: Pre-melted	18 months			Store in original packets and keep cool.
Chocolate: Semisweet	18 months	18 months	18 months	Keep cool.
Chocolate: Unsweetened	1 year	1 year	1 year	Keep cool.
Chocolate Syrup	1 year	1 year		Refrigerate after opening.
Clams: Live		1 day		Cover with a wet cloth.
Clams: Shucked		1 day	3 months	Cover tightly.
Cocktail Sauce	12–18 months			
Cocktail Sauce: AO	1 month	6 months		Refrigerate for longer storage.
Cocoa: Baking Chocolate	18 months			Keep cool.
Cocoa Mix: Beverage	1 year			
Coconut: Canned: Shredded	1 year			
Coconut: Canned: Shredded: AO		5–7 days	6 months	Wrap or cover tightly.
Coconut: Dried: Shredded	6 months			
Coconut: Dried: Shredded: AO		3–4 weeks	6 months	Wrap or cover tightly.
Coconut: Fresh: Cut		4–5 days	6 months	Wrap tightly.
Coconut: Fresh: Shredded			6 months	Wrap tightly.
Coconut: Fresh: Whole	1 week	3–4 days		
Coconut Milk or Water		2 days		Cover tightly.
Coffee: Brewed		1 day		Cover tightly.
Coffee: Ground: Canned	1–2 years			
Coffee: Ground: Canned: AO		2 weeks	2 weeks	Store in airtight container.
Coffee: Instant	1 year			
Coffee: Instant: AO	2–3 months			Cover tightly.
Coffee Beans: Ground		1 week	2 weeks	Store in airtight container.
Coffee Beans: Whole: Roasted	1–2 weeks	3–4 weeks	3–4 months	Beans keep longer if stored in vacuum bag.
Cold Cuts: AO or Deli-Wrapped		2–5 days	NR	Refer to labels for storage instructions. Overwrap in plastic and store in coldest part of refrigerator.

PRODUCT	PANTRY	REFRIG.	FREEZER	COMMENTS
Cold Cuts: Vacuum-Packed		5–7 days ASD	NR	Keep in original packaging or plastic and store in coldest part of refrigerator.
Cookies	1–2 weeks	1–2 weeks	9–12 months	Wrap tightly or store in airtight container.
Corn: Canned	1 year			
Corn: Canned: AO		2–3 days		Cover tightly.
Corn: Fresh		1 day	10–12 months	Refrigerate in plastic. If you have to store corn more than 1 day, cook it first, and then cut it off the cob.
Corned Beef: Cooked		3–5 days	2 months	Wrap in plastic or foil.
Corned Beef: Uncooked		1 week ASD	1 month	Store in vacuum pack or wrap in plastic or foil.
Cornmeal: Masa Harina	6–9 months	1 year	1 year	Keep tightly closed. Refrigerate for longer storage.
Cornmeal: Stone-ground	1 month	2–3 months	2–3 months	Keep tightly closed. Refrigerate for longer storage.
Cornstarch	18 months			Keep tightly closed.
Corn Syrup	USD			
Corn Syrup: AO	4–6 months			Cover tightly.
Crab: Canned	6 months			
Crab: Cooked		1–2 days	3 months	Wrap tightly.
Crab: Live		1 day		Store in special insulated carton.
Crab: Vacuum-Packed		1 month		
Cracker Crumbs		1 year		Seal tightly in plastic bag
Crackers and Crisp Breads	6 months			
Crackers and Crisp Breads: AO	1 month	3–4 months		Seal tightly or store in airtight container.
Cranberries: Cooked		1 month		Store in covered container.
Cranberries: Fresh		1 month	10–12 months	Store in plastic bag.
Cream: Half and Half		1–4 days ASD	4 months	Do not pour leftover cream back into carton.
Cream: Ultra-pasteurized		3–4 days ASD	NR	
Cream: Ultra-pasteurized: AO		1–4 days	NR	Cover tightly.
Cream: Whipped: Aerosol: Dairy		3–4 weeks ASD	NR	Do not freeze.
Cream: Whipped: Aerosol: Non-dairy		2–3 months ASD	NR	Do not freeze.
Cream: Whipped: Homemade		1 day	1 month	Freeze in dollops and store in plastic.
Creamer: Non-dairy: Liquid		2–3 weeks	1–2 years	Cover tightly after opening.
Creamer: Non-dairy: Powdered	2 years			Refrigeration not necessary.
Creamer: Non-dairy: Powdered: AO	1 year			Refrigeration not necessary.
Cream of Tartar	1 year			Keep tightly covered in a cool, dry place.
Crème Fraîche: Commercial		3–4 weeks		Cover tightly.
Crème Fraîche: Homemade		7–10 days		Cover tightly.
Crenshaw Melon: Cut		2–3 days	10–12 months	Wrap cut pieces in plastic.
Crenshaw Melon: Whole	Until Ripe	1–2 weeks		Refrigerate after ripe.
Cucumbers		4–5 days	NR	Wrap in plastic.
Currants: Fresh		1–2 days	10–12 months	Refrigerate uncovered. Freeze in plastic bag.
Custard: Homemade		2–3 days		Refrigerate covered.
Danish Pastry	2–3 days	2–3 days	3 months	Store in tightly closed plastic bag.
Dates: Hard		1 year	Several years	Store in tightly closed plastic bag.
Dates: Soft		2–3 weeks	1 year	Store in tightly closed plastic bag.
Deli Meats: AO or Deli-Wrapped		2–5 days	1 month	Refer to labels for storage instructions. Overwrap in plastic and store in coldest part of refrigerator.

PRODUCT	PANTRY	REFRIG.	FREEZER	COMMENTS
Deli Meats: Vacuum-Packed		5–7 days ASD	2 months	Store in original package or plastic.
Dough: Biscuit (Canned)		USD	NR	Do not freeze.
Dough: Biscuit (Commercially Frozen)			3–4 weeks	
Dough: Bread (Commercially Frozen)			USD	Store in original packaging.
Dough: Cookie (Commercial)		USD	AMI	Freeze only if manufacturer recommends.
Dough: Cookie (Homemade)			9–12 months	Wrap tightly.
Doughnuts: Yeast	2–3 days	2–days	3 months	Wrap tightly.
Dressing: See Salad Dressing; Stuffing				
Duck (Commercially Packaged)		2 days	6 months or USD	Store in original packaging.
Eggnog: Commercial		3–5 days ASD	6 months	Keep chilled.
Eggnog: Homemade		1 day	6 months	Keep chilled.
Eggplant	1–2 days	3–4 days	6–8 months	Refrigerate in plastic.
Eggs: Hard-cooked: Peeled		5 days	NR	Store in covered container.
Eggs: Hard-cooked: Unpeeled		1 week	NR*	Store uncovered. *Do not freeze.
Eggs: In Shell		3 weeks ASD	NR*	*Do not freeze. Discard cracked eggs. Store with pointed ends down. Do not wash before storing.
Eggs: Out of Shell: Whole		2–3 days	9 months	Store in covered container. To freeze, pierce yolks and stir gently to mix with whites.
Egg Salads and Stuffed Eggs		1 day		Cover tightly.
Egg Substitutes		1 week	1 year	
Egg Substitutes: AO		3 days	NR	Cover tightly.
Egg Whites		7–10 days	1 year	Store in covered container.
Egg Yolks		2–3 days	9 months	Cover with water; then cover and store. To freeze, pierce yolks and stir gently.
Egg Yolks: Hard-cooked		4–5 days	NR	Store in airtight container.
Endive: Belgian		1 day	NR	Wrap in damp paper towel and then in plastic bag. Rinse before serving.
Endive: Curly		3–5 days	NR	Rinse; dry thoroughly. Wrap in plastic with a paper towel to absorb moisture. Store away from apples.
Escarole		3–5 days	NR	Rinse; dry thoroughly. Wrap in plastic with a paper towel to absorb moisture. Store away from apples.
Extracts	6 months			
Fennel		7–10 days	10–12 months	Wrap in plastic.
Figs: Canned		1 year		
Figs: Canned: AO			1 week	Cover tightly.
Figs: Fresh		1–2 days	10–12 months	Refrigerate in plastic.
Fish: Canned	12–18 months			
Fish: Canned: AO		2–3 days	2–3 months	Cover tightly.
Fish: Cooked		2 days	3 months	Cover tightly.
Fish: Dried or Pickled		1 week	6 months	Wrap tightly.
Fish: Smoked: Sliced		3–4 days		Wrap tightly.
Fish: Smoked: Whole		1–2 weeks		Wrap tightly.
Fish: Uncooked: Fatty		1 day	3 months	Wrap tightly.
Fish: Uncooked: Lean		1 day	6 months	Wrap tightly.
Fish Salad		1 day	NR	Cover tightly.
Flour: White	6–8 months	1 year	1 year	Refrigerate for longer storage.

PRODUCT	PANTRY	REFRIG.	FREEZER	COMMENTS
Flour: White: AO	6–8 months	1 year	1 year	Refrigerate after opening for longer storage.
Flour: Whole Wheat	1 month	6–8 months	1 year	Best to refrigerate.
Flour: Whole Wheat: AO		6–8 months	1 year	Cover tightly.
Formula: Infant	12–18 months			
Formula: Infant: AO		2 days		Cover tightly. Discard leftovers after feeding.
Frankfurters		5–7 days ASD	2 months	
Frankfurters: AO		1 week	2 months	Keep in original packaging or wrap in plastic.
Fruit: Canned: Citrus	6–12 months			
Fruit: Canned: Citrus: AO		3–5 days		Cover tightly.
Fruit: Canned: Non-citrus	12–18 months			
Fruit: Canned: Non-citrus: AO		3–5 days		Cover tightly.
Fruit: Dried	1 month	6–12 months		Wrap tightly after opening.
Fruit: Pickled	12–18 months			
Fruit: Pickled: AO		4–8 weeks		Cover tightly.
Fruit Preserves	12–18 months			Refrigerate after opening.
Fruit Preserves: AO		6 months		Cover tightly.
Game		1–2 days	6–9 months	Wrap tightly.
Game Birds		1–2 days	6–9 months	Wrap tightly.
Garlic: Chopped or Minced		2–3 months	NR	Keep in a small glass jar. If homemade, cover with oil.
Garlic: Whole	1–8 weeks	Not necessary	NR	Store in cool, dry place. Discard bitter green parts.
Gelatin: Flavored	1 year			
Gelatin: Unflavored	3 years			
Giblets		1 day	2–3 months	Store in airtight container.
Ginger: Fresh	6 months	2–3 weeks	1 month	Will last for 6 months at room temperature in a jar submerged in white wine or sherry.
Goose (Commercially Packaged)		2–3 days or USD	4–6 months or USD	Store in original packaging.
Gooseberries		2–3 days	10–12 months	Cover with plastic and store in a rigid container.
Grapefruit: Cut		2–3 days	10–12 months	Wrap tightly in plastic.
Grapefruit: Whole	1 week	Up to 2 weeks		Refrigerate in perforated plastic bag.
Grapes	1 day	3–5 days	10–12 months	Sort; remove decayed grapes. Wrap in plastic, but do not wash until ready to serve.
Gravy		1–2 days	2–3 months	Cover tightly.
Greens: Collard, Mustard, Turnip		1–2 days	10–12 months	Refrigerate in plastic.
Grits	1 year			
Guavas	Until ripe	7–10 days	10–12 months	Refrigerate in vegetable crisper after ripe.
Ham: Canned	6–12 months			
Ham: Canned: AO		5–7 days	1 month	Wrap in plastic or foil.
Ham: Dry-Cured: Sliced		3–5 days	1 month	Country Ham, Smithfield Ham, Virginia Ham
Ham: Dry-Cured: Whole		6–12 months		Country Ham, Smithfield Ham, Virginia Ham
Ham: Sugar-Cured: Half or Whole: Cooked		3–5 days	1 month	Wrap in plastic or foil.
Ham: Sugar-Cured: Half or Whole: Uncooked		1 week	3 months	Wrap in plastic or foil.
Ham Salad		2–3 days		Cover tightly.
Herbs: Dried: Ground or Crushed	6 months			Store in cool, dark place.
Herbs: Dried: Whole	1 year			Store in cool, dark place.

PRODUCT	PANTRY	REFRIG.	FREEZER	COMMENTS
Herbs: Fresh		Up to 1 week	2–4 months	Refrigerate in plastic or place the stems in a small jar of water, covered with a plastic bag secured with a rubber band.
Honey	Indefinitely			
Honey: AO	6 months			
Honeydew Melon: Cut		3–5 days	10–12 months	Wrap cut pieces in plastic.
Honeydew Melon: Whole	Until Ripe	1 week		Refrigerate after ripe.
Horseradish: Fresh		2–3 weeks	NR	Refrigerate in plastic.
Horseradish: Prepared		USD		
Horseradish: Prepared: AO		2–3 months		Prepared horseradish loses its potency as it ages.
Hot Dogs		5–7 days ASD	2 months	
Hot Dogs: AO		1 week	2 months	Keep in original packaging or wrap in plastic.
Ice Cream and Frozen Desserts			1–2 months	Keep frozen solid.
Jam and Jelly	1 year			
Jam and Jelly: AO		6 months		Cover tightly.
Jerusalem Artichokes (Sunchokes)		1–2 weeks	NR	Wrap in plastic.
Jícama		1–2 weeks	NR	Wrap in plastic.
Juice: Bottled: Citrus	1 year			
Juice: Bottled: Citrus: AO		7–10 days		Store in covered container.
Juice: Bottled: Non-citrus	1 year			
Juice: Bottled: Non-citrus: AO		7–10 days		Store in covered container.
Juice: Canned: Citrus	6 months			
Juice: Canned: Citrus: AO		7–10 days		Transfer to covered glass or plastic container.
Juice: Canned: Non-citrus	1 year			
Juice: Canned: Non-citrus: AO		7–10 days		Transfer to covered glass or plastic container.
Juice: Carton:		3 weeks	8–12 months	
Juice: Carton: AO:		7–10 days		Store in covered container.
Juice: Frozen			8–12 months	
Juice: Frozen: Prepared		7–10 days		Store in covered glass or plastic container.
Juice Boxes	4–6 months		8–12 months	
Juice Boxes: AO		7–10 days		Store in original container.
Kale		2–3 days	10–12 months	
Ketchup	1 year			
Ketchup: AO	1 month	6 months		Refrigerate for longer storage.
Kiwi Fruit	Until Ripe	2 weeks	10–12 months	Refrigerate after ripe.
Lamb: Ground		1 day	3–4 months	Refrigerate in store wrap. Freeze in freezer wrap.
Lamb Chops, Ribs, and Roasts		3 days	6–9 months	Refrigerate in store wrap. Freeze in freezer wrap.
Lamb Stew Meat		1–2 days	3–4 months	Refrigerate in store wrap. Freeze in freezer wrap.
Lard	1 year			
Leeks		1–2 weeks	10–12 months	Refrigerate in plastic.
Lemon Juice (Commercially Frozen)			8–12 months	Keeps in the refrigerator for 2 months after thawing.
Lemons	5–7 days	2–3 weeks	NR	Refrigerate in plastic.
Lentils: Dried	1 year			Some varieties last longer.
Lettuce: Butterhead Varieties		3–4 days	NR	Rinse; dry thoroughly. Wrap in plastic with a paper towel. Store away from fruits, which will cause browning.

PRODUCT	PANTRY	REFRIG.	FREEZER	COMMENTS
Lettuce: Iceberg		1–2 weeks	NR	Remove core and wilted leaves. Rinse well, shake out excess moisture. Store in a lettuce container or tightly closed bag, away from fruits.
Lettuce: Loose Leaf Varieties		7–10 days	NR	Rinse; dry thoroughly. Wrap in plastic with a paper towel. Store away from fruits, which will cause browning.
Lettuce: Romaine		7–10 days	NR	Rinse; dry thoroughly. Wrap in plastic with a paper towel. Store away from fruits, which will cause browning.
Limes	NR	2–3 weeks	NR	Refrigerate in plastic.
Lobster: Cooked		1 day	2 months	Wrap tightly.
Lobster: Live		1 day		Store in special insulated carton.
Lobster: Vacuum-Packed		1 month		
Lunch Meats: AO or Deli-Wrapped		3–5 days	2 months	Keep in original packaging or wrap in plastic.
Lunch Meats: Vacuum-Packed		5–7 days ASD	2 months	Store in original packaging.
Macadamia Nuts: Shelled		6 months	9–12 months	Store in airtight container.
Mangoes	Until Ripe	2–3 days	10–12 months	Refrigerate in plastic. Freeze only cut fruit.
Maple Syrup	2 years			
Maple Syrup: AO		1 year	Indefinitely	Cover tightly.
Margarine: Diet		2–3 months	1 year	Cover tightly.
Margarine: Regular or Soft		4–5 months	1 year	Cover or wrap tightly.
Marshmallow Creme	3–4 months			Refrigerate after opening.
Marshmallow Creme: AO		2 weeks		Cover tightly.
Marshmallows	2–3 months			Keep in airtight container.
Mayonnaise: Commercial	2–3 months ASD			
Mayonnaise: Commercial: AO		2 months	NR	Cover tightly.
Meat: Canned	12–18 months			
Meat: Canned: AO		2–3 days	2–3 months	Wrap in plastic or foil.
Meat: Cooked		3 days	2–3 months	Refrigerate or freeze immediately after cooking.
Meat: Cooked: in Gravy		1–2 days	2–3 months	Refrigerate or freeze immediately after cooking.
Meat Entrées: Carry-Out		1 day		Cover tightly.
Meat Entrées: Frozen			2–3 months	Store in original packaging.
Meat Entrées: Frozen: Prepared		1–2 days		Cover tightly.
Meat Salad (other than Ham Salad)		1–2 days		Cover tightly.
Melon	Until Ripe	4–5 days	10–12 months	Refrigerate after ripe. Wrap cut pieces in plastic.
Melon Balls		2–3 days	10–12 months	Wrap in plastic.
Milk: Canned: Evaporated	6 months			Invert cans every 2 months.
Milk: Canned: Evaporated: AO		3–5 days	NR	Cover tightly.
Milk: Canned: Sweetened	4 months or USD			Invert cans every 2 months.
Milk: Canned: Sweetened: AO		3–5 days	NR	Cover tightly.
Milk: Dry: Nonfat: Mixed		3–5 days		Cover tightly.
Milk: Dry: Nonfat: Unmixed	1 year			Store in cool, dry place.
Milk: Dry: Whole: Mixed		3–5 days		Cover tightly.
Milk: Dry: Whole: Unmixed	3 months			Store in cool, dry place.
Milk: Fresh		1–5 days ASD	3 months	Do not pour leftover milk back into carton.
Milk-Based Food: Pudding, etc.		2–4 days	NR	Cover tightly.

PRODUCT	PANTRY	REFRIG.	FREEZER	COMMENTS
Molasses	1 year			
Molasses: AO	6 months			Cover tightly.
Muffins	1–2 days	1 week	3 months	Wrap in plastic or airtight container.
Mushrooms: Canned	1 year			
Mushrooms: Canned: AO		5–7 days		Drain and store in a covered container.
Mushrooms: Dried	6 months			Store in a cool, dark, dry place.
Mushrooms: Fresh	NR	2–3 days	10–12 months	Store unwashed in paper bag or cardboard container.
Mussels: Live		1 day		Cover with a wet cloth.
Mussels: Shucked		1 day	3 months	Cover tightly.
Mustard	1 year			
Mustard: AO	1–2 months	1 year		Refrigerate for longer storage.
Nectarines: Cut		1–2 days		Wrap tightly in plastic.
Nectarines: Whole	Until Ripe	5–7 days	NR	After ripe, refrigerate in plastic.
Noodles	6–18 months			
Nuts: Canned	1 year			
Nuts: Canned: AO		3–6 months		Cover tightly.
Oatmeal	1 year			
Oil: Olive	4–12 months	6–12 months		Store tightly covered in a dark place.
Oil: Sesame	2 months	4 months		Store tightly covered in a dark place.
Oil: Vegetable, Corn, Peanut	1 year			Store tightly covered in a dark place.
Oil: Vegetable, Corn, Peanut: AO	4–6 months			Store tightly covered in a dark place.
Oil: Walnut		2 months	4 months	Store tightly covered in a dark place.
Okra: Cooked		3–4 days		Cover tightly.
Okra: Fresh		2–3 days	10–12 months	Refrigerate in plastic. Be sure it is very dry first.
Olives	1 year			
Olives: AO		2–4 weeks		Completely submerge in liquid. Discard if soft.
Onions: Dry: Cut		2–3 days	10–12 months	Sweet onions are slightly more perishable.
Onions: Dry: Uncut	2–3 weeks	See note		Store in cool, dark, dry place with good air circulation, away from potatoes. Do not refrigerate or freeze unless cut.
Onions: Green or Scallions		5–7 days	10–12 months	Refrigerate in plastic. Wash just before using.
Orange Juice: Fresh		2–3 days	3–4 months	Cover tightly.
Oranges: Fresh: Cut		2–3 days		Wrap in plastic.
Oranges: Fresh: Whole	3–5 days	2–3 weeks	10–12 months	Freeze only sections.
Oranges: Mandarin: Canned	6 months			
Oranges: Mandarin: Canned: AO		1 week		Cover tightly.
Oysters: Live		1 day		Cover with a wet cloth.
Oysters: Shucked		1 day	3 months	Cover tightly.
Pancake Mix	15 months			
Pancake Mix: AO	USD			Seal or cover tightly.
Pancakes		1 day	2–3 months	Cover tightly.
Papayas	Until Ripe	7–10 days	10–12 months	After ripe, refrigerate in plastic. Freeze only cut fruit.
Parsley		Up to 1 week		Wash and dry well. Wrap in dry paper towels to absorb excess moisture. Then wrap in plastic.

PRODUCT	PANTRY	REFRIG.	FREEZER	COMMENTS
Parsnips		7–10 days	10–12 months	Remove leafy tops. Refrigerate in plastic.
Passion Fruit	Until Ripe	1–2 days	10–12 months	
Pasta: Cooked		4 days	2 months	Freeze only in sauce.
Pasta: Dried	2 years			
Pasta: Fresh		1–2 days	2 months	Cover tightly.
Peaches: Canned	1 year			
Peaches: Canned: AO		1 week		Cover tightly.
Peaches: Fresh: Cut		2 days	10–12 months	Refrigerate in plastic.
Peaches: Fresh: Whole	Until Ripe	3–5 days		After ripe, refrigerate in plastic.
Peanut Butter: Commercial	1 year			
Peanut Butter: Commercial: AO	1 month	3–4 months		Cover tightly.
Peanut Butter: Homemade		10 days		Cover tightly.
Peanuts: Raw: In Shell	2 months	6 months	9–12 months	Store in airtight container.
Peanuts: Roasted: In Shell	1 month	6 months	9–12 months	Store in airtight container.
Peanuts: Roasted: Shelled		3 months	6 months	Store in airtight container.
Pears: Cut		1–2 days	10–12 months	Wrap in plastic.
Pears: Whole	Until Ripe	7–10 days		After ripe, refrigerate in plastic. Freeze only cut fruit.
Peas: Dried	1 year			Some varieties keep longer.
Peas: English, Snow, Sugar Snap		3–4 days	10–12 months	Refrigerate in plastic.
Pecans: In Shell	2–3 months	6 months	1 year	Store in airtight container.
Pecans: Shelled		6 months	1 year	Store in airtight container.
Pectin: Liquid: AO		1 month		Recap tightly.
Peppers: All Types: Canned	1 year			
Peppers: All Types: Canned: AO		1 week		Cover tightly.
Peppers: All Types: Dried	1 year			Store in cool, dry place.
Peppers: All Types: Fresh: Cut		2 days	6–8 months	Wrap in plastic.
Peppers: All Types: Fresh: Whole		4–5 days		Refrigerate in a paper or plastic bag.
Peppers: All Types: Pickled	1 year			
Peppers: All Types: Pickled: AO		4–6 weeks		Cover tightly.
Persian Melon: Cut		1–2 days	10–12 months	Wrap cut pieces in plastic.
Persian Melon: Whole	Until Ripe	4–5 days		Refrigerate after ripe.
Persimmons		1–2 days	10–12 months	Freeze only cut fruit.
Pickles	1 year			
Pickles: AO		1–2 months or USD		Discard if liquid turn cloudy or scummy.
Pie: Chiffon		2–3 days	NR	Cover loosely with foil or plastic.
Pie: Cream		2–3 days	NR	Cover loosely with foil or plastic.
Pie: Custard		2–3 days	NR	Cover loosely with foil or plastic.
Pie: Fruit		4–5 days	6 months	Cover loosely with foil or plastic.
Pie: Pecan-type		4–5 days	6 months	Cover loosely with foil or plastic.
Pie: Pumpkin		2–3 days	2 months	Cover loosely with foil or plastic.
Pie Crust: Baked		2–3 days	4–6 months	Wrap tightly in plastic or heavy foil.
Pie Crust: Unbaked		1 day	2 months	Wrap tightly in plastic or heavy foil.
Pimientos	1 year			
Pimientos: AO		10 days		Cover tightly.
Pineapple: Canned	1 year			

PRODUCT	PANTRY	REFRIG.	FREEZER	COMMENTS
Pineapple: Canned: AO		1 week		Cover tightly.
Pineapple: Fresh: Cut		1 week	10–12 months	Wrap or cover tightly.
Pineapple: Fresh: Whole	1–2 days	3–5 days		Refrigerate cut pieces in plastic.
Pine Nuts		1 month	6 months	Store in airtight container.
Pistachios		3 months	1 year	Store in airtight container.
Plantains	Until Ripe	3–5 days	NR	
Plums	Until Ripe	3–5 days	10–12 months	After ripe, refrigerate in plastic.
Pomegranates		2–3 weeks	10–12 months	
Pomegranate Seeds		2 weeks	1 year	Store in tightly covered jar.
Popcorn: Popped	2–3 months			This refers to commercial, bagged popcorn.
Popcorn: Popped: AO	1–2 weeks			Wrap tightly.
Popcorn: Unpopped: Plain	1–2 years, or USD			
Popcorn: Unpopped: Plain: AO		2 weeks		Cover tightly.
Popcorn: Unpopped: with Oil	2–3 weeks, or USD			
Popcorn: Unpopped: with Oil: AO		2 weeks		Cover tightly.
Pork: Ground		1 day	1–2 months	Refrigerate in store wrap. Freeze in freezer wrap.
Pork Chops, Ribs, and Roasts		3 days	3–6 months	Refrigerate in store wrap. Freeze in freezer wrap.
Pork Stew Meat		1–2 days	1–2 months	Refrigerate in store wrap. Freeze in freezer wrap.
Potatoes	2–3 weeks			Store in cool, dry place with good air circulation, away from onions. Do not refrigerate or freeze unless cut. If pre-bagged, remove any that are damaged before storing.
Potatoes: Canned	1 year			
Potatoes: Canned: AO		3–5 days		Cover tightly.
Potatoes: Cooked		3–5 days	10–12 months	Cover tightly. Mashed or stuffed baked potatoes are the only type of cooked potatoes that freeze well.
Potatoes: Frozen: Commercial			1 year	
Potatoes: Instant	1 year			After opening, seal in plastic bag.
Potatoes: New		3–4 days		Store in cool, dry place, as for mature potatoes.
Poultry: Canned	12–18 months			
Poultry: Canned: AO		2–3 days	2–3 months	Cover tightly.
Poultry: Cooked		3 days	2 months	Cover tightly.
Poultry: Cooked in Sauce		1–2 days	6 months	Cover tightly.
Poultry Entrées: Carry-Out		1 day		Cover tightly.
Poultry Entrées: Frozen			2–3 months	
Poultry Entrées: Frozen: Prepared		1–2 days		Cover tightly.
Poultry Salad		2–3 days		Cover tightly.
Preserves	1 year			
Preserves: AO		6 months		Cover tightly.
Prickly Pears	Until Ripe	3 days	10–12 months	Refrigerate after ripe.
Prunes: Fresh	Until Ripe	3–5 days	10–12 months	After ripe, refrigerate in plastic.
Pudding: Commercial	USD*	USD*		*Store as purchased: pantry, refrigerator or freezer.
Pudding: Frozen			4–6 weeks	Keep frozen.
Pudding: Homemade		2–3 days		Keep refrigerated.
Pudding Mix	1 year			Keep cool and dry.
Pumpkin: Uncut	Up to 1 month	2–3 months		Store in cool, dark, dry place, or refrigerate.

PRODUCT	PANTRY	REFRIG.	FREEZER	COMMENTS
Pumpkin Seeds	2–3 months	1 year	1 year	Store in airtight container.
Quinces	Until Ripe	2–3 weeks	10–12 months	Wrap in plastic.
Radicchio		3–5 days	NR	Rinse well; dry thoroughly. Store in plastic with a paper towel. Store away from apples.
Radishes		1–2 weeks	NR	Remove leafy tops. Wrap in plastic.
Raspberries		1–2 days	10–12 months	Remove decayed fruit. Store uncovered, without washing. To keep from bruising, store in single layer.
Rhubarb		3–5 days	10–12 months	Wrap in plastic.
Rice: Brown	1 month	6 months		
Rice: Cooked		1 week	6–8 months	Cover tightly.
Rice: White	2 years			
Rice: Wild	Indefinitely			
Rice: Mix	6 months			
Rolls	2–4 days	4–7 days	3 months	Wrap tightly in plastic or foil.
Salad Dressing: Commercial	6 months ASD			
Salad Dressing: Commercial: AO		3 months		Cover tightly.
Salad Dressing Mix	18 months			
Salad Dressing Mix: Prepared		2 weeks		Cover tightly.
Salami: Sliced		5–7 days	1 month	Wrap tightly in plastic or foil.
Salami: Whole		2–6 weeks		Wrap tightly in plastic or foil.
Salsa: Commercial	1 year			
Salsa: Commercial: AO		1 month		Cover tightly.
Salt	Indefinitely			Seasoned salt keeps for 1 year.
Salt Pork		1 month		Wrap tightly in plastic or foil.
Sauces: Canned	12–18 months			Acid-based sauces keep longer than other types.
Sauces: Canned: AO		2–5 days		Cover tightly.
Sauerkraut: Canned	6 months			
Sauerkraut: Canned: AO		4–5 days		Cover tightly.
Sauerkraut: Fresh		Up to 1 week		Cover tightly.
Sausage: Breakfast		5–7 days ASD	2 months	Store in original packaging.
Sausage: Breakfast: AO		5–7 days		Wrap in plastic.
Sausage: Cooked or Smoked		4–7 days	2 months	Store in original packaging.
Sausage: Dry: Sliced		1 week	1 month	Wrap tightly in plastic or foil.
Sausage: Dry: Whole		2–6 weeks		Wrap tightly in plastic or foil.
Sausage: Fresh		1–2 days	1–2 months	Wrap tightly in plastic or foil.
Scallops		1 day	3–6 months	Refrigerate on ice, or poach and then freeze.
Seafood Cocktail Sauce	12–18 months			
Seafood Cocktail Sauce: AO	1 month	6 months		Refrigerate for longer storage
Seafood Salad		1 day	NR	Cover tightly.
Shallots	Up to 1 month			Store in cool, dark, dry place.
Shortening: Solid Vegetable	8 months			
Shortening: Solid Vegetable: AO	6 months			Cover tightly.
Shrimp: Cooked		1 day	2 months	For freezing, pack in sturdy containers.
Shrimp: Raw		1 day	3–6 months	Refrigerate on ice. Freeze in sturdy containers.
Soft Drinks	1 year			

PRODUCT	PANTRY	REFRIG.	FREEZER	COMMENTS
Soft Drink Mix	2 years			
Soft Drink Mix: AO	2–3 months			Cover tightly.
Soft Drink Mix: Prepared		7–10 days		Store in covered glass or plastic container.
Sour Cream		1–2 weeks ASD .. NR		Before opening, invert container to keep surface from drying out. Pink or green scum indicates spoilage.
Soybeans		1–2 days		Refrigerate in plastic bag.
Soy Sauce	1 year			
Soy Sauce: AO		1 year		Cover tightly.
Spices: Ground	1–2 years			Store in cool, dark place.
Spices: Whole	2–3 years			Refrigerate poppy seeds and sesame seeds.
Spinach: Fresh		2–3 days	10–12 months	Refrigerate in plastic. If spinach is purchased pre-packaged, remove any wilted leaves before storing.
Sprouts		7–10 days	NR	Refrigerate in plastic.
Squab		1 day	4–6 months	Store in original packaging.
Squash: Summer	NR	5–7 days	10–12 months	Refrigerate in plastic.
Squash: Winter: Cut		2–4 days	10–12 months	Wrap tightly in plastic.
Squash: Winter: Whole	1 week	2 weeks		Store in cool, dark, dry place, or refrigerate.
Star Fruit	Until ripe	Up to 1 week	10–12 months	After ripe, refrigerate in plastic.
Steak Sauce	1 year			
Steak Sauce: AO	1 year			Cover tightly.
Stock		1–2 days	4–6 months	Store in tightly covered container.
Strawberries		3–5 days	10–12 months	Sort and remove damaged or decayed fruit. Do not wash until ready to serve. Cover with plastic.
Stuffing: Prepared		1–2 days	1 month	Always freeze stuffing separately from poultry.
Stuffing Mix	6 months			
Sugar: Brown	12–18 months			
Sugar: Granulated	2–3 years			
Sugar: Powdered	18 months			
Sugar Substitutes	2–3 years			
Sunflower Seeds: Shelled	2–3 years	1 year	1 year	Store in airtight container.
Sweet Potatoes: Canned	1 year			
Sweet Potatoes: Canned: AO		3–5 days		Cover tightly.
Sweet Potatoes: Fresh	Up to 2 weeks	NR	NR	Store in cool, dark, dry place. They bruise easily, so handle them carefully. Do not allow them to freeze.
Sweet Rolls	2–4 days	4–7 days	3 months	Store in tightly closed plastic bag.
Swiss Chard		2–3 days	10–12 months	Wrap in plastic.
Syrups	1 year			Keep tightly closed. Refrigerate to extend storage.
Tabasco Sauce	1 year			
Tabasco Sauce: AO	1 year			Cover tightly. Discard if it turns brown.
Taco Sauce	2 years			
Taco Sauce: AO		1 month		Cover tightly.
Taco Shells	6 months			
Taco Shells: AO	1 week			Seal tightly in plastic bag.
Tamarillos	Until Ripe	7–10 days	NR	
Tamarind Paste		2–3 weeks	NR	
Tangerines	1–2 weeks	Up to 1 month		Refrigerate in plastic bag.
Tapioca	1 year			
Tea: Brewed		4–6 hours	2–3 days	Store in covered container.
Tea: Herbal	6–9 months			
Tea: Instant	3 years			
Tea: Loose	2 years			
Tea Bags	1 year			

PRODUCT	PANTRY	REFRIG.	FREEZER	COMMENTS
Toaster Pastry	2–3 months			Keep in airtight package.
Tofu		3–5 days ASD	2 months	Refrigerate in covered container, submerged in water. Change water daily.
Tomatillos	Up to 2 weeks		10–12 months	
Tomatoes: Canned	6 months			
Tomatoes: Canned: AO		1 week		Cover and store in non-metal container.
Tomatoes: Fresh	Until ripe	NR	2 months	Refrigeration destroys flavor. Use frozen tomatoes for soups and sauces.
Tomatoes: Sun-dried		6–9 months		Cover tightly.
Tomato Paste or Puree	12–18 months			
Tomato Paste or Puree: AO		1 week	2 months	Cover tightly.
Tomato Sauce	12–18 months			
Tomato Sauce: AO		4–5 days	2 months	Cover tightly.
Tortillas	2–4 days	4–7 days ASD	4 months	Wrap tightly in plastic or foil.
Tuna Salad		2–3 days		Cover tightly.
Turkey: Smoked		1 week	6 months	Wrap in plastic or foil.
Turkey: Whole		2–3 days	6–12 months	Wrap in plastic or foil.
Turkey Parts		1–2 days	3–6 months	Wrap in plastic or foil.
Turnips		5–7 days	8–10 months	Refrigerate in plastic.
TV Dinners			3–4 months	
Uglifruit: Cut		2–3 days		Wrap tightly in plastic.
Uglifruit: Whole	1 week	2 weeks	10–12 months	Refrigerate in perforated plastic bag. Freeze only sections.
Variety Meats		1 day	1–4 months	Wrap loosely in plastic or foil.
Veal: Ground		1 day	3–4 months	Refrigerate in store wrap. Freeze in freezer wrap.
Veal Chops, Ribs, and Roasts		3 days	6–9 months	Refrigerate in store wrap. Freeze in freezer wrap.
Veal Cutlets		1–2 days	3–4 months	Refrigerate in store wrap. Freeze in freezer wrap.
Veal Stew Meat		1–2 days	3–4 months	Refrigerate in store wrap. Freeze in freezer wrap.
Vegetables: Canned	12–18 months			
Vegetables: Canned: AO		4–7 days		Cover tightly. See individual listings for exceptions.
Vegetables: Cooked		3–4 days		Cover tightly.
Vegetables: Pickled	12–18 months			
Vegetables: Pickled: AO		4–8 weeks		Cover tightly.
Vinegar	1 year			
Vinegar: AO	6 months			Slightly cloudy appearance doesn't affect quality.
Waffles		1 day	2–3 months	Wrap tightly in plastic or foil.
Walnuts: In Shell	2–3 months	1 year	1year	Store in airtight container.
Walnuts: Shelled		1 year	1 year	Store in airtight container.
Water: Bottled	2 years			
Water Chestnuts: Canned	1 year			
Water Chestnuts: Canned: AO		1 week		Store covered, in their own liquid.
Watercress		2–3 days	NR	Wrap in plastic.
Watermelon: Cut		3–4 days	10–12 months	Refrigerate in plastic.
Watermelon: Whole	2–3 days	1 week		
Wheat Germ		2–3 months	2–3 months	
Whipped Topping Non-dairy: Aerosol		2–3 months		Do not freeze.
Whipped Topping Non-dairy: Carton		1–2 weeks	1 year	
Worcestershire Sauce	1 year			
Worcestershire Sauce: AO	1 year			Cover tightly.
Yeast: Dry	USD	USD		
Yeast: Fresh		USD		
Yogurt		1 week ASD	4–6 weeks	Before opening, invert container to keep surface moist.
Zucchini		3–4 days		Wrap in plastic.

Food Terms

■ ■ ■

How terms are alphabetized:

■ Entries are arranged alphabetically, without regard to spaces or hyphens.

A

Acid foods—Foods with a pH of less than 7, including tomatoes, vinegar, lemon juice, and wine. See *Non-reactive pan.*

Acidulated water—A solution of water and an acidic ingredient, such as Fruit Fresh, lemon juice, or vinegar, used to prevent food such as cut fruit from discoloring. The standard proportion is 1 teaspoon of the acid ingredient to 1¼ cups water.

Adjust the seasoning—To taste food before serving, in order to determine if additional condiments, herbs, or spices need to be added. Also called "correct the seasoning."

Al dente—Italian for "to the tooth." Descriptive term for food (usually pasta) cooked just until tender: firm, slightly chewy, but not soft or flabby.

Allspice—A spice that tastes like a blend of cinnamon, cloves, and nutmeg, available either whole or ground.

Amandine—Served with almonds.

Anise seed—An aromatic spice with a mildly sweet flavor, similar to licorice; related to parsley.

Antipasto—A plate of assorted meats, vegetables, and cheeses, served as the first course of an Italian meal.

Arborio rice—Italian short-grain rice used to make risotto.

Aromatic rice—A term for varieties of rice with a nutty flavor and aroma.

Arrowroot—A thickening agent similar to cornstarch.

Aspic—A gelatin mixture congealed in a mold or used to glaze food.

Au gratin—Term for food browned in the oven or under the broiler, with a crusty topping, such as buttered bread crumbs or shredded cheese.

B

Baguette—A long, slender loaf of French bread.

Bake—To cook food in the oven using dry heat.

Balsamic vinegar—Aged Italian vinegar made from Trebbiano grape juice.

Barbecue—To cook over coals, sometimes basting with a sauce. Also written *Barbeque, Bar-B-Q,* or *BBQ.*

Bard—To cover uncooked meat with strips of fat meat, such as bacon, to improve its flavor and prevent it from drying out as it cooks.

Basil—An herb of the mint family, with a flavor similar to bay leaves and oregano, somewhat like minty licorice. Available as fresh leaves or as crushed dried leaves.

Basmati rice—Fragrant, Indian long-grain rice with a nutty flavor.

Baste—To moisten or glaze a food by brushing, spooning, or pouring liquid over it while it cooks. Different liquids may be used: pan drippings, broth, melted butter, etc. This helps to prevent the food from drying out, and adds flavor and color.

Batter—A thick liquid mixture, usually made of eggs, milk, and flour. This mixture can be poured or dropped from a spoon. Batter is sometimes used to coat food such as chicken, fish, or vegetables before frying.

Batter bread—A bread containing yeast, made without kneading, distinguished from a quick bread, which is made without yeast.

Bay leaf—An aromatic herb of the laurel family, with a strong, woodsy flavor, which is added to food during cooking, but removed before serving.

Beat—To stir a mixture rapidly, incorporating air into it, using an over-and-under motion, rather than an around-and-around motion. One minute with an electric mixer equals about 100 strokes by hand.

Beau monde seasoning— A blend of spices, sold commercially, including celery salt and onion powder.

Béchamel sauce—A white sauce made from butter, flour, and milk. One of the basic French sauces, including "Espagnole," "Hollandaise," "Mayonnaise," "Velouté," and "Vinaigrette" (see entries).

Beignet—A square fritter, fried in hot oil, and dusted with powdered sugar.

Betty—A pudding-type dessert made of layers of fruit and buttered bread crumbs, such as apple betty.

Beurre manié—French term for "kneaded butter," which is a mixture of equal parts butter and flour, creamed together, and used to thicken sauces.

Bind—To add a substance, called a "binding ingredient," to a mixture, so that it thickens and clings together in a mass. Egg yolks are added to bind hollandaise sauce. Tapioca is used to bind certain puddings or fruit pies. Gelatin is used to bind congealed salads or desserts.

Biscotti—Twice-baked, crunchy Italian cookies, often used for dipping.

Bisque—A thick cream soup or purée, often made with shellfish.

Blacken—A method of preparation in which a food, such as fish, is seasoned with a spicy mixture, and then fried in a hot skillet until it is blackened on both sides.

Blanch—A process in which food is plunged briefly into boiling liquid, then immediately into cold water to stop the cooking process Blanching tomatoes and peaches for about 30 seconds causes the skin to slip off easily. Blanching green vegetables helps to set a brilliant color. Blanching can also remove excess saltiness from foods such as bacon. See *parboil.*

Blend—To mix ingredients together, in order to obtain a uniform texture.

Boil—To cook liquid until it reaches 212° (at sea level). When liquid boils, bubbles form quickly, rise to the surface of the liquid, and break.

Bok choy—Crisp Chinese cabbage, similar to Swiss chard.

Bone—To remove bones from meat, poultry, or fish. Sometimes called "debone."

Bouillabaisse—A seafood stew.

Bouillon—See *Stock.*

Bouquet garni—A combination of herbs (usually including parsley, thyme, and bay leaf) tied together in cheesecloth and used to flavor food while cooking. The bouquet is removed before the food is served.

Braise—A two-step cooking process in which food is browned on the stove in fat and then covered and cooked slowly until done, either on top of the stove or in the oven. A little liquid is frequently added before covering the pan. This is a good cooking technique for less tender cuts of meat. See *Pot roast.*

Bran—The outer husk of a grain.

Bread—To coat a food with crumbs before cooking. To help crumbs adhere, the food is often dipped first in flour, and then in beaten egg or some type of thick liquid before it is rolled in the crumbs.

Brine—A strong saltwater solution used to preserve certain types of food, such as olives.

Brisket—A cut of beef usually barbecued or used to make corned beef.

Broccoflower—A cross between broccoli and cauliflower, and milder than either.

Broil—To cook a food directly under a source of heat, such as in an oven under the broiling element, or over a source of heat, such as on a grill. When foods are broiled in an oven, they are usually placed on a rack, to allow any accumulated greases to run off. Also see *Brown* and *Pan-broil*.

Broiler—A size classification for chicken from 7–9 weeks old, weighing from 1½–2 pounds.

Broth—See *Stock*.

Brown—To cook food quickly, at a fairly high heat, so that the surface of the food browns. This can be done in a pan on top of the stove (see *Sauté*), in the oven (see *Toast*), or under the broiler (see *Broil*).

Bruise—To crush or pound an ingredient slightly (such as mint leaves) in order to release the flavor.

Bruschetta—A traditional Italian garlic bread, drizzled with olive oil, and sprinkled with salt and pepper.

Brush—To use a pastry brush to spread a liquid (such as melted butter) over the surface of a food.

Buckwheat—Kernels similar to grain. When hulled and crushed, they are called groats, which can be cooked like rice. When ground into grits and toasted, they are called kasha. They can also be milled into flour, sometimes used in pancakes.

Bulb baster—A utensil that resembles a giant eyedropper, used to baste meat as it cooks.

Bulgur—Wheat kernels with some of the bran removed, which have been steamed, dried, and crushed. Used for Tabbouleh (see page 183).

Bundt pan—Brand name for a fluted tube pan, with curved sides and indentations that give foods prepared in it a sculptured appearance.

Butter—To spread some type of fat, such as butter, oil, or non-stick spray, on a cooking utensil, to prevent food from sticking to it. Also see *Grease*.

Butterfly—To cut food down the center, almost all the way through, leaving both halves attached, and spreading them out to resemble a butterfly or an open book.

C

Cajun—A type of cuisine marked by French and Southern influences, with a decidedly "country" flavor, relying heavily on spices and fats. Jambalaya is a traditional Cajun dish.

Cake turntable—A device that resembles a lazy Susan on a pedestal, used to hold a cake while it is being decorated. Since the turntable revolves, the cake can be decorated more evenly and easily.

Calzone—A small stuffed pizza.

Canapés—Small crackers or cutouts of bread, toast, or pastry topped with a spread or garnish, and served as appetizers.

Candy thermometer—A thermometer used to check the temperature of candy as it cooks. It registers

from 100°–400°. (It cannot be used interchangeably with a meat thermometer, since each type registers a different range of temperatures.)

Caper—An unopened flower bud from the caper bush, with a peppery flavor. Usually pickled, and frequently flavored with tarragon.

Capon—A neutered rooster, 16–20 weeks old, weighing from 6–9 pounds.

Caramelize—(1) To melt sugar in a pan until it liquifies and turns a caramel color; (2) To cook a food until the natural sugars in the food begin to turn brown. (3) A stage in cooking candy, from 310°–321°, in which sugar melts, turns golden, and forms a brittle ball when dropped into water.

Caraway Seeds—An aromatic spice in the carrot family, with a pungent, licorice flavor. Available as whole or ground seeds.

Cardamom—A spice in the ginger family, with a sweet, lemony, ginger-like flavor. Available as whole or ground seeds.

Carryover cooking—The residual cooking that occurs in food after it is removed from the oven. The internal temperature will rise from 5°–10°.

Cassia—Chinese cinnamon, whose flavor is not quite as delicate as true cinnamon, but has more of a "bite."

Cayenne—A small, hot, dried chile pepper, frequently used in its ground form. Sometimes called "red pepper."

Celery seeds—A spice available as whole or ground seeds, and also mixed with salt ("celery salt") which resembles fresh celery in flavor.

Chafing dish—A serving container with a source of heat (such as a candle or Sterno) beneath it.

Chantarelle—A wild mushroom with a thick stem and a wavy cap, a nutty flavor, and a chewy texture.

Char—To seal flavor and juices in a food by blackening the surface quickly.

Chard—See *Swiss chard.*

Cheesecloth—Loosely-woven, soft fabric used to wrap various foods, such as a bouquet garni. Also used to strain foods.

Chervil—A delicate herb similar to parsley, whose flavor resembles anise. Available as fresh or dried leaves.

Chicory—(1) A leafy vegetable related to endive, with a bitter flavor; (2) The bitter root of certain varieties of chicory, sometimes roasted and used to flavor coffee.

Chili powder—A strong and peppery powdered blend of ground chile peppers and spices. Not as hot as cayenne.

Chill—To refrigerate food until it is cold throughout. Also see *Cool.*

Chinois—A sieve with extremely fine mesh or perforations, shaped like a cone, which is used to purée or strain food. Sometimes called a "China cap."

Chive—An herb related to the onion, garlic, and leek, with slender, hollow stems, and a mild onion flavor. Available fresh, dried, or frozen.

Chop—(1) To cut food into small pieces, using a knife, food processor, or food chopper. (2) A thin cut of pork, lamb, or veal, served with a small amount of bone.

Chorizo—Pork sausage made with peppers and garlic.

Chunk—To cut food into bite-size pieces, usually larger than 1".

Chutney—A spicy condiment containing fruits or vegetables, sugar, vinegar, and spices.

Cilantro—A leafy, aromatic herb, also known as Chinese parsley, Mexican parsley, or coriander, with a pungent, soapy taste. Available as fresh or dried leaves. Also see *Coriander.*

Cinnamon—A spice made from the dried bark of a tropical tree, available in stick or ground form.

Citron—A citrus fruit similar to the lemon, but larger and milder in flavor.

Clarified butter—Unsalted butter that has been melted, and from which the milk solids have been removed. Also called "drawn butter."

Clarify—To remove impurities. Clarified butter is made by melting it, and then skimming the milk solids from the clear liquid. Stock is clarified by adding broken cooked egg shells, simmering, and straining out the shells.

Clove—A spice with a warm, pungent flavor, made from the dried buds of a tropical tree, available either whole or ground. Also see *Garlic clove.*

Coat—To cover the surface of a food completely, such as with a sauce, glaze, icing, or crumbs.

Coat a spoon—A test to determine if a sauce or custard containing eggs is done. When the back of a spoon is placed on the surface of the mixture and lifted, the thickened mixture should adhere to the spoon.

Cobbler—A fruit dessert similar to a deep-dish pie. It has no bottom crust, and has a biscuit-like topping.

Coddle—To cook food, such as eggs, in individual, covered containers, set in simmering water.

Colander—A bowl-shaped, perforated container, used to drain foods such as pasta.

Combine—To blend ingredients into a uniform mixture.

Comino—Ground cumin seeds.

Compote—A combination of fresh or cooked fruits, served hot or chilled.

Condiment—Any accompaniment to food, such as sauce, relish, chutney, mayonnaise, mustard, etc., that imparts added seasoning or flavoring.

Conserve—A combination of two or more fruits, cooked with sugar and sometimes raisins and nuts.

Consommé—Stock or broth that has been clarified to remove any sediment or impurities. See *Clarify.*

Cookie press—A cylinder that holds cookie dough. with a patterned disk on one end, through which the dough is extruded. On the opposite end is a plunger or trigger, used to press the dough through the cylinder.

Cool—To allow a cooked food to stand at room temperature until it is no longer warm to the touch. See *Chill.*

Core—To remove the inedible center of a fruit or vegetable.

Coriander—An aromatic herb of the parsley family, with a faint citrus flavor, grown for its seeds and leaves, each of which has a distinct flavor. The leaves are also known as Chinese parsley and cilantro.

Corn salad—A salad green also known as "mâche" and "lamb's lettuce."

Correct the seasoning—See *Adjust the seasoning.*

Cos lettuce—Another name for romaine lettuce.

Coulis—A thin fruit or berry sauce.

Court bouillon—A savory bouillon made from fish stock, used for poaching fish, or as a base for fish sauces.

Couscous—Cooked bulgur wheat which is served much as rice would be served, sometimes as a salad.

Crab boil—A mixture of spices used to flavor water in which seafood (such as crab, shrimp, or lobster) is cooked.

Cracklings—Crisp pieces of cooked fatty pork or poultry.

Cream—To mix two or more foods vigorously, such as butter and sugar,

until the resulting consistency is smooth, fluffy, and creamy.

Cream, coffee—Another term for *light cream.* See *Cream, light.*

Cream, half and half—See *Half and half.*

Cream, heavy—Heavy whipping cream with a fat content of 36–40 percent, generally available only in specialty markets. See *Cream, whipping.*

Cream, light—Cream with a fat content somewhere between 18–30 percent, usually about 20 percent. Another term for "coffee cream" and "table cream."

Cream, table—Another term for *light cream.* See *Cream, light.*

Cream, whipping—Cream that is generally sold for whipping purposes, but which is not quite as high in fat as heavy cream. Its fat content is between 30–36 percent.

Cream sauce—See *Béchamel sauce.*

Cream of tartar—A white powder that is added to egg whites before beating, to increase volume and maintain stability.

Crème Anglaise—A rich custard sauce, often served over fruit or cake.

Crème fraîche—Thickened cream similar to sour cream, made from heavy cream and buttermilk, or heavy cream and sour cream. It can be boiled without curdling.

Creole—A type of cuisine marked by French, Spanish, and African in-

fluences, which relies heavily on tomatoes and peppers for flavoring. Gumbo is a well-known Creole dish.

Crêpe—A thin French pancake.

Crimp—To join and seal the layers of pie or pastry crust, by pinching the edges together, or by pressing them with a fork or other tool.

Crisp—(1) To make foods such as salad greens crisp, by plunging them into ice water; (2) To make foods such as hard rolls crisp, by heating them in the oven.

Croissant—A French roll made of puff pastry and shaped like a crescent.

Croquettes—Minced or ground cooked foods, such as salmon, mixed with a thick cream sauce, and formed into balls, patties, logs, or cones, and then fried.

Croustades—Edible crust-like containers that can be filled with food.

Croutons—Small seasoned cubes of bread toasted in butter or oil.

Crudités—Raw vegetables cut into bite-sized pieces and served as appetizers, frequently with a dip.

Cruet—A small container used to make or store salad dressing or ingredients used in salad dressing.

Crumb—To break up food into small pieces. See *Crumble.*

Crumble—To break up food into small pieces. See *Crumb.*

Crumpet—A type of round, flat bread, similar to an English muffin, which is not split before toasting.

Crush—To mash or break food into pieces, or to bruise the leaves of fresh herbs to release their flavor.

Cube—(1) To cut food into small cubes, about ½"–1"; (2) To tenderize meat with a utensil that makes cube-shaped imprints.

Cube steak—A cut of round steak that has been mechanically tenderized.

Cumin—An aromatic seed, with a warm, pungent, salty-sweet flavor similar to caraway. Available whole or ground, and often used in Latin American, Oriental, and Indian cuisine.

Curdle—To cause curds to form; to coagulate. Often refers to the undesirable separation of milk and eggs in a custard or sauce.

Cure—To preserve food, usually meat or fish, by pickling, smoking, drying, salting, or storing in a brine.

Curry—An Indian method of food preparation.

Curry powder—A powdered blend of a variety of herbs and spices, with a somewhat exotic flavor.

Custard—A dessert-like pudding, made with eggs, milk, and sugar, which can either be cooked on top of the stove, or baked in the oven.

Cut—To sever food using a knife or scissors.

Cut in—To incorporate shortening or butter into dry ingredients, using a pastry blender or 2 knives. As shortening or butter is cut into tiny bits, the dry ingredients adhere to them.

Cutlet—A small, thin, boneless piece of meat, such as veal or chicken.

D

Dash—A very small amount (less than ⅛ teaspoon). See *Pinch*.

Debone—See *Bone*.

Deep-fry—To cook food in hot fat, so that food floats in or is covered by the fat while it cooks.

Deglaze—To add liquid (such as broth or wine) to a pan in which food has been cooked, so as to loosen and dissolve the remaining encrusted bits of food. This technique is frequently used to make gravy or sauce.

Degrease—To remove melted fat from the surface of a liquid. This can be done by skimming the surface with a spoon, using a fat-separating pitcher, or refrigerating the liquid in its container, allowing the fat to rise to the top and congeal.

Devein—(1) To remove the vein from the back of a shrimp, using a knife or a tool designed specifically for this purpose; (2) To remove ribs from peppers.

Deviled—Highly seasoned, often with pepper, mustard, or Worcestershire sauce.

Dice—To cut food into cubes of uniform size and shape, from ⅛"–¾".

Dill—An herb with a mild flavor faintly similar to caraway. Cultivated for its seeds and feathery leaves; also called "dill weed."

Disjoint—To separate poultry at the joints.

Dissolve—To allow a dry ingredient to become completely mixed with a liquid in a solution, so that bits of the dry ingredient are no longer visible in the liquid.

Dollop—A spoonful of a soft food, such as whipped cream or sour cream, sometimes added as a garnish to a food before serving.

Dot—To place small bits of an ingredient, such as butter, on the surface of a food.

Double boiler—A double-decker saucepan used to cook custard, chocolate, or any food that needs protection from direct heat. Water is placed in the lower pan. Unless the recipe states otherwise, the upper pan is placed over the water—not in it.

Dough—A mixture of ingredients, such as those used for making bread or cookies, which is thick enough to roll out or knead, but too thick to pour.

Drain—(1) To remove the excess liquid from a food, such as cooked pasta, using a colander or sieve; (2) To allow food, such as bacon, to stand on paper towels, or to blot it with paper towels, so as to remove the excess grease.

Draw—To remove the entrails from fish or poultry.

Drawn butter—See *Clarified butter*.

Dredge—To coat food with a dry mixture before cooking, either by sprinkling, rolling, or shaking the food in a bag with the dry mixture.

Dredger—A cup with a mesh or perforated top, used to sprinkle dry ingredients, such as flour or powdered sugar.

Dress—(1) To cover with a sauce, such as a salad; (2) To stuff poultry or meat before cooking; (3) To garnish; (4) To prepare fish or poultry for cooking by removing scales, feathers, etc.

Dressing—(1) A sauce applied to salads or vegetables, usually tossed with the food to distribute it evenly; (2) A mixture used to stuff the cavity of another food, such as poultry, before cooking. Sometimes this mixture is cooked separately from the food, and is served with the food. See *Stuffing*.

Drippings—Liquefied fat and juices that accumulate in a pan in which meat is cooked.

Drizzle—To pour a liquid over food in a very fine stream.

Drop—To release a food, such as pancake batter, from a spoon onto a surface.

Dust—To coat a food lightly with flour, sugar, cocoa, or some other fine, dry ingredient.

Dutch oven—A large, deep, cooking pot or kettle with a tight-fitting lid, which can be used to cook on top of the stove or in the oven. Sometimes the lid, instead of being almost flat, is quite deep, and resembles another pot turned upside down.

E

Egg wash—A mixture of beaten egg and water, which is brushed onto food, such as pastry, before baking.

Elephant garlic—Large garlic whose flavor is much milder than ordinary garlic. Often roasted and served as an hors d'oeuvre.

Emulsion—A mixture of two liquids that do not normally mix smoothly, such as eggs and oil, in which one liquid is added very slowly to the other liquid while the mixture is beaten rapidly.

En brochette—Cooked on a skewer.

En croûte—Baked in a crust.

Endive—A family of leafy green vegetables, including Belgian endive, curly endive, and escarole. It is related to chicory.

En papillote—Cooked in an envelope of parchment, paper, or foil.

Espagnole sauce—A brown sauce made from butter, flour, and brown stock. One of the basic French sauces, including "Béchamel," "Hollandaise," "Mayonnaise," "Velouté," and "Vinaigrette" (see entries).

Extract—A concentrated flavoring extracted from foods. Also called "Essence."

F

Fatback—Fat from the back of a pig, used as flavoring.

Fell—A membrane that covers some cuts of meat, such as a leg of lamb. See *Silver skin.*

Fennel—An aromatic plant. One type is cultivated for its bulb, prepared as a vegetable. Another is cultivated for its seeds, available whole or ground.

Filberts—See *Hazelnuts.*

Filé powder—A seasoning powder made of sassafras leaves, traditionally used in Creole cuisine.

Fillet—A boneless piece of meat or fish. *Filet* is the French spelling.

Filo pastry—See *Phyllo.*

Filter—To strain, usually through cheesecloth.

Fines herbes—A blend of finely-chopped herbs, including chives, parsley, tarragon, basil, and chervil.

Five spice powder—A Chinese seasoning blend that includes cinnamon, cloves, fennel seed, ground star anise, and Szechuan peppercorns.

Flake—To pull food apart into small pieces, using 1 or 2 forks.

Flambé—To pour a warm alcoholic liquid over a food and then ignite it.

Flan—(1) Caramel custard; (2) A round pastry tart.

Floret—A small cluster of flowers, such as those produced by broccoli.

Flour—To coat with flour.

Fluff—To toss with a fork to remove any lumps and to make a food light and fluffy.

Flute—To make a decorative scalloped edge for a pie crust, by pressing and pinching the dough around the rim with the thumb and forefinger.

Foie gras—Fatty liver from geese or ducklings.

Fold (fold in)—To incorporate a light substance, such as beaten egg whites or whipped cream, into a heavier substance, by using a spatula or spoon to fold one substance gently over and into the other one.

Fondant—A mixture of sugar, cream of tartar, and water, which is cooked to 234°–240° (the "soft-ball" stage). It is then beaten and kneaded. It is used as a filling for candy and also as a pliable material for decorating cakes.

Fondue—A method of food preparation, whereby bite-sized pieces of food are cooked in a pot at the table.

Frappé—A fruit juice mixture with a slushy texture.

Free-range—A term for poultry that is allowed to roam and feed without being confined. Its flavor is usually superior to that of other poultry.

Freezer burn—A loss of moisture that occurs in foods when they are improperly wrapped for freezing, evidenced by a dry surface with white or gray patches.

French—To cut a food, such as green beans, lengthwise into very thin strips.

French fry—To cook a food, such as strips of potatoes, in deep fat.

Fricassee—To cook small pieces of sautéed meat in a small amount of liquid or sauce.

Frittata—An Italian dish made of scrambled eggs mixed with other ingredients. The ingredients in a frittata are incorporated into the eggs, rather than being folded into the center, as in an omelet.

Fritter—A cake-like concoction made of chopped food, which is dipped in batter and then deep-fried.

Frizzle—To fry food, usually thin slices of meat, until the edges curl.

Frost—To apply icing, frosting, glaze, or sugar to a cake, fruit, or other food.

Frosting—A sugary mixture used to coat cakes, pastries, and various baked goods. Another term for icing.

Fry—To cook food uncovered in some type of hot fat.

Fryer—A size classification for chicken from 9–12 weeks old, weighing from 3–4 pounds.

G

Ganache—A rich, creamy, whipped icing used to frost a cake or torte.

Garlic—A bulb that is a close relative of chives, onions, and shallots.

Garlic clove—An individual piece of garlic (sometimes called a "pod" or "toe") that can be broken away from a whole head (called a "bulb").

Garnish—To decorate a food, or the dish on which it is served.

Gel—See *Jell.*

Giblets—The heart, liver, gizzard, and neck of poultry.

Ginger—A gnarled root used as a spice, with a peppery, spicy, penetrating, slightly sweet flavor, available either fresh and whole, dried and ground, or crystallized.

Glaze—To cover a food with a mixture that adds a glossy finish.

Goulash—A Hungarian-type stew, usually served with egg noodles.

Grate—To cut food, usually with a grater, into thin shreds.

Gratin—Food with a crusty topping of cheese or crumbs, which is browned before the food is served.

Gratin dish—A shallow dish or pan, usually round or oval.

Grease—To spread butter, oil, fat, or non-stick cooking spray on a cooking utensil, to prevent food from sticking to it. Also see *Butter.*

Grenadine—A sweet, red syrup made from pomegranate juice.

Grill—To cook food on a rack directly over a source of heat.

Grind—To pulverize food, such as coffee, peppercorns, or other hard spices, into fine pieces, frequently using a mill of some sort.

Grits—Hominy ground to a coarse texture. Popular in the South, it is boiled and served for breakfast, or as a starchy side dish.

Gumbo—A Creole stew, usually including tomatoes, onions, and okra.

Gyro—A Greek dish made from chopped meat that is pressed and formed into a cone. It is then cooked on a revolving vertical spit, sliced thin, and served stuffed into pita bread.

H

Half and half—A mixture of half milk and half cream, with a fat content of 10–12 percent.

Haricots verts—French for "green beans." Usually quite small.

Hash—A dish made from finely-chopped meat, potatoes, and frequently other vegetables, such as onions, cooked in a skillet.

Hazelnuts—Sweet, rich nuts, often chopped or ground, and added to various desserts. Also called "filberts."

Headspace—The amount of space allowed at the top of a container for expansion of food when it is frozen or processed.

Herbes de Provence—A mixture of dried herbs, usually made from a combination of basil, fennel seed, lavender, marjoram, rosemary, sage, savory, and thyme.

Herbs—The fragrant leaves of various plants, which are used to flavor foods. See *Spices.*

Hollandaise sauce—An emulsified sauce, similar to mayonnaise, made from egg yolks and butter, and frequently flavored with lemon juice or vinegar. One of the basic French sauces, including "Béchamel," "Espagnole," "Mayonnaise," "Velouté," and "Vinaigrette" (see entries).

Hot water bath—A technique, used in the oven or on top of the stove, in which the container of food to be cooked is placed inside a larger pan that contains hot water, so that the food is surrounded with gentle heat while it cooks or is kept warm. Also called "bain-marie" and "water bath."

Hull—The inedible outside layer of various vegetables, nuts, or seeds.

Husk—See *Shuck.*

I

Ice—(1) To decorate food with icing; (2) To chill until hard and icy.

Icing—A sugary mixture used to coat baked goods. Another term for frosting.

Immersion blender—A hand-held blender, similar to a portable mixer with a single beater, which is placed directly into the container (such as a saucepan) that holds the food to be blended.

Infuse—To immerse herbs, spices, or other flavoring ingredients, such as tea leaves, in a hot liquid, in order to extract the flavor.

Instant-read thermometer—A thermometer used to check the temperature of meat as it cooks. It registers temperatures up to 220°, and gives a reading in a few seconds. It is not usually left in the meat as it cooks, but rather towards the end of the cooking time. (Cannot be used in place of a candy thermometer.)

Invert sugar—A type of sugar with a very fine crystal structure, frequently used in making candies. It can usually be purchased in a jar in specialty stores.

Italian seasoning—A blend of dried herbs, sold commercially, including some combination of oregano, basil, rosemary, thyme, sage, marjoram, and red pepper.

J

Jalapeño—A small, very hot, green chile pepper.

Jam—A condiment made from mashed fruits, sugar, and sometimes pectin.

Jambalaya—A Cajun dish similar to paella, prepared with meat, seafood, and rice.

Jell—To congeal.

Jell point—The temperature at which a food will thicken properly.

Jerk seasoning—A hot-sweet seasoning native to Jamaica.

Jícama—A root vegetable with a crunchy texture and a mildly sweet flavor, similar to an apple.

Jigger—A liquid measure containing 1½ fluid ounces.

Julienne—To cut food into slender, matchstick-size strips, about ⅛" x ⅛".

K

Kalamata olives—Greek olives, purplish in color, with a fruity flavor.

Kielbasa—Seasoned Polish sausage.

Kitchen twine—White string, usually made of linen, used for such jobs as trussing a stuffed roast during cooking. It is food-safe and holds together in high temperatures.

Knead—To work dough so that it becomes smooth and elastic. This is achieved by pressing the dough with the heels of the hands, while stretching it out, then folding it over itself, turning it a quarter of a turn, and repeating the process several times.

Kosher—Food prepared according to traditional Jewish dietary laws.

L

Lard—(1) Pork fat that has been rendered and clarified; (2) To insert strips of fat into uncooked lean meat, in order to tenderize and add flavor to the meat as it cooks.

Leavening—An ingredient, such as yeast or baking powder, that causes cooked foods to rise.

Legume—A type of vegetable bearing seeds in pods, such as beans and peas.

Line—To layer the bottom of a pan with parchment paper, to keep food from sticking, or with an edible substance, such as ladyfingers.

Liqueur—An alcoholic drink, usually sweet and served after dinner, flavored with aromatic ingredients, such as "crème de banana" (banana-flavored liqueur), "crème de menthe" (mint-flavored liqueur), etc.

Loaf pan—A rectangular pan used most often for baking bread or meatloaf. Its size can vary from quite small to large, with the standard size measuring about 9" x 5" x 3".

Lobster boil—See *Crab boil.*

M

Mace—A sweet, aromatic spice with a warm flavor, made from the ground outer husk of the nutmeg, whose flavor it strongly resembles.

Macerate—To soften or flavor a food by soaking it in a liquid, such as fruit soaked in brandy. When food is macerated, there is an exchange of flavors between the food and the liquid.

Mâche—A salad green, also called corn salad, with rounded leaves, and a slightly nutty flavor.

Maraschino cherries—Preserved cherries, sold with or without stems.

Marinade—A seasoned liquid in which food is soaked in order to tenderize it and add flavor.

Marinate—To allow food to stand in a liquid mixture, in order to cause it to become more tender or flavorful.

Marjoram—An herb with a slightly minty flavor, somewhat resembling sage and oregano. Usually available as dried leaves.

Marmalade—A condiment which contains the peel of citrus fruit.

Marrow—The soft, fatty tissue found in the cavities of bones.

Marsala—A fortified Italian wine.

Marzipan—A sweet almond paste made with sugar, ground almonds, and egg whites.

Masa—A type of flour made from corn, used widely in Mexican cuisine. Sometimes called "masa harina."

Mash—To crush a food (such as cooked potatoes) until smooth and even-textured.

Mayonnaise—An emulsified sauce (similar to hollandaise), made from egg yolks, oil, and lemon juice. It is one of the basic French sauces, including "Béchamel," "Espagnole," "Hollandaise," "Velouté," and "Vinaigrette" (see entries). Mayonnaise is distinguished from "salad dressing," which is a similar, but sweeter sauce, made without eggs.

Mealy—Resembling the texture of coarse meal; crumbly.

Meat thermometer—A thermometer used to check the temperature of meat as it cooks. It registers temperatures up to 220°. (It cannot be used interchangeably with a candy thermometer, since each type of thermometer registers a different range of temperatures.)

Medallion—A small, round cut of fish or meat.

Melt—To heat a solid food, such as butter or shortening, until it becomes liquefied.

Meringue—A confection made of stiffly beaten egg whites and sugar, used as a topping, or baked separately and used as a decoration or as a holder for fruit or ice cream.

Mesclun—An assorted blend of baby lettuces and salad greens, often referred to as a "gourmet blend."

Mince—To chop or cut food into very small pieces, ⅛" or less.

Minestrone—A thick, hearty soup, flavored with meat, and made with vegetables, pasta, and beans.

Mint—An herb with a fresh, fruity flavor. Available as fresh or dried leaves.

Mix—To blend ingredients together.

Mocha—A flavor that combines chocolate and coffee.

Mold—To pour a food into a form, allowing it to stand (usually refrigerated) until it is set.

Morel—A variety of wild mushroom with a crinkly, cone-shaped, brown cap. They are prized for their smoky, nutty flavor.

Mortar and pestle—A bowl and heavy, blunt instrument used to pulverize herbs or seasonings.

Moussaka—A traditional Greek dish whose ingredients include lamb or beef, eggplant, and tomatoes.

Mousse—A sweet or savory dish served hot or cold, usually made with egg whites or whipped cream, which give it an airy texture.

Muddle—To crush ingredients (such as mint leaves) in a liquid.

Muffin pan—A metal baking pan with individual cups, used to bake muffins or cupcakes. The standard size pan has 6–12 cups, while the miniature size (sometimes called a "gem" pan) has 12–24 cups.

Mull—To flavor a beverage, such as cider or wine, by heating it with various spices and flavoring ingredients.

Mustard—(1) A spice with a sharp, pungent flavor, available as whole or ground seeds; (2) A condiment prepared with this spice.

N

Nonpareils—Tiny hard candies, sometimes called "shot," used to decorate cakes and cookies.

Non-reactive pan—A nonporous pan that does not produce a chemical reaction when it comes into contact with acid foods. A pan made of glass, stainless steel, enamel, or glazed ceramic is non-reactive. An aluminum pan is reactive. See *Acid foods.*

Nutmeg—An aromatic spice with a warm, faintly sweet, spicy flavor, available either in ground form, or as whole, nut-shaped seeds.

O

Oregano—An herb similar in flavor to marjoram, but slightly more pungent. Available as fresh or crumbled dried leaves.

Oyster mushroom—A mushroom with a smooth cap, shaped like a shell or a fan, and with a mild flavor resembling oysters.

P

Paella—A traditional Spanish dish containing saffron-flavored rice and a variety of meat and seafood.

Pan-broil—To broil food in a skillet or heavy pan on top of the stove, using as little additional fat as possible. Drip-

pings that accumulate are poured or spooned off, so that there is no accumulation of fat. Also see *Broil.*

Pan-fry—To cook food in a skillet, uncovered, in a small amount of fat.

Paprika—A ground spice traditionally used in Hungarian cuisine, red in color, with a slightly peppery flavor ranging from mild to pungent and hot.

Parboil—To partially cook a food in boiling liquid, which is a step further than blanching.

Parch—To dry a food by roasting.

Parchment paper—A heavy paper used for lining baking pans, or for wrapping foods. It is grease-resistant and moisture-resistant.

Parcook—To cook a food partially by any method.

Pare—To cut the skin or rind off a food.

Parsley—An herb with a fresh, slightly sweet flavor, available as fresh leaves or dried flakes. The flat-leaf Italian variety has a smoother, more mellow flavor, while the curly variety has a slightly bitter flavor, and is best used as a garnish.

Partially set—A descriptive term for gelatin which has been chilled until it has reached the consistency of thick egg whites.

Passion fruit—A tropical fruit with a purplish-brown rind, juicy yellow flesh, and an intense, citrus flavor. It has small, teardrop-shaped segments filled with seeds.

Pasta—Any of a wide variety of noodles, made from a basic dough consisting of durum wheat flour and a liquid, usually water or milk. The dough can also include eggs and/or oil. It is available in a wide variety of shapes, sizes, and flavors, and is also available either fresh or dry. Refer to the "Pasta" chapter for descriptions of different types of pasta.

Pastry bag—A cone-shaped bag, made of cloth or plastic, that can be fitted with a variety of decorating tips. The large end is filled with icing or soft food (such as mashed potatoes), and the bag is squeezed, forcing the contents through the tip attached to the small end.

Pastry blender—A utensil used for cutting fat, such as shortening, into flour. Its shape is similar to a stirrup, with a straight handle on the top, attached to several U-shaped wires.

Pastry cloth—A piece of fabric which provides a non-stick surface for rolling out pastry. Some cloths are marked with concentric circles, which can be used as guidelines for rolling out various sizes of pie crusts.

Pastry wheel—A tool with a handle and a rolling blade, used to cut out pastry.

Pâté—A paste-like mixture of finely sieved liver, fish, seafood, or ground meat and herbs, baked in a pastry crust or mold, and served with crackers or toast as an appetizer.

Pâte à choux—See *Puff pastry*.

Patty—A round, flat piece of food (such as a hamburger patty) or candy (such as a peppermint patty).

Patty shell—An edible cup made of pastry, used to hold food such as creamed chicken.

Pectin—A substance used for preparing foods such as jams and jellies, which causes them to thicken and gel.

Pepper—Members of the Capsicum genus, peppers can be either sweet (for example, bell peppers), or hot (also known as chile peppers). Chile peppers can range in flavor from mild (poblano) to hot (jalapeño and serrano) to fiery (habanero and chipotle). These are not to be confused with the peppercorn berry, from which we get black pepper.

Peppercorn—A berry that grows on a vine plant. The black peppercorn, from which we get black pepper, is available whole, cracked, or ground. The white peppercorn is the milder, dried inner kernel of the ripe berry. The fresh green peppercorn, less common, is usually packed in brine.

Petit four—A bite-sized tea cake, usually square or diamond-shaped, with fancy icing and often decoration.

Phyllo—Greek pastry made up of tissue-thin layers of dough. (Sometimes spelled "Phylo," "Filo," or "Fillo.")

Pickle—To use a salty brine or vinegar mixture to preserve foods, such as vegetables or fruits. The most common type of pickle is made from cucumbers.

Pickling spice—A blend of spices, sold commercially, usually including mustard seed, cinnamon, bay leaves, black pepper, cardamom, allspice, ginger, turmeric, and mace.

Pierce—To prick with a sharp fork or the point of a knife.

Pie weights—Pellets about the size of small beans, which are placed on a piece of foil or parchment, and then set into an unfilled pie crust before baking, to keep the empty crust from buckling up as it cooks. Rice or dried beans can also be used for this purpose.

Pilaf—A seasoned rice dish in which rice is first browned in oil or butter, before the liquid is added to the recipe. This dish can also be prepared with bulgur and is sometimes called "pilau."

Pimiento—A sweet red pepper added to dishes to enhance the flavor and color.

Pinch—A very small amount (less than 1/8 teaspoon), or the amount that can be held between the thumb and forefinger. See *Dash*.

Pine nuts—Blanched seeds of pine cones (traditionally used to prepare pesto), and sometimes referred to as "pignoli."

Pipe—To squeeze icing or soft food through a pastry bag, in order to produce a decorative design.

Piquant—A term for food with a tangy or highly seasoned flavor.

Pit—To remove the seed of a fruit or berry.

Pita—Middle Eastern flat bread, sometimes called "pocket bread."

Pith—A white, fibrous membrane (usually bitter) that surrounds some vegetables and citrus fruits.

Plank—To cook on a wooden board.

Pluck—To remove the feathers from poultry.

Plump—To cause a food (such as raisins) to soften and increase in size by soaking in a liquid.

Poach—To cook a food gently in a simmering liquid.

Pone—Food that is flat and round in shape, such as a corn pone.

Popover pan—A baking pan similar to a muffin pan, with cups which are slightly deeper than muffin cups.

Poppy seeds—Tiny, blue-black seeds with a nutty flavor, often sprinkled on buns, or added to breads and cakes.

Porcini—A large wild mushroom with a smooth, rounded cap and a thick stem. They are known for their meaty, earthy flavor.

Port—A sweet Portuguese wine.

Portobello—A very large, dark brown mushroom, sometimes as large as 6" in diameter, known for its meaty flavor and dense texture.

Pot de crème—A creamy, custard dessert served in a tiny individual cup, which sometimes has its own lid.

Pot-roast—To cook meat by first browning it, and then braising it in a small amount of liquid, in a tightly covered container. It can be cooked in the oven or on top of the stove.

Poultry seasoning—A blend of herbs and spices, sold commercially, including sage, celery seed, black pepper, thyme, savory, onion, and marjoram.

Pound—To strike food with a heavy instrument, to flatten or tenderize it.

Praline—A confection made with caramelized sugar and pecans.

Precook—To cook a food partially or completely before it is reheated and served.

Preheat—To allow the oven or skillet to heat to a certain temperature before adding the food to be cooked.

Prepared pan—A pan that has been greased and/or floured.

Preserves—A thick mixture of whole or coarsely cut fruit, sugar, and sometimes pectin.

Pressure-cook—To cook food under pressure in steam.

Prick—To make small holes in the surface of a food, such as a pie crust.

Primavera—A descriptive term for food seasoned with fresh vegetables.

Proof—(1) To set a mixture containing yeast in a warm, dry place to rise; (2) A term referring to alcoholic content, where 1 percent = 2 proof and 100 percent = 200 proof.

Prosciutto—Italian-style ham which has been salt-cured and air-dried, usually sliced very thin. Cooked prosciutto is referred to as "cotto," and raw, as "crudo."

Provençale—A descriptive term for food seasoned with olive oil, garlic, fresh herbs, and sometimes tomatoes.

Puff pastry—A rich, multilayered French pastry, made with flour, butter, eggs, and water, such as that used to make cream puffs or croissants. Also called "pâte à choux."

Pull—To separate cooked meat, such as barbecue, into shreds.

Punch down—To use the fists to mash down a dough, allowing the gases to escape, and thereby reducing its volume.

Puree—To blend, process, or pass a cooked food through a sieve, until it has the consistency of baby food.

Q

Quiche—A pastry shell filled with a custard-type filling and various other ingredients. It is usually baked in a flat, round pan with straight, fluted sides.

Quick bread—A bread made with a leavening agent other than yeast, such as baking powder or baking soda.

Quinoa—A kernel which behaves much like a grain, and can be substituted for rice in many instances. It has a mild flavor, a light texture, and a high nutritional value.

R

Rack—A cut of meat which contains the ribs, such as rack of lamb.

Radicchio—A red-leaf variety of chicory, slightly bitter, often mixed with salad greens.

Ragoût—A hearty stew, usually made with a brown sauce.

Ramekin—A small, individual-size baking dish, similar to a miniature soufflé dish.

Ramen—A type of narrow Asian noodle.

Rancid—A descriptive term for fat or a fat product that has spoiled.

Ratatouille—A stew made of eggplant, tomatoes, and squash.

Ream—To extract juice from citrus fruit.

Reconstitute—To cause a dehydrated product to return to its original consistency, by soaking it in liquid.

Reduce—To cause a liquid to evaporate partially by simmering it uncovered, in order to thicken it, reduce its volume, and intensify its flavor.

Refresh—To cool food that has been blanched or parboiled, by holding it under cold running water or plunging it into ice water, in order to stop the cooking process.

Render—To melt down fat from a piece of meat. Also called "try out."

Rest—To allow dough to stand for a period of time without disturbing it.

Rib—One branch of a bunch of celery. Sometimes called a "stalk."

Ribbon—A descriptive term for egg yolks that have been beaten with sugar, so that when the beater is held high over the bowl, the consistency of the mixture that falls back into the bowl resembles a thick ribbon.

Rice—To press potatoes, or other cooked food, through a utensil called a ricer, which causes them to come out in long strands.

Rind—The tough outer covering or skin of a food.

Ring mold—A pan with a tube in the center, used either as a baking pan or a mold. The tube is slightly larger than that of a standard tube pan, and the sides are usually not as high.

Risotto—Rice that is first sautéed in butter, and then cooked and stirred, as broth is added slowly.

Roast—To cook food in the oven uncovered, without adding any liquid.

Roaster—A size classification for chicken from 10–20 weeks old, weighing over 5 pounds.

Rock Cornish hen—A hybrid miniature chicken, from 4–5 weeks old, weighing from 1–1½ pounds.

Roe—Fish eggs.

Rolling boil—A fast boil.

Rolling pin—A cylinder-shaped utensil used to roll dough to a uniform thickness. It can be made of wood, nylon, or marble. The American style has handles on the ends and is straight. The French style does not have handles, and can be either straight or tapered on the ends.

Roll out—To use a rolling pin to flatten dough to a specified thickness.

Rosemary—An herb with a fresh, pungent, pine flavor, whose leaves resemble pine needles.

Rotisserie—A device that rotates and cooks food impaled on a spit.

Roux—A mixture of fat (such as butter) and flour, blended and cooked slowly over low heat, and used as a base for thickening sauces, gravies, and soups. Depending on what type of fat is used, and how long it is cooked, the roux can range in color from pale to dark. However, the flour should always be cooked for at least 3–5 minutes, so that any pasty taste is removed. Roux is a staple in Creole cuisine.

Rusk—A crisp, browned piece of bread (usually twice-baked), such as Holland Rusk.

S

Saddle—A cut of meat including both loins in one piece, such as a saddle of veal.

Saffron—One of the costliest of all spices, made from the stigmas of the crocus flower. It imparts a yellow color and a pungent, exotic flavor, and is available both as whole threads and in powdered form.

Sage—An herb with gray-green leaves and a warm, pungent, musty flavor. Available as fresh leaves or dried, rubbed leaves.

Salad herbs—A blend of various herbs used to flavor salads.

Salsa—Spanish for "sauce," and a staple in Southwestern cuisine. It can be uncooked ("salsa cruda") or cooked. Green salsa is called "salsa verde," and its main ingredients are usually tomatillos, cilantro, and green chiles.

Sauté—To cook a food quickly on top of the stove in a shallow pan, until the food is browned, using a small amount of fat. Also see *Brown*.

Sauté pan—A wide, shallow pan with straight sides, used to sauté, stir-fry, and brown foods. Its straight sides help to keep the fat from spattering. It differs from a skillet, which has sloping sides.

Savory—(1) An herb of the mint family, whose flavor resembles sage and thyme. Available as whole fresh leaves or dried crushed leaves; (2) A descriptive term for a dish with a piquant, rather than sweet taste.

Savoy—Curly, soft cabbage. Always served cooked.

Scald—(1) To heat a liquid in a pan on the stove, until just before it reaches a boil. Tiny bubbles form at the edge of the pan, but do not rise and break on the surface of the liquid; (2) To rinse food with boiling water.

Scale—To remove scales from fish.

Scallion—A member of the onion family, whose bulb is immature and undeveloped. Sometimes referred to as a "green onion."

Scallop—(1) To cook in a thick sauce; (2) To make an ornamental border around food. (3) A type of seafood.

Scant—Not quite full.

Score—To cut slashes in the surface of a food (such as the edges of a steak, the surface of a ham, or the skin of a cucumber), to keep it from curling, to help it to cook evenly, or to decorate it.

Scramble—To mix until well blended.

Scrape—To remove the outer layer of a food, such as the kernels from an ear of corn, by stroking with an edged instrument, such as a knife.

Sear—To seal the juices in a food (frequently meat) by browning it quickly in a pan on top of the stove over high heat, without burning it.

Season—To add flavoring to a food to improve its taste, with ingredients such as salt, pepper, herbs, and spices.

Seasoned flour—Flour that has been seasoned, usually with salt and pepper, and sometimes with paprika.

Seed—To remove seeds from a food.

Seize—A term used to describe melted chocolate that has hardened and become lumpy. This occurs when any moisture, such as condensed steam, comes into contact with the chocolate. For this reason, chocolate should never be covered during cooking.

Separate—(1) To divide the white from the yolk of an egg. (2) A term referring to an undesirable condition, in which the ingredients of a sauce come apart and do not stay combined.

Sesame oil—An oil made from pressed sesame seeds that is used for flavoring foods.

Sesame seeds—Seeds that have a crisp texture and a nutty flavor when toasted. Often sprinkled on buns and breads.

Set (set up)—To congeal.

Shallot—A bulb-shaped vegetable related to the onion and garlic, but with a milder flavor than either.

Shell—To remove the hard outer covering of a food, such as eggs or nuts.

Shiitake—A mushroom with a large, dark brown, meaty cap and a smoky flavor. These are frequently used in Oriental cuisine, and are also known as black forest mushrooms.

Shirr—A method of cooking whole eggs, whereby they are placed in ramekins, covered with cream or milk, and sometimes crumbs, and baked until they are softly set.

Short—A term describing a food that has a high fat content, such as shortbread.

Shred—To cut food into long, thin slivers, usually using a grater.

Shrimp boil—See *Crab boil*.

Shuck—To remove the husk or shell, such as from an ear of corn.

Sieve—A metal utensil with mesh or perforations, through which soft food is pressed (such as cooked fruit), to remove any lumps.

Sift—To pass dry ingredients through a very fine sieve or sifter to separate the fine from the coarse particles, and to cause the ingredients to become fluffier and more uniform in texture.

Silver skin—The thin, pearl-colored membrane covering certain meats, such as leg of lamb and tenderloin. See *Fell.*

Simmer—To cook a liquid on top of the stove until just before it boils, or about 180° at sea level. Small bubbles form around the edges of the pan, but do not rise to the surface and break.

Singe—To burn the hairs off poultry that has been plucked.

Size of a walnut—A measure for butter, equal to about 2 tablespoons.

Skewer—A sharply-pointed metal or wooden rod onto which chunks of food are threaded, and then broiled or cooked over a grill.

Skillet—A wide, shallow pan with sloping sides, used to fry foods. It differs from a sauté pan, which has straight sides.

Skim—To remove the fat, foam, or scum from the surface of a liquid, such as soup, using a spoon, ladle, or special device for that purpose.

Skin—To remove the outer covering of a food by peeling.

Sliver—To cut food into thin, even strips.

Smiling—A quaint term used to describe liquid, usually water, that is just barely simmering.

Smoke—To preserve a food by drying it in an enclosed area, where it is exposed to wood smoke.

Smoke point—The temperature at which heated fat begins to smoke. Fat with a higher smoke point is better for frying. Each time fat is reheated, its smoke point becomes lower. Clarified (drawn) butter has a higher smoke point than plain butter.

Snip—To cut or gash with scissors.

Soak—To immerse in liquid or allow something to stand in liquid.

Soft peaks—A descriptive term for egg whites or cream beaten until soft points form when the beater is removed from the mixture. The tops of the points curl over and droop slightly. They will not point straight up.

Sorbet—A frozen confection made of ice, fruit syrup, and egg whites.

Soufflé—A casserole-type dish in which beaten egg whites are incorporated with other ingredients, and cooked to make a light, airy concoction.

Spices—Aromatic seasonings derived from parts of a plant other than its leaves. See *Herbs.*

Spit—A sharply pointed rod used to hold food as it cooks.

Spit-roast—To cook food on a rod, turning it as it cooks over a hot fire.

Springform pan—A round baking pan, with sides somewhat higher than a layer cake pan, and with a clamp that releases the sides from the base, allowing the contents to be released intact. Cheesecake is most often baked in a pan of this type.

Squab—A young, domesticated pigeon, weighing 1 pound or less.

Squab chicken—A small chicken, weighing less than 1½ pounds.

Star anise—A dried seed head with a pungent flavor similar to fennel.

Steam—To cook food using steam, by placing it in a perforated basket or on a rack over boiling or simmering liquid, and then covering it. The food does not touch the liquid.

Steep—To soak in liquid, in order to soften a food or extract flavor or impurities from it.

Stew—To cover a food with liquid, and then simmer it either on top of the stove or in the oven, for an extended period of time. A variety of vegetables and flavorings are often added to stew.

Stewing chicken—A size classification for chicken over 10 months old, weighing from 4–6 pounds.

Stiff but not dry—A descriptive term for egg whites or heavy cream beaten to stiff peaks, which still appear moist and glossy.

Stiff peaks—A descriptive term for egg whites or heavy cream beaten until stiff points form when the beater is removed from the mixture. The tops of the points will not curl over, but will point straight up.

Stir—To combine ingredients in a container by moving a spoon in circular motions through the mixture.

Stir-fry—To sauté quickly in a large pan, using very little fat, stirring or tossing the food constantly.

Stock—Strained broth in which meat, poultry, fish, or vegetables have been cooked, in order to extract their flavor. Also called "broth" and sometimes called "bouillon."

Stockpot—A deep pot with high, straight sides and handles on each side, used for slow cooking of stocks.

Straight pack—A term describing frozen produce, such as fruit, that is processed without any added sugar.

Strain—To remove solid particles from a liquid by pouring it through a strainer, sieve, or colander.

Straw mushrooms—Small, light brown mushrooms whose caps resemble umbrellas, with a slippery texture and a mild flavor.

Stud—To insert bits of flavoring (such as slivers of garlic) into food.

Stuff—To place dressing into the cavity of poultry or meat before cooking.

Stuffing—A mixture used to stuff a cavity of another food, such as poultry, chops, or vegetables, which is cooked with the food or separately from the food. See *Dressing.*

Suet—Animal fat, usually beef.

Sweat—To cook food over low heat in its own juice, using a small amount of fat. The food is tightly covered with foil or parchment paper, and then covered with the pan lid, so that the food softens but does not brown.

Swirl—To whirl gently in a pan.

Swiss chard—A root vegetable grown for its leaves.

T

Tahini—A paste prepared from ground sesame seeds, with a taste resembling peanut butter.

Tarragon—An herb with a slightly bitter flavor resembling licorice. Available as fresh or dried leaves.

Tart—A filled pastry without a top crust.

Tartar sauce—A sauce made from a mayonnaise base, often served chilled with fish.

Tart pan—A shallow pan with straight, fluted sides. It often has a removable, tray-like bottom that can be pushed up through the sides, allowing the contents to be removed undisturbed. Tart pans can be round or oblong.

Teakettle—A cooking vessel usually made of some kind of metal or enamel, and used to boil water.

Teapot— A container usually made of china, ceramic, or pottery, in which tea is brewed and served.

Temper—(1) To stabilize the texture of chocolate by a melting and cooling process; (2) To heat beaten raw eggs gradually, so that they don't curdle, before adding them to a hot soup or sauce. This is done by adding some of the hot mixture to the eggs little by little, and then incorporating the egg mixture back into the hot mixture.

Tenderize—To make food more tender, either by using a mallet or other utensil to break up connective tissue, or by using a chemical agent, such as a commercial meat tenderizer or marinade.

Terrine—A deep, covered baking dish, often made of earthenware.

Test with a straw or toothpick—To insert a thin wire, skewer, broom straw, or toothpick into the center of a cake to test for doneness. When the straw comes out clean, without any batter adhering to it, the cake is done.

Thicken—To cause a liquid to become more dense, either by adding flour, starch, or eggs, or by boiling it to reduce its volume.

Thin—To cause a liquid to become less dense by adding more liquid.

Thyme—An herb whose pungent flavor resembles cloves and sage, available as fresh or dried leaves.

Timbale—(1) A drum-shaped mold used to bake various foods; (2) Foods baked in such a mold.

Toast—To brown a food using dry heat. See *Brown.*

Tofu—A creamy cake made of bean curd, a soybean product, often used in Oriental cuisine. It is frequently used as a vegetarian meat substitute.

Tomatillo—A fruit resembling a green cherry tomato, with an acid flavor. Frequently used as the basis for green salsa ("salsa verde").

Torte—A fancy decorated cake of several layers.

Toss—To mix foods (such as salads), using a gentle lift-and-drop motion.

Tostada—A crisp, fried tortilla.

Trifle—A dessert made of macaroons or sponge cake, fruit, and whipped cream.

Truss—To hold a food together with string or skewers (such as poultry or a stuffed roast), so that it maintains a compact shape during cooking.

Try out—To melt down fat from a piece of meat. Also called "render."

Tube pan—A round, deep baking pan with a center tube, especially used for baking angel food cake.

Turkey, fryer-roaster—A classification for a turkey less than 16 weeks old, weighing from 4–8 pounds.

Turkey, mature—A classification for a turkey over 15 months old, weighing from 12–25 pounds.

Turkey, young hen— A classification for a female turkey from 14–22 weeks old, weighing from 7–15 pounds.

Turkey, young tom—A classification for a male turkey from 14–22 weeks old, weighing from 15–25 pounds, or more.

Turmeric—A spice related to ginger, with a warm, mellow flavor, sometimes used in place of saffron. Available dried and ground. It imparts a golden-yellow color.

Turn—(1) To turn food over in a pan; (2) To flute the edges of a food.

Turn out—To unmold food onto a serving dish.

U–V

Unmold—To remove food from the mold in which it was formed.

Vanilla—A spice with a warm, aromatic, sweet flavor. Available as dried beans or as a liquid extract.

Variety meats—Organ meats, such as liver, kidneys, heart, and tongue.

Velouté sauce—A white sauce made from butter, flour, and light-colored stock. One of the basic French sauces, including "Béchamel," "Espagnole," "Hollandaise," "Mayonnaise," and "Vinaigrette" (see entries).

Vinaigrette—A sauce, used as a salad dressing, made from oil, vinegar, herbs, and other seasonings. One of the basic French sauces, including "Béchamel," "Espagnole," "Hollandaise," "Mayonnaise," and "Velouté" (see entries).

W–X

Water bath—See *Hot water bath.*

Whey—The liquid that separates from the curds during the cheese-making process.

Whip—To incorporate air into a mixture using an egg beater, electric mixer, or wire whisk. This increases its volume, and changes its texture and consistency.

Whisk—(1) A wire utensil made of loops joined at the handle, which is used to whip ingredients such as egg whites; (2) To use such a utensil to whip food.

Wok—A metal pan with a rounded bottom and a handle, used for stir-frying.

Work—(1) To mix with the hands; (2) To knead.

Y–Z

Yuca—A large root with tough, brown skin and crisp, white flesh. Used in Caribbean and Latin American cuisine.

Zest—The outer skin (not the white pith) of a citrus fruit. This portion of the fruit is rich in aromatic oils.

Food Math

■■■

HOW MUCH TO BUY AND PREPARE

Quantities and yields are approximate.

Tips on looking up entries:

▪ Entries are arranged alphabetically, without regard to spaces or hyphens. Entries more than one word long are alphabetized as though there were no spaces between the words.

▪ If a particular food, such as "rice," appears in this list in more than one form, such as "brown," "instant," etc., all the forms are listed together before the next food is listed, which would be "Rice Chex cereal."

▪ If you can't find something under the general or generic listing, look for it under the specific or brand name listing.

FOOD	QUANTITY	YIELD
Alcoholic beverages	1 fifth	25.6 oz.; 17 jiggers (1½ oz. each)
Alcoholic beverages	1 liter	33.8 oz.; 22 jiggers (1½ oz. each)
Alfalfa sprouts	1 lb.	6 cups
Allspice, ground	1 oz.	4½ Tbsp.
Almond paste	8-oz. can	¾ cup
Almonds, ground	1 lb.	2⅔ cups

FOOD	QUANTITY	YIELD
Almonds, in shell	1 lb.	1 cup nutmeat; 5–6 oz. nutmeat
Almonds, sliced	2¼ oz.	½ cup
Almonds, slivered	2 oz.	⅓ cup
Almonds, whole	2½ oz.	½ cup
Anchovy fillets	1 fillet	1 tsp. anchovy paste
Anchovy fillets	2-oz. can	12 anchovies; 3 Tbsp. mashed
Anchovy paste	2-oz. tube	4 Tbsp.
Angel hair pasta, fresh	9-oz. pkg.	3¾ cups cooked
Apple pie filling	21-oz. can	2⅓ cups
Apples, dried	6-oz. pkg.	1 cup dried; 2⅔ cups cooked; equivalent to 1½ lbs. fresh; makes 1 (8″) pie or 3 cups applesauce
Apples, fresh	1 med.	¾ cup chopped; 1 cup diced or sliced
Apples, fresh	1 lb.	3 med.; 2½ cups peeled, diced, or sliced; 3 cups unpeeled, diced, or sliced
Apples, fresh	2 lbs.	makes 1 (9″) pie; 1 cup applesauce
Applesauce	16-oz. jar	2 cups
Apple slices, canned	20-oz. can	2 cups drained
Apricots, canned	16-oz. can	2 cups drained halves; 6–8 whole
Apricots, dried	6-oz. pkg.	1 cup dried; 2 cups cooked

FOOD	QUANTITY	YIELD
Apricots, fresh	2 med.	½ cup sliced
Apricots, fresh	1 lb.	2 cups halves or slices; 8–12 med.
Arrowroot	1 Tbsp.	thickens as 2½ Tbsp. flour
Artichoke bottoms	14-oz. can	5–10 pieces
Artichoke hearts	15-oz. can	1 cup chopped
Artichokes	1 sm. (baby)	2–3 oz.
Artichokes	1 med.	8–10 oz.
Artichokes	1 lg.	15–20 oz.
Arugula, fresh	½ oz.	½ cup
Asparagus, canned, cut	15-oz. can	1¾ cups
Asparagus, canned, spears	15-oz. can	12–18 spears
Asparagus, fresh	1 lb.	16–20 med. spears; 3 cups trimmed (2" pieces); 2½ cups cooked pieces
Asparagus, frozen	10 oz.	2 cups cut; equivalent to 1¼ lbs. fresh
Avocados	1 lb.	2 med.; 1½ cups pulp
Bacon, fatback	¼ lb.	1 cup cracklings
Bacon, sliced	1 lb.	10–15 thick, 16–24 avg., or 25–30 thin slices
Bacon, sliced, center cut	12 oz.	25–30 thin slices
Bacon, sliced, cooked	1 slice	1 Tbsp. crumbled
Bacon, sliced, cooked	1 lb.	1–1½ cups cooked and crumbled
Baked beans	4½ quarts	25 servings
Baking powder	7-oz. can	1¼ cups
Baking soda	16-oz. box	2⅓ cups
Bamboo shoots, canned	8-oz. can	1 cup drained
Bananas, dried, sliced	1 lb.	4–4½ cups
Bananas, fresh	1 med.	1 cup sliced
Bananas, fresh	1 lb.	3 sm. or 2 lg.; 1½ cups mashed; 2 cups sliced
Barbecue	7½ lbs.	25 servings
Barley, pearl, quick-cooking	1 lb.	2½ cups uncooked; 8 cups cooked
Basil, dried	1 oz.	¾ cup
Basil, fresh	½ oz.	1 cup chopped leaves
Bay leaves, dried	1 whole	¼–½ tsp. broken; ⅛–¼ tsp. crushed
Bay leaves, dried	1 oz.	about 200 leaves
Bean puree	1 lb.	2½ cups
Beans, canned	15-oz. can	1¾ cups

FOOD	QUANTITY	YIELD
Beans, dried	1 lb.	2–2½ cups dried; 5½–6 cups cooked
Bean sprouts, canned	16-oz. can	2 cups drained
Bean sprouts, fresh	1 lb.	3–4 cups raw; 2 cups cooked
Beef, brisket, uncooked	6 lbs.	3 lbs. cooked
Beef, cooked, diced	1 lb.	3 cups
Beef, dried, sliced	5 oz. jar	24 slices; 2 cups shredded
Beef, flank steak	1 avg.	1¼–1½ lbs.
Beef, ground, raw	1 lb.	2 cups; 12 oz. cooked
Beef, ground, raw	8–10 lbs.	25 servings for hamburgers
Beef, roast	1 lb. cooked	makes 4–5 sandwiches
Beef, tenderloin	5 lbs.	12–18 servings
Beer	1 pony keg	7¾ gallons; ½ full-size keg; equivalent to 82 (12-oz.) cans, and pours 100 (12-oz.) cups with a ½" head
Beer	1 full-size keg	15½ gallons; equivalent to 165 (12-oz.) cans, and pours 200 (12-oz.) cups with a ½" head
Beet greens, fresh	1 lb.	8 oz. leaves; 6 cups raw; 1½ cups cooked
Beets, canned	8-oz. can	1 cup sliced
Beets, fresh	1 lb.	10 (2") beets; 2 cups cooked and sliced or diced
Berries (see also other listings)	1 pint	2–3 cups
Berries (see also other listings)	1 quart	makes 1 (9") pie
Bisquick	60-oz. box	14 cups
Blackberries, canned	15-oz. can	1¾ cups
Blackberries, fresh or frozen	1 lb.	3½ cups
Black-eyed peas, canned	15-oz. can	1½ cups drained
Black-eyed peas, dried	1 cup	7 oz. dried; 2½ cups cooked
Black-eyed peas, dried	1 lb.	2–2½ cups dried; 5–6 cups cooked
Black-eyed peas, frozen	10-oz. pkg.	1½ cups
Black-eyed peas, in pod	1 lb.	1¾ cups shelled
Black-eyed peas, shelled	1 lb.	2⅓ cups

FOOD	QUANTITY	YIELD
Blueberries, canned	15-oz. can	1½ cups
Blueberries, fresh or frozen	1 lb.	3½ cups; makes 1 (9″) pie
Blueberry pie filling	21-oz. can	2⅓ cups
Bok choy (see Cabbage)		
Bouillon, cube	1 cube	1 cup prepared
Bouillon, granules	1 tsp.	1 cup prepared
Bouillon, liquid concentrate	2 tsp.	¾ cup prepared
Bouillon, soup base paste	¾ tsp.	1 cup prepared
Bouillon, soup base paste	1 Tbsp.	1 qt. prepared
Boysenberries, canned	17-oz. can	2 cups
Boysenberries, fresh	1 pint	12 oz.; 1¾ cups
Bran flakes	16-oz. pkg.	8½ cups
Bread	1 lb. loaf	16–18 regular slices; 30 thin slices; 12 cups croutons
Bread	1¼-lb. loaf	19–21 regular slices
Bread	1½-lb. loaf	24 regular slices; 30 thin slices
Bread	2-lb. loaf	28 regular slices; 36 thin slices
Bread	3 (1-lb.) loaves	25 servings
Bread, dry	3 slices	1 cup fine crumbs
Bread, French	1-lb. loaf	16 (¾″) slices
Bread, fresh	2 slices	1 cup coarse crumbs; 1½ cups cubes
Bread, party-size	8-oz. loaf	30–32 slices
Bread, pita (see Pita bread)		
Bread, toasted	2 slices	½ cup crumbs; 1 cup cubes
Bread crumbs commercial	8 oz.	2 cups
Broccoli, fresh	1 lb.	2 cups florets
Broccoli, fresh	1 bunch	1¼ lbs.; 3 cups chopped, cooked
Broccoli, frozen	10-oz. pkg.	1½ cups chopped
Broth, beef or chicken	10½-oz. can	1¼ cups
Broth, beef or chicken	14½-oz. can	1¾ cups
Brussels sprouts, fresh	1 lb.	4 cups cooked
Brussels sprouts, fresh	1 quart	1¼ lbs.
Brussels sprouts, frozen	10-oz. pkg.	18–24 sprouts; 1½–2 cups cooked
Bulgur wheat, uncooked	1 lb.	2¾ cups uncooked; 8 cups cooked

FOOD	QUANTITY	YIELD
Buns	5 (8-bun) pkgs.	25 servings
Butter	2 Tbsp.	"the size of a walnut"
Butter	¼-lb. stick	½ cup; 8 Tbsp.; 12–16 pats; ⅓ cup clarified butter
Butter	½ lb.	25 servings
Butter	1 lb.	2 cups; 4 sticks
Butter, soft	8-oz. tub	1 cup
Butter, whipped	1 lb.	3 cups
Butter Buds sprinkles	½-oz. packet	makes 4 oz. liquid
Butter Buds sprinkles	2½-oz. jar	¾ cup dry
Butter Buds sprinkles	4-oz. box	8 (½-oz.) packets
Buttermilk powder	12-oz. can	3¾ cups; makes 3¾ quarts
Butterscotch morsels	12-oz. pkg.	2 cups
Cabbage, bok choy, raw	1 lb.	4–5½ cups shredded or sliced; ¾ cup cooked
Cabbage, green, cooked	1 lb.	1½–2 cups shredded; 2–2½ cups wedges
Cabbage, green, raw	1 med. head	1¼–1½ lbs.; 4–6 cups shredded
Cabbage, green, raw	1 lb.	12 oz. after trimming
Cabbage, red, raw	1 med. head	2 lbs.; 4 cups cooked
Cabbage, Savoy, raw	1 lb.	13 oz. after trimming
Cake mix	18½-oz. box	5–6 cups batter; 2 (9″-round) layers; 2 (8″-square) layers; 1 (13″ x 9″ x 2″) cake; 1 cartoon character cake; 24 cupcakes
Cake, sheet (9″ x 13″)	1½ cakes	25 servings
Cake, two-layer (9″)	2–2½ cakes	25 servings
Candied fruit	8-oz. pkg.	1½ cups chopped
Cannellini beans, dried	1 lb.	2–2½ cups dried; 5–6 cups cooked
Cantaloupe	1 avg. (6″ diam.)	3 lbs.; 4½ cups cubed; 25 (⅞″) balls
Cardamom	1 pod	18–20 seeds; 1 tsp. ground
Carrots, canned	16-oz. can	2 cups sliced
Carrots, cooked	1 lb.	1⅓ cups puréed
Carrots, frozen	10-oz. pkg.	1½–2 cups
Carrots, frozen	16-oz. pkg.	equivalent to 2 lbs. fresh, raw, untrimmed

FOOD	QUANTITY	YIELD
Carrots, raw	1 lb.	24–36 baby; 12–14 sm.; 5–7 med.; 14 oz. peeled; 12 oz. cooked; 2½–2¾ cups cooked or diced; 2½–3 cups shredded or sliced
Cashews, canned	6¼-oz. can	1⅓ cups
Cashews, shelled	1 oz.	14 lg. or 18 med.
Cashews, shelled	1 lb.	3¼ cups
Cauliflower, fresh	1 med. head	1¾–2¼ lbs.
Cauliflower, fresh	1 lb.	9 oz. after trimming; 7½ oz. cooked; 1½ cups cut up
Cauliflower, frozen	10-oz. pkg.	2 cups cut up
Cauliflower, frozen	16-oz. pkg.	2 lbs. fresh, raw (before trimming)
Caviar	1 oz.	1½–2 Tbsp.; 3 canapés
Celeriac (Celery root)	1 lb.	3 cups grated or julienned; 1 cup cooked and pureed
Celery	1 med. rib	¼ cup celery flakes
Celery	2–3 med. ribs	1 cup chopped, diced, or sliced
Celery	1 med. bunch	1 lb. untrimmed; 12 oz. after trimming; 2 cups diced or sliced
Celery flakes	1 oz.	¾ cup
Celery salt	1 oz.	2 Tbsp.
Celery seeds	1 oz.	4 Tbsp.
Cereal, All Bran	13.8-oz. pkg.	6½ cups
Cereal, Corn Chex	12-oz. pkg.	11 cups
Cereal, cornflakes (see Cornflakes)		
Cereal, Rice Chex	12-oz. pkg.	11 cups
Cereal, Wheat Chex	16-oz. pkg.	7 cups
Champagne, 187 ml.	1 split	6.3 oz.
Champagne, 750 ml.	1 bottle	5 (5-oz.) servings
Champagne, 750 ml.	1 case	60 (5-oz.) servings
Chayote squash (Mirliton)	1 avg.	1 lb.
Cheese	3–5 lbs.	25 servings
Cheese, cold pack	8-oz. carton	⅞ cup
Cheese, crumbled (blue, etc.)	4 oz.	1 cup
Cheese, firm (Cheddar, etc.)	16 oz.	4 cups shredded
Cheese, hard (Parmesan, etc.)	8 oz.	1½ cups grated

FOOD	QUANTITY	YIELD
Cheese spread	5-oz. jar	1 cup
Cheese spread, pressurized	8-oz. can	⅞ cup
Cheesecake	2 lbs.	8″ cake
Cheesecake	3 lbs.	10″ cake
Cheez Whiz	8-oz. jar	⅞ cup
Cheez Whiz	16-oz. jar	1¾ cups
Cherries, canned, tart	16 oz. pitted	1½ cups drained
Cherries, dried, tart	3-oz. pkg.	½ cup
Cherries, fresh, sweet	1 lb. unpitted	1 quart; 1¾ cups
Cherries, frozen, tart	1 lb. pitted	2 cups
Cherries, frozen, tart	26-oz. pkg.	makes 1 (9″) pie
Cherries, maraschino	10-oz. jar	25 cherries with stems; 33 cherries without stems
Cherry pie filling	21-oz. can	2⅓ cups
Chestnut puree	8¼-oz. can	1 cup
Chestnuts, canned	10-oz. can	about 25 whole chestnuts
Chestnuts, in shell	1½ lbs.	35–40 lg.; 1 lb. peeled; 2½ cups peeled; 2 cups puréed
Chex snack mix	14-oz. pkg.	8 cups
Chicken, bone in	3 lbs.	2½–3 cups cooked meat
Chicken, bone in	12½ lbs.	25 servings
Chicken, boneless	1 lb.	3 cups cooked and diced
Chicken, breasts, bone in	1 lb.	¾–1 cup cooked meat
Chicken, breasts, boneless	10 oz.	¾–1 cup cooked meat
Chicken, breasts (half)	1 avg.	scant ½ cup cooked, chopped meat
Chicken broth	13¾-oz. can	1¾ cups
Chicken, canned	5-oz. can	½ cup drained
Chicken, canned	10-oz. can	1 cup drained
Chicken, capon, whole	5 lb.	2¼ lbs. cooked meat
Chicken, whole	2–3 lbs.	2–3 cups cooked, chopped meat
Chicken, whole	4–5 lbs.	5 cups cooked, chopped meat
Chickpeas, dried	1 cup	2½ cups cooked
Chiles, green, chopped	4½-oz. can	½ cup
Chiles, green, chopped	7-oz. can	1 scant cup
Chiles, green, whole	4-oz. can	3 whole chiles
Chili powder	1 oz.	3½ Tbsp.
Chili sauce	12-oz. bottle	1¼–1½ cups
Chinese noodles (wide) (also see Chow mein noodles)	5-oz. can	2½ cups

FOOD	QUANTITY	YIELD
Chives, freeze-dried	1 oz.	about 3 cups
Chives, fresh	1 Tbsp.	1 tsp. freeze-dried
Chives, fresh	1 bunch	½ cup snipped
Chocolate, bar or square	1 oz.	3 Tbsp. chopped or grated
Chocolate, bar or square	9 oz.	1⅝ cups chopped or grated; 1 cup melted
Chocolate, unsweetened	1 oz.	1 square; 4 Tbsp. grated
Chocolate, unsweetened	1 oz.	1 envelope liquid
Chocolate bits, M&M	12-oz. pkg.	1½ cups
Chocolate drink powder	14½-oz. tin	3¼ cups powder; makes 6½ quarts
Chocolate kisses (mini)	10-oz. pkg.	209 pieces
Chocolate morsels	12-oz. pkg.	2 cups
Chocolate syrup	24-oz. bottle	2⅛ cups
Chocolate wafers	20 wafers	1 cup fine crumbs
Chocolate wafers	2½-oz. pkg.	scant ⅔ cup fine crumbs
Chow mein noodles	3-oz. can	1½ cups
Chow mein noodles	5-oz. can	2½ cups
Chutney	8-oz. jar	1 cup
Cilantro, dried	1 oz.	1 cup
Cinnamon, ground	1 oz.	4 Tbsp.
Cinnamon, stick	1" part of stick	1 tsp. ground
Cinnamon, stick	1 oz.	8–10 (5"-long) sticks
Cinnamon candy dots	1-lb. pkg.	2¼ cups
Citron, chopped	6½-oz. jar	1 cup
Clam juice	8-oz. bottle	1 cup
Clams, canned	6½-oz. can	¾ cup
Clams, fresh, in shell	8 quarts	3 doz.; 4 cups (1 quart) shucked
Clams, shucked	1 quart	2–3 cups chopped
Cloves, ground	1 oz.	4 Tbsp.
Cloves, whole	1 tsp. whole	¾ tsp. ground
Cloves, whole	3 oz.	1 cup
Club crackers	16-oz. box	32 (4-section) crackers
Cocktail sauce	9-oz. jar	1⅛ cups
Cocktail sauce	12-oz. bottle	1½ cups
Cocoa, baking	8-oz. tin	2⅔ cups
Cocoa hot drink mix	10-oz. tin	2 cups
Coconut, flaked	3½-oz. can	1¼ cups
Coconut, flaked	7-oz. pkg.	2½ cups
Coconut, flaked	14-oz. pkg.	5⅓ cups
Coconut, fresh	1 lb.	1 med.; 3 cups grated or chopped
Coconut milk, canned	15 oz.	1⅞ cups

FOOD	QUANTITY	YIELD
Coffee, freeze-dried	2-oz. jar	¾ cup dry; 30–36 (6-oz.) cups prepared
Coffee, ground	1 lb.	5 cups (80 Tbsp.) grounds; 40–60 (6-oz.) cups prepared
Coffee, instant	4-oz. jar	2½ cups dry; 120 (6-oz.) cups prepared
Coffee, prepared	2½–3½ gal.	serves 25 people
Cole slaw	3¼ quarts	25 servings
Collard greens, canned	15-oz. can	2 cups
Collard greens, fresh	1 lb.	6–7 cups raw; 1½ cups cooked
Collard greens, frozen	10-oz. pkg.	1½ cups cooked
Congealed salad	3 quarts	25 servings
Consommé	10½-oz. can	1⅓ cups
Coriander seeds	½ cup	1¼ oz.
Corn, canned, creamed	12-oz. can	1½ cups
Corn, canned, creamed	16-oz. can	2 cups
Corn, canned, kernels	15¼-oz. can	1¾ cups drained
Corn, canned, kernels	17-oz. can	2 cups drained
Corn, fresh ears	2–3 med.	1 cup cut kernels
Corn, frozen	10-oz. pkg.	1¼ cups kernels
Corn, frozen	16-oz. pkg.	1⅔ cups kernels
Cornbread	8" square pan	4 cups crumbs for stuffing
Cornbread	9" round pan	4 cups crumbs for stuffing
Corned beef hash	15-oz. can	2 cups
Cornflake crumbs	21-oz. pkg.	6¾ cups
Cornflakes	16-oz. pkg.	16 cups
Cornflakes	3–4 cups	1 cup crushed
Cornflakes	4 oz.	1 cup crumbs
Corn husks (for tamales)	1 lb.	40 leaves
Cornish game hen	1 med. hen	1¼ lbs.
Cornmeal, uncooked	1 lb.	3 cups uncooked; 16 cups cooked
Cornstarch	1 Tbsp.	thickens same as 2 Tbsp. flour
Cornstarch	1 oz.	3 Tbsp.
Cornstarch	1 lb. pkg.	3½ cups
Corn syrup	16 oz.	2 cups
Cottage cheese	8 oz. (½ pt.)	1 cup
Couscous, uncooked	1 cup	7 oz. uncooked; 2½–3 cups cooked
Crab, Dungeness	1 avg.	2–3 lbs. in shell
Crab, in shell	1 lb. whole	6–7 oz. meat; ⅔ cup flaked

FOOD	QUANTITY	YIELD
Crabmeat, canned	6½-oz. can	1 cup flaked
Cracker meal	14-oz. box	2¾ cups
Crackers, graham	16-oz. box	33 (2½″ x 5″) crackers
Crackers, graham	15 (2½″ sq.)	1 cup fine crumbs
Crackers, graham, crumbs	13½-oz. box	3¾ cups; makes 3 pie shells
Crackers, Ritz	24 crackers	1 cup fine crumbs
Crackers, Ritz	1 roll	35 crackers; 1½ cups fine crumbs
Crackers, Ritz	1-lb. pkg.	140 crackers; 6 cups fine crumbs
Crackers, saltines	30 crackers	1 cup fine crumbs
Crackers, saltines	16-oz. pkg.	130–140 (2″ x 2″) crackers; 4½ cups fine crumbs
Crackers, saltines	1½ lbs.	25 servings
Crackers, Triscuits	13-oz. box	84 crackers
Crackers, Wheat Thins	16-oz. box	256 crackers
Cranberries, dried	6-oz. pkg.	1⅓ cups dried
Cranberries, fresh	12-oz. pkg.	3 cups
Cranberries, fresh	1-lb. pkg.	4 cups; 3 cups cooked sauce
Cranberry relish	12-oz. carton	1¼ cups
Cranberry relish	16-oz. jar	1¾ cups
Cranberry sauce, jellied	16-oz. can	2 cups
Crayfish	1 lb. in shell	10 crayfish; ¾ cup meat
Cream, heavy	½ pint	1 cup unwhipped; 2 cups whipped
Cream, heavy (unwhipped)	¾ pint	25 servings
Cream, light (half-and-half)	1 pint	2 cups; 16 coffee servings
Cream, whipped, pressurized	7-oz. can	1⅞ cups
Cream cheese	3-oz. pkg.	⅓ cup
Cream cheese	8-oz. pkg.	1 cup
Cream cheese spread	8-oz. carton	⅞ cup
Cream cheese spread	12-oz. carton	1⅜ cups
Creamer, non-dairy	11-oz. jar	3⅛ cups; 150 servings (1 tsp. each)
Creamer, non-dairy, flavored	8-oz. jar	1⅔ cups; 20 servings (4 tsp. each)
Cream of Rice	14-oz. box	2¼ cups uncooked
Cream of tartar	1 oz.	3 Tbsp.

FOOD	QUANTITY	YIELD
Cream of Wheat, quick	1 lb.	2½ cups uncooked; 16 cups cooked
Cucumbers	1 lb.	2 med.; 15 oz. after peeling; 11 oz. without seeds; 2½–3 cups peeled and sliced or chopped
Cumin seeds, ground	1 oz.	4½ Tbsp.
Cumin seeds, whole	1 tsp.	½ tsp. ground
Currants, dried	10-oz. pkg.	2 cups
Currants, dried	1-lb. pkg.	3 cups
Currants, fresh	1 quart	3¾ cups
Curry paste	5 oz.	½ cup
Curry powder	1 oz.	4 Tbsp.
Dandelion greens	1 lb.	2¾ cups cooked
Dates, diced, sugared	1 lb.	2⅔ cups
Dates, dried, pitted	8-oz. pkg.	54 dates; 1¼ cups chopped
Dates, dried, with pits	1 lb.	60 dates; 2½ cups pitted
Dill seeds	1 oz.	4½ Tbsp.
Dill weed, dried	1 oz.	¾ cup
Dill weed, fresh	½ oz.	½ cup; ¼ tsp. dill juice
Dip, refrigerated	16-oz. carton	1¾ cups
Durkees dressing	10-oz. bottle	1⅛ cups
Eggplant	1 med.	1¼ lbs.; 8 (¼″ thick) slices; 3 cups diced; 2½ cups cooked
Eggplant, baby	1 avg.	¼ lb.
Egg roll wrappers	16-oz. pkg.	14 wrappers
Eggs, large	1 whole egg	6 hard-cooked slices
Eggs, large	4 whole eggs	1 cup hard-cooked eggs, chopped
Eggs, large	1 cup	5–7 whole eggs; 8–10 whites; 12–14 yolks
Egg substitute	16-oz. carton	2 cups; 8 eggs
Egg whites, unbeaten	½ cup	up to 4 cups beaten
Endive, Belgian	1 med. head	10–16 leaves
Endive, curly	1 med. head	12 oz.; 3–4 cups torn up
Equal	1 envelope	sweetens as 2 tsp. sugar
Equal Measure	¼ tsp.	sweetens as 2 tsp. sugar
Equal tablets	1 tablet	sweetens as 1 tsp. sugar
Escarole	1 med. head	8 oz.; 6–7 cups torn up; 4 salad servings
Farina, quick-cooking	1 lb.	2½ cups uncooked; 16 cups cooked

FOOD	QUANTITY	YIELD
Fava beans, canned	20-oz. can	2 cups
Fava beans, dried	1 lb.	8–9 servings; 2 cups dried; 4½ cups cooked
Fava beans, fresh, in pod	1 lb.	1–1½ cups shelled
Fava beans, fresh, in pod	5 lbs.	6–8 servings
Fennel bulb	1 lb.	3 cups sliced
Fennel seeds, dried	1 oz.	4 Tbsp.
Feta cheese	8-oz. pkg.	4–6 salad servings
Fettuccine, fresh	9-oz. pkg.	3¾ cups cooked
Figs, canned	16-oz. can	12–16 med.
Figs, dried	1 lb.	40–45 med.; 3 cups chopped; 4 cups cooked
Figs, fresh	1 lb.	12 sm.; 9 med.; 2⅔ cups chopped
Filberts (see Hazelnuts)		
Filo pastry (see Phyllo pastry)		
Fish, boneless	1 fillet	4–6 oz.
Fish, boneless	1 steak	5–8 oz.
Flour, all-purpose	1 lb.	3½ cups unsifted; 4 cups sifted
Flour, all-purpose	5-lb. bag	20 cups sifted
Flour, bread	1 lb.	4 cups sifted
Flour, bread	5-lb. bag	20 cups sifted
Flour, buckwheat	1 lb.	3¼ cups sifted
Flour, cake	1 lb.	4⅛ cups unsifted; 4⅝ cups sifted
Flour, corn	1 lb.	4 cups sifted
Flour, gluten	1 lb.	3¼ cups sifted
Flour, instant	1 lb.	3⅝ cups unsifted
Flour, pastry	1 lb.	4 cups unsifted; 4½ cups sifted
Flour, potato	1 lb.	4 cups sifted
Flour, rice	1 lb.	3 cups unsifted; 3½ cups sifted
Flour, rye (dark)	1 lb.	3½ cups sifted
Flour, rye (light)	1 lb.	5 cups sifted
Flour, seasoned	10-oz. box	2¼ cups unsifted
Flour, self-rising	1 lb.	4 cups sifted
Flour, soy (full fat)	1 lb.	7½ cups sifted
Flour, soy (low fat)	1 lb.	5½ cups unsifted
Flour, whole wheat	1 lb.	3½ cups stirred
Flour, whole wheat	5-lb. bag	18 cups stirred
Frankfurters	16-oz. pkg.	8–10 frankfurters
Frankfurters	6¼ lbs.	25 servings
Frosting, canned	16 oz.	1¾ cups
Fruit, candied	1-lb. pkg.	3 cups chopped
Fruit, canned	16-oz. can	2 cups fruit and liquid; 1½ cups drained
Fruit, dried	1 lb.	3 cups
Fruit, frozen	10-oz. pkg.	1¼ cups drained
Fruit cocktail	16-oz. can	2 cups
Fruit pectin, liquid	3-oz. pkg.	thickens 3–4 cups fruit or 2–4 cups juice
Fruit pectin, powdered	1¾-oz. box	thickens 4–8 cups fruit or 3–6 cups juice
Fruit peel, candied	1 lb.	2½–3 cups chopped
Fruit puree	1 lb.	2 cups
Fruit salad	3¼ quarts	25 servings
Garbanzo beans, canned	15-oz. can	2 cups drained
Garbanzo beans, dried	1 lb.	2–2¼ cups dried; 5–5½ cups cooked
Garbanzo beans, fresh	1 lb.	3 cups cooked
Garlic	1 sm. clove	½ tsp. minced
Garlic	1 med. clove	¾ tsp. minced; ⅛ tsp. garlic powder
Garlic	1 lg. clove	1½ tsp. minced
Garlic	1 oz.	6 lg. cloves; 3 Tbsp. minced
Garlic	1 bulb (head)	8–15 cloves
Garlic, chopped	4¼-oz. jar	½ cup
Garlic, elephant	1 clove	2 cloves regular garlic
Garlic, minced	1 tsp.	1–2 med. cloves
Garlic, minced	4¼-oz. jar	½ cup
Garlic powder	1 oz.	3 Tbsp.
Garlic salt	1 oz.	2 Tbsp.
Gelatin, fruit-flavored	3¼-oz. pkg.	7 Tbsp. powder; will gel 1 pt. liquid
Gelatin, unflavored	1 (¼-oz.) envelope	1 Tbsp. granules; will gel 1 pt. liquid
Gelatin, unflavored	8-oz. box	32 envelopes
Ginger, candied, chopped	1 oz.	2 Tbsp.
Ginger, crystallized	1 Tbsp.	1 tsp. ground
Ginger, fresh	1 Tbsp. chopped	1 tsp. ground
Ginger, fresh	1½"–2" piece	2 Tbsp. grated or chopped
Ginger, fresh	4 oz.	1 med. root; ½ cup peeled and finely chopped

FOOD	QUANTITY	YIELD
Ginger, ground	½ tsp.	1 tsp. fresh chopped
Ginger, ground	1 oz.	4 Tbsp.
Gingersnap cookies	15 cookies	1 cup fine crumbs
Goose	1 med.	10–12 lbs.
Gooseberries, canned	16-oz. can	2 cups
Gooseberries, fresh	1 lb.	3 cups
Grains	1 cup	3 cups cooked uncooked
Granadillas (see Passion fruit)		
Grapefruit, canned	16-oz. can	2 cups sections
Grapefruit, fresh	1 lb.	1 medium; 10–12 sections; 1¼–1¾ cups sections; ⅔–¾ cup juice; 3–4 Tbsp. grated peel
Grapefruit, frozen	14-oz. pkg.	1½ cups sections
Grape leaves	16-oz. jar	40 leaves
Grapes, canned	8-oz. can	1 cup drained
Grapes, seedless	1 lb.	15 oz. without stems; 2½–3 cups halved
Grapes, with seeds	1 lb.	14½ oz. without stems; 2¼ cups halved
Gravy, canned	12-oz. can	1⅓ cups
Gravy, canned	18-oz. can	2 cups
Gravy mix (brown)	3 Tbsp.	makes 1 cup gravy
Gravy mix (brown)	5¼-oz. jar	1½ cups mix; makes 8⅓ cups gravy
Great Northern beans, dried	1 lb.	2 cups dried; 6–7 cups cooked
Green beans, canned	16-oz. can	1¾–2 cups
Green beans, fresh	1 lb.	14 oz. trimmed; 3 cups trimmed; 3 cups cut or frenched; 2½ cups cut and cooked
Green beans, frozen	10-oz. pkg.	1½ cups
Green peas, canned	16-oz. can	2 cups
Green peas, fresh, in pod	1 lb.	1 cup shelled
Green peas, frozen	10-oz. pkg.	1½–2 cups
Green peas, split, dried	1 lb.	2⅓ cups uncooked; 5 cups cooked
Greens, fresh, raw	1 lb.	3 cups cooked
Greens, frozen	10-oz. pkg.	1½ –2 cups
Grenadine syrup	12-oz. bottle	1½ cups
Grits, quick-cooking	1 cup	3⅓ cups cooked

FOOD	QUANTITY	YIELD
Grits, quick-cooking	1 lb.	3 cups uncooked; 10 cups cooked
Half-and-half (see Cream)		
Ham, canned, boneless	1 lb.	12 oz. lean meat
Ham, cooked	1 lb.	3 cups diced; 2 cups ground
Ham, deviled, canned	2½ oz.	4½ Tbsp.
Ham, deviled, canned	4½ oz.	½ cup
Ham, slice	1" thick	1¼–1½ lbs.
Hazelnuts, in shell	1 lb.	½ lb. nutmeat; 1½ cups nutmeat
Hazelnuts, nutmeat	1 lb.	3½ cups
Hearts of palm	14-oz. can	5–6 average stalks
Hearts of palm	24-oz. can	8–9 average stalks
Herbs, dried	1 tsp.	1 Tbsp. fresh
Herbs, fresh, chopped	1 Tbsp.	1 tsp. dried, crushed
Hominy, canned	15-oz. can	1¾ cups
Hominy, cooked	1 cup	8½ oz.
Hominy, uncooked	1 cup	4½ cups cooked
Hominy, uncooked	1 lb.	2½ cups uncooked
Hominy grits (see Grits)		
Honey	16-oz. jar	1⅓ cups
Honeydew melon	1 avg.	4 lbs.; 4 cups diced; 35 (⅞") balls
Horseradish, fresh	1 Tbsp.	2 Tbsp. bottled
Horseradish, fresh	1½ lbs.	2¾ cups peeled and grated
Horseradish, prepared	1 oz.	2 Tbsp.
Horseradish, prepared	5-oz. jar	⅝ cup
Horseradish, prepared	6½-oz. jar	¾ cup
Horseradish sauce	8-oz. jar	1 cup
Hot Dogs (see Frankfurters)		
Hot pepper sauce	4½-oz. bottle	½ cup
Ice	1 lb.	allow for each guest; fills 3–4 water glasses
Ice	10 lbs.	chills 1 case wine
Ice cream	1 quart	4 cups
Ice cream	3¼–4⅝ quarts	25 servings
Jam or jelly	18-oz. jar	1⅔ cups
Jam or jelly	1½ lbs.	25 servings
Jerusalem artichokes	1 lb.	12 medium; 2½ cups peeled and sliced
Jícama, fresh	1 lb.	4 cups shredded
Juniper berries	4 berries	½ tsp. crushed
Kale, fresh	1 lb.	6–7 cups raw leaves; 1¼ cups cooked leaves

FOOD	QUANTITY	YIELD
Ketchup	14-oz. bottle	1½ cups
Kidney beans, canned	16-oz. can	2 cups
Kidney beans, dried	1 lb.	2–2½ cups dried; 5–6 cups cooked
Kiwi	1 med.	5–6 slices; ½ cup slices
Kohlrabi	2 lbs.	1 bunch; 4 med. bulbs; 3½ cups cubed and cooked
Lamb	1 lb.	about 2 chops, ¾″ thick
Lamb	1 leg	5–7 lbs. with bone; 3 lbs. boneless
Lamb	1 rack	6 lbs.
Lard	1 lb.	2½ cups
Lasagna, uncooked	1 lb.	16–24 noodles (2¼″ x 9½″)
Leeks	1 bunch	1 lb.; 8 oz. trimmed; 2 lg. or 3 med.; 1½–2 cups chopped or sliced raw (white portion only); 1 cup chopped cooked
Lemonade	1½ gal.	25 servings
Lemon grass	2 stalks	1 Tbsp. finely chopped
Lemons	1 med.	2–3 Tbsp. juice; 1 Tbsp. grated peel; 7–10 med. slices
Lemons	1 lb.	4–6 med.; ⅔–1 cup juice
Lentils, dried	1 lb.	2¼ cups dried; 5 cups cooked
Lettuce, Bibb	1 med. head	12 oz.; 4 cups torn up
Lettuce, Boston	1 med. head	12 oz.; 4 cups torn up
Lettuce, butterhead	1 med. head	12 oz.; 4 cups torn up
Lettuce, iceberg	1 med. head	18 oz.; 6–8 cups torn up; 4 cups shredded; 5–6 lg. leaves; 4 salad wedges
Lettuce, iceberg	6 med. heads	25 salad servings
Lettuce, leaf	1 med. bunch	12 oz.; 25–30 leaves; 4–6 cups torn up
Lettuce, mesclun	4 oz.	6 cups torn, loosely packed
Lettuce, romaine	1 med. head	14 oz.; 6 cups torn up
Lettuce, salad mix	4-oz. pkg.	4–6 cups torn up
Lima beans, canned	15-oz. can	2 cups
Lima beans, dried	1 lb.	2 cups dried; 5 cups cooked
Lima beans, fresh, in pod	1 lb.	6 oz. shelled; ¾–1 cup shelled

FOOD	QUANTITY	YIELD
Lima beans, fresh, shelled	1 lb.	3 cups
Lima beans, frozen	10-oz. pkg.	1¾ cups cooked
Limes	1 med.	1½–2 Tbsp. juice; 1–2 tsp. grated peel
Limes	1 lb.	6–8 med.; ½–1 cup juice
Linguine, fresh	9-oz. pkg.	3¾ cups cooked
Lobster, in shell	1 avg.	2½ lbs.; 2 cups cooked meat
Macadamia nuts, canned	5-oz. can	1 cup whole
Macadamia nuts, jar	7-oz. jar	1½ cups
Macadamia nuts, nutmeat	1 lb.	3⅓ cups nutmeat
Macaroni, uncooked	1 cup	2 cups cooked
Macaroni, uncooked	1 lb.	4 cups uncooked; 8 cups cooked
Macaroons (2½″)	9–10	1 cup fine crumbs
Mace, ground	1 oz.	4½ Tbsp.
Mackerel, canned	16-oz. can	2 cups
Malted milk powder	13-oz. jar	2¾ cups; 15 servings
Mangoes	12 oz.	1 med.; ¾ cup pulp
Manicotti	1 lb.	9–12 pieces
Maple syrup	12-oz. bottle	1½ cups
Margarine	¼-lb. stick	½ cup; 8 Tbsp.; 12–16 pats
Margarine	½ lb.	25 servings
Margarine	1 lb.	2 cups; 4 sticks
Margarine, soft	8-oz. tub	16 Tbsp.
Margarine, whipped	1 lb.	3 cups
Marinara sauce	15-oz. carton	1¾ cups
Marjoram, dried leaves	1 oz.	¾ cup
Marjoram, fresh	½ oz.	½ cup leaves
Marshmallow creme	7-oz. jar	2⅛ cups
Marshmallow creme	13-oz. jar	3⅞ cups
Marshmallows, mini	1 cup	2 oz.; 8 regular; 80 mini
Marshmallows, mini	10½-oz. pkg.	5½ cups
Marshmallows, regular	1 regular	¼ oz.; 10 mini
Marshmallows, regular	1 cup	11 regular
Marshmallows, regular	10½-oz. pkg.	45 regular
Marshmallows, regular	16-oz. pkg.	65 regular
Marzipan	7-oz. tube	⅞ cup
Mayonnaise	1½ cups	25 servings
Mayonnaise	32-oz. jar	4 cups
Meat, boneless	1 lb.	2 cups ground or minced
Meatballs	¾–1 oz.	1 cocktail-size meatball

FOOD	QUANTITY	YIELD
Meatballs	1½–2 oz.	1 dinner-size meatball
Melon balls, frozen	12-oz. pkg.	1½ cups
Milk	1 quart	4 cups
Milk, evaporated	5-oz. can	⅔ cup
Milk, evaporated	12-oz. can	1½ cups
Milk, instant nonfat dry	⅓ cup	1 cup reconstituted
Milk, instant nonfat dry	9.6-oz. pkg.	4 cups dry; 3 quarts reconstituted
Milk, sweetened, condensed	14-oz. can	1¼ cups
Millet	1 cup	3½ cups cooked
Mincemeat	27-oz. jar	2⅔ cups
Mincemeat, condensed	9-oz. box	½ cup
Mint, fresh leaves	1 cup	¼ cup dried leaves
Mixed vegetables, canned	16-oz. can	2 cups
Mixed vegetables, frozen	10-oz. pkg.	2 cups
Molasses	12-oz. bottle	1½ cups
Monosodium glutamate (MSG)	1 oz.	2 Tbsp.
Mushrooms, canned	4-oz. can	3 oz. drained weight; ⅔–¾ cup whole or sliced; 6–8 oz. fresh
Mushrooms, dried	2½–3 oz.	1 lb. fresh (after reconstituting)
Mushrooms, fresh	1 lb.	1 quart whole, raw; 30–40 sm.; 18–20 med.; 12–14 lg.; 7–10 extra lg.; 4–5 cups raw; 2 cups sliced, sautéed; equivalent to 12 oz. canned
Mussels, unshucked	1 quart	1½ lbs.; 25 mussels; 1 cup meat
Mustard, dry	1 tsp.	1 Tbsp. prepared
Mustard, dry	1 oz.	5 Tbsp.
Mustard, ground, dry	½ lb.	2¼ cups dry
Mustard, prepared	1 oz.	2 Tbsp.
Mustard, prepared	8 oz.	1 cup
Mustard, seeds	1 oz.	2½ Tbsp.
Mustard greens, canned	15-oz. can	1¼–1½ cups
Mustard greens, fresh	1 lb.	6–7 cups leaves; 1½ cups cooked
Mustard greens, frozen	10-oz. pkg.	1¼–1½ cups
Navy beans, dried	1 lb.	2½ cups dried; 5½ cups cooked

FOOD	QUANTITY	YIELD
Nectarines	1 lb.	3–4 medium; 2½ cups sliced; 1¾ cups diced; 1½ cups puréed
Noodles, uncooked	1 cup	1¼ cups cooked
Noodles, uncooked	1 lb.	10 cups uncooked; 12 cups cooked
Nutmeg, ground	1 oz.	3½ Tbsp.
Nutmeg, whole	1 whole	2–3 tsp. grated
Nutra Sweet Spoonful	2-oz. jar	sweetens like 2⅓ cups sugar
Nuts, in shell	1 lb.	½ lb. shelled; 4 cups chopped; 3 cups ground
Oatmeal, quick-cooking	18-oz. pkg.	6 cups uncooked; 10½ cups cooked
Oatmeal, uncooked	1¼ cups	1 cup oat flour
Oats, rolled	1 cup	1¾ cups cooked
Oats, rolled	1 lb.	5 cups uncooked
Oats, steel-cut, uncooked	1 cup	3 cups cooked
Oil, vegetable	16-oz. bottle	2 cups
Okra, canned	16-oz. can	1¾ cups chopped or sliced
Okra, fresh	1 lb.	35 average pods; 1½–2 cups sliced
Okra, frozen	10-oz. pkg.	1¼ cups chopped or sliced
Olives, ripe, chopped	4½-oz. can	⅔ cup
Olives, ripe, chopped	6-oz. can	1⅓ cups
Olives, ripe, pitted	15 lg. or 36 sm.	1 cup chopped
Olives, ripe, pitted	6-oz. can	1⅔ cups whole
Olives, ripe, sliced	2¼-oz. can	½ cup
Olives, ripe, whole	5¾–6 oz. can	18 super colossal; 25 colossal; 55 med.
Olives, Spanish, stuffed	7-oz. jar	about 65
Olives, Spanish, whole	5-oz. jar	about 20
Onion powder	1 oz.	3 Tbsp.
Onions, canned	16-oz. can	2 cups
Onions, dehydrated	¼ cup	1 cup chopped raw
Onions, dehydrated	4 oz.	1½ cups dry
Onions, french fried	2.8-oz. can	1⅜ cups
Onions, french fried	6-oz. can	3 cups
Onions, frozen, chopped	10-oz. pkg.	2½–3 cups
Onions, green, white part	1 bunch	⅓ cup chopped
Onions, green, with tops	1 bunch	5–8 stalks; 1 cup sliced
Onions, white or yellow	1 sm.	3 oz.; ½ cup chopped

FOOD	QUANTITY	YIELD
Onions, white or yellow	1 med.	4½ oz.; ½–⅔ cup chopped
Onions, white or yellow	1 lg.	6 oz.; 1 cup chopped; 4 tsp. juice
Onions, white or yellow	4 oz.	1 cup sliced
Onions, white or yellow	1 lb.	2 lg. or 3 med.; 2–2½ cups chopped
Onion salt	1 oz.	2½ Tbsp.
Onion soup mix	1 envelope	⅓ cup dry mix; 4 cups reconstituted
Orange juice, frozen	6-oz. can	6 cups reconstituted
Oranges	1 med.	⅓–½ cup juice; 10–12 sections; ⅓–½ cup sections; 4–5 tsp. grated peel
Oranges	1 lb.	3 medium; 1 cup juice; 1–1½ cups sections; 4–5 Tbsp. grated peel
Oranges, mandarin	11-oz. can	1¼ cups
Oranges, mandarin	15-oz. can	1¾ cups
Oregano, dried leaves	1 oz.	¾ cup
Oregano, fresh	½ oz.	½ cup chopped
Oreo cookies	12 cookies	1 cup fine crumbs
Oreo cookies	1-lb.-4-oz. pkg.	51 cookies
Orzo	2 oz.	⅓ cup uncooked; 1 cup cooked
Ovaltine	12-oz. jar	4 cups; 16 servings (4 Tbsp. each)
Oxtail	1 tail	1½–2 lbs.
Oysters, canned, smoked	3.7-oz. can	26 petite or 20 medium oysters
Oysters, canned, smoked	8-oz. can	⅔ cup drained
Oysters, shucked	1 lb.	12 med.; 1 pint
Pancake batter	1 cup	5 med. (5″) pancakes
Pancakes	1 med.	3 Tbsp. batter
Pancake syrup	1½–2 quarts	25 servings
Papaya	1 lb.	1 medium; 2 cups sliced or cubed
Paprika	1 oz.	4 Tbsp.
Parsley, dried flakes	1 tsp.	2 sprigs fresh
Parsley, dried flakes	1 oz.	1⅓ cups
Parsley, fresh	1 oz.	¾ cup
Parsley, fresh	1 bunch	2 oz.; 1½ cups chopped
Parsnips, without tops	1 bunch	1 lb.; 3–4 med.; 2 cups cooked and diced

FOOD	QUANTITY	YIELD
Passion fruit	1 avg.	3 oz.
Passion fruit	5–6 whole	½ cup pulp
Pasta (also see listings for individual types)		
Pasta, dry, uncooked	3¼ lbs.	25 side dish servings
Pâté	1 lb.	12 appetizers
Pea beans, dried	1 lb.	2½ cups dried; 5½ cups cooked
Peaches, canned, halves	16-oz. can	6–10 halves
Peaches, canned, sliced	16-oz. can	2–2½ cups drained
Peaches, dried	1 lb.	3 cups dried; 5¼ cups cooked
Peaches, dried, low-moisture	1 lb.	8 cups cooked
Peaches, fresh	1 lb.	3–4 med.; 2 cups peeled and sliced or diced; 1½ cups pulp
Peaches, fresh	2 lbs.	makes 1 (9″) pie
Peaches, frozen	10 oz.	1 cup slices drained; 1¼ cups slices with juice
Peach pie filling	21-oz. can	2⅓ cups
Peanut butter	18-oz. jar	2 cups
Peanuts, honey-roasted	5-oz. bag	1⅔ cups
Peanuts, nutmeat	1 lb.	3 cups nutmeat
Peanuts, in shell	1 lb.	⅔ lb. shelled; 2⅓ cups nutmeat
Peanuts, Spanish	7-oz. bag	1¼ cups nutmeat
Pears, canned, halves	16-oz. can	6–10 halves
Pears, canned, sliced	16-oz. can	2–2½ cups drained
Pears, dried	1 lb.	2¾ cups dried; 5½ cups cooked
Pears, fresh	1 lb.	3–4 med.; 2 cups sliced or cooked
Peas (see varieties, such as "Black-eyed," "Green," "Sugar snap," etc.)		
Pecans, chips or pieces	2-oz. pkg.	½ cup
Pecans, chips or pieces	6-oz. pkg.	1½ cups
Pecans, nutmeat	1 cup	4 oz.
Pecans, nutmeat	1 lb.	4 cups halved; 3¾ cups chopped or pieces
Pecans, in shell	1 lb.	½ lb. nutmeat; 2¼ cups nutmeat
Pepper, ground (red or black)	1 oz.	4 Tbsp.
Peppercorns	1 oz.	3 Tbsp.
Pepperoni, sliced	3½-oz. pkg.	50–54 slices; enough for 1 extra large pizza

FOOD	QUANTITY	YIELD
Peppers, roasted	15 oz.	2 cups drained; 1¾ cups chopped
Peppers, sweet, fresh	1 sm.	¼ cup chopped or minced
Peppers, sweet, fresh	1 med.	½ cup chopped or minced
Peppers, sweet, fresh	1 lg.	6–8 oz.; 1 cup chopped or minced
Peppers, sweet, fresh	1 lb.	3 lg. or 5 med.; 3–4 cups chopped
Peppers, sweet, frozen	10-oz. pkg.	2¼ cups diced or in strips
Persimmons	1 avg.	4 oz. edible flesh
Persimmons	9 oz. whole	¾ cup pulp
Pesto sauce	7-oz. carton	⅞ cup
Pheasant, whole	1 avg. (female)	3 lbs.
Phyllo pastry	1 lb. thin	26 (12″ x 17″) sheets
Phyllo pastry	1 lb. med.	20 (12″ x 17″) sheets
Phyllo pastry	1 lb. thick	18 (12″ x 17″) sheets
Pickapeppa sauce	5-oz. bottle	½ cup
Pickles	1-oz. whole	2½ Tbsp. chopped
Pickles	¾–1 lb.	25 servings
Pickles	1 lb.	3 cups chopped
Pie (9″–10″)	3–4 pies	25 servings
Pie crust mix	11-oz. box	2⅔ cups; makes 2 single crusts
Pie filling	20–21-oz. can	makes 1 (9″) pie
Pimientos, diced	2-oz. jar	¼ cup
Pimientos, diced	4-oz. jar	½ cup
Pineapple, chunks	8-oz. can	¾ cup + ¼ cup juice
Pineapple, chunks	20-oz. can	2 cups + ½ cup juice
Pineapple, crushed	8-oz. can	¾ cup + ¼ cup juice
Pineapple, crushed	20-oz. can	2 cups + ½ cup juice
Pineapple, fresh	1 med.	2 lbs.; 3 cups chunks or cubes
Pineapple, sliced	8-oz. can	4 slices
Pineapple, sliced	20-oz. can	10 slices; 2½ cups crushed or chunks
Pine nuts	5 oz.	1 cup
Pinto beans, canned	15-oz. can	1½ cups
Pinto beans, dried	1 lb.	2 cups dried; 5 cups cooked
Pistachios, nutmeat	1 cup	4½ oz. nutmeat
Pistachios, nutmeat	1 lb.	3½–4 cups nutmeat
Pistachios, in shell	1 oz.	20 nuts
Pistachios, in shell	1 cup	½ cup nutmeat

FOOD	QUANTITY	YIELD
Pistachios, in shell	1 lb.	3½–4 cups; 2 cups nutmeat
Pita bread	14-oz. pkg.	6 pieces
Pizza sauce	8-oz. jar	¾ cup
Pizza sauce	15-oz. jar	1¾ cups
Plantains	1¼ lbs.	2 med.; 1 lb. after peeling; 2½ cups cooked slices
Plums, canned	16-oz. can	10–14 plums
Plums, fresh	1 lb.	8–10 sm.; 6 med.; 4–5 lg.; 2–2½ cups halved and pitted; 2 cups cooked
Pomegranates	1 med.	½ cup pulp and seeds
Pomegranates	3–4 lg.	5 lbs.; 1 quart juice
Popcorn, microwave	1¾-oz. (snack) bag	4 cups popped
Popcorn, microwave	3½-oz. (reg.) bag	8 cups popped
Popcorn, unpopped	3 Tbsp.	1½ oz. kernels; 4 cups popped
Popcorn, unpopped	8 oz.	1 cup unpopped
Popcorn, unpopped	30-oz. jar	4 cups unpopped
Popcorn, unpopped	2-lb. bag	4 cups unpopped; 25 servings
Popcorn, unpopped	4-lb. bag	8 cups unpopped
Poppy seeds	1 oz.	3 Tbsp.
Pork, boneless	4 oz. raw	3 oz. cooked
Pork, boneless	1 lb.	2 cups ground
Pork, loin roast, bone in	2 lbs.	1 lb. cooked meat
Potato chips	4 oz.	2 cups coarsely crushed
Potato chips	1 lb.	4–5 quarts
Potato chips	1½ lbs.	25 servings
Potatoes, instant flakes	⅓ cup flakes	½ cup prepared
Potatoes, instant flakes	13¾-oz. pkg.	5⅔ cups flakes; 8½ cups prepared
Potatoes, mashed	4½ quarts	25 servings
Potatoes, new	1 lb.	9–12 sm.
Potatoes, red	1 lb.	7–9 sm.; 5–6 med.
Potatoes, russet or white	1 med.	1 cup grated
Potatoes, russet or white	1 lb.	3 medium; 14 oz. peeled; 1¾ cups mashed; 2 cups french fries; 3 cups cubed; 2¼ cups peeled and diced; 3 cups shredded
Potatoes, sweet (see Sweet potatoes)		

FOOD	QUANTITY	YIELD
Potato salad	4½ quarts	25 servings
Potato sticks, shoestring	1½-oz. can	1 cup
Poultry seasoning, ground	1 oz.	6 Tbsp.
Prickly pears	1 lg.	½ cup chopped or puréed
Prickly pears, jar, chopped	16-oz. jar	2 cups drained
Prunes, canned, whole	9-oz. can	24 prunes
Prunes, dried, pitted	12-oz. pkg.	2½ cups dried; 1½ cups paste; 54 prunes; 64 bite-size prunes
Pumpkin, canned	16 oz.	2 cups; makes 1 (9″) pie
Pumpkin, fresh	1 lb.	4 cups pared and cubed; 1 cup cooked and mashed; 11 oz. pulp
Pumpkin, fresh	5 lbs.	1 med.; 4½ cups cooked and puréed
Quail	1 avg.	3–6 oz.
Quinces	1 lb.	3–4 med.; 1½ cups chopped
Quinoa, uncooked	1 lb.	3 cups uncooked; 9 cups cooked
Rabbit	1 avg.	2 lbs.; 1½ cups cooked meat
Radicchio	1 med. head	8 leaves
Radishes	1 bunch	12–13 radishes; 8 oz. without leaves; 1 cup sliced
Raisins, muscat	15-oz. pkg.	2½ cups
Raisins, seedless	1-lb. pkg.	3 cups
Raspberries, fresh	1 pint	1¾ cups
Raspberries, frozen	10-oz. pkg.	1 cup with syrup
Ravioli, fresh	9-oz. pkg.	3 cups cooked
Red beans, dried	1 lb.	2½ cups dried; 6 cups cooked
Rhubarb, fresh	1 lb.	4–8 stalks; 2 cups chopped and cooked
Rhubarb, fresh	2½ lbs.	makes 1 (9″) pie
Rhubarb, frozen	12-oz. pkg.	1½ cups chopped or sliced and cooked
Rice, aromatic, uncooked	1 cup	3 cups cooked
Rice, brown, uncooked	1 cup	4 cups cooked
Rice, instant, uncooked	1 lb.	4 cups uncooked; 8 cups cooked
Rice, long grain, converted	2 lbs.	4¾ cups uncooked; 14 cups cooked
Rice, wild, uncooked	1 lb.	3 cups uncooked; 9–10 cups cooked
Ricotta cheese	8 oz.	1 cup
Rolls	4 doz.	25 servings
Rosemary, dried leaves	1 tsp. leaves	¾ tsp. crushed leaves
Rosemary, dried leaves	1 oz.	9 Tbsp.
Rosemary, fresh	½ oz.	⅓ cup leaves
Rosemary, fresh	4″ stem	¼ tsp. dried leaves
Rutabagas	1 avg.	2–3 lbs.; 5 cups cubed
Saffron, whole	4–6 threads	¼ tsp. crushed powder
Saffron, whole	1½ grams	1 Tbsp. crushed powder
Sage, dried	1 oz.	¾ cup
Sage, fresh	1 Tbsp.	1 tsp. dried chopped
Sage, fresh	½ oz.	½ cup leaves
Sage, fresh	12 leaves	1 tsp. dried
Sage, rubbed	1 oz.	⅔ cup
Salad dressing	16-oz. bottle	2 cups
Salad dressing	2–3 pints	25 servings
Salad dressing mix	1.4-oz. dry pkg.	2 cups prepared
Salad greens, mixed	4 oz.	6 cups torn, loosely packed
Salmon, canned	6-oz. can	⅝ cup drained
Salmon, canned	14¾-oz. can	1¾ cups
Salmon, smoked	4 oz.	12 canapés
Salsa, tomato	12-oz. jar	1½ cups
Salsa, tomato	16-oz. jar	2 cups
Salsa, tomato	24-oz. jar	3 cups
Salsify, fresh	1 lb.	4–5 roots without leaves
Salt	1 oz.	1½ Tbsp.
Salt	1 lb.	1¾ cups
Salt pork	¼ lb.	1 cup cracklings
Sandwiches	38	25 servings
Sandwich filling	1¼–1½ quarts	25 servings
Sardines	3¾-oz. can	20 sardines
Sauerkraut	14-oz. can	1¾ cups
Sauerkraut	32-oz. jar	4 cups
Scallions (white part only)	1 bunch	⅓ cup chopped
Scallions (with tops)	1 bunch	6–8 scallions; ½ cup chopped; 1 cup sliced

FOOD	QUANTITY	YIELD
Scallops, bay	1 lb.	.75 scallops; 2 cups
Scallops, sea	1 lb.	30 scallops; 2 cups
Sesame seeds	1 oz.	3 Tbsp.
Shallots, fresh	1 med.	½–1 oz.; 1 Tbsp. minced
Shallots, fresh	4 oz.	4–6 med.; 10–12 sm.; 1 cup chopped; ¾ cup minced
Shallots, fresh	1 lb.	2¼ cups coarsely chopped; 2 cups minced
Shell peas, fresh, in pod	1 lb.	1 cup shelled
Shortening, solid	1-lb. can	2½ cups
Shortening, sticks	20-oz. pkg.	3 sticks, 1 cup each
Shrimp, canned	4½-oz. can	½ cup
Shrimp, in shell	1 lb.	less than 10 extra-colossal; 10–15 colossal; 21–25 jumbo; 26–30 extra-lg.; 31–35 lg.; 43–50 med.; 51–60 sm.
Shrimp, raw, in shell	1½ lbs.	¾ lb. cooked in shell and peeled; 2 cups cooked
Snow peas, fresh	4 oz.	1½ cups trimmed
Snow peas, frozen	6-oz. pkg.	1½ cups
Sorrel, fresh	½ oz.	⅔ cup
Soup	5–6 quarts	25 side dish servings
Soup	6–9 quarts	25 main dish servings
Soup base paste	¾ tsp.	1 cup prepared
Soup base paste	1 Tbsp.	1 quart prepared
Sour cream	8 oz. (½ pint)	1 cup
Soybeans, dried	1 cup	3 cups cooked
Soybeans, dried	1 lb.	2 cups dried
Spaghetti, uncooked	1 lb.	4 cups uncooked; 7–8 cups cooked
Spinach, canned	15–16-oz. can	1½–2 cups
Spinach, fresh, loose	1 lb.	9–10 oz. trimmed; 7–8 cups lightly packed raw leaves; 3 cups torn leaves; 1¼ cups cooked; ½–¾ cup cooked and squeezed very dry
Spinach, fresh, packaged	10 oz.	8 oz. trimmed; 6 cups leaves; ⅔ cup cooked and squeezed very dry
Spinach, frozen	10-oz. pkg.	1½ cups
Split peas, dried	1 lb.	2⅓ cups dried; 5 cups cooked

FOOD	QUANTITY	YIELD
Squab	1 avg.	12–16 oz.
Squash, spaghetti	2 lbs.	4 cups cooked "spaghetti"
Squash, summer, fresh	1 lb.	3–4 med. or 6 sm.; 2½–3 cups sliced, raw; 2 cups sliced, cooked; 1⅔ cups cooked and mashed
Squash, summer, frozen	10-oz. pkg.	1½ cups sliced
Squash, winter, canned	16-oz. can	2 cups
Squash, winter, fresh	1 lb.	1 cup cooked and mashed
Squash, winter, frozen	12-oz. pkg.	1½ cups sliced
Strawberries, fresh	1 cup whole	4 oz.; ½ cup puréed
Strawberries, fresh	1 pint	2½ cups whole; 1¾ cups sliced; 1¼ cups puréed; 12 lg., 24 med., or 36 sm.
Strawberries, frozen, sliced	10-oz. pkg.	1 cup drained; 1¼ cups with syrup
Strawberries, frozen, whole	20-oz. pkg.	4 cups whole; 2¼ cups puréed
Strawberry pie filling	21-oz. can	2⅓ cups
Strudel leaves (see Phyllo pastry)		
Stuffing mix	8-oz. pkg.	4 cups dry; 2¼ cups finely crushed; enough to stuff 16 lbs. boned fish, 16 chops, or 5–9 lbs. poultry
Suet (beef fat)	1 cup chopped	4½ oz.
Suet (beef fat)	1 lb.	3¾ cups chopped
Sugar, brown	1 lb.	2¼ cups packed
Sugar, brown granulated	14-oz. box	2¾ cups
Sugar, confectioners'	1 lb.	3¾ cups unsifted; 4¼ cups sifted
Sugar, granulated	1 lb.	2¼ cups
Sugar, granulated	5-lb. bag	11¼ cups
Sugar, instant-dissolving	11-oz. box	1⅝ cups
Sugar, superfine	1 lb.	2¼ cups
Sugar cubes	1 (½") cube	½ tsp. sugar
Sugar cubes	1-lb. box	96 cubes
Sundae syrup	20-oz. bottle	1¾ cups
Sunflower seeds, kernels	3¾-oz. pkg.	¾ cup kernels
Sunflower seeds, in shell	3-oz. pkg.	1½ oz. kernels
Sunflower seeds, in shell	7-oz. pkg.	2½ cups in shell; ¾ cup nutmeat
Sweet and sour sauce	9-oz. jar	1⅛ cups

FOOD	QUANTITY	YIELD
Sweet potatoes, canned	16 oz.	1¾–2 cups
Sweet potatoes, fresh	1 lb.	2 lg. or 3 med.; 12 oz. peeled; 2 cups cubed or sliced; 1¾–2 cups mashed
Swiss chard	1 lb.	8–9 oz. stems plus 6–7 oz. leaves; 4 cups stems plus 5–6 cups leaves; 1½ cups cooked stems plus 1 cup cooked leaves
Syrup, maple (see Maple syrup)		
Syrup, pancake (see Pancake syrup)		
Taco sauce	16-oz. jar	2 cups
Taco seasoning, dry	1¼-oz. pkg.	4 Tbsp. dry
Tangerines	1 lb.	4 average tangerines; 2 cups sections
Tapioca, quick-cooking	8-oz. pkg.	1½ cups; 3¾ cups cooked
Tarragon, dried leaves	1 oz.	1 cup
Tarragon, fresh	½ oz.	⅓ cup
Tartar sauce	9-oz. jar	1⅛ cups
Tea, bags	3 reg. bags	1 family-size bag
Tea, bags	1¼ oz.	16 bags
Tea, bags	8 oz.	100 bags
Tea, iced	1½ gal.	25 servings
Tea, instant	3 oz.	2½ cups dry; 24 quarts prepared
Tea, loose	1 tsp.	¾–1 cup iced; 1–2 cups steeped; 2 tea bags
Tea, loose	4 oz.	1½ cups; 40–45 cups iced; 75 cups steeped
Thyme, dried leaves	1 oz.	½ cup
Thyme, fresh	1 sprig	½ tsp. dried
Thyme, fresh	½ oz.	⅓ cup leaves
Thyme, fresh, chopped	1 oz.	6 Tbsp.
Tofu, firm	1 lb.	2½ cups cubed; 2 cups crumbled; 1¾ cups puréed
Tofu, soft	1 lb.	1¾ cups puréed
Tomatillos	1 lb.	12–16 med. tomatillos
Tomatoes, canned	16-oz. can	2 cups pulp and juice
Tomatoes, canned	28-oz. can	2 cups drained
Tomatoes, canned, diced	16-oz. can	2 cups pulp and juice
Tomatoes, with chiles	14½-oz. can	1¾ cups
Tomatoes, cooked	2 lbs.	1½ cups
Tomatoes, fresh	3–5 lbs.	25 salad or sandwich servings

FOOD	QUANTITY	YIELD
Tomatoes, fresh	8–12½ lbs.	25 side dish servings
Tomatoes, fresh	1 med.	1 cup chopped
Tomatoes, fresh	1 lb.	2 lg., 3 med., or 4 sm.; 1–1½ cups peeled, seeded, and chopped; ¾ cup cooked; equivalent to 12 oz. canned
Tomatoes, fresh, cherry	1 lb.	1 pint; 25–35 tomatoes
Tomatoes, fresh, plum (Roma)	1 lb.	7–8 tomatoes
Tomatoes, stewed	14½-oz. can	1½ cups
Tomatoes, sun-dried	1 oz.	10 tomatoes
Tomato paste	4½-oz. tube	5–7 Tbsp.
Tomato paste	6-oz. can	¾ cup
Tomato purée	16-oz. can	2 cups
Tomato sauce	8-oz. can	1 cup
Tortellini, fresh	9-oz. pkg.	2¼ cups cooked
Tuna, canned	6–6¼-oz. can	⅔ cup drained
Tuna, canned	9–9¼-oz. can	1 cup drained
Turkey, bone in	12–18 lbs.	25 servings
Turkey, canned	5-oz. can	½ cup drained
Turkey, whole hen	8–16 lbs.	6¼–12½ lbs. uncooked meat
Turkey, whole roaster	5–9 lbs.	3¾–6¾ lbs. uncooked meat
Turkey, whole tom	16–24 lbs.	13–19½ lbs. uncooked meat
Turmeric	1 oz.	4 Tbsp.
Turnip greens, canned	16-oz. can	2 cups
Turnip greens, fresh	1 lb.	6–7 cups raw leaves; 1 cup cooked leaves
Turnip greens, frozen	10-oz. pkg.	1½ cups cooked
Turnips	1 lb.	3–4 med.; 2½–3 cups cooked and mashed; 2–2½ cups diced
Turtle beans, dried	1 lb.	2–2⅓ cups; 5 cups cooked
Vanilla bean, scraped	1" bean	1 tsp. extract
Vanilla extract	1 oz.	2½ Tbsp.
Vanilla wafers	30 wafers	1 cup fine crumbs
Vanilla wafers	12-oz. box	88 cookies
Vegetable purée	1 lb.	2 cups
Vegetables, canned	8-oz. can	1 cup
Vegetables, canned	12-oz. can	1½ cups

FOOD	QUANTITY	YIELD
Vegetables, canned	16–17-oz. can	2 cups
Vegetables, canned	20-oz. can	2¼–2½ cups
Vegetables, canned	29-oz. can	3¼–3½ cups
Vegetables, canned	6-lb.-8-oz. can	25 servings (1 #10 can)
Vegetables, frozen	10-oz. pkg.	1½ cups
Vegetables, frozen	16-oz. pkg.	2–2¾ cups
Vegetables, frozen	20-oz. pkg.	3–4 cups
Vienna sausages	5-oz. can	7–8 links
Vinegar	12-oz. bottle	1½ cups
Vinegar	16-oz. bottle	2 cups
Waffle batter	5 oz.	1 (7″) waffle
Walnuts, chopped	1 lb.	3½ cups
Walnuts, halves	2½-oz. pkg.	⅝ cup
Walnuts, halves	7-oz. pkg.	1¾ cups
Walnuts, halves	1 lb.	4 cups
Walnuts, pieces	2-oz. pkg.	⅓ cup
Walnuts, pieces	2½-oz. pkg.	½ cup
Walnuts, in shell	1 lb.	½ lb. nutmeat; 2 cups nutmeat
Walnuts, whole	1 lb.	4 cups
Water chestnuts	5-oz. can	15–17 water chestnuts
Water chestnuts	8-oz. can	1 cup sliced
Watercress	1 bunch	4 oz.; 2 cups chopped
Watermelon (with rind)	22 lbs.	22 cups cubes or balls
Watermelon (with rind)	40 lbs.	25 servings
Wax beans, canned	16-oz. can	1¾–2 cups
Wax beans, fresh	1 lb.	14 oz. after trimming; 3 cups trimmed; 3 cups cut or frenched; 2½ cups cut and cooked
Wax beans, frozen	10-oz. pkg.	1½ cups
Wheat, cracked, uncooked	1 cup	3–3½ cups cooked
Wheat berries, uncooked	1 cup	3 cups cooked
Wheat germ	12-oz. jar	3 cups
Whipped topping, frozen	8-oz. carton	3½ cups
Whipped topping mix	1.4-oz. pkg.	2 cups whipped topping
White beans, dried	1 lb.	2–2½ cups dried; 6 cups cooked
Wine, 187 ml.	1 split	6.3 oz.
Wine, 750 ml.	1 bottle	5 (5-oz.) servings
Wine, 750 ml.	1 case	60 (5-oz.) servings
Wine, 1 liter	1 bottle	6 (5-oz.) servings
Wine, 1.5 liter	1 magnum	9 (5-oz.) servings

FOOD	QUANTITY	YIELD
Wine, 1.75 liter	1 bottle	11 (5-oz.) servings
Wonton wrappers	1-lb. pkg.	60 wrappers
Yeast, active dry	¼-oz. pkg.	2¼ tsp.; enough to make 1 loaf of bread
Yeast, active dry	4-oz. jar	14 Tbsp.; enough to make 16 loaves of bread
Yeast, compressed cake	0.6-oz. cake	equivalent to ¼-oz. pkg. dry
Yeast, compressed cake	2-oz. cake	equivalent to 3 (¼-oz.) pkgs. dry
Yogurt	8 oz. (½ pint)	1 cup
Yogurt	3 cups	1 cup yogurt "cheese"
Ziti, uncooked	2 oz.	1 cup; 1½ cups cooked
Zucchini	1 lb.	3 med.; 1 cup sliced

Food Substitutions

...

IF YOU NEED THIS	SUBSTITUTE THIS
1 tsp. ....Allspice (ground)........	½ tsp. ....Ground cinnamon + ¼ tsp. ....Ground cloves + ¼ tsp. ....Ground nutmeg
1⅓ cups......Almond paste.............	1¾ cups ....Ground almonds + 1½ cups ....Powdered sugar + 1 ....Egg white + 1 tsp. ....Almond extract + ¼ tsp. ....Salt
2 Tbsp..........Almonds, ground....... (for flavoring)	¼ tsp. ....Almond extract
1 ....Anchovy, mashed......	1 tsp. ....Anchovy paste
1 tsp. ....Apple pie spice.........	½ tsp. ....Ground cinnamon + ¼ tsp. ....Ground nutmeg + ⅛ tsp. ....Ground allspice + ⅛ tsp. ....Ground cardamom
1 Tbsp..........Arrowroot	2 Tbsp..........All-purpose flour or 4 tsp. ....Cornstarch
1 strip..........Bacon, cooked .... and chopped	1 Tbsp.......Bacon bits
1 tsp. ....Baking powder, ... double-acting	¼ tsp. ....Baking soda + ½ tsp. ....Cream of tartar
1 tsp. ....Baking powder, ... double-acting	¼ tsp. ....Baking soda + ½ cup ....Buttermilk (Reduce other liquid in recipe by ½ cup.)
1 Tbsp..........Beau monde	2 tsp. ....Onion powder + 1 tsp. ....Celery salt

IF YOU NEED THIS	SUBSTITUTE THIS
2¼ cups......Biscuit mix.................	2 cups ....Flour, sifted with + 1 Tbsp.......Baking powder + 1 tsp...........Salt + ¼ cup ....Shortening (cut in)
1 cup...........Bread crumbs,........... commercial (for breading foods with a coating)	1 cup...........Cornflake crumbs or 1 cup...........Corn chip crumbs or 1 cup...........Cracker crumbs or 1 cup...........Matzo meal or 1 cup...........Ground rolled oats or 1 cup...........Potato chip crumbs
1 cup...........Bread crumbs, soft.....	¾ cup ....Cracker crumbs or 1⅓ cups ....Oatmeal (uncooked)
1 cup...........Broth: beef, chicken, . vegetable, etc.	1 cup...........Boiling water + 1.................Bouillon cube + 1 tsp. ....Bouillon crystals
10½ oz ....Broth: beef, ... chicken, etc. (canned)	1⅓ cups ....Boiling water + 1⅓.............Bouillon cubes or 1⅓ tsp. ......Bouillon crystals
14½ oz ....Broth: beef, ... chicken, etc. (canned)	1¾ cups ....Boiling water + 1¾.............Bouillon cubes or 1¾ tsp. ......Bouillon crystals
1 cup...........Butter or margarine ... (for baking)	⅞ cup ....Shortening + ½ tsp. ....Salt
1 cup...........Butter or margarine ... (for reducing fat in baking)	8 tsp. ....(1 envelope) Butter Buds + ½ cup Liquid + ½ cup ....Butter or margarine
1 cup...........Butter or margarine ... (for sautéing)	1⅓ cups ....Whipped butter

IF YOU NEED THIS		SUBSTITUTE THIS	
1 cup	Buttermilk	1 Tbsp. ⅞ cup + 1 Tbsp.	Lemon juice or white vinegar + Whole milk (Let stand for 10 minutes.)
1 cup	Buttermilk	1 cup 1¾ tsp.	Whole milk + Cream of tartar
1 cup	Buttermilk	1 cup ¼ cup	Water + Buttermilk powder
1 cup	Buttermilk (for baking)	1 cup 1 cup	Plain yogurt *or* Sour cream
1 tsp.	Cardamom, ground	1 tsp.	Ground cinnamon
1 Tbsp.	Carob powder	1 Tbsp.	Cocoa powder
⅛ tsp.	Cayenne	4 drops	Tabasco sauce
½ cup	Celery (1 rib)	¼ cup	Celery flakes
1 tsp.	Celery salt	¾ tsp. ¼ tsp.	Salt + Crushed celery seed
1 Tbsp.	Celery seed (for pickling)	1 Tbsp.	Dill seed
1 cup	Cheddar, sharp	1 cup ⅛ tsp. ¼ tsp.	Cheddar (mild) + Dry mustard + Worcestershire sauce
1 Tbsp.	Chervil, chopped	1 Tbsp.	Parsley, chopped
1 Tbsp.	Chili powder	2 tsp. 1 tsp. 1 tsp. ½ tsp.	Cumin + Cayenne + Oregano + Garlic powder
1 cup	Chili sauce	1 cup	Ketchup
1¼ cups	Chili sauce	1 cup ½ cup 2 Tbsp.	Tomato sauce + Sugar + Vinegar
1 Tbsp.	Chives, fresh	1 tsp.	Freeze-dried chives
6 oz.	Chocolate, morsels	9 Tbsp. 7 Tbsp. 3 Tbsp.	Cocoa powder + Sugar + Butter or margarine
2 oz.	Chocolate, semisweet	⅓ cup	Chocolate chips
1 oz.	Chocolate, semisweet	½ oz. 1 Tbsp.	Unsweetened chocolate + Sugar
1 oz.	Chocolate square, unsweetened	3½ Tbsp. 2 tsp.	Cocoa powder + Butter or shortening

IF YOU NEED THIS		SUBSTITUTE THIS	
1 oz.	Chocolate square, unsweetened	3 Tbsp. 2 Tbsp.	Carob powder + Water
1 cup	Cinnamon sugar	⅞ cup 2 Tbsp.	Granulated sugar + Ground cinnamon
1¼ cups	Cocktail sauce	1 cup 3 Tbsp. 1 Tbsp. 2 tsp.	Ketchup or chili sauce + Horseradish + Lemon juice + Worcestershire sauce
1 cup	Coconut, grated	1⅓ cups	Coconut, flaked
1 cup	Coconut milk, fresh	3 Tbsp. ⅞ cup	Cream of coconut + Water or low-fat milk
1 cup	Coconut milk, fresh	1 cup ½ tsp. ½ tsp.	Heavy cream + Coconut extract + Sugar
1 cup	Cornmeal, self-rising	1 cup 1 tsp. ½ tsp.	Plain cornmeal + Baking powder + Salt
1 Tbsp.	Cornstarch	2 Tbsp.	All-purpose flour
1 Tbsp.	Cornstarch	2 Tbsp.	Tapioca
1 Tbsp.	Cornstarch	2½ tsp.	Arrowroot
1 cup	Corn syrup, dark	¾ cup ¼ cup	Light corn syrup + Light molasses
1 cup	Corn syrup, light	1¼ cups ⅓ cup	Light brown sugar + Liquid (water or any liquid used in recipe)
1 cup	Crabmeat (fresh)	6½ oz.	Canned crabmeat
1 cup	Cracker crumbs	1 cup	Dry bread crumbs
1 cup	Cream, heavy (for cooking, not whipping)	¾ cup ⅓ cup	Whole milk + Butter
1 cup	Cream, light	½ cup ½ cup	Heavy cream + Whole milk
1 cup	Cream, light (for cooking)	⅞ cup 3 Tbsp.	Whole milk + Butter
1 cup	Cream, light (for cooking)	1 cup	Evaporated milk
1 cup	Cream, whipped, sweetened	4 oz.	Whipped topping
1 cup	Cream, whipped, sweetened	1¼ oz.	Dessert topping mix, prepared

IF YOU NEED THIS		SUBSTITUTE THIS	
1 cup	Cream, whipping	⅔ cup	Evaporated milk +
		4 tsp.	Lemon juice or vinegar
1 cup	Cream, whipping	½ cup	Nonfat dry milk +
		⅓ cup	Water +
		1 Tbsp.	Lemon juice
1 tsp.	Cream of tartar	1 tsp.	Lemon juice or vinegar
1 cup	Currant jelly	1 cup	Raspberry jelly
1 cup	Currants, dried	1 cup	Raisins or chopped dates
1 Tbsp.	Curry powder	½ tsp.	Ground cardamom +
		½ tsp.	Cayenne +
		½ tsp.	Ground coriander seed +
		½ tsp.	Cumin +
		½ tsp.	Ground ginger +
		½ tsp.	Turmeric
1 cup	Dates, chopped	1 cup	Dried currants *or*
		1 cup	Chopped figs *or*
		1 cup	Chopped prunes *or*
		1 cup	Chopped raisins
1	Egg (for baking)	1	Egg yolk +
		1 Tbsp.	Water
1	Egg, large	3½ Tbsp.	Mixed egg yolks and whites, stirred together
1	Egg, large	3½ Tbsp.	Liquid egg substitute (For best results, do not use this this substitute for more than 2 of the total number of eggs called for in a recipe.)
1	Egg, whole (for cooked recipes)	2½ Tbsp.	Powdered egg +
		2½ Tbsp.	Water
6	Eggs, whole (for cooked recipes)	1 cup	Powdered egg +
		1 cup	Water
1	Egg white	2 Tbsp.	Egg whites, stirred
1	Egg yolk	1½ Tbsp.	Egg yolks, stirred
2	Egg yolks (for custards or sauces)	1	Whole egg
1 cup	Farmer cheese	1 cup	Cottage cheese, dry or drained
1 tsp.	Fennel seeds	1 tsp.	Caraway seeds
⅓ cup	Fines Herbes	3 Tbsp.	Parsley flakes +
		2 tsp.	Dried chervil +
		2 tsp.	Dried chives +
		1 tsp.	Dried tarragon

IF YOU NEED THIS		SUBSTITUTE THIS	
5 tsp.	Five-Spice Powder (Chinese)	1 tsp.	Ground anise +
		1 tsp.	Ground fennel +
		1 tsp.	Ground cloves +
		1 tsp.	Ground cinnamon +
		1 tsp.	Ground pepper
2 Tbsp.	Flour, all-purpose (for thickening)	1 Tbsp.	Arrowroot
1 Tbsp.	Flour, all-purpose	1 Tbsp.	Corn flour
2 Tbsp.	Flour, all-purpose (for thickening)	1 Tbsp.	Cornstarch
1 cup	Flour, all-purpose	⅞ cup	Rice flour
1 cup	Flour, all-purpose, (for baking breads)	Use up to ½ cup	Bran, whole wheat flour, or cornmeal, plus enough all-purpose flour to make 1 cup
1 cup	Flour, all-purpose, sifted	1 cup + 2 Tbsp.	Cake flour, sifted
1 cup	Flour, cake, sifted	⅞ cup	All-purpose flour +
		2 Tbsp.	Cornstarch
1 Tbsp.	Flour, corn	1 Tbsp.	All-purpose flour
13 Tbsp.	Flour, gluten	1 cup	All-purpose flour
1 Tbsp.	Flour, masa harina	1 Tbsp.	Cornmeal
1 Tbsp.	Flour, potato	2 Tbsp.	All-purpose flour
1 Tbsp.	Flour, potato	1 Tbsp.	Cornstarch
⅞ cup	Flour, rice	1 cup	All-purpose flour
1¼ cups	Flour, rye	1 cup	All-purpose flour
1 cup	Flour, self-rising, sifted	1 cup	All-purpose flour +
		1½ tsp.	Baking powder +
		¼ tsp.	Salt (Mix and substitute measure-for-measure for self-rising flour. Omit any additional baking powder and/or salt called for in the recipe.)
1 cup	Flour, whole wheat, coarse	⅞ cup	All-purpose flour
1 cup	Flour, whole wheat, fine	1 cup	All-purpose flour
1½ cups	Fruit, fresh, cut up	16 oz.	Canned fruit, drained
1¼ cups	Fruit, fresh, cut up	10 oz.	Frozen fruit, drained
¼ tsp.	Fruit Fresh (Ascorbic acid crystals)	1 tsp.	Lemon juice

IF YOU NEED THIS	SUBSTITUTE THIS		IF YOU NEED THIS	SUBSTITUTE THIS
1 clove........Garlic (med.).............⅛ tsp. ....Garlic powder *or*			1 cup.............Leeks, sliced................1 cup........Shallots, sliced	
	¾ tsp. ....Minced garlic *or*		1 tsp. ....Lemon or lime juice ...1 tsp. ....Vinegar or white	
	½ tsp. ....Garlic salt *or*		(for acidulation)	wine
	½ tsp. ....Garlic juice *or*		1 tsp. ....Lemon or lime ....1 tsp. ....Lemon or lime peel,	
	1 tsp. ....Garlic paste		peel, fresh	dried
½ cup ....Garlic butter..............½ cup ....Butter (1 stick) +			1 tsp. ....Lemon or lime peel, ..2 Tbsp......Lemon or lime juice	
	1 clove.......Garlic, minced		fresh (for flavoring)	
	(or equivalent)		1 tsp. ....Lemon or lime peel, ..½ tsp. ....Lemon or lime extract	
⅛ tsp. ....Garlic powder............½ tsp. ....Garlic juice *or*			fresh (for flavoring)	
	1 tsp. ....Garlic paste *or*		1 cup.............Lobster meat...............6 oz.........Frozen lobster meat	
	½ tsp. ....Garlic salt		1 tsp. ....Mace, ground ....1 tsp. ....Ground nutmeg	
½ tsp. ....Garlic salt ....½ tsp. ....Garlic juice			1.................Marshmallow, reg. ....10..........Mini marshmallows	
	1 clove.......Garlic, minced *or*		2½ cups.......Marzipan..................2 cups......Almond paste +	
	⅛ tsp. ....Garlic powder			1 cup..........Powdered sugar +	
1 Tbsp.........Ginger, ...⅛ tsp. ....Powdered ginger				2 Tbsp........Corn syrup
fresh chopped			1 cup.............Mayonnaise, ...1 cup..........Cottage cheese	
1 cup............Half and half ....⅞ cup ....Whole milk +			commercial	(Process in blender until smooth)
	1½ tsp. ......Butter		1 cup.............Mayonnaise, ...½ cup.........Mayonnaise +	
1 cup............Half and half ....½ cup ....Light cream +			commercial	½ cup.........Plain yogurt
	½ cup ....Whole milk		1 cup.............Mayonnaise, ...1 cup..........Commercial	
1 tsp. ....Herbs, dried leaf........¼ tsp. ....Herbs, powdered			homemade	mayonnaise +
1 Tbsp.........Herbs, fresh...............1 tsp. ....Herbs, dried				1 tsp. ....Lemon juice +
1 cup............Honey ....1¼ cups ....Sugar +				1 tsp. ....Prepared mustard
	¼ cup ....Liquid		1 cup.............Milk, condensed ....1 cup..........Nonfat dry milk +	
1 cup............Honey ....1 cup........Corn syrup			(sweetened)	½ cup..........Boiling water +
2 Tbsp.........Horseradish, ...1 Tbsp.......Horseradish, dried +				⅔ cup.........Sugar +
bottled	1 Tbsp........Vinegar +			3 Tbsp........Melted butter	
	1 Tbsp........Water			(Process mixture in blender	
1 Tbsp.........Horseradish, fresh ......2 Tbsp........Horseradish, bottled				until smooth.)
2 Tbsp.........Italian seasoning........1 tsp. ....Dried basil +			1 cup.............Milk, evaporated........1 cup..........Cream	
	1 tsp. ....Dried marjoram +		1 cup.............Milk, skim.................¾ cup.........Water +	
	1 tsp. ....Dried oregano +			⅓ cup.........Nonfat dry milk	
	1 tsp. ....Dried thyme +		1 cup.............Milk, sour ....1 Tbsp. ......Lemon juice or white	
	1 tsp. ....Dried rosemary +			vinegar +	
	1 tsp. ....Dried sage			⅞ cup +	
6 oz............Jícama ....6 oz...........Water chestnuts				1 Tbsp......Milk
1 cup............Ketchup ....1 cup........Chili sauce			(Let mixture stand for 5 minutes.)	
1¼ cups......Ketchup ....1 cup........Tomato sauce +			1 cup.............Milk, whole ....½ cup.........Evaporated milk +	
(for cooking)	¼ cup ....Sugar +			½ cup.........Water	
	2 Tbsp.......Vinegar +		1 cup.............Milk, whole ....1 cup..........Skim milk +	
	¼ tsp. ....Ground cloves			1 Tbsp........Melted butter	
1 cup............Lard..........................1 cup........Shortening			1 cup.............Milk, whole ....1 cup..........Nonfat milk +	
				2½ tsp. ......Butter	

IF YOU NEED THIS		SUBSTITUTE THIS	
1 cup	Milk, whole	1 cup	Water +
		4 Tbsp.	Dry whole milk
1 quart	Milk, whole	1 quart	Skim milk +
		3 Tbsp.	Cream
1 cup	Molasses (for baking)	¾ cup	Sugar +
		¼ cup	Water
1 lb.	Mushrooms, fresh	12 oz.	Canned mushrooms *or*
		3 oz.	Dried mushrooms, reconstituted
1 tsp.	Mustard, dry	1 Tbsp.	Mustard, prepared
1 Tbsp.	Mustard, prepared	1 Tbsp.	Dry mustard +
		1 tsp.	Vinegar +
		1 tsp.	Water, milk, or cream +
		1 tsp.	Sugar
1 tsp.	Nutmeg, ground	1 tsp.	Ground mace
¼ cup	Onion, chopped	1 Tbsp.	Instant minced onion *or*
		1 Tbsp.	onion flakes *or*
		1 tsp.	Onion powder
2 Tbsp.	Onion juice	¾ tsp.	Instant minced onion or onion flakes
1 tsp.	Onion powder	1 Tbsp.	Instant minced onion
2 Tbsp.	Onion soup mix (dry)	1 Tbsp.	Instant minced onion +
		1	Beef bouillon cube
1 tsp.	Orange peel, fresh	1 tsp.	Orange peel, dried
1 tsp.	Orange peel, fresh	½ tsp.	Orange extract
1 tsp.	Orange peel, fresh (for flavoring)	2 Tbsp.	Orange juice
1 tsp.	Oregano, dried	1 tsp.	Marjoram, dried
1 tsp.	Parsley, dried	1 tsp.	Dried chervil
1 Tbsp.	Parsley, fresh, chopped	1 tsp.	Parsley flakes
1 tsp.	Pepper flakes, hot	½ tsp.	Cayenne
2 Tbsp.	Pepper, sweet bell (any color)	1 Tbsp.	Sweet bell pepper flakes
1 Tbsp.	Pepper flakes, red sweet, rehydrated	2 Tbsp.	Chopped pimiento
1 oz.	Pepperoni	1 oz.	Salami
8 cups	Pie crust mix	6¼ cups	Flour, mixed with +
		1 Tbsp.	Salt +
		2½ cups	Shortening (cut in)

IF YOU NEED THIS		SUBSTITUTE THIS	
1 lb.	Potatoes, mashed	1⅓ cups	Instant mashed potatoes, prepared
1⅓ tsp.	Poultry seasoning	¾ tsp.	Sage +
		¼ tsp.	Thyme +
		⅛ tsp.	Ground cloves +
		¼ tsp.	Pepper
1 tsp.	Pumpkin pie spice	½ tsp.	Ground cinnamon +
		⅛ tsp.	Ground nutmeg +
		⅛ tsp.	Ground mace +
		⅛ tsp.	Ground ginger +
		⅛ tsp.	Ground cloves
1 cup	Raisins	1 cup	Dried currants or chopped dates
1 cup	Ricotta cheese	1 cup	Cottage cheese
1 cup	Romano cheese	1 cup	Parmesan cheese
¼ tsp.	Saffron, powdered	¼ tsp.	Turmeric
1 oz.	Salami	1 oz.	Pepperoni
4 tsp.	Salt, seasoned	2 tsp.	Salt +
		½ tsp.	Sage +
		½ tsp.	Parsley flakes +
		½ tsp.	Onion powder +
		¼ tsp.	Marjoram +
		¼ tsp.	Paprika
¼ cup	Shallots, chopped	¼ cup	Onions, chopped
1 cup	Sour cream (for baking)	¾ cup	Sour milk or buttermilk +
		⅓ cup	Butter
1 cup	Sour cream (for baking)	1 cup	Plain yogurt +
		1 tsp.	Baking soda
1 cup	Sour cream (for baking)	1 Tbsp.	Lemon juice +
		⅞ cup +	
		1 Tbsp.	Evaporated milk
1¼ cups	Sour cream (for dips)	1 cup	Cottage cheese +
		¼ cup	Plain yogurt or buttermilk
			(Blend in processor.)
1¼ cups	Sour cream (for dips)	1 cup	Cottage cheese +
		1 Tbsp.	Lemon juice +
		¼ cup	Milk or water +
		⅛ tsp.	Salt
			(Blend in processor.)
1¼ cups	Sour cream (for dips)	8 oz.	Cream cheese +
		¼ cup	Milk
			(Blend in processor.)

IF YOU NEED THIS	SUBSTITUTE THIS
1 cup............Stock, any	2 tsp...........Stock base + 1 cup...........Water
1 cup............Stock, fish	1 cup...........Clam juice (Reduce salt in recipe.)
1½ tsp. ....Stock base, any	1 ....Bouillon cube
1 cup............Stuffing mix	1 cup...........Croutons
1 ....Sugar, cube	½ tsp. ....Granulated sugar
1 cup............Sugar, granulated (for sweetening only; not for baking)	24 pkg. ......Equal
1 cup............Sugar, granulated	⅞ cup ....Honey (Reduce liquid by 3 Tbsp.)
1 cup............Sugar, granulated	½ cup ....Maple syrup + ¼ cup ....Corn syrup (Reduce liquid by 2 Tbsp.)
1 cup............Sugar, granulated	¾ cup ....Maple syrup (Reduce liquid by 3 Tbsp.)
1 cup............Sugar, granulated	1¾ cups ....Powdered sugar, packed
Any amt. ......Syrup, pancake	Any amt.....Jelly + water to thin
4 drops........Tabasco sauce	⅛ tsp. ....Cayenne or ¼ tsp. ....Black pepper
1 pkg............Taco seasoning (1¼-oz. size)	4 tsp...........Instant minced onion + 2 tsp...........Chili powder + 2 tsp...........Salt + 1 tsp...........Garlic powder + 1 tsp...........Cornstarch + 1 tsp...........Ground cumin + 1 tsp...........Cayenne
2 tsp.............Tapioca (for puddings or pies)	1 Tbsp.......All-purpose flour
½ cup ....Tartar sauce	6 Tbsp........Mayonnaise + 2 Tbsp........Pickle relish
1 lb................Tomatoes, cooked and seasoned	8 oz............Can tomato sauce
1 cup............Tomato juice (for cooked recipes)	½ cup ....Tomato sauce + ½ cup ....Water
½ cup ....Tomato paste	1 cup...........Tomato sauce or purée (Simmer until reduced to ½ cup.)
1 cup............Tomato puree	½ cup ....Tomato paste + ½ cup ....Water

IF YOU NEED THIS	SUBSTITUTE THIS
1 cup............Tomato sauce	1 cup...........Tomato purée
1 cup............Tomato sauce	½ cup ....Tomato paste + ½ cup ....Water
1 can............Tomato soup (10¾ oz.) (for cooking)	1 cup...........Tomato sauce + ¼ cup ....Water
1 oz..............Truffles	1 oz............Shiitake mushrooms
1 tsp.............Turmeric	1 tsp...........Dry mustard
1 tsp.............Vinegar, any type	1 tsp...........Lemon juice
1 tsp.............Vinegar, Chinese (black)	1 tsp...........Balsamic vinegar
4 Tbsp..........Vinegar, red wine (for salad dressing)	3 Tbsp........Cider vinegar + 1 Tbsp........Red wine
1 cup............White sauce	10¾ oz. .....Canned cream-style soup (undiluted)
½ cup ....Wine (for cooking)	½ cup ....Apple juice or cider
½ cup ....Wine (for marinade)	¼ cup ....Vinegar + ¼ cup ....Water + 1 Tbsp........Sugar
1 Tbsp..........Worcestershire sauce	1 Tbsp........Soy sauce + 4 drops......Tabasco sauce + ⅛ tsp. ....Lemon juice + Dash...........Sugar
1 cake ....Yeast, compressed	1 pkg..........Yeast, Active dry
1 pkg............Yeast, Active dry	1 Tbsp........Yeast, Active dry
1 cup............Yogurt	1 cup...........Sour cream

Container Capacities

. . .

WHEN YOU NEED	USE ONE OF THESE
½-cup container	4" x 1¼" Tart Pan
	2¾" x 1⅜" Muffin Cup
1½-cup container	8" x 1" Tart Pan
2-cup container	5" x 3" x 2" Loaf Pan
(1 pint)	5" x 2" Soufflé Dish
3-cup container	8" x 1¼" Pie Pan
(¾ quart)	7" x 5½" x 2" Rectangular Pan
	5¾" x 2¾" Soufflé Dish
4-cup container	9" x 1½" Pie Pan
(1 quart)	8" x 1½" Round Layer Cake Pan
	8¼" x 2¼" Ring Mold
	7⅜" x 3⅝" x 2¼" Loaf Pan
	6" x 3" Soufflé Dish
	6½" x 6½" x 2" Corning Casserole
5-cup container	6½" x 3" Soufflé Dish
(1¼ quarts)	
6-cup container	9" x 2" Pie Pan (Deep Dish)
(1½ quarts)	10" x 1½" Pie Pan
	9" x 1½" Round Layer Cake Pan
	7½" x 3" Fluted Tube Cake Pan
	10½" x 7" x 1½" Roasting Pan
	9½" x 6" x 2" Rectangular Pan
	8½" x 3⅝" x 2⅝" Loaf Pan
	8½" x 4½" x 2½" Loaf Pan
	6½" x 3½" Soufflé Dish
	7" x 3" Soufflé Dish
	6½" x 6½" x 2¾" Corning Casserole
	7" x 5½" x 4" Melon Mold
	9½" Round Savarin Mold

WHEN YOU NEED	USE ONE OF THESE
7-cup container	10½" x 7½" x 1½" Roasting Pan
(1¾ quarts)	8½" x 2½" Soufflé Dish
	6" x 4½" Charlotte Mold
8-cup container	8" x 8" x 2" Square Cake Pan
(2 quarts)	9" x 9" x 1½" Square Cake Pan
	9¼" x 2¾" Ring Mold
	15¼" x 10¼" x ¾" Roasting Pan
	11" x 7" x 2" Rectangular Pan
	9" x 5" x 3" Loaf Pan
	7" x 3½" Soufflé Dish
	8" x 3" Soufflé Dish
	8" x 8" x 2½" Corning Casserole
	9½" x 3½" Brioche pan
9-cup container	9" x 3½" Fluted Tube Cake Pan
(2¼ quarts)	
10-cup container	9" x 9" x 2" Square Cake Pan
(2½ quarts)	11¾" x 7½" x 1¾" Baking Pan
	17¼" x 11½" x 1" Roasting Pan
	10" x 10" x 2" Corning Casserole
	15" x 10" x 1" Jelly Roll Pan
12-cup container	9" x 3" Tube Cake Pan
(3 quarts)	10" x 3½" Fluted Tube Cake Pan
	8" x 3" Springform Pan
	12½" x 8½" x 1½" Roasting Pan
	13½" x 8½" x 2" Baking Pan
	13" x 9" x 2" Rectangular Pan
	9" x 4" Soufflé Dish
	8" x 8" x 3¾" Corning Casserole

WHEN YOU NEED	USE ONE OF THESE
16-cup container (4 quarts)	9″ x 3″ Springform Pan 10″ x 4″ Fluted Tube Cake Pan 14½″ x 10″ x 2″ Roasting Pan 15″ x 11″ x 2″ Rectangular Pan
18-cup container (4½ quarts)	10″ x 4″ Tube Cake Pan

THIS CONTAINER HOLDS	CUPS	QUARTS
Custard Cups:		
Small	¾	−¼
Large	1¼	+¼
Muffin Cups:		
Miniature	⅛	
Standard	⅓	
Jumbo	¾	
Tart Pans:		
4″ x 1¼″	½	
8″ x 1″	1½	
Pie and Quiche Pans:		
8″ x 1¼″	3	¾
9″ x 1½″	4	1
9″ x 2″	6	1½
10″ x 1½″	6	1½
Layer Cake Pans:		
8″ x 1½″ Round	4	1
9″ x 1½″ Round	6	1½
8″ x 8″ x 2″ Square	8	2
9″ x 9″ x 1½″ Square	8	2
9″ x 9″ x 2″ Square	10	2½
Tube Pans:		
7½″ x 3″ Fluted	6	1½
9″ x 3½″ Fluted	9	2¼
9″ x 3½″ Tube	12	3
10″ x 3½″ Fluted	12	3
10″ x 4″ Fluted	16	4
10″ x 4″ Tube	18	4½
Ring Molds:		
8¼″ x 2¼″ Ring Mold	4½	1+
9¼″ x 2¾″ Ring Mold	8	2
Springform Pans:		
8″ x 3″	12	3
9″ x 3″	16	4

THIS CONTAINER HOLDS	CUPS	QUARTS
Roasting Pans and Flat Pans:		
10½″ x 7″ x 1½″	6	1½
11¾″ x 7½″ x 1¾″	10	2½
12½″ x 8½″ x 1½″	12	3
14½″ x 10″ x 2″	16	4
15¼″ x 10¼″ x¾″	8	2
17¼″ x 11½″ x 1″	10	2½
Rectangular Pans:		
5½″ x 7″ x 2″	3	¾
9½″ x 6″ x 2″	6	1½
11″ x 7″ x 2″	8	2
13″ x 9″ x 2″	12	3
15″ x 10″ x 2″	16	4
Loaf Pans:		
5″ x 3″ x 2″	2	½
7⅜″ x 3⅝″ x 2¼″	4	1
8½″ x 3⅝″ x 2⅝″	6	1½
8½″ x 4½″ x 2½″	6	1½
9″ x 5″ x 3″	8	2
Soufflé Dishes:		
3″ x 1½″ Ramekin	½	
3½″ x 1½″	¾	
4¾″ x 1¾″	1	¼
5″ x 2″	2	½
5¾″ x 2¾″	3	¾
6″ x 3″	4	1
6½″ x 3″	5	1¼
7″ x 3″	6	1½
7″ x 3½″	8	2
8½″ x 2½″	7	1¾
8″ x 3″	8	2
9″ x 4″	12	3
Corning Casseroles:		
5″ x 5″ x 1½″	1½	¼+
5″ x 5″ x 2¼″	2¾	½+
6½″ x 6½″ x 2″	4	1
6½″ x 6½″ x 2¾″	6	1½
8″ x 8″ x 2½″	8	2
8″ x 8″ x 3¾″	12	3
10″ x 10″ x 2″	10	2½
Miscellaneous:		
7″ x 5½″ x 4″ Melon Mold	6	1½
9½″ Round Savarin Mold	6	1½
7″ x 4″ Charlotte Mold	8	2
9½″ x 3½″ Brioche Pan	8	2
6″ x 4½″ Charlotte Mold	7½	1⅞

Measurement and Conversion Charts

■ ■ ■

RECIPE CONVERSION
■ ■ ■

In the center column, locate the amount of ingredient called for in your recipe. To divide it in half, trace the amount to the left column. To double it, trace the amount to the right column.

HALF THE AMOUNT	ORIGINAL AMOUNT	TWICE THE AMOUNT
Dash	⅛ tsp.	¼ tsp.
Pinch	⅛ tsp.	¼ tsp.
⅛ tsp.	¼ tsp.	½ tsp.
¼ tsp.	½ tsp.	1 tsp.
½ tsp.	1 tsp.	2 tsp.
⅝ tsp.	1¼ tsp.	2½ tsp.
¾ tsp.	1½ tsp.	1 Tbsp.
⅞ tsp.	1¾ tsp.	3½ tsp.
1 tsp.	2 tsp.	4 tsp.
1¼ tsp.	2½ tsp.	5 tsp.
1½ tsp.	1 Tbsp.	2 Tbsp.
2¼ tsp.	1½ Tbsp.	3 Tbsp.
1 Tbsp.	2 Tbsp. (⅛ cup)	¼ cup
4½ tsp.	3 Tbsp.	6 Tbsp.

HALF THE AMOUNT	ORIGINAL AMOUNT	TWICE THE AMOUNT
2 Tbsp.	4 Tbsp. (¼ cup, or 2 fl. oz.)	½ cup
2 Tbsp. + 2 tsp.	⅓ cup	⅔ cup
¼ cup	½ cup (4 fl. oz.)	1 cup
⅓ cup	⅔ cup	1½ cups
3 Tbsp.	¾ cup	1½ cups
½ cup	1 cup (½ pint)	2 cups (1 pint)
½ cup + 2 Tbsp.	1¼ cups	2½ cups
10 Tbsp. + 2 tsp.	1⅓ cups	2⅔ cups
¾ cups	1½ cups	3 cups
½ cup + ⅓ cup	1⅔ cups	3⅓ cups
¾ cup + 2 Tbsp.	1¾ cups	3½ cups
1 cup	2 cups (1 pint)	4 cups (1 quart)
1¼ cups	2½ cups	5 cups
1½ cups	3 cups (1½ pints)	6 cups (1½ quarts)
1¾ cups	3½ cups	7 cups
2 cups (1 pint)	4 cups (2 pints, or 1 quart)	8 cups (½ gal.)
2¼ cups	4½ cups	9 cups
2½ cups	5 cups (1¼ quarts)	10 cups (2½ quarts)
2¾ cups	5½ cups	11 cups
3 cups (1½ pints)	6 cups (1½ quarts)	3 quarts
3½ cups	7 cups (1¾ quarts)	14 cups
4 cups (1 quart)	8 cups (2 quarts, or ½ gal.)	1 gal.
5 cups	10 cups (2½ quarts)	5 quarts
6 cups (1½ quarts)	3 quarts (¾ gal.)	1½ gal.
7 cups	14 cups (3½ quarts)	7 quarts
½ gal.	1 gal.	2 gal.
1 gal.	2 gal.	4 gal.

Converting from U.S. to Metric Measures
...

WHEN YOU KNOW	MULTIPLY BY	TO FIND
ounces (oz.)	28.35	grams (g)
pounds (lbs.)	0.454	kilograms (kg)
teaspoons (tsp.)	4.93	milliliters (ml)
tablespoons (Tbsp.)	14.79	milliliters (ml)
fluid ounces (fl. oz.)	29.57	milliliters (ml)
cups (c.)	236.59	milliliters (ml)
cups (c.)	0.236	liters (l)
pints (pts.)	473.18	milliliters (ml)
pints (pts.)	0.473	liters (l)
quarts (qts.)	946.36	milliliters (ml)
quarts (qts.)	0.946	liters (l)
gallons (gal.)	3.785	liters (l)
inches (in.)	2.54	centimeters (cm)
inches (in.)	25.4	millimeters (m)

Converting from Metric to U.S. Measures
...

WHEN YOU KNOW	MULTIPLY BY	TO FIND
grams (g)	0.035	ounces (oz.)
kilograms (kg)	2.202	pounds (lb.)
milliliters (ml)	0.203	teaspoons (tsp.)
milliliters (ml)	0.068	tablespoons (Tbsp.)
milliliters (ml)	0.034	fluid ounces (fl. oz.)
liters (l)	4.237	cups (c.)
liters (l)	2.114	pints (pts.)
liters (l)	1.057	quarts (qts.)
liters (l)	0.264	gallons (gal.)
centimeters (cm)	0.394	inches (in.)
millimeters (m)	0.039	inches (in.)

U.S. and Metric Abbreviations
...

U.S. MEASURE	METRIC MEASURE
teaspoon = tsp.	milliliter = ml
tablespoon = Tbsp.	centiliter = cl
pint = pt.	deciliter = dcl
quart = qt.	liter = l
gallon = gal.	decaliter = dkl
peck = pk.	kiloliter = kl
bushel = bu.	milligram = mg
ounce = oz.	gram = g
pound = lb.	kilogram/kilo = kg
inch (") = in.	millimeter = mm
foot (') = ft.	centimeter = cm
yard = yd.	meter = m

Equivalent Measures for Weight
...

U.S. OUNCES	U.S. POUNDS	METRIC
.035 oz.		1 g
.25 oz.		8 g
.5 oz.		15 g
1 oz.		28.35 g
1¾ oz.		about 50 g
2 oz.	⅛ lb.	57 g
3 oz.		85 g
3½ oz.		about 100 g
4 oz.	¼ lb.	113 g
5 oz.		142 g
6 oz.	⅜ lb.	170 g
7 oz.		198 g
8 oz.	½ lb.	227 g
8¾ oz.		about 250 g = ¼ kg
10 oz.	⅝ lb.	284 g
12 oz.	¾ lb.	340 g
14 oz.	⅞ lb.	397 g
16 oz.	1 lb.	454 g
17½ oz.		about 500 g = ½ kg
18 oz.	1⅛ lbs.	510 g
20 oz.	1¼ lbs.	567 g
22 oz.	1⅜ lbs.	624 g
24 oz.	1½ lbs.	680 g
26 oz.	1⅝ lbs.	737 g
26½ oz.		about 750 g = ¾ kg
28 oz.	1¾ lbs.	794 g
30 oz.	1⅞ lbs.	851 g
32 oz.	2 lbs.	907 g
34 oz.	2⅛ lbs.	964 g
35¼ oz.		about 1,000 g = 1 kg

EQUIVALENT MEASURES FOR LIQUIDS
■ ■ ■

U.S. MEASURE	FLUID OZ.	METRIC
¼ tsp.		1.23 ml
½ tsp.		2.46 ml
¾ tsp.		3.7 ml
1 tsp.		4.93 ml
1¼ tsp.		6.16 ml
1½ tsp.		7.39 ml
1¾ tsp.		8.63 ml
2 tsp.		9.86 ml (about 1 cl)
1 Tbsp.	½ oz.	14.79 ml
2 Tbsp.	1 oz.	29.57 ml
3 Tbsp.	1½ oz.	44.37 ml
¼ cup (4 Tbsp.)	2 oz.	59.15 ml
⅓ cup	2⅔ oz.	79 ml
⅜ cup	3 oz.	88 ml
6 Tbsp. + 2 tsp.	3⅓ oz.	100 ml = 1 dl
½ cup	4 oz.	118.3 ml
⅝ cup	5 oz.	148 ml
⅔ cup	5⅓ oz.	158 ml
¾ cup	6 oz.	177 ml
⅞ cup	7 oz.	207 ml
1 cup	8 oz.	236.59 ml
1¼ cups	10 oz.	300 ml
1⅓ cups	10⅔ oz.	315.42 ml
1½ cups	12 oz.	360 ml
1⅔ cups	13⅓ oz.	394.29 ml
1¾ cups	14 oz.	420 ml
2 cups (1 pt.)	16 oz.	473.18 ml
2 cups + 2 Tbsp.	17 oz.	500 ml
2½ cups	20 oz.	591.4 ml
3 cups (1½ pts.)	24 oz.	709.77 ml
3 cups + 3 Tbsp.	25.5 oz.	750 ml
3½ cups	28 oz.	827.96 ml
4 cups (1 quart)	32 oz.	946.36 ml
1 qt. + ¼ cup	33.8 oz.	1,000 ml = 1 liter
1½ qts.	48 oz.	1.419 liters
1½ qts. + ⅜ cup	51 oz.	1.5 liters
2 qts. (½ gal.)	64 oz.	1.89 liters
2 qts. + 6 Tbsp.	67 oz.	2 liters
2½ qts.	80 oz.	2.365 liters
3 qts. (¾ gal.)	96 oz.	2.84 liters
3 qts. + 9 Tbsp.	100½ oz.	3 liters
3½ qts.	112 oz.	3.312 liters
4 qts. (1 gal.)	128 oz.	3.785 liters
1 gal. + ¾ c.	134 oz.	4 liters
2 gal.	256 oz.	7.57 liters
2½ gal. + 2¼ cups	338 oz.	1 dkl

WATER FACTS
■ ■ ■

- 1 pt. of water weighs 1 lb.
- At sea level, water freezes at 32° Fahrenheit / 0° Celsius.
- At sea level, water simmers at 180° Fahrenheit / 82° Celsius.
- At sea level, water boils at 212° Fahrenheit / 100° Celsius.

CONVERTING FROM FAHRENHEIT TO CELSIUS
■ ■ ■

1. Subtract 32° from Fahrenheit temperature.
2. Multiply the result by 5.
3. Divide the result by 9.

OVEN TEMPERATURES
■ ■ ■

FAHRENHEIT	DESCRIPTION	CELSIUS
200°	Very cool	95°
225°	Cool	110°
250°	Very slow	120°
275°	Slow	135°
300°	Slow	150°
325°	Warm	165°
350°	Moderate	175°
375°	Moderately hot	190°
400°	Fairly hot	200°
450°	Very hot	230°
475°	Very hot	245°
500°	Extremely hot	260°
525°	Extremely hot	275°

Measurement Equivalents

■■■

- A "Pinch" or "Dash" contains less than ⅛ teaspoon.
- A "Jigger" contains 1½ fluid ounces.
- Butter "the size of a walnut" equals about 2 tablespoons.

FLUID OZ.	TSP.	TBSP.	CUPS	QUARTS
60 drops	1	⅓		
¼	1½	½		
⅓	2	⅔		
½	3	1		
⅔	4	1⅓		
1	6	2	⅛	
1⅓	8	2⅔		
1½	9	3		
1⅔	10	3⅓		
2	12	4	¼	
2⅓	14	4⅔		
2⅔	16	5⅓	⅓	
3	18	6	⅜	
3⅓	20	6⅔		
3⅔	22	7⅓		
4	24	8	½	⅛
5	30	10	⅝	
5⅓	32	10⅔	⅔	
6	36	12	¾	
7	42	14	⅞	
8	48	16	1	¼
10		20	1¼	
10⅔		21⅓	1⅓	
12		24	1½	⅜
13⅓		26⅔	1⅔	
14		28	1¾	
16		32	2	½
18			2¼	
20			2½	⅝
22			2¾	
24			3	¾
26			3¼	
28			3½	⅞
30			3¾	
32			4	1
36			4½	1⅛
40			5	1¼
44			5½	1⅜
48			6	1½
56			7	1¾
64			8	2
72			9	2¼
80			10	2½
88			11	2¾
96			12	3
112			14	3½
128			16	4

Canned Goods Sizes

■■■

CAN	WEIGHT	CUPS	SERVINGS	USES
#¼	4 oz.	½	1	Individual
#⅜	6 oz.	¾	1	Juices
#½	8 oz.	1	2	Tomato sauce
#1 picnic	10½ oz.	1¼	2–3	Soup, fruit
#211 cylinder	12 oz.	1½	3–4	Corn
#300	13½ oz.	1¾–2	3–4	Pork and beans
#303	15½ oz.	2	4	Fruits, vegetables
#2	20 oz.	2½	5	Pineapple, juices
#2½	28½ oz.	3½	7	Tomatoes
#3	33½ oz.	4¼	8	Family size
#3 cylinder	46 oz.	5¾	10–12	Large juice
#5	56 oz.	7	14	Institutional
#10	103½ oz.	13	25	Institutional

Scoop Sizes

■■■

The scoop # indicates how many scoops per quart.

SCOOP SIZE	LEVEL MEASURE	SCOOP SIZE	LEVEL MEASURE
#6	⅔ cup	#20	1½ fluid oz.
#8	½ cup	#24	1⅓ fluid oz.
#10	3 fluid oz.	#30	2 Tbsp.
#12	⅓ cup	#40	0.8 fluid oz.
#16	¼ cup	#60	1 Tbsp.

Ladle Sizes

■■■

LADLE SIZE	MEASURE	# PER QUART
1 oz.	⅛ cup	32
2 oz.	¼ cup	16
2⅔ oz.	⅓ cup	12
4 oz.	½ cup	8
6 oz.	¾ cup	5⅓

Index

...

BEANS (cont.)
fava
preparing, 191, 322
selecting, 322
storing, 322, 344
when to buy, 322
yield, 322, 383
garbanzo, yield, 383
great Northern, yield, 384
green
Amandine, 212
boiling, 211
with Cream Cheese Sauce, 213
with Honey Mustard Sauce, 212
preparing, 211, 322
Salad, 213
Red, White and, 213
selecting, 322
in Sour Cream, 213
Southern-Style, 212
steaming, 211
storing, 322, 344
Sweet and Sour, 212
testing for doneness, 212
yield, 322, 384
Italian
preparing, 322
selecting, 322
storing, 322, 344
when to buy, 323
yield, 322
kidney, yield, 385
lima
Casserole, 194
with Dill, 194
preparing, 191, 322
selecting, 322
storing, 322, 344
Succotash, 209
when to buy, 322
yield, 322, 385
Mixed Bean Soup, 86
navy, yield, 386
pea beans, yield, 387
pinto, yield, 388
puree, yield, 378
red
Red, White, and Green Bean Salad, 213
and Rice, 195
yield, 389
shell. See cranberry beans
sprouts, yield, 378
turtle, yield, 391
wax
preparing, 322
selecting, 322
storing, 322, 344
when to buy, 323
yield, 322, 392

BEANS (cont.)
White, 195
Soup, 87
yield, 392
Béarnaise Sauce, 252
beat, 360
BEAU MONDE SEASONING, 360
substitutions, 393
Béchamel Sauce, 250, 360

BEEF
brisket,
102,
360
Barbecued, 103
yield, 378
chipped beef
Creamed, 96
Dip, 77
chuck, 102
Roast, 103
Marinated, 104
corned beef
hash, yield, 381
storing, 348
cuts of beef, 102
Enchiladas, 111
Fajitas, 107
Filet Mignon, 107
grilling guidelines, 106
flank, 102
Grilled Steak, 108
grilling guidelines, 106
grilling guidelines, 106
ground beef
Chili, Texas-Style, 110
Enchiladas, 111
grilling guidelines, 106
Hamburgers, 98
and Macaroni, 112
Meatballs, 113
Meatloaf, 113
and Noodles, 111
Stroganoff, 112
Tacos, 113
Salad, 114
Hash, Roast Beef, 108
marinating, 103
Minute Steaks, 107
oxtail, yield, 387
porterhouse steak, grilling guidelines, 106
pot roast
Old-Fashioned, 104
Slow Cooker, 104
rib, 102
-eye roast, roasting guidelines, 104
-eye steak, grilling guidelines, 106
roast, roasting guidelines, 104
Standing Rib Roast, 106

BEEF (cont.)
roasting guidelines, 104
round, 102, 104
eye of, roasting guidelines, 104
top, roast, roasting guidelines, 104
shank, 102
shish kebabs, grilling guidelines, 106
short loin, 102
short plate, 102
sirloin, 102
steak, grilling guidelines, 106
tip roast, roasting guidelines, 104
Soup, Vegetable, 94
Stir-Fried Beef and Broccoli, 109
storing, 344
Stroganoff, 109
T-bone steak, grilling guidelines, 106
tenderloin, 102, 104
Classic, 106
Grilled, 105
roasting guidelines, 104
yield, 378
BEER
-Batter-Fried Fish, 144
Biscuits, 259
Cheese Soup, 87
Muffins, 259
yield, 378
BEETS
Baked, 196
boiling, 196
greens. See Greens
Harvard, 197
with Horseradish, 196
preparing, 196, 323
Salad, 197
selecting, 323
with Sour Cream, 196
storing, 323, 344
testing for doneness, 196
when to buy, 323
yield, 323, 378
beignet, 360
BERRIES. See also specific varieties
preparing, 323
selecting, 323
storing, 323, 344
varieties, 323
when to buy, 323
yield, 323, 378
betty, 360
beurre manié, 360
BEVERAGES
Bloody Marys, 73
cocoa. See also Chocolate
Microwave, 71
mix, hot drink, yield, 381
Mix, Instant, 71
Old-Fashioned, 71
storing, 347

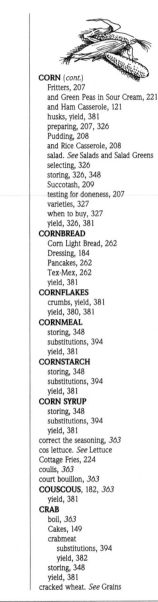

CRACKERS
Club, yield, 381
crumbs
storing, 348
substitutions, 394
graham, yield, 382
meal, yield, 382
Ritz, yield, 382
saltines, yield, 382
storing, 348
Triscuits, yield, 382
Wheat Thins, yield, 382
cracklings, *363*

CRANBERRIES
Bread, 263
preparing, 323
Relish, 242
yield, 382
Salad, 243
sauce, yield, 382
selecting, 323
storing, 323, 348
when to buy, 323
yield, 323, 382
crayfish, yield, 382

CREAM, *363*
coffee, *363*
cheese. *See* Cheese
creamer, non-dairy. *See* Creamer
Gravy, 250
half and half, *367*
substitutions, 396
yield, 382
heavy cream, *363*
substitutions, 394
yield, 382
light cream, *363*
substitutions, 394
yield, 382
sauce. *See* Béchamel Sauce
sour cream. *See also* Sour Cream
storing, 357
substitutions, 397
yield, 390
storing, 348
table, *363*
Whipped, 312
storing, 348
substitutions, 394
yield, 382
whipped topping. *See* Whipped Topping
whipping, *363*
substitutions, 395
yield, 382

CREAMED DISHES
Chipped Beef, 96
Corn, 207
Eggs, 155
Ham and Asparagus, 120
Spinach, 228

CREAMER, NON-DAIRY
storing, 348
yield, 382

CREAM OF TARTAR, *363*
storing, 348
substitutions, 395
yield, 382

CREAM SOUPS
Basic, 89
Chicken with Cheese, 88
Mushroom with Rice, 90
Tomato, 92
Vichyssoise, 95
Quick, 95
Creamy Glaze, 286
crème Anglaise, *363*

CRÈME FRAÎCHE, *363*
storing, 348
Crenshaw melon. *See* Melons
Creole, *363*
crêpe, *363*
crimp, *363*
crisp, *363*
croissant, *363*

CROQUETTES, *363*
Salmon, 147
Crostini Crisps, 78
croustades, *363*
croutons, *363*
crudités, *363*
cruet, *363*
crumb, *363*
Crumb Cake, 278
crumble, *363*
crumpet, *363*
crush, *364*

CUBE, *192, 364*
steak, *364*

CUCUMBERS
and Onions, 210
preparing, 209, 327
Salad, 243
selecting, 327
in Sour Cream, 209
storing, 327, 348
Stuffed, 209
when to buy, 327
yield, 327, 382

CUMIN, *364*
yield, 382
curdle, *364*
cure, *364*

CURRANTS, 323
jelly, substitutions, 395
storing, 348
substitutions, 395
yield, 382

CURRY, *364*
Baked Curried Fruit, 244
paste, yield, 382
powder, *364*
substitutions, 395
yield, 382
Sauce, 254

CUSTARD, *364*
Baked, 312
Caramel (Flan), 312
Pie, 304
storing, 348
Vanilla Sauce, 310
cut, *364*
cut in, *364*
cutlet, *364*

D

Daiquiris, Frozen, 73
Danish pastry, storing, 348
dash, *364*

DATES
chopped, substitutions, 395
storing, 348
yield, 382
debone, *364*
deep-fry, *364*
deglaze, *364*
degrease, *364*
demitasse, 70

DESSERTS AND DESSERT SAUCES
Apple Crisp, 310
Baked Custard, 312
Banana Pudding, 310
Bananas Foster, 310
Bread Pudding, 311
Butterscotch Sauce, 316
cake. *See* Cake
candy. *See* Candy
Cantaloupe Rings, 314
Caramel Custard (Flan), 312
Chocolate Pots de Crème, 311
cookies. *See* Cookies
Fruit Crisp, 314
Frozen Lemon Dessert, 313
Hot Fudge Sauce, 310
Ice Cream and Liqueur, 314
Ice Cream Balls, 314
ice cream ideas, 314
Lemon Sauce, 312
Long Island Peaches, 315
Meringue Shells, 314
Mocha Cream Dessert, 314
pies and cobblers. *See* Cobblers; Pies

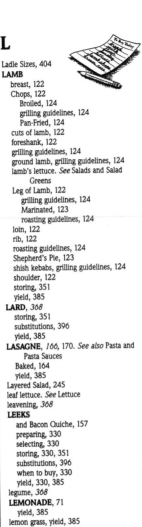
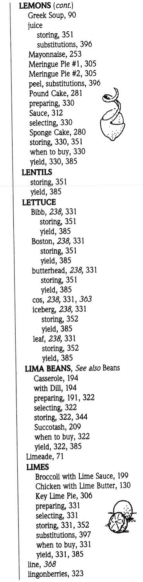

MILK
condensed, substitutions, 396
evaporated, substitutions, 396
skim, substitutions, 396
sour, substitutions, 396
whole, substitutions, 396–397
storing, 352
yield, 386
millet. *See* Grains
mince, *192, 368*
mincemeat, yield, 386
minestrone, *369*
Mini Pizzas, 80
MINT, *190, 369*
yield, 386
Minute Steaks, 107
mix, *369*
Mixed Bean Soup, 86
Mixing, Baking, and Food Preparation Center, 28–29
MOCHA, *369*
Butter Cream Frosting, 284
Café, 70
Cream Dessert, 314
Frosting, 287
Swiss Mix, Instant, 70
MOLASSES
storing, 353
substitutions, 397
yield, 386
mold, *369*
Molded Pineapple Salad, 247
Monkey Bread, 266
morel. *See* Mushrooms
Mornay Sauce, 254
mortar and pestle, *369*
MOSTACCIOLI, *164,* 170. *See also* Pasta and Pasta Sauces
with Cream Sauce, 167
with Ham and Tomato Sauce, 168
moussaka, *369*
mousse, *369*
Mousseline Sauce, 254
MSG, yield, 386
muddle, *369*
MUFFINS
Beer, 258
Blueberry, 259
Bran, 260
muffin pan, *369*
storing, 353
mull, *369*

MUSHROOMS
Artichoke Hearts with, 188
Baked, 214
chantarelle, *362*
Chicken with, 132
Green Peas and, 221
Marinated, 216
morel, *369*
oyster, *369*
porcini, *371*
portobello, *371*
preparing, 214, 332
Rice with, 180
Sautéed, 215
sautéing, 214
selecting, 332
shiitake, *373*
Soup with Rice, Cream of, 90
with Sour Cream, 215
Steamed, 215
steaming, 214
storing, 332, 353
straw, *375*
Stuffed, 216
substitutions, 397
testing for doneness, 214
Veal and, 114
when to buy, 332
yield, 332, 386
muskmelon. *See* Cantaloupe; Melons
MUSSELS
storing, 353
yield, 396
MUSTARD, *369*
dry
substitutions, 397
yield, 386
Green Beans with Honey Sauce, 212
greens. *See* Greens
Honey Horseradish Sauce, 252
Mayonnaise Dressing, 253
Sauce, 254
seeds, yield, 386
storing, 353
substitutions, 397
yield, 386

N

Nacho Layered Dip, 79
navy beans. *See* Beans
NECTARINES
preparing, 242, 333
selecting, 333
storing, 333, 353
when to buy, 333
yield, 332, 386
new potatoes. *See also* Potatoes
in Parsley Butter, 224
yield, 388
nonpareils, *369*

non-reactive pan, *369*
NOODLES, *166,* 170. *See also* Pasta and Pasta Sauces
Amandine, 168
Chinese, yield, 380
chow mein, yield, 381
with Cream Cheese, 169
Ground Beef and, 111
with Mozzarella, 169
Parmesano, 169
Ring, 168
with Sour Cream, 169
Tuna Casserole, 148
yield, 386
NUTMEG, *369*
substitutions, 397
yield, 386
Nutra Sweet, yield, 386
NUTS. *See also* specific varieties
and Bolts, 80
Crumb Pie Crust, 306
Pastry, 300
storing, 353
yield, 386

O

OATMEAL
Cookies, 295
storing, 353
yield, 386
oats, yield, 386
oblique cut, *192*
oil, storing, 353
OKRA
Batter-Fried, 216
boiling, 216
French-Fried, 217
preparing, 216, 333
selecting, 333
steaming, 216
storing, 333, 353
testing for doneness, 216
and Tomatoes, 217
when to buy, 333
yield, 333, 386
OLIVES
kalamata, *367*
oil, storing, 353
storing, 353
yield, 386
Omelet for One, 154

ONIONS
canned, yield, 386
dehydrated, yield, 386
Dry Onions
  Caramelized, 218
  Cucumbers and, 210
  French Soup, 92
  Fried Rings, 219
  Parmesan, 218
  preparing, 217, 333
  red, 333
  selecting, 333
  storing, 333, 353
  varieties, 333
  Vidalia, Roasted, 218
  when to buy, 333
  yield, 333, 386–387
french fried, yield, 386
frozen, yield, 386
Green Onions (Scallions), *373*
  preparing, 217, 333
  selecting, 333
  storing, 333, 353
  when to buy, 333
  yield, 333, 386, 389
juice, substitutions, 398
powder
  substitutions, 398
  yield, 386
salt, yield, 387
scallions. See green onions
soup mix
  substitutions, 397
  yield, 387
substitutions, 397
ORANGES
Butter Cream Frosting, 284
juice
  storing, 353
  yield, 387
Mandarin
  storing, 353
  yield, 387
Pecan Rice, 181
peel, substitutions, 397
preparing, 244, 334
selecting, 333
storing, 334, 353
varieties, 334
when to buy, 334
yield, 334, 387
OREGANO, *190, 369*
substitutions, 397
yield, 387

OREO COOKIES
Oreo Cookie Pie Crust, 306
yield, 387
organizing kitchen, 6–7, 17–40
ORIENTAL
Chicken, 133
Chicken Salad, 140
Ovaltine, yield, 387
oxtail. See Beef
OVEN
about, 56
Cooking Center, 25–27
Mixing, Baking, and Food Preparation
  Center, 28–29
Temperature Conversion, 403
thermometer, 27
OYSTERS
Dressing, 184
oyster mushroom. See Mushrooms
storing, 353
yield, 387

P

paella, *369*
pan-broil, *369*
PANCAKES, 266
batter, yield, 387
mix, storing, 353
Quick, 266
storing, 353
syrup. See also Maple Syrup
  substitutions, 398
  yield, 387
yield, 387
pan-fry, *369*
PANTRY
kitchen master list, 52–54
stocking shelves, 35–39
uncluttering counters and cabinets, 14
PAPAYA
preparing, 334
selecting, 334
storing, 334, 353
when to buy, 334
yield, 334, 387
paprika, *369*
parboil, *369*
parch, *369*
parchment paper, *369*
parcook, *369*
pare, *369*
PARSLEY, *190, 369*
New Potatoes in Parsley Butter, 224
preparing, 335
selecting, 334
storing, 335, 353
substitutions, 397
varieties, 335

PARSLEY (*cont.*)
when to buy, 335
yield, 334, 387
PARSNIPS
preparing, 335
selecting, 335
storing, 335, 354
when to buy, 335
yield, 335, 387
partially set, *369*
PASSION FRUIT, *369*
storing, 354
yield, 387
PASTA AND PASTA SAUCES, *370*
acini di pepe, *168*, 170
agnolotti, *168*, 170
anelli, *164*
Angel Hair with Ham and Artichokes, 163
bavettini, *166*
bucatini, *166*, 170
cannelloni, *164*, 170
capelli d'angelo, *166*, 170
capellini, *166*, 170
cappelletti, *168*
cavatappi, *164*, 170
cavatelli, *168*
Chicken Salad, 141
conchiglie, *168*, 170
conchigliette, *168*
conchiglioni, *168*, 170
cooking charts for dried, 170
ditali, *164*, 170
ditalini, *164*
farfalle, *168*, 170
farfalline, *168*, 170
fedelini, *166*
fettucce, *166*
fettuccelle, *166*, 170
fettuccine, *166*, 170
  Alfredo, 163
  yield, 383
fischietti, *164*
fusilli, *166*, 170
gemelli, *166*, 170
gnocchi, *168*, 170
Ground Beef and Noodles, 111
lasagne, *166*, 170
  Baked, 164
  yield, 385
linguine, *166*, 170
  Florentine, 164
  with Ham Sauce, 165
  with Shrimp, 165
  yield, 385

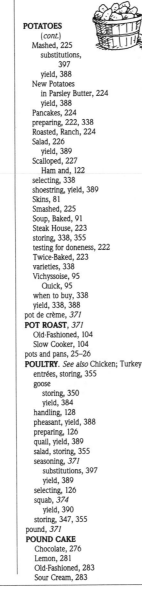

Q

R

ROSEMARY, *190, 372*
  Chicken, 136
    yield, 389
rotisserie, *372*
rounds, vegetable, *192*
roux, *372*
Royal Icing, 287
RUM
  Cake, 284
  Daiquiris, Frozen, 73
  Glaze, 286
  Sauce, 316
rusk, *372*
RUTABAGAS
  preparing, 339
  selecting, 339
  storing, 339
  when to buy, 339
  yield, 339, 389

S

saddle. *See* Meats
SAFFRON, *372*
  substitutions, 397
  yield, 389
SAGE, *190, 372*
  yield, 389
SALAD DRESSINGS
  Buttermilk, 250
  Caesar, 250
  Durkee's, yield, 382
  French, 251
  Herb, 252
  Mayonnaise, 253
    Cayenne, 253
    Lemon, 253
    Mustard, 253
  mix
    storing, 356
    yield, 389
  Mustard, 253
  Poppy Seed, 254
  Sour Cream, 254
  storing, 356
  Sweet and Sour #1, 255
  Sweet and Sour #2, 255
  Thousand Island, 255
  vinaigrette, *376*
    Basic, 256
    Creamy, 256
    Walnut, 256
  yield, 389

SALADS AND SALAD GREENS
  Apple Waldorf, 240
  arugula, *238,* 331
    storing, 343
    yield, 378
  Baby Greens with Apples, 240
  Beet, 197
  Bibb lettuce, *238,* 331
    storing, 351
    yield, 385
  Boston lettuce, *238,* 331
    storing, 351
    yield, 385
  Brown Rice, 179
  butterhead lettuce, *238,* 331
    storing, 351
    yield, 385
  Caesar, 241
  Carrot and Raisin, 204
  chicken salad
    with Grapes, 139
    Pasta, 141
    Spread, 96
    storing, 347
    and Wild Rice, 140
  chicory, 331, *362*
    storing, 347
  Club, 242
  Cobb, 242
  Congealed
    Cranberry, 243
    Cucumber, 243
    Pineapple, Molded, 247
    Tomato Aspic, 248
    yield, 381
  corn, *238, 363*
  cos lettuce, *238,* 331, *363*
  Creamy Cole Slaw, 202
  dock, 331
  Double Hearts Vinaigrette, 244
  Egg Spread, 97
    storing, 349
  endive, *365*
    Belgian, *238,* 327
    curly, *238,* 327
    preparing, 328
    selecting, 327
    storing, 327, 349
    varieties, 327
    when to buy, 328
    yield, 327, 382
  escarole, *238,* 327
    storing, 349
    yield, 382

SALADS AND SALAD GREENS (*cont.*)
  fish salads, storing, 349
  Fruit, 244
  Grapefruit and Avocado, 245
  Green Bean, 213
  Green Pea, 221
  ham, storing, 350
  herbs, *372*
  iceberg lettuce, *238,* 331
    storing, 352
    yield, 385
  lamb's lettuce, *238*
  Layered, 245
  leaf lettuce, *238,* 331
    storing, 352
    yield, 385
  mâche, *238, 368*
  Macaroni, 165
  mesclun, *238, 368*
    yield, 385
  mix, yield, 385
  mixed greens, yield, 389
  Oriental Chicken, 140
  Pasta, with Cheese, 173
    Pasta, with Tuna, 172
  Potato, 226
  preparing greens, 240, 331
  radicchio, *238,* 327, *371*
    storing, 356
    yield, 389
  Red, White, and Green Bean, 213
  rocket, *238,* 331
  romaine lettuce, *238,* 331
    Romaine with Mandarin Oranges, 247
    Romaine, Sweet and Sour, 248
    storing, 352
    yield, 385
  seafood, storing, 356
  selecting, 330
  sorrel, 331
    yield, 390
  spinach. *See also* Spinach
    as a salad green, *238*
    Salad, 228
      Wilted, 228
    storing, 331, 351, 352, 358
  Sweet and Sour Cole Slaw, 202
  Taco, 114
  tuna salad
    storing, 358
    Tuna and Rice, 150
    Tuna Spread, 100
    Tuna with Water Chestnuts, 150
  types of greens, 238
  varieties, 331
  watercress, *238,* 331
    storing, 358
    yield, 392
  when to buy, 331
  yield, 330

variety meats. *See* Meats

VEAL
  breast, 114
  Cutlets, Breaded, 114
  cuts of veal, 114
  leg, 114
  loin, 114
  marinating, 114
  and Mushrooms, 114
  Parmesan, 115
  Piccata, 115
  rib, 114
  shank, 114
  shoulder, 114
  storing, 358

VEGETABLES. *See also* specific varieties
  canned, yield, 392
  cooking, 186
  cutting up, 192
  and Dip, 74
  frozen, yield, 392
  mixed, yield, 386
  pickled, storing, 358
  preparing, 186
  puree, yield, 391
  selecting, 186
  Soup, Beef, 94
  storing, 358
Velouté Sauce, 254, *376*
vermicelli. *See* Pasta and Pasta Sauces

VICHYSSOISE, 95
  Quick, 95
Vidalia onions. *See* Onions
Vienna sausages, yield, 392

VINAIGRETTE, *376. See also* Salad
  Dressings
  Asparagus Vinaigrette, 190
  Basic, 256
  Creamy, 256
  Double Hearts Vinaigrette Salad, 244
  Walnut, 256

VINEGAR
  storing, 358
  substitutions, 398
  yield, 392
Volume Measurements, Equivalent, 404

W–X

WAFFLES, 270
  batter, yield, 392
  Quick, 266
  storing, 358
Waldorf Salad, Apple, 240

WALNUTS
  Broccoli with Bacon and, 198
  size of a walnut, *374*
  storing, 358
  Vinaigrette, 256
  yield, 392

WATER
  bath. *See* Hot Water Bath
  bottled, storing, 358
  Facts, 403

WATER CHESTNUTS
  storing, 358
  yield, 392
watercress. *See* Salads and Salad Greens
watermelon. *See* Melons
wax beans. *See* Beans
Weight Measurements, Equivalent, 402
wheat berries. *See* Grains
wheat, cracked. *See* Grains

WHEAT GERM
  storing, 358
  yield, 392
whey, *376*
whip, *376*

WHIPPED TOPPING. *See also* Cream
  mix, yield, 392
  storing, 358
  yield, 392
whisk, *376*

WHITE BEANS, 195
  Soup, 87
white rice. *See* Rice
White Sauce, 250
wild rice. *See also* Rice
  Chicken and Wild Rice, 139
  Chicken and Wild Rice Salad, 140
  Ham and Wild Rice Casserole, 122
  Wild Rice Soup with Turkey, 94
Wilted Spinach Salad, 228

WINE
  Cooler, Citrus, 73
  substitutions, 398
  yield, 392
wok, *376*
wonton wrappers, yield, 392

WORCESTERSHIRE SAUCE
  storing, 358
  substitutions, 398
work, *376*

WORK CENTERS. *See* Cooking Center;
  Food Service Center; Mixing, Baking
  and Food Preparation Center;
  Refrigerator and Freezer center; Sink
  Center
  designing, 18–21

Y–Z

YEAST
  storing, 358
  substitutions, 398
  yield, 392

YOGURT
  storing, 358
  substitutions, 398
  yield, 392
Yorkshire Pudding, 183
yuca, *376*
zest, *376*

ZITI, *164,* 170. *See also* Pasta and Pasta
  Sauces
  Baked, 174
  yield, 392

ZUCCHINI
  and Bacon, 236
  boiling, 236
  Pie, 84
  Pineapple Bread, 270
  preparing, 236, 342
  selecting, 342
  steaming, 236
  storing, 342, 358
  testing for doneness, 236
  when to buy, 342
  yield, 342, 392